Clothing
FASHION, FABRICS & CONSTRUCTION

Fourth Edition

Jeanette Weber, CFCS

Glencoe
McGraw-Hill

New York, New York   Columbus, Ohio   Chicago, Illinois   Peoria, Illinois   Woodland Hills, California

Glencoe/McGraw-Hill

A Division of The **McGraw·Hill** *Companies*

Send all inquiries to:
Glencoe/McGraw-Hill
3008 W. Willow Knolls Drive
Peoria, IL 61614-1083

ISBN 0-07-829006-6

Printed in the United States of America

7 8 9 10   071   07 06

CONTENTS IN BRIEF

CONTRIBUTING WRITER

Anne Marie Soto
Fashion and Sewing Specialist
AMS Associates
Teaneck, New Jersey

TEACHER REVIEWERS

Abbie W. Brockwell, CFCS
Monmouth Regional High School
Tinton Falls, New Jersey

Katherine M. Chimini
Central High School
Bridgeport, Connecticut

Suzan P. Close
Pahokee Middle/Senior High School
Pahokee, Florida

Denise S. Geller, CFCS
Homestead High School
Fort Wayne, Indiana

Michelle Good
Niles North High School
Skokie, Illinois

Marsha Grothusen
Oregon Trail Junior High School
Olathe, Kansas

Jane Eastman Halladay
Johnson City High School
Johnson City, New York

DeAnn Hebert
East High School
Des Moines, Iowa

Deborah L. Hopper
Glenwood Middle School
Chatham, Illinois

Suzanne Howell
LaPorte High School
LaPorte, Indiana

Beth King
Holland Christian High School
Holland, Michigan

Jacqueline Merkerson
Hialeah High School
Hialeah, Florida

Karol Rademacher
Roosevelt High School
San Antonio, Texas

Shannon Rasmussen
Logan High School
Logan, Utah

Phyllis A. Stewart
Lincoln High School
Vincennes, Indiana

Melanie Tabor
Swain County High School
Bryson City, North Carolina

Susan C. Teelin
Camden Middle School
Camden, New York

Sheryl Tumbleson
Proviso East High School
Maywood, Illinois

Karen I. Voelz
Milton School District
Milton, Wisconsin

Judy Wenger
Shawnee Mission North High School
Overland Park, Kansas

Shannon Wilson
Lawrence Kansas Public Schools
Lawrence, Kansas

Linda Zabek
Frontier Regional School
South Deerfield, Massachusetts

CONTENTS

SEWING AND SERGING HANDBOOK CONTENTS

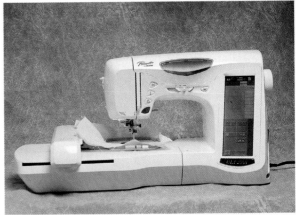

Careers

Trends in TECHNOLOGY

How To...

Charts

Highlighted Topics

Serging Techniques

UNIT 1
Clothing and Society

23

Influences on Clothing

OBJECTIVES

- Describe the basic functions that clothing fulfills.

- Explain personal influences on clothing choices.

- Compare the influence of family and friends on clothing choices.

- Evaluate the media's impact on clothing.

- Explain how societal changes influence clothing.

KEY TERMS

adornment	society
media	status
modesty	status symbols
peer group	values

W HO DECIDES WHAT CLOTHING YOU wear? Do you? "Well, sure," most teens might say, "I always decide." That's a reasonable answer, but there might be more to it than you think. As you'll soon see, something as routine as the weather or as complex as the media can have impact on the clothing decisions you make. See *Fig. 1-1.*

CHOOSING WHAT TO WEAR

What happens when you sleep longer than you should on a school morning? If you went to bed knowing what tomorrow's outfit would be, the clothing decision has already been made. If not, you probably rush to the closet and grab something.

Whether you quickly choose boots instead of athletic shoes when getting dressed or carefully pick an outfit that makes you look your best, something is behind your decisions. What might that be? People choose the clothes they wear for a number of reasons.

Your Basic Needs

You might not realize it, but the clothing you choose meets certain basic needs that all people share. While serving the functions shown in *Fig. 1-2* on pages 26-27, clothing meets many needs. Some are physical—for comfort, protection, and safety. Clothing covers the body and protects it from the weather, harm, and injury.

Other needs are intellectual, emotional, and social. Clothes can communicate lots of information about people and their lives. Clothes can make you feel attractive and self-confident. Clothes can also help you identify with other people and feel like part of a group.

Your Activities

Clothing choices are linked to how and where you spend your time. A hiker or shopper chooses comfortable shoes for walking. Many sports enthusiasts need protective gear. Bike riders, skateboarders, and football and hockey players wear helmets. Soccer players wear shin guards.

Even the people you'll be with influence what you wear. Weekend activities with family and friends may call for either casual or dress-up outfits. Wearing something similar to your friends can make you feel more comfortable.

1-1 How do you decide what to wear? Sometimes an outfit that works for you one day just doesn't seem right on another. Why is that?

1-2 • Basic Functions of Clothing

Throughout history, clothing has fulfilled these basic functions.

Protection. Clothing insulates from the cold and keeps the sun from burning and dehydrating the body in the heat. Special clothing protects people from harm in sports and certain occupations. Construction workers, firefighters, and police officers need special clothing for safety. Workers in hospitals and restaurants wear sanitary clothing and hair coverings to prevent the spread of germs. People who produce medical products wear gloves and facemasks to prevent contamination.

Identification. Clothing and accessories can identify people as members of a group. Uniforms provide instant recognition of police officers, firefighters, and members of the military. Uniforms create a special image for hotel staffs and airline personnel. Uniforms also identify athletic teams, with striped shirts and shorts in rugby and tight, one-piece singlets in wrestling. Badges, emblems, and pins on jackets and caps show participation in athletics, scouts, and community organizations.

A check of the weather guides many clothing choices. The right garments can insulate your body against extremely hot or cold temperatures. Many warm-weather clothes feature light colors that reflect sunlight and loose styles that allow warm air from the body to escape. Cold-weather clothing has multiple layers and heavy or bulky fabrics that trap warm air from the body, creating an insulating layer of warmth for outdoor activities.

Your activities often allow you to make choices about what to wear, but sometimes the decision isn't up to you. A school, for example, may set up rules about what can be worn. On a part-time job you might have to wear a uniform or clothes of a certain style and color. Fast-food workers must wear hats or hairnets to prevent hair from falling into the food they prepare or serve.

Activities are as varied as people. What activities influence the clothing choices that you make each day?

Your Personal Preferences

Everyone has likes and dislikes. That's why clothes come in many colors, fabrics, and styles. Clothing likes and dislikes are determined by your **values**, beliefs about what's important, desirable, or worthwhile. By examining your values, you can discover your overall attitude toward clothing. This is your clothing philosophy, and it affects what you decide to wear.

Modesty. Clothing provides **modesty**, a belief about the proper way to cover the body with clothes. Modesty may vary for the occasion. Bathing suits and bare feet are fine for the beach but not in schools, offices, and most restaurants. Modesty also varies in history. In Victorian times, women wore bathing outfits that covered them from elbows to knees. Today, the bikini is common.

Status. Clothing and accessories can show a person's **status**, a position or rank within a group. Kings and queens, even now, wear crowns to set them apart from subjects. Leaders of marching bands stand out with tall fur hats. Members of the military wear insignias to indicate rank. The captain of an athletic team might also wear an insignia. Deans of universities wear colorful scarves or hoods over their robes to show status in the school.

Adornment. People wear clothing and jewelry to enhance their appearance and attract attention. As **adornment**, these decorations express uniqueness and creativity and bring admiration and recognition. As a result, people feel good about themselves. Throughout history, people have adorned their bodies with cosmetics, body paint, and tattoos in addition to clothing and jewelry.

What do you look for in clothes: comfort, durability, low cost, easy care, status, the latest style? As you answer, your values about clothes become clearer.

People who want comfort choose clothes that feel good. For durability, they want clothing that wears well over a long period of time. Those who value low cost look for special sales and bargains. To preserve their free time, some people want clothing that takes little care. Individuals who value status select clothes and accessories that look, or are, expensive or have the name of a designer or celebrity. If having the latest styles, colors, and accessories is important, a person might sacrifice comfort and practicality in order to wear up-to-date fashions.

Your likes and dislikes also include how you feel about your appearance. Do you like to stand out in a group or blend in? Do you like to be a trendsetter? Perhaps you prefer a middle-of-the-road approach. Some people dress in a certain way so others will notice them. Other people use their clothing choices as a way to blend in with the crowd. The more you understand your personal preferences, the easier it is to make the best clothing choices for every occasion.

OTHER INFLUENCES

Some influences on clothing decisions are less obvious than the ones you've just read about. Family, friends, and the media also have impact on fashion choices.

Influence of Family

Since the family is such a constant presence in most people's lives, its impact may go unnoticed. When clothing decisions are made, however, the family does make a difference. Where the family lives and favorite activities influence what is worn. Families who live in northern climates, for example, need heavy coats, mittens, and boots for snowy winter days. Families who enjoy outdoor activities might need clothing for camping, hiking, or water sports. See *Fig. 1-3*.

Influence of Friends

A **peer group** consists of people with a similar background, social status, and age. Your peer group is your friends and classmates. An adult's peers are friends and job associates. A peer group can have a big influence on how people dress and act.

During the teen years, young people usually have a strong need to be accepted by peers. The group may decide what clothing is "in," whether high-top athletic shoes with untied laces, a baseball cap turned backwards, or a brand of clothing. Acceptance hinges on wearing the "approved" style.

Following the course set by peers is not necessarily good or bad. It depends on the circumstances. Problems arise when the group's idea of "right" conflicts with the individual's beliefs as well as the family's. In another chapter, you'll see that deciding when to go along with the crowd can be a measure of your own identity and values.

Impact of the Media

Through the **media**, messages are communicated to a large audience. You'll find the media all around you. Almost everyone watches television, listens to the radio, goes to the movies, or rents videos. People also read magazines and newspapers, browse through catalogs, and surf the Internet. All of these impact clothing choices.

Many product messages are communicated through the media. When you read a magazine article on the season's latest fashion trends, you get ideas about what to buy and wear. Advertisements, however, are the main method used to promote products. When you buy a cer-

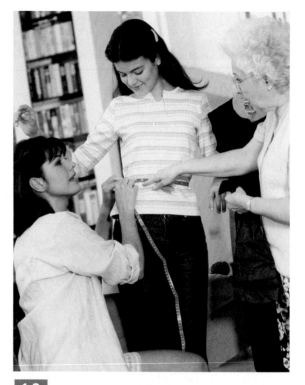

1-3 Clothing choices are influenced by the family. Often family members work together to take care of individual needs.

tain jacket brand that you saw advertised, your decision has been influenced by the media.

Advertising

If it weren't for advertisements, how would you know which stores carry the clothes you want and how much they cost? Advertising is very useful to consumers, but you have to remember that the main purpose is to sell a product, image, or idea. Advertising is very powerful because of its ability to persuade people to buy. An ad for a premium ice cream talks about the good taste but doesn't mention the high fat content. A television commercial for a luxury car doesn't mention its poor gas mileage. An ad for clothing or accessories shows the item on a gorgeous model, with no information about the product.

When you see such ads, look for the facts. Many ads appeal strictly to emotions. They create vague but positive feelings for the product. Often, the goal is to make you think that this item will make your life—and you—more interesting, more exciting, more attractive, more popular, and ultimately happier.

If you read, look, and listen to each ad carefully, you can separate the facts from the emotional appeal. Advertising should be only one of the many influences on your clothing choices.

Celebrities

Have you heard anyone say, "Imitation is the sincerest form of flattery?" When you admire someone, it's easy to allow that person to influence the choices you make, often about clothing. Subconsciously, people think that if they look or act like a particular person, some of the admired characteristics will rub off.

Entertainers, especially on stage, screen, and television, influence clothing, hairstyles, and makeup. They may influence fashion through the styles they wear themselves or the costumes of the characters they portray. In the 1960s, people copied the haircuts and the collarless suits worn by the Beatles. Later, Madonna started a trend by wearing lingerie as outerwear. More recently, people have copied the hairstyles and casual, urban clothing of the leads in the television show, *Friends*.

Celebrities from the sports world also inspire fashion trends. Some famous athletes endorse brand products. Michael Jordan has done ads for Air Jordan athletic shoes and Tiger Woods for Nike sportswear. Other athletes inspire particular styles, such as the colorful tennis outfits worn by Serena and Venus Williams.

Models, politicians, religious leaders, television personalities, and heroes can all motivate people to copy their style of clothing. As the television host of *Who Wants to Be a Millionaire*, Regis Philbin started a fashion craze for matching shirts and ties. After the rescue operations that followed the destruction of the World Trade Center in New York City, people wore caps, jackets, and T-shirts inscribed with FDNY and NYPD, the insignias of New York's fire and police departments. What other heroes and celebrities influence fashion trends?

Fashion Facts

TRENDSETTERS. Media stars and fashion trends have a long history together. Rudolph Valentino, the dashing movie idol of the silent film era, popularized an accessory not worn by men until that time: the wristwatch. In the 1950s, actors James Dean and Marlon Brando turned the black leather jacket into standard "rebel" attire with their film portrayals of alienated teens and outlaws. When John F. Kennedy was President of the United States in the early 1960s, his wife Jacqueline could start a trend just by wearing a certain style to a televised interview. Her hats, purses, and even the muff she wore to warm her hands were all copied.

Status Symbols

Many fashion designers, sports figures, and other celebrities have their names, initials, or symbols on clothes and accessories. Through exposure in the media, such items can become **status symbols**, which give the wearer a special feeling of importance or wealth. See *Fig. 1-4* on page 30.

What status symbols have you noticed on clothing? A small alligator adorns LaCoste's shirts. The YSL initials appear on Yves St. Laurent's accessories, and Tommy Hilfiger's name is on sweatshirts. The Nike "swoosh" symbol appears on sportswear.

For some people, status symbols are important. By wearing these clothes and accessories, people try to look special. They may want to show that they can afford something expensive, or they just like wearing something that is "in." As long as you understand the reason for status symbols, and the ones you choose fit your budget, these items may have a place in your wardrobe. If status symbols mean nothing to you, you can still look just fine without them.

A CHANGING SOCIETY

Society influences what people wear. A **society** is a group of individuals who live together in a

1-4 You could buy a certain brand of athletic shoes because they last well and are comfortable. You could also choose a brand because all your friends are wearing them and they are linked to a famous athlete. Which situation describes a status symbol?

particular area, sometimes as a nation or community. Together, the people share certain traditions, institutions, and interests. The United States is a society of people who live together under one form of government. Although many variations exist in the way Americans dress, in the society as a whole there are similarities.

In the U.S., change is inevitable and ongoing. What happens in one part of the country can quickly influence other parts. Where clothing is concerned, five major trends influence the choices people make. These trends are introduced here, but you'll read more about them later.

More Casual Living

At one time, American society was more formal. Many clothing rules existed. Hats and gloves were a regular part of a woman's wardrobe. Most men wore business suits. People dressed up when they traveled on an airplane, went shopping, or ate in restaurants. Many restaurants prohibited women from wearing slacks or pantsuits; men had to wear jackets and ties. There were other

rules too. For example, women never wore white shoes before Memorial Day or after Labor Day. Black was the only acceptable color to wear for funerals. Black was never worn for weddings.

Today, most restaurants welcome customers in casual clothes. While traveling, people dress for comfort. Wedding guests and even bridesmaids frequently wear black. Most workplaces permit employees to wear casual attire. See *Fig. 1-5*. With more emphasis on leisure time, sports, and exercise, wardrobes reflect these interests. Women, in particular, no longer accept uncomfortable and constricting clothes or shoes just to follow the dictates of fashion designers.

Rapid Communication

Technological changes have brought societies around the world in close contact. Societies today share goods, services, and information quickly and easily. Like other news, fashion news transmits rapidly via computer, television, fax, and videos. The same television shows and movies are seen in many different countries. Concerts and sporting events are telecast live via satellite TV. The Internet and its commercial on-line services, such as CompuServe, America Online, and Prodigy, offer new ways to communicate, advertise, and sell to suppliers and customers.

As a result, similar fashions are available for sale at the same time in many parts of the world. Teens in Japan and the United States can wear the same style of jeans even though they're manufactured in a third country. People around the world can access the Internet to purchase goods from almost anywhere.

Multiple Shopping Options

If you like to shop for clothes, you're living at the right time, since opportunities are every-

1-5 Many businesses today allow employees to dress more casually than in the past. What advantages do employees have with this practice?

where. Stores are still a favorite shopping option. Although stores are not all the same, their differences are less obvious than they once were. Today, the price at a discount store might be higher than buying on sale somewhere else.

Many stores are conveniently grouped together in malls. Some are found in small "strip centers," where the stores are lined up in a row. Large indoor malls feature at least two large stores, a collection of smaller stores, and a food court. Mega-malls have over 400 stores, many restaurants, and even entertainment areas, as you can see on page 32.

People who don't have the time or desire to go to a store can order almost anything at home via computer, fax, or phone. They can download pictures of merchandise over modem lines and place orders or ask questions through e-mail. No matter where you live, you can now shop 24 hours a day—as long as your budget holds up.

Consumer Power

While designers drove the fashion world of yesterday, consumer influence is felt today. The time when a designer's revolutionary new style spread rapidly across the country no longer exists. Now designers are more likely to focus on new colors and fabrics than on radical new styles. They draw inspiration from what people are already wearing—at parties, clubs, sporting events, and on the street.

As consumers, people have become more educated. Their knowledge and skills have grown with rapid communication. As a result, consumers know what they want, and they want it all: rock-bottom prices, the best quality, good service, and the least hassle. They shop where these demands will be met. If a new store or shopping concept comes along, consumers are willing to give it a try. Loyalty to a store or brand name is less likely. All of these changes have made consumers more powerful, which makes sellers listen.

Global Marketplace

You might not have traveled around the world, but it's possible that something in your closet did. A well-traveled shirt could have begun its journey in another country, where someone created a design. At the same time, a fabric design was in the works somewhere else. After the fabric was produced in a third country, it was sent to a fourth country, where the shirt was manufactured. The thread, buttons, and trim were shipped in from other parts of the world. Once the shirt was assembled, the finished garment was shipped to a store, where it became yours.

Today, a garment that's entirely made in one country is the exception rather than the rule. Developing nations have become key players in the fashion industry, mostly as sources of materials and production. Clothing made around the world can be sold almost anywhere in the world.

Fashion capitals have also expanded across the globe. In the 1940s and 1950s, the major high-fashion designers were based in Paris. All the ready-to-wear designers were based in New York City. In the 1960s and 1970s, London, Rome, and

Trends in TECHNOLOGY

»SHOPPING AS ENTERTAINMENT

Malls are not just for shopping these days. Are you familiar with these?

- Multiplex movie theaters, bowling alleys, skating rinks, amusement parks, indoor playgrounds, and arcades.

- Multiple TV screens, banking a wall and playing videos or sporting events.

- Mini basketball courts, skateboard ramps, and rock climbing walls in sporting goods stores.

- Temporary video arcades with computer game technology on giant screens and private consoles for stop-and-play fun.

- Celebrities appearing in person for autographs and demonstrations.

- Computer stations for surfing the Internet, and photo booths.

- How-to classes and early-morning walking groups.

- Comfortable lounge chairs and piano music for customers.

- Special fairs about health, jobs, weddings, proms, antiques, and crafts.

- Food courts and "sidewalk" cafes, for eating as well as people watching.

INVESTIGATION ACTIVITY
What entertainment is available at malls near you?

Milan also became important fashion capitals. Today, Tokyo, Germany, Spain, Scandinavia, Canada, and Hong Kong have joined the list of places where the fashion industry thrives. The marketplace is truly global.

LOOKING AHEAD

While clothes mean little to some and more to others, there's no denying that clothing has great impact. In this course, you'll see how fashions reflect history and how technology has brought change. You'll explore the way clothing expresses culture as well as your own personality.

If you like, you can tap your creativity while you study clothing. You'll learn about color and design and how to choose styles that make the best of your appearance. Perhaps you'll create designs of your own.

This course will also give you practical knowledge. Can you evaluate well-made clothing? Can you identify different fabrics? Do you know the best methods of clothing care? Would you like to sew a garment or accessory? These skills will help you as a consumer. Using the process on page 33, you'll learn to make sound decisions about clothing choices and management. As you study each unit, you'll also explore career possibilities for your future. Whatever your interests and goals as you complete this course, you'll discover that the world of fashion is exciting and ever-changing.

How To... MAKE DECISIONS

To make the best clothing choices, you need good decision-making skills. The six steps shown here can guide you through decisions. Each time you use them, you'll become better prepared for future decisions.

Step 1: State the situation.

Clearly identify the problem or situation.

You need a nice outfit to wear to a job interview.

Step 2: List various options.

What choices do you have?

- **Should you buy something new?**
- **Could you sew a new garment?**
- **Should you make do with something you already own?**
- **Could you borrow a garment from a relative or friend?**
- **What other options do you have?**

Step 3: Evaluate the options.

What are the pros and cons of each option? Evaluate all your choices before deciding.

- **How much money can you spend on something new?**
- **Can you wait for a sale?**
- **Do you have the skills to sew a garment?**
- **Will you look presentable without something new?**
- **Would a borrowed garment fit well and look good?**

Step 4: Consider your values.

What is most important to you? Consider money, time, practicality, appearance, and creativity.

Step 5: Select the best option.

Based on your evaluation of each option, which choice is best? When you've made your decision, follow through on it. The sooner you act, the sooner the problem will be solved.

If this were your decision, what choice would you make?

Step 6: Evaluate the results.

Take time to evaluate your decision. Answer these questions: Why did you make the decision that you did? What important fact helped in making your decision? In the long run, did you make the right choice?

Exploring **Decisions**

What clothing decision do you have to make in the near future? Apply the six steps to make a choice.

Review

CHAPTER SUMMARY

- Clothing is often chosen to meet certain basic functions and needs.

- People make clothing choices based on activities as well as personal preferences.

- Values, family, and friends influence a person's clothing choices.

- Influences on clothing choices reach consumers in several ways through the media.

- Rules about clothing have relaxed in the United States, creating more choices for consumers.

- Advances in technology have greatly increased the variety of clothing available.

- Studying clothes and fashion can help you make satisfying choices about your wardrobe, and even your career.

USING KEY TERMS

Create a true-false quiz based on the Key Terms. Exchange quizzes with a classmate and complete.

RECALLING THE FACTS

1. Describe ways that clothing serves basic functions.

2. Give two examples of how clothing offers protection from the weather.

3. Why do people want clothing choices in many different styles, colors, and fabrics?

4. Give examples of how individual values can affect clothing choices.

5. How do family and peers affect decisions about clothing?

6. Describe a helpful approach when using the information in advertisements.

7. Why might a designer jacket worn by a movie star become popular with some people?

8. Do all people value status symbols? Explain.

9. List three situations in which formal dress has been replaced by more casual wear.

10. How have advances in communication technology affected the fashion world?

11. How have changes in shopping options affected clothes buying?

12. What influence do consumers have on the fashion world today?

13. In what sense might some garments be called "world travelers"?

and Activities

THINKING CRITICALLY

1. Predict what might happen if people in certain occupations no longer wore uniforms. Give examples.

2. Would you follow the fashion example set by a celebrity? Explain.

3. Some people are offended when they dress up for dinner at a nice restaurant and other diners are wearing jeans and casual wear. What is your point of view?

APPLYING YOUR KNOWLEDGE

1. **Identifying values.** In writing, identify at least five personal values that you use when choosing clothes for your wardrobe.

2. **Identifying influences.** List five garments or outfits in your wardrobe. For each one, explain what influenced you to buy or wear that item. Choose from the influences described in the chapter.

3. **Fashion inspiration.** Work with a few classmates to identify how celebrities, movies, and television programs inspire current fashion. Collect magazine photos and write descriptions for a bulletin board or poster display that illustrates this inspiration.

4. **Status symbols.** Choose an activity or organization that's familiar to you. Describe or draw articles that identify different ranks or positions of people in that group. Explain what each item signifies.

5. **Looking ahead.** In the last passage of this chapter, you read about what you'll gain from this course. List five topics or skills to be explored. As a preview of the course ahead, scan the table of contents and identify chapters related to the topics and skills you listed. Which ones will be most helpful to you?

CREATIVE SOLUTIONS

Your clothing class has been encouraged to submit design ideas for new school band uniforms. The band director and the head of the family and consumer sciences department will evaluate the designs, with input from band members themselves. The top suggestions will be sent to the principal and school board for consideration. You and several classmates decide to pool your ideas. At your first meeting, you decide to identify some general concerns and points to consider as a guide in developing your design.

Think Creatively

What factors will you and your group consider when creating a design for the uniforms?

Cultures and Customs

OBJECTIVES

- **Explain how clothing reflects cultures.**

- **Give examples of clothing symbols.**

- **Discuss clothing customs and expectations in the U.S. culture.**

- **Describe appropriate outfits for certain occasions.**

KEY TERMS

appropriate	expectations
culture	heritage
customs	roles
dress code	standards

Adapting to new cultures.

Today, increasing numbers of people spend time living or working in countries outside their homeland. Some relocate permanently. In these situations the question of clothing arises. Some people continue to wear the traditional garments of their own culture wherever they go. They feel most comfortable in the clothing they have always worn and believe that others should respect that choice. Some prefer to wear the styles of the culture where they are living. They want to fit in well and eliminate potential barriers.

What do you think?

Do people need to adopt a culture's clothing styles in order to fit in? Are other behaviors more important for acceptance?

WITH EVERY PASSING YEAR, PEOPLE say the world grows smaller. Of course, that's not literally true, but what do they mean? They mean that people now communicate across continents and travel to other lands with greater ease. Places that once seemed far away and remotely different are now more familiar. As diverse people share ideas and products around the world, they become closer, which is changing the way people view other cultures.

CLOTHING REFLECTS CULTURES

Each society has its own **culture**, the collected ideas, skills, beliefs, and institutions of a society at a particular time in history. Food, entertainment, art, religion, politics, and technology—all are elements of a society's culture. Cultural differences are what set one society apart from another.

Every culture has something special and unique about its clothing. The garments that people wear—the fabrics, designs, and colors—tell so much about the way people think and live. They reveal part of that people's story, much as each piece in a puzzle contributes to the finished picture. See *Fig. 2-1*.

National Costumes

Over the centuries, many cultures have developed their own distinctive clothing style, or national costume. Most national costumes had very practical beginnings.

Ancient Celts in the highlands of Scotland wove clan blankets with special plaid patterns to identify each clan. In the sixteenth century, they started wrapping these plaid blankets around the body to form a short, belted-on, all-purpose garment called a kilt. The extra fabric was pulled up over the shoulder from the back and pinned in

2-1 Contemporary fashions can be inspired by traditional ethnic garments and fabrics. This garment reflects the African culture through the style, bright colors, and interesting pattern.

place. Today Scotsmen still wear plaid kilts for special occasions. See *Fig. 2-2.*

In Middle Eastern countries, where the desert is very hot during the day and very cold at night, the turban became a common clothing item. It absorbed sweat and also insulated from the cold. The turban continues to serve these practical functions in many cultures. See *Fig. 2-3.*

Over the years, some cultures developed garments with a similar shape, which was comfortable and easy to make. The Hawaiian muumuu, the North African caftan, and the Arabian kibr, a hooded robe with sleeves, are all loose-fitting garments that are still worn today.

Some national costumes, such as the Indian sari and Japanese kimono, feature beautiful fabric designs in colorful silks. Other national costumes have unique forms of ornamentation. Traditional Hungarian clothes, for example, are decorated with leather. Colorful, embroidered designs

2-3 Turbans are common in many parts of the world, from North Africa, across the Middle East, and into Central Asia. The narrow cloth that creates a turban can be as long as 12 feet.

accent Scandinavian clothing. Native American garments feature colored beads, arranged in special patterns and sewn to soft leather. See *Fig. 2-4.*

In some parts of the world, people still wear distinctive national costumes as part of their everyday dress. The African tribal robe and Indian sari, for example, have changed little over the centuries.

Global Trends

In your school, how similar are the clothes students wear? How do these styles compare to those worn across the country? What about teens in China, Italy, Ghana, Brazil, India, or Australia? If you could travel the world, you would probably see many teens dressed like you.

Today, many people wear similar clothing styles in countries around the world. The Chinese businessman in Beijing wears the same type of suit as the American businessman in New York City. Mass communication and global distribution of the latest fashions have produced this effect.

There are exceptions, however. People who live in countries with very hot or cold climates may

2-2 In its original form, the kilt needed no tailoring and didn't need to be replaced as often as breeches. Today the kilt is worn proudly and considered the national dress of Scotland.

2-4 Beautiful woven fabrics and designs are typical of Native American costumes. Handcrafted beads, belts, and other adornments add to the beauty of the costume.

has many symbolic meanings. Clothing can tell you about a person's heritage, occupation, role, gender, and values.

Heritage

Every person has a special **heritage**, the cultural background and ethnic traditions handed down from ancestors. Heritage defines identity and produces pride. To celebrate heritage, people participate in ethnic festivals and holidays, often wearing colorful costumes. On Chinese New Year, people don new clothes in "lucky" orange or red, as brilliant as the fireworks that mark the day. At the Navajo Nation Fair, Native Americans display stunning traditional garments, worn with feathered headdress, beaded bracelets, and leather moccasins.

2-5 National costumes worn for special occasions in Mexico are bright and colorful. Although the bride at a Mexican wedding usually wears white, red is a popular color among the guests. Colorful flowers in the hair complement the dress this woman wears.

find greater comfort in their traditional clothing. Others, such as those in developing countries, may not have the means or the desire to wear Western styles.

In many cultures, national costumes are now worn only for festive occasions, such as holidays, parades, weddings, and dances. Wedding guests in Germany, Korea, or Mexico may celebrate by wearing traditional outfits that have been worn for generations. See *Fig. 2-5*. This is one way for people to reflect their cultural pride in a modern world.

CLOTHING AS SYMBOLS

Why does a bride in the U.S. traditionally wear a white gown? In the American culture, the color white symbolizes innocence, faith, and purity. By contrast, brides in China wear red garments because red symbolizes joy and permanence. Throughout the cultures of the world, clothing

Many clothing styles have come to symbolize a particular cultural background. A kimono is associated with Japan, a sari with India, and leather lederhosen with Germany. See *Fig. 2-6.* Colorful fabrics wrap the heads of African women. South Americans wear distinctive striped ponchos.

Because the United States is a culturally diverse society, no single clothing style symbolizes heritage. Although basic clothing styles were inherited from Europe, many cultures have contributed special items. The mandarin collar comes from China, for example, and the caftan

2-7 People often wear clothing that symbolizes their occupation. Even in a different setting, you would probably know what work these people do. How can you tell?

2-6 Although the classic Indian sari is made with six yards of fabric, a nine-yard version can be draped to form pants rather than a flowing gown. The graceful, feminine sari can be made from shimmering silk or gauzy cotton in beautiful pastels. Some have bright floral prints.

comes from Africa. Native Americans have contributed highly prized turquoise and silver jewelry.

Within the United States, regional differences show. A Texan may wear cowboy boots with his business suit. People in Hawaii and Florida usually wear brighter colors than those worn in Minnesota. Can you think of reasons for these regional differences in clothing?

Occupation

In a courtroom drama on television, how do you identify the judge? You probably notice the traditional black robe. In the same way, clothing identifies many professions. Ministers, priests, and other clergy members usually wear special robes or shawls when conducting religious services. Uniforms clearly symbolize the police force, fire department, and military. Many people in service occupations, including restaurant workers, delivery people, and postal workers, also wear special uniforms for quick identification.

Clues to professions are all around you. Examples are a doctor's white coat, a priest's collar, and a chef's hat. What other clothing symbols are linked to careers? See *Fig. 2-7.*

Roles

For high school graduation, you'll probably wear a long robe and mortarboard hat. These symbolize your role as a graduate. Clothing identifies many **roles**, the different positions people have in society.

A bride is distinguished from her attendants by the wedding gown, veil, and special dresses worn. A baby's heirloom gown, passed down through generations, symbolizes baptism. Athletes and members of marching bands wear distinctive uniforms. Many high school athletes wear special "letter" jackets that show participation in sports, as well as positions and honors. Roles are easily identifiable because of the many special garments that act as symbols.

Gender

For many years in Western society, clothing symbolized gender. Women wore skirts and men wore pants. Since pants are accepted clothing for both genders today, slight differences in design now make distinctions. Compare the buttons on men's and women's shirts. What difference do you notice?

In other cultures, clothing styles worn by males and females have evolved quite differently. For centuries in some parts of the world, pants have been worn by both genders. In Lapland, north of the Arctic Circle, both men and women wear pants to protect against subzero temperatures. In Southeast Asia, such as Vietnam and Thailand, men and women wear pants for work and leisure activities.

In other parts of the world, males wear skirts or long robes just as females do. Men in the South Pacific wear a wrapped skirt called a sarong. Arab men wear long, flowing robes. In many African societies, males wear colorful, wrapped skirts of various lengths. Chinese and Japanese men have worn silk robes for centuries. See *Fig. 2-8.*

Values

Clothing and accessories can reflect the values of a culture or specific group. A few examples show how.

Membership in a particular religious group might be symbolized by jewelry with crosses, stars, or other religious symbols. Through dark-colored clothing in simple styles, the Amish show regard for their ancestor's way of living. See *Fig. 2-9* on page 42. Some Jewish men wear a cap called a yarmulka (YAH-muh-kuh) at all times; others wear it only for special occasions and religious services. Followers of Hasidism (HA-suh-dih-zum) stand out from others in the Jewish community with their long coats and dark hats. Seik men, who don't cut their hair, wrap their heads in a turban. Many Muslim women wear a long, scarf-like cloth, called a hijab, to cover the hair and frame the face.

Clothing also reflects cultural views of modesty. In some cultures of the world, wearing very little clothing is acceptable, perhaps only a loincloth for men. In others, women must wear a long veil that completely covers them in public. In

2-8 In oriental countries, robes have been common attire throughout history. Designs, colors, fabrics, and styles have been modified to suit the culture and the purpose. What versions of the oriental robe have you seen?

2-9 In an Amish household, the mother usually sews clothing for the family. She makes bonnets, dresses, aprons, and capes, as well as pants and shirts for the males in the family.

Europe, men of all ages swim in very brief bathing suits, and some women don't wear tops. In the United States, most swimwear is less revealing. On the other hand, Americans are more likely to wear shorts in public, while many Europeans don't believe that shorts are proper street attire.

CLOTHING CUSTOMS

Every society has certain **customs**, long-established practices that regulate social life. See *Fig. 2-10*. While some customs cover etiquette, others relate to clothing. A clothing custom is

2-10 The clothing people choose for a date or to wear to a restaurant is influenced by the customs in a society. How would you dress for such occasions?

born when people adopt a way of dressing for a specific situation. Wearing shorts to a rock concert may be one custom, while wearing dress-up clothes to a symphony concert is another. Knowing the clothing customs in society can help you make decisions about what to wear for different occasions.

Understanding Expectations and Standards

Many people have certain clothing **expectations**, or thoughts about what is reasonable or justified for people to wear. Custom in American society says that males don't wear skirts. Business suits are out of place on a construction site, just as jeans are out of place in many offices. Swimsuits belong on the beach, but not in school classrooms.

Teens often become aware of what others expect of them. A parent's ideas about clothing, hairstyle, and makeup may differ from what the teen likes. An employer, friend, or team members may have certain expectations about how you should dress. An employer expects a well-groomed appearance. See *Fig. 2-11*. As a team leader you might be expected to set an example that shows other members how to dress.

When the majority of people share the same expectations in a society, standards form. **Standards** are the guidelines and principles that set forth what's **appropriate**, or suitable, to wear. Standards may be written or unwritten, and they can change over time.

Dress Codes

On the doors of businesses, you've probably seen signs that warn, "No shirt, no shoes, no service." This statement is a simple **dress code**, a set of rules that describe acceptable or required clothing. Most restaurants require customers to wear shoes and shirts because of health laws. If you don't follow these rules, the restaurant can refuse to serve you.

Many schools and offices have dress codes for students and employees. A general list of clothing items tells what may not be worn, such as no torn jeans, no bared midriffs, no low-cut tops, no hats, and no T-shirts with inappropriate images or messages. Most schools have formal dress codes, which are written. Informal codes are unwritten,

but people are still expected to understand and follow them. When a business has an informal dress code, an employee can usually determine what it is by noting how supervisors dress.

Differing Standards

If you've ever moved from one part of the country to another, you may have noticed that clothing standards differ among communities and regions. Ideas of appropriateness are not always the same.

In an urban area a man might need to wear suits and ties more often than someone who lives in a small community. For women, dresses and pantsuits may be the standard for social events in some communities, while casual sportswear can be worn in others. In resort areas, both men and women may wear brightly colored casual wear for all types of activities.

Choosing Appropriate Styles

Matching clothing to the occasion can be to your advantage. When you need acceptance and approval, the "right" clothing makes a difference. It can make you feel comfortable, relaxed, and self-assured, especially in new situations. By following standards in dress, people feel that they fit in better and the group or community accepts them.

2-11 What does an employer expect concerning clothing and appearance? Here, a clean uniform, confined hair, and personal cleanliness are all likely expectations. Following them contributes to job success.

Job Interviews

On a job interview, a good impression counts. The way you dress for an interview sends a message about the kind of employee you'll be.

Dress for the interview, not the job. Even if employees wear jeans, you should wear clothes suitable for a special dinner out. Dress conservatively—no extreme outfits, heavy makeup, or elaborate hairstyles. With flattering colors and styles, you'll feel more confident. Clean and neat hair, hands, clothes, and shoes create a good impression. You'll find more tips on dressing for a job interview on page 386. By following these guidelines, you can focus the interviewer's attention on your skills and less on your appearance. See *Fig. 2-12.*

On the Job

The trend toward casual clothing has spread to many workplaces. At first, summer Fridays became casual days. Males didn't have to wear business suits and ties to the office on Fridays. Women could wear sportswear and flats instead of tailored outfits and heels. Soon magazines, newspapers, and stores featured casual fashions for office wear. More recently, "business casual," described on page 45, has become acceptable throughout the year in many offices.

Despite changes, most businesses still have dress standards. In some companies, employees wear casual clothes for office work, but traditional business attire when meeting clients or giving presentations. Typically, employees shouldn't look as though they're headed for a picnic or a formal dance. A good general rule is to wear nothing extreme—not too tight, too short, too low, too thin, too bold, too fancy, or too bright. Such inappropriate clothing distracts others and creates wrong impressions.

Special Occasions

Weddings, funerals, and religious services have special clothing expectations and standards. For most weddings held in a church, temple, hotel, or club, guests are expected to wear special-occasion clothes. This means dresses or pantsuits for women, and jackets and ties for men. For some ceremonies, long gowns and tuxedos may be expected. At funerals, people should dress conservatively in darker colors and tailored styles. Wearing dark colors shows respect for the family's loss.

Some religions have special clothing requirements for their services. For example, a head covering may be expected. Others may require that the shoulders be covered. For all religious services, conservative clothes are a good choice.

When going to a fancy party, males usually wear a suit and tie, and females wear dressy clothes. A formal dance may request "black tie."

2-12 If you were an employer considering two equally qualified candidates, would you hire the person who is neat and presentable or the one who is not? Most employers are influenced by an interviewee's appearance. "Putting your best foot forward" can help you get the job.

How To . . . SELECT BUSINESS CASUAL ATTIRE

"Business casual?" the new employee said. "What's that?" Business casual is a dress code used to describe appropriate clothing for many workplaces. Most companies define the code as half way between traditional business attire (suits and ties) and casual clothes (jeans, T-shirts, and athletic wear). Not every workplace interprets "business casual" in exactly the same way, but the ideas listed here are typical. If no written dress code exists, ask your employer what to wear, or notice what leading employees wear.

Acceptable "Business Casual"

Collared shirts

Sweaters

Khakis or slacks

Skirts or casual dresses (women)

Laced or slip-on shoes (loafers, flats, low heels)

Blazer or jacket for presentations and conferences

Jeans and athletic shoes (sometimes acceptable if clean and neat)

Unacceptable Business Attire

Faded, worn, or ripped jeans

T-shirts

Sweatshirts and pants

Cropped tops

Micro-mini skirts

Shorts, cutoffs, and swim trunks

Spandex

Athletic shoes, clogs, and sandals

Any item that isn't clean and neat

Exploring Business Casual

Ask employed adults about business casual policies. What clothing is worn? Compare results in class.

This means a tuxedo for men and formal gowns or fancy dresses for women. See *Fig. 2-13*. With the trend toward more casual clothing, some men are not wearing a tie with a tuxedo or suit. Instead, they might choose a banded shirt or a collarless sweater. High-fashion styles are very acceptable at parties and formal events.

Some fine restaurants require a jacket for men and clothing that is not casual for women. These requirements help create a more formal atmosphere within the restaurant. However, strict dress standards are changing. Now very few restaurants require a tie and many no longer require jackets. This reflects the general trend in society to dress more casually.

Respecting Customs

For some teens, following society's clothing customs may not always seem necessary. An individual style appeals to them, or they want the look shared by a group of friends. Teens often use people in movies and music videos as role models, copying their clothing styles. These performers wear outfits chosen for theatrical effect, however, and what works in the entertainment industry might not work in the real world.

Clothing choices can have negative effects. What problems might unconventional clothing choices cause for a teen at home, school, work, or elsewhere? For teens and adults, doing what's expected makes life go more smoothly. Maturity shows when people follow certain clothing customs because they know they need to get along well with others. See *Fig. 2-14*.

2-13 For some special occasions, a male might wear a tuxedo. Is that customary for the prom at your school? What do females wear?

2-14 The students in this classroom are wearing conventional clothing styles, as expected in their school. Unconventional and inappropriate styles can cause problems that interfere with learning. What might some of those problems be?

Trends in TECHNOLOGY >>FASHION WEB SITES

When you're looking for fashions, Web sites are both shopping tools and virtual fashion magazines. Look what you can find.

- **A virtual fitting room.** You can match body characteristics to such images as broad shoulders, narrow hips, and short legs. After creating your body image, the computer "dresses" it with the garment you choose. The site may suggest other suitable garments. When you input hair color, eye color, and skin tone, flattering color combinations display.

- **Outfit suggestions.** If you order a top, other items to complete the outfit are suggested.

- **Order memory.** Remembering your last order, the site suggests new products that might interest you.

- **Customizing services.** After providing your body measurements, you can select the style, fabric, and fashion details for a custom-made shirt, suit, or jeans. These are usually expensive. Check the cost and read the return policy before ordering.

- **Special information and activities.** You might find grooming tips, prom fashions, polls about what's in and what's not, and live interactive chats with celebrities.

- **E-mail announcements.** Once you've ordered on-line, e-mails provide special announcements and discount offers.

INVESTIGATION ACTIVITY

Find Web sites that offer the features described here. Which would be most useful to you?

Handling Clothing Mistakes

What can you do if you don't know what to wear for a particular occasion? If you know the standard attire for a similar event, you can feel safe wearing that. Otherwise, ask someone. Parents and teachers may know what's acceptable. Friends who have been to similar events might have suggestions. For a party, you can call the host or hostess or ask other guests what they plan to wear. Avoiding extremes—too casual or too dressy—is a good moderate approach.

Suppose you walk into an event and discover you aren't dressed right. That can feel awkward. If you concentrate on talking with other people and getting involved in the activities, the awkward feelings usually lessen. Can you find humor in the situation? Maybe you can joke with someone else who missed the dress "rules." Everyone makes clothing mistakes once in a while, but these are good learning experiences.

Review

CHAPTER SUMMARY

- As an element of culture, clothing often reflects how people think and live, as well as their history.

- Different cultures can often be identified by specific garments.

- Clothing has symbolic meanings related to heritage, occupations, roles, gender, and values.

- A society's clothing customs, expectations, and standards dictate what is considered acceptable to wear in specific situations.

- Following standards for dress in a society can be confusing. Avoiding extremes in attire is the most successful approach.

USING KEY TERMS

Work with a partner. For each Key Term, take one minute to create a list of ideas or examples that describe or relate to that term.

RECALLING THE FACTS

1. In general, how can clothing be a clue to what a society is like?

2. Describe two national costumes.

3. Why is the clothing people wear in many countries similar today?

4. Is there one clothing style that reflects the United States culture? Explain.

5. List ways that clothing symbolizes occupations and roles.

6. How is clothing as a symbol of gender similar and different in different cultures?

7. Describe ways that clothing can reflect a society's values.

8. How do clothing customs and dress codes differ?

9. What results when people in society share similar clothing expectations?

10. In general, how do you "dress for the interview, not the job"?

11. How does "business casual" compare to traditional business clothes?

12. Identify appropriate dress for three special occasions.

13. What problem related to society's clothing standards do some teens face? What is a wise response?

14. How can you minimize the awkwardness of choosing the wrong clothes for an occasion?

and Activities

THINKING CRITICALLY

1. Do ethnic differences in clothing ever cause people to judge others incorrectly? Explain.

2. Some Asian and African countries are developing their economies through trade with the West. Many people in these societies fear that this contact causes them to lose ethnic identity. Is this an unavoidable result of economic improvement? Explain your answer.

3. Why do you think some workplaces have adopted more casual dress codes?

APPLYING KNOWLEDGE

1. **Ethnic costumes.** Working with a small group, look through magazines and newspapers for illustrations of people in ethnic garments. Create a display that identifies each country or region and describes its costume.

2. **Sharing clothing heritage.** Along with other class members, locate ethnic garments and accessories. Show these to the class, demonstrating how they are worn and for what purposes.

3. **Personal heritage.** Research clothing styles worn by people of your cultural background. Write a description of a typical garment, explaining its history and special features.

4. **Costume design.** Design a national costume for the United States. Share your design and explanation with the class.

5. **Wearing pants.** Research who and what influenced women to begin wearing pants in the U.S. You might start by locating information on Amelia Bloomer and Susan B. Anthony.

6. **Following the code.** Locate the section on student dress in your school handbook. Compare that description to what students wear. How closely is the code followed?

CREATIVE SOLUTIONS

A new friend of yours has confided in you. She is a foreign exchange student in your school and comes from a country where the traditional dress is quite different. During the weeks that she has been in your school, she has started to wear American clothing styles much more often. She likes wearing them and feels good about fitting in with the other students, but she feels a sense of guilt and disloyalty to her own culture. She wonders how her family would feel if they knew what she is doing.

Think Creatively

How would you respond to your new friend? What ideas might be helpful to her?

Clothing and Families

OBJECTIVES

- Explain why clothing needs differ among families.

- Explain how family values affect clothing decisions.

- Describe tools and techniques that help families with clothing management.

- Describe ways families can share clothing responsibilities.

KEY TERMS

budget
compromise
delegate
family life
    cycle

management
    process
multiple roles
priorities
resource

WHILE SPENDING A WEEK WITH HER grandparents, a teen and her grandmother browsed through a trunk in the attic, looking at all the old clothing and accessories that had been saved over the years. The styles, fabrics, and colors were fascinating. The teen and her grandmother laughed together over some of the "old-fashioned" looks and admired the beauty of other items. The stories her grandmother told about the items showed the teen how times and families have changed, and yet how much is still the same. The clothing had much to "teach" that day.

FAMILY CLOTHING NEEDS

How do you think family clothing needs have changed over the years? Some things never change. Like your family, your grandparents' families would have needed clothing for protection from the weather as well as clothing for certain occasions. Because society is ever-changing,

however, what your family needs today isn't the same as it was years ago.

Even today, clothing needs differ among families. That's because no two families are exactly alike. What do you think influences the clothing choices that families make? Everything from where they live, to their activities, to the way they earn a living has impact. See *Fig. 3-1*.

Location and Activities

When one teen's family moved from the Sun Belt to a northern state, their clothing needs changed dramatically. While warm weather clothes and only a few sweaters and jackets were suitable year-round before their move, the family had to add a winter wardrobe afterwards. Obviously, families around the country have dif-

3-1 The way a family lives affects their clothing needs. A special dinner might call for dress-up clothes in one family, while more casual clothes work well for another family.

ferent clothing needs. What clothing might a family need for life in a big city? What might they need for rural life in a small town or on a farm?

Often families share activities that call for specific garments. Families that take regular camping and fishing trips might invest in clothing for the outdoors. If they attend cultural events, such as concerts and plays, they need appropriate garments to wear. How does time spent at home reading, playing games, and watching television affect their clothing choices?

Many clothing needs in families are individual. A young dancer in one family needed a leotard and special shoes. A skier in the family wanted a parka, hat, and gloves for skiing. Another family member needed a reflective vest and other garments for jogging. Looking for ways to satisfy individual clothing needs can be challenging in a family.

Multiple Roles

Every family member has **multiple roles**, meaning more than one. These roles include a person's place in the family. A teen could be a son or daughter, brother or sister, niece or nephew, grandchild, and possibly a great-grandchild. See *Fig. 3-2*. Roles also include what people do outside the family. For example, you have roles as a student and a friend. You could also have a role on a sports team or as a part-time employee. Others in your family have outside roles related to work, leisure activities, and community involvement.

If you had only one role in life, clothing decisions might be easier. The fact is multiple roles create multiple clothing needs. A teen who plays team sports probably couldn't wear athletic clothes to an awards banquet. An outfit worn to

3-2   Family members have roles that influence their clothing needs. What roles are indicated here? How are they linked to clothing choices?

school probably wouldn't work for weeding the family garden. What roles in your life affect the clothes you need?

Clothing for work roles is often a high priority in a family. Depending on the occupation, uniforms, suits, casual clothes, or heavy work clothes might be purchased. While the person who works in a store or office may want variety in clothing styles, someone who wears a uniform or works at home is less likely to have this concern.

Stages of Life

If you peeked into the closets of a family with young children and compared the contents to the closets in their grandparents' home, you would find many differences. In part, that's because the people are in different stages of life.

Families are often described as going through stages known as the **family life cycle**. The standard stages are the beginning years when a couple starts out. They have no children at this point. The parenting stage is next, when children are born into the family and raised. At the launching stage, children leave home to go out on their own. The cycle completes with the retirement stage, when the couple are by themselves again. Of course, life isn't quite this simple. Many variations take place, but as the cycle shows, a basic pattern exists.

As explained on the next page, clothing needs change as people move through the stages of family life. You can probably add to the examples that show how each stage has its own impact.

- **Single people and couples with no children.** Fewer family obligations may mean more ability to spend money on clothing. Sometimes clothing is high priority for these individuals.
- **Families with children.** The clothing needs of children must be balanced with adult needs. Because young children grow quickly, outgrown clothing must be replaced regularly. Children often need special clothing for sports, scouts, 4-H, hobbies, and similar activities, which can be costly. Clothing for teens is typically expensive.
- **Empty nest families.** As adult children become self-supporting, the family typically has more money for other expenses.
- **Retirement.** At this stage a couple may be able to refocus on their own needs. If more leisure time is available, casual clothing may replace business clothes. With advanced age and a fixed income, people typically buy fewer new garments. An elderly person may have special clothing needs, seeking comfortable styles that make dressing and undressing easier.

Family Values

Every family has its own set of values, which identify what's important to them. The adults in a family take the lead in establishing basic values. These values then influence the many clothing decisions made by the family and its members.

For any decision, values provide a guide. Suppose a family is buying new school clothes. As busy people who want to spend their limited free time doing something fun, this family chooses easy-care fabrics that are washable and require no ironing. How did values influence their decision?

Values are apparent in many clothing decisions. One family buys clothing on sale because they care about saving money. Another chooses designer labels because they like to look fashionable. A family that values physical activity might own more sportswear than a less active family.

Even clothing gifts show values. Is a hand-knitted sweater more or less appreciated than a more expensive one from the store? Will a family be pleased to receive hand-me-downs for a rapidly growing baby, or do they want only new clothes for the child? When family values are understood, decisions are more easily made.

CLOTHING MANAGEMENT

To manage a household, families consider everything involved—from repairing the sink to cooking meals. Clothing care is a large part of the process. Think about what's involved: making decisions about clothing and budgets; buying clothes; home laundering; taking items to be cleaned to the dry cleaner; storing clothes; ironing; and repairing clothes. In some households sewing clothes is another task.

When family members have multiple roles, managing responsibilities can be a challenge. Sharing family responsibilities is a good way to make sure that no one is overburdened. Resentment can build when one family member has more to do than anyone else, and stress is a common outcome. A bad mood, anger and frustration, and illness are a few signs of stress. To prevent stress, families need to find ways to manage responsibilities effectively.

A useful tool for families to use is the **management process.** Just as a business manager plans how to use resources to achieve goals, family

3-3 • The Management Process

	STEP	PROCEDURE
1	Planning	Assess the situation, develop a list of tasks, identify resources, and set priorities.
2	Organizing	Develop a schedule and gather needed resources.
3	Implementing	Put the plan into action and monitor progress.
4	Evaluating	Evaluate the plan and identify any future changes.

members can do the same. Some situations can be handled much more effectively when guided by the basic, four-step process shown in *Fig. 3-3*.

Setting Clothing Priorities

As part of the management process, a family sets **priorities** by ranking the importance of items or options. Suppose each member in a family can identify a personal clothing need. If money isn't available for everything, priorities are set. A mother's new coat may be higher on the list than a father's new suit. A snowsuit for an infant may be higher priority than a sibling's athletic shoes.

Values contribute heavily when prioritizing. Although each person has a personal point of view, the interest of the entire family can't be overlooked. If a new suit could help the father get a job that pays more, making the suit a high priority may be the best decision, even if that disappoints someone. When families discuss such decisions, all members understand the priorities and goals better.

Identifying Resources

After prioritizing, families need to identify available resources. A **resource** is anything used to reach a goal or manage life. Time, talent, and money are resources. The tools needed for a task, as well as the people who can teach how to use tools, are other resources.

How can resources help when prioritizing clothing needs? The creative family finds many answers to this question. Sewing garments or

accessories might save money that could be spent on something else. To have more money for clothing, is a part-time job possible? Could an item be borrowed? Hunting for the best prices on-line, at a sale, or at a secondhand store might enable the family to buy two or more items. Sharing items with family members is a no-cost way of expanding wardrobes.

Budgeting for Clothes

In most families, income is a limited resource that must be distributed for many expenses. To control spending and cover all expenses, families use a spending plan or schedule called a **budget**. Budgets can be created for the month or year and be written or unwritten. Individuals also use them to manage personal expenses, as you can do with the information on page 56.

Clothing is only one item covered in a family budget. Other items are food, housing, transportation, recreation, medical expenses, and personal expenses for each family member. See *Fig. 3-4*. When itemized, clothing expenses add up. Costs are not just for outfits; they're for underwear, socks, accessories, and shoes too. Cleaning and repair costs must also be included. Careful analysis tells the budget creator what percentage of income can be allotted for clothing.

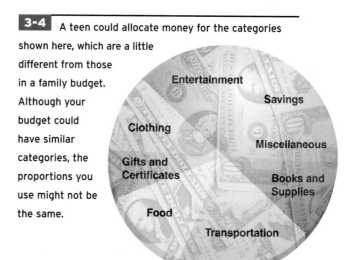

3-4 A teen could allocate money for the categories shown here, which are a little different from those in a family budget. Although your budget could have similar categories, the proportions you use might not be the same.

Entertainment
Savings
Clothing
Miscellaneous
Gifts and Certificates
Books and Supplies
Food
Transportation

Computers are a valuable tool for families. They enable people to write letters, plan a budget, and even design clothing. Record keeping is easier with software that stores data, creates charts, and calculates numbers. Saving files on a backup disk and updating regularly prevents loss if the computer "crashes."

A computer also provides access to the largest resource center in the world. Internet Web sites have information about almost everything. Because anyone can publish information, evaluate

Internet sources carefully. Ask the following questions:

Is the site produced by qualified experts? Read about the authors or host organization and look for credentials. Is the information up-to-date? When were revisions made? Is the purpose to provide information, sell a product, or promote a cause? Is the information inaccurate, incomplete, or biased? Check other sources.

Internet rumors, or "urban legends," are frequently posted on Web sites and passed via e-mails. These rumors often concern a defect in a company's product, an unusual crime, or an unpopular cause that a company is said to promote.

INVESTIGATION ACTIVITY
Some Internet sites offer the truth about urban legends. Search for a site and report on the truth behind urban legends.

Sometimes items in other categories take priority over clothing items. That means limiting clothing expenses. If the family needs a new car, for example, less money might be spent on clothes.

If children and teens receive an allowance, they may be expected to pay for certain needs. Accessories, grooming aids, and minor clothing purchases might be their responsibility. A major item, such as a new coat, could be part of the family budget. Sometimes a teen's allowance or earnings cover all clothing expenses.

Budgeting methods are not right or wrong. Each family determines what works best for them. Through communication, family members become familiar with budget limitations and understand their own spending responsibilities.

Sharing Responsibilities

Clothing takes time and effort to select, clean, store, and repair. Families need to manage these responsibilities.

In some families, each family member may shop for his or her own clothes. In other families, one person may do the clothes shopping for all family members. Responsibilities for clothing care may be handled by one person or shared among family members.

Can you list the roles and responsibilities of each person in your family? Listing your own is easy, but you're likely to overlook items on someone else's list.

How To... MAKE A BUDGET

If you practice budgeting as an individual, you'll learn skills for family budgeting. As shown here, budgeting helps keep spending under control by distributing income among all potential expenses.

Step 1: Determine income. Estimate monthly income by adding all possible sources: paycheck, allowance, and gifts.

Step 2: Keep a record. Record all expenses in a notebook every day for one or two months. Include the cost and a brief description of the expense.

Step 3: Analyze spending. Determine what you spent for clothing, food, entertainment, personal items, transportation, and other expenses. Analyze where the money goes. Are there examples of wasteful spending?

Step 4: Plan expenses. Based on past spending, list how much money you can spend monthly for each category in your budget, including savings. The total should not exceed your estimated income.

Step 5: Use and evaluate the plan. Keep track of spending. Since your objective is to spend no more than was budgeted for each category, limit spending in any category that might go over. If you need more money in a category, raise the budgeted amount, but remember that you have to lower the amount in one or more other categories by an equal amount. Revising the categories is fine as long as the total budgeted amount never exceeds your income.

Exploring **Budgets**

Make a budget that would work for you. Try following it for a period of time.

Delegating and Scheduling

Sharing family responsibilities is a good way to make sure that no one carries too much of the load. Many families delegate tasks to family members. To **delegate** means to assign responsibility to another. For example, one person could be assigned to do the same task all the time. Another option is to rotate responsibilities on a weekly or monthly basis. In some families, each person is responsible for his or her own clothing. In other families, one person does the laundry and others iron and put away their own things. Families can experiment to find a method that works well for them.

Keeping track of responsibilities is easier with schedules. A chart showing each person's assignment and when it should be done keeps the family on track. Many families post charts on a bulletin board or in another visible location.

The approaches families take to clothing management differ according to their standards. One family might want garments carefully folded or hung out of sight after use. Another might not mind that a jacket is draped over the back of a chair for a while.

If roles change, standards may change. Suppose a stay-at-home mother has always done the family laundry. If she becomes employed outside the home, other family members make her life easier by taking on laundering responsibilities.

To make the sharing of responsibilities work, each family member needs to participate, making sure duties are fulfilled. See *Fig. 3-5*. Family bonds grow stronger when people can be trusted to do their part and are thoughtful of others.

Settling Disagreements

Sometimes disagreements occur over priorities and responsibilities. Understanding other points of view takes effort. It can be hard to accept that a sibling's outfit could be more important than the one you need. Sometimes it may seem as though you've been given more responsibilities than others. Unfortunately, such decisions don't always seem fair. Since unfairness is part of life, however, it's usually better to go along, and maybe the next time the advantage will swing in the other direction.

To help resolve disagreements, families can turn to a helpful tool called **compromise**. Through compromise, each person gives up something in order to get something else in return. One teen said, "I can wait a few months for my new jacket, especially since I'll be able to get the one I really want." Another teen said, "I'll do the laundry this month so my sister can practice for her recital. She told me she'd do it for me next month." Both comments show compromise.

At times, compromise isn't obvious. A parent might decide, "What I need can wait for a while." Other family members don't always know that such sacrifices were made.

Compromise isn't an option in every situation. An adult may have the final say, sometimes for reasons that aren't clear to others. Children and teens who learn to be understanding earn the respect of family members.

3-5 Family members share responsibilities to distribute the burden. That can mean taking care of your own clothes and helping others as well.

CHAPTER 3

CHAPTER SUMMARY

- A family's clothing needs depend on where they live, what they do, and the roles of family members.

- Clothing needs change as a family moves through the family life cycle.

- Clothing decisions made within a family are based on each family's set of values.

- Setting priorities and identifying resources are part of the management process.

- A budget is a valuable tool for seeing how clothing needs fit in with a family's other expenses.

- Each family needs to agree on how clothing care tasks are assigned.

- Tasks are often shared in a family, based on each member's roles and responsibilities.

USING KEY TERMS

For each Key Term, write one statement that describes how the term relates to your study of clothing. Write a second statement showing how the term relates to a different field.

RECALLING THE FACTS

1. In what ways do location and activities affect clothing needs in a family?

2. How do roles affect a family's clothing needs?

3. Why is the family life cycle a factor in a family's clothing needs?

4. How are family values useful when making clothing decisions?

5. List clothing responsibilities that a family must manage.

6. Describe the management process.

7. Why is creativity useful when identifying resources?

8. How can computer software help with family management?

9. What clothing-related expenses need to be included in a useful budget?

10. Suppose someone asks, "What is the best way to set up a family budget?" How do you answer?

11. How is delegation useful for meeting family clothing responsibilities?

12. Is compromise the solution to every family problem? Explain.

13. Why is willingness to "go the extra mile" a valued trait for family management?

and Activities

THINKING CRITICALLY

1. Should teens who buy clothes with money earned from a job have more say in clothing choices than teens whose spending money comes from an allowance? Why or why not?

2. Should teens in a family be role models for younger family members in the way they dress? Explain.

APPLYING KNOWLEDGE

1. **Comparing clothing.** Ask adults of your parents' generation to describe the clothing they wore as teens. Ask them to share photos, if possible. What did their parents think of the fashions? Do these adults feel that clothing styles today are significantly different from those of their own teen years? If so, in what ways? Discuss their responses in class.

2. **Interpreting family values.** The following are some values a family might have: (a) spending time together; (b) concern for the environment; (c) saving money. For each value, explain how the family's clothing choices might be affected by that value. Include specific examples.

3. **Stress research.** Locate information on stress. What are the signs of stress and suggestions for managing it?

4. **Delegating duties.** Create a schedule that shows how a fictional family might share clothing responsibilities. Include at least one teen in the family. What tasks must be included? Who will do them and when?

5. **Borrowed clothes.** A teen borrows clothes from a sibling without asking, often returning them dirty or damaged, and sometimes even forgets to return them. What should the sibling do to correct this situation effectively?

6. **Creating consensus.** Plan and present a skit between a teen and a parent about a clothing-related disagreement. Present both points of view and include a resolution. Discuss whether the situation was resolved effectively.

CREATIVE SOLUTIONS

A friend of yours has developed a pattern of behavior that concerns you. Often when she is going out with friends, sometimes to a party, she changes clothes after she leaves her home. She carries with her the clothes that her family finds distasteful and changes at a friend's house. You've noticed that the clothing she chooses has become increasingly immodest, and you're worried about what problems this may cause for her and her relationship with her family.

Think Creatively

Can you approach this situation with your friend? If so, how?

CHAPTER 4

Clothing and Self-Expression

OBJECTIVES

- **Evaluate the importance of first impressions.**

- **Describe how personality can be expressed through clothing.**

- **Compare the effects of conformity and individuality on clothing choices.**

- **Explain how personal style develops.**

KEY TERMS

body language
conformity
impression
individuality
nonverbal
  messages

peer pressure
personality
self-concept
stereotype
verbal
  messages

CLOTHING IS A TOOL USED for self-expression. It can send messages about a person, sometimes accurate and sometimes not. You can use clothing to express your personality, emotions, and individual style.

CREATING IMPRESSIONS

Suppose you were a costume designer for theater productions. For a comedic melodrama about the Old West, you're designing costumes for a hero, a heroine, and a villain. The director wants the audience to be able to distinguish these characters easily from the rest. How would you create the desired effects through costuming?

Just as clothing creates an impression on the stage, it does the same for people in everyday life. An **impression** is an image that forms in the minds of others.

When you walk into a room or are introduced to someone, you create an impression. Judgments are often made quickly. A first impression, usually formed within a minute or two, can be remarkably powerful. It sometimes determines whether a person gets a chance to make a second impression. See *Fig. 4-1.*

How can people form impressions so quickly? They interpret what they see and hear rapidly and with little thought. Visual and verbal clues link to assumptions that may or may not be true. Clothing offers clues, but people usually take in more. Words, behavior, and physical appearance add to a first impression.

Appearance

Often people notice what a person is wearing before they see the face or hear the voice. The style, color, fit, and neatness of clothing influence opinions. An impression, however, is based on a combination of clothes, grooming, and general health.

Good grooming gives the finishing touch to a pleasing appearance. To do a checkup, look at your hair, skin, hands, and teeth. Does your hair shine from being washed and brushed regularly?

4-1 Do you think a positive first impression is more valuable in some situations than others? If so, when might that be?

4-2 Hair looks good when it's clean and shiny. What else contributes to a positive appearance?

Is your skin clean and healthy-looking? Are your hands clean and your nails trimmed neatly? Have you brushed your teeth? Is your breath fresh? Your skin, hair, hands, and mouth all need daily attention to look your best. See *Fig. 4-2*.

Good general health is best promoted with proper eating habits and exercise. Paying attention to these has an impact on appearance too.

Behavior

Have you heard the saying "Actions speak louder than words"? A person's behavior, especially toward others, speaks loud and clear. Suppose a waiter drops a plate full of food in a restaurant. One coworker yells at the waiter; a second coworker helps pick up the mess. What impression does the behavior of each employee make on the customers?

The way a person behaves toward others shows much about the person. Politeness gives one impression, while rudeness sends another. Manners usually have a strong influence on whether an impression is favorable or unfavorable.

Behavior is conveyed through verbal and nonverbal messages. **Verbal messages**, communication with words, are easy to observe. The tone of voice and the specific words spoken quickly add to an impression. **Nonverbal messages**, or communication without words, are also noticeable.

Body Language

People send nonverbal messages with **body language**. This consists of eye contact, facial expressions, posture, arm and leg positions, and even distance from others. Many feelings and attitudes are expressed, consciously or subconsciously, through body language. If you've watched a mime perform, you've seen a dramatic example of how a person can communicate with only the face and body rather than words.

By noticing body language, people form opinions. The following observations are common:

- **Eye contact.** Looking directly at another person shows interest, warmth, and self-confidence. Averting the eyes shows disinterest, shyness, or nervousness.
- **Facial expression.** The face has many muscles that control expressions. Much of what goes on in a person's mind finds expression in the face. See *Fig. 4-3*.
- **Posture.** A straight, comfortable posture shows self-assurance and a positive attitude. Sloping shoulders and slumping posture give a negative appearance.

4-3 Raised eyebrows show surprise; frowns show disappointment. A smile suggests happiness or friendliness, and a down-turned mouth seems sad. What do the facial expressions say here?

Body language and tone of voice clarify messages. Without these clues, written communication can be misunderstood. Since on-line contact is common today, remember the following guidelines:

- If they're understood, abbreviations or acronyms can shorten a message. Popular ones include FYI (for your information), BTW (by the way), TNX (thanks), and SYL (see you later).

- Be cautious about typing words in all capital letters. This is the electronic equivalent of shouting.

- If understood, symbols called *emoticons* can express feelings. Sideways, emoticons look like a face.

:-)	= happy	:-...	= broken hearted
:-(	= sad	;-)	= just kidding
:-@	= angry		(wink)
%-)	= confused	:-!	= foot in mouth
:-e	= disappointed	:^D	= Great! I like it!

- Avoid discussing personal or sensitive issues that you wouldn't want others to read. A misplaced click can forward such messages to others.

- In an on-line chat group, avoid criticism, called "flaming."

- If your message can't be said face-to-face, don't put it in an e-mail.

INVESTIGATION ACTIVITY

Talk with people who use e-mail regularly to gather examples of misunderstood Internet communication.

- **Arm and leg positions.** Open and relaxed positions of the arms and hands demonstrate receptiveness and friendliness. Closed and clenched positions show anger, discomfort, and nervousness. Legs planted squarely or comfortably relaxed show that the person is secure in the situation. Tapping the fingers or a foot probably means that the person is nervous, bored, or impatient with what's going on.
- **Distance.** How far a person sits or stands from another can indicate feelings. Everyone is surrounded by "personal space." Coming too close to an individual and invading that space

may make the person feel uncomfortable. Close friends usually stand only 6 to 8 inches (15 to 20 cm) apart. Other people stand farther apart but may slowly move closer together to show friendliness.

Accuracy of First Impressions

No matter who they are, people are judged by first impressions. What first impressions have you formed lately about different people you've met?

First impressions affect your judgment of others, just as your own appearance and behavior affect what others think about you. Unfortunately,

Fashion Facts

first impressions can be misleading. Suppose a new student sits next to you at lunch. Her eyes are red and puffy. She sniffs often, and barely touches her food. She seems upset. You're about to ask if you can do anything to help when she sighs and says, "I just can't shake this cold."

What impression might you make about someone who is wearing a soiled sweatshirt, baggy pants, and dirty shoes? Perhaps the person has a smudged face and messed-up hair. Is the person really sloppy and unkempt, or has he just finished washing a car? Perhaps he has just returned from a five-mile run. In all fairness, you should stop and evaluate your impression of another person before you make a quick judgment.

Another risk of judging too quickly is forming an incorrect impression through stereotyping. A **stereotype** is a simplified and standardized image of a person or group. A stereotype tries to sum up another person's entire character based on a few obvious traits, such as race, age, size, or gender. People are also stereotyped by the way they look and the type of clothes they wear. An unusual hairstyle, for example, may make people think that a teen is a rebel. A letter sweater or jacket makes some people think the wearer excels at sports. These are two examples of stereotyping through appearance. What other examples come to mind?

While judging on appearance may be a natural first reaction, the thoughtful person looks past differences in clothes and focuses instead on the person who wears them. It is a sign of maturity to understand that words and actions are truer signs of character than clothing styles, especially when given the test of time.

WHAT CLOTHING COMMUNICATES

Why do people pay attention to the messages sent by clothing? They tend to focus on clothes because, unlike height and eye color, clothing is a choice. Wearing an inappropriate outfit to a job interview, for example, reflects on the person who decided to wear it. It calls attention to that person's judgment. It makes the interviewer wonder about qualities like attitude, awareness, and sensibility.

By learning what clothing communicates, you can become more aware of how others might react to the clothing you choose to wear. Your clothing selections can help you manage those reactions. You'll be better able to send the messages about yourself that you truly want to send.

What can clothing convey? Clothing tells people about your personality. It can connect you with a group of people or set you apart in some way. While first impressions can change, lasting impressions grow from the clothing styles you regularly wear.

Personality

When Clark Kent ducked into a phone booth to become Superman, he traded his business suit for a cape, mask, belt, and boots. This change of clothing symbolized his personality change from mild-mannered reporter to super hero.

Personality is an individual's unique combination of mental, emotional, and social qualities. You express your personality through your attitudes, emotions, and behavior. Are you outgoing and talkative, or quiet and shy? Are you self-confident or unsure of yourself? Do you like to be unique in your clothing selections? The answers to these questions reveal your personality.

Your personality influences the clothing styles you prefer. In turn, your clothing choices can reflect your changing moods and self-image. You can deliberately express your personality through the clothes you wear. See *Fig. 4-4*.

Emotions

Have you ever wondered why you don't feel like wearing a particular item of clothing at certain times? Maybe it doesn't match your mood.

Emotions can affect clothing choices. If you're happy and cheerful, you may reach for bright, bold colors. If you're feeling down, you may subconsciously select dark colors. You may even choose a favorite article of clothing that gives you a sense of comfort and security.

4-5 Self-concept is more visible than you might think. How does it show here?

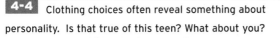

4-4 Clothing choices often reveal something about personality. Is that true of this teen? What about you?

Clothing is also useful for communicating emotions. Wearing clothes that you like can inspire self-confidence and communicate that assurance to others. If you're nervous about presenting an oral report to the class, for example, choose an outfit that makes you feel good. Wearing a favorite outfit can do much to boost your confidence.

Self-Concept

Have you ever looked at a photo or video of yourself and said, "That doesn't look like me"? What you saw didn't fit the image you have of yourself—your **self-concept**. Thoughts about who you are and what you're like can be positive, negative, or somewhere in between.

Self-concept can actually influence how a person looks. If you see yourself as friendly and cheerful, that's how you'll act. See *Fig. 4-5*. You project positive feelings. A warm, friendly smile and a ready handshake suggest a positive self-concept. People with a positive self-concept often have a sense of pride in appearance that influences what clothing they decide to wear and how they take care of it. They want to look presentable. A negative self-concept can be projected too—through mannerisms as well as clothing. Looking presentable may not feel like a worthy goal to someone with a negative self-concept.

You may wonder what image you project. To find out how others see you, notice their reactions to you. Ask a close friend and a relative how they see you. Could you present a more positive image? Making positive changes can actually improve self-concept. Because appearance is an important part of image, especially in the teen years, flattering clothes contribute to a positive self-concept. During this course, you'll learn how to select colors, fabrics, and styles that will help you make the best of your appearance—and boost your self-concept.

Conformity

To feel good about themselves, most people want approval from others. For teens this feeling can be strong. They identify with peers and want to wear what others in their group wear. Through **conformity**, a teen goes along with certain standards, attitudes, or practices followed by the group. Conformity brings a sense of identity, belonging, and security. The teen feels accepted as part of the group. See *Fig. 4-6.*

Within a peer group, appearance may be regulated by written or unwritten rules. Specific clothing styles, brands, and colors may be approved or disapproved. Usually there is an "in" way of dressing. Certain accessories may be important to the group, which identifies the "right" shoes, boots, belts, hats, or backpacks to own.

Peer Pressure

Sometimes members of a peer group are expected, and even pressured, to dress in the approved way. The peer group's push to conform is called **peer pressure**. Clothing that doesn't fit the group's standards may be criticized. The person may be talked about, laughed at, or teased.

Some peer pressure is gentle and used to help members develop a sense of belonging and togetherness. Group members can benefit from such positive peer pressure. For example, conforming to school and community customs can bolster a teen's self-confidence. It can help a new employee fit in with coworkers and feel more at ease on the job.

Peer pressure can be strong and cruel, however, forcing people to conform or be excluded from the group. To resist negative peer pressure, you need confidence that comes from a clear understanding of your own self-concept and values.

When imposing a dress code, a peer group can be highly critical, sometimes thoughtlessly so, of anyone who fails to meet the code. Name-calling, labeling, and exclusion from the group and its activities can follow. Such behavior often reflects a lack of self-confidence. People who are insecure or unhappy with their own identity may feel threatened

4-6 Many teens like the feelings of security and belonging that come when they wear similar clothing.

by someone who doesn't follow the peer group's standards. Undermining the other person's identity helps reassure them of their own.

Handling Peer Disapproval

Almost everyone experiences peer disapproval at some time, and clothing is an obvious target. Understanding the source of criticism and its motivation reveals how to handle it. Is it the opinion of a friend who has your best interests at heart, or does it come from someone you barely know? Does it concern the appropriateness of your outfit, or is it about your appearance? For example, "The saying on that T-shirt will hurt a lot of people" deserves more consideration than "No one wears that color anymore."

If a remark was intended to be helpful, try to accept it that way. If it was meant as a joke, laugh it off. If it was designed to be cruel, consider the reasons for such destructive behavior, and walk away.

Keep the same advice in mind when you're tempted to comment on someone's outfit. Ask yourself: Are my views wanted and helpful? What is the worst that could happen if I say nothing?

Even if your opinion is specifically requested, be sensitive to another's feelings. If someone asks, "What do you think of this sweater?" you might comment that it fits well or has an interesting pattern. You don't need to mention that the hot orange color is painful to look at. With practice, you'll find that truth doesn't have to hurt.

Individuality

Almost everyone has a strong desire to be part of a group. On the other hand, people feel the need to be original in some way. As a teen's self-confidence grows, the need to express individuality increases. **Individuality** is the total combination of characteristics that set one person apart from another. See *Fig. 4-7.* Clothing styles, colors, and accessories contribute to individuality when they are different from the norm. Expressing individuality can start a trend when others want to dress the same way.

The desire to express individuality can conflict with the desire to conform. Wanting to satisfy both impulses can be confusing. You may want to dress like your peers in order to belong. At the same time, you may want your clothes to represent you, not everybody else.

If you have a conflict between individuality and conformity, the middle ground provides a good comfort zone. If everyone in your group wears jeans of a certain style or brand, you could go ahead and wear them too. Then show individuality by completing your outfit with a unique shirt or sweater that suits you. As you do this more often, you may find that your peers are less concerned with what you wear than you thought.

DEVELOPING YOUR PERSONAL STYLE

"Try this on! It looks just like you!" Have you ever been shopping with friends who said this to

4-7 Clothes offer a way for a teen to show individuality through color, pattern, and style choices. Are you more comfortable with conformity or individuality?

you? What did they mean? Your friends were trying to say they know something about you. They have some definite ideas about the kind of clothes that match your personality. Did you agree with their selection, or were you amazed that they picked out something you didn't like at all?

As you decide what clothing to buy and wear, your own personal style evolves. Some people have a strong desire to dress exactly like a friend or someone they admire. When people imitate others by wearing the same hair and clothing styles, they become a "copy." They lose their own distinctiveness.

People who adopt extreme clothing styles create a false image. They may dress in ways that are too old, too young, too extreme, or too bizarre. Some are trying to be something that they aren't. Some are trying to fulfill a need for attention.

Putting too much emphasis on appearance is usually a mistake. Time, effort, and money spent to look "just right" take away from other interests and activities. On the other hand, showing no interest in appearance and clothes causes problems. Always looking sloppy or wearing the same clothes everywhere can interfere with relationships. Either too much or too little concern with clothes may limit experiences in life.

Choices and Consequences

Every decision has consequences, even decisions about clothing. Decisions that are thoughtfully made are likely to bring satisfying results. Poor decisions, however, lead to conflicts, disapproval, and missed opportunities. What difficulties might result from the following clothing decisions made by a teen?

- Regularly wears clothes disapproved by parents.
- "Lives" in jeans and T-shirts without owning any dressy clothes.
- Wears the same colors and styles worn by gangs.
- Buys only trendy fashions.

The consequences of these clothing choices can be simple or serious. Personal safety could even be at stake. What consequences might come from the clothing decisions you make? Mature teens recognize possible consequences and take steps to prevent problems. They learn from mistakes and make corrections.

Searching for the "Real" You

The teen years are a time to look inward and evaluate who you are and who you want to be. As part of this exploration, some teens experiment with clothes by trying new styles, colors, and fabrics. One teen wore only black and white clothing for a while. Another experimented with hair color. Still another decided to change her "look" every few months.

Exploration allows you to learn more about yourself—how you look, how you want to look, and how others see you. You will discover what you like and what is best for you. See *Fig. 4-8.* By the time you reach adulthood, you'll probably have a clearer image of yourself.

Although many teens experiment with their appearance, some search in different ways, perhaps through hobbies, friendships, and other exploration. Wherever your road to adulthood takes you, evaluate your choices carefully to avoid long-lasting negative impacts on your life. Staying in charge of your exploration will help you stay in charge of your life.

4-8 A teen who likes to be bold and trendy one time might experiment with a different look later. That's part of exploration during the teen years.

How To... CHOOSE ACCESSORIES

Accessories complete an outfit. Whether the item is expensive or not, consider how it will go with the clothes in your wardrobe. Some information that helps when buying accessories is provided here.

Jewelry. There are two basic types of jewelry. Fine jewelry is made from gold, silver, or platinum and may contain precious or semiprecious stones, such as diamonds, emeralds, jade, and turquoise. Costume jewelry is made of metal, plastic, leather, beads, or other materials. Some is coated with gold or silver and set with imitation stones to look like fine jewelry.

Shoes. When choosing shoes, a good fit is essential. Ill-fitting shoes can cause poor posture and painful foot disorders, such as bunions, blisters, and corns. Most shoes have a number and letter to indicate size—the larger the number, the larger the shoe. Some come in half sizes, such as 8½. The letter indicates width—from AAA (very narrow) to EEE (very wide). Because sizes vary among manufacturers, always try on both shoes.

Wear socks or hosiery similar to what will usually be worn with the shoes. Shop late in the day when feet are largest. Many athletic shoes are designed for specific sports or activities; others are multi-purpose.

Socks and hosiery. Socks are sized 8 to 13, according to foot length. Wearing the wrong size can be uncomfortable and cause ingrown toenails. Stretch socks fit any foot size. Panty hose and tights are sized by height and weight. Consult the chart on the package.

Backpacks and handbags. Available in a wide variety of sizes, shapes, and materials, these items should have smooth seams, sturdy straps or handles, secure fasteners, and handy compartments for storing items. Try backpacks on to check comfort.

Exploring Accessories

Hats are another accessory. Find out how they are sized and determine your hat size.

Review

CHAPTER SUMMARY

- All aspects of a person's appearance and behavior combine to create an impression on others.

- First impressions are often misleading and should not be the basis for judgments about a person.

- Clothing can communicate an individual's personality, emotions, and self-concept.

- Handling pressure to conform, especially from peers, takes a clear self-concept and sense of values.

- People develop a personal style to satisfy the need to express their individuality.

- Clothing decisions carry consequences, which mature people consider when choosing how to dress.

USING KEY TERMS

Choose one Key Term and try to communicate it nonverbally. You might demonstrate the term, draw a cartoon, or find pictures that illustrate it. Have classmates identify the term.

RECALLING THE FACTS

1. Explain how people form impressions of others.

2. Is a flattering outfit enough to create a pleasing appearance? Why or why not?

3. What body language might show that a person is worried about something?

4. What is a stereotype? What problem does it cause?

5. Why is it worthwhile to know what clothing communicates to others?

6. How can clothing choices relate to emotions?

7. How can self-concept affect personal appearance?

8. A friend says, "I finally found these shoes at the third store I tried. They cost a lot and the style's not my favorite, but I had to have them." What might have caused your friend's actions?

9. If someone criticizes your clothes, how should you respond?

10. Describe one way to meet both the need for conformity and individuality in clothing choices.

11. What difficulties do some teens have in trying to develop a personal style?

12. What problems may come from making clothing decisions without thinking about consequences?

13. Why do teens often experiment with different clothing styles and looks?

and Activities

THINKING CRITICALLY

1. What do you focus on when forming impressions of other people? Evaluate your fairness and accuracy.

2. What type of clothing might threaten a teen's safety? Why?

APPLYING KNOWLEDGE

1. **First impressions.** From a magazine or newspaper, cut out three pictures of people. Write your impression of each person based on the clothing worn. Exchange pictures with a friend or classmate and repeat the activity. Compare descriptions. What does this activity suggest about first impressions?

2. **Mistaken impressions.** In writing, complete the following: "I remember when my first impression of someone was wrong. This happened when . . ." Add information to explain why you formed the impression and what made it change. What do the overall experiences of classmates suggest about first impressions?

3. **Body language.** Locate an article that gives additional information on interpreting body language. Summarize the main points for the class.

4. **Fashion expressions.** Hold a fashion expressions day. Bring or wear a garment that you think shows your personality well or that indicates an emotion you sometimes have. Describe for the class how this garment is a tool for self-expression.

5. **Self-image.** On a piece of paper, write a self-portrait. Explain how you see yourself, including your appearance, voice, talents, interests, social skills, and emotional traits. Then ask two people who know you well to write their own description of you. Compare the three views. What might explain any differences?

6. **Peer pressure.** Suppose a good friend of yours associates with a group of peers who wear clothing that often conflicts with your school's dress code. Your friend wants you to be part of the group, but you don't want trouble. You also don't want to lose a friendship. What would you do?

CREATIVE SOLUTIONS

You've overheard some classmates making fun of the unusual styles that a new student wears. The student doesn't seem to notice the impression these clothes create. You respect your new classmate's right to dress according to individual tastes. At the same time, you think that if you were in that person's position, you'd like to know how others are reacting to your appearance.

Think Creatively

What action, if any, do you take in this situation? Why?

Careers
Fashion Promotion

A S MANY SHOPPERS HAVE SAID, "This looks too good to resist—I'll take it." In the world of fashion promotion, these words are music to the ears, and cash in the bank. When someone decides to buy a garment, the professionals who promote the product are largely responsible. That includes people who work in marketing, advertising, and public relations.

In the competitive field of fashion, eye-catching images, catchy phrases, and creative techniques can mean the difference between selling and not selling. Where have you seen examples of fashion promotion? In magazines, newspapers, and brochures? On a fashion Web site? At a mall fashion show? Someone has to plan and carry out all these efforts.

Fashion promotion starts with careful research into what consumers want and at what price. To convince the public that they "must" have certain clothes, a team might develop a special campaign. In one career, a person might study sales figures. Someone might travel far and wide to persuade retailers to carry a line of clothing. If anything can be done to sway the consumer to choose one product over another, someone in fashion promotion is probably doing it.

IS THIS FIELD FOR YOU?

Understanding fashion is useful but not essential to start a fashion promotion career. These statements are better indicators that a person might fit well in the field.

- I have plenty of physical and mental energy.
- I have confidence in my ideas.
- I'm not upset by changes in plans or routine.
- I enjoy travel.
- I'm not afraid to take risks.
- I enjoy working with different people.
- I respect other people's views and concerns.
- I can argue my side of an issue persuasively.
- I can predict people's expectations and reactions in a given situation.

A catalog that is carefully written and has eye appeal helps sell clothing. These copywriters must be accurate but creative when describing merchandise.

Education and Training

Specialized training after high school is an advantage in fashion promotion. What you need varies with the career. Basic computer skills are expected in almost every area since record keeping is common. As the fashion trade continues to expand around the world, foreign language skills are valued. A market researcher may have a master's degree in business administration, with a good grounding in math and statistics. A bachelor's degree in graphic arts or journalism could launch an advertising career. For models, courses in dance and public speaking teach grace and poise.

Some firms hire new graduates, who go through a formal training program. Others offer internships, where classroom studies are rounded out with work experience. Newer workers train under older ones and learn from their experience. To encourage advancement, employers may sponsor continuing education programs that build job skills. Paying to send a sales manager to an international marketing seminar, for example, can increase both the employee's and the company's earnings.

Possible Career Paths

Career paths in fashion promotion are as varied as the starting points. In public relations, a research assistant could become a public relations specialist, then a manager, and finally a vice president. A copywriter might rise through the advertising ranks to copy chief, then creative director, and ultimately advertising manager. Using modeling as a stepping-stone, a model might become a fashion editor.

Because similar skills are needed for some jobs in fashion promotion, moving between careers is possible. With a gift for expression, a copywriter in the advertising department could become a speechwriter in public relations.

Sales representatives need good communication skills, whether selling fabrics to a store or handbags to a boutique.

THE SKILLS YOU NEED

A confident, outgoing personality is needed for fashion promotion. In addition to genuinely enjoying the company of others, successful people should have the following skills:

- Communication
- Organization
- Management
- Analytical thinking
- Creativity
- Enthusiasm

Choosing a *Fashion Promotion Career*

ART/CREATIVE DIRECTOR | COPYWRITER | DISPLAY DESIGNER | *FASHION MODEL* | FASHION PROMOTION SPECIALIST | *GRAPHIC DESIGNER* | MARKET ANALYST | PUBLIC RELATIONS SPECIALIST | *SALES REPRESENTATIVE*

Market Analyst

As a teen, do you pay more attention to magazine or radio ads? Market analysts want to know. To make sound decisions, businesses need the information that analysts gather. Market analysts develop and interpret opinion polls. They study consumer needs and attitudes, using telephone surveys, in-store interviews, "mystery shoppers," and discussions with selected "focus groups."

Marketing analysts look at past sales patterns to make predictions for the future. With the information they provide, a company can pinpoint how many shirts to ship to a particular part of the country. They may even determine whether a designer's new line will be profitable for the company.

Sales Representative

Without sales representatives, the fashion world couldn't survive. Using their persuasive skills, sales reps convince people to buy. A textile mill's rep might sell stain-resistant fabric to a uniform manufacturer. In turn, the manufacturer's rep offers the stain-resistant uniforms to a restaurant chain's buyer.

Knowing a product well makes selling easier. Sales reps build loyalty by advising clients on how to reduce costs and increase sales.

They report to the employer, on market conditions, buyers' concerns, and competitors' activities. Travel, between towns or across oceans, is part of selling.

Public Relations Specialist

How does a shoe company become involved in sponsoring a road race? How does a fashion reporter learn about a designer's new collection? Often, a public relations (PR) specialist is at work.

PR specialists get the word out to consumers and the media. They invite reporters to press conferences, plan promotional events, and arrange factory tours. They also coordinate with marketing and advertising personnel to announce and organize grand opening events.

As part of their work, public relations specialists set up and manage events. They prepare promotional materials that include press releases and pamphlets.

Fashion Model

Not all fashion models walk on high-fashion runways or appear on magazine covers. Some are simply the feet in a shoe ad or the unknown model in a clothing catalog. Most models sign with agencies that send them to auditions, or "go-sees," in search of jobs. The job often means striking poses for hours under hot studio lights, while remaining patient, poised, and enthusiastic. Job insecurity and constant attention to appearance can add stress.

Building a reputation as reliable and cooperative leads some models to success. Only a few, however, earn the pay-offs of travel, fame, and fortune. The right "look," combined with initiative, perseverance, and luck, makes the difference.

Models with an eye for design may become consultants to leading designers or develop their own line of clothing. Since work is uneven and popularity can fade, smart models plan for a second career and invest wisely.

Models work in many areas of fashion promotion. Someone with an interest in modeling could start by finding opportunities to model at local fashion shows.

Graphic Designer

In the fashion industry, a picture may be worth more than a thousand words. Graphic designers are in demand wherever illustrations are needed to add color and interest. Working with art directors, graphic designers develop company Web sites, magazine ads, promotional pamphlets, and clothing catalogs. With input from market analysts and fashion designers, they create logos that appear on different clothing lines.

Graphic designers also contribute behind the scenes. Sales reports, which are often used to attract investors, are more effective with a design that adds life to pages of statistics. A bold, trendy design in company newsletters and other public relations literature reflects well in a business where "image is everything."

CAREER APPLICATIONS

1. **Market Research.** Develop a twenty-item questionnaire designed to gather data about color preferences in clothing. Distribute copies of your survey to a certain group, such as classmates or older adults. Analyze responses and record them in a chart or table. How might such information be used in the fashion industry?

2. **FCCLA.** Select a career in fashion promotion. Plan an Applied Technology Project that studies and demonstrates how computers are used in the career. What tasks are done? What software is needed? How does it operate? Include a software demonstration as part of the project.

3. **Professionalism.** You're a copywriter for an ad agency. You've been directed to write copy for a fashion campaign, but you're worried that the campaign might offend some consumers. The campaign idea originated with the director of the agency. How will you handle the situation?

UNIT 2
The Fashion World

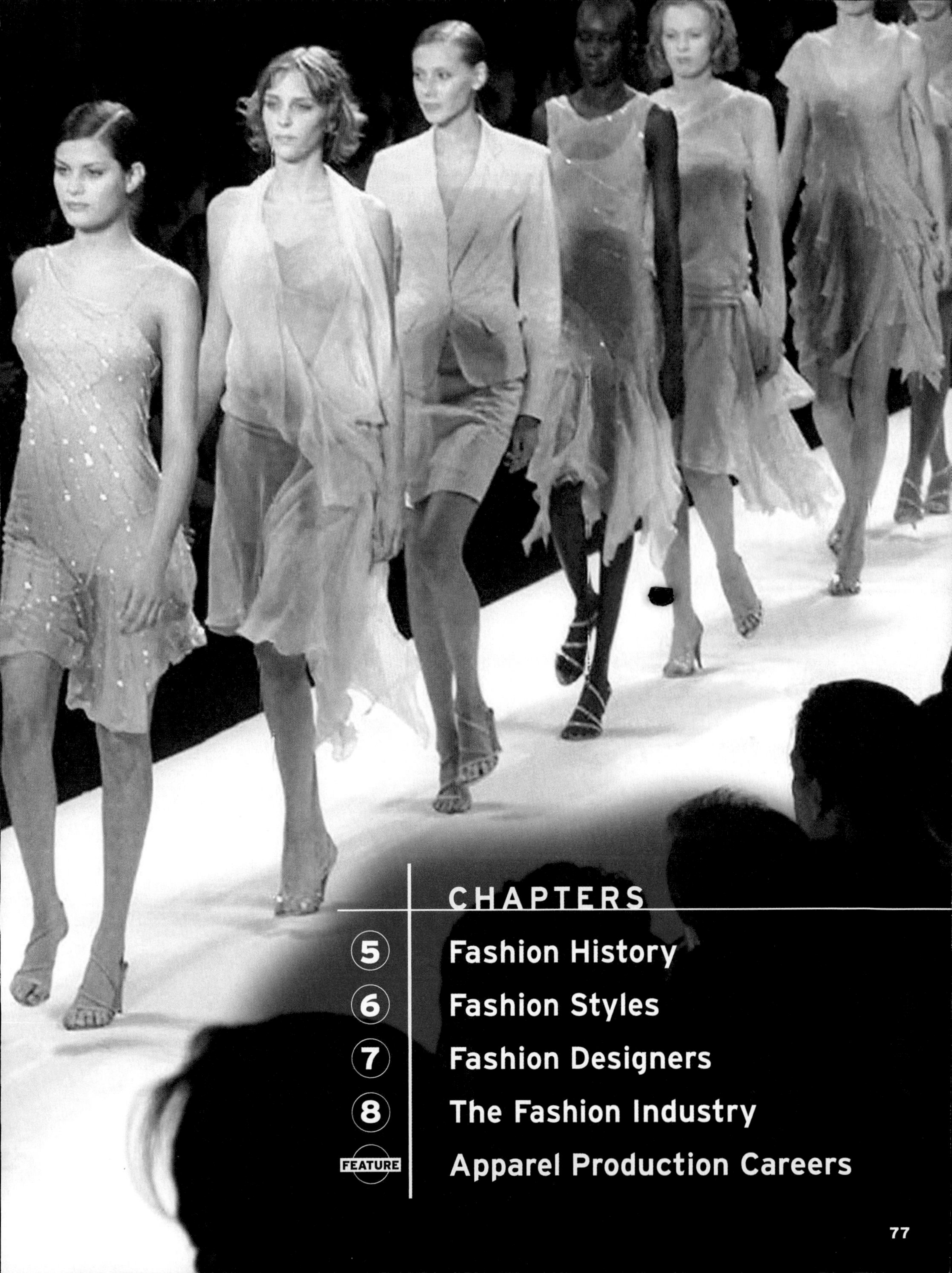

CHAPTERS

Fashion History

OBJECTIVES

- Explain how the first clothes and fabrics were made and worn.

- Describe the evolution of fashions from early civilizations to the nineteenth century.

- Discuss factors that influenced fashion history.

- Give examples of clothing styles in the twentieth century.

KEY TERMS

barter	sumptuary
cellulose	laws
Industrial	sweatshops
Revolution	technology
ready-to-wear	

WHEN YOU SLIP ON A FAVORITE PAIR of blue jeans, do you stop to think that a coal miner born 150 years ago appreciated the same sturdy, riveted denim construction? When you put on running shoes, do you realize that a Briton sheepherder laced his boots in the same crisscross pattern 1500 years ago? Throughout history, garment styles have reappeared. They may look the same or they may be changed slightly to reflect new needs and new technology.

THE EARLIEST CLOTHING

Thousands of years ago, people learned to make clothing from natural resources as protection from weather. Animal skins and hair, plants, grasses, and tree bark were some of the materials used. Because ancient people left visual records, people today know what early clothes were like. Drawings in caves and ancient Egyptian tombs provide records. Surviving sculptures of the Greeks and Romans also show clothing styles of the times.

The First Clothes and Fabrics

The earliest clothing was very simple in construction and design. Looking for food and shelter left little time to decorate clothes.

In northern Europe, where cold weather stretches from early fall to late spring, cave dwellers dressed in animal skins. For comfort these may have been worn hair side in. See *Fig. 5-1.*

In Africa, the South Pacific, and parts of Asia, people needed protection from the sun and rain. They laced grasses together to form woven fabric, probably used at first for mats and baskets rather than clothing. Parts of plants, such as the bark of trees, were soaked and treated until soft enough for cloth. Fragments of textiles dating back to about 7500 B.C. have been unearthed in southern Turkey.

As early as 5000 B.C., people in Egypt made linen cloth from flax plants that grew along the

5-1 Early people stitched animal skins together to make garments. After rubbing the skins with stones or beating them with sticks to soften them, they punched holes in the leather. Using sinews, string-like tendons from animals, and special tools made from bones, they laced the holes.

Nile River. A few thousand years later, inhabitants of present-day India and Pakistan, and possibly the Americas, produced fabric made of cotton. At about the same time in China, silkworms were raised for their silken cocoons.

Fashions of Early Civilizations

As civilizations developed, people learned to raise animals and grow crops.

While refining the arts of spinning, weaving, and dyeing, they began to cut fabric into garments. The earliest, simplest garment was a rectangle of fabric wrapped or draped about the body. This was the most convenient way to make a garment. A rectangle of fabric was easy to wash and could be smoothed out to dry.

Ancient Egypt

The Egyptian civilization has flourished in northern Africa's Nile River valley for thousands of years. Early garments, made from lightweight linen and cotton, were well suited to the hot climate. Drawings, mummy cases, and actual fabrics discovered in the tombs of Egyptian pharaohs

5-2 In ancient Greece a himation was often worn over a chiton. The himation, a rectangular piece of fabric, was draped with an end over one shoulder and the other end over the opposite arm.

ATHENIANS CONVERSING.

reveal the fashions of the day. Men wore knee-length skirts tied in front. A sleeved, shirt-like garment completed the outfit. Women wore long, straight dresses that tied behind the neck or at the shoulder. Some had short sleeves. A short shawl was often tied around the shoulders. Both men and women wore wide collars made of beads or semiprecious stones.

Minoan Contribution

The Minoan civilization was distanced from the Egyptians by the Mediterranean Sea—and about 3000 years. Minoan society reached its peak around 1700 B.C. on the island of Crete.

The women wore some of the first recorded examples of fitted garments. Their full skirts were stretched into a bell shape, possibly over hoops made of wood or rushes. Jackets were short and formfitting, with elbow-length sleeves. The colorful fabrics featured geometric designs or nature prints. Small hats were popular.

Ancient Greece

If you've ever seen pictures of centuries-old Greek vases and life-size statues, you're familiar with the clothing of ancient Greece. Detailed descriptions have been found in carefully written accounts. The Greeks fashioned their garments by elaborately wrapping, draping, and pinning long, rectangular pieces of fabric, which took dozens of square feet of fabric.

Both men and women wore a garment called a chiton (KY-tun). It consisted of two fabric rectangles joined at the shoulders and held in place by jeweled pins. The fabric was folded to fall in pleats from the shoulders to the hem. Sometimes a himation (hih-MA-tee-ahn) was worn as a cloak, as shown in *Fig. 5-2*.

Early Greek garments were woolen. With the conquests of Alexander the Great around 330 B.C., linen and silk became available to wealthier classes. A very fine himation might have a colorful design of red, purple, yellow, and blue.

Roman Empire

As Roman rule spread from present-day Italy into Greece, many elements of Greek culture,

5-3 Because the Roman toga was made from a long piece of fabric, the wearer frequently needed help with wrapping the garment.

including clothing styles, were adopted. The Greek himation became the basis for the Roman toga.

The long piece of toga fabric was cut into a rectangle or semicircle. It was then wrapped around the body, always exposing the right arm and usually covering the left arm. See *Fig. 5-3*. Different colors identified various occupations and class ranks. Only the emperor could wear a purple toga.

A tunic was worn underneath the toga. It fell over the shoulders and down the arms, forming sleeves. Many men wore gold rings and bracelets.

Women wore a stola, a long, belted robe similar to the Greek chiton. Over the stola a wrap called a palla was worn. This Roman copy of the Greek himation was worn in much the same manner. Jewelry included necklaces, brooches, earrings, and gold wedding rings.

China and Japan

In ancient times, China was a region of many different nations. In 221 B.C., the Qin dynasty unified most of China. Gradually, clothing styles became similar throughout the country. Women wore a coat and a long skirt; men wore a long robe. Later on, both genders began to wear trousers.

Both the coat and robe were simple shapes with straight lines. A common style featured a high, narrow collar and fastened diagonally from the center of the neckline to just under the right arm and down the right side of the body. In the winter, these garments were padded with cotton or silk for warmth. Although the shapes were simple, the garments often featured very elaborate silk embroidery. Some designs symbolized beliefs and customs; others provided information about the wearer's status.

In the Manchu region of China, women wore a slim, fitted dress called a cheongsam (CHAWNG-sahm). This high-collared dress, which buttoned on the right side and had long side slits, is still popular today.

As far back as the fourth century in Japan, the kimono (kuh-MOH-noh) was the standard dress for both men and women. See *Fig. 5-4*. The first kimonos were made from one piece of linen and

5-4 The kimono is a traditional garment style in Japan. It is still worn today for special occasions.

wrapped to fit the body. Later, two-piece kimonos made from silk were common. By the 700s, the kimono included various inner and outer layers, as well as a wide decorative sash, called an obi (OH-bee). The rank of the wearer and the formality of the occasion were indicated by the fabric, the colors, and the arrangement of the layers.

THE EVOLUTION OF FASHION

Many years ago, fashion changed very slowly. People often wore the same clothing style for life. A particular style could continue past a lifetime. An outfit for special occasions was often handed down from one generation to another.

Until the fourteenth century, European clothes were loose-fitting and draped. People from different cultures wore similar clothes. Around 1350, people started wearing more fitted styles. From then on, regional differences in garments began to develop in Europe. Eventually, European settlers in America influenced the clothing styles worn in the United States and Canada.

5-5 These garments are representative of the clothing worn during the Middle Ages.

In Africa and Asia, societies were not strongly influenced by Europe. As a result, clothing styles in these countries reflected their own unique cultures.

Middle Ages

The Middle Ages spanned from about 400 to 1400 and marked gradual change in clothing styles. See *Fig. 5-5*. These developments are recorded in paintings, religious statues, and illustrated manuscripts of the times.

Early in the medieval period, men wore simple wool or linen tunics and long stockings. Women wore tunics over long gowns. Goatskin and sheepskin outer garments provided protection in cold weather.

As a prosperous middle class developed, distinguishing a rich commoner from a rich nobleperson was difficult. Men wore knee-length pants called breeches; women's gowns had a fitted bodice, a very full skirt, and long, full sleeves. Garments of both men and women were trimmed with embroidery and decorative edgings.

Because the established nobility felt threatened when the middle class imitated upper-class clothing tastes, **sumptuary laws** were created. These regulations controlled what each social class could wear. Only the wealthy could enjoy silk garments trimmed with ermine fur and real silver accents. Peasant clothes were limited to certain colors and fabrics. Punishment for dressing above one's social class included fines, imprisonment, and death.

Renaissance Splendor

During the Renaissance, clothing styles in Italy, France, and Spain featured elaborate designs, beautiful fabrics, and elegant decorations. See *Fig. 5-6*. The exploration of the New World in the fifteenth and sixteenth centuries brought great wealth to Europe. Gold threads were woven into fabrics. Jewels, lace, and furs decorated garments.

The wealthier classes set the standard for fashion, a trend still seen today. The upper classes favored bright colors and large prints, elaborately layered. Men wore a tight-fitting shirt called a

5-6 Renaissance clothing was very elaborate. Wealthier classes set the standards for these elegant fashions.

doublet under a sleeveless, skirted garment called a jerkin. A short gown with very full sleeves topped these garments. Long stockings and puffed breeches completed the outfit.

Women's dresses featured a fitted bodice and very wide skirt. A metal, wood, or whalebone frame, called a farthingale, held the skirt out from the body. Skirts were sometimes split to show off fancy petticoats.

Both men and women wore ruffs—stiff, pleated collars that framed the face—and shoes trimmed with buckles and bows. Slashing, in which an upper garment was slit and a lower one pulled through in small puffs, was popular.

The Seventeenth Century

During the reign of Louis XIV in the seventeenth century, France became the world's fashion leader. The Royal court at Versailles set the style. Lace became an important decoration on men's garments. Breeches were trimmed with lace at the hem. Shirts with long, full sleeves were embroidered or trimmed with little ribbon bows. A cravat (kruh-VAT), or lace-edged piece of linen, circled the neck and tied in a knot or bow. Near the end of the century powdered wigs became popular. See *Fig. 5-7.*

During this time, women discarded hoops and frames to let their gowns fall naturally from the waist to the hem. Stiff ruffs gave way to standing lace collars and then lace-trimmed bodices. Necklines became lower, and hairstyles became higher. Beauty marks were applied to the face.

The Eighteenth Century

Fig. 5-8 on page 84 shows styles of the eighteenth century. In the early 1700s, fashions for both men and women in France were very elegant, with laces, ribbons, and colorful silks. Madame de Pompadour influenced fashion by

5-7 In seventeenth-century France, powdered wigs became fashionable. Lace was common on both men's and women's garments.

5-8 Typical fashions of the eighteenth century are shown here.

trimming her gowns with bows, edging her neckline with lace, and wearing a frilled neckband. Her hairstyle, lifted and combed straight back, is known as the pompadour.

Men wore a suit coat with a fitted waist and flared hem, the forerunner of today's suit coat. As the century progressed, the coat became thigh-length and had less lace trimming. Shirts with narrow turned-over collars were worn under the coat. Wigs became less popular.

In the late eighteenth century, people were very interested in Greek sculpture. As the French Revolution began, French commoners rebelled against the extravagances of the wealthy. Many women started wearing loose, flowing muslin dresses based on classical Greek garments. These dresses were very different from the wide skirts, rich fabrics, and elaborate trims worn by royalty. Because these soft dresses had no room for pockets, women began to carry purses. Hairstyles featured soft, ringlet curls.

In America the 1700s brought colonization, followed by the Revolutionary War. As Europeans settled in America, they brought their fashion styles with them.

The Nineteenth Century

After the French Revolution (1789-1799), France changed from a monarchy to a democracy. Dressing like royalty and upper classes was frowned on throughout Europe. Social change and

the rise of the middle class meant that many people could afford to buy new clothes more often.

Men's fashions of this period included the cut-away jacket, which evolved into the tailcoat, then shortened to the knee-length frock coat by mid-century. Gone were bright colors and lace trims. Men in Europe and the United States began wearing trousers, ending a 200-year tradition of knee breeches. An important trend began mid-century with the matching of the coat, vest, and trousers. Previously, each garment was a different color.

Women's fashions in Europe and the United States in the early 1800s featured a raised waistline inspired by Empress Josephine, wife of Napoleon. This dress style came to be known as empire (AHM-pihr).

Gradually, dresses became fuller and more elaborate. Stiff petticoats (fancy underskirts with ruffled or lace edges), crinolines (full, stiff underskirts), or hoops supported the skirts. Some

HAIR CARE IN 1800. In days when hair salons and blow dryers were unknown, a cap was a basic item in a woman's wardrobe. Women living in the United States around 1800 tucked their long hair under a simple head covering as protection against dirt and dust. That way they could wash their hair less often. A more stylish hat was worn over the cap for social outings.

5-9 How do these fashions of the nineteenth century differ from those of the preceding century?

dresses had leg-of-mutton sleeves (full at the top and narrow at the bottom). Necklines widened until the shoulders were bared. Tightly laced corsets were essential undergarments.

In the Victorian society of the late 1800s, clothes were designed more for appearance than practicality. This reflected the idea that women were fragile, delicate creatures. By the 1870s, full skirts gave way to back bustles (fullness on the back of a skirt). The overskirt was pulled up and attached at the bustle to expose the long under-skirt. Dresses had high necklines and long, fitted or leg-of-mutton sleeves.

In the 1890s, young women who worked in factories and offices began to wear simple skirts and tailored white blouses, called shirtwaists. The style was called the Gibson girl look, named after illustrations drawn by Charles Dana Gibson, an American artist. This and other fashions of the nineteenth century are shown in *Fig. 5-9*.

INFLUENCES ON FASHION HISTORY

Throughout history, trade, politics, religion, and technology have influenced fashion. Each has brought distinctive changes.

Trade

As societies traded goods with each other, they also exchanged ideas that influenced their clothing. Sailors and merchants brought back fabrics and trimmings to their own countries. Soldiers returning from foreign wars told how others lived and dressed. Missionaries taught their European clothing customs to others. The twelfth-century Crusaders opened trade routes to Western Europe, the Middle East, and the Orient.

Queen Victoria reigned in England from 1837 to 1901. She influenced the time in many ways, so much so that the era became known as Victorian England.

The exchange of fashions was quickened by the practice of **barter**, trading without money. Goods were exchanged, along with ideas and techniques. A thirteenth-century Spanish merchant might at first import silks and damasks. As demand for these fineries grew, a textile manufacturer would learn how the fabrics were made in order to produce them in Europe.

Politics and Power

For many centuries, kings, queens, and lesser nobility set the style. They could afford the luxurious fashions made by tailors and dressmakers. The vast majority of people wore only what they could make themselves. Thus, fashion trends spread slowly.

The most dominant nations spread their influence to others. During the Renaissance, when Spain and Portugal were at the height of power, their fashions influenced styles throughout Europe. Since the reign of the powerful and extravagant Louis XIV, France has been a fashion leader.

With the emergence of the middle class, royalty and wives of political leaders became fashion leaders. England's Queen Victoria popularized full-skirted dresses supported by hoops and petticoats. See *Fig. 5-10*. France's Empress Eugénie introduced the bolero jacket, felt hat, and Scottish tartan.

Meanwhile, Asian and African societies were thriving. European traders returned from Asia with beautiful silk fabrics. The styles of ancient Egypt were fashionable after Napoleon's campaigns in Northern Africa.

Religion

Clothing can be a statement of religious beliefs. The sixteenth century Reformation movement in Germany, Switzerland, Holland, and England encouraged dark colors, simple styles, and little decoration. This was in sharp contrast to the splendor of the Renaissance in France, Spain, and Italy.

The English Puritans believed in humility and simplicity in life. They chose very plain clothing styles to show that they didn't conform to worldly standards.

Technology

From the first stitches that pieced together animal skins, people have used technology to change and improve fabrics and clothing. **Technology**, which uses scientific knowledge to develop something new, has had great influence on fashion.

For most of human history, making clothes was labor intensive. See *Fig. 5-11* on page 88. Materials were limited to natural fibers. New clothes were time-consuming to make and expensive to buy, so most people used a garment until it wore out. The Industrial Revolution would change all that.

The Industrial Revolution

Around 1760 Scottish inventor James Watt developed the steam engine and began what is

Trends in TECHNOLOGY

>>EARLY INVENTIONS

Throughout fashion history, inventions have revolutionized the production of yarns, fabrics, and garments.

- **Flying shuttle.** Invented in 1733 by John Kay, an Englishman, the flying shuttle could be released from a box on one side of the loom and "fly" across the loom to a box on the other side.

- **Spinning jenny.** Developed in 1767 by Englishman James Hargreaves, this tool was named in honor of his wife. The spinning jenny had eight spindles so eight yarns could be spun at the same time.

- **Cotton gin.** This invention of Eli Whitney in 1793 separated cotton fibers from the seeds. As a result, much more cotton fabric could be produced.

- **Spinning mule.** Invented in 1797 by Englishman Samuel Crompton, this machine could produce as much yarn as 200 hand spinners.

- **Sewing machine.** In 1845 Elias Howe, from Boston, devised a practical sewing machine with a lockstitch similar to today's home machines. The Singer Sewing Machine Company added the first electric motor to sewing machines in 1889.

- **Paper pattern.** A Massachussetts tailor, Ebenezer Butterick, developed a paper pattern that his wife used to make his shirts. By 1865 the Buttericks had moved to New York City and were selling paper patterns by mail to customers all over the world. In 1870 James McCall, a tailor and author of a system for drafting patterns, began to manufacture dress patterns in New York City.

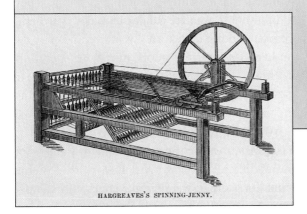

HARGREAVES'S SPINNING-JENNY.

INVESTIGATION ACTIVITY
Learn more about these and other similar inventions. Report your findings.

---

known as the **Industrial Revolution**—the rapid changes that resulted from the invention of power-driven machines. People could weave fabric and sew garments a hundred times faster than working by hand. Well-made clothing cost less to manufacture and buy, and people could buy clothes from catalogs and stores.

The Industrial Revolution also influenced clothing styles. Earlier, an English gentleman's clothes were as elaborate as those of an English lady. Both wore light colors and delicate fabrics. Machinery in the new factories, however, created dark and dirty smoke. As a result, middle-class businessmen began to wear darker colors and sturdier fabrics.

Development of Factories

The first factories in the United States were built in New England after 1790. Most were located in such seaport cities as Boston and New York. Others were near railroad lines and rivers. Many were textile mills—dark, noisy, dirty, unpleasant, and overcrowded places to work.

Cotton was shipped from the South to the northern mills for spinning and weaving into fabric. The first loom for weaving silk was set up in a factory in Paterson, New Jersey, in 1842. Paterson remained the silk center of the world until the early 1930s.

At first, garment manufacturers employed women who lived close to the textile mills to sew garments at home. Soon factories were established to make garments. These dark, airless, uncomfortable, and unhealthful places to work were sometimes called **sweatshops**. Most workers were women and children. See *Fig. 5-12*.

After the Civil War, people started to build textile mills in the South to be closer to the cotton fields. Then, finished fabrics were shipped to fac-

5-12 Early garment factories were unpleasant places to work.

tories in the North to be made into garments. Today, the majority of textile mills in the United States are still located in the South.

Growth of Ready-to-Wear

The first men's clothing factory specialized in making sailor's uniforms. Sailors, miners, and pioneers needed simple, durable clothing. They didn't want to wait for a tailor to make a garment. People working in factories were becoming a new middle class and had more money to spend on clothing. The market for men's ready-to-wear grew very quickly. **Ready-to-wear** describes clothing made in advance for sale to any purchaser.

Women's ready-to-wear grew more slowly. Fashions for women changed frequently and were more difficult to sew. The first ready-to-wear items for women were simple capes and shawls. Then, garments that wouldn't go out of fashion quickly, such as petticoats and underwear, began to be manufactured.

Shirtwaists, worn in the 1890s by women in factories and offices, were easy to manufacture in varied sizes. Soon many clothing styles were being manufactured for women. By 1900, New York City had about 475 shirtwaist factories that employed over 18,000 workers.

The growth of ready-to-wear created the growth of large stores. When clothing was still made at home, people bought their fabric, thread,

5-11 Before the Industrial Revolution and the rise of factories, fabrics were hand woven on small looms, and garments were sewn by hand. Both processes were time-consuming.

How To... PRESERVE TEXTILES

What do you do with an expensive wedding gown that was worn only once? Many brides save their gown as a sentimental heirloom. Christening gowns, special uniforms, quilts, and antique linens can also be saved. Some dry cleaners will clean and pack an item in a special storage container. Make arrangements to inspect the item after cleaning but before storing. If you want to preserve an item yourself, follow these steps:

1. Clean and repair the item, since dust, dirt, and stains can damage fabric over time. Some items need dry cleaning. Washable items shouldn't be starched or ironed.

2. Wrap the item in clean, white, cotton cloth, such as an old sheet or pillowcase, clean muslin, or special acid-free tissue paper. No direct contact with wood, cardboard, regular tissue paper, or other wrapping paper should be made, as these materials contain acid that damages textiles.

3. If folding is needed, pad folds with clean muslin or acid-free tissue paper to prevent fibers from breaking along the folds. As another option, loosely roll the item around an acid-free cardboard tube or one that has been wrapped first with muslin or white cloth.

4. Store the item flat, if possible, in an acid-free box or as the top layer in a dresser drawer or storage trunk. Choose a location with good air circulation away from heat, humidity, and sunlight. Avoid hot attics and damp basements. Never use airtight plastic bags or containers, which trap moisture that causes mold and mildew. Sturdy items can be hung on well-padded hangers with several layers of polyester fiberfill. Wrap the entire item with clean, unbleached muslin. Once a year examine and rewrap with fresh materials.

Exploring Textile Preservation

Bring a textile to class and demonstrate the proper preservation storage technique. If possible, preserve an item that you want to save.

and ribbon at dry-goods stores. As stores began to sell clothing made in the factories, the stores carried more merchandise. All shirts were sold in one area, all trousers in another, and so on. By 1850, the department store was born. Special marketing techniques, such as "sales" and "specials," were first used by a large store in Boston. The method spread quickly. Catalog and mail-order selling became a popular way to reach people in rural areas.

Invention of New Fibers

In 1889, a French chemist created quite a sensation at the Paris Exhibition with fabrics made of artificial silk. These were the first fabrics not made of natural fibers.

For many years, researchers had experimented with dissolving the fibrous inner bark of mulberry trees. This produced **cellulose**, the main component of such plants as cotton and flax. Creating fibers from the dissolved bark proved difficult, however. Finally researchers tried forcing the solution through fine holes, as a silkworm does to make silk. This technique produced long, threadlike fibers.

In 1910 this new textile fiber was introduced to the United States; in 1924 it was given a name: rayon. Through technology many new fibers and fabrics have been developed, making a huge impact on fashions in the twentieth century.

FASHIONS OF THE TWENTIETH CENTURY

During the last century, fashion has changed far more quickly than in the past. Clothing styles have reflected the changing roles and interests of men and women.

1900 to 1950

At the turn of the century, times were changing. By 1912, petticoats were abandoned for long, straight skirts. During World War I, more women worked in shops, offices, and factories, so more practical clothing developed. Looser garments, such as sweaters and middy blouses with sailor collars, became popular.

5-13 The look of the 1920s was marked by a straight silhouette, dropped waist, and shorter skirt length. Hair was bobbed and covered by a domed hat called a cloche.

5-14 Garments of the 1930s

After World War I, people's excitement showed in their fashions. The "flapper dress" of the 1920s was straight and short, adorned with fringe or flounces, and worn with a long string of beads. See *Fig. 5-13*. By the 1930s, women became active in sports. They began wearing wide trousers and

5-15 During the 1940s, garments for both men (top left) and women (top right) featured padded shoulders.

5-16 Garments of the 1950s included these styles.

military uniforms and equipment. Women's skirts became slimmer and shorter, due to fabric rationing. Nylon stockings were almost impossible to get, so women wore cotton stockings. Slacks and jumpsuits became the standard work clothes for women as they replaced men in factories.

After World War II, styles changed radically. People were tired of the clothes they had worn during the war. Fabric was easily available again. Christian Dior, a French designer, introduced the "New Look" for women. Almost overnight, women started to wear dresses and suits with very full, long skirts.

The 1950s

The 1950s saw fashions influenced by designers, movies, and television shows. See *Fig. 5-16.* Dior introduced the A-line silhouette for women. Full skirts were worn with crinolines and paired with sweater sets. Pants were rolled up or cropped for casual wear.

Men's fashions featured the gray flannel business suit—single-breasted and loosely fitted, with narrow lapels and natural shoulders. It was worn with a button-down oxford shirt and a narrow, striped tie for the Ivy League look. Dress shirts could be pale blue or yellow, instead of only white.

The T-shirt came out from under the dress shirt, influenced by actors Marlon Brando and James Dean. This former undershirt was now worn on its own with blue jeans. Leather jackets and the pompadour hairstyle of Elvis Presley became popular with young men. Young women wore a man's shirt over a pair of cuffed jeans. Saddle shoes or white bucks completed the look.

The 1960s

In the 1960s, the influence of fashion designers declined. They were replaced by cultural events, such as the Beatles, Woodstock, and rock concerts. First Lady Jacqueline Kennedy became an important fashion leader for women, popularizing the Chanel suit and pillbox hat.

Many young men started wearing colorful fabrics and jewelry. Soon men of all ages wore mul-

above-the-knee shorts to participate in these events. Evening gowns were long, formfitting, and often cut on the bias. See *Fig. 5-14.*

By comparison, men's clothing went almost unchanged in this same period. Both single- and double-breasted suits were popular. By 1940, both men and women wore tailored suits with broad, padded shoulders. See *Fig. 5-15.*

During World War II, a shortage of fabric occurred because so many textiles were used for

5-17 During the 1960s, females wore short skirts and males wore jackets with wide lapels.

5-18 Pantsuits for women and the unisex look were both part of the fashion scene in the 1970s.

ticolored, striped or checked shirts with their business suits. Jacket lapels widened and pants were flared or bell-bottomed. Men grew long sideburns, mustaches, or beards to go with longer hair lengths.

Women's fashions focused on the miniskirt, which kept rising throughout the decade. Pantyhose were introduced, and boots became the "in" accessory. Sleeveless, A-line dresses were worn year round. See *Fig. 5-17*.

The "double-knit revolution" strongly influenced garment styles. Polyester double knits were widely used because they were washable, didn't wrinkle, and were inexpensive. These fabrics were more suitable to simple, straight designs, however, than to softly draped garments.

African-Americans rediscovered traditional African garments made of kente cloth. Afro hair-styles and cornrow braids were widely worn by both men and women. The 1960s also saw the hippie look for males and females. Jeans and

shirts were decorated with patches, paint, and embroidery.

The 1970s

By 1970, the midi- and maxi-length skirts were introduced. These longer lengths flopped as women refused to be dictated to by designers. Instead, women turned more and more to pantsuits, which slowly gained acceptance for all occasions. See *Fig. 5-18*.

The unisex look was very popular throughout the 1970s. Men and women wore the same styles in the same fabrics and colors. Women wore pantsuits, styled like menswear, with a tailored shirt and necktie, to the office.

The two-piece, polyester leisure suit gained popularity with men. It consisted of slacks and a jacket with a large collar and topstitching. A bright floral shirt was usually worn without a tie. The shirt collar rolled over the jacket collar for a casual look.

Jeans became very fashionable. T-shirts had slogans printed on the front. Hip hugger pants were worn. The layered look featured several pieces of clothing worn one on top of the other. Such movies as *Grease, Annie Hall,* and *Saturday Night Fever* created popular looks. By the end of the decade, clothes were more casual and comfortable.

The 1980s

Styles in the 1980s featured broad, padded shoulders, reminiscent of the 1940s. Skirt lengths ranged from long to short; pant legs could be wide or narrow.

The increase of women executives created the need for business suits for women that were equal to men's in quality and design. The result was the power suit—a tailored jacket and medium-length skirt worn with a tailored blouse.

Designer jeans became a status symbol. Warm-up suits were worn for jogging and for streetwear. The standard outfit for young people consisted of jeans, a shirt or sweater, and athletic shoes. Styles were influenced by entertainers, including Madonna, Cyndi Lauper, Prince, and Michael Jackson. See *Fig. 5-19.*

Fashion trends emerged from around the world. Italian designers contributed superbly tailored suits. Japan offered uniquely layered designs. England's Princess Diana set trends with her haircut and clothing. The television show *Dallas* and the movie *Flashdance* popularized elegant clothing and torn sweats. By the end of the decade, freedom of choice dominated.

The 1990s and Beyond

In the 1990s, as shown on page 94, fashions for both men and women became more natural in shape. Gone were the padded shoulders and poufed skirts. Styles ranged from baggy pants to tight leggings and from oversized shirts to skinny tops. No longer did one style dominate.

Styles from past decades re-emerged in the middle 1990s. Consumers were attracted to updated versions of the fitted jackets from the 1950s, sheath dresses from the 1960s, and wrap dresses and hip hugger pants from the 1970s.

5-19 Celebrities helped shape the fashion looks of the 1980s.

Casual business attire created a new clothing category for men. Many companies permitted men to wear khakis or slacks with a shirt and no tie to the office. Even executives exchanged their traditional business suits for more casual wear.

Leisurewear in the 1990s consisted of jeans, leather jackets, and work shoes—often worn with a baseball cap. The hip-hop style, with baggy pants and a T-shirt, appealed to many young people. Activewear, once worn only for sports, became another type of leisurewear.

In the twenty-first century, the trend has been toward more casual clothing. Both males and females dress less formally for school, work, travel, parties, and recreation. People want clothes that are comfortable and versatile and can be worn at work as well as home. Outfits that can go everywhere are desired.

With all the influences on fashion styles, something new is always on the horizon. What trends do you think will mark the century ahead?

CHAPTER SUMMARY

- Earliest garments were woven or sewn from native plants and animals to protect against the local climate.

- Ancient Greeks and Romans formed garments by draping or wrapping fabric.

- From the 1500s to the 1700s, the elaborate styles and rich fabrics of the wealthy classes and nobility were fashionable.

- Garments changed gradually between the Renaissance and the French Revolution.

- Fashions have been influenced by trade, politics, and other societal forces, including the Industrial Revolution.

- Throughout the twentieth century, fashions have grown more casual, with many reflecting personal tastes.

USING KEY TERMS

Write the Key Terms on a sheet of paper. Then explain how each one influenced the history of fashion. Include specific examples.

RECALLING THE FACTS

1. From what materials did the earliest human beings make their clothing?

2. Describe two ways that the Romans adapted Greek styles.

3. Why did the upper classes of the Middle Ages pass sumptuary laws?

4. Describe a common garment of Japanese men and women in the 700s.

5. How did women's dresses change between the fifteenth and the seventeenth centuries?

6. How did dress reflect people's feelings during and after the French Revolution?

7. How can trade influence clothing and fashion?

8. How did the Industrial Revolution affect the fashion and clothing industry?

9. How did the rise of ready-to-wear change the way people bought clothes?

10. Briefly, how did women's fashions change between 1900 and 1930?

11. Contrast the styles favored by young men and businessmen in the 1950s.

12. Describe four major developments in fashion in the 1960s.

13. Describe three fashion trends of the 1970s.

14. Give examples of the casual fashions of the 1980s and 1990s.

and Activities

THINKING CRITICALLY

1. How were fashions of ancient Greece and Rome similar to those in China and Japan at that time? How were they different?

2. Why do you think most of today's garments are fitted rather than draped?

3. Compare the types of clothes that were fashionable during the Renaissance with those of today. Why do you think they are so different?

APPLYING KNOWLEDGE

1. **Draped designs.** With another classmate, design a draped or wrapped garment using a square or rectangular piece of fabric. Demonstrate and model your design.

2. **History parade.** Imagine that the historical society has asked your class to plan a fashion show, "Through the Ages." Work with classmates to plan the fashions and write the script.

3. **Fashion migration.** On a world map, locate countries and areas where fibers or clothing styles originated. Trace on the map how the fibers and clothing styles spread to other countries.

4. **Asia and Africa.** Research clothing styles worn in an African or Asian country. Explain what you learned about the culture from the fashions.

5. **More fashions.** Research fashions of a time or place not discussed in the chapter. What, for example, was the Baroque style of dress? The Regency? When and why was the Amalia dress popular?

6. **Fashion favorites.** People often find the fashions of a certain era or location appealing. If you had lived at a time or place when fashions were quite different, which would you choose and why?

CREATIVE SOLUTIONS

Suppose you're gathering information about your family history when you come across an old photo of an unidentified couple in what looks like dress clothes. The photo isn't dated. More information about when the photo was taken might help you determine who the people are.

Think Creatively

What clues in the clothing might help you determine the era in which the photo was taken?

Fashion Styles

OBJECTIVES

- Define fashion terms, including style, classic, fad, avant-garde, and retro.

- Describe a fashion cycle.

- Explain fashion swings.

- Distinguish between styles of necklines, collars, and sleeves.

- Identify styles of dresses, shirts, skirts, pants, jackets, and coats.

KEY TERMS

avant-garde	kimono sleeve
classics	raglan sleeve
cowl	retro
fad	set-in sleeve
fashion	style
fashion cycle	

you couldn't wait to buy last year look old to you now? Why do the clothes in pictures of your parents as teens look old-fashioned, yet some of the clothes your grandparents wore seem more attractive? Why do some fashions last much longer than others? To answer these questions, you need to understand some basic fashion terms.

Style

When her friend admired a dress in a store window, one teen commented, "That style would look great on you!" **Style** refers to the characteristics that distinguish one particular item of clothing from another. Jeans are a specific style of pants. Straight, A-line, and circular are all skirt styles. Set-in, raglan, and kimono are all styles of sleeves.

In this chapter, you'll learn to recognize these and many other garment styles. Some styles may

N EVER BEFORE HAVE SO MANY clothing choices been available to you. Surprisingly, a small number of basic garment styles are the springboards for hundreds of variations today. Styles you see in stores and magazines have colors, patterns, textures, and unique features added to the basics. Whether you like jeans and a T-shirt or feathers and glitter, most garments embody the styles you'll read about in this chapter.

WHAT IS FASHION?

Fashion is the particular style that is popular at a given time. Anything that's "in" is part of current fashion. Fashion usually means clothes, but there are fashions in hairstyles, home decoration, and even foods. See *Fig. 6-1*. While few people ate yogurt years ago, this dairy item has become quite a "fashionable" food choice today.

Fashion Terms

When thinking about fashion, some interesting questions come to mind. Why does an outfit

6-1 Hairstyles and hair accessories are subject to fashion too. Who knows? This interesting style of the past could be back in fashion someday.

How To ... **WRITE FASHION COPY**

"I like to write, but I've never written about fashions before," a high school student said when talking about his latest assignment. In preparing to write the script for a student fashion show, he wondered just what the task would take.

Whether writing a script or producing ads, catalog copy, press releases, or reports, fashion writers focus on "what's new" in fashion. They describe fashions, sometimes evaluate them, and often motivate consumers to buy.

With a good fashion vocabulary, a writer can accurately describe styles, fabrics, colors, and details. Descriptive words add flair and drama to the message. When copy space is limited, the writing must be creative, simple, and brief.

Persuasive copy must appeal and convince. First, it catches the reader's attention with a statement or perhaps a question. Next, it answers the reader's question, "What's in it for me?" Finally, it motivates the reader to respond.

Here are some tips for writing effective fashion copy.

- Become familiar with the product, the designer or manufacturer, the store, and the targeted customer. The more a writer knows, the more effective the writing.

- Understand the purpose or objective to express it clearly.

- Use familiar words in creative and clever ways.

- Don't overuse "in" words, current idioms, or catchy phrases.

- Be honest. Write copy that's believable and credible.

- Avoid too much copy. Most readers want just the facts, not a long dissertation.

- Create interest and excitement. Make the copy come alive.

Exploring **Fashion Writing**

Try your hand at fashion writing. Choose a fashion style that's new. Then write a fashion magazine article that introduces the look to the public.

6-2 Some styles are considered classics. Why do you think people are often willing to spend more for a classic?

Other examples are polo shirts, turtleneck sweaters, cardigan sweaters, sweatshirts, trench coats, and tuxedos. Classic accessories are the pearl necklace, loafer shoes, and clutch purse. These styles have been around for years. Do you have clothing that would be considered classic?

Fad

Some fashions are "here today and gone tomorrow." A fashion that is very popular for only a short time is called a **fad**. A color, such as mauve or chartreuse, can be a fad. Such accessories as rhinestone jewelry and platform shoes can be too. See *Fig. 6-3*. Fads in clothing are common. Short miniskirts and low-slung, baggy pants are examples. Fads can even be a certain look, such as "punk-rock," "safari," or "grunge."

Fad items are usually less expensive than others. For example, "pop-it" plastic necklaces and cinch belts were fads in the 1950s. White go-go boots and Nehru jackets, named for India's prime minister, swept in and out of fashion in the 1960s. While hot pants and leisure suits were worn in the 1970s, the 1980s saw fluorescent socks, leg warmers, and pouf skirts. In the 1990s young people wore low-slung, baggy pants, and people of all ages wore boxer shorts as outerwear.

be very fashionable today. Others may be outdated this year, but "in" the next. Such is the ever-changing world of fashion.

Classic

Certain styles stay in fashion for a long time. These are known as **classics**. Styles that become classics are usually simpler and less innovative than others.

The navy blue blazer jacket is a classic. See *Fig. 6-2*. Although the blazer may feature narrow lapels with metal buttons one year and wide lapels with navy buttons a year later, the basic blazer style never dies.

Many other styles have also become classics. Blue jeans and the tailored shirt are both classics.

6-3 Fads don't last long, but sometimes they reappear as a new, revised version of an old idea. Although these shoes are from the past, do they look familiar?

6-4 Part of the fun of wearing authentic retro clothes comes with finding them. Where else might you find such garments?

ahead of fashion. Clothes described this way are daring and unconventional. Because they're "far out," they don't appeal to most people. Certain avant-garde features, however, may become generally accepted after a few years.

Some people choose clothing, hair, and makeup styles that are avant-garde. These styles call attention to the wearer. Cut-out clothing, green or orange hair, and black lipstick are examples of avant-garde looks.

Retro

Like the line from a song, "Everything old is new again," an old-fashioned look can be revived. Today the **retro** look, which brings back styles of an earlier time, is fashionable. Clothing styles from the 1950s, 1960s, and 1980s can be seen in recent fashions. Examples are twin sweater sets, V-neck sweaters, and wrap dresses. Pointed pumps and sheath dresses, reminiscent of Audrey Hepburn's character in *Breakfast at Tiffany's*, have made a comeback.

Some people prefer wearing original clothes, not updated versions. Thrift shops and attics are popular sources for such retro garments. See *Fig. 6-4.*

Sometimes a fad returns when discovered by another generation. Platform shoes go in and out of fashion. Mood rings, popular with young people in the 1970s, came back again in the 1990s. Large plaids and flower prints from the 1970s reappeared in the late 1990s.

Many fads, such as wearing slashed jeans or untied shoelaces, are popular mainly with teens. Fads help teens express two important needs: to feel a sense of belonging among peers and to express individuality. You can probably point out current fads that serve these purposes for teens.

Avant-Garde

In the clothing industry **avant-garde** (ah-vahn-GARD) is a French expression that means

Fashion Facts

RETURN TO THE PAST.
Ancient Greek and Roman philosophers and mathematicians wore wraparound garments. When Shakespeare composed his greatest works of literature, men's styles looked more like panty hose than pants. Eighteenth-century Scottish warriors rode into battle wearing kilts. Noting how men of great learning and courage never wore trousers, some people today want to bring back male skirts, or "unbifurcated (undivided) garments." Supporters of this idea note that in some cultures men still wear such styles.

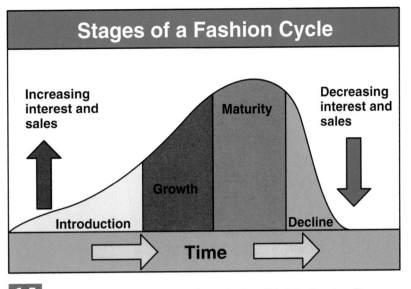

Stages of a Fashion Cycle

Increasing interest and sales

Maturity

Decreasing interest and sales

Growth

Introduction

Decline

Time

6-5 A style moves through stages from the time it is introduced until consumer interest in the style ends. The time lapse for this cycle is not the same for every style.

Fashion Cycles

Every fashion has a **fashion cycle** as it is introduced, grows, matures, and declines. See *Fig. 6-5*. Some fashion cycles are very short-lived, such as those for fads. Others take a long time before their popularity declines. Classics, for example, have very long fashion cycles. Recognizing the different stages of a fashion cycle is important to both store buyers and consumers.

- **Introduction stage.** A fashion is born when it's worn for the first time. Models, celebrities, and others who like to wear the latest designs introduce the garment to the public. Most new fashions are introduced in small quantities at higher prices.
- **Growth stage.** As interest in a fashion builds and people gradually accept it, variations are sold at lower prices.
- **Maturity stage.** When many people wear a fashion, it reaches the peak of its popularity. The style is produced in large quantities at prices that most consumers can afford.

- **Decline stage.** Eventually, people tire of a particular style. Although they may continue to wear it, sales rapidly decline. Remaining items are reduced in price. The style starts to look old-fashioned. Usually the decline stage is shorter than the introduction stage.

Fashion Swings

Although basic styles of clothes and accessories remain the same, certain details change according to fashion. Skirt lengths go up or down, and jackets become longer or shorter. Sometimes jacket lapels are wide; other times they're narrow. Rather than introducing a brand new fashion, many designers change styling details from season to season to create "fresh" looks.

Few examples demonstrate fashion swings better than the yo-yo action of skirt lengths. Until World War I, floor length was fashionable for every woman and every occasion. During the 1920s, hems rose to the knees. In the 1930s, they fell to the calf. With fabric in short supply during

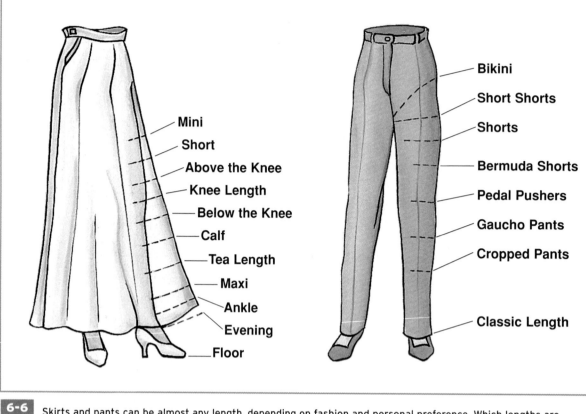

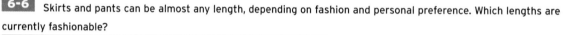

6-6 Skirts and pants can be almost any length, depending on fashion and personal preference. Which lengths are currently fashionable?

World War II, knee length returned. In the 1960s, a variety of fashion lengths were introduced— mini, midi (midcalf), and maxi. Since then, many different lengths continue to be popular at the same time.

Like skirts, pant lengths have been through fashion swings. See *Fig. 6-6*. Even when fashion brings back a particular length, the name for the style may be different. For example, in the 1990s, the cropped pants of earlier times came back into fashion. Over the years, these pants, which fall between the knee and ankle, have been called clam diggers, Capri pants, toreador pants, and pedal pushers. The name could be something else the next time around. See *Fig. 6-7*.

Fashion details in trousers and pants also swing back and forth. Trouser tops are sometimes tight across the hips. At other times they have pleats for added fullness. The width of pant legs can change from wide to medium to narrow, and then back again. Sometimes trouser legs have cuffs and sometimes they're plain.

Men's neckties are another good example of fashion swings. In the 1940s, very wide ties balanced the wide lapels on double-breasted suits. When Ivy League suits were stylish in the 1960s, ties became very skinny, and diagonal stripes were popular. As suits with wider lapels came back again in the mid-1970s, ties got wider too. See *Fig. 6-8*. In the 1980s, they narrowed to a medium width, with stripes, tiny prints, and dark colors. Later, in the early 1990s, wider ties returned, with more color. Fabrics featured flowers, cartoon characters, and other bold designs. By the late 1990s, solid-color ties, often the same color as the shirt, were worn. These changes usually happen gradually, although a new "look" may suddenly become popular.

6-7 Pants that fall between the knee and ankle have been in and out of fashion over the years. What else have cropped pants been called?

6-8 Fashions change for many reasons. Designers want to create something new, manufacturers want to sell something new, and people want to wear something new. Why do you think the cycle of change is faster today than it used to be?

FASHION FEATURES

Not every fashion detail is used by designers every season. A certain type of collar may appear on many garments one year; the next year another style is popular. Garment features—necklines, collars, and sleeves—can be combined to create many different looks. Some combinations, however, are more pleasing and practical than others.

Neckline Styles

The neckline is the area around the neck and shoulders. Before the twentieth century, garments

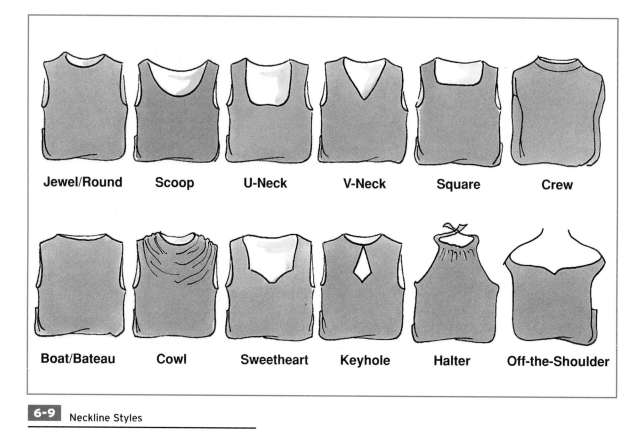

Jewel/Round   **Scoop**   **U-Neck**   **V-Neck**   **Square**   **Crew**

Boat/Bateau   **Cowl**   **Sweetheart**   **Keyhole**   **Halter**   **Off-the-Shoulder**

6-9   Neckline Styles

from the same period all had similar necklines. Today many different types appear in a season. You're likely to see those described here and in *Fig. 6-9.*

- **Jewel.** This high, rounded neckline is so named because it provides a good background for a necklace or pin.
- **Crew.** Also high and round, the crew neckline is finished with a knit band. This style was originally on sweaters worn by rowing crews.
- **Cowl.** The **cowl** is a softly draped neckline on a dress or blouse. Because it's cut on the bias, which is the diagonal grain of the fabric, soft folds form. *Cowl,* which means softly draped, was originally the term for a hooded robe worn by monks.
- **Bateau.** This neckline resembles the outline of a long, low boat resting on the water. *Bateau* is the French word for boat.

- **Sweetheart.** This neckline is moderately low in front and forms a point, similar to a heart shape.
- **Halter.** With this neckline, a drawstring or band holds a sleeveless garment front in place at the neck. The shoulders and back are bare.

Collar Styles

A collar is a separate piece of fabric attached to the neckline. It can be small or large, soft or stiff, stand up or fold over. Although most collars are sewn onto the garment, some are detachable. Removable collars change a garment's look and can be cleaned separately. They can be held in place with buttons, snaps, hook-and-loop fasteners, or basting stitches. see→ p 556

Classic collar styles include the shirt, button-down, convertible, notched, and shawl collar. See *Fig. 6-10.* Some collars are joined to a lapel, the front part of a shirt or jacket that is folded back on the chest. The notched collar forms a point where the collar and lapel meet. In contrast, the shawl collar joins the lapel in a continuous line. Some curiously named collars are explained below.

- **Peter Pan.** The Peter Pan collar is small and flat, with rounded corners. The name is taken from the play *Peter Pan,* written in 1904 by James M. Barrie. The costumes in the play had this collar style.
- **Sailor, or middy.** This collar was copied from those on a sailor's uniform. A middy, or midshipman, is a student at a naval academy.
- **Mandarin.** The stand-up style of a mandarin collar is seen in the traditional dress worn in China. The term *mandarin* is the name of the dialect spoken in many parts of China, including Beijing.
- **Tuxedo.** This collar has turned-down points and is usually worn with a bow tie and tuxedo jacket, named after Tuxedo Park, NY.
- **Chelsea.** The chelsea collar first became popular in the Chelsea section of London.
- **Puritan.** Named for the Puritans of the sixteenth century, this collar imitates the style they wore.
- **Ruff.** A small, stand-up ruffle identifies the ruff collar. It's less frilly than the stiff white ruffs worn by men and women at the turn of the seventeenth century.
- **Jabot.** This is a small, standing collar with a lacy, ruffled, or pleated trimming attached at the front. The trimming is called a jabot (zha-BOH).

6-10 Collar Styles

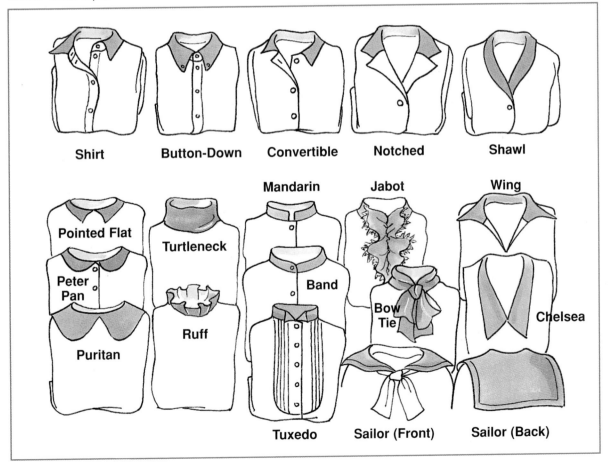

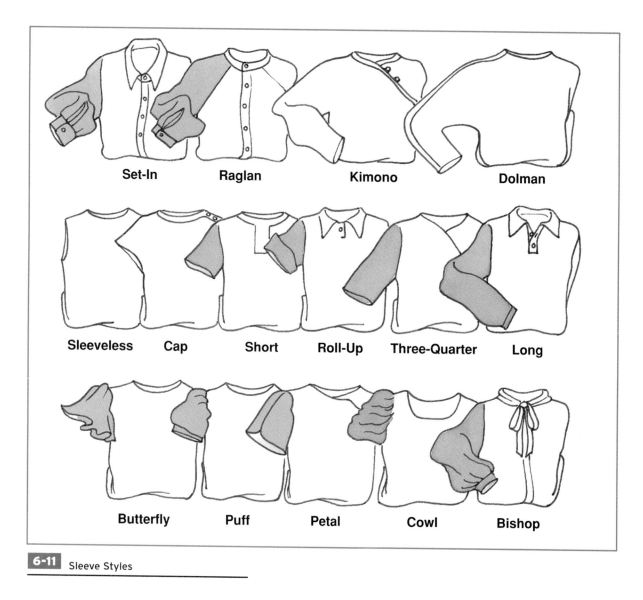

Sleeve Styles

The sleeve has come a long way from its beginning as an overhang of material draped about the shoulders. Sleeves today range from a tiny cap to a full, flounced attachment. See *Fig. 6-11*. There are three basic sleeve styles. see→ p 559

- **Set-in.** The **set-in sleeve** is joined to the garment by an armhole seam that circles the arm near the shoulder.
- **Raglan.** A front and back diagonal seam that extends from the neckline to the underarm identifies the **raglan sleeve**.

- **Kimono.** A **kimono sleeve** is cut in one piece that includes the garment front and back. It is then sewn together along the outer arm and the underarm.

All other sleeves are variations of the three basic styles. Some interesting types include the following:

- **Dolman.** A variation of the kimono sleeve, this type is narrow at the wrist and wide at the underarm.
- **Puff, or baby doll.** As a type of set-in sleeve, this style is popular for babies' and children's clothes.

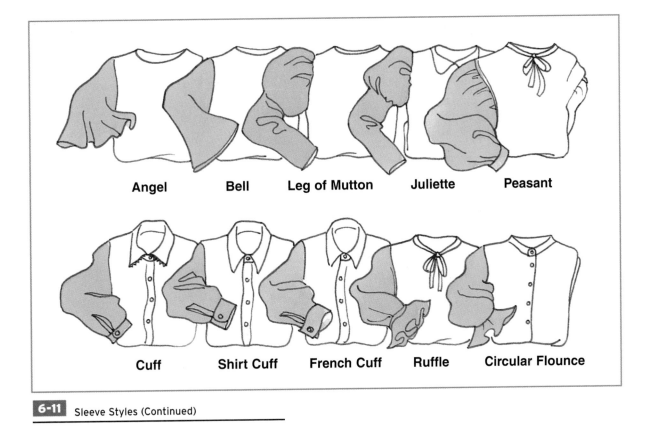

Angel   Bell   Leg of Mutton   Juliette   Peasant

Cuff   Shirt Cuff   French Cuff   Ruffle   Circular Flounce

6-11 Sleeve Styles (Continued)

- **Leg of mutton.** This set-in sleeve was very fashionable in the Victorian era. The name comes from its resemblance to a cooked leg of lamb.

GARMENT STYLES

Imagine a teen putting on her robe to go out for a special dinner. Long ago a female might have done just that, because what people call a dress today was once called a robe. History shows that many garments have changed in name as well as style over the years.

From medieval times until the eighteenth century, most dresses were actually separate skirts and bodices. Persian and Anglo-Saxon men have worn pants since ancient times. The term *pants* wasn't used, however, until the late 1800s, when it meant outer garments worn by men and boys. The word *coat* comes from the English word *cloak*. This large piece of fabric was wrapped around the body over other clothing for warmth.

Jacket is a modern form of the Old French *jaquette*, or "little coat." Today a jacket is typically an outer layer of clothing of more or less hip length. It may also be worn under a coat.

Some garment styles today are described by names that link to the past. Other connections are made to the garment's shape. Once learned, the names give you a way to distinguish one garment from another.

Dress Styles

Dress styles can be divided into those that have a waistline or horizontal seam and those that lack one. See *Fig. 6-12* on page 108. Classic styles without waistlines are described here.

- **Sheath.** This dress is close fitting and shaped by darts.
- **Shift, or chemise.** A loose-fitting dress, this one became popular in the 1920s.

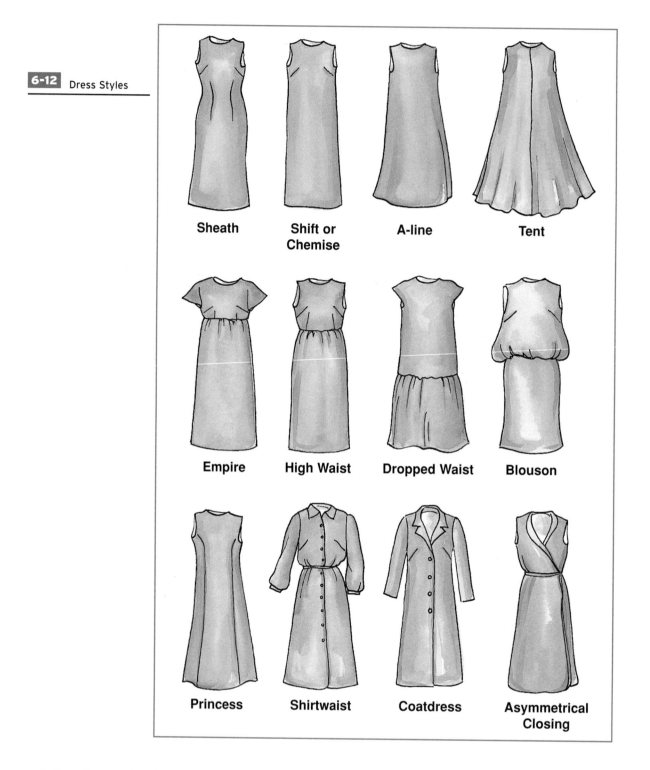

Sheath	Shift or Chemise	A-line	Tent

Empire	High Waist	Dropped Waist	Blouson

Princess	Shirtwaist	Coatdress	Asymmetrical Closing

- **A-line.** Due to the shape that flares out to the hemline, this dress is called an A-line. It was introduced by Christian Dior in 1955.
- **Princess.** The vertical seams give the close-fitting, flared princess dress its shape.

Other dress styles have a bodice and skirt joined at, above, or below the natural waistline. These styles include the empire, high-waist, dropped waist, blouson, and shirtwaist. A two-piece dress consists of a separate, matching skirt and top.

Shirt Styles

The term *shirt* usually refers to a top that is more tailored than a blouse. Many styles are made to fit both women and men. Some popular shirt and blouse styles are described below and shown in *Fig. 6-13*.

- **Dress.** The dress shirt is a traditional man's shirt that is worn with a suit and necktie.
- **Sport.** Sport shirts are more casual and usually worn without a tie.
- **Polo.** This knit shirt is similar to those worn by polo players in the 1920s.
- **Hawaiian, or aloha.** This sport shirt is made of floral fabric in tropical colors.
- **Henley.** Crew teams that competed in the Henley rowing regatta in England wore collarless shirts that inspired the name of this style.
- **Tuxedo.** Tuxedo shirts have a pleated front and a small wing or banded collar.
- **Tank top.** This shirt resembles a man's undershirt. The name comes from the bathing suit that was worn in the first indoor pools, which were originally called tanks.
- **Tunic.** Inspired by the ancient Roman garment, the tunic is a loose-fitting top that is hip length or longer.

6-13 Shirt Styles

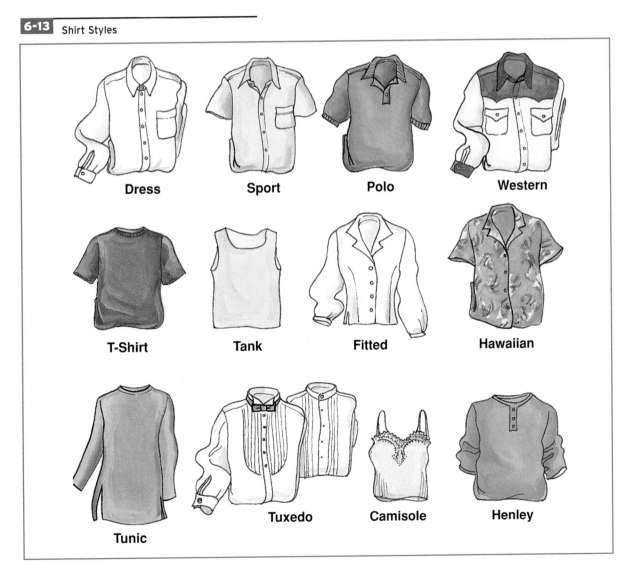

Dress   Sport   Polo   Western

T-Shirt   Tank   Fitted   Hawaiian

Tunic   Tuxedo   Camisole   Henley

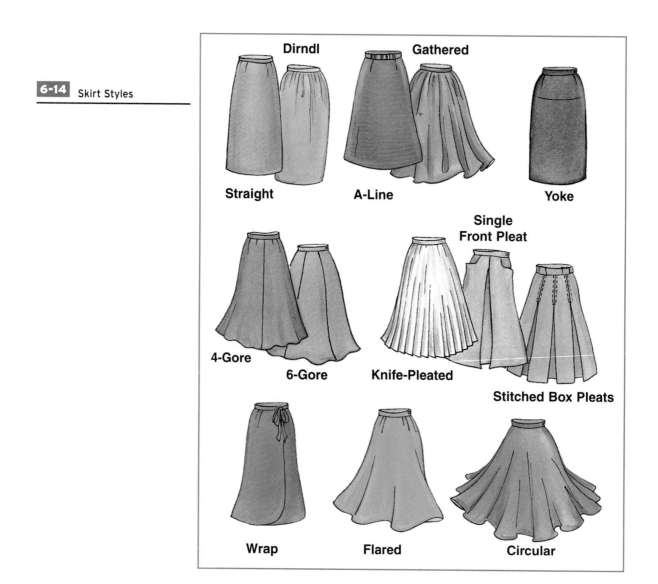

Skirt Styles

A skirt is a separate piece of clothing that can be worn with any top. See *Fig. 6-14*. Skirts can be straight, flared, or full. Darts, seams, pleats, and gathers create the shapes. Straight skirts often have a slit or pleat in the back seam to allow for movement. Variations of basic skirt shapes include the following:

- **Dirndl.** This straight skirt has extra fullness gathered at the waistline.
- **Gored.** Shaped sections called gores form this skirt. It fits at the waistline and flares at the hem. Four-gore and six-gore skirts are most common, but a twenty-four-gore skirt is possible.

- **Wrap.** This skirt wraps around the body and fastens with buttons or ties. A kilt, the traditional attire for men in Scotland, is a pleated wrap skirt.

Pants Styles

Pants styles vary in length as well as width. See *Fig. 6-15*. They can be short or long, full or fitted. Fashion dictates which are most popular and how they are worn. The waistline usually falls at the natural waistline but can be higher or lower. Pants that begin at the hip, rather than the waist, are called hip huggers. The following are common pants styles:

- **Straight.** Straight pants are the same width from knee to hem.
- **Tapered.** Tapered pants are narrower at the hem than at the knee.
- **Flared.** Flared pants are wider at the hem than at the knee. Bell-bottoms form a wide flare from the knee down.
- **Bermuda shorts.** Named for the island of Bermuda, these above-the-knee pants are worn there as men's streetwear.
- **Culottes.** These pants are cut to resemble a skirt.
- **Palazzo.** Also called pajama pants, these flowing pants are long, wide culottes.
- **Leggings.** Leggings are close-fitting, knitted pants.
- **Warm-ups.** These knit pants have an elastic or drawstring waist and ribbing or elastic at the ankles.
- **Jumpsuit.** The jumpsuit is a one-piece garment that combines pants with a bodice.

6-15 Pants Styles

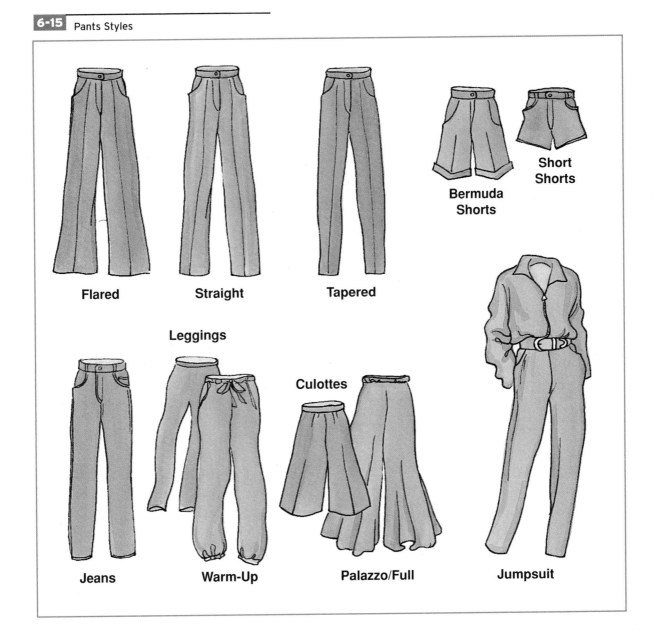

CHAPTER 6 Fashion Styles • 111

| Blazer | Double-Breasted | Boxy | Fitted | Vest |

| Tuxedo | Cardigan | Bolero | Chanel | Safari |

| Bomber/ Varsity | Windbreaker | Parka | Pea | Poncho |

| Trench | Polo | Chesterfield | Wrap | Cape |

6-16 Jacket and Coat Styles

Jacket and Coat Styles

Jackets and coats can be either single- or double-breasted. A single-breasted garment has one row of buttons down the center-front opening. A double-breasted garment has a wider front overlap and two rows of buttons. Among the styles you'll see are those described here and illustrated in *Fig. 6-16.*

- **Blazer.** This classic, solid-color jacket may be single- or double-breasted. When first worn in England in the 1890s, it was single-breasted and deep red or red-and-white striped.
- **Cardigan.** A collarless jacket or sweater, this garment buttons down the front. It's named for the 7th Earl of Cardigan, who added its extra layer of warmth to his military uniform in 1854.

>>SPREADING THE FASHION MESSAGE

As new fashion styles have been created over the years, people have been introduced to them in fashion shows. Only those who were invited to the shows, however, got the first look at the latest styles. Everyone else had to wait until photographs appeared in newspapers and fashion magazines. Times have changed. With the help of today's technology, the latest styles can be seen immediately after the shows.

- **Internet.** Through Web sites and on-line fashion magazines, consumers can download pictures from a fashion show that has just taken place on another continent. With new "walk around" technology, consumers can go behind the scene to a model's fitting session. The model can be spun around on the computer screen to see the clothing from any angle.

- **Cable television.** Networks on cable television send cameras and reporters to record the fashion shows. The tapes, along with interviews with the designers, are broadcast right away to viewers all over the world.

- **Videotapes.** Many designers produce videotapes of their fashion shows. Retailers show these videos in the stores next to the designer's clothes. The consumer can see a detailed picture of the clothes, accessories, hairstyles, and makeup that are part of the designer's current fashion look.

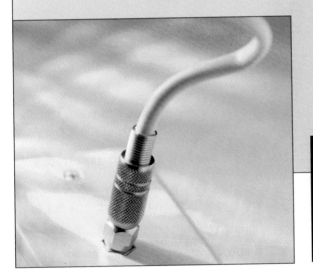

INVESTIGATION ACTIVITY

Obtain fashion videotapes from different years. After viewing, compare how styles were similar and different in those years.

- **Bolero.** This short jacket is styled after those worn by Spanish bullfighters.
- **Tuxedo.** A tuxedo jacket is a semiformal garment with a satin collar. It's named for the country club in Tuxedo Park, New York, where it was first worn.
- **Chesterfield.** The 6th Earl of Chesterfield, a fashion leader in the mid-1800s, wore this coat style that was named for him. The style usually has a black velvet collar.
- **Trench.** This all-purpose coat is made of water-repellent fabric. It is so named because British military officers wore it in the trenches during World War I.
- **Pea.** The pea coat was copied from the hip-length coats worn by sailors.

Review

CHAPTER SUMMARY

- A garment is identified by its style and by its variation of that style.

- A style may be described as classic, avant-garde, retro, or a fad.

- Fashion cycles occur as styles become more popular after being introduced and later decline in popularity.

- Fashion swings occur when style details change back and forth.

- A garment's style is determined by its features, including neckline, collar, and sleeves.

- Different style names are given to dresses, skirts, shirts, pants, and coats and jackets.

USING KEY TERMS

Give a specific fashion example that illustrates each Key Term. Your examples might be garments you've seen in magazines, ones that other people wear, or ones you own. Describe how each example fits the definition of the term.

RECALLING THE FACTS

1. What is meant by the term style?

2. Does a classic style ever change? Explain.

3. Why might fads be especially appealing to teens?

4. How is a fad different from an avant-garde style?

5. What is meant by the retro look?

6. What are the stages of a fashion cycle? Give an example of a recent fashion cycle.

7. Describe two examples of fashion swings.

8. How does a crew neckline differ from a bateau?

9. How are mandarin and ruff collars similar and different?

10. How is a set-in sleeve different from a dolman?

11. Why would a Hawaiian shirt look out of place at a formal dinner?

12. A catalog describes a skirt as gored. What does that mean?

13. List these pants styles from most full to least full: tapered, palazzo, leggings.

14. Compare the collars found on a chesterfield coat, a tuxedo jacket, and a cardigan sweater.

and Activities

THINKING CRITICALLY

1. Can a person have both a need to belong and a need for individuality? How can fads address these emotional needs?

2. Why do you think some styles are more classic than others?

3. Compare waistlines in various dress styles. What effects do they create and why?

4. Why do you think the decline stage of a fashion cycle is typically shorter than the introduction stage?

APPLYING KNOWLEDGE

1. **Garment styles.** Go through your own wardrobe and list the styles you see. What neckline, collar, and sleeve styles can you identify?

2. **New names.** Working with a partner, choose ten clothing styles described in the chapter and come up with new names for them. Choose names that indicate the style in some way.

3. **Garment lengths.** Review the illustration on page 102, which compares different garment lengths. Names for specific lengths can change periodically. Which terms are unfamiliar to you, if any? Why? Do you know these lengths by other fashion names?

4. **Today's trends.** Look through magazines and catalogs for pictures of garments that are currently in fashion. Arrange the illustrations on posters as a display of today's trends. Label the styles shown.

5. **Historical styles.** Many of the styles in this chapter may not make you think of the historical ones you saw in Chapter 5. That's because historical fashions combined styles and details in special ways. Browse the photos in Chapter 5 and other historical pictures to identify the styles used in those fashions. What made the garments different from today's use of similar styles?

6. **New styles.** Choose four different collar and sleeve styles. Combine these features to create shirt and blouse styles. How many different designs can you create? Which ones do you prefer? Show your designs to the class.

CREATIVE SOLUTIONS

Suppose you win a clothing store contest. The prize is your choice of two new outfits. You want to select garment styles that will make your wardrobe more versatile, perhaps with styles suitable for school, for fun, and also for special occasions. You'd like the clothes to last, but you enjoy trendy looks too.

Think Creatively

What styles will you choose for two outfits that can take you through many situations?

Fashion Designers

OBJECTIVES

- Explain the role of fashion designers in the apparel industry.

- Identify the names and achievements of famous fashion designers.

- Describe the design process.

- Compare couture and pret-a-porter collections.

KEY TERMS

atelier

collection

computer-aided design (CAD)

couture

couturiers

croquis

draping

haute couture

knock-offs

licensing

pret-a-porter

royalty

sloper

MANY PEOPLE BELIEVE FASHION designers lead very glamorous lives, surrounded by beautiful people, gorgeous fabrics, and wealthy customers. For most designers, this isn't true. Although the career has many rewards, designers work very hard, and most lead a less exotic life than you might imagine.

THE ROLE OF FASHION DESIGNERS

Fashion designers produce designs for clothing that will be sold in a particular market. They use design principles, fabrics, and construction techniques to transform their ideas to reality.

Designers work at different levels within the fashion industry. Some have gained national and world recognition, while others create designs, but without acclaim. Many provide support as they assist higher-level designers or work with existing designs.

Specialization is common in the design world. Those who create designs might concentrate on only one type of garment, such as swimwear, lingerie, bridal gowns, maternity, or children's clothes. Some specialize in jewelry, shoes, or other accessories. See *Fig. 7-1*. Other designers work in such fashion-related fields as cosmetics and fragrances and home furnishings.

To be successful, fashion designers must be aware of their target market—those who are likely to buy their designs. After all, if no one buys the clothing, a designer will soon be out of work.

High-Fashion Designers

When you walk through a clothing department, the names of certain designers are apparent. High-fashion, or "name," designers create garments that carry their name when sold. These designers are very influential in establishing the fashionable looks for each season. How many of the name designers on pages 126-131 do you recognize?

Some high-fashion designers own their own firm or are financed by partners. Others, such as Ralph Lauren and Donna Karan, are publicly

7-1 Designers create more than just clothing fashions. Home furnishings and such accessories as eyeglasses also begin with design.

7-2 The company owned by a high-fashion designer is often called a fashion house.

owned companies listed on the stock exchange. The companies of high-fashion designers are typically called fashion houses. See *Fig. 7-2.*

Famous designers may be known for a special style or look. Ralph Lauren's designs have classic elegance. Jil Sander creates a simple, spare look. The fine tailoring of Giorgio Armani and the casual, street-smart style of Tommy Hilfiger are also recognized. All are famous for both women's wear and menswear designs.

At least twice a year, and sometimes three or four, designers turn out a collection. A **collection** is the group of clothes designed and produced for a specific season. It may have 50 to 70 items.

Some designers have collections for different customers, such as men's apparel and women's apparel. Different collections may also be developed for different price ranges, using names like designer, better, and moderate.

Top designers are responsible for most of the fashion company's creative decisions. They search for new ideas, design garments, choose fabrics and colors, and establish an image. Business management is often part of the job as they set prices, meet with buyers and clients, and promote the fashions. They also approve the licenses of other products that are manufactured and sold under the designer's name. The fashion industry looks to name designers to develop new trends that will inspire everyone to buy new clothes.

Apparel Industry Designers

Most designers in the fashion industry don't have name recognition. They work for garment manufacturers that produce clothing for a particular brand or store label. See *Fig. 7-3.*

Like high-fashion designers, many designers who work for manufacturers also create original designs. They must develop the clothing collections that their company will produce.

The industry also employs designers called stylists. These people adapt designs created by others, often high-fashion designs. By modifying designs, stylists enable manufacturers to produce less expensive versions. The copies are called **knock-offs.** To reduce costs, the stylist selects a less-expensive fabric and changes some details.

Whether working on an original design or adapting one, designers in the industry must understand garment construction, the manufacturing process, and their firm's production capability. They may work closely with buyers of major stores to produce fashions that will sell.

The fashion industry also uses the services of freelance designers. These people work inde-

7-3 Much of the clothing people buy has been designed by professionals who don't have name recognition.

7-4 Designers might like to draw only what they like themselves, but they have to keep customers in mind. Designs that don't sell can be costly.

pendently, selling original designs or adaptations to manufacturers. The designs may have to follow a manufacturer's detailed specifications. These designers are self-employed and not involved in the manufacturer's business decisions.

The Business of Designing

When you see a runway model wearing a designer's latest creations, it's easy to forget that fashion is a complicated business. Designers create hundreds of styles each season, yet many never make it to the stores. Manufacturers and store buyers select only the styles they think will be successful. Styles that don't sell reduce the profit for everyone, from designer to seller. According to a saying in the garment industry, "a designer is only as good as the last collection." The customer makes the final decision. See *Fig. 7-4.*

In the business of fashion, success once depended on high prices. Now an inexpensive garment may be just as fashionable as an expensive one. Upper income consumers may buy low-cost garments too. Those on a tight budget may splurge on a costly item. Consumers also combine items to create a fashionable outfit regardless of each item's price. For example, an inexpensive cotton T-shirt could be worn with an expensive leather skirt, or an expensive silk blouse with an inexpensive pair of jeans. Today's fashions are available in all price ranges.

THE DESIGN PROCESS

Turning out many designs under the pressure of deadlines is typical in the design field. Before a design can even be started, however, a designer needs an idea. Once that challenge has been met, the actual design steps can begin.

Finding Inspiration

Designers are constantly on the lookout for something new. They need fresh ideas on a regular basis. Have you ever wondered why different designers come up with similar ideas at the same time? In this world of rapid communication, whatever inspires one can also inspire another.

Fashion ideas come from art exhibits, theater productions, movies, newspapers, magazines, and travel. See *Fig. 7-5.* Historical clothing and textile collections are another resource. Sometimes ethnic clothing and street fashions provide inspiration.

7-5 Art has long inspired fashion designers. The Winged Victory of Samothrace, a Greek statue housed in the Louvre, is just one example.

How To . . . CREATE A DESIGN SKETCH

Do you like to draw? If so, you might like to try your hand at doing a fashion sketch. To get started, use the basic procedure described here.

1 A good drawing controls proportion. First, draw a light vertical line down the center of your paper, making it the height you want the figure to be.

2 Then divide the line into eight equal segments, using light horizontal lines. Note how the parts of a figure fit within those eight segments. For example, the top segment shows the correct height for the head. Next, draw the figure over the lines you've prepared.

3 Once you're able to draw a figure with correct proportions, practice drawing figures in different poses.

4 Finally, choose a pose for your fashion figure and add an original design.

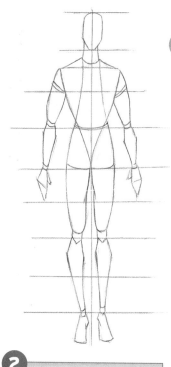

Exploring Fashion Drawing

Create a fashion design of your own. To improve your skills, find more information on fashion drawing.

New fabric textures, patterns, and prints also give ideas. Special trims and fasteners can become the focus of a new design. New fibers and fabric finishes offer fresh thoughts about styling, comfort, and performance.

Designers also notice how people live. Seeing more casual ways of living, a designer might focus on khaki pants, denim jeans, flannel shirts, and barn jackets. Another designer might create mix-and-match separates that can be worn for school, work, and leisure activities. The latest hi-tech fabrics could be used in sportswear, activewear, and rainwear.

Sketching Designs

With an idea in mind, the designer makes a sketch. Most garment sketches are very rough, with little detail. Some may be drawn on a body silhouette; others are sketched flat like a technical drawing. Color may be added by using colored markers or pencils.

A preliminary design sketch is called a **croquis** (kro-KEY). As the garment is developed, the croquis is revised to include all the garment's details, including yokes, pockets, collars, belts, and fasteners. It may even include construction notes.

Computer-aided design (CAD) software programs often take the place of hand sketching today. These systems create a three-dimensional drawing directly on the computer screen, as described on page 123.

Draping

Some designers prefer working with fabric to create a design rather than sketching. They begin by draping the fabric on a dress form. The process of **draping** means arranging fabric into graceful folds and attractive lines. Some high-fashion designers drape their creations on a live model.

The draping process allows the designer to see the actual silhouette, proportion, and details of a design. It shows whether a certain print, plaid, or striped fabric will be suitable. The fabric can be rearranged many times until the desired result is achieved. Although draping allows room for cre-

Fashion Facts

FASHION THEORIES.
Centuries ago royalty set fashion trends for the middle class to copy. High-fashion designers often set trends today. When manufacturers produce inexpensive versions of designs, the styles move from high fashion to mass fashion. This is called the "trickle down" theory of fashion. Designers are subject to influence too. When celebrities in movies, music videos, television shows, and even sporting events impact what high-fashion designers create, this is called the "trickle up" theory of fashion.

ativity, it usually takes much more time than sketching or designing on a computer.

Some ready-to-wear designers work with muslin, a coarse, cotton fabric, instead of the fashion fabric. Although muslin may not have the same hand or drape, it's inexpensive.

Selecting Fabrics and Trims

When selecting fabrics, designers consider the particular silhouette and details of a design. They also pay attention to fabric costs so the retail price of the garment will be affordable for customers. Some high-fashion designers work with fabric mills to develop fabrics for their exclusive use.

A swatch of the intended fabric is attached to each design sketch or detailed drawing. If the design has trim, a trim swatch is also included.

Making Sample Garments

The next step is developing a pattern for the sample garment. At this point, the designer usually works with a person who makes patterns. A preliminary pattern is usually made with a **sloper**. This basic pattern fits a certain body shape and has been used successfully in the past. If the new design is completely different from previous designs, a new sloper is created.

7-6 A sample garment must be made and refined before the design is ready to be included in a collection.

of high-fashion clothing. The dressmaking industry that creates the most fashionable, expensive, and exclusive designer clothing is called **haute couture** (oht koo-TOOR). The word *haute*, which is French for "high," means high class or fancy.

Designers create their haute couture collections for fashion-conscious customers. The clothes are original designs that can cost thousands of dollars. Many construction techniques are still done by hand in the designer's workroom, or **atelier** (a-tul-YAY). The fabrics are the finest available. They are often one-of-a-kind fabrics created exclusively for the designer. The garments are custom-made to fit each client's measurements exactly. Very few people today can afford true haute-couture fashions.

History of Haute Couture

Haute couture began in Paris several hundred years ago. In the 1770s, the French dressmaker Rose Bertin started sending what became known as "fashion babies" to London. These dolls were dressed in detailed copies of Queen Marie

Once made, the preliminary pattern is used to cut out a sample garment. At this stage, the trial garment may be made from a piece of the actual fabric or from muslin. Then the fabric pieces are sewn together by a sample maker and tried out on a model. The garment may be revised many times until the designer is satisfied that it can go into the collection. See *Fig. 7-6*.

DESIGNER COLLECTIONS

At one time, each garment was designed specifically for the client who would wear it. These became truly one-of-a-kind designs. When a designer presents a collection today, individual clients or retail buyers can order the clothes. Some designers create both couture and ready-to-wear collections, others only ready-to-wear.

Couture

Couture (koo-TOOR), the French word for dressmaking, is the designing, making, and selling

7-7 Charles Worth established the House of Worth, which existed for almost a century. He may have been the first dressmaker to label his designs.

Computer-aided design (CAD) systems are rapidly replacing the hand-sketching process. Designers work with a digital, or on-screen, three-dimensional, dress form that corresponds to the master pattern size. New designs are sketched directly onto the dress form. To make adjustments on the front, back, and sides of the garment, the designer simply "turns the dress form around."

Changes take only minutes to make, and experimenting with different collars and necklines is quick and easy. The designer can also try different colors and fabrics. After a design is finalized, the computer converts it into flat pattern pieces. Seam allowances and other details are added. Then the computer figures how much fabric is needed and what the production cost will be.

CAD makes the design process more cost-efficient in many ways. Because the computer stores old designs, updating a garment for the new season doesn't necessarily mean starting from scratch.

INVESTIGATION ACTIVITY
Use CAD software to create a fashion design of your own.

Antoinette's latest clothes. Dressmakers in London used the dolls to duplicate the style, fabric, and construction techniques of the original garments.

Other **couturiers** (koo-TOOR-ee-ays), or designers who make fashionable, custom-made clothes, copied this idea. They began to send dolls to potential customers around the world. Early American dressmakers studied the dolls to copy the original French designs and learn French construction techniques. This practice continued until newspapers and fashion magazines became an important method of fashion communication.

Charles Worth was a young Englishman who started his design career in London. See *Fig. 7-7.*

In 1845, he went to Paris to work for a firm that specialized in fabrics and shawls. Thirteen years later he opened his own highly successful fashion house. He had many wealthy and prominent clients, including Empress Eugenie and the court of France's Second Empire. Worth was the first designer to present gowns on live models. He was the first to sell sample gowns to be copied in the United States. He was the first designer to market a perfume under his own name. Because of these and other innovations, Worth is considered the father of haute couture.

Until World War II, everything that was significant in fashion started in Paris. During World War

7-8 High-fashion collections are introduced twice a year at elaborate runway shows.

II, many of the Paris fashion houses had to close. Retailers and fashion-conscious customers in the United States began to pay more attention to talented American designers. These included Claire McCardell, Norman Norell, and Charles James. After the war, such French designers as Coco Chanel, Christian Dior, and Cristobal Balenciaga helped Paris regain its place of importance.

Today, fashion designers in the United States, Italy, England, and Japan have also established couture houses. As a result, many cities are now influential in the fashion industry.

Fashion Shows

Twice a year, high-fashion designers and couture houses present their collections with fashion shows. They are held in July for the fall-winter collections and in January for the spring-summer collections. Retailers, the fashion press, celebrities, and wealthy private clients attend these by-invitation-only events. The major events take place in Paris, New York, and Milan. Collections are also shown in London, Tokyo, Montreal, and other major cities. See *Fig. 7-8*.

These shows are very elaborate events where the designer can be as imaginative as possible. Some of the clothes on the runway are purely fantasy. The designer aims to attract attention and get the fashion press to write about the collection. The major goal, however, is to get orders from retail buyers and private clients for garments in the shows.

Designer Ready-to-Wear

At one time, everyone in the fashion world eagerly awaited the Paris collections. American manufacturers sent representatives overseas to attend the fashion shows. Then the representatives rushed back to America and copied the designer originals. Ready-to-wear copies were

7-9 Top designers also produce collections that sell for less than their original designs. These collections help them compete with the many garment manufacturers who sell knock-offs and designs of their own.

mass-produced in factories and shipped to stores as soon as possible.

In time, talented American designers began to produce expensive, ready-to-wear clothes with a distinctly American point of view. Many fashion leaders began to appear in clothes by American designers. The Paris fashion houses soon realized they would need to find other ways to make money, so they decided to do the same thing the Americans were doing. They created their own ready-to-wear collections. See *Fig. 7-9.*

Today the French couture houses present two **pret-a-porter** (PRET-a-por-TAY), or deluxe ready-to-wear, collections per year. These clothes are more practical and not quite as expensive as the couture collections. The fabrics may not be quite as unique. There is very little, if any, hand sewing. The pret-a-porter collections, as well as other business ventures, including fragrances and accessories, earn money for the couture houses.

Today many European couture designers sell their pret-a-porter clothes in major department stores in the United States and other countries. Some have opened their own boutique stores in New York City and other cities. These specialty stores carry the latest ready-to-wear collections of the designers.

Top designers in New York, Milan, and other cities also hold showings of their ready-to-wear collections. These may be held in hotels, museums, tents, or the individual designer's showroom. Large design or industrial groups sponsor many of these showings. They may last for a week or more. Retail buyers place their orders, and the press reports the new fashion directions of each designer. Videos of these showings are broadcast around the world. Everyone gets to see the clothes as they looked on the runway, with the makeup, hairstyles, and accessories that give them the look the designer intended. Clothes and accessories by top American designers are sold in Paris, London, Rome, and other cities around the world.

Licensing

In the fashion world, **licensing** means giving legal permission to use your name to promote a

7-10 Many designers, such as Karl Lagerfeld, market more than just fashions. Perfume is another product sometimes linked to designer names.

product. In return, the person is paid a fee and a percentage of the profits, called a **royalty**. The licensee is the manufacturer who buys the rights to the name. The licensor is the person or company who sells the name. Common licensors include fashion designers, celebrities, sports figures, and cartoon or other fictional characters.

Fashion designers have licensed their names to everything from perfume to automobiles. See *Fig. 7-10.* Beauty products, accessories, and home furnishings are particularly popular. In some cases, the designer makes suggestions about the product and approves designs done by someone else. This is often someone who technically understands the final product better than the designer. In other cases, the designer is responsible for the actual product design.

Licensing of moderately priced items has enabled many more customers to buy designer products. It has also become a major source of profit for fashion designers and couture houses all over the world.

FAMOUS DESIGNERS

JOSEPH ABBOUD (American designer, 1950-). Designs classic clothes for men and women that combine European styling with American practicality; of Lebanese descent; also licenses accessories, fragrances, and home furnishings.

ADOLFO (American designer, 1929-). Born in Cuba; known for elegant knit suits inspired by Chanel's famous tweed suits; Nancy Reagan, as first lady, was often photographed in Adolfo's clothes.

LINDA ALLARD (American designer, 1940-). Began as an assistant design director at Ellen Tracy, a manufacturer of career clothes; became design director in 1964, and her name was added to the label in 1984.

GIORGIO ARMANI (Italian designer, 1936-). Known for unconstructed jackets, finely tailored menswear, and women's suits with menswear details; credited with reintroducing linen to menswear and women's wear.

CRISTOBAL BALENCIAGA (French couturier, 1895-1972). Born and raised in Spain; a major influence from the end of World War II until he retired in 1968; trained many other designers, including Courreges, Ungaro, and Givenchy. Innovations included narrow rolled collars, evening gowns with a slight train, patterned hosiery in heavier fibers, and cocoon coats.

GEOFFREY BEENE (American designer, 1927-). Designs beautiful, couture quality clothes; also licenses many products, including shoes, gloves, hosiery, eyewear, home furnishings, and perfume.

BILL BLASS (American designer, 1922-2002). Known for classic sportswear in menswear fabrics, elegant mixtures of fabrics, and glamorous evening clothes; licensed many products, including automobiles and chocolates; received Coty Hall of Fame Award in 1970.

CALLET SOEURS (French couture house, 1895-1935). Fashion house founded by three sisters and considered one of the greatest dressmaking establishments of its time; famous for delicate lace blouses, richly embroidered floral patterns, and the use of chiffon, georgette, and organdy.

PIERRE CARDIN (French designer, 1922-). Born in Italy and worked for Schiaparelli and Dior before opening his own couturier house in 1950; first Paris couturier to sell his own ready-to-wear; first designer to license his name and once held over 500 licenses.

BONNIE CASHIN (American designer, 1915-). One of the first American designers not influenced by Paris couturiers; known for comfortable country and travelling clothes, such as hooded jersey dresses, ponchos, and soft, knee-high boots; also designed costumes for the theater, ballet, and movies.

GABRIELLE "COCO" CHANEL (French couturier, 1883-1971). Perhaps the most famous of all French couturiers; her many contributions include slacks for women, the classic "little black dress," and suits with boxy, collarless jackets trimmed in braid. The House of Chanel continues today under the direction of Karl Lagerfeld.

LIZ CLAIBORNE (American designer, 1930-). Born in Belgium and raised in New Orleans; designed for Jonathan Logan before beginning her own company; known for dresses, coordinated sportswear, and petite collections; also licenses many accessories.

ANDRE COURREGAS (French designer, 1923-). Called the "space age designer" because of his forward-looking designs made of all white fabrics and accessorized by white tights and white boots; introduced industrial zippers in jumpsuits and other clothing.

OSCAR DE LA RENTA (American designer, 1932-). Born in the Dominican Republic; known for elegant, feminine daywear and "for evening" wear that features luxurious fabrics, such as taffeta, organza, and tulle; also designed the couture collection for the House of Balmain in Paris.

CHRISTIAN DIOR (French couturier, 1905-1957). In 1947, introduced "The New look," which featured a closely fitted bodice and long, full skirt; created inner construction methods to shape dresses in an A, H, or Y silhouette. After Dior's death, Yves Saint-Laurent headed the House of Dior; today Gianfranco Ferré heads it.

DOMENICO DOLCE (1958-) and **STEFANO GABBANA** (1962-) (Italian designers). Joined forces in Milan in 1982; their clothes are often described as modern-romantic, with many historical references and pieces designed to be worn in different ways; D & G is their lower-priced collection.

PERRY ELLIS (American designer, 1940-1986). Known for young, adventurous clothes, natural fibers, neutral colors, and hand-knitted sweaters for men and women. After his death, the Council of Fashion Designers of America began the "Perry" award to recognize new design talent.

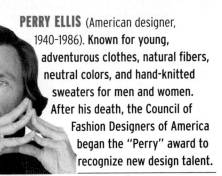

GIANFRANCO FERRÉ (Italian designer, 1945-). Studied architecture, which influences his creations; first designed furniture, then accessories for other designers; replaced Marc Bohan as design director for Christian Dior in 1989.

MARIANO FORTUNY (Italian designer, 1871-1949). Known for long, delicate, pleated gowns inspired by Greek statues; his unique pleating technique remains a mystery.

JEAN-PAUL GAULTIER (French designer, 1952-). Began as an assistant to Pierre Cardin; designs unusual, controversial, and expensive ready-to-wear clothing for a younger market; inspired by street fashions to create overly tight garments and unisex styling.

RUDI GERNRICH (American designer, 1922-1985). Known in the 1960s for daring clothes, such as topless swimsuits and see-through blouses, as well as knit minidresses and knee-high leggings worn with tunic tops.

HUBERT DE GIVENCHY (French designer, 1927-). Worked for several French designers, including Schiaparelli; known for simple, elegant designs worn by his favorite movie actress, the late Audrey Hepburn; his many licensing agreements include hosiery, eyewear, sportswear, and home furnishings; now headed by Alexander McQueen.

FAMOUS DESIGNERS

ALIX GRÈS (French designer, 1903-1993). **First desire was to be a sculptor; known for draped and molded jersey dresses; business closed during World War II but reopened after the war and continued until the mid 1980s.**

HALSTON (American designer, 1932-1990). **Known in the 1970s for his ultra-suede dresses and suits; popular designer for many celebrities, including Elizabeth Taylor and Liza Minelli.**

EDITH HEAD (American designer, 1899-1981). **Costume designer who won eight Oscars; designed movie wardrobes for such screen stars as Grace Kelly, Mae West, Paul Newman, Robert Redford, and Elizabeth Taylor.**

CAROLINE HERRERA (American designer, 1939-). **Born in Venezuela; moved to the U.S. in 1980; designs dresses, ball gowns, and wedding gowns, plus made-to-order clothes for private clients; has her own fragrances.**

TOMMY HILFIGER (American designer, 1952-). **As a teen, drove to New York City to use his life savings ($150) to buy trendy jeans; resold them to upstate friends; owned ten specialty stores by age twenty-six; known for his All-American casual look; heads a fashion empire with collections and licenses in apparel, accessories, and home fashions.**

CHARLES JAMES (American couturier, 1906-1978). **Raised in Chicago but operated dressmaking salons in London and Paris; also ran a custom-order business; considered an equal by top Paris couturiers.**

BETSEY JOHNSON (American designer, 1942-). **Designs funky, youthful fashions that have a sense of humor, such as a vinyl slip dress and the "Basic Betsey"—a limp, clinging T-shirt dress in many lengths.**

WOLFGANG JOOP (German designer, 1944-). **Known for technical knowledge and fabric research; designs for men and women; says his label stands for "quality and taste, but the ability to be a little bit tacky."**

NORMA KAMALI (American, 1945-). Inspired to be a designer by her mother, who sewed; first recognized for adventurous, body-conscious fashions; has used unusual fabrics, such as silk parachute cloth and quilted mover's blankets.

DONNA KARAN (American designer, 1948-). **One of the most successful designers today; has own design firm and specializes in simple, well-made sportswear; first designer to popularize the bodysuit; has many licensed products, including shoes, jewelry, hosiery, and eyewear; her DKNY collection is a popular department in many stores.**

REI KAWAKUBO (Japanese designer, 1945-). **Born and educated in Japan; known as a trend-setting, French, ready-to-wear designer; his garments are a happy combination of textures and patterns, usually based on traditional Japanese clothing.**

ANN KLEIN (American designer, 1923-1974). **Revolutionized junior-size clothes, giving them an adult look; pioneered sportswear as uniquely suited to the American woman.**

CALVIN KLEIN (American designer, 1942-). **Famous for creating Calvin Klein jeans; designs simple, sophisticated sportswear with architectural lines; uses natural fabrics, mostly in earth tones; has created controversy over his daring advertising campaigns.**

MICHAEL KORS (American designer, 1959-). Creates designer sportswear; designs individual pieces first, then combines them into outfits.

CHRISTIAN LACROIX (French designer, 1951-). Opened his own couture and ready-to-wear business in 1987; introduced dresses with fitted tops and short bubble skirts for a special evening look; occasionally designs costumes for the ballet and theater.

KARL LAGERFELD (French designer, 1939-). Born in Germany; designs garments under his own name and for the House of Chanel; designs furs for Fendi; designs shoes for Mario Valentino and Charles Jordan.

HELMUT LANG (Austrian designer, 1956-). Experiments with unusual, high-tech fabrics to create rumpled looks and subtle layers; some see him as a prophet of fashion, while others think his clothes are anti-fashion.

RALPH LAUREN (American designer, 1939-). Famous for his Polo collection of menswear; also designs women's wear, children's clothes, home furnishings, accessories, and cosmetics; designs are influenced by the American West and an idealized version of traditional English apparel and décor; his company owns many stores that bear his name.

CLAIRE MCCARDELL (American designer, 1906-1958). Considered the top all-American designer in the 1940s and 1950s; specialized in practical clothes for the average woman; used sturdy fabrics, such as denim, gingham, and wool jersey; introduced bareback summer dresses, bolero jackets over halter dresses, and ballet slippers as streetwear.

MARY MCFADDEN (American designer, 1936-). Known for hand-painted tunics; garments feature luxurious fabrics, pleating, and braid and rope trim.

NICOLE MILLER (American designer, 1952-). Gained attention with men's ties, then boxer shorts and menswear linings in bold graphic prints; clothes are youthful and midpriced.

MISSONI (Italian designers, **ROSITA**, 1931-, **OTTAVIO**, 1921-). Husband and wife team known for simple knit garments designed by Rosita that are made in startling geometric and abstract patterns created by Ottavio.

ISSEY MIYAKI (Japanese designer, 1938-). Worked as an assistant to Givenchy and Geoffrey Beene; has his own design business in Tokyo and also shows in Paris; his work combines Japanese fashion attitudes with the exotic fabrics he designs.

ISAAC MIZRAHI (American designer, 1961-). Worked with Perry Ellis and Calvin Klein before starting his own business at age twenty-six; designs young, inventive clothes in unexpected colors and fabrics for women and men; occasionally designs costumes for the ballet. In 1995, Mizrahi was the subject of *Unzipped*, a popular movie documentary about the fashion industry.

CLAUDE MONTANA (French designer, 1949-). Recognized for leather fashions, as well as bold, well-defined silhouettes and broad, exaggerated shoulders for men and women.

NORMAN NORRELL (American designer, 1900-1972). Sometimes called "the American Balenciaga" for the precise tailoring and timeless elegance of his clothes; remembered for many designs, including trouser suits for town, slinky sequined sheaths, and sweater tops with luxurious skirts. He was the first designer elected to the Coty Hall of Fame, and was founder and president of the Council of Fashion Designers of America.

FAMOUS DESIGNERS

TODD OLDHAM (American designer, 1961-). Self-taught; first fashion job was in an alterations department; uses simple shapes with offbeat prints and trims; runway shows are elaborate events; has worked on productions with MTV.

PAUL POIROT (French designer, 1880-1944). Considered the father of the French fashion industry and one of the greatest designers of all time; banished the corset and introduced the hobble skirt, turbans, and kimono tunics in the early 1900s; many French artists designed his fabrics.

MIUCCIA PRADA (Italian designer, 1950-). Family firm produces high quality leather goods; took over from her mother as director in 1978; first success was a black nylon backpack; first ready-to-wear collection was in 1989; creates soft, comfortable shapes that come alive on the body.

EMILIO PUCCI (Italian designer, 1914-1992). Was a member of Italy's Olympic ski team; fashion career began when a photographer noticed his ski clothes; known for lightweight jersey dresses in bright, bold geometric prints.

MARY QUANT (English designer, 1934-). In the mid 1950s, London was the center of the fashion world and Quant was its most important designer; credited with starting the Mod Look, featuring miniskirts, hip hugger pants, body stockings, and hot pants.

TRACY REESE (American designer, 19__-). Graduated from Parsons School of Design. Both of her lines—*Tracy Reese* and *plenty*—are known for bright colors, unusual prints, and intricate patterns. While whimsical and breezy, her designs combine modern technology with vintage flair to create a look of her own.

YVES SAINT LAURENT (French designer, 1936-). Worked for Christian Dior and, after Dior's death, became head of the House of Dior at age twenty-one. Known for many designs, including the trapeze dress, pea jackets, Mondrian dresses, coat dresses, the safari look, and Russian-inspired designs; opened a series of pret-a-porter boutiques called Rive Gauche; his many licenses are often identified by the initials YSL.

JIL SANDER (German, 1943-). Began as a fashion journalist; opened one of the first boutiques in Germany; creates fluid, well-proportioned designs with little decoration; now heads a fashion empire with boutiques all over the world.

ELSA SCHIAPARELLI (French couturier, 1890-1973). Considered one of the most creative and unconventional couturiers of the 1930s and 1940s; first to design fitted sweaters with collars, bows, and other details knitted in; introduced the color "shocking pink"; loved unusual details, such as brightly colored zippers.

WILLI SMITH (American designer, 1948-1987). Started his own firm, WilliWear Ltd., at age twenty-eight; designed youthful clothes for men and women in a style he described as "real clothes."

ANNA SUI (American designer, 1955-). An avid sewer since junior high school; designs moderately priced, unconventional, adventurous clothes for young customers.

RICHARD TYLER (American designer, 1948–). Born and studied in Australia where he apprenticed with his mother, a seamstress who created costumes for the Australian ballet; designed in Europe and now in Los Angeles.

EMANUEL UNGARO (French designer, 1933–). Born in France to Italian parents; worked for Balenciaga and Courregas; early designs were structured and ultramodern; known today for soft, body-conscious designs.

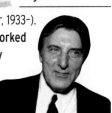

VALENTINO (Italian designer, 1932–). Shows couture collection in Rome and pret-a-porter collection in Paris; many of his clothes and accessories have his signature initial V marked in the seams or incorporated into the design.

GIANNI VERSACE (Italian designer, 1946–1997). Designed for several pret-a-porter firms and then designed a menswear collection under his own name; created sophisticated and elegant designs for women's wear as well as costumes for the opera and the ballet. Versace boutiques around the world feature clothing and accessories now designed by his sister Donatello.

MADELEINE VIONNET (French couturier, 1876–1975). Considered one of the three greatest couturiers, along with Chanel and Balenciaga, of the 20th century; famous for bias-cut dresses, handkerchief hems, cowl and halter necklines, and art deco embroideries.

ADRIENNE VITTADINI (American designer, 19__–). Born in Hungary, but grew up in Philadelphia; specializes in hand- and machine-knit garments, usually in vibrant colors; has a collection of fragrances and hand-knitting yarns.

DIANE VON FURSTENBERG (American designer, 1946–). Born in Brussels, educated in Europe, and moved to New York in 1969. Her knit jersey wrap dress was a "uniform" for career women in the 1970s; operates a design studio and is a popular designer on the QVC shopping network.

VERA WANG (American designer, 1949–). Childhood figure-skating champion who designed costumes for the 1994 Winter Olympics; famous for expensive bridal gowns and evening dresses.

CHARLES FREDERICK WORTH (French couturier, 1826–1895). Known as the father of haute couture; in 1858 opened his own fashion house, which remained the most important fashion house in Paris for 50 years; dressed many famous women, including Empress Eugenie of France and Empress Elizabeth of Austria; his perfume, Je Reviens, is still sold today.

Here Willi Smith works with a model wearing one of his skirt designs in New York in 1987.

CHAPTER SUMMARY

- Designers use their understanding of design, fabric, and construction to create new fashions.

- High-fashion designers assume complete control for producing some of the most creative and expensive clothing in the industry.

- After inspiration from many sources, designers perfect their ideas through sketches, draping, and sample garments.

- Haute couture fashions are most expensive. Ready-to-wear and pret-a-porter collections are moderately priced.

USING KEY TERMS

Write ten fill-in-the-blank statements that use at least ten Key Terms in the blanks. Exchange papers with a classmate and fill in the blanks. When completed, return the papers for checking. Discuss any difficulties either of you had with the statements.

RECALLING THE FACTS

1. What are some of the responsibilities of a high-fashion designer?

2. How do stylists contribute to the clothing industry?

3. Is it good business sense for a store buyer to choose garments from a variety of price ranges? Why or why not?

4. Summarize the design process in five steps.

5. List at least six sources of inspiration for new fashion designs.

6. Why does a designer sketch a croquis?

7. What are some advantages and disadvantages of draping?

8. What role did fashion babies play in the history of haute couture?

9. What current fashion business practices were pioneered by Charles Worth?

10. Describe a fashion show that presents high-fashion designs.

11. What gave rise to pret-a-porter fashions?

12. How do pret-a-porter fashions compare with haute couture designs?

13. How does licensing affect designers and consumers?

14. Compare the designs of Oscar de la Renta and Calvin Klein.

and Activities

THINKING CRITICALLY

1. From a designer's point of view, what are some advantages and disadvantages of a stylist creating knock-offs of a collection?

2. Which do you think is more important for a fashion house today: couture collections, ready-to-wear collections, or licensing agreements? Explain your answer.

3. Do you think a designer's style can be translated into such items as home furnishings, perfume, and makeup? Explain.

APPLYING KNOWLEDGE

1. **Designers.** Research a famous fashion designer. Give a presentation on the designer's life, creations, and influence. If possible, include illustrations of his or her fashions.

2. **Adapting designs.** Look through high-fashion magazines for a style that is not worn by most people. Suggest ways that the look could be modified to have greater appeal.

3. **New designs for teens.** If you were a designer, where would you look for inspiration when creating new fashions for teens today? Write an explanation of your ideas.

4. **Licensing.** Using magazines, newspapers, and visits to stores, list fashions and related products that are promoted by designers, celebrities, and sports figures. Share the results in class. How do you explain the length of the lists?

5. **International language.** Using information in fashion publications, this chapter, and previous chapters, list foreign terms used in the fashion industry. Create a glossary by including definitions.

CREATIVE SOLUTIONS

You and a classmate have been asked to organize a teen fashion show as a fundraiser for a school club. To create the atmosphere of a high-fashion runway show, you plan to talk with local stores about obtaining fashions for the show.

Think Creatively

What designers and fashions will you include in the show? Will high fashion be part of the show? How will you handle affordability and variety?

The Fashion Industry

OBJECTIVES

- List ways that fibers and fabrics are used other than in clothing.

- Explain how the textile industry operates.

- Describe the manufacturing process for clothing.

- Explain what's involved in fashion merchandising.

- Describe promotion methods used by designers, manufacturers, and retailers.

KEY TERMS

assembly line	forecasting
chain	services
contractors	line
converters	market week
copy	marketing
fashion	mass-produced
merchandising	retail
fashion	wholesale
promotion	

Did you know that the United States produces enough fabric to stretch to the moon and back 23 times? Creating that much fabric is easier than it once was. Because of today's technology, procedures that used to take several months can now be done in minutes. Textile production, of course, is just one part of the huge fashion industry. The road from fibers, to fabrics, to garments, to stores takes many steps and millions of employees, as you'll soon see.

THE TEXTILE INDUSTRY

Fiber and fabric producers make up the textile industry. This industry, one of the oldest and largest in America, provides fiber and fabric for many purposes.

Uses of Fibers and Fabrics

The largest percentage of the textiles manufactured in the United States—almost 40 percent—goes into clothing. The remaining fibers are used for home furnishings and other uses. See *Fig. 8-1.*

While clothing is an obvious use of fibers and fabrics, others might surprise you. Did you know that a felt-tip pen has a nylon point? Were you aware that the covering on a tea bag is a textile product? Fibers and fabrics are also found in luggage, flags, and ropes. *Fig. 8-2* on page 136 gives examples of the many uses of fibers and fabrics.

From Fiber to Fabric

In the textile industry, fiber producers begin the process that creates fabric. Farmers grow plants that provide cotton fibers. Ranchers raise sheep that provide fleece for wool. Scientists work for chemical companies that develop and manufacture fibers. All of these fibers are eventually spun into yarns and then made into fabrics by textile mills.

After buying the finished fabrics, manufacturers create many different products. Apparel manufacturers cut and sew fabric into garments. Fabric stores buy textiles to sell to home sewers.

8-1 Percentages of Fiber Used for Different Purposes

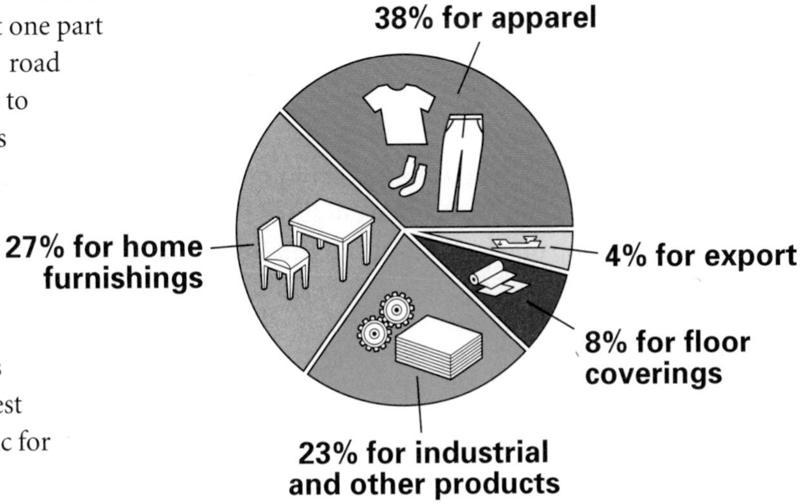

- **38% for apparel**
- **4% for export**
- **8% for floor coverings**
- **23% for industrial and other products**
- **27% for home furnishings**

HOME DECORATION			
Curtains Draperies Slipcovers Upholstery	Rugs Carpets Table linens	Lampshades Sheets Pillowcases	Blankets Bedspreads Towels
MEDICINE			
Disposable surgical gowns Disposable masks	Disposable sheets	Disposable bandages	Lining for arti- ficial hearts
RECREATION			
Artificial foot- ball turf Tennis racket strings	Backpacks Tents Sails Fishing lines	Carbon-fiber, reinforced plastics in fishing rods, golf clubs, ski poles	Carbon-fiber, reinforced plastics in hulls of sail- boats, canoes
INDUSTRY			
Filters Polishing cloths	Conveyor belts	Buildings with fabric "skins"	Napped sur- face on paint rollers
TRANSPORTATION			
Tires Vehicle seat belts Vehicle wall coverings	Vehicle seat covers Vehicle flooring Spacesuits	Spacecraft interiors Booster rockets	Space shuttle heat shield

knitted fabrics in many types and weights. Some produce only woven fabrics, while others make only knits. Some large mills manufacture both.

The design department of a textile mill works closely with the research department to develop new weaves, patterns, prints, and colors. New fabrics created by fabric designers often inspire new clothing styles. These designers are working today on fabrics that will appear in the stores in one or two years.

Once fabrics are dyed or printed with a design, additional treatments give the fabrics special qualities. For example, one finish makes a fabric repel water. Brushing creates a fuzzy surface on another fabric.

Through quality control, finished fabrics are inspected and tested to be sure they meet specific standards of quality and performance. Apparel manufacturers, retailers, and independent labs also do testing.

How do you think different companies produce clothing and home furnishings in coordinating colors each season? Many fabric mills and manufacturers work with **forecasting services**. These services predict color, fabric, and fashion trends two or more years in advance. They

Fiber Companies

The backbone of the textile industry is research and development. These departments develop new fibers and the equipment for making them. Through testing, they evaluate a new fiber's strength, dyeability, and reaction to special finishes.

The new fibers, including nylon and polyester, are created from chemicals. They are produced by such chemical companies as DuPont and Hoechst Celanese, which sell their fibers to textile mills.

Textile Mills

Textile mills spin fibers into yarns and convert them into fabric. See *Fig. 8-3*. Some of the largest textile mills are Burlington Industries, Dan River, Fieldcrest Cannon, Springs Industries, and Milliken & Company. Mills produce woven and

8-3 Fibers are transformed to yarns and fabric in textile mills.

How To...

EXPLORE FASHION CAREERS

The outfit you see in a store window has come a long way from fiber to fashion. People in design, production, retailing, marketing, and promotion all made contributions. Would you like to be part of the process? At the end of each unit in this text, you'll find fashion career information. Using the suggestions on this page, you can investigate careers to see whether there's a good match for you in the fashion world.

Step 1: Identify Career Goals

Careers impact the way people live. Do you want to live where you do now, or are you willing to move? Would you work nights and weekends? Do you want to travel? Which of these sounds appealing: a formal or casual workplace; a relaxed or hectic pace; part-time or full-time work? Find out how the careers you're considering would meet your expectations.

Step 2: Evaluate Personal Qualities and Skills

You'll get more enjoyment and success from a career that fits your qualities and skills. In the fashion industry, some careers take creativity and originality while others take an interest in research, science, manufacturing, or business. In all fields, dependability, flexibility, and a positive attitude are valued. Do you get along well with others? Do you like to write, sew, sketch, take photos, or use a computer? Compare your qualities and skills with those needed in fashion careers.

Step 3: Research Career Paths

The direction a career takes as you change positions is called a career path. By gaining experience and taking on more responsibility, you can advance to higher positions. That's called moving up on the career ladder. If you apply experience in one field to a new field, your career path takes a different direction. Find out what education, training, and experience are needed for paths in the careers you're exploring.

Step 4: Explore Job Possibilities

The more you know about a career, the easier it is to evaluate it. You could work part-time as a sales associate to learn about retailing. You might sample a career by taking an entry-level position. You can talk to people who work in certain careers. What opportunities are there in your area to learn about careers that interest you?

Exploring Fashion Careers

Investigate a fashion career, writing a response for each step described here.

develop special reports, color cards, and fabric swatches for their clients. Forecasting enables companies to produce matching items.

Textile Converters

Textile **converters** are companies or individuals who serve as middle agents between textile mills and apparel manufacturers. Converters buy unfinished fabrics, called greige (GRAY) goods, from the mills and have them dyed, printed, and finished to meet the specifications of designers and manufacturers. They have more flexibility than large mills to fulfill orders on short notice.

Today's Locations

For years, the southeastern United States has been the center of textile manufacturing, as well as research and development. About 70 percent of textile employment is located in this region, primarily near small urban communities.

Many of the industry's related businesses, such as sales and marketing, are located in New York City. There, mills and converters have showrooms where apparel designers and manufacturers can see fabric samples. Showrooms are also located in Los Angeles, Dallas, Atlanta, and Chicago.

THE APPAREL INDUSTRY

The shirt with the "in" style, the special clothes for playing sports, and even the gloves you wear in winter are all products of the apparel industry. See *Fig. 8-4.* This important segment of the fashion industry accounts for more companies, employees, and sales volume than any other segment.

The apparel industry is also known as the garment industry or the rag trade. This fast-paced field is very complex. Since ideas about what is fashionable change from season to season, they are hard to predict. Manufacturers risk making mistakes. Although some companies have been in business for many years, others go in and out of business almost overnight. Ready-to-wear manufacturers can make a large profit one season with a "hot" line that sells well. They can lose heavily next season if they guess incorrectly about what will sell.

From Fabrics to Garments

Apparel manufacturers buy fabrics from textile mills and converters, design and produce a clothing collection, or **line**, and sell the finished garments to stores. Some companies do all the production themselves; others hire different companies to do various steps. The factories where clothes are made are located in many cities and countries.

Almost all of today's clothes are **mass-produced**. This means that many garments are made at the same time, with machines doing most of the work. Hems are usually machine-made. Even buttons can be sewn on by machine. As a result, garments can be made faster and cheaper than ever before. See *Fig. 8-5.*

Types of Manufacturers

Apparel is divided into three main categories: women's wear, menswear, and children's wear. Women's wear receives the most publicity, has the greatest designer recognition, and is the most competitive segment of the fashion industry.

8-4 Because of the huge apparel industry, you can choose from many garments when shopping.

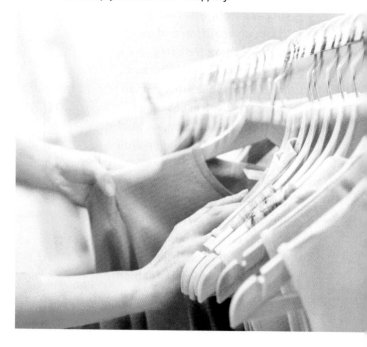

When garments are mass-produced, workers often specialize in certain tasks.

Each category is further subdivided into garment types. Women's wear, for example, includes dresses, blouses, sportswear, outerwear, eveningwear, bridal, maternity wear, and intimate apparel.

Small manufacturers usually specialize in one or two garment types in a certain price range. Large firms may produce apparel under many different labels in several price ranges. Most manufacturers of accessories and home furnishings also specialize in one or two areas.

Garment Manufacturers

Manufacturers handle all phases of a garment's production—from design, to production, to shipping. See *Fig. 8-6.* Most produce two lines of clothing per year. These lines are designed at least six months ahead of a season. Clothes shown to store buyers and the press in the spring will be in the stores in the fall. Clothes shown in the fall will be available in the stores the following spring.

Contractors

Although some manufacturers do all production in their own factories, many hire **contractors**. These are companies that specialize in sewing certain garments for a specific price. They may be located in the United States or in other countries, such as India or Korea. Contractors produce the garment according to the manufacturer's designs and specifications.

Accessories Manufacturers

Accessories include shoes, hosiery, jewelry, watches, scarves, neckties, gloves, hats, belts, handbags, and small leather goods. Many companies specialize in manufacturing only one type of accessory. Others manufacture several types. Many name designers have licensing agreements with manufacturers for accessories that complete the designer's fashion look.

Although the manufacturing of accessories has many of the same steps as garments, production techniques are specialized. Shoes are formed on a foot-shaped mold, called a *last.* Stones are inserted into jewelry. Hosiery is knitted to the shape of the legs and feet. Felt hats are shaped, ties are lined, and handbags may have detachable straps.

The Manufacturing Process

The steps for manufacturing ready-to-wear are very similar to those used by home sewers. As described here, they begin with design and end with distribution.

Have you ever received the wrong item in a shipment? If so, you can appreciate careful packaging.

The manufacturing process begins with designing the line to be produced.

1. **Designing the line.** The fashion designer or design department plans the line. For each item, they determine the design, select the colors and fabrics, and add the details. See *Fig. 8-7.* As you saw in Chapter 7, stylists create less expensive versions of designer fashions. For this reason, two manufacturers might produce garments with similar styles but different prices. Most countries, except for France, have no laws against line-for-line copies.

2. **Making samples.** To check the styling, appearance, and fit of each design, a sample garment is made. The sample may be changed and reworked many times until the design and marketing departments believe the design will sell. Specifications are written for each garment.

3. **Establishing costs.** The **wholesale** price of each item must be figured. This is what stores pay to manufacturers when buying goods to sell. The wholesale price is determined by adding all expenses for fabric, lining, trims, fasteners, labor, packaging, and shipping. Then additional business expenses, such as rent and advertising, are added. The cost for each and every component must be established since the slightest error could result in losses instead of profits. Some manufacturers double their costs to arrive at the wholesale price. See *Fig. 8-8.*

4. **Taking orders.** Sales representatives show sample garments to store buyers in the manufacturer's showrooms. Items that are ordered go into production.

5. **Ordering materials.** All fabrics, trims, and fasteners are ordered from vendors, or suppliers. Large manufacturers buy fabrics directly from major textile mills. Smaller companies, unable to order in large quantities, are usually restricted to smaller fabric suppliers.

8-8 • Computing the Price of a Pair of Pants				
MANUFACTURING EXPENSES	**QUANTITY NEEDED**	**UNIT COST**	**COST PER PANTS**	**TOTALS**
Material Fabric Interfacing	 1.6 yds. .2 yd.	 $2.50/yd $ .55/yd.	 $4.00 $ .11	 $4.11
Trims and Supplies Buttons Zipper	 2 1	 $2.00/gross $ .15	 $ .03 $ .15	 $ .18
Labor (Computed for all processes)			$5.10	$5.10
Other Packaging; tags; shipping; etc.			$ .60	$ .60
Total Cost to Manufacture				$9.99
Wholesale Price for Retailers (often doubles manufacturing cost)				$19.99
Retail Price for Consumers (often doubles wholesale cost)				$39.99

Have you ever wondered how the bar code on a price tag works? The widths and lengths of the lines and spaces indicate numbers and letters that identify a specific product. When a bar code is scanned, a computerized database with product information is accessed. The user gets information about the product. If a sale is made, records adjust immediately.

Bar code technology is one tool used by a management system called Quick Response (QR). With this system, fiber producers, fabric mills, apparel manufacturers, and retailers link electronically to do business faster and more efficiently. QR has many advantages for businesses.

- Increases speed of design and production with computer-aided design (CAD) and computer-aided manufacturing (CAM) systems.
- Increases efficiency by allowing companies to reorder and communicate electronically.
- Accurately tracks sales and inventory to avoid overstocking goods.
- Reduces amount of time that goods spend in transit or warehouses.
- Decreases time needed to restock merchandise, avoiding out-of-stock items.

Ultimately, QR saves time at all stages, from fiber manufacture to retail sales. Retail reorders are smaller and more frequent. Even though inventories are lower, fewer items are out of stock. Best of all, producers, manufacturers, and retailers enjoy greater profits.

INVESTIGATION ACTIVITY
Use the Internet and other resources to learn more about how QR works.

---

6. **Creating production patterns.** The master pattern must be "graded" up and down into other sizes. The manufacturer's sample size 8, for example, will be produced in sizes 4 to 16. Today, most garment manufacturers use computers for pattern grading.

7. **Creating layouts.** Developing a layout is like doing a giant jigsaw puzzle. All the pattern pieces must fit onto the smallest amount of fabric possible to minimize costs. When a manufacturer produces thousands of garments, a financial savings of just a few fabric inches per garment can be substantial. A marker, a long piece of paper with outlines of all pattern pieces on the layout, is created. Both the layout and marker can be created by computer. see→ p 492

8. **Cutting fabric.** Special machines stack as many as 500 layers of fabric sixty feet long, so many garments can be cut out at the same

Heavy-duty sewing machines designed for specialized tasks are used in manufacturing garments.

time. The marker is placed across the top as a guide for the cutting knives. Some companies have a computer-aided manufacturing (CAM) system that does the layout and cutting automatically. The fabric pieces are then sorted by sizes, tied into bundles, and sent to sewing operators located on the premises or in contractor's shops.

9. **Assembling garments.** On an **assembly line**, each worker specializes in a certain task and then passes bundles of items to the next worker. On a shirt, for example, one person may stitch the sleeve, another may attach the collar, and another may sew the buttonholes. Specialized industrial sewing machines are designed for each task. See *Fig. 8-9.* Some machines, especially those used for inexpensive apparel, are automated. Garment pieces may be moved by a conveyor system from one workstation to the next. At the end of the assembly line, the garment is completed. Today, only very expensive garments are assembled by one individual.

10. **Finishing garments.** Buttons, snaps, hooks and eyes, shoulder pads, beading, and other ornaments are attached by hand or specialized machines. After threads are trimmed, each garment is pressed, buttoned, and folded or hung on a hanger.

11. **Inspection.** Finished garments are inspected. Otherwise, stores return merchandise, which affects the firm's profits. Some manufacturers check all items; others do spot checks. Many manufacturers check quality throughout production instead of just at the end. This is called Quality Assurance, or QA. Fabrics are scanned, either visually or by computerized equipment, for flaws or color variations when they arrive from textile mills. Cutting is checked for sizing and pattern matching. Stitching is checked for stitch type, stitch length, and seam finish. Such components as thread, buttons, and zippers are also checked for quality.

12. **Distribution.** After attaching sales tickets, bar codes, and hangtags, the finished garments are shipped to stores by truck, rail, or air. If a style is successful, reorders are filled. Items that are not reordered are pulled from the line.

The poor working conditions in early sweatshops led to unionization.

A crowded sweat-shop on the top floor of a rear building

Meanwhile the designer or design team is busy creating the next collection, and the entire process begins again.

The Role of Unions

At one time, the average garment worker labored 10 to 12 hours per day, six days per week. The wages were so low that workers often took extra work home to do at night and on Sundays. Conditions in the first garment factories were so bad that workers began to organize into unions. See *Fig. 8-10.*

Labor unions formed to obtain better working conditions, better pay, and such benefits as medical insurance, sick pay, and vacation pay for workers. As a result, garment workers in the United States are among the best paid in the world. Their wages allow them to maintain an average standard of living. Many manufacturers, however, have garments made in other countries where the cost of labor is lower.

Today, the Union of Needletrades, Industrial, and Textile Employees (Unite) represents over 300,000 garment workers. It was formed in July of 1995, when the International Ladies' Garment Workers' Union (ILGWU) and the Amalgamated Clothing Workers of America (ACWA) merged. Unite puts a union label in every item made by its members. The union has sponsored an advertising campaign to remind people to look for the union label, which shows that the clothes were made in America.

Fashion Centers

The "heart" of the garment industry is in New York City, where most major manufacturers have offices. Known in the trade as Seventh Avenue, the garment district includes over 4,500 showrooms and factories.

The most hectic times in the garment district are when store buyers come for **market week** to purchase merchandise. These are the primary times when designers and manufacturers introduce their new lines. New York City hosts five market weeks and many trade promotions each year.

8-11 Apparel marts like this one in Dallas are located in several major U.S. cities. Buyers can visit manufacturers' showrooms and place orders.

Until the early 1990s, most companies manufactured goods in New York City. Today production has shifted to many cities and towns throughout the United States, primarily in the South, and to foreign countries.

Los Angeles has become the headquarters for the garment industry on the West Coast, specializing in sportswear. Chicago, Dallas, and Atlanta have large apparel marts, where manufacturers have showrooms and sales offices. See *Fig. 8-11.* Some manufacturers also have regional showrooms in Miami, San Francisco, and Seattle. To help promote their fashion industries, cities hold special fashion fairs and exhibitions. Some focus on sportswear, menswear, or children's wear. Others promote such specialties as knits, silks, tweeds, beading, and leather goods.

FASHION MERCHANDISING

After apparel manufacturers produce goods, they sell the items to retail stores who sell them to you, the customer. **Retail** means the sale of goods in small quantities to consumers.

Fashion retailers sell clothes and accessories. They decide what styles, fabrics, colors, and sizes to sell and at what prices. Another look at *Fig. 8-8*

Retailers do all they can to convince you to buy. What techniques do you think are most effective?

on page 140 will show you how retail cost is determined. Retailers display, advertise, promote, and sell the items, choosing techniques they hope will entice people to buy. All of this is called **fashion merchandising**, a critical and exciting component of the fashion industry. See *Fig. 8-12.*

Retail Stores

The success of designers and manufacturers ultimately rests in the hands of fashion retailers. Retailers range from small, one-owner stores to large corporations with hundreds of stores. One way to classify them is by type, such as department store, specialty store, off-price retailer, discount store, and outlet. Chapter 17 explains more about these stores.

Another way to classify retailers is by their position in the fashion field.

- **Fashion leaders.** Such stores as Neiman/Marcus and Nordstrom feature newly introduced styles that are usually expensive.
- **Traditional retailers.** Macy's, Dillards, and the May Company are examples of stores that offer many fashions at moderate prices.
- **Mass merchants.** Such stores as JC Penney and Sears carry widely accepted styles at moderate to lower prices. At the low-price end of the mass market are the discounters, like Wal-Mart and Kmart.

Today many stores are part of a **chain**, a large retail company with stores in many cities and towns all over the country. Chains have headquarters, a central office where all merchandising decisions are made. All stores in a chain carry similar items, have similar prices, and look very much alike. Popular chains are The Limited, Gap, Old Navy, Talbots, Abercrombie & Fitch, Sears, JC Penney, Target, Kmart, and Wal-Mart.

Direct Retailers

Many companies reach customers through direct retailing that bypasses stores. Department stores regularly send out catalogs to promote new fashions and sales. Some retailers, including L.L. Bean and Lands' End, sell almost entirely through catalogs. Others offer catalog items not found in their stores. Customers can order by mail, phone, or fax without visiting a store. See page 324 for information on ordering from a catalog.

Many retailers now sell on the Internet. Even small firms have set up Web sites to sell their products directly to customers. Two other methods of direct retailing are cable television and at-home selling. The advantages and disadvantages of these are covered in Chapter 17.

Retail Operations

Both large and small retailers have an organizational structure, ranging from sales associates and stock clerks to buyers and merchandise managers. Large stores need a number of employees with different responsibilities, while small stores typically manage with one person doing several jobs.

Sales associates sell merchandise to customers, while stock clerks work behind the scene. Buyers purchase all merchandise. They must decide what styles, fabrics, colors, and sizes will sell best. Buyers for large chains work with managers of individual stores to finalize selections.

Merchandise managers oversee the operation of several departments within a store. At the top is the store's general merchandise manager who determines the dollar allocations for each division and oversees the store's fashion image.

Every store has a fashion image that it presents to customers. The fashion office gathers information about upcoming trends and shares that knowledge with everyone in the store's organization. This helps buyers make purchasing decisions and helps the advertising and display departments reflect the store's fashion image.

FASHION PROMOTION

In the competitive world of fashion, people are always looking for ways to promote sales. Clever words and illustrations make an advertisement stand out from all others. Eye-catching window displays make people stop and notice. In-store displays and fashion shows attract attention. Catalogs and Web sites bring merchandise information into customers' homes. **Fashion promotion** includes all these efforts to inform people about what's new in fashion and to convince them to buy.

Marketing

How do designers, manufacturers, and retailers decide how to promote products? Marketing research and analysis can help.

Marketing is concerned with developing, promoting, and selling products. People who work in marketing conduct surveys that focus on consumer needs and attitudes. They want answers to many questions. How much will customers pay? What colors will sell best? What fibers and fabrics are most desired? Should a garment be washable? How many items can be sold?

A careful analysis of surveys and past sales can help predict what will sell in the future. This information is used to develop new products, organize production and shipping schedules, and develop advertising campaigns. Marketing and forecasting are important for a company's success.

Promotion Methods

To promote a product or service, marketers have many resources. Some promotions are directed toward retail buyers, others toward consumers. See *Fig. 8-13.*

- **Advertising.** Advertising appears in newspapers, magazines, and direct mail pieces and on radio, television, the Internet, and outdoor billboards. Some companies have an in-house advertising department; others hire an outside advertising agency. Most ads feature fashion photographs or illustrations, often drawn in a stylized manner. Advertising **copy**, the words and sentences used, helps communicate the fashion message.

  Most of a store's promotional budget typically goes for advertising—primarily in newspapers—to announce a sale or highlight new

8-13 Professionals often work together to decide how to promote a fashion line.

Fashion

merchandise. Large retailers also develop direct mail pieces to reach potential customers. These include special catalogs, coupons, and inserts in monthly bills.

Designers, manufacturers, and textile mills advertise in trade publications to reach store buyers and in magazines and on television to appeal to consumers. They may announce a new fiber or fabric, promote a designer's collection, or "sell" their image. They also do cooperative advertising with retailers by helping to pay for store ads that feature their name or product.

- **Publicity.** While advertising is costly, publicity is usually free. Some large companies have their own public relations (PR) department to handle publicity. Others hire outside PR firms. PR people distribute kits with information about products and store events or photos of a designer's collection to fashion editors and writers. Any resulting newspaper articles and magazine photo displays appear without charge. The goal is to get as much publicity as possible through various news media.
- **Visual displays.** Displays in store windows and within stores are forms of fashion promotion. See *Fig. 8-14.* Eye-catching displays encourage customers to buy not just the garment but the accessories too. Mannequins, props, color, and lighting transform a display into an exciting message. Many stores also display merchandise in attractive and creative ways on tables and shelves.

- **Special events.** "Spring in January," "Vive la France!" and many other special themes attract customers to stores. Fashion shows and in-store demonstrations may be part of these events. Both designers and manufacturers hold fashion shows to promote their collections. Formal runway shows are held for buyers during market weeks; traveling trunk shows present lines to store customers and sales associates.
- **Fashion publications.** Fashion magazines, including *Vogue, Glamour, Seventeen, Ebony,* and *GQ (Gentlemen's Quarterly),* carry articles and ads for readers to enjoy. Some magazines research fashion trends as a service to advertisers. These reports predict the styles, colors, and fabrics that people will wear next season. Newspapers also have articles about fashion trends and clothing care, interviews with designers, and photos of fashion collections.
- **Trade publications.** A trade publication is a magazine, newspaper, newsletter, or book devoted to a specific industry. The most influ-

8-14 A visual display in a store window catches the eye and draws people in to buy.

ential fashion trade publication is *Women's Wear Daily*, called *WWD* by many. It covers all aspects of the industry—from fibers and fabrics, to apparel and accessories, to fashion trends and business notices. People interested in textiles and menswear read the *Daily News Record*, known as *DNR*. Both newspapers are published by Fairchild Publications, based in New York City.

Trade Associations

Trade associations are organizations of manufacturers, designers, retailers, and other people involved in a particular industry. In the United States, many trade associations help spread information about the fashion industry. The following trade associations represent designers, apparel manufacturers, and retailers:

- **American Apparel Manufacturers Association (AAMA).** As the umbrella trade association for apparel companies, AAMA publishes forecasts and educational materials and sponsors the largest trade show for the apparel industry.
- **The Fashion Association (TFA).** TFA represents hundreds of design, textile, manufacturing, and retail firms. It prepares press kits, videos, newsletters, and on-line information for members and the media.
- **National Retail Federation.** This association represents major department stores and specialty chains, sponsors meetings on retailing concerns, and publishes *Stores* trade magazine.

- **Council of Fashion Designers of America (CFDA).** So that designers can show their new collections to retailers and the fashion press, CFDA organizes the famous tent shows, "Seventh on Sixth," in New York City's Bryant Park. See *Fig. 8-15*. CFDA recognizes designers who have made special contributions to the fashion industry with prestigious awards.
- **National Association of Men's Sportswear Buyers (NAMSB).** This association promotes all categories of menswear. Trade shows during market weeks involve over 1,000 menswear lines.
- **The Fashion Group.** This professional organization of women executives in fashion and related fields puts together special reports on American ready-to-wear collections and European pret-a-porter and couture collections. It also honors people who have made important contributions to the fashion industry.
- **Fédération Française de la Couture.** Along with its branch, Chambre Syndicale, this association represents many French couture houses.

Other trade associations promote the fiber and textile industries. These include the American Fibers Manufacturers Association (AFMA), Cotton Incorporated, National Cotton Council, Wool Bureau, American Textile Manufacturers Institute (ATMI), and Leather Industries. The accessories and home furnishings fields also have many trade associations.

8-15 The CFDA offered support after the September 11, 2001, tragedy at the World Trade Center. Here Ralph Lauren, Donna Karan, and model Carolyn Murphy wear a limited edition T-shirt sold to raise funds.

Review

CHAPTER SUMMARY

- The textile industry supplies fabric for many home and commercial uses besides garment making.

- Textiles begin as fibers, which are spun into yarns and woven or knitted into fabrics at textile mills.

- Apparel manufacturers buy textiles, design and create garments, and sell them to retail stores.

- Fashion merchandising and promotion include all the activities and businesses involved in presenting clothes to consumers and encouraging them to buy.

- Manufacturers and retailers use various methods to promote their fashions.

USING KEY TERMS

For each Key Term, tell whether it is most closely related to the manufacturing, wholesale, or retail end of the fashion industry. Explain the link in each case.

RECALLING THE FACTS

1. Name four industries besides the garment trade that rely on textiles.

2. Describe what happens as fibers are transformed to fabric in textile mills.

3. Where in the United States are the centers of textile manufacturing, sales, and marketing?

4. How are converters and contractors similar and different?

5. What types of specialization are found among apparel manufacturers?

6. How are sample garments used to make and sell clothing?

7. In what steps of the manufacturing process is mass production used?

8. How have unions affected the garment industry in the United States?

9. Where are the fashion centers of the garment industry?

10. Describe two types of direct retailing.

11. How does the fashion office influence a retailer's operations?

12. What role does marketing play in the garment industry?

13. Describe one way that a public relations department gains "free advertising."

14. What information is found in fashion and trade publications?

15. Identify four services that trade associations provide for members.

and Activities

THINKING CRITICALLY

1. You've read that segments of the fashion industry are centered in different parts of the United States. What do you think is the reason for the location of each center?

2. Why is a reliable forecasting service so important to a manufacturer's success?

3. What are the advantages and disadvantages of producing garments on an assembly line?

APPLYING KNOWLEDGE

1. **Textile uses.** In writing, complete a paragraph that begins with this opener: "Textiles are used for more than just apparel. My life would be different without other textile uses because . . ."

2. **Local industries.** Working with classmates, make a list of textile companies and apparel manufacturers in your city or state, including addresses, Web sites, and telephone numbers. Compile a master list as a classroom resource.

3. **Manufacturing process.** Describe the process of creating a garment, from design to distribution.

4. **Manufacturing careers.** Choose six steps in the manufacturing process, and describe a career needed to accomplish each one. Include career titles.

5. **Manufacturing math.** An employee at an apparel factory redesigns the pattern layout for cummerbunds (special waist-bands that go with tuxedos). Using the new layout, the manufacturer gets four cummerbunds per yard of fabric, rather than three. If a tuxedo rental company orders 120 cummerbunds, how many yards of fabric will the manufacturer save by using the new layout? If the fabric costs $6.50 per yard, how much money will the manufacturer save on fabric for this order alone?

6. **Unions.** Research some aspect of unions, their role, or their operation. Possible topics include historical events, important figures, and impact on legislation. Present a report to the class.

7. **Careers in the industry.** Interview someone who works in an area of the textile or apparel industries. Ask about job responsibilities, likes and dislikes, educational background, and experiences. Report what you learned.

CREATIVE SOLUTIONS

To make some extra money, two of your cousins have started a small appliqué business. They design and make personalized appliqués, and sew them to customers' garments. They want to promote their business but don't have a large advertising budget.

Think Creatively

What low-cost means could your cousins use to promote their business?

Careers

Apparel Production

I N THE POCKET OF A GARMENT, have you ever found a small sticker that read "Inspected by 79"? What does that mean? Actually, number "79" is probably one of a small army of apparel production workers who take a garment from an idea to something wearable.

In the most modern apparel production environments today, overhead conveyors and other automated systems carry partially assembled garments between workstations. Computer-operated robots pick finished garments off the assembly line and arrange them for packing and shipping. Telecommunication systems, such as bar code tracking, allow clothing manufacturers to quickly produce the garments most in demand.

With modular apparel manufacturing, machine operators work in groups, or modules. They specialize in one task but learn to run other machines as well. A good understanding of the production process allows workers to create efficient schedules and meet quality goals. For higher productivity, they earn higher pay.

While technology and new methods are taking hold, manual work and assembly lines are still common in apparel production, especially with small manufacturers. Computerization and teamwork, however, are gaining importance as effective ways to lower production costs and improve quality.

IS THIS FIELD FOR YOU?

What type of person is suited for work in apparel production? The statements below profile a successful worker.

- I pay attention to detail.
- I appreciate the way parts of a process fit together.
- I take pride in doing quality work.
- I'm confident about giving my input on a project.
- I enjoy learning new skills.
- I believe that even small tasks are important.
- I have a talent for helping people work well as a group.

In apparel production many workers handle the same task at the same time. They may specialize in one operation but learn others as well.

Education and Training

Careers in apparel production have traditionally started with on-the-job training after high school. With further education from a community college or technical school, however, workers can advance more quickly. Since the industry uses computerized machinery, basic computer skills in data entry and word processing help workers stay current. Courses in communication, management, and even psychology are well used by workers where apparel production is modular.

Specialized training is an advantage. Particularly useful is a two-year, associate-of-science degree in apparel production. Studies include fabric behavior and construction, the workings of mass production equipment, and the basics of design. Certificates of proficiency in such areas as electronic grading and marking are also available.

Possible Career Paths

Combined with higher education, apparel production careers can be a starting point for other careers. By studying design, a patternmaker might become an assistant designer and eventually head designer. Courses in management and production principles can lead a line worker to a supervisory position. A supervisor, in turn, might advance to production manager. A hand sewer could combine work experience with courses in small business operation to start a custom tailoring service. Retailers and dry cleaners also need experienced, knowledgeable people to alter or mend clothing.

THE SKILLS YOU NEED

With changes in the production workplace, interpersonal skills are becoming as important as manual skills. A combination of skills, which includes the following, is most helpful:

- Hand-eye coordination
- Mental concentration
- Communication
- Teamwork
- Flexibility
- Computer

The sewing machines used on the floor of a garment-making facility are state of the art. They quickly adjust stitch type and stitch length for any change in fabric.

Choosing an Apparel Production *Career*

INSPECTOR | MACHINE MANUFACTURER REPRESENTATIVE | *PATTERNMAKER* | SAMPLE MAKER | SENIOR MILL ASSISTANT | *SEWING MACHINE OPERATOR* | *SHIPPING AND RECEIVING CLERK* | *SUPERVISOR* | PRODUCTION MANAGER

Patternmaker

Whether you buy or make a shirt, it starts in the same way—with a pattern. A patternmaker translates the approved sample garment into a paper pattern. Patternmakers may work in the sample room of a fashion house or in a clothing manufacturer's product engineering department.

With a process called grading, the patternmaker increases and decreases the size of all pattern pieces to correspond to garment sizes. Each garment manufacturer has its own standard measurements for different sizes. Formerly done by hand, grading has been simplified by using a computer and digitizer tablet, a device that electronically records dimensions in a graphics program.

Inspector

The job of inspector, or quality controller, is vital today. While automation has taken over some inspection duties, in the garment trade the trained human eye is highly valued.

The inspector whose number you find on a piece of clothing checks finished garments for secure stitching, correct colors, and correct sizes. An earlier inspection might mark a flaw in uncut fabric, alerting the cutter to avoid that spot. Another inspector may correct an error in a partly completed article or return it to a worker for repairs. Inspector-worker teams get more involved in preventing and spotting errors on assembly lines.

Sewing Machine Operator

Professional sewing machine operators account for almost half of all workers in apparel production. Mass-producing a garment takes operations that can't be done on one machine. Instead, each operator uses a customized machine, programmed to perform a specific function. One embroiders, another attaches collars, and a third finishes buttonholes.

Operators are expected to take full advantage of a machine's capabilities—in other words, they have to keep up. Because of the trend toward work modules, sewers often learn to use multiple machines. In teams, they take an active role in problem solving.

As part of apparel production, a sample cutter cuts fabric to make a prototype of the garment that will be produced.

When sewing a garment, you need to press seams and iron the completed garment. Certain workers in industrial apparel production also have these responsibilities.

Supervisor

Any issue affecting smooth production during apparel assembly is probably a supervisor's concern. Are the machines working safely? If not, have repairs been arranged? Are employees satisfied with schedules? Are excellent workers rewarded and less productive ones advised on better work habits? With responsibilities like these, supervisors often put in more than 40 hours a week. They may work rotating shifts to get to know all workers.

As workers' roles have changed, so has the supervisor's job. Supervisors today are less likely to tell workers to increase production to meet management demands. They are more likely to ask for suggestions on improving a module's productivity, help carry out changes, and evaluate results.

Shipping and Receiving Clerks

Shipping clerks assemble and pack orders for shipping. Some drive forklifts that take packages to the shipping dock. Using computerized shipping or manifest systems, clerks create labels and paperwork for routing merchandise. They make sure records are forwarded to other departments.

Receiving clerks perform similar duties. They compare an order against the invoice and check contents for damage. After notifying other departments of receipts, they route the goods to appropriate areas. They may also schedule deliveries and deal with lost or damaged shipments.

In a small company clerks may perform both shipping and receiving tasks. Hand-held scanners and computers are used for record keeping.

CAREER APPLICATIONS

1. **Career Preparation.** Choose an apparel production job that sounds interesting. Review the job duties and recommended training and education. Then list three actions you could take now to help prepare for this job.

2. **FCCLA.** With a few classmates, plan an Interpersonal Communications Project. Research and present the qualities needed for successful teamwork. Include a skit that demonstrates problems apparel production employees could have as they work together in a module and how they might solve the problems. A possible problem would be an uncooperative team member who slows the module down.

3. **Professionalism.** Locate definitions of the word professionalism. Consult individuals, dictionaries, and industry groups, which often post a code of ethics on Web sites. Based on your investigation, explain in writing how workers in production jobs can practice professionalism, regardless of their job title.

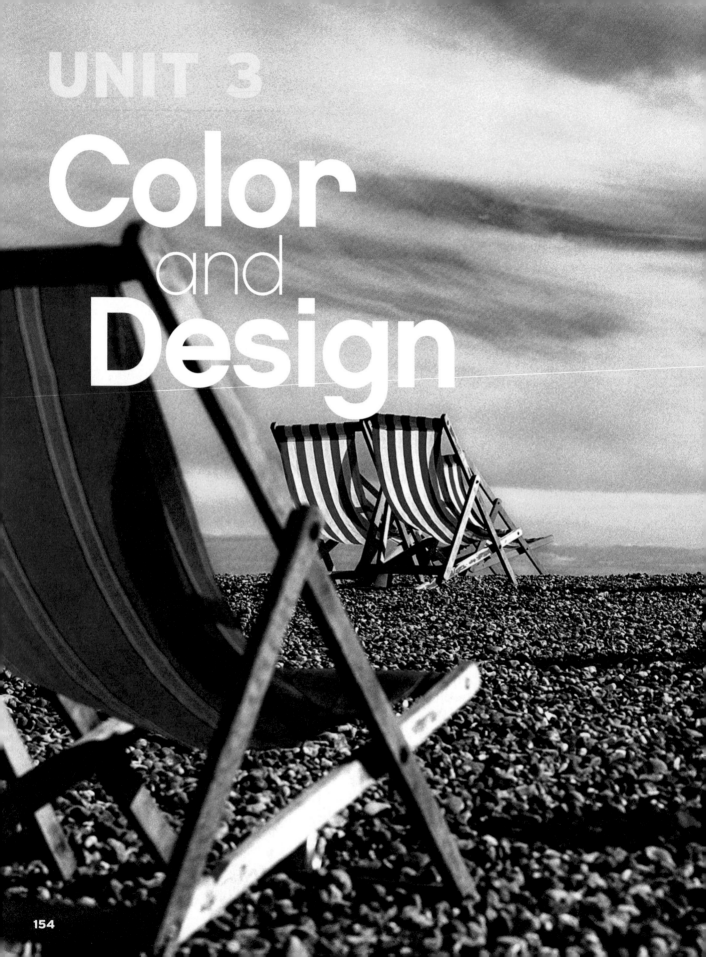

UNIT 3
Color
and
Design

154

Understanding Color

OBJECTIVES

- Describe the impact of color.
- Identify primary, secondary, and intermediate colors on the color wheel.
- Describe color schemes that work well together.
- Choose colors that are flattering to you.

KEY TERMS

color scheme	pigments
complementary color	primary color
hues	secondary color
intensity	shade
intermediate color	tint
	value

or away from certain areas of your body, color can help. Color can emphasize a special feature, such as the color of your eyes. Color can also create illusions in height and size. The better you understand color, the easier it will be to use this design element to your advantage when sewing a garment, buying clothes, or putting an outfit together. See *Fig. 9-1*.

THE IMPACT OF COLOR

Before you work with color, think about how it can work for you. Colors have many impacts. They act as symbols and communicate feelings. Some colors suggest coolness, while others

HOW MANY COLORS DO you think people can see? You might be surprised to learn that the human eye sees as many as six to seven million colors. Is it any wonder that color has such high impact?

All the colors around you make life more interesting. Meals are more tempting with colorful foods and dishes. Theater, television, and computer screens entertain with colorful images. Homes and offices blend colors to create special effects. Colors can provide beauty, attract attention, and even affect a person's mood.

COLOR AND CLOTHING

What's the first thing you notice about the clothing in a store display? For many people, it's the color. As one of several elements of design, color is often noticed first. The other elements—line, shape, space, and texture—have impact, but nothing like color.

Learning about color is useful in many ways, especially when making the clothing decisions that shape your wardrobe. With an understanding of color, you can choose clothes that help you look your best. If you want to draw attention to

9-1 By learning about color, you can choose clothing colors that help you look your best.

appear hot. Some fade into the background, while others stand out. Optical tricks can even cause colors to vibrate. As *Fig. 9-2* shows, colors also send special messages.

Colors as Symbols

A traffic light at an intersection sends a message without words. The light's colors—red, yellow, and green—are symbols of stop, caution, and go. Anyone who doesn't understand the message can get into serious trouble.

Certain colors symbolize special holidays. Stores are decorated with red for Valentine's Day and green for St. Patrick's Day. Rust, gold, and other harvest colors carry the Thanksgiving theme. Red and green are associated with Christmas; blue and white with Chanukah; and black, red, and green with Kwanzaa.

Colors are also associated with ceremonies and celebrations. In the American culture, baptismal outfits, first communion dresses, and bridal gowns are traditionally white. Mourners at funerals usually wear black. Decorations at a baby shower may be pastel pink and blue.

Colors can represent groups and countries, from high school athletic teams to the flags of nations. Red, white, and blue make Americans think of the United States; to a Parisian, they are the colors of France. Red and white are the colors of both the Canadian and the Japanese flags. What are your school's colors? What are the colors of your favorite college or professional team?

Even in language, colors represent something more than their literal meaning. Suppose you're looking over your finances. You may *feel blue* if you're *in the red*, because you're in debt. If you're *in the black*, on the other hand, others may be *green with envy*. Can you think of other common phrases that use colors?

Colors and Temperature

In a similar way, colors suggest temperatures by their associations with nature. Red, orange, and yellow look like fire and the sun. These are considered warm colors. Blue is the color of deep waters, clear skies, and the sparkle of snow. Green recalls grassy lawns and shade trees. Violet is seen in the shadows of a cool evening. Such colors are said to be cool colors.

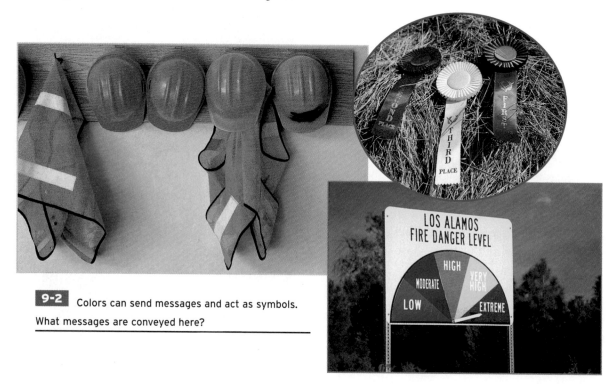

9-2 Colors can send messages and act as symbols. What messages are conveyed here?

COLORS OF DISTINCTION.

"Basic black" is considered a classic in fashion colors, but it has a rival in the color purple–specifically, Tyrian purple. Before synthetic dyes were developed, purple dye was extracted from the shells of sea snails living in the Mediterranean and Aegean Seas. Thousands of the tiny animals were needed, making purple garments too costly for all but the wealthiest people–usually the nobility. To this day, the color is associated with royalty, power, and prestige.

These associations often make people seek cool, crisp colors on a hot day. Many spring and summer clothes are offered in blues, blue-greens, and greens. In fall, colors turn more to warm colors—red, orange, gold, and brown. These colors may make people feel warmer on a cold morning.

The association between color and temperature is sometimes practical as well as psychological. White and light-colored clothes are a more comfortable choice in hot weather because they reflect the sunlight. Since black and dark colors absorb light, they are worn more often in colder weather.

Colors and Movement

The next time you're grocery shopping, scan the shelves of the cereal aisle. While all the cereal boxes compete for your attention, the ones that use bright red, yellow, or orange probably stand out the most. In the competitive world of cereal selling, manufacturers know that warm colors are noticeable. They tend to advance or move toward you. Cool colors, on the other hand, tend to recede or move away from you. See *Fig. 9-3.*

This is why warm colors are used to attract attention. Red flags and yellow traffic signs are easy to see. At a road construction site, the signs, traffic cones, and safety vests worn by the con-struction crew are bright orange. A red or yellow fire engine is more visible than a white or green one.

The same is true with clothing. Compare two outfits in the same style, one bright red and the other dark brown. Which would stand out more?

Colors and Mood

Imagine waking on a rainy day after a month-long heat wave. You might say, "I feel like wearing my dark blue sweater." Then after a week of rainy weather, you might reach for your bright yellow sweatshirt.

Both responses show color's ability to influence your mood. Blues, greens, and violets have a subduing effect. They give a sense of calm and relaxation, like the relief of a cooling rain. Reds, oranges, and yellows express excitement and stimulate action. They encourage you to be cheerful, which you may need after a week without sunshine.

These feelings and qualities are important when planning a home or business, as well as a wardrobe. The bright, cheerful colors in a restaurant invite you to order the deluxe meal. In the doctor's office and hospital, shades of blue and green evoke feelings of restfulness.

Some colors inspire confidence by implying solidity and level-headedness. Think of the steel-gray business suit of a lawyer or investment broker, for example. On the other hand, what colors would you pick for a children's entertainer?

9-3 When you glance quickly at the two circles, which one seems larger? The yellow one appears to "jump out," giving the illusion of greater size. Both circles are actually the same size. Since warm colors tend to advance and cool colors tend to recede, you see the circles differently.

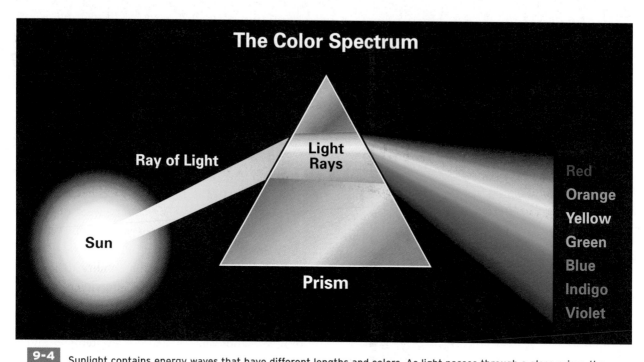

The Color Spectrum

Ray of Light

Light Rays

Sun

Prism

Red
Orange
Yellow
Green
Blue
Indigo
Violet

9-4 Sunlight contains energy waves that have different lengths and colors. As light passes through a glass prism, the waves bend and produce a band of blended colors, called a spectrum. Red rays are on one side of the spectrum. These rays are the longest and they bend the least. The shortest rays bend the most, creating violet on the other side of the spectrum. In between are waves that produce the other colors shown in the drawing.

THE LANGUAGE OF COLOR

Have you ever owned a box of crayons that offered more colors than you knew existed, with names that were just as imaginative? A crayon might be cherry, ruby, or flame. A more precise way to describe colors is with the specific names that identify them, such as red, green, and blue. These are called **hues**.

What Is Color?

Color has amazing versatility, but where does it actually come from? Without light, you wouldn't see the various hues. Sir Isaac Newton determined this fact in the mid-1600s when he showed that light is the source of all color. By passing sunlight through a prism, he produced a rainbow of colors from the bending light rays. See *Fig. 9-4.*

All objects contain **pigments**, substances that absorb some light rays and reflect others. When light strikes an object, you see only the colors that

reflect, or bounce back, to your eyes. See *Fig. 9-5.* When light rays are absorbed, those colors are not seen. If a fabric looks blue, for example, that's because only the blue rays are reflected. The pigment in the fabric dye absorbs the other light rays, along with their colors.

The Color Wheel

To work with color, you need a system that organizes hues into a logical pattern. Such a system can help you manage the many possible color combinations and determine how colors work together. The color wheel is a system that places colors around a circle. Positions on the wheel show how the colors relate to each other. See *Fig. 9-6.*

- **Primary colors.** Red, yellow, and blue are the three **primary colors**, the basic colors from which all other colors are made. These three colors are equally spaced from each other on the wheel.

Seeing Color

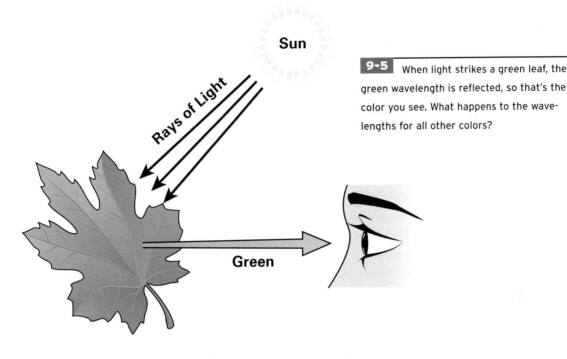

Sun

Rays of Light

Green

9-5 When light strikes a green leaf, the green wavelength is reflected, so that's the color you see. What happens to the wavelengths for all other colors?

- **Secondary colors.** Combining equal amounts of two primary colors creates a **secondary color**. These three colors appear halfway between the three primary colors. Blue and yellow make green. Blue and red make violet, which is often called purple. What secondary color is made from red and yellow?

- **Intermediate colors.** If you combine a primary color with a neighboring secondary color, an **intermediate color** is created. Blue and green combine to make blue-green. Red combines with orange to make red-orange. What are the other intermediate colors on the color wheel?

- **Complementary colors.** Colors that are directly opposite each other on the color wheel are called **complementary colors**. They include some unexpected pairings. Many people think of blue and red as complementary, but the actual complement of blue is orange. What is red's complement?

9-6 The color wheel shows the colors from which all others are made. The colors are arranged in a specific order with yellow at the top. Which are the primary, secondary, and complementary colors on the wheel?

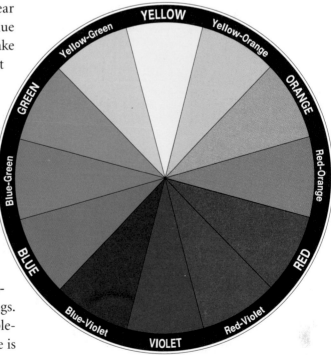

Color Variations

On a color wheel, the colors are very bright and vivid. Most colors that you see around you, however, are lighter, darker, or softer than the hues on the color wheel. These variations differ in two ways—value and intensity.

Value

Adding white or black to a color changes its **value**. This describes the lightness or darkness of a color. Adding white lightens a color, and adding black darkens a color.

A color that is lightened by adding white is called a **tint**. The pastels of pink, mint green, and baby blue are tints. A color that is darkened by the addition of black is called a **shade**. Navy blue is a shade of blue; brown is a shade of orange.

Every color has a wide range of value, from very light to very dark. See *Fig. 9-7*. Red, for example, can go from a very pale pink to a dark burgundy. How would you describe the value range of the color blue?

Intensity

Intensity is the brightness or dullness of a color. Bright colors are deep and vivid. Because they contain the most color pigment, they are very color intense. Jewel tones, such as emerald green and ruby red, are examples of high-intensity colors. See *Fig. 9-8*.

Dull colors, despite the term, are not necessarily boring or drab. Colors like dusty rose and khaki green are softer, muted, or subdued. You can reduce the intensity of a color by adding gray or its complementary color. Adding gray to yellow, for example, creates beige.

Like pure colors, tints and shades can also have different intensities. The pink of a rose petal can be very soft and pale, while pink nail polish may be fluorescent bright.

9-8 Have you ever heard that some colors in a room or an outfit are "tiring" to look at? That's what happens when colors of equal brightness are used together. Look at this shape and the words within for several seconds. As both colors fight for attention, your eyes strain to focus on the words. The image almost seems to vibrate.

VIBRATION HARD TO READ

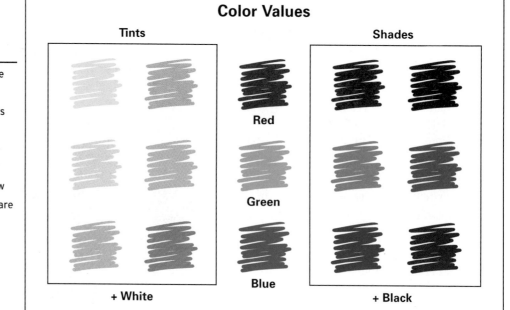

Color Values

9-7 Tints are made by adding white to a color. Shades are colors darkened with black. Color values can range from very light to very dark, depending on how much white and black are used.

Tints   +White

Red   Green   Blue

Shades   +Black

Neutral Colors

You may wonder why black and white are not on the color wheel. In technical terms, they are not true colors because they don't have color pigment. You see them because of what happens to light. When all light rays are absorbed by a surface, you see the surface as black. When all light rays are reflected from a surface, you see white.

Black and white are called neutral colors. Gray, a combination of black and white, is also a neutral. Sometimes tints and shades of beige are considered neutrals, but they aren't true neutrals because they have a yellow or green base.

Neutral colors are very useful. You've already seen how they can change the value and intensity of a color. Adding white to orange produces a peach tint. Adding gray to orange softens the intensity to buff.

Trends in TECHNOLOGY

>>CORRECTING COLOR BLINDNESS

"I thought you wanted to buy a blue shirt," one teen said to his friend. "This is blue," the friend replied. "Well, it looks green to me," the first teen responded. Obviously, not everyone sees color the same way.

How does the eye perceive color? The retina contains millions of cells called rods and cones, which are sensitive to light. With rods you see black and white when light is dim. Cones mix colors so you can see them accurately.

If the chemicals in cones aren't correct, a deficiency occurs in the way a person sees color. This condition is called color blindness. About nine percent of humans, usually males, experience color blindness.

A color-blind person sees some colors but often has trouble distinguishing certain ones. Red-green color blindness is the most common form, and blue-yellow is less common.

Although color blindness can't be cured, a new eyeglass lens helps. The lens is coated with a color filter that changes light waves as they enter the eye. Different coatings match different types of color blindness. Soft contact lenses may soon have similar benefits. When wearing special lenses, a person can distinguish colors more easily, although shades are still difficult to see.

Another innovation is a computer filter that allows those with normal vision to view images as though they were color-blind. Architects, interior designers, engineers, and graphics professionals who work on projects for people who are color-blind find this useful.

INVESTIGATION ACTIVITY

Find and take a test for color blindness. You may be able to locate one on the Internet. How might a color-blind person benefit by knowing of the condition?

CREATING A COLOR SCHEME

Suppose a young family member puts on an orange and blue shirt with a pair of dark red pants. You might decide to suggest a color combination that is more pleasing to the eye.

Knowing what colors work well together takes an understanding of color and the differences between the many values and intensities. To make it easier, experts have identified several color schemes that can be used as guidelines. A **color scheme** is a plan for using a color or a combination of colors—to decorate a room or put together an outfit.

Monochromatic

"Mono" is a prefix meaning one. "Chromatic" refers to color. Thus, a monochromatic color scheme uses the values and intensities of just one color. See *Fig. 9-9.*

In a monochromatic color scheme, you can choose values that contrast greatly or very little. For example, wearing a pale blue shirt with navy blue slacks creates strong contrast between the upper and lower halves of the body. The same slacks paired with a darker, indigo blue shirt have little contrast, creating a more continuous look.

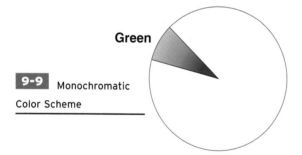

9-9 Monochromatic Color Scheme

Analogous

An analogous (uh-NAL-uh-gus) color scheme uses two or more colors that are next to each other on the color wheel. See *Fig. 9-10.* Yellow, yellow-orange, and orange are analogous. A blue-green shirt with blue shorts is an outfit based on analogous hues.

When using an analogous color scheme, remember that colors blend better if they are close in value and intensity. Red and red-violet are more harmonious than pink and red-violet. Pink would mix better with pink-lavender. What other combinations do you like?

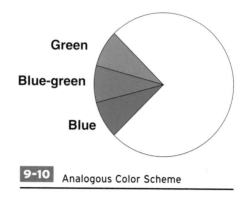

9-10 Analogous Color Scheme

Complementary

A complementary color scheme combines direct opposites on the color wheel. See *Fig. 9-11.* Examples are red and green, and orange and blue.

When complementary colors of equal intensity are used together, a very bold color scheme results. Each color emphasizes the other. Wearing an outfit of two bright complements will certainly attract notice.

A softer effect can be obtained by using different values and intensities. Try pairing pink with forest green, instead of pure red with pure green. Choose a rust and navy plaid, instead of orange and blue.

Another method is to use one of the complementary colors as an accent. A yellow blouse with violet trim or a red tie with a narrow green stripe is eye-catching but not overwhelming.

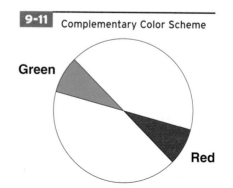

9-11 Complementary Color Scheme

Split-Complementary

One color used with the two colors on each side of its direct complement makes up a split-complementary color scheme. See *Fig. 9-12*. This combination is more common and easier to wear than a complementary color scheme. The effect is not as bold.

You often find a split-complementary scheme in a plaid or print fabric. A blue-and-green plaid accented with a stripe of red-orange uses this color scheme.

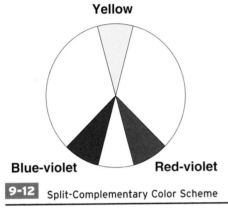

9-12 Split-Complementary Color Scheme

Triadic

Three colors that are equally distant from each other on the color wheel create a triadic color scheme. See *Fig. 9-13*. The primary colors of red, yellow, and blue make up one example. Orange, violet, and green create another example. As you can imagine, with this much contrast in hues, a triad of high-intensity colors would be very bold. A combination of softer, muted colors would be easier to wear.

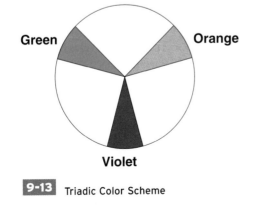

9-13 Triadic Color Scheme

Accented Neutral

Since neutrals have no hue, they combine well with any color. Matching white, black, or gray with a smaller amount of a color results in an accented neutral color scheme. The accent color brightens up the neutral color. A gray suit might be accented with a yellow tie or scarf, or a blue handkerchief.

An accented neutral scheme is often used to create a focal point, or point of interest. The eye is drawn to the accent color, making that area more noticeable.

SELECTING COLORS FOR YOU

Of the many hues in the color spectrum, which ones look best on you? Should you choose the warm reds, oranges, and yellows or the cool blues, blue-violets, and greens? Some color experts say that everyone can wear every color, as long as it has the right value and intensity.

It's always best to evaluate colors in natural light, because other types of light can alter the way they appear. Incandescent light may add a touch of yellow, while fluorescent light adds blue. Some light bulbs are "soft pink," adding a subtle pink tone. Natural sunlight, though, reflects an object's true colors.

When selecting colors for your wardrobe, consider your personal coloring, your body shape, and your height. The right values and intensities of a color will complement these features. See *Fig. 9-14*.

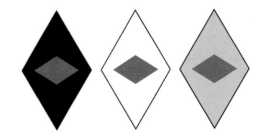

9-14 A color's intensity changes when placed against different backgrounds. How does this explain why colors look different on people? What happens when you put different garments together in an outfit?

9-15 The colors you wear can make your hair and eye colors stand out.

Personal Coloring

Your personal coloring consists of the color of your skin, hair, and eyes. See *Fig. 9-15*. Some of these colorings can change. Sunshine causes some skins to tan and hair to lighten. Hair color may darken as a person grows older, until a certain point where it may start to go gray. Many people change their hair color, sometimes with striking effects.

Skin Tones

Skin tones vary widely, from cream, to honey, to olive, to ebony. All tones, however, have either yellow or blue undertones, subtle traces of color seen through the skin. To determine the color of your undertone, look at the skin on the inside of your wrist. If possible, compare it with other people's to see the difference between warm and cool undertones. Skin with a more yellow, gold, or peach cast has warm undertones. A blue or pink trace indicates cool undertones.

Analyzing Colors

To find out which colors look best on you, compare various colors to your personal coloring. Stand at a mirror and hold colors underneath your chin. You can use clothing, pieces of fabric, or even colored paper. Remember to use natural daylight rather than artificial lighting if possible. Have one or more friends or relatives help with your evaluation.

As you hold up a color, watch for changes in your eyes and face. A good color accents your eyes or hair and seems to give them sparkle. Your complexion looks healthy and glowing. Your face appears softer; any laugh lines or circles under your eyes are diminished. In contrast, another color may make your face appear hard and sad, and your eyes lackluster. You and others will notice the difference.

If you have a light complexion, does your face look more red or yellow with certain colors? If you have darker skin, how do different colors impact your skin tone? Overall, does the color enhance or overpower you?

As you continue your analysis, you may need to switch back and forth among colors to compare the effects. Try to discover whether some colors are more flattering than others. Do you look better in cool or warm colors, in brighter or softer hues? Do you look best in a clear red, blue-red, or orange-red? Is your best green an olive green, a blue-green, or a true green? Is pure white or ivory more attractive on you? Some people use the seasonal approach to selecting colors, as shown on page 167.

How To ... CHOOSE YOUR COLORS

How can you decide what colors look best on you? One color analysis system is based on the four seasons, as shown below. Skin, hair, and eye color link a person with a season, which has a set of corresponding colors. Note how a hue changes slightly for each season. Green is true green for winter, blue-green for summer, yellow-green for spring, and earthy green for autumn.

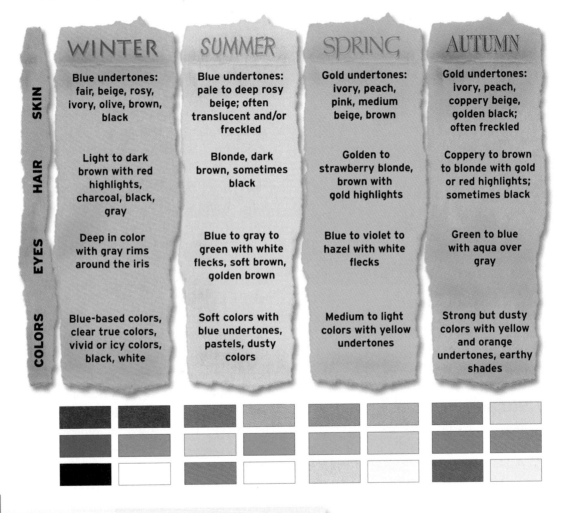

	WINTER	SUMMER	SPRING	AUTUMN
SKIN	Blue undertones: fair, beige, rosy, ivory, olive, brown, black	Blue undertones: pale to deep rosy beige; often translucent and/or freckled	Gold undertones: ivory, peach, pink, medium beige, brown	Gold undertones: ivory, peach, coppery beige, golden black; often freckled
HAIR	Light to dark brown with red highlights, charcoal, black, gray	Blonde, dark brown, sometimes black	Golden to strawberry blonde, brown with gold highlights	Coppery to brown to blonde with gold or red highlights; sometimes black
EYES	Deep in color with gray rims around the iris	Blue to gray to green with white flecks, soft brown, golden brown	Blue to violet to hazel with white flecks	Green to blue with aqua over gray
COLORS	Blue-based colors, clear true colors, vivid or icy colors, black, white	Soft colors with blue undertones, pastels, dusty colors	Medium to light colors with yellow undertones	Strong but dusty colors with yellow and orange undertones, earthy shades

Exploring Seasonal Colors

Work with a partner to determine what season applies to each of you. Use the information on skin, hair, and eye color to decide. Then find the colors that work best for you, using colored paper, fabric swatches, or actual garments.

9-16 A color that looks good on one person may be less effective on someone else. How would you evaluate these color choices in clothing?

The white one would, but why? All the light that reflects from the white object makes it look larger. On the other hand, the black cube absorbs all light, making the cube look smaller.

In the same way, colors can create illusions that change how you look. The right color or combination of colors can help you look larger or smaller, taller or shorter.

Suppose you want to make your shoulders appear broader. Would you wear a dark green shirt or a bright red one? To de-emphasize the hips, would a pair of light yellow or blue-gray pants be more effective?

Guided by what you know about the effects of different colors, you can probably figure the better choices. You know that warm colors seem to advance, bright colors draw attention, and light colors add size. Thus, the bright, warm hue of the red shirt would emphasize the shoulders better than the dark, cool green.

To minimize an area, you need the opposite effect. Hips would be less noticed in a receding, cool blue-gray than in yellow. *Fig. 9-17* suggests how colors can be used for different effects on size.

Remember that your goal in choosing colors is to achieve a look of good health. If a color makes you look pale or harsh, it's not a good color for you, no matter how trendy it may be. See *Fig. 9-16*.

Body Shape

If you looked at a white cube and a black cube of identical size, which one would appear larger?

9-17 • Color Effects on Size			
WHAT DO YOU WANT TO DO?	**USE THESE . . . HUES**	**USE THESE . . . VALUES**	**USE THESE . . . INTENSITIES**
Increase size or draw attention to an area	Warm hues, such as reds, oranges, and yellows	Light, high values; light tints; strong contrasts in value	High intensities: pure, strong, brilliant, saturated with color
Decrease size or take attention away from an area	Cool hues, such as blues, blue-greens, and blue-purples	Low, middle values; dark shades; weak or no contrasts in value	Low intensities: weak or grayed colors

Height

An unbroken block of color gives the illusion of added height. Dressing from neckline to hem in a single color or in clothes that are close in value and intensity helps make you look taller. See *Fig. 9-18.*

On the other hand, broken blocks of color detract from height. Wearing sharply contrasting items, either in hue, value, or intensity, makes you look shorter. You might combine a light blue sweater with navy pants or a shamrock green shirt with tan pants.

Emphasis

Color can also be used to emphasize certain areas and diminish others. A scarf or collar that contrasts with the shirt draws attention toward the face and away from the body. To minimize a waistline, choose a belt that matches the dress or pants. Wearing a belt in a bright, contrasting color will make it the center of attention.

Your Favorite Colors

In one clothing class, students completed a color analysis. Later someone said, "I never knew blue was my best color, but it's always been my favorite. I've got lots of blue clothes." People with an eye for color often choose what looks good on them—without even trying. The mirror tells them that some hues look better than others. Compliments from friends and family also reinforce the notion that certain colors are more flattering.

Does that mean you shouldn't wear other colors? Not necessarily. You can wear the "right" colors when you want to look your best, or just use them as accents. You can keep your special colors in mind as you shop, but you don't have to skip over a good buy just because the color isn't on your list. Wearing colors simply because you like them puts your personality on center stage, and that can be fun.

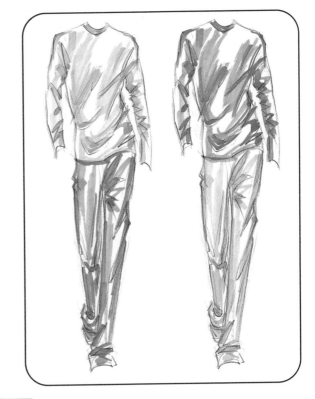

9-18 Colors can make you look taller or shorter. They also affect how size is seen. What illusions do these outfits create?

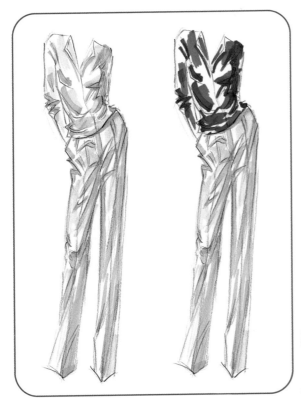

Review

CHAPTER SUMMARY

- Colors can be used as symbols to communicate messages.

- Colors can draw or deflect attention by suggesting temperature and movement.

- The three primary colors—red, yellow, and blue—are used to make all others, including secondary and intermediate colors.

- Adding black or white creates variations of colors on the color wheel.

- Colors can be used in color schemes to create different visual effects.

- The best colors for you are those that enhance your natural coloring.

- You can use color to help accent or minimize physical features.

USING KEY TERMS

Cut out two attractive outfits from a magazine or catalog and glue them to a large piece of paper. Label each with the color scheme used. Use other Key Terms to label and describe the colors included in the outfits.

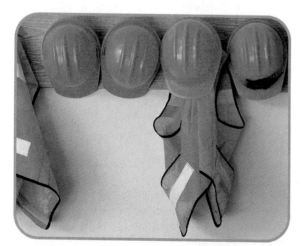

RECALLING THE FACTS

1. Why is it valuable to understand the impact of color?

2. Give four examples of how colors are used as symbols.

3. Why are some colors called "warm" and others "cool"? Give examples.

4. Which color would be better for a library's walls, mint green or deep gold? Why?

5. How do pigments determine an object's apparent color?

6. How are secondary colors related to primary colors?

7. How do you find the complement of a color on the color wheel?

8. How is a tint of blue related to a shade of blue?

9. How can colors be varied in a monochromatic color scheme?

10. Give two tips for creating a pleasing complementary color scheme.

11. How are neutrals useful in creating colors? In creating color schemes?

12. Describe how a color that looks good on you affects your appearance.

13. Which colors are better for minimizing features, shades or tints? Why?

and Activities

THINKING CRITICALLY

1. The symbolism of colors varies among different cultures. People in India wear white to mourn the dead; in the United States, the traditional choice is black. How do you think such differences arise?

2. One teen thought the colors in a dress were flattering when she tried it on in the store's fitting room. When she modeled it at home, however, she didn't like the colors. What do you think happened?

3. Lime green clothes may be "in" one year and "out" the next. Why do you think such color trends occur?

4. Of the color schemes described in the chapter, which do you think would be easiest to use when coordinating an outfit? Which would be most difficult? Why?

APPLYING KNOWLEDGE

1. **Color creation.** Choose one of the primary colors. From this color, create a dulled intensity variation, a secondary color, an intermediate color, a tint, and a shade. Use water-based paints.

2. **Color schemes.** Choose one of the color schemes described in the book. Starting with a skirt, pants, or dress, create an outfit of three pieces or more that is based on that color scheme. Write a description of your outfit, identifying the scheme and the colors selected.

3. **Skin tones.** Evaluate your skin tone for either blue or yellow undertones. Cut a 2-inch (5-cm) circle from a sheet of white paper and place it over the skin of your lower inner arm. Compare with classmates. Are your undertones cool (blue) or warm (yellow)? How can you use this demonstration to guide you in choosing colors for your wardrobe?

4. **Accents.** Experiment with complementary and neutral accents, using large and small fabric samples. Which colors combine for pleasingly dramatic effects? How might these combinations be worn?

5. **Personal colors.** Follow the directions on page 167 to determine the most flattering colors for you.

CREATIVE SOLUTIONS

Your friend has a new job at A-1 Restaurant. He asks for your advice when choosing a uniform shirt. His options are either a deep green with the collar, trim, and restaurant name in gold or a gold shirt with green trim and lettering. He can then wear pants of any color that goes well with the shirt. Your friend is fair-skinned with pale blue eyes and bright red hair. He stands a lanky six-foot-two.

Think Creatively

Which shirt design should your friend choose to make the most of his features? What color pants? Why?

Understanding Design

OBJECTIVES

- Describe ways to determine body shape and size.

- Define the elements of design.

- Define the principles of design.

- Demonstrate the use of design elements and principles in choosing and creating fashions.

KEY TERMS

asymmetrical balance	rhythm
balance	shape
emphasis	silhouette
harmony	space
line	symmetrical balance
proportion	texture

THE PROFESSIONAL FASHION DESIGNER uses design knowledge to create clothes that people want to buy. Other people can use this knowledge too. After learning about design, many people discover how to choose clothes and put together outfits that help them look their best. The garments that you prefer to wear—your favorites—probably

10-1 A special garment can make you feel good about the way you look. Why is it sometimes difficult for people to tell what looks good on them?

have designs that suit you well, making you feel good about your appearance. To expand the list of favorites in your closet, the study of design in this chapter may be just what you need.

Using design knowledge to your advantage is not about changing what you are. People need to become comfortable with their own appearance, recognizing that physical qualities alone don't make a person. If learning to use design to make the best of appearances makes someone feel more comfortable, however, then the ideas are worth exploring. While a new outfit can't change physical characteristics, the right design can bring out the best in anyone. See *Fig. 10-1*.

SHAPE AND SIZE

To choose clothing that emphasizes their best features, people need to keep body height, shape, and size in mind. They can use three methods to determine these.

- **Frame.** Two people of the same height and weight may look very different because of their frame. Body frame, the skeletal structure of the bones, is usually described as small, medium, or large. A person with a large frame typically looks bigger than someone with a small frame. As *Fig. 10-2* shows, wrist size can be used to estimate frame size.

10-2 Measure around the wrist with a tape measure and compare to chart.

Using Wrist Size to Estimate Body Frame Size			
HEIGHT	WRIST SIZE FOR SMALL FRAME	WRIST SIZE FOR MEDIUM FRAME	WRIST SIZE FOR LARGE FRAME
Females under 5'2"	Less than 5.5"	5.5" to 5.75"	Over 5.75"
Females 5'2" to 5'5"	Less than 6"	6" to 6.25"	Over 6.25"
Females over 5'5"	Less than 6.25"	6.25" to 6.5"	Over 6.5"
Males over 5'5"	5.5" to 6.5"	6.5" to 7.5"	Over 7.5"

Comparing Areas of the Body

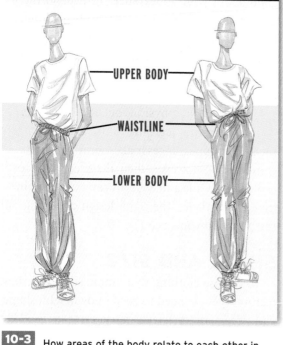

UPPER BODY

WAISTLINE

LOWER BODY

10-3 How areas of the body relate to each other in size influences appearance. Who appears to be taller, someone with a high waistline or a lower one?

- **Size ratios.** Comparing areas of the body is another way to look at stature. In *Fig. 10-3* you see how the waist divides the upper and lower portions of the body. Two people of equal height may not have the same size ratio between these two areas. While one person may have a long upper body and short legs, another may have a short upper body and long legs. People of the same height can also have arms of different lengths. One person's arm length may be longer in comparison to total height.

- **Geometric shape.** A common way to think about body shape is geometrically, as shown by the basic body shapes below. Of course, with so many different heights and sizes possible, these shapes can have many variations among people.

  Triangle: narrow shoulders and wide hips.

  Inverted triangle: wide shoulders and small hips.

  Rectangle: about the same width at shoulders, waist, and hips.

  Hour-glass: about the same at chest and hips and smaller at the waist.

Whatever your body height, shape, and size may be, clothing can change your appearance with design illusions. As you've learned, illusions make things appear different than they actually are. A person who wants to look thinner in the thighs can choose a clothing design that helps create that illusion. Someone who wants to look more broad-shouldered can also use illusions to gain that appearance.

As you study design in this chapter, you'll relate the information to clothing and discover ways to create a number of illusions. Some of them may be ideas you'd like to try as you add to your wardrobe.

Your study of design will be twofold. First, you'll become familiar with the elements of design. Then you'll learn how a few general principles guide the use of these elements. For years, designers have used the elements and principles of design, listed in *Fig. 10-4*, to create appealing

10-4 What is good design?

LINE
SHAPE
SPACE
TEXTURE
COLOR

+

BALANCE
PROPORTION
EMPHASIS
RHYTHM
HARMONY

= Good Design

fabric patterns and garment designs. Soon you'll be able to use them, too, as you put together outfits that you'll feel good about wearing.

THE ELEMENTS OF DESIGN

When you look for new clothes, are some designs more appealing? While an outfit with a very simple design might attract one person's attention, someone else may like a more elaborate look. What may surprise you is that all designs, from simple to complex, come from only a few basic design elements.

Whether an artist, architect, or fashion designer, the person who studies design in any part of the world uses the same basic tools, called the elements of design. These are color, line, shape, space, and texture. Color was covered in the last chapter, and the other design elements are discussed here. All of these elements can be used individually and in combination to create different visual effects, whether in a fabric pattern, a painting, a home's décor, or an item of clothing. See *Fig. 10-5*.

Understanding Line

A **line** is a series of points connected to form a narrow path. How many basic line types do you see around you? Straight and curved are the main ones. A zigzag line is a variation made by com-

LINES IN ART. When you view a line on a computer screen, what do you see? You're actually looking at many dots too small for your eye to discern. A famous painting illustrates how dots can create lines. In the 1800s the French artist Georges Seurat used a technique called pointillism to paint a famous work of art titled "Sunday Afternoon on the Island of La Grande Jatte." Seurat covered his canvas with tiny dots, never using a continuous line. When you get very close to the painting, the dots are visible. As you stand back, the dots blend visually to form the lines that define the shapes of the people and objects in the work.

bining straight lines. By putting different lines together, many patterns can be formed.

Whether curved, straight, or a variation, a line takes one of three basic directions. Vertical lines go up and down, horizontal lines go across, and diagonal lines rest at an angle. Eyes tend to follow lines in the directions they go. The types of lines and their directions are shown in *Fig. 10-6*.

10-5 With just a few basic design elements, an endless number of design possibilities exist. How are lines handled in these designs?

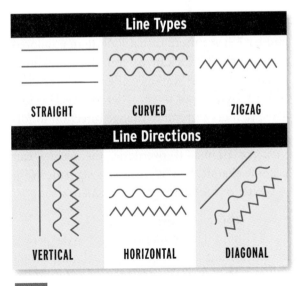

Line Types		
STRAIGHT	CURVED	ZIGZAG
Line Directions		
VERTICAL	HORIZONTAL	DIAGONAL

10-6 A line is defined by its path and length. The eye tends to follow both of these, sending an impression to the brain.

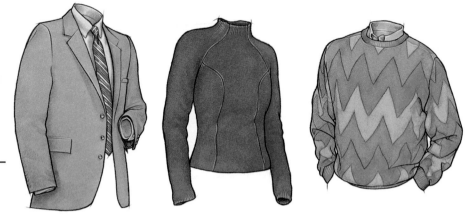

10-7 Designers use lines to create different effects. How would you describe the effects of line in each of these garments?

Line is the most essential element of design because it divides areas into shapes and spaces.

How Designers Use Lines

Clothing designers use lines for different effects, as you can see in *Fig. 10-7*. Straight lines, which provide a crisp, formal look, often appear in classic or conservative designs. Business suits commonly have clean, straight lines at the shoulders, sleeves, pockets, cuffs, and hems. Straight lines are seen in striped and plaid patterns.

Curved lines, which can be circular or waved, give a feeling of movement to a design. By adding softness and roundness to a garment, curved lines are often used to create a casual image. A western-style shirt with a curved seam across the chest and back has a more casual look than a tailored shirt. Curved lines can be found in necklines, lapels, ruffles, and scalloped edges.

With zigzag lines, a very different effect occurs. The eye must constantly change direction to follow such lines, which builds a feeling of excitement or drama. If overdone, the feeling can become chaotic. You might see zigzag patterns in a sweater or in the design of a garment's trim.

Lines and Illusion

In fashion design, illusions can't make people disappear, but they can create a bit of visual "magic." The illusion of line can emphasize or minimize portions of a person's body. Lines and their direction may even help camouflage a body feature that you want to be less noticeable.

- **Vertical lines.** Vertical lines lead the eyes up and down, giving the illusion of more height and less width. Therefore, you can use vertical lines to create a taller, thinner look. To do this, choose lines that are long and unbroken. Notice this effect in *Fig. 10-8*. Vertical lines give a feeling of strength, dignity, and formality. Narrow panels, raised collars, and V necklines emphasize the vertical look. Where else might you see vertical lines?
- **Horizontal lines.** As they explore horizontal lines, the eyes move from side to side, giving

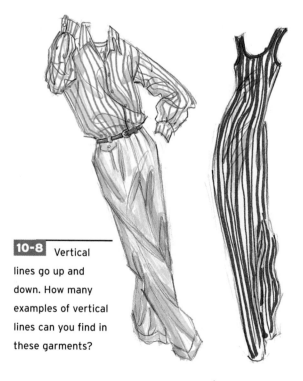

10-8 Vertical lines go up and down. How many examples of vertical lines can you find in these garments?

the illusion of width rather than height. See *Fig. 10-9*. Therefore, using horizontal lines in particular locations gives that area a shorter or wider look. For example, with the right use of horizontal lines, you can add width to shoulders, chest, or hips. Broad collars, full sleeves, and large pockets give a widening effect, although more subtle than an obvious horizontal stripe. Two-piece outfits and contrasting belts divide body length with a horizontal line. Horizontal lines tend to create a feeling of stability and restfulness.

- **Diagonal lines.** In *Fig. 10-10*, the slanted lines add movement and excitement to the clothing. The extent of the effect from diagonal lines depends partly upon whether the lines slant more vertically or horizontally. Zigzag diagonal lines create the most excitement. Due to their dramatic impact, diagonal lines are often chosen for high-fashion clothes and sportswear.

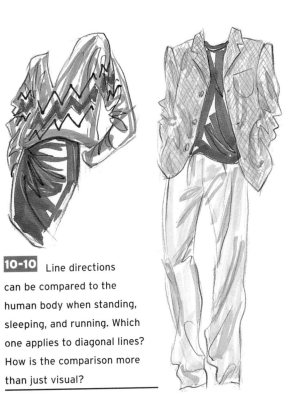

10-10 Line directions can be compared to the human body when standing, sleeping, and running. Which one applies to diagonal lines? How is the comparison more than just visual?

10-9 Horizontal lines go across. How does the effect of the stripes on these garments compare to the effect of the stripes in Fig. 10-8?

In looking for a line to follow in a garment, the eye naturally finds the dominant line, which might be a center seam, a waistline, a curved neckline, or a bold stripe. Whatever it is, that line or combination of lines has the most influence. For example, a bold horizontal stripe across the hip or waist makes each look larger.

Direction isn't all that creates illusion. The thickness of the lines and the amount of space between them are other contributors. Widely spaced vertical stripes may actually give the impression of added width. This is because the eye moves sideways across the lines. Widely spaced horizontal stripes have the opposite effect, causing the eye to move up and down instead of sideways.

How can you take advantage of line illusions when choosing clothes? Look at the illusions shown in the illustration on page 178. When you learn how lines work, you can apply what you know to clothing choices.

Understanding Shape

When you see the shadow of an object on the wall, you're looking at its shape. **Shape** is the out-

How To...

CREATE DESIGN ILLUSIONS

Designers use lines to create the effects they want, of length and width, in particular. Whether you want to add or subtract visual height or width to your own body image, lines can help. Here's how.

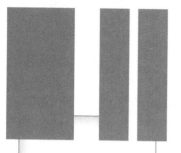

Which rectangle looks taller and thinner? The vertical line breaks the space and leads the eye up and down, making the one on the right look taller. Vertical lines in a garment suggest height and are slimming.

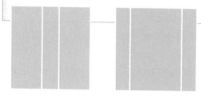

A change in the location of lines can change the apparent size of an area. What would the effect be if these lines were on a skirt or shirt?

Which vertical line is longer? Actually, they're the same. If these were dress styles, which one would make a person look shorter?

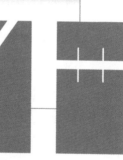

Which lines make the rectangle look thinner? What fashion styles might use these lines?

Which rectangle looks wider? The horizontal bar adds width to the rectangle on the right. What does this tell you about the effect of stripes in a garment?

Exploring **Illusions**

With a partner, look through magazines, catalogs, and books to find examples of garments that show the illusions described. Create a poster that illustrates these links.

line that forms when one or more lines come together to enclose an area. Sometimes this is called a **silhouette**. Notice what lines trace the silhouette of the dress in *Fig. 10-11*.

As you look at garments, how many different shapes can you identify? You may see skirts and pants that are straight and narrow, yet notice others that flare with a bell shape. Do you see actual waistlines? Is one shape more common than the others? To pick out a shape quickly, some people find they can block out the detail and see the shape by squinting.

Most clothes fit four basic shapes: natural, tubular, bell, and full. See *Fig. 10-12* on page 180. When worn, each shape can make the body shape underneath more or less noticeable.

- **Natural.** The natural shape follows your body's outline. Clothes of this shape fit close to the body and emphasize the natural waistline. This shape is the most classic and is worn most easily on average body sizes.
- **Tubular.** The tubular shape is rectangular with vertical emphasis. The dominant lines go up and down. The waistline is not usually defined. A T-shirt dress, straight-leg pants, and a tailored business suit are examples of tubular shapes. This shape appears to add height and thinness to the body.
- **Bell.** Both diagonal and horizontal lines combine in the silhouette of a bell shape. A-line skirts and dresses and flared pants and jackets are all bell shapes. This shape can cut height and add contour to a figure. Depending on where the top and bottom of the bell hit, the shape can add or subtract width.
- **Full.** Full shapes have more horizontal and curved lines than other shapes do. Gathered skirts and dresses, full sleeves, and pants with wide legs are examples of full shapes. Full shapes tend to make the body look larger.

10-11 The outer lines of a garment define its shape. The simple and graceful lines of this dress make the shape easy to identify.

Fashion trends influence which shapes are in style during a fashion season. Usually silhouettes change gradually from year to year, but occasionally fashion designers introduce an abrupt switch to a different shape. Styles may suddenly swing from full to tubular when designers, magazines, and stores promote a new look.

Understanding Space

When a shape is created, another design element forms. The area inside that shape is known as **space**. As a design element on a garment, space is just as important as the silhouette, because what goes on within the spaces contributes to the visual effect of the garment.

Many decisions are made as space is considered in design. How will the space be divided? What will the relationship between spaces be? What will go in each space? Each answer contributes to the final design.

Typically, internal lines, either structural or decorative, divide the space on a garment. In *Fig. 10-13* on page 181, these lines turn a shape into something with visual appeal. As part of a garment's structure, seams produce inner spaces. You see this effect when a seam divides the back of a shirt to form a yoke. Decorative stitching and trims can also divide space, as you see in the lace down the front of a blouse.

When lines divide space, the number of lines and their size and arrangement make a difference. Too much activity can be tiring. Too little may be boring.

NATURAL
Follows the body's outline

TUBULAR
Rectangular shape with vertical emphasis

BELL
Combines vertical and horizontal lines in bell shape

FULL
Wider than other shapes, with more horizontal and curved lines

Shape is the outline, or silhouette, of a garment. **Space** is the area within that shape.

Structural lines are framed by sewing the different parts of a garment together. They include seams, darts, tucks, gathers, pleats, necklines, armholes, waistlines, and hems.

Decorative lines are created by adding trims, such as braid, edgings, lace, and buttons, to a garment.

As you read earlier, strong illusions are possible with lines. That's why you'll want to note where the structural and decorative lines fall on your body when you buy or sew clothes. For example, pants and skirts with fitted yokes emphasize the hipline. Usually, the fewer lines within the space of a garment, the less attention they attract. By contrast, more lines, especially bold ones, draw attention.

Understanding Texture

Texture describes the surface characteristics that determine the look and feel of an object. Fabric texture results from the fiber, yarn, construction, and finish used. Texture determines how a fabric moves when worn. See *Fig. 10-14.*

Fabric textures include soft or crisp, smooth or nubby, and dull or shiny. Heavy work pants might have a rough texture. Depending on the yarn

10-14 The term *drape* describes the way a fabric hangs in folds. Why do fabrics drape differently?

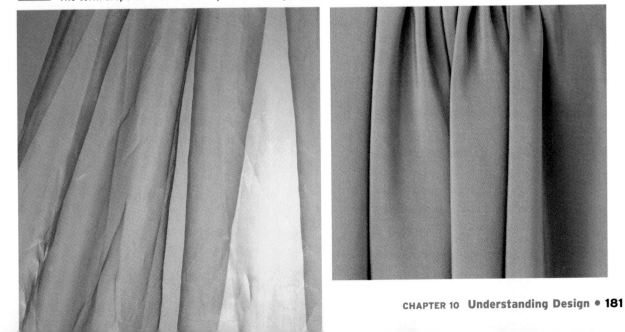

used, a sweater might feel nubby or smooth. An evening gown often feels soft and silky. How would you describe the textures of the clothing you're wearing now?

Texture affects the way a garment looks. To test this idea, imagine that one of your favorite shirts had been made of fabrics with different textures. What would the shirt be like if made with a heavy wool, a crisp cotton, a soft nubby knit, or a shiny satin? Each result would be totally different.

Texture and Illusion

Just as color and line create different illusions, textures create different impressions too. By making careful choices, you can use texture to suggest a taller, shorter, larger, or smaller look.

- **Soft and clingy fabrics.** Such soft and clingy fabrics as jersey and chiffon hug the body and emphasize figure irregularities. When draped into soft silhouettes, however, these fabrics can be very flattering to most body shapes.

- **Moderately crisp fabrics.** Corduroy, denim, and other crisp fabrics stand away from the body just enough to conceal body shapes. Some add size.

- **Extra-crisp fabrics.** Taffeta and vinyl are fabrics that may create a firm outer shell, making the body seem larger.

- **Smooth fabrics with a dull finish.** These fabrics do not seem to create illusions about size and shape. Some examples of smooth fabrics are flannel, broadcloth, gabardine, and wool jersey.

- **Nubby and bulky fabrics.** Fabrics of this type typically add dimension, making a person appear larger; however, they can also hide features. Such fabrics as wide-wale corduroy, mohair, and heavy tweeds look best on a slim to average body size of medium to tall height.

- **Dull fabrics.** When fabrics have a dull texture, they absorb light and tend to make a figure look smaller. Flannel, denim, and gingham all have dull surfaces.

- **Shiny fabrics.** These fabrics reflect light and give the impression of added size. Some shiny

fabrics are satin, polished cotton, nylon, and vinyl. Sequined and metallic fabrics also have shiny surfaces.

In addition to illusion, fabric textures create different moods. Rough, bulky fabrics lend a casual air. Delicate and glittery fabrics are more formal. Despite these general principles, designers often mix textures in a garment, and you may want to do a little blending within an outfit yourself. See *Fig. 10-15.* At one time fashion had "rules" about mixing different fabrics. Today many creative combinations are possible, from mixing velveteen with tweed to combining denim with satin.

Understanding Pattern

When the elements of design are brought together on a fabric, a pattern results. Patterns come in great variety—stripes, plaids, geometrics, florals, scenics, borders, and more. Patterns

10-15 Texture differences can make an outfit interesting. What different textures are shown here?

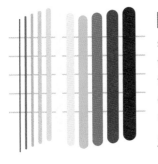

10-16 The size and intensity of a pattern affects the way you see it. Which side of this pattern catches your eye? Is that side larger? What does this tell you about fabric patterns?

can be large or small, even or uneven, light or dark, spaced or clustered, muted or bold. All of these affect how a fabric looks on you.

As you think about patterns, notice what happens with those of different sizes and intensity. A small pattern tends to decrease apparent size, while a large pattern increases it. Similarly, a bold pattern adds size, yet a subtle pattern typically doesn't. Look at what happens as the pattern size and boldness increase in *Fig. 10-16*.

Trends in TECHNOLOGY

>>FABRICS BY COMPUTER

Imagine having 16 million colors to use in a design, all right at your fingertips. With some advanced CAD programs (computer-aided design), this huge range of color options is possible. No wonder designers can create so many fabric patterns.

Just look at all the fabric designs around you. You may see plaids, stripes, polka dots, floral prints, geometric patterns, or simply solid colors in different textures and hues. Each was created when a fabric designer arranged color, yarn, and weaving pattern to suit a plan. All of this can be done right on a computer.

A fabric designer uses a special pad, called a tablet, for sketching by computer. A stylus serves as a pen. The designer chooses yarns and weaves on the computer and experiments with color combinations. In order to duplicate an existing color, the designer can use special equipment that analyzes the color and identifies the formula for reproducing it in different yarns and fabrics.

Once complete, the final design and any variations are saved on the computer. An approved fabric design is sent from the designer's computer directly to the computer at the fabric mill.

The computer can also do calculations that answer production questions. What will each version of a fabric cost? How much yarn and dye will be needed? Once answers are provided, manufacturers are prepared to make decisions and move on to production, where the design becomes reality.

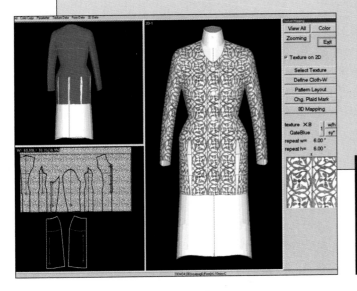

INVESTIGATION ACTIVITY

Locate CAD programs that are used in fabric design. If possible, use the elements and principles of design to create a simple CAD design of your own.

Other characteristics of a pattern can also create illusions. A widely spaced design can make you seem larger as it draws the eye across the distances from one part of the pattern to another.

THE PRINCIPLES OF DESIGN

Have you ever had this experience? You're getting ready to go somewhere, and you keep trying on clothes in order to find an outfit that works. You see the color, line, shape, space, and texture in the garments, but you just can't seem to find the right combination. You might need some guidelines to help you make decisions.

The principles of design are artistic guidelines for using all the design elements. Fashion designers use them in designing clothes. You can use them too when you sew a garment or put an outfit together. The principles are balance, proportion, emphasis, rhythm, and harmony.

Understanding Balance

When two children of the same weight sit on a seesaw, what happens? The seesaw will probably

10-17 Here is an example of symmetrical balance in a garment. What do you think prevents this type of balance from making a garment look uninteresting?

balance. With design, the principle of balance is similar. A design has **balance** when the spaces on both sides of a central line, real or imagined, appear equal. For example, what you see on the left side of a shirt balances visually with what's on the right side. A balanced design gives a feeling of stability.

Do the two sides of a shirt have to be identical to be in balance? Not necessarily. Balance can be achieved in different ways.

Symmetrical Balance

When the spaces on each side of a garment look just the same, balance is symmetrical. A shirt with two identical sides divided by a center front closing has **symmetrical balance**. Notice how balance is shown in the jacket in *Fig. 10-17*.

A simple skirt with a center front seam that divides two similar sides is another example of symmetrical balance. This type of balance usually gives a formal or tailored look to a garment.

Asymmetrical Balance

Some designers like to add an element of interest or a sense of excitement to a garment by surprising the eye with differences. Clothes with an asymmetrical design don't look the same on each side of the real or imagined central line. A wrap skirt has this look because of the vertical or slanted line that is off-center in the front.

Even when the sides of a garment are visually different, the design can still be in balance. How can that be? Design elements have varying visual "weights." By putting the right combinations together, designers achieve what is known as **asymmetrical balance**. Balance can make asymmetrical designs visually pleasing. A warm or dark color, for example, seems heavier than a cool or light color. Knowing this, a designer might balance a large white space with a smaller black space to produce visual balance. A shirt with a colorful pocket on one side might be balanced asymmetrically by placing two vertical stripes on the other side. Even an accessory, such as a scarf or pin, can help balance the spaces in a garment. How was asymmetrical balance achieved in the garment in *Fig. 10-18*?

10-18 With asymmetrical design, the sides of a garment don't match exactly. How does the designer still achieve a sense of balance?

Creativity results in variations to the traditional 3-to-5 ratio, as *Fig. 10-20* on page 186 indicates. Some designs invert the ratio used, placing the larger portion on the top. A long jacket over a short skirt is an example.

Clothing looks best when it's in proportion to your own size. When following this principle, a short or small-framed person might avoid such large, overpowering details as wide lapels and collars and huge pockets and bows. Likewise, a tall or large-framed person might avoid tiny details. When the parts don't relate well to each other or to your body size, they're said to be out of proportion.

Asymmetrical balance has an informal look. Garments with asymmetry are often more difficult and more costly to make because both sides must be handled differently.

Understanding Proportion

Proportion describes how separate parts of a garment relate to each other and to the whole in size. Proportion is also called scale. Throughout history people have studied proportion, concluding that parts with somewhat unequal sizes look best together. To visualize this, imagine a floral arrangement with flowers all the same height. What might look better?

In fashion design, a 3-to-5 ratio has been commonly used. For example, a well-proportioned dress in a classic style might have a 3-to-5 ratio between blouse and skirt lengths. See *Fig. 10-19*. This ratio gained favor because it provides a flattering look that equates to body structure. Typically, about ⅜ of a person's total height is above the waist, and ⅝ is below.

10-19 Uneven proportions, considered ideal, were first used in the art and architecture of early Egypt and Greece. In this outfit an uneven proportion exists between the lengths of the top and bottom. How might a dress with a natural waistline achieve the same proportion?

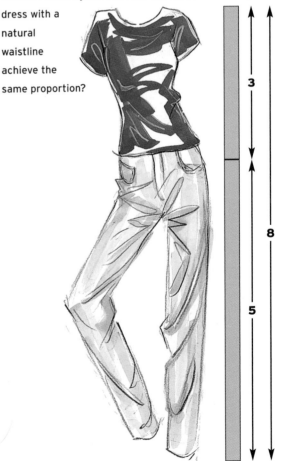

Designers vary proportions to create different looks. Which of these outfits might be best for a tall person? What about someone who is short? Why?

Understanding Emphasis

When you look at an outfit, what catches your eye first? The focal point of a design, the part that draws attention, is known as **emphasis**. On a garment, emphasis may be used for effect—to make an outfit more interesting or unique. Emphasis can also be used to highlight your best features and draw attention away from figure problems.

Emphasis can be accomplished with color, line, texture, design details, trims, and accessories. For example, a colorful belt emphasizes the waistline. A contrasting collar draws attention toward the face. A bright tie or shiny buttons make a plain outfit more appealing. When lines cross, attention goes to that area.

Well-planned emphasis leads the eye quickly to the center of interest. See *Fig. 10-21*. Poorly planned emphasis confuses the eye so that it doesn't know where to focus. What would happen if wide, contrasting trim outlined all the edges of an outfit?

Understanding Rhythm

When you think of rhythm, you might think of a regular drumbeat in music. In design, **rhythm** is visual, carrying the eye through a regular pattern produced by design elements. On a garment, rhythm moves the eye gently from one area of the garment to another. Rhythm, which ties a design together, can be achieved in several ways. Three are described here. See *Fig. 10-22*.

- **Repetition.** A pattern repeats, as with rows of stripes. A pointed shirt collar repeats the point of a jacket lapel.
- **Radiation.** Lines or patterns flow from a central location. The gathers in a skirt show this effect.
- **Gradation.** A pattern changes gradually, as in a change of size or color.

Good rhythm is apparent when the lines of an outfit work well together. For example, a curved pocket complements the curve of a jacket hem. Poor rhythm upsets the look of a garment. Stripes and plaids that don't match at seam lines, for example, break rhythm. Conflicting lines, such as curved seams and striped fabric, also break the rhythm of an outfit.

10-21 Where is the emphasis in this young man's outfit?

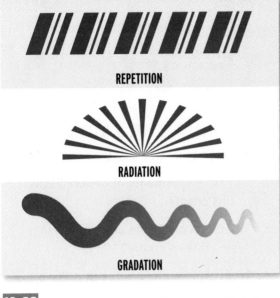

REPETITION

RADIATION

GRADATION

10-22 How many different rhythms are you likely to hear in a song? How many different design rhythms are you likely to see in a garment? Why?

Understanding Harmony

Harmonious music pleases the ear because all parts blend well together. Similarly, a design has visual **harmony** when design elements complement each other. The elements relate in a unified way to convey a single theme. You can see harmony in the outfit in *Fig. 10-23*.

Fashion shows harmony in garment design as well as in entire outfits. The bride who carefully puts together a harmonious look for her wedding day considers everything from dress, to hair, to jewelry, to shoes. Besides matching her outfit to the style of wedding she plans, her choices also suit her personality and physical stature.

When harmony exists, each part looks like it belongs. The parts can be varied to prevent a boring look, but they aren't just thrown together. Harmonious looks are usually planned, and the results are often eye-catching.

INDIVIDUALITY

Just a look around at fashions will tell you that the "rules" about design are flexible. Not everyone follows them all the time. Designers often gain attention by taking unconventional approaches

to design. Military boots with a sheer skirt? A floor-length jacket over pants? Knowing the principles enables designers to use them selectively and creatively or to surprise you by apparently ignoring all the "rules" in coming up with something quite unusual.

On a personal level, the outfits you put together may not all be design masterpieces. Like some designers, you might enjoy putting outfits together that express your own individuality in some unique way. When you want to look your very best, however, knowing how to use the design principles can be a real advantage.

10-23 When all the principles of design come together appropriately in a garment, the result is harmonious. How would shoes, accessories, and hairstyle affect the harmonious look of this outfit?

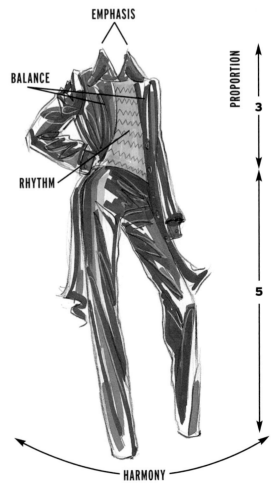

CHAPTER SUMMARY

- Keeping body height, shape, and size in mind can help you decide what clothing designs might be best for you.

- The elements of design are color, line, shape, space, and texture.

- Design elements in fashion can be handled in ways that create optical illusions.

- Design illusions can help emphasize, minimize, or camouflage body features.

- Most clothes are one of four basic shapes: natural, tubular, bell, or full.

- The principles of design are balance, proportion, emphasis, rhythm, and harmony.

- Effective use of design elements is guided by the principles of design.

USING KEY TERMS

With a partner, plan a presentation on two design elements or principles, as listed in the Key Terms for this chapter. Include visuals that show how each element or principle is used. Label the Key Terms on your visuals.

RECALLING THE FACTS

1. How are body size and shape determined?

2. Define the elements of design discussed in this chapter.

3. What look or feeling do the two main types of lines create?

4. What effects are created by a line's direction?

5. How would you recognize the four basic clothing shapes?

6. What's the difference between structural lines and decorative lines in a garment?

7. How can texture create different illusions? Include three examples.

8. Define the five principles of design.

9. What is the difference between symmetrical and asymmetrical balance?

10. Why is the 3-to-5 ratio significant in fashion?

11. Describe three ways to create rhythm in a design.

12. Compare musical and visual harmony.

and Activities

THINKING CRITICALLY

1. Compare the effects created by the following fabric textures: clingy, crisp, smooth, and bulky.

2. According to what you've learned about design, determine which of the following would be flattering on a small person: a wide belt; a bow tie; a wide-brimmed hat; a vertical-striped shirt; a shirt with a large floral print. Explain your reasoning.

3. Why do you think a cartoonist might create a very thin character with a huge hat?

APPLYING KNOWLEDGE

1. **Effects of lines.** Collect illustrations of clothes with different line types and directions. Use felt-tipped pens to highlight the dominant lines. Describe the effect of the lines in each garment.

2. **Illusion solutions.** Make a list of five problems in body shape and size that people might want to address with clothing illusions. Describe in writing what you, as a fashion consultant, would suggest for each person. Include drawings when appropriate.

3. **Emphasis.** Find an illustration of a simple garment. Describe how emphasis might be added to the garment design.

4. **Textures and patterns.** Collect fabric swatches with different textures and design patterns. According to design, which ones would be best for people of varying heights? Why?

5. **Design in business.** Use the elements and principles of design to create an effective brochure that a store might use to promote an upcoming fashion show that will present the new fall styles.

6. **Everyday design.** Observe how the elements and principles of design are used in your school and surroundings. Describe the effects that you see.

CREATIVE SOLUTIONS

A few weeks before Homecoming, your friend's cousin gave her a party dress that had been worn only once. Your friend wanted a dress for the dance but didn't have the money for a new one, so this seemed like the perfect answer.

She loved the beautiful, deep lavender color, but when trying the floor-length dress on, your friend saw that the hem was too short on her. Without a waistline seam, the dress made her feel too tall and thin. The long vertical seams and darts drew added attention to her height. Your friend wondered how she might alter the dress.

Think Creatively

What do you think your friend could do to make the dress more suitable for her?

Careers

Design

THROUGHOUT THE ROOM, STUDENTS cluster around a rainbow of shimmering party dresses, aiming pins into fabric. "Angle the pins," the instructor directs. "That will give you better control over the fabric." After the instructor demonstrates on one ice-blue dress, students remove their pins and restick them, frowning in concentration.

The scene is a design school lab, and the students, aspiring fashion designers. Placing pins just right may seem tedious, yet this is the grounding that future designers need. During their training, students will learn to drape fabric on dress forms and fit garments. They will master working with fabrics of all types, from slippery silks to heavy denims. As they study the history of fashion, they'll see how styles have changed.

Eventually, as graduates, the students will be ready to work in the fashion industry. There they will select fabrics, cut out patterns, and stitch seams. If dreams come true, they may someday see their own designs in shops and stores throughout the country.

IS THIS FIELD FOR YOU?

How many of these statements apply to you? If most do, you might be a budding fashion designer.

- I like to shop for clothing.
- I like to read fashion magazines and articles.
- New fashion designs catch my eye.
- I have strong opinions about clothing styles.
- I notice the colors around me.
- I have a knack for putting outfits together.
- People often compliment me on my clothing.
- I enjoy working with fabric.
- I have a talent for sketching.

Part of a design student's study involves making patterns and samples. Here the student outlines her pattern on fabric. Instead of pins, how is the pattern held in place?

Education and Training

Most design students complete a three- or four-year program in fashion design, but a two-year degree is also available. Core classes include sketching, computer graphics, draping, pattern making, and sewing skills. Some students explore the specialty of costume design. Studies also include the social and psychological importance of clothes and fashion.

Working with established designers is an exciting feature in some top schools. Senior students might stage a fashion show that is judged and attended by professional designers. This contact is an advantage as new graduates start a career. Some schools provide opportunities for study in foreign countries.

Competition for admission to design schools is stiff. Since directors look for creative portfolios, art classes are good preparation. A few exceptionally talented individuals earn internships to fashion houses on their portfolios alone.

Possible Career Paths

"Working your way up" is the typical route for success in fashion design. An intern may pick up pins and put away supplies, but experience can lead to becoming a sketcher, sample maker, or design assistant. These jobs, which don't always require additional education, can be satisfying careers in themselves or steps to other positions.

Designers who achieve fame and fortune are rare, but they offer inspiration. As a sales rep for a neckwear company, Ralph Lauren sold his modest tie collection to a New York City department store. Today, his Polo empire includes a vast line of clothing, luggage, cologne, home decorations—and ties.

An original, appealing idea is no guarantee of success. Aspiring designers may work many years before getting a chance to present original designs. Some sell clothing in their own boutique, hoping to break into larger markets and move closer to recognition.

THE SKILLS YOU NEED

What skills will help you in the design field? Whether a first-year fashion design student or an established professional, you'll need to demonstrate the following skills and qualities:

- A "passion for fashion"
- Communication
- Creativity
- Design knowledge
- Artistic ability
- Sewing skills
- Teamwork
- Strong work ethic

Today's fashion designers learn to use such technology as CAD systems to make designing faster and easier.

Choosing a **Design** *Career*

ACCESSORIES DESIGNER | *APPAREL DESIGNER* | **APPAREL STYLIST**
| *DESIGN ASSOCIATE* | *FABRIC DESIGNER* | **FABRIC LIBRARIAN**
| **FABRIC STYLIST** | **SKETCHER** | **TEXTILE COLORIST**

Apparel Designer —

A line of clothing starts with a designer, who decides on each garment's style, fabric, and ornamentation. Inspiration may come from travels, a movie, an art exhibit, or the work of other designers.

Design success depends on having an understanding of fabrics and styling techniques, as well as input from other professionals: colorists, market experts, and, sometimes, a team of assistants. Many apparel designers specialize in one type of clothing, such as sportswear, swimwear, lingerie, bridal gowns, or children's clothes.

While creativity is a large part of a designer's job, so is self-discipline. Developing fresh, new ideas while working against deadlines can be challenging. Computer graphics can create a virtual sample of the finished design faster than an actual sample can be produced. Computer-aided design (CAD) skills are essential in today's market.

Twice a year or more, top designers must produce a collection of 50-70 items, then submit it for critique by reporters, retailers, and the buying public. Economic trends, constant competition, and the unpredictable tastes of fashion experts and shoppers add to the challenge of a designer's work.

Apparel Stylist ——

That "designer" outfit in the store window may not be quite what it seems. It could be the work of an inventive apparel stylist. A stylist creates moderately priced adaptations of expensive designer originals.

Ideally, adaptations are not simply inexpensive copies. Rather, the stylist modifies the basic style to produce clothes that are fashionable, as well as affordable, to more people. Suppose the original design includes a lined silk jacket with 12 mother-of-pearl buttons. The stylist's version might have a lined rayon jacket with 12 acrylic buttons. Besides economy, an apparel stylist must also think about how the garment will fit the image of the company and the overall clothing line.

Choosing the right colors for garments is part of an apparel designer's job. Why do you think clothing colors change as new fashion lines are developed?

Technology is also useful when designing fabrics. Many variations can be made until the design is right.

Design Associate

Fabric design staffs need people to carry out daily tasks and manage data. As the design department creates fabric patterns, design associates record instructions that the production department will need. Associates store and update electronic files in the firm's fabric pattern library.

As the production of a new fabric begins, design associates scan artwork into the computer, translating images into digital data. They also prepare the pattern printout, which serves as a sample of the actual fabric. During the design process, associates may also help fabric designers by creating different versions of a fabric pattern, using computer-aided design (CAD) programs.

Fabric Designer

Without fabric, an apparel designer wouldn't get very far. Fabric designers try to predict what fibers, textures, and colors will be popular and then design suitable fabrics. These professionals are not only creative artists, but they're also technical experts and merchandisers. They may work closely with the textile company's research and development (R&D) department on weaves, knits, patterns, prints, and colors.

While working out their ideas on computer, fabric designers experiment with different yarns, textures, and color combinations. Once a design is approved, they transmit it directly from their computer to the computer at the fabric mill for production. Since new fabrics often inspire clothing designs, a fabric designer's work may influence fashion trends.

CAREER APPLICATIONS

1. **Creating adaptations.** Find photographs of three different high-fashion garments. For each one, describe in writing what you would do to create an adaptation. Include references to the elements and principles of design.

2. **FCCLA.** Research a fashion design career that interests you and plan an Illustrated Talk on that career. Include a job description; the skills, personal qualities, and education needed; salary range; and job market outlook. Use charts, photographs, or other helpful visuals to clarify your information and add interest to your presentation.

3. **Professionalism.** You're an assistant designer who is asked by a head designer to frame some sketches for a presentation. You realize that some of the designs are identical to those done by another assistant who recently left the company. What is a professional approach to this situation?

UNIT 4

Fibers and Fabrics

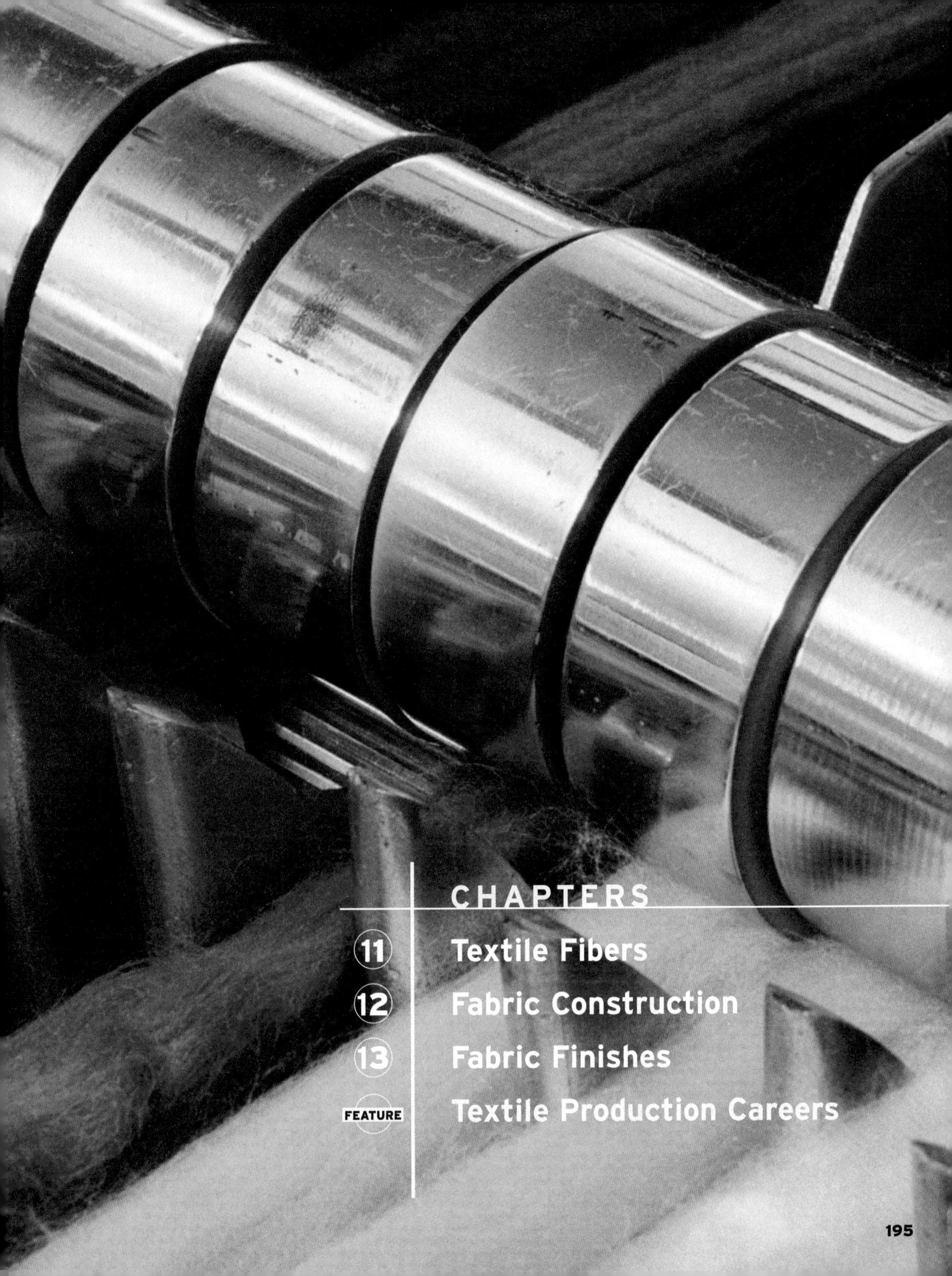

CHAPTERS

Textile Fibers

OBJECTIVES

- Explain how fibers are classified.

- Describe the fiber characteristics needed for use in fabrics.

- Explain how manufactured fibers are made.

- List the various fibers and describe their characteristics.

KEY TERMS

abrasion	microfibers
absorbent	natural fibers
fiber	pill
generic name	resilient
luster	tensile
manufactured fibers	strength
	trade name

EXAMINE THIS ISSUE

Fiber preferences. As you read this chapter, you'll learn about fibers that have a natural origin and those that are manufactured. People often have different viewpoints when it comes to which fibers they prefer. One person may love the natural feel and look of cotton, whereas someone else is totally happy wearing a garment made from a soft, stretchy fabric of manufactured fibers.

What do you think?

When you choose clothes, does fiber make a difference to you? Why do you think some people have preferences?

B EFORE YOU BEGIN THIS CHAPTER, unravel a fabric scrap to find a single thread or yarn. Then untwist the yarn and pull out one hairlike unit. It will be so fine that you can scarcely see it. That's a fiber.

Examine the fiber closely to see its characteristics. Is it long or short, straight or crimped? Is it dull or shiny, smooth or coarse? When you pull on the fiber, does it break easily? Does it spring back when stretched or stay extended? If you look through a microscope, you'll see many more features of this tiny fiber.

WHAT ARE FIBERS?

A **fiber** is the basic unit that makes fabric. It's similar to a very fine strand of hair. Fibers are usually grouped and twisted together to form a continuous strand, called a yarn. See *Fig. 11-1.* By weaving or knitting yarns together, different textiles can be made.

To understand them more easily, fibers are classified, or grouped, according to their source or origin. **Natural fibers** come from natural sources, such as plants and animals.

Scientific experimentation and development have produced "test tube" fibers, called **manufactured fibers**. These are made from such substances as wood pulp, petroleum, natural gas, air, and water.

In many publications and advertisements, you'll see manufactured fibers referred to as man-made. Sometimes the term synthetic is used, although not all manufactured fibers are produced from chemicals.

FIBER NAMES

Fibers are also classified by name. Each fiber has a **generic name**, which indicates a general classification of fibers of similar composition. Cotton, wool, nylon, rayon, and polyester are examples of generic names. According to the Textile Fiber Products Identification Act, a fiber's generic name must be listed on the label of all textile products.

Fiber companies also have a **trade name** for each manufactured fiber they produce. These names are registered as trademarks and are protected by law. No other company can legally use the same name for the same type of product. For example, polyester is a generic name for a manufactured fiber. Its trade name may be Dacron®, a

11-1 When fibers are twisted together, they make yarns. Yarns can be woven or knitted together to make fabric.

DuPont product; Acrilan®, a Solutia product; or Fortrel®, a Wellman product.

FIBER CHARACTERISTICS

How does a manufacturer decide what fibers to use in a fabric? The characteristics, or properties, of each fiber suit it to a particular fabric. The fabric's appearance and performance depend on the following characteristics:

- **Strength.** Is the fiber strong enough for fabric? Different fibers have different **tensile strengths**, the ability to withstand tension or pulling. See *Fig. 11-2.*
- **Durability.** Will the fiber resist wear and decay? With greater durability, you get longer wear and use from garments and other items.
- **Resiliency.** Is the fiber **resilient**, able to spring back into shape after crushing or wrinkling? Resilient fibers in a wool carpet flatten underneath a piece of heavy furniture but bounce back into shape by steaming the carpet.
- **Elasticity.** When the fiber is stretched, does the original length return? Swimwear, some exercise clothing, and other close-fitting garments need this characteristic.
- **Abrasion resistance.** Will the fiber resist abrasion? **Abrasion** is a worn spot that can develop when fibers rub against something. The inside of a collar that rubs the back of your neck can become abraded. Some fibers **pill**, or form tiny balls of fiber on the fabric. As a result, the garment looks less attractive.
- **Wrinkle resistance.** Do the fibers resist wrinkling? Polyester is very wrinkle-resistant, but cotton and rayon wrinkle easily.
- **Shape retention.** Will the fiber keep its shape after wearing or cleaning? Some fibers stretch when the garment is worn; others shrink when exposed to water or heat.
- **Luster.** How will the fiber affect fabric appearance? Just as fiber shape and length have an effect, so does shine. Some fibers have **luster**, or sheen, created by the amount of reflected light. Fibers that reflect larger amounts of light produce fabrics with high luster. Luster doesn't affect a fabric's performance. See *Fig. 11-3.*
- **Absorbency.** Is the fiber **absorbent**, or able to take in moisture? Some fibers, such as cotton and wool, are very absorbent. Other fibers, such as polyester and nylon, are not. That's why you can dry yourself faster with a terrycloth towel of 100-percent cotton than with a cotton-and-polyester blend.
- **Wicking.** Does the fiber draw moisture away from the body? This ability to pull moisture through spaces between the yarns is called wicking. Some athletic wear makes use of this quality. Since the fabric allows body moisture to evaporate, a jogging suit with wicking ability doesn't feel clammy.

11-2 Spacesuits must protect wearers from extreme temperatures and radiation. The fabrics and fibers in these garments must be flexible enough for movement, yet strong enough to withstand hits by particles of dust and rock traveling at high rates of speed.

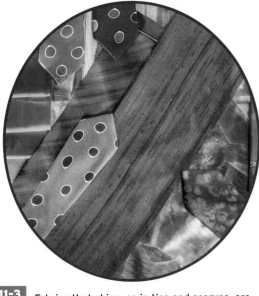

11-3 Fabrics that shine, as in ties and scarves, are said to have luster.

• **Washability.** Can the fiber be washed or must it be dry-cleaned? This characteristic helps determine the care a fabric needs.

NATURAL FIBERS

Natural fibers come from plants and animals. Cotton, flax, and ramie are plant fibers. They are made from cellulose, a fibrous substance found in plants. Wool and silk are animal fibers made of protein. Wool comes from sheep, and silk is spun by silkworms. Other animal fibers include such specialty fibers as cashmere and angora. *Fig. 11-4* summarizes information on the most widely used natural fibers.

All natural fibers, except silk, are staple fibers. These are short fibers measured in inches or centimeters. Silk is a filament fiber, a long fiber measured in yards or meters.

11-4 • Information on Natural Fibers			
ADVANTAGES	**DISADVANTAGES**	**CARE**	**USES**
Cotton *Sources: United States, China, India, Egypt*			
Extremely versatile; strong and durable; comfortable and soft; absorbs moisture; doesn't cling or pill; dyes easily.	Not resilient or elastic; wrinkles unless treated; shrinks in hot water unless treated; will mildew; flammable.	Easily laundered at high temperature; can be ironed at high temperature.	Shirts, sweaters, dresses, jeans, underwear, socks, diapers. Towels, sheets, placemats, napkins, curtains, upholstery.
Flax *Sources: Russia, Poland, the Netherlands, Belgium, France*			
Stronger than cotton; comfortable; absorbs moisture; durable; lint-free; dries faster than cotton.	Not resilient; wrinkles easily; shrinks unless treated; will mildew; hard-to-remove creases.	Easily laundered; can be ironed at high temperature.	Blouses, dresses, pants, suits, handkerchiefs. Towels, tablecloths, napkins, draperies.
Wool *Sources: Australia, New Zealand, South Africa, United States (for apparel);Russia, China, Argentina, Turkey (for carpets)*			
Very versatile; provides warmth; durable; very resilient; resists wrinkling; absorbs moisture; resists abrasion; naturally flame-resistant.	Damaged by moths and other insects; shrinks and mats; may pill; absorbs odors.	Usually dry-cleaned; sometimes washable; iron at low temperature.	Coats, suits, slacks, sweaters, socks. Blankets, rugs, carpets.
Silk *Sources: China, India, South Korea, Brazil*			
Natural luster; strong yet lightweight; smooth; absorbs moisture.	Weakened by sunlight, perspiration, high iron temperature; may yellow with age; may water spot.	Usually dry-cleaned; sometimes washable; iron at low temperature.	Blouses, dresses, lingerie, scarves, ties, bridal gowns. Draperies, upholstery.

11-5 The Seal of Cotton™ symbol (left) identifies 100-percent cotton products. The Natural Blend ™ symbol (right) indicates durable-press products containing a percentage of cotton. These are registered trademarks of Cotton Incorporated.

Cotton

Cotton is the most widely used fiber in the world. Often it's combined with other fibers, such as polyester. You can identify cotton by looking on product labels for the seals shown in *Fig. 11-5*.

Cotton comes from the boll, or seed pod, of the cotton plant. After the seedpods are harvested, the cotton fiber is separated from the seeds and processed. Under a microscope, a cotton fiber looks like a twisted ribbon. Some cotton plants produce seed bolls with fibers as long as 2 inches (5 cm). These are known as long staple fibers and are used for fine-quality, cotton fabrics. See *Fig. 11-6*.

People who lived in the areas known today as Pakistan and northern India probably made the first cotton cloth. In the fourth century B.C., the armies of Alexander the Great introduced cotton to northern Africa. The Nile Valley in Egypt became a center for raising the cotton plant. Cotton was introduced into Europe during the Crusades. When Spanish conquistadors arrived in the New World, they found fine cotton textiles in Peru, Mexico, and the southwestern part of North America.

People like cotton because it's strong, absorbent, and comfortable to wear, even in hot weather. It doesn't cling or pill. Cotton can be washed in high temperatures and with strong soaps or detergents. It accepts dyes very easily.

On the negative side, cotton wrinkles and can shrink. It mildews easily, is flammable, and isn't resilient or elastic. Special finishes give cotton fabrics wrinkle resistance, shrinkage control, mildew resistance, and flame retardance.

Flax

The fiber called flax comes from the inside of the stem of the flax plant. Under a microscope, a flax fiber looks like a bamboo pole. When flax is made into fabric, it's called linen. See *Fig. 11-7*.

11-6 The cotton garments you wear began with the cotton plant. The cotton boll bursts open to expose the fluffy white cotton fibers. The cotton is then plucked from the plant by a mechanical picker and later spun into yarn.

11-7 The stalks of flax plants furnish long fibers that are made into linen fabric. The flax fibers can be separated from each other by soaking the stems in chemically treated water.

In the ancient world, flax was plentiful along the Nile River. The Egyptians wove it into linen fabric that was light, cool, and easy to launder. This fabric was particularly suited to their climate. Pieces of linen have been found in Egyptian tombs more than 4,000 years old.

Flax is stronger than cotton and very absorbent. It's lint-free and dries more quickly than cotton. You can wash, bleach, and iron flax at high temperatures without scorching. This versatile fabric can be soft and lightweight for a handkerchief, crisp and smooth for a suit, or thick and heavy for draperies.

Flax, however, is not very resilient and wrinkles easily. Thus, linen fabric is often used for garments with a wrinkled or unpressed look. To reduce its natural tendency to wrinkle, linen is often given a wrinkle-resistant finish. The fiber may shrink and be damaged by mildew.

Wool

Wool comes from the fleece of sheep. Wool from sheep younger than eight months old is called lamb's wool. The quality of the wool depends on the breed of sheep and the climate where the animal was raised. Sheep are sheared once or twice a year. See *Fig. 11-8.*

The Sumerians, who lived in the valley of the Tigris and Euphrates Rivers, learned to make fine woolen cloth over 5,000 years ago. They were great traders, who exported wool to other parts of the world. The Romans introduced sheep into Spain in 150 B.C. and crossbred them with the African ram. This produced merino sheep, which are valued for their fine wool.

Wool is a comfortable, durable, and versatile fiber. If you look at a wool fiber through a microscope, you'll see a covering of scales. The fiber also looks wavy and crimped. Wool fibers trap air,

11-8 After sheep are sheared, the fleece is washed and carded to remove impurities and straighten the fibers.

Pure New Wool

11-9 Certain international symbols are used to show how much wool a fabric contains. Two are shown here. Manufacturers who make products that meet the performance standards set by The Woolmark Company can use these registered trademark symbols.

which in turn prevents the loss of body heat. Wearing wool, you feel warm in cold weather. The overlapping scales help shed raindrops, yet wool absorbs moisture from the air or body and still feels dry.

Wool is resilient. The fiber is very springy and elastic and returns to its original shape and size after stretching. That's why wrinkles and creases hang or steam out easily. Wool wears well and resists abrasion. It's naturally flame-resistant, so a wool blanket can be used to smother a fire.

When heat and moisture are applied to wool, the scales spread and soften slightly. This is called felting. If the fabric is rubbed or pressed hard, the scales interlock and the fabric mats and shrinks. Traditionally, most wool fabrics had to be dry-cleaned or washed gently by hand in warm water, but modern-day treatments mean that a number of wool products and garments can be safely machine-washed.

Moths, carpet beetles, and other insects can damage wool by eating holes in the fabric. Special finishes can be applied to wool for moth resistance.

All-wool fabrics made from fibers that have never been used before are labeled "pure new wool" or "virgin wool." Fibers can be taken from existing wool fabrics to produce "recycled wool" fabric. Wool can also be combined with other fibers. *Fig. 11-9* shows two symbols used on product labels to identify how much wool is in the fabric.

Silk

When silkworms spin their cocoons, the silk fiber forms. See *Fig. 11-10*. Amazingly, the continuous filament can be as long as one mile. Cocoons are harvested before the silk moths emerge. If a moth breaks through the wall of the cocoon, the single filament would be broken into many shorter fibers.

According to ancient written records, silk was produced in China as far back as 2640 B.C. The Chinese kept the process of making silk, called sericulture, a secret for many centuries. Punishment for revealing this carefully guarded secret was torture and death. Eventually, the secret process was smuggled into Japan via Korea. Later, it was smuggled into Western countries by monks, who hid the little silkworms in their bamboo canes.

Silk feels very soft and smooth. Under a microscope, the fiber looks like a glass rod with an irregular surface. The surface texture provides a superb luster.

Silk is strong, yet comfortable to wear. It has elasticity, resists wrinkling, is absorbent, and drapes easily. Silk can be dyed in brilliant colors and prints.

11-10 Silkworms grow by eating mulberry leaves. When fully grown, they spin a cocoon. After two or three weeks, the cocoon is unwound by hand or machine to collect the silk thread.

Silk fabrics range from lightweight sheers to heavy textures. They are usually dry-cleaned, but some can be hand-washed. Strong soaps, bleaches, perspiration, deodorants, and high ironing temperatures can weaken or discolor silk fabrics.

Other Natural Fibers

Although the most common natural fibers are cotton, flax, wool, and silk, you'll also find other fibers used for clothing and home furnishings. Some come from plants, others from animals.

- **Ramie.** When seen under a microscope, this fiber, with a natural silk-like luster, is very similar to flax. It comes from the stems of China grass, grown primarily in Southeast Asia. One of the strongest fibers known, ramie is also very resistant to insects and mildew. Since the fiber is stiff and brittle, however, and has poor elasticity and resiliency, it's usually combined with other fibers, sometimes cotton or flax. Ramie is used in sweaters, knitted tops, shirts, placemats, and upholstery.

- **Specialty animal fibers.** These fibers include alpaca, camel hair, cashmere, llama, mohair, and vicuna. Most come from animals raised in South America, Turkey, China, Tibet, and other areas of Asia. Because of limited availability, these fibers are expensive. Their characteristics are similar to those of sheep's wool, but the fibers are usually softer, finer, and more lustrous. They may be used alone or with sheep's wool for sweaters, suits, coats, shawls, and blankets. See *Fig. 11-11*. Dry cleaning is usually recommended.

- **Natural rubber.** This fiber is made from latex, a milky liquid that comes from rubber trees. It's used to waterproof coats, hats, boots, gloves, and aprons and can provide elasticity for waistbands. Rubber also makes a backing for rugs and recreational items. Today, the use of spandex, a manufactured fiber, has many more advantages than rubber.

MANUFACTURED FIBERS

Although people thought about making artificial fibers as early as the 1600s, successful attempts didn't come until the late 1800s. Today chemical engineers transform such substances as wood pulp and petroleum into many different fibers with specific characteristics. Manufactured fibers are long, filament fibers unless they have been cut into staple lengths. There are two basic types of manufactured fibers.

- **Cellulosic fibers.** The four cellulosic fibers are rayon, lyocell, acetate, and triacetate. They are produced from wood pulp, with a minimum of chemical steps.

- **Noncellulosic fibers.** All other manufactured fibers are made from carbon, hydrogen, nitrogen, and oxygen molecules rather than wood pulp. The molecules are linked together into long chains called polymers.

Since 1910, when the first manufactured fiber was produced in the United States, a total of 26 generic, manufactured fibers have been developed. Not all are currently produced. Each generic fiber differs significantly in its chemical composition.

11-11 Sheep's wool, as from this Shetland sheep, may be used alone or with other animal fibers to produce fabrics.

Making Manufactured Fibers

Fiber manufacturing, shown in *Fig. 11-12*, begins with a raw material, such as cellulose—in the form of wood chips—or chemical polymers. The material is dissolved in a solvent or melted with heat to produce a thick, syrupy liquid.

Next, the liquid solution is extruded, or forced through a spinneret, a metal plate with tiny holes, similar to a showerhead. Each hole forms one fiber. The fibers can be thin or thick, depending on hole size. Different hole shapes, such as round, oval, and triangular, create different fiber characteristics.

After emerging from the spinneret, the liquid hardens into a long filament. Some filaments go into a chemical bath, where they become solid. This process is called wet spinning. Others go into warm air, where the solvent evaporates and the fibers harden. This process is called dry spinning. Filaments that have been created by melting with heat are passed through cool air to harden them. This process is called melt spinning.

After spinning, the filaments are stretched to align the molecules and increase strength and elasticity. Some filaments are twisted into yarns and stored on spools. Others are cut into short lengths for spinning into yarns later.

Today, fiber research is focused on improving the performance of manufactured fibers. The changed fibers, or variants, are sometimes called second- and third-generation fibers. Fibers can be engineered to produce fabrics with specific qualities, such as elasticity, flame resistance, or a luxurious feel.

Specific Manufactured Fibers

Many manufactured fibers resemble natural fibers, but each generic fiber has its own unique properties. Characteristics are continually modified to improve performance and care. The manufactured fibers described here are commonly used for clothing, furnishings, and household items. *Fig. 11-13* on page 206 summarizes the characteristics, care, and uses of many manufactured fibers. *Fig. 11-14* on page 207 lists their trade names.

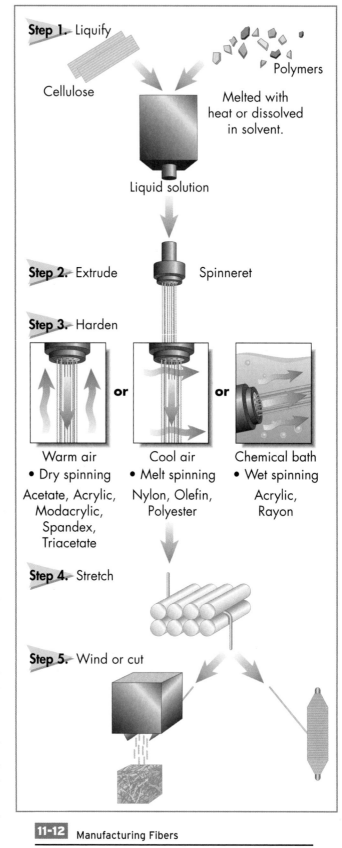

11-12 Manufacturing Fibers

>>MICROFIBERS

What is twice as thin as the finest silk fiber and 100 times finer than a strand of human hair? The answer is the amazing **microfiber**, one of the newest developments in fiber research. Most microfibers are made from polyester or nylon, but some are rayon and acrylic. They can be used alone or blended with other natural or manufactured fibers.

When packed together very tightly, microfibers create yarns with a greater fiber surface area than those made with other fibers. Because the yarns are denser and stronger than others of similar weight, fabrics are durable. Microfiber fabrics are also comfortable due to their light weight and ability to wick away moisture. Since they resist wrinkles and keep their shape well, the fabrics take little care. They look good because of their luxurious, silk-like hand and drape. Since the fibers absorb dyes well, fabrics can have deep, rich colors.

The major drawback of microfibers is heat sensitivity, so a very low temperature is needed to press fabrics. With so many positive qualities, however, microfiber use is growing rapidly.

INVESTIGATION ACTIVITY

Conduct your own investigation to see what microfiber garments are available in stores. Look for "microfiber" on garment labels. You'll see something like "100-percent polyester microfiber." List the garments you find and the composition of the microfibers.

Rayon

The first manufactured fiber was rayon. This cellulosic fiber is made primarily from wood pulp. Rayon can be produced in many variations for different uses. Rayon can be combined with most other fibers.

Like cotton and linen, rayon is absorbent and comfortable to wear. It's soft, drapes easily, and has a nice luster. Rayon dyes well and can be printed with bright designs. Some rayon fabrics are washable, but most must be dry-cleaned.

Rayon wrinkles easily and can shrink. It's also weak when wet and can be weakened by long exposure to light and high temperatures. Special finishes, however, improve these performance qualities.

11-13 • Information on Manufactured Fibers

FIBER NAME	ADVANTAGES	DISADVANTAGES	CARE	USES
Acetate	Silk-like appearance; soft and drapable; dries quickly; resistant to shrinking, moths, mildew.	May wrinkle; low abrasion resistance; heat-sensitive; damaged by acetone.	Usually dry-cleaned; iron at low temperature.	Blouses, dresses, wedding and party clothes, linings. Draperies, upholstery.
Acrylic	Soft, warm, wool-like; lightweight; wrinkle-resistant; resistant to moths and sunlight.	May pill; may accumulate static electricity; heat-sensitive.	Dry-cleaned or laundered; iron at low temperature.	Wool-like sweaters, pants, socks, hats, mittens, and other garments. Blankets, carpets, upholstery.
Lyocell	Exceptional strength; lustrous; soft drape; very absorbent; resists abrasion; dyes beautifully.	Wrinkles; susceptible to mildew and silverfish.	Washable; iron at low temperature.	Suits, dresses, jackets, coats. Specialty papers, medical dressings, conveyor belts.
Modacrylic	Soft and warm; resilient; resists abrasion and flames; fast drying; resistant to moths, mildew, and sunlight.	Very heat-sensitive; may accumulate static electricity.	Dry-cleaned or laundered; iron at very low temperature.	Pile fabrics, fake furs, children's sleepers, wigs.
Nylon	Very strong; resilient; lustrous; dries quickly.	May yellow or gray; heat-sensitive; low moisture absorbency.	Easily laundered; iron at low temperature.	Lingerie, pantyhose, swimsuits, blouses, jackets. Carpets, tents, car tires.
Olefin	Unique wicking properties; strong and lightweight; quick drying; resistant to abrasion, soil, mildew, weather, and perspiration.	Doesn't absorb moisture; heat-sensitive.	Washable; iron at low temperature.	Shirts, underwear, socks for activewear. Indoor-outdoor carpeting, upholstery, disposable diapers, protective clothes.
Polyester	Excellent wrinkle resistance; strong; resistant to abrasion; dries quickly; blends well with other fibers; retains heat-set pleats and creases.	Absorbs oily stains; low absorbency of moisture.	Easily laundered; needs little or no pressing.	100% or blends for shirts, pants, suits. Sheets, tablecloths, fiberfill in parkas and comforters.
Rayon	Soft and comfortable; high moisture absorbency; drapable.	May wrinkle or shrink unless treated; may mildew.	Usually dry-cleaned; sometimes washable.	Blouses, shirts, and linen-like garments. Draperies, upholstery.
Spandex	Excellent elasticity and recovery; stronger and more durable than rubber; lightweight; resistant to body oils.	Damaged by chlorine bleach; damaged by heat.	Washable.	Elastics, underwear, swimwear, active sportswear.
Triacetate	Can be permanently pleated; wrinkle-resistant; shrink-resistant; crisp finish.	Heat-sensitive (but not as much as acetate).	Easily laundered.	Dresses, skirts, sportswear.

11-14 • Trade Names of Manufactured Fibers			
FIBER	**TRADE NAMES**	**FIBER**	**TRADE NAMES**
Acetate	*Celanese acetate, Chromspun®, Estron®, MicroSafe®*	Olefin	*Essera®, Spectra®*
Acrylic	*Acrilan®, BioFresh®, Creslan®, Duraspun®, MicroSupreme®, Pil-Trol®*	Polyester	*A.C.E.®, CoolMax®, Dacron®, ESP®, Fortrel®, MicroMattique®, Polyguard®, Sensura®, Ultura®*
Lyocell	*Lenzing lyocell, Tencel®*	Rayon	*Fibro®, Galaxy®, Viscose®, Zantrel®*
Modacrylic	*SEF Plus®*	Spandex	*Cleerspan®, Glospan®, Lycra®*
Nylon	*Anso IV®, Antron®, Hydrofil®, Micro Touch®, Supplex®, Tactel®*	Triacetat	*(Not Currently Produced in U.S.)*

Polyester

One of the most widely used manufactured fibers is polyester. This strong, high-performance fiber is used alone or blended with many fibers, especially cotton. Both woven and knitted fabrics of various weights are used for clothing and home furnishings.

Polyester has excellent resilience and outstanding wrinkle resistance. It doesn't stretch or shrink. It also washes easily, dries quickly, and needs little or no pressing. Polyester fabrics retain heat-set creases and pleats better than other fabrics do. When combined with other fibers, polyester adds strength and wrinkle resistance. Polyester fiberfill is warm, lightweight, and remains fluffy when wet, unlike down.

Polyester is not very absorbent. Thus, 100-percent polyester fabrics may feel hot and uncomfortable in warm weather. Recent developments have improved moisture-absorbency properties.

Some polyester and polyester-blend fabrics have a tendency to pill. Polyester also attracts and holds oil-based soil unless the fabric is pretreated with a soil-releasing agent.

Nylon

In 1939 nylon was introduced as a "miracle fiber" due to its excellent strength, elasticity, and washability. Made from petroleum chemicals, it was the first noncellulosic fiber.

Nylon is very strong, lightweight, and lustrous. It's resilient, doesn't stretch or shrink, and can be blended with many other fibers. Nylon is a very versatile fiber, with many consumer and industrial uses.

Because nylon doesn't absorb moisture well, it can feel uncomfortably warm in hot weather and cool in cold weather. Unless specially treated, it also collects static electricity.

Nylon is easy to wash, quick drying, and needs little or no pressing; however, it may yellow or gray after a period of time. Some nylon fabrics absorb and hold oil stains. Because of heat sensitivity, nylon must be ironed at low temperatures.

Fashion Facts

FIRST NYLON IN FASHION. As commercial production of nylon began in 1939, a new product took the fashion world by storm–nylon stockings. With World War II, however, nylon was diverted to making parachutes, tents, and ropes for military use. During the early 1940s, stockings that sold for $1.25 a pair sold for $10 on the black market. Shortly after the war ended in 1945, thousands of women rushed to department stores to buy the stockings that were available again.

Lyocell

Lyocell, the newest generic fiber, is made from wood pulp. Compared to other cellulosic fibers, it's stronger, has better abrasion resistance, and shrinks less.

Lyocell is breathable, absorbent, and generally comfortable to wear. Other characteristics are luster and soft drapability. These make it popular for garments traditionally made from silk. See *Fig. 11-15*.

Fabrics made from lyocell tend to wrinkle. Generally, light ironing or hanging the garment in a steamy bathroom removes the wrinkles. These fabrics are also susceptible to damage from mildew and silverfish, small wingless insects.

Lyocell blends well with other fibers, including cotton, linen, wool, silk, nylon, rayon, and polyester. Expensive garments are more likely to have lyocell because production is more costly than for some other fibers.

11-16 Clothes made of acrylic provide the warmth of wool but are washable and can be worn by people who are allergic to wool.

Acrylic and Modacrylic

Acrylic is a soft, resilient fiber that resists wrinkling. See *Fig. 11-16*. It has high bulking power and offers warmth without added weight. It's often substituted for wool because it has similar characteristics but is washable and nonallergenic.

Acrylic fibers resist sunlight. Thus, they are suitable for curtains, draperies, and upholstery. Some acrylic fabrics, however, pill or collect static electricity.

Acrylic fabrics can be washed or dry-cleaned, but they may hold oil-based stains. Because the fiber is heat-sensitive, fabrics should not be dried or ironed at high temperatures.

Modacrylic fibers share many of the characteristics of acrylic fibers.

Acetate

Since acetate is a cellulosic fiber, some of its characteristics are similar to those of rayon. It's

11-15 Lyocell is similar to rayon, but it's washable and wrinkles less. The fiber can be made to look like silk, suede, and even denim.

absorbent and dries faster than rayon. Although it can be dyed and printed, special dyes must be used.

Acetate has a silky appearance. It can be soft or crisp and drapes well. It's resilient and holds creases well. Acetate is also resistant to shrinking, moths, and mildew.

Because acetate is heat-sensitive, ironing at low temperatures is best. It can also be dissolved by acetone, which is contained in nail polishes and polish removers. Unless treated with an antistatic finish, acetate may cling to the body.

Many different fabrics are made from acetate. Some common ones are satin, taffeta, and silk-like fabrics. Usually acetate fabrics are dry-cleaned, but some may be washed, depending on care instructions. Acetate is frequently blended with other fibers. See *Fig. 11-17*.

Triacetate

Triacetate and acetate have many similar properties. Both are drapable and have a silky feel.

11-17 Acetate gives this suit a silky feel and look.

Both are resilient and hold creases well. They also have low resistance to abrasion.

By contrast, triacetate is not as sensitive to heat as acetate. Therefore, triacetate fabrics can be permanently pleated when the fibers are heat-set. Triacetate is also stronger and more shrink-resistant than acetate as well as easily laundered.

One unique characteristic of triacetate is that white fabrics stay white better than most other fibers. Triacetate is used in light to heavyweight fabrics that usually have a crisp finish.

Olefin

Olefin is strong, lightweight, and quick drying. It has good resistance to abrasion, perspiration, soil, and mildew. Hard-to-remove stains, such as ink and grease, can be easily removed from olefin fibers.

Olefin, however, is sensitive to heat and light. It doesn't absorb moisture and is difficult to dye.

Many outdoor garments and exercise wear are made from polypropylene (pah-lee-PRO-puh-leen), a type of olefin fiber. Since it doesn't absorb moisture and wicks perspiration away from the skin, polypropylene keeps the body warm and dry in cold or damp weather. Skiers and runners like the wicking property for shirts, underwear, and socks.

Spandex

Spandex is an elastic fiber with excellent stretchability and recovery. See *Fig. 11-18* on page 210. Even after repeated stretching, elasticity continues. Because of resistance to sunlight, perspiration, oil, and abrasion, this fiber has replaced rubber in most clothing uses. Spandex can be covered with other yarns or left uncovered.

Using high temperatures when washing or machine-drying can cause this fiber to discolor and lose some of its stretching power. Chlorine in bleach and swimming pools can damage the fiber.

Metallic

Metallic fibers are added to fabrics mostly for decoration. Some are made entirely of metal, and some are combined with plastic.

The ability to stretch makes spandex useful. It's often combined with other fibers to make garments more comfortable to wear. The spandex fiber, in general, can stretch more than 500 percent without breaking.

Metal can be bonded to the surface of another textile fiber to give the fiber new characteristics. For example, if silver is used, the new fiber resists odor-causing bacteria and can transfer heat away from the body. Because silver conducts electricity, a small amount of this fiber can also eliminate electrical static.

Aramid

Aramid fibers have exceptional strength and heat and flame resistance. Even at high temperatures, these fibers maintain their shape and form. They are also very resistant to abrasion. With these qualities, the fiber is often found in the protective clothing worn by firefighters.

IDENTIFYING FIBERS

To work with fibers, people must be able to distinguish them. Product developers, retail buyers, buying offices, and independent labs use fiber identification tests to identify fibers and verify the fiber content of products.

Many textile fibers can't be identified merely by sight or touch. Instead, testing helps tell one fiber from another. Some tests are easy; others require special testing apparatus. You can conduct some simple tests of your own by following the directions on page 211 and comparing results to the characteristics described in *Fig. 11-19.*

11-19 • Identifying Fibers in the Lab			
FIBER	**VISUAL**	**CHEMICAL**	**BURNING**
Cotton and Flax	Staples		Burn readily to fine gray ash; odor of burning paper.
Wool	Staple	Dissolves in NaOH	Burns briefly to black crushable ash; odor of burning hair or feathers.
Silk	Filament or staple	Dissolves in NaOH	Burns briefly to black crushable ash; odor of burning hair or feathers.
Polyester and Nylon	Filament or staple		Melt and burn only in flame, leaving hard, tan bead; sweet chemical odor.
Rayon and Lyocell	Filament or staple		Burn readily to fine gray ash; odor of burning paper.
Acrylic	Filament or staple		Melts and burns readily, forming hard black bead; acrid chemical odor.
Acetate	Filament or staple	Dissolves in acetone	Melts and burns readily, forming hard black bead; acrid chemical odor.

How To... IDENTIFY FIBERS

With a few simple tests in the lab, you can identify fibers. Collect four or more fabric samples that contain 100 percent of a given fiber, including manufactured and natural. Exchange samples (but not fiber identities) with a partner. Then assemble the following: *a magnifying glass or microscope, tweezers, two glass dishes, 5-percent sodium hydroxide (or bleach), acetone (or nail polish remover), a candle (votive) in a nonburnable holder, tin foil, and a fire extinguisher.* Follow the instructions under "Exploring Fiber Identification."

Visual Observations: Length of Fiber

1. Cut or pull a yarn from a fabric sample. You may need to separate or unwind the yarn to view a fiber clearly.
2. Using a magnifying glass or microscope, study a single fiber.
3. Note whether the fiber is a short staple or a long filament.

Burning Observations: Burning Rate, Odor, and Type of Ash or Residue

1. Cut or pull a yarn from a fabric sample. Don't use the same yarn used for chemical testing.
2. Place a candle in a low candleholder on a 12-inch square piece of tinfoil. Light the candle.
3. Holding the yarn with tweezers, move it near the candle's flame. Stand back from the flame. Watch to see whether anything happens to the yarn.
4. Place the end of the yarn in the flame. Watch to see what happens. Note the burning rate. To determine odor, fan the vapors toward you rather than leaning over the candle.
5. Note the type of ash or residue that remains.

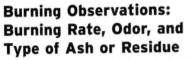

Chemical Observations: Reaction to Sodium Hydroxide and to Acetone

Caution: Do not splash the chemicals or get them on your hands or clothing. Bleach discolors or dissolves some fabrics. Acetone dissolves acetate and removes nail polish and acrylic nails. Acetone is highly flammable so never use near an open flame.

1. Cut or pull two yarns from a fabric sample. Untwist to separate the fibers.
2. Pour a small amount of sodium hydroxide (NaOH) or bleach into a glass dish. Repeat with acetone or nail polish remover in another glass dish.
3. Using tweezers, carefully place the fibers from one yarn in the sodium hydroxide. Place the fibers from the other yarn in the acetone. Let them soak for five minutes.
4. Check to see whether the fibers have dissolved.

Exploring Fiber Identification

Using the fabric samples provided by your partner and the procedures on this page, make the visual, chemical, and burning observations described. Write down your observations. What fiber might each sample contain?

Review

CHAPTER SUMMARY

- Fibers, the basic material of fabrics, are either natural or manufactured.

- Cotton, flax, wool, and silk are the most widely used natural fibers.

- Manufactured fibers are made by liquefying cellulose or polymers, then forcing the liquids through forms to create filaments.

- Each fiber has certain properties, which affect a fabric's performance, appearance, and care.

USING KEY TERMS

On a piece of paper, list these forms of the Key Terms: abrasion resistant, absorbent, lustrous, tendency to pill, resilient, and tensile strength. Beside each term identify natural and manufactured fibers that have the quality. Explain what the quality means.

RECALLING THE FACTS

1. How are natural fibers different from manufactured fibers?

2. You're told that Lycra® is a trade name for spandex. What does that tell you?

3. How are the traits of resiliency and elasticity similar and different?

4. Why would wicking be an important quality in a fabric for athletic socks?

5. What qualities might make cotton a good choice for a child's play clothes? Why?

6. How do the drawbacks of cotton compare with those of flax?

7. How does the wool fiber's structure affect its ability to hold heat?

8. What is the difference between lamb's wool, virgin wool, and recycled wool?

9. How do cellulosic and noncellulosic fibers differ from one another?

10. How does a spinneret affect the characteristics of a manufactured fiber?

11. What qualities make polyester a popular choice for fabrics?

12. For what natural fibers are lyocell and acrylic sometimes substituted? Why?

13. Why might olefin fabrics be a good choice for a road crew worker on a cold morning?

14. On page 206, what disadvantage is common to most manufactured fibers? How does this affect their care?

and Activities

THINKING CRITICALLY

1. Why do you think manufactured fibers have become an important part of the textile industry?

2. A friend recommends that you should always look for garments made with manufactured fibers because they are scientifically designed to be more durable. How do you respond?

APPLYING KNOWLEDGE

1. **Fiber usage.** In a clothing catalog, choose three garments of the same type, such as dresses or men's shirts. Read the garment descriptions. List the natural and manufactured fibers used in each one. Compare your list with those of classmates. What can you conclude about the use of various fibers? About the use of natural fibers compared to manufactured?

2. **Favorite fibers.** Look through clothes in your own wardrobe. List the fiber content, as found on the garments' care labels. Which fibers appear most often? Why do you think they are so common in your wardrobe?

3. **Fiber prices.** In a catalog, locate two similar garments: one made of a natural fiber and the other made of a commonly substituted manufactured fiber—for example, a silk scarf and a rayon scarf, or wool and acrylic sweaters. Compare the prices. Compile your findings with those of classmates. What can you conclude about how natural and manufactured fibers affect the price of fabrics?

4. **Fiber family.** Research the history of one manufactured fiber. Report your findings to the class.

5. **Microscope investigation.** Examine a silk fiber and another natural fiber under a microscope. Sketch and make notes on what you see. Mount both sketches and write a paragraph based on your notes. How does what you saw relate to the properties of each fiber?

CREATIVE SOLUTIONS

Your aunt is starting a new job as a sales representative for a firm that creates CAD software for garment makers. The job involves a lot of travel, up to a week at a time, and giving presentations to buyers. She mentions that she's trying to decide which clothes from her current wardrobe she can wear on sales trips.

Think Creatively

What qualities do you think your aunt should focus on when evaluating clothes for her new job? Based on your knowledge of fibers, which fibers would you suggest she look for on clothing labels to best fill these needs?

Fabric Construction

OBJECTIVES

- Explain how yarns are formed.

- Describe the four distinguishing characteristics of fabrics.

- Compare the characteristics of woven and knitted fabrics.

- Describe other methods of fabric construction.

KEY TERMS

blends	selvage
filament yarns	spun yarns
filling yarns	texturing
grain	warp yarns
knitting	weaving
pile	yarns
ply	

TRY THIS EXPERIMENT. From a small cotton ball, loosen and pull out several fibers. As you tug on them, note their strength. Now twist them together with your fingers as you pull. The twisted yarn has become stronger than the loose fibers. Suppose you had many of these yarns and you began to interlace them or loop them together. Skillfully done, you could produce something quite useful—fabric.

YARNS

Most fabrics are made from **yarns** that have been created from fibers twisted together or laid side by side. The fibers may be natural, manufactured, or a combination of both. Because of the many yarns available today, you can choose from fabrics that vary greatly in design, texture, and performance. See *Fig. 12-1*.

Types of Yarns

Yarns can be made entirely from one type of fiber or from different ones. By twisting two or more yarns together, yarns of different textures and colors can be produced. The varieties are almost limitless.

Spun Yarns

A yarn made of staple fibers is called a **spun yarn**. You'll recall that staple fibers are short and measured in inches or centimeters. All natural fibers, except silk, are staples. Manufactured fibers can be cut into staple lengths to give fabrics the appearance of cotton, linen, or wool. The staple fibers are twisted together to form a single yarn long enough to make into fabric.

12-1 Fibers are twisted together to make yarns of many colors and variations.

12-2 Spun Yarn

Spun yarns are fuzzier and more irregular than filament yarns. The short ends of the staple fibers create a rough surface on the yarns. See *Fig. 12-2*.

Filament Yarns

A yarn made entirely of filament fibers is called a **filament yarn**. Filament fibers are long, continuous fibers measured in yards or meters. Silk is a filament. Unless they've been cut, manufactured fibers are also filaments.

Filament yarns are smoother and more lustrous than spun yarns. A monofilament yarn has only one strand, as seen in nylon sewing thread and fishing line. When two or more filaments are combined during the manufacturing process, a multifilament yarn forms. See *Fig. 12-3*.

Ply Yarns

Manufacturers usually twist two or more single yarns together to make a ply yarn. Since **ply** tells the number of strands used, you'll find yarn that's two-ply, three-ply, or more. Several ply yarns twisted together form a cord or cable. See *Fig. 12-4*.

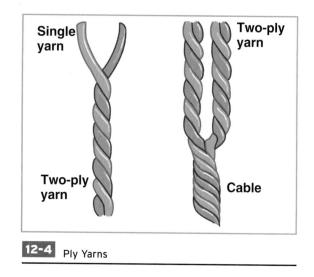

12-4 Ply Yarns

To understand ply, look closely at some different yarns. Knitting and embroidery yarns are good examples to compare. How many plies does each yarn have? How tightly are they twisted? The amount of twist affects the yarn's appearance, feel, and behavior.

High-twist yarns are firm, strong, dull in texture, and relatively fine in size. A twist that's too tight, however, can weaken a yarn. Low-twist yarns are softer, weaker, more lustrous, and less compact than high-twist yarns.

Novelty Yarns

Some clothing in your wardrobe may have fabric with unusual textures and colors. These are made with novelty yarns. See *Fig. 12-5*. Two or more yarns that are not alike in type or size are combined to construct such yarns. They often have loops or different thicknesses. Twisting a thin and shiny filament yarn with a spun yarn that is thick and fuzzy can create thickness variations. Sometimes three yarns are used. One yarn is the base yarn, another creates the decorative effect, and a third acts as a tie or binder, as shown in *Fig. 12-6*.

Texturing and Blending

Yarns can be treated to create different textures. If specific characteristics are desired in a

12-3 Filament Yarns

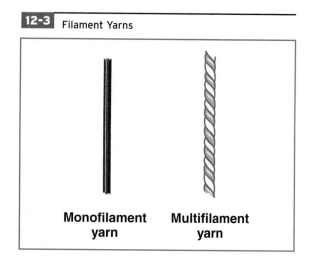

Monofilament yarn   **Multifilament yarn**

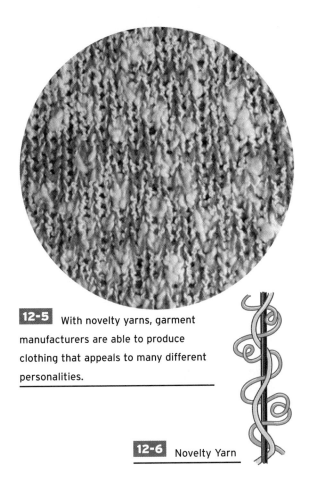

12-5 With novelty yarns, garment manufacturers are able to produce clothing that appeals to many different personalities.

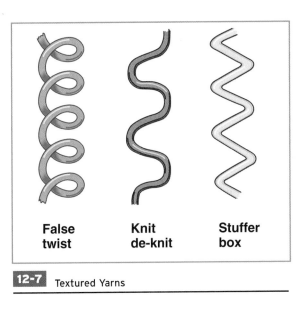

12-7 Textured Yarns

yarns have more space between the filaments than regular filament yarns. Thus, fabric made of textured yarns has more breathability and is more comfortable to wear. The texturing process also helps prevent static buildup in the fabric.

Blended Yarns

Just as "two heads are often better than one," two fibers can also be better. By combining different fibers into one yarn, **blends** are created. The best qualities of different fibers are brought together in a new yarn. See *Fig. 12-8.* A textile mill might combine just natural fibers, only manufactured fibers, or put both types together in one

12-6 Novelty Yarn

yarn, two or more fibers can be blended to obtain qualities from each fiber. Both of these processes are described here.

Textured Yarns

Filament yarns made of manufactured fibers can be permanently set into ripples, waves, zig-zags, or twists. This **texturing** process uses chemicals, heat, or special machinery to turn the straight, rod-like filaments into coiled, looped, or crimped yarns. *Fig. 12-7* shows different shapes of textured yarns.

Texturing increases the yarns' bulk, giving a softer feel to the finished fabric. It also increases the stretch and recovery of the yarns. Textured yarns have improved wrinkle resistance and wash-and-wear properties.

Adding bulk to filament yarns helps overcome some of the disadvantages of the fiber's original characteristics. For example, textured filament

12-8 Different fibers are often blended together to form fabric that has the best characteristics of each fiber.

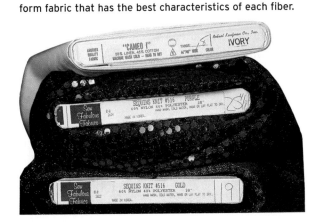

How To...
EVALUATE FABRIC CHARACTERISTICS

To find out whether a fabric is right for your purposes, try the tests described here.

- **Wrinkle resistance.** Will a garment crease or wrinkle during wear? Grab a fistful of fabric and squeeze for about 20 seconds. Release and check for wrinkles. Shake the fabric several times or smooth it with your hand. Wait about 40 seconds. Are the wrinkles disappearing?

- **Drapability.** Does the fabric fall into soft, natural folds, indicating it drapes well? Hold the fabric between your hands. Move your hands together while slowly gathering the fabric. Are the folds sharp and crisp or soft and flowing?

- **Strength.** Does the fabric resist tearing? High tearing strength is useful in children's clothes, work clothes, and activewear. Make a scissors cut in the edge of the fabric (not a garment). Then try to tear the fabric by hand. Does the fabric tear easily?

- **Shape retention.** Will knitted fabric keep its shape after wearing? Stretch a knitted garment with your hands, looking for reasonable resistance. If it stretches too easily, the shape may not come back, as on baggy sweater elbows and knees of pants.

- **Air permeability.** Will the fabric allow air to pass through? Fabrics that "breathe" have high air permeability for more comfort in hot or humid weather. In cold or windy weather, fabric needs low air permeability. Hold the fabric tightly against your mouth and exhale. Evaluate the amount of pressure needed to blow air through.

- **Cover.** Does light shine through the fabric? A fabric with low cover is somewhat translucent. A navy shirt shouldn't show through when tucked into light colored pants. Place a light colored fabric over one with a darker color. If the lighter fabric has adequate cover, the darker fabric won't be visible.

Exploring Fabric Characteristics

Conduct one or more tests on three fabrics to check the characteristics of each. Demonstrate your findings for the class.

yarn. Which combination would each of the following be: wool and silk; nylon and acetate; cotton and polyester?

Fibers are usually blended to improve fabric performance. Why is polyester often combined with cotton? The cotton offers comfort, softness, and absorbency. The polyester adds strength, wrinkle resistance, shrink resistance, mildew resistance, and quick drying.

Fibers can also be blended for appearance. Adding an angora fiber to wool gives more texture and softness to a sweater. Silk may be included for shine or luster.

FABRIC CHARACTERISTICS

Fabric characteristics distinguish one fabric from another. *Fig. 12-9*, shown on pages 228-231, gives many examples of fabrics with different qualities. Typical uses are included with the examples. Examining construction, texture, hand, and weight will help you identify the many fabrics available.

- **Construction.** Fibers and yarns become fabric when they are joined by a construction method. The two most common methods are weaving and knitting. **Weaving** interlaces two sets of yarns that are at right angles to each other. **Knitting** loops yarns together. Other methods used to make a few fabrics include interlocking, fusing, bonding, twisting, and looping. Construction easily identifies some fabrics. You can recognize terrycloth by its loops. Velvet has a raised surface, while corduroy has rows of cut threads. A special weave produces the shiny look of satin, and felt has interlocked fibers matted together.
- **Texture.** How does the surface of a fabric look and feel to the touch? Smooth, rough, dull, shiny, nubby, fuzzy, and combinations of these all describe a fabric's texture.
- **Hand.** How does a fabric react as you handle it? Is it soft and pliant, firm, stiff, or crisp? You can learn how a fabric behaves by draping it over your hands.

- **Weight.** The yarns and fabric construction determine the weight of a fabric. Fabrics range in weight from very light to very heavy.

WOVEN FABRICS

As a child, you may have woven strips of paper together to create an art project. This same basic process is used to weave fabric by interlacing lengthwise and crosswise yarns on a loom. The yarns that run the length of the fabric are called **warp yarns**. The crosswise yarns are **filling yarns**. They are woven or interlaced into the warp yarns, following a specific pattern. See *Fig. 12-10*.

Along both edges of a woven fabric is a **selvage**. This self-edge forms when the filling yarn turns to go back in the other direction. The selvage is usually a little stiffer and firmer and won't ravel. see→ p 490

The direction that yarns run in a woven fabric is known as the **grain**. The warp yarns form the lengthwise grain. The filling yarns form the cross-

12-10 These terms help in understanding the construction and characteristics of woven fabrics. How do the selvages form when fabric is produced? What makes bias grain true?

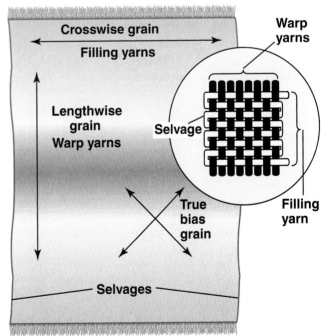

Crosswise grain
Filling yarns

Warp yarns

Lengthwise grain
Warp yarns

Selvage

Filling yarn

True bias grain

Selvages

Trends in TECHNOLOGY

>>SMART PERFORMANCE FABRICS

Fabrics no longer simply look good and offer protection. With new technology, they have some added qualities that may surprise you.

- **Climate sensitivity.** With encapsulation technology, fabrics can help maintain a person's body temperature as the outside temperature changes. Encapsulation means each fiber or yarn is coated with a substance that breaks, changes, or disappears under certain conditions. For example, a paraffin coating changes from liquid to solid as the temperature changes. Encapsulation provides long-term protection that won't peel off or wash away. Used for sweaters, gloves, and socks, these climate-sensitive fabrics save or give off body heat.

- **Aroma enhancement.** Imagine a fabric that smells as great as it looks. When you touch a fabric with encapsulated fragrance, a small amount of the scent escapes. Scents can also be stored in a perfume reservoir incorporated in the lining of a garment. As electronic sensors in the garment react to changes in the body, the scent travels to the cuffs and neckline and escapes into the air.

- **Odor prevention.** Fabrics can help fight odors, too. During manufacturing, antibacterial agents are introduced into fibers. The resulting fabrics help protect against bacteria, fungi, and yeast, as well as fight odors. They are particularly useful for active sports apparel, intimate apparel, and hosiery, as well as products for babies and children. Other applications exist in the healthcare and medical fields for such items as uniforms, mattresses, and pillow coverings.

INVESTIGATION ACTIVITY

Find more examples of "smart" clothing. What other capabilities might clothing of the future provide?

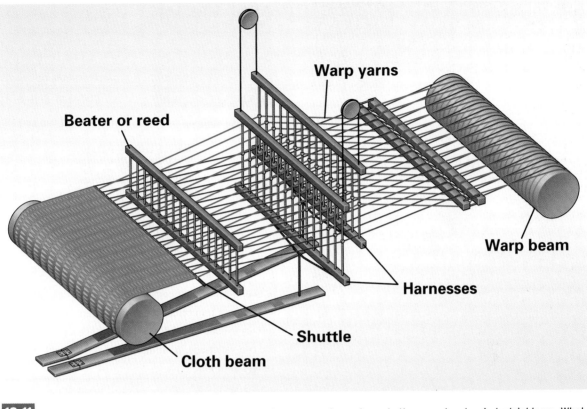

Warp yarns

Beater or reed

Warp beam

Harnesses

Shuttle

Cloth beam

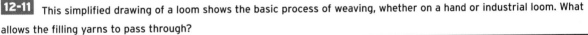

12-11 This simplified drawing of a loom shows the basic process of weaving, whether on a hand or industrial loom. What allows the filling yarns to pass through?

wise grain. The bias grain runs diagonally across the fabric. True bias has the greatest amount of stretch. see→ p 490

The Weaving Process

Fabric can be woven on a small hand loom or a huge computerized loom. Either way, the basic process is the same. See *Fig. 12-11*. Warp yarns are positioned on the loom first. They are attached to a warp beam at the back of the loom and then stretched through one or more frames, called harnesses. Warp yarns are usually stronger than filling yarns.

The filling yarn is wound onto a bobbin, which is placed in a container called a shuttle. The shuttle draws the filling yarn over and under the warp yarns. As the shuttle goes back and forth, the harness goes up and down to make room for it. This space is called the shed. One harness goes up, the shuttle passes through the shed, and the harness goes back down. Then the filling yarn is pushed into place at the front of the loom by a beater or reed. As the shuttle comes back through to the original side, another harness goes up. As these up-and-down and back-and-forth motions continue, the finished fabric rolls onto the cloth beam at the front of the loom.

High-speed, computerized looms can produce over 100 yards of fabric per hour. Instead of a shuttle, these looms use a stream of water or an air jet to carry the filling yarn across the shed at very high speeds. The yarn travels as fast as 200 miles per hour. The harnesses and beaters on these looms move faster than the eye can follow. See *Fig. 12-12* on page 222.

12-12 Computerized looms in industry can produce fabrics at amazing speeds. They can be programmed to create many complex patterns.

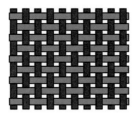
Plain weave

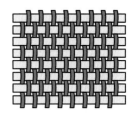
Ribbed weave

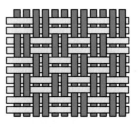
Basket weave

12-13 As the most common weave in fabrics, the plain weave has a firm construction that wears well. The plain surface is good for designs. Here you see a plain weave and two variations. What makes the ribbed and basket weaves different?

Basic Weaves

Think of all the fabrics you've seen in clothing and home furnishings. These are evidence that woven fabrics come in many variations. They range from very lightweight, open-mesh fabrics to heavy, firm, tightly woven fabrics.

If you examine a woven fabric closely, you can see the weave that was used. The three basic weaves are plain, twill, and satin. Almost all woven fabrics are based on these three weaves.

Plain Weave

The plain weave is the simplest of all weaves. The filling yarns pass over and under each warp yarn. The yarns alternate in each row to form an even, balanced weave. Plain-weave fabrics have no right and wrong sides unless they are printed or finished differently. The yarns can be tightly or loosely woven.

Some examples of plain weaves are muslin, voile, broadcloth, percale, taffeta, and crepe. Plain-weave fabrics are used for shirts, handkerchiefs, and sheets.

A ribbed weave is a variation of the plain weave. Using filling yarns that are thicker than the warp yarns creates the rib. Poplin and faille are ribbed fabrics.

A basket weave is another plain-weave variation. Two or more yarns are grouped side by side in each direction and woven as one. Oxford cloth is a basket weave. *Fig. 12-13* shows a plain weave and two variations.

Twill Weave

You can recognize a twill weave by the parallel, diagonal ridges on the fabric surface. In a twill weave, filling yarns pass over and under one or more warp yarns. Each successive row shifts to the right or left to give the diagonal line, as shown in *Fig. 12-14*.

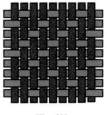

Twill

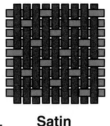

12-14 Twill weaves create diagonal lines on fabric. Manufacturers can make these lines stand out by using plied yarns and other techniques.

12-15 Many fabrics are made with the satin weave, including wool, polyester, cotton, and linen. Note how yarns pass over several other yarns to produce the floats on the top.

Satin

Twill weaves are firmer, heavier, and more durable than plain weaves. Denim, chino, and gabardine are examples of twill weaves. Twill weaves are often used for strong, sturdy work clothes.

Satin Weave

A satin weave has yarns that float on the surface to give it a luster or shine. Either the warp or the filling yarns pass over four to eight yarns at a time. The long floats appear on the right side of the fabric. See *Fig. 12-15*.

The satin weave creates a smooth surface with lots of sheen. Satin weaves, however, snag easily. Satin fabrics are used for blouses, eveningwear, and bed linens.

12-16 A pile weave is produced with three yarns. In addition to the warp and filling yarns, another yarn is added. This yarn creates loops on the surface. When cut, they form the pile.

Other Weaves

By changing the way the yarns are interlaced, different textures, patterns, and designs can be woven in fabric. Examples are pile, leno, jacquard, and dobby weaves.

- **Pile weave.** A raised surface of loops or yarn ends characterizes a **pile** weave. The weaving process uses three sets of yarns. See *Fig. 12-16*. The extra yarns are brought to the fabric surface as loops. For terrycloth the loops are left uncut. They are cut to form corduroy, velvet, velveteen, and velour. The back of the fabric can be a plain, twill, or satin weave. The surface loops of velvet and velveteen can be sculptured when cut to form a decorative surface texture. In most corduroy, the pile yarn is woven in a striped effect to create the rows. The width of the pile can range from narrow pinwale to wide-wale corduroy.

- **Leno weave.** In this weave the warp yarns cross and twist between the filling yarns, as shown in *Fig. 12-17*. Because the filling yarns cannot shift, the open or sheer fabrics that result have good stability. Leno weaves are used to make open-weave curtains and draperies, thermal blankets, and netting.

- **Dobby weave.** Small geometric designs are woven with a dobby attachment on the loom. In order to produce a more complex pattern,

12-17 With a leno weave, the filling yarns are held tightly in place by the twists in the warp yarns. To keep the warp yarns from shifting, an adhesive is used when finishing some fabrics.

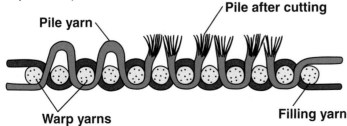

Pile yarn

Pile after cutting

Warp yarns

Filling yarn

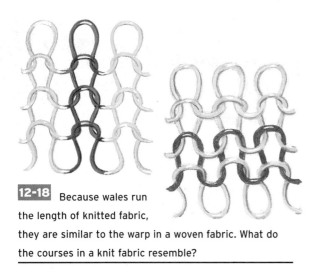

12-18 Because wales run the length of knitted fabric, they are similar to the warp in a woven fabric. What do the courses in a knit fabric resemble?

the dobby controls which harnesses are raised or lowered. Piqué fabrics are an example of a dobby weave.

- **Jacquard weave.** The Jacquard weave produces very elaborate and detailed designs. Special looms, controlled by computers, produce the intricate designs and combinations of weaves. Fabrics woven with jacquard designs include brocade, damask, and tapestry. These fabrics are used for table linens, draperies, and upholstery.

KNIT FABRICS

Like woven fabrics, knit fabrics have a lengthwise and crosswise direction. In a knit, the lengthwise rows of stitches are called wales. The crosswise stitches are called courses. See *Fig. 12-18*. A knit usually has a greater degree of stretchability in one direction. Most knits stretch more in the crosswise direction.

Because of their stretchability, knits move with the body. As a result, they are comfortable to wear. Knits are easy to care for and don't wrinkle easily. They can be made in various fibers and weights and with different constructions.

The Knitting Process

When fabric is knitted, loops of yarn are pulled through other loops of yarn to create interlocking rows. One yarn can form the entire fabric or gar-

ment. Varying the stitches, or loops, creates different textures and patterns.

Knitting machines can duplicate hand-knitting stitches and patterns. While hand knitting uses only two needles, a knitting machine uses many more. Each wale in a knitted fabric is produced by its own needle. A 45-inch-wide fabric could have as many as 675 wales. This means it would take 675 needles to produce the fabric.

Knitting machines are of two types: flat and circular. Flat knitting machines produce fabric with two, long, finished edges, like the selvage edges on a woven fabric. Compared to circular machines, flat knitting machines can make more complex fabrics, such as cable knits. They can also produce more complex shapes. Full-fashion sweaters, which follow the contour of the body more closely, are an example. Where narrowing occurs, as in the shoulder area, a mark results when stitches transfer to adjacent needles.

Circular knitting machines produce tubes of knitted fabric. See *Fig. 12-19*. The diameter of the

12-19 A sweater that you wear may have been produced on a circular knitting machine.

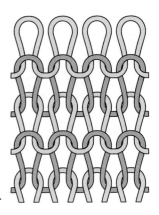

12-20 Jersey knits, the most common weft knits, have all loops drawn to one side of the fabric. These fabrics stretch about equally in both directions.

12-21 Purl knits are weft-knit fabrics. The courses have an alternating pattern that draws some stitches to the front and some to the back.

tube depends on the fabric's end use. A hosiery machine, for example, has a smaller diameter than a sweater machine. Some circular machines knit the complete item, as done with socks and pantyhose. A circular machine produces fabric faster than a flat machine. Circular knits can also be cut open and used as flat fabric.

Types of Knits

The two basic knits are weft and warp. Weft knits are made with only one yarn. Warp knits are made with several yarns. Both knits have many variations.

Weft Knits

When you knit by hand, you're making a weft knit. In the industry, weft knits can be made on either a flat or circular knitting machine. Most weft knits have two-way stretch in both the lengthwise and crosswise directions; however, they can get lengthwise "runs" from broken threads because of their single-yarn construction.

The following are three, basic, weft-knit fabrics:

- **Jersey knits.** These are the most common weft knits, sometimes called plain knits or single knits. See *Fig. 12-20*. The front and back have different appearances. The right side has vertical wales; the wrong side has crosswise courses. Because single knits are made with one set of needles, they have a tendency to curl at the edges. T-shirts, sports shirts, dresses,

sweaters, and pantyhose are made of jersey-knit fabrics.

- **Purl knits.** Purl knits are the same on both sides. See *Fig. 12-21*. They have crosswise courses like the wrong side of a jersey knit. Purl knits stretch in both the lengthwise and crosswise directions. They are thicker than jersey knits and lie flat without curling at the edges. Most purl knits are used for sweaters.

- **Rib knits.** Vertical ribs, or columns of stitches, alternate on the front and back of these knits. See *Fig. 12-22*. Rib knits are used as neck, wrist, and bottom bands on sweaters and jackets. They lie flat and have greater elasticity in their width than their length.

12-22 Rib knits are weft-knit fabrics. The wales have an alternating stitch pattern. In this particular example, the first two wales are the same, but the second two are different.

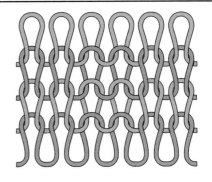

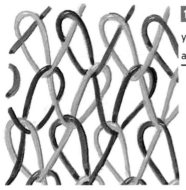

12-23 Warp knits are made with multiple yarns that interlock. These knits account for about 25 percent of knit fabrics.

Specialized weft-knit fabrics include imitation furs, knitted terry, and knitted velour. The two specialized knits described below are quite common:

- **Interlock knits.** These are a variation of rib knits. Because the columns of wales are directly behind each other, the fabrics are smooth and more stable. They don't stretch out of shape. Interlock knits are popular for blouses, dresses, and dressy T-shirts.
- **Double knits.** Two yarns and two sets of needles are used to make these knits. The loops are drawn through from both directions. Heavier, firmer, and sturdier than other knits, double knits won't run or ravel. They're used for a variety of garments.

Warp Knits

Warp knits are made with several yarns on flat knitting machines. The fabric is constructed by looping the multiple warp yarns so they interlock. See *Fig. 12-23*. Thus, each loop is made with two yarns. The fabric is usually run-resistant.

- **Tricot knits.** These knits have very fine, vertical wales on the right side and crosswise courses on the back. They are stable, lie flat, and don't run or ravel. Tricot knits are used primarily for lingerie, underwear, loungewear, and uniforms. Tricot knitting machines can produce fabric much faster than weaving or any other type of knitting.

- **Raschel knits.** An extra yarn can create a textured or patterned design in these knits. Fabrics range from lacy knits, to thermal underwear, to heavy blankets. Raschel knits with extra spandex yarns are used in swimwear and foundation garments.

OTHER FABRIC CONSTRUCTIONS

Some fabrics are constructed with heat and moisture, adhesives, or bonding agents. Others are created with special yarns, designs, or layers.

- **Nonwoven fabrics.** Interlocking fibers with heat and moisture or with an adhesive substance produces nonwoven fabrics. These fabrics don't ravel or fray. They are flexible and have good shape retention. They may have weak areas, however, and may tear easily. Most nonwoven fabrics are inexpensive to produce.

Fashion Facts

ELECTRONICS. If you seldom go anywhere without carrying an electronic gadget, maybe your clothing can help. Manufacturers now make a jacket with a cell phone and MP3 player built in. Just put on the headphones and talk into the collar. The microphone is there, and a concealed remote provides control.

Eventually, you may be able to buy a jacket that doubles as a wearable wireless computer. The fabric feels like cloth but acts as a digital display. Do you need to know the weather forecast? Just check the small, interactive screen—on your sleeve.

As perhaps the oldest known textile, felt is made by applying heat, moisture, and pressure to wool fibers or a combination of wool and other fibers. The process depends on the natural ability of wool fibers to shrink and lock together to form a mat. Felt is used primarily for hats, craft projects, and industrial purposes.

Manufactured fibers can be joined or fused together with an adhesive or bonding agent. These nonwoven fabrics are used for sew-in and fusible interfacings, disposable surgical gowns, and disposable diapers.

- **Laces and nets.** Twisting or looping threads or yarns together produces laces and nets. Special machines make very intricate lace designs for garments and home furnishings.
- **Stretch fabrics.** Both woven and knitted fabrics can be made with yarns that have increased stretchability. These stretch fabrics use textured yarns or yarns that have been wrapped around an elastic core. Spandex or rubber can also be used. Stretch fabrics can be designed to stretch in the warp direction, the filling direction, or both. Two-way stretch fabrics are especially suitable for swimsuits, exercise wear, and active sportswear.
- **Bonded fabrics.** Fabrics can be bonded to other fabrics, vinyl, clear films, or rubberized coatings. The fabric gains more body or a special surface. To make simulated leather, vinyl is bonded to a woven or knitted base. Rubberized coatings can be added to fabrics for water repellency.
- **Laminated fabrics.** These fabrics have a layer of foam between an outer fabric and a backing fabric. They give additional warmth to outerwear.
- **Quilted fabrics.** These fabrics consist of two layers of fabric with a batting between them. See *Fig. 12-24*. The three layers of fabric can be held together with machine stitching in a decorative pattern or in rows.

Pinsonic quilting holds the layers of fabric together by heat fusion instead of stitching. This method has no stitching threads that can break; however, holes can develop in the fabric at the point of the heat fusion. Pinsonic quilting is used for bedspreads, mattress pads, and placemats.

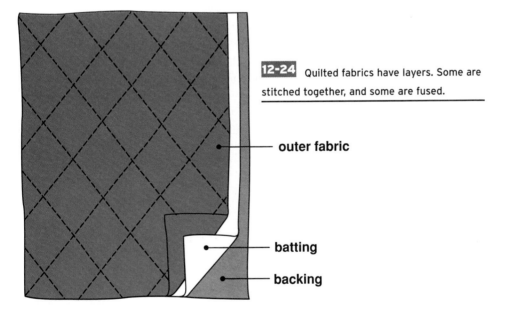

12-24 Quilted fabrics have layers. Some are stitched together, and some are fused.

outer fabric

batting

backing

FABRIC DICTIONARY

◀ BATISTE
Soft, sheer plain-weave fabric, usually a cotton blend; *blouses, children's wear, nightwear.*

BOILED WOOL ▶
Wool knit fabric, rubbed and shrunk; warm and flexible but not stretchable; *jackets.*

◀ BROADCLOTH
Closely woven, plain-weave fabric of cotton, wool, or silk; *shirts, sportswear, suits, coats.*

BROCADE ▶
Jacquard-woven fabric with an elaborate design raised slightly above the firmly woven background; *evening dresses, upholstery.*

◀ BURLAP
Coarse, rough-textured fabric made of jute; *accessories.*

CALICO ▶
Lightweight, plain-weave fabric with a small printed design; *sportswear.*

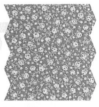

◀ CANVAS
Strong, heavyweight, plain-weave fabric of cotton or manufactured fibers; *sportswear, accessories, recreational items.*

CHALLIS ▶
Lightweight, plain-weave fabric with a slightly fuzzy, soft finish and a small floral print; *blouses, dresses.*

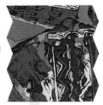

◄ CHAMBRAY
Plain-weave, cotton fabric with colored warp and white filling yarns that create a pastel color; *shirts, sportswear.*

CHARMEUSE ►
Lightweight, satin-weave, silk-like fabric with a shiny surface; *dresses, blouses, pajamas.*

◄ CHENILLE
Fabric made from chenille yarns, fuzzy yarns with a surface that resembles a caterpillar; *jackets, bathrobes, slipcovers, blankets.*

CHIFFON ►
Soft, very sheer, plain-weave fabric of silk or manufactured fibers; *dressy clothes, scarves.*

◄ CHINO
Sturdy, medium-weight, twill-weave fabric of cotton or cotton blends; *pants, sportswear, uniforms.*

CHINTZ ►
Plain-weave, glazed-cotton fabric; *clothing, curtains, slipcovers.*

◄ CORDUROY
Cut-pile fabric of cotton or manufactured fibers, usually with rows of pile that vary from narrow to wide; *sportswear, suits, upholstery.*

CREPE ►
Fabric with a crinkled surface created by highly twisted yarns or a special finish; *blouses, dresses, lingerie.*

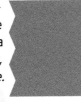

◄ DAMASK
Heavy, firm, Jacquard-woven fabric with a slightly raised, glossy design that is the same on both sides of the fabric; *tablecloths, napkins, draperies, upholstery.*

DENIM ►
Strong, twill-weave fabric of cotton or cotton blend, with colored warp and white filling yarns; *jeans, sportswear.*

◄ DOTTED SWISS
Crisp, sheer fabric with woven dots; *dresses, curtains.*

DOUBLE KNIT ►
Sturdy, knitted fabric made with two sets of needles to produce a double thickness of fabric; *sportswear, dresses, suits.*

◄ DUCK
Durable, plain-weave, cotton fabric; *sportswear, upholstery.*

EYELET ►
Embroidered fabric with open-work patterns; *blouses, dresses, curtains.*

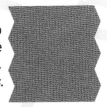

◄ FAILLE
Crosswise-ribbed fabric; *dresses, draperies.*

FAKE FUR ►
Pile fabric, usually of modacrylic fibers; looks like animal fur; *coats, hats, upholstery, stuffed toys.*

FABRIC DICTIONARY

◄ FELT
Nonwoven fabric created by matting wool or other fibers with moisture, heat, and pressure; *hats, crafts.*

FLANNEL ►
Soft, napped fabric of cotton, wool, or rayon; *shirts, dresses, nightwear, sheets.*

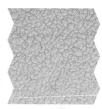

◄ FLEECE
Warm, lightweight fabric with a thick, soft pile or nap; *jackets, sweat suits, hats.*

GABARDINE ►
Strong, medium-weight to heavyweight, twill fabric of wool or manufactured fibers; *sportswear, suits, coats.*

◄ GINGHAM
Lightweight to medium-weight, plain-weave cotton fabric made of dyed yarns to create plaids, checks, and stripes; *shirts, dresses, curtains.*

JERSEY ►
Smooth, lightweight knit; matte jersey has a dull surface; *dresses, shirts, sportswear, underwear.*

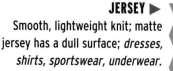

◄ LACE
Decorative, open-work fabric; *fancy blouses, dresses, trims, curtains, tablecloths.*

◄ LAMÉ
Shiny, metallic fabric made from yarns that are all metal, metal wound around a core yarn, plastic-coated metal, or metal-coated plastic; *eveningwear, accessories.*

MADRAS ►
Plain-weave, cotton fabric in plaid, checks, or stripes with non-colorfast dyes that bleed for a faded look; *sportswear.*

◄ MUSLIN
Firm, plain-weave, cotton fabric in a variety of weights; *dresses, sheets, draperies.*

NET ►
Open-mesh fabric formed by twisting yarns together; *evening dresses, veils, curtains.*

◄ ORGANDY AND ORGANZA
Crisp, sheer, plain-weave fabrics; organdy is made from cotton, organza from silk or rayon; *dressy clothes, curtains.*

OXFORD CLOTH ►
Medium-weight, basket-weave or plain-weave fabric with colored warp and white filling yarns; *shirts.*

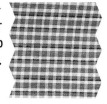

◄ PERCALE
Firm, smooth, plain-weave fabric of cotton or cotton/polyester blend that is similar to muslin but woven of finer yarns; *shirts, dresses, sheets.*

◄ PIQUÉ. Medium-weight fabric in a dobby weave with small geometric designs, such as bird's-eye and honeycomb; *dresses, children's wear.*

POPLIN ▶
Medium-weight, finely ribbed fabric that is slightly heavier than broadcloth; *sportswear, dresses.*

◄ SAILCLOTH
Very strong, durable, cotton fabric originally used for sails; *sportswear.*

SATEEN AND SATIN ▶
Smooth, shiny fabrics woven in a satin weave; sateen is made from cotton, satin from silk or acetate; *blouses, dresses, evening dresses, draperies.*

◄ SEERSUCKER
Plain-weave cotton or cotton-blend fabric with puckered stripes; *summer suits, sportswear.*

SHANTUNG ▶
Plain-weave fabric of silk or manufactured fibers with a nubbed surface; *dresses, suits, draperies.*

◄ SUEDE CLOTH
Woven or knitted fabric with a napped finish that looks like suede; *coats, jackets, upholstery.*

TAFFETA ▶
Crisp, plain-weave fabric that has a sheen and rustles when it moves; *dressy clothes, ribbon.*

◄ TERRYCLOTH
Woven or knitted pile fabric with uncut loops on one or both sides; *robes, beachwear, towels.*

TRICOT ▶
Drapable warp knit with fine vertical wales on the front and crosswise ribs on the back; *shirts, dresses, lingerie.*

◄ TULLE
Fine, lightweight net; *bridal veils, formal gowns.*

TWEED ▶
Sturdy, plain- or twill-weave fabric with a nubby surface made from wool or wool-blends; *jackets, suits, skirts, coats, upholstery.*

◄ VELOUR
Soft, woven or knitted fabric with a thick pile surface; *coats, sportswear, casual wear.*

VELVET AND VELVETEEN ▶
Lustrous, cut-pile fabrics; velvet is made of silk or manufactured fibers, velveteen of cotton; *jackets, dressy clothes, robes, draperies, upholstery.*

◄ VINYL
Woven or knitted fabric coated with vinyl to look like leather or rubber; *coats, rainwear, upholstery.*

VOILE ▶
Soft, very sheer, plain-weave fabric similar to organdy and batiste; *blouses, dresses, curtains.*

CHAPTER 12 Review

CHAPTER SUMMARY

- Fibers are spun into yarns, which are inter-laced or looped to create fabric.

- A fabric's characteristics are affected by the type and number of yarns used.

- Fabrics are distinguished by their look, feel, and construction.

- Weaving and knitting are the two most common methods of fabric construction.

- Woven fabrics are made by interlacing lengthwise and crosswise yarns.

- Weaving patterns can be varied to produce different qualities in fabrics.

- Knit fabrics are made by looping yarns into interlocking rows.

- The type of knit used affects the qualities of the fabric.

- Other fabrics are formed by joining fibers and yarns with heat, moisture, adhesives, or stitching.

USING KEY TERMS

Demonstrate five of the Key Terms for the class, using one or more fabric samples. Choose fabric samples that can be cut to separate the yarns as needed.

RECALLING THE FACTS

1. How can you tell a spun yarn from a filament yarn?

2. Identify four basic types of yarn and explain how each is formed.

3. How does texturing improve a fabric's feel and performance?

4. What is the main advantage of blending fibers?

5. Describe four characteristics you can use to identify fabrics.

6. What determines a fabric's weave?

7. Why is a satin weave a better choice for a dressy blouse than a hiking shirt?

8. How does a pile weave differ from the basic weaves?

9. How are courses and wales related to fill-ing yarns and warp yarns?

10. How does a purl knit differ from a jersey knit?

11. Why are double knits sturdier than single knits?

12. Why are warp knits more run-resistant than weft knits?

13. Identify and describe four ways to make fabrics other than knitting and weaving.

and Activities

THINKING CRITICALLY

1. Compare knitting and weaving. How are they similar and different?

2. Why is it important to know what weave or knit is used in a fabric?

APPLYING KNOWLEDGE

1. **Fabric profiles.** Collect a variety of fabric swatches. Mount each on an index card. On the back of the card, write the fabric's name, fibers, and type of construction. Use the cards for a classroom game of "Name that Fabric" before adding them to a class bulletin board.

2. **Looking at yarns.** Examine different garments under a magnifying glass. Try to identify the weave or knit and the presence of textured or novelty yarns.

3. **Weaving samples.** Using paper strips or pieces of yarn or string, demonstrate how to create different weaves.

4. **Stretchability test.** Cut different fabric samples of equal sizes. Include weaves, knits, and fabrics made with other constructions. Test each sample for stretchability, both lengthwise and crosswise. Record the results in a bar graph.

5. **Shrinkage and wrinkling.** Cut three 4-by-4-inch samples of different fabrics. Soak one swatch of each fabric in hot water and one swatch in cold water for several minutes. Dry flat. Soak the third swatch in warm water and dry in a dryer. Compare shrinkage and wrinkle resistance of the samples. What conclusions can you make from your observations?

6. **Choosing fabrics.** Refer to the Fabric Dictionary on pages 228-231. Based on those descriptions and on what you know about fibers, explain which clothing fabrics you would choose for these purposes: yard work; school; lounging; athletics; and prom.

7. **Fabric costs.** Visit a fabric store to compare costs of different fabrics. Report your findings to the class. Why do you think some fabrics are more costly than others?

CREATIVE SOLUTIONS

You've found a sweater that you want to buy at a thrift shop, but the garment label is missing. Without it, you don't know the sweater's fiber content and all the useful information this knowledge provides.

Think Creatively

What simple observations or tests could help you identify the sweater's fabric? What could this information tell you about the sweater's wear and care?

Fabric Finishes

WHEN FABRIC FIRST COMES FROM THE loom, it looks nothing like the finished fabric you see in a shirt, jacket, or towel. Many of the fabrics have no color; they are gray or off-white. The warp yarns may have been stiffened to withstand the strain of weaving. The fabric may be limp, fuzzy, dull, or very shiny. How then are fabrics transformed into the beautiful, colorful, and comfortable materials that you want to buy and wear? The answer is by adding finishes.

FINISHING PROCESSES

Finishes are any special treatments applied to improve a fabric's appearance, texture, or performance. Every fiber and fabric have certain favorable and unfavorable qualities. Finishes can be added to reduce the undesirable characteristics and improve the desirable ones.

Some finishes are added to create a specific design, such as a stripe or print. Other finishes offer a softer, firmer, or smoother hand. Many finishes add a specific property or quality to the fabric, such as wrinkle resistance. See *Fig. 13-1.* Fabric finishes may be permanent or temporary. While a permanent finish lasts throughout the life of the fabric, a temporary finish may last through only one or two cleanings.

COLOR AND DESIGN FINISHES

When fabric first comes from the loom, the lack of color gives it the name **gray goods**. The fabric must be cleaned to remove any oils, resins, gums, or soil that would prevent a finish from penetrating the fabric. Manufacturers then alter the appearance of gray goods by dyeing or printing the fabric.

Dyeing Textiles

Dyes are compounds that penetrate and color fibers. They can color the entire fabric or create special designs. For centuries, natural dyes were obtained from plants, insects, shellfish, and minerals. The first synthetic dye was discovered by

13-1 You can learn about the finish on a garment's fabric by reading the labels and hangtags.

13-3 Here, yarns are dyed before they are woven into fabric. Most dyes are mixed by computer to produce uniform colors.

accident in 1856. Then a whole new industry developed for textiles.

Textile colorists are continually seeking better dyes for different fibers and blends. Today they use computers to develop exact formulas for dyeing different fibers a certain color.

Five different methods are used for dyeing. See *Fig. 13-2*. With *stock dyeing*, natural fibers can be dyed before they're spun into yarns. This permits the spinning of tweed and multicolored yarns. *Solution dyeing* is used when manufactured fibers are produced. Dye is added to the liquid solution that goes through the spinnerets. The color becomes a permanent part of the manufactured fiber. In *yarn dyeing*, the yarns are dyed before

weaving or knitting. See *Fig. 13-3*. This is used for plaids, checks, and stripes. In *piece dyeing*, fabric is dyed after weaving or knitting. Manufacturers store undyed fabric and then dye it a specific color. With *garment dyeing*, the fabric is cut and sewn into the finished product. Then the entire garment or item is dyed.

Colorfastness

Buying a bright green shirt only to have it fade to a dull green is disappointing. If the shirt had been **colorfast**, however, the fabric color wouldn't have changed. Whether washed or exposed to chlorine or sunlight, a colorfast fabric doesn't fade. The fastness of the color depends on the type of dye, the chemical structure of the fiber, and the method of application. See *Fig. 13-4*.

Most dyes aren't colorfast to everything. Some are more affected by washing, dry cleaning, sunlight, or perspiration. Some dyes may crock, or rub off onto your skin or other clothing.

Always read the label or hangtag for information about colorfastness. You can't tell how stable a color is by looking at the fabric.

Manufacturers select dyes that are most suitable to the fiber content and the intended use of a fabric. Children's clothes and sportswear, for example, need to hold their color through many washings. For draperies, upholstery, and carpets,

13-2 What dyeing method do you think was used for this fabric?

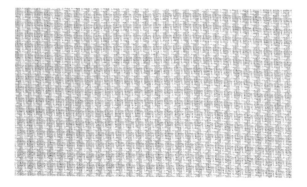

13-4 This textile lab technician is testing the color-fastness of dyes.

fastness to sunlight is important. Swimwear needs to be colorfast with exposure to sunlight, washing, and chlorine.

On the other hand, some fabrics are designed to fade or bleed. Many buyers like the denim jeans that are meant to lighten when washed. Madras, a woven plaid fabric, is supposed to bleed so the plaid becomes softer and less distinct.

Printing Textiles

What makes a fabric beautiful? For many people it's the design. Through **printing**, color is transferred to the surface of a fabric to form a pattern. Fabrics can be printed in a number of ways. Some printing techniques are very old and still used by crafts people today. The textile industry, however, uses high-speed, electronic machines for textile printing. See *Fig. 13-5*. Some specialty fabrics, such as scarves and evening gowns, may be printed by hand.

Four of the most common printing methods are screen, rotary screen, roller, and heat transfer.

Other methods, which you can try yourself, are tie-dyeing and painting. See page 238.

- **Screen printing.** With this method, fabric or metal mesh screens are stretched on frames. A separate screen is prepared for each color in the design. Once the design is traced onto a screen, all areas that aren't part of the color to be printed are blocked out with a special coating. The colors are then pressed through the screens onto the fabric, using a squeegee or roller. Large designs, especially those used on fabrics for home furnishings, can be printed this way.

- **Roller printing.** A roller printing press contains circular rollers, or printing plates, one for each color in a design. Each roller is chemically etched with the pattern part for a particular color, leaving high and low areas on the rollers. The raised sections of the roller pick up the desired color. As the fabric passes through the press and makes contact with the raised sections of each roller, the pattern prints. The different areas of color combine to form the completed design.

13-5 Fabric patterns can be designed by computer and automatically programmed into the printing press.

How To . . . CREATE PRINTED FABRIC

Machines print fabric with colors and designs, but you can too. Painting and tie-dying are popular hand-printing techniques that produce beautiful results. Both can be done on flat fabric or finished garments.

Painting Fabric

Fabric paints include glitter, glow-in-the-dark, flat, and three-dimensional. Brush-on paints give a soft look. Squeeze-tube paints provide an outline effect. Marker paints are easy to use. Follow these guidelines:

- Check paint instructions for fabric recommendations. Many paints work best on cotton-and-polyester blends.

- Wash the fabric, but don't use a fabric softener.

- For a work surface, cover a piece of cardboard with a plastic trash bag or dry cleaner's bag. Place the covered cardboard inside the garment to prevent paint from seeping through to the reverse side. Hold the cardboard in place on the inside of the garment with masking tape.

- Follow the paint manufacturer's instructions for garment care. Waiting at least 48 hours before laundering a newly painted fabric is typical.

Tie-Dye Patterns

Different patterns result from the way you tie fabric.

- **Large sunburst pattern.** Pull up the center section of fabric and space the ties a few inches apart down the length of the fabric.

- **Small designs.** Space the ties evenly around the fabric.

- **Special effect.** Push the center of each knot through to the other side before tying.

- **Wide band.** Use many strings or rubber bands close together.

Tie-Dyeing Fabric

To tie-dye, fabric is bound with string or rubber bands in certain places, then dipped into dye. The dye doesn't penetrate the spots where the fabric is held tightly together. After dyeing the first color, the fabric can be retied and dipped in a different color. Repeating creates more complicated designs. Fabrics made of 100-percent cotton work best, but a blend of cotton and polyester can be used successfully.

Exploring **Hand-Printing**

Try painting or tie-dying a T-shirt. Create your own original design or use an existing one for inspiration.

- **Rotary screen printing.** This method combines the advantages of screen printing and roller printing. It's faster than screen printing and can produce more than 3,500 yards per hour. The rotary screens, made from metal foil, are less costly than the copper engraved rollers used in roller printing.
- **Heat-transfer printing.** With this method, designs, insignias, and words are transferred onto fabric. First, a paper pattern for the design is printed with heat-sensitive dyes. The design appears in reverse on the pattern. When the pattern is placed face down on the fabric and heat is applied, the design transfers to the fabric. See *Fig. 13-6.*

TEXTURE AND PERFORMANCE FINISHES

A pair of jeans may be comfortable enough to wear all day long. A party dress has a sheen that sparkles in the moonlight. A shirt goes right from the dryer to the hanger, with no need for ironing. All of these result from special fabric finishes that affect both texture and performance, making garments more enjoyable to wear.

Texture Finishes

Most fabrics have some type of finish that improves surface texture and hand. Additional benefits are improving the comfort and performance of the fabrics.

- **Calendering.** Fabric passes between two heated rollers that smooth the fabric and improve the luster.
- **Glazing.** A resin is applied during calendering to produce a high polish or glaze on the surface of the fabric. Chintz is a glazed fabric.
- **Embossing.** Fabric is given a raised design on the surface when it's calendered with rollers engraved with the design.
- **Ciré (suh-RAY).** A super-glossy finish is obtained by applying wax or some other substance before calendering. Ciré nylon is sometimes used for lightweight jackets.
- **Moiré (mwah-RAY).** A watered or wavy pattern is obtained by calendering two layers of fabric slightly off grain. Moiré fabric is used for eveningwear.
- **Napping.** Rotating wire brushes raise the short fiber ends of staple yarns to create a soft and fuzzy surface called **nap**. The nap looks different when viewed from different directions. Flannel is a napped fabric. ▌see→ **p 494**
- **Stone washing and acid washing.** Pumice stones, sometimes dampened with an oxidizing bleach, are added to a mass-production, laundering process. They provide the abrasion that makes denim garments appear worn and partially faded. The garments also become softer and more comfortable to wear. See *Fig. 13-7.*

13-6 Transfer printing uses heat to switch a design from the paper to the fabric. How does the design on the pattern compare to the finished design?

13-7 Many people like the look and feel of stone-washed jeans.

- **Mercerization.** This finish gives cotton added luster, strength, and drapability. It also improves the fiber's affinity for dye. Fabrics and yarns are treated with a caustic soda or lye solution. This is one of the few finishes applied before dyeing.
- **Sizing.** Starches or resins are added to the fabric for extra body. Sizing is usually only a temporary finish.

Performance Finishes

Sometimes a fabric's performance results from the fibers used. For even better performance, however, many different finishes are applied to fabrics. Read care labels and follow manufacturer's recommendations so that a fabric's finish is not diminished or destroyed.

- **Antibacterial or antiseptic.** This finish checks the growth of bacteria and fungi, such as mold and mildew. Germs that cause odor, disease, and infection are reduced or even prevented. Brand names include Sanitized® and Pacificate®.
- **Antistatic.** Some fabrics cling due to static electricity. By absorbing small amounts of moisture from the air, this finish reduces the fabric dryness that causes static electricity.
- **Crease-resistant.** Commonly known as CRF, these resin finishes help fabrics resist wrinkling. They are most often applied to fabrics made from fibers that wrinkle easily, including cotton, rayon, and flax.
- **Durable press.** This is a descriptive term for garments that maintain a pressed appearance despite repeated washings and wearings. Through heat setting, resin curing, or an ammonia process, the fabric fibers are stabilized. The fabric resists wrinkling during wear, and the garment maintains its shape, pleats, and creases. When washed and dried by machine, the garment needs little or no ironing. Any wrinkles tend to flatten or disappear after the garment hangs for a while. Apparel made of 100 percent cotton and treated by this process may be described as "wrinkle free," "wrinkle-resistant," or "no iron."

In advertisements and articles, you may see the term permanent press used, especially for cotton and polyester blends. Fabric experts prefer the term durable press. This means that with proper care, the fabric or garment will perform as expected. If care instructions are not followed, however, some wrinkling may occur. The word permanent implies that wrinkling never occurs.

- **Flame-resistant and flame-retardant.** These finishes reduce flaming and burning in fabrics that have been exposed to a flame or high heat. They are used on children's sleepwear and other clothing. See *Fig. 13-8*. Special care may be needed to maintain the finish.
- **Mothproof.** To repel moths and other fiber-eating insects, this finish is widely used on wool fibers. It's added when fabric is dyed.
- **Shrinkage control.** These finishes don't guarantee that no shrinkage will occur. Instead, shrinkage should be minimal, even after repeated launderings. The term Sanforized® assures that the fabric won't shrink more than one percent in washing. Washable wool fabrics have been treated to prevent shrinkage when laundered as directed on the label. If a fabric is labeled as preshrunk, a shrinkage process has been applied. ◼see→ p 490

13-8 Federal law requires flame-retardant fabrics for children's sleepwear.

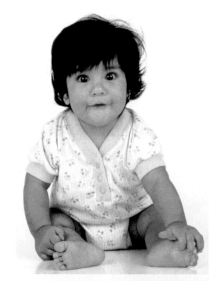

>>HIGH-PERFORMANCE FINISHES

What's new in fabric finishes? The latest developments are fascinating.

- **Nonstick garments.** A Teflon® surface on fabrics helps repel dirt and water, making it useful for outerwear. The finish forms a molecular bond with the fiber. Teflon® yarns in socks and hosiery reduce friction between sock and skin.

- **Speed enhancement.** Competitive swimmers like the neck-to-ankle bodysuits that improve performance. One specially designed fabric is a Lycra® spandex blend that is fed through compression rollers to make it thinner and lighter.

Heating the fabric provides a smooth, flat finish. Finally, the fabric is coated with a water-repellent finish that minimizes drag.

- **Sun protection.** Some fabric finishes shield from prolonged exposure to the sun. A special chemical technology reduces penetration by harmful ultraviolet rays. For fabrics without this protection, you can get a laundry detergent that adds UV protective chemicals when clothes are washed.

- **Allergy protection.** Eventually, an anti-dust-mite fabric impregnated with a small amount of a special pesticide may be available. Potential uses are sheets, pillowcases, and quilts.

INVESTIGATION ACTIVITY

One manufacturer coats fabric to make it change color according to your mood. Find other examples of how finishes are expanding the functions of fabric.

- **Soil release.** Fabrics made from manufactured fibers or treated with a durable-press finish often retain soil and oily stains. With soil-release finishes, dirt and stains remove more easily from fabrics. Most are durable through 40 or 50 launderings.

- **Water- and stain-repellent.** These finishes help fabrics repel water- and oil-based stains. The yarns are coated with a chemical that resists water and other liquids. Drops remain on the fabric surface in a small bead rather than being absorbed immediately, as shown on page 242. Because the repellent is applied to the yarns, rather than the whole fabric, the fabric remains porous so air and body moisture can pass through. The fabrics, however, eventually become wet. The repellent finish may need renewal when the garment is dry-cleaned. In addition to clothing, these finishes are often used on table linens and upholstery fabrics. A widely used repellent is Scotchguard®.

- **Waterproof.** These finishes keep the fabric and the wearer dry. Waterproof fabrics have been coated or treated so that no water penetrates. Since the fabric has been made nonporous, it may be uncomfortable to wear. New, microporous, waterproof finishes allow body moisture to escape, while not allowing water to penetrate. GoreTex® is a widely used, breathable, waterproof fabric.

CHAPTER 13

Review

CHAPTER SUMMARY

- Finishes are applied to improve a fabric's appearance, texture, and performance.

- Some finishes are permanent and some are temporary.

- Some finishes add color or designs to fibers or fabrics.

- Texture finishes change a fabric's look, feel, and hand.

- Performance finishes make fabrics easier to care for and more useful.

- Some finishes can be diminished or destroyed by improper fabric care.

USING KEY TERMS

Working with a partner, list the Key Terms in a column on a sheet of paper. For each Key Term, point out ways that it is demonstrated in the fabrics you see around you. Note specific examples. Which Key Term will have no examples? Why?

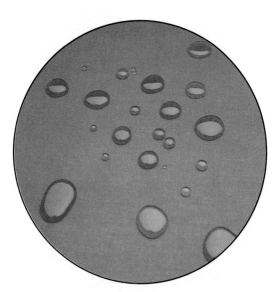

RECALLING THE FACTS

1. What is the difference between a permanent and a temporary finish?

2. Why are gray goods cleaned before finishing?

3. Name and describe five dyeing processes.

4. When is coloring added in stock dyeing? In piece dyeing?

5. Do colorfast fabrics ever fade? Explain.

6. How are screens used in screen printing?

7. What are the advantages of rotary screen printing, compared to other methods?

8. How are glazing and ciré similar and different?

9. How is a fabric texture changed in embossing? In napping?

10. Why are fabrics mercerized before dyeing?

11. What are the benefits of applying a durable-press finish?

12. What is the difference between water-repellent and waterproof?

13. How has technology improved water-proof finishes?

242 ● UNIT 4 **Fibers and Fabrics**

and Activities

THINKING CRITICALLY

1. Why do you think a temporary finish might be added to a fabric?

2. What finishes would be most useful for a pair of sweat socks? Why?

3. Why is it useful to know the type of finishes applied to a garment when shopping for clothes?

APPLYING KNOWLEDGE

1. **Finishes and care.** Bring in examples of fabric descriptions and care instructions from fabric bolts. Share and discuss these in class. What relationships can you see between certain finishes and the care needs of the fabric?

2. **Choosing finishes.** Cut a shirt shape from a large note card or draw one on paper. Decide what type of shirt this will be. Then choose a fiber content and finishes that suit the garment's use. Explain your choices to the class.

3. **Colorfast testing.** Dip unused fabric samples in hot water. Observe swatches for color loss. What conclusions can you draw about colors, fabrics, and colorfastness? Record your results and conclusions in a chart.

4. **Water repellency.** Collect different types of outdoor apparel, including sweatshirts, jackets, windbreakers, and umbrellas. Using an eyedropper or small measuring spoon, place droplets of water on each item. How does the water behave on each article? How long does it take for any water to be absorbed? Summarize your observations in a short paper.

5. **Name research.** Using library resources, find out how some generic and trade names for finishes, including mercerized and Sanforized®, were chosen.

CREATIVE SOLUTIONS

You're helping a friend choose a fabric to make a Western-style shirt. The pattern shows the shirt made with blocks of fabric in different colors. As the two of you look at solids and prints that might look good together in the shirt, your friend mentions that different blocks of red, black, and white would look great. Then your friend remembers a formerly owned red shirt that turned the wash water pink.

Think Creatively

If the red and black dyes in the fabric your friend likes aren't colorfast, they might run on the white after the shirt is made and washed. What should your friend do?

Careers

Textile Production

MAGINE LOOKING IN ON A MODERN textile mill. Row after row of colorful cones hold yarns that twine through the intricate machinery. At rapid speeds the yarns are drawn into the weaving or knitting machines, where fabrics in beautiful patterns swiftly emerge to be used for apparel, accessories, or home fashions.

Weaving and knitting are not the only jobs handled by textile mills today. Many are vertically integrated, which means they produce the yarns and apply the finishes, in addition to manufacturing the fabrics. Most textile mills in the United States stretch through the New England states and down into the Carolinas. Many exist in other countries.

The people who work in textile production make up the largest segment of the textile industry. People typically rotate on the various shifts to keep the mill running around the clock. Careers that cover a wide range of responsibilities contribute to the mill's operation—everything from chemists in laboratories to those who keep the machinery whirring.

IS THIS FIELD FOR YOU?

Textile production encompasses a wide range of careers. If you asked what qualities each person brings to the job, however, workers in these fields are apt to agree with the statements below.

- I pay attention to detail.
- I'm interested in the process by which things happen.
- I have a strong sense of self-direction.
- I like to take charge of my environment.
- I enjoy seeing how my efforts contribute to a group's success.
- I can balance several tasks at once.

Think about all the fabrics you see around you every day, and you will realize the scope of textile production. In textile mills, machines run at high speeds turning out fabrics in a wide array of colors and patterns.

Education and Training

Although a high-school diploma lands some jobs in textile production, employers often look for technical training or related experience. For a machine operator, an associate's degree that focuses on computer skills and electronics is useful. A textile engineer prepares with a bachelor's degree, studying textile machinery and the effects of mechanical forces on fibers. A textile scientist may have a doctorate in analytical chemistry and possibly years of teaching and research experience.

Many firms have management training programs for new employees, starting with summer internships for promising college seniors. A course in company management methods is first. By rotating assignments in different areas of the plant, a candidate learns about the jobs and machinery. Seminars with experienced managers and technicians further prepare employees for leadership positions.

Possible Career Paths

In textile production a person's career path can branch in different directions. A machine operator with a two-year degree might advance to line supervisor. By adding a four-year degree in chemical engineering, the operator could become a manufacturing

production engineer who supervises an entire range of production processes. With sales training, a person who has line and supervisory experience could take a different path. By becoming a machinery manufacturer's representative, the employee could train line operators to use new equipment.

Similar paths run through other areas of textile production. A chemical engineer may work on a new process for extruding polyester. Some years later that person may be the product engineer who oversees such a project, from research and development, to patenting, to marketing.

Higher education increases the chances for moving a career forward, since advanced skills transfer more readily to related fields. A textile chemist, for example, may leave the laboratory to work as a county extension agent who advises consumers on clothing care.

THE SKILLS YOU NEED

Running heavy machinery and running scientific experiments may seem like vastly different jobs; however, both are likely to require the following common skills:

- Problem solving
- Analytical thinking
- Communication
- Teamwork
- Eye-hand coordination
- Record keeping
- Attention to detail

Effective communication between supervisors and employees helps keep textile production going.

Choosing a *Textile* Production *Career*

CHEMICAL TECHNICIAN | ENVIRONMENTAL ENGINEER | MACHINE OPERATOR | PROCESS ENGINEER | PRODUCT DEVELOPMENT MANAGER | RESEARCH SCIENTIST | TEXTILE CHEMIST | TEXTILE CONVERTER | YARN TECHNICIAN

Textile Chemist —

By studying the molecular structure of fibers, textile chemists learn how fibers behave when woven, dyed, finished, and washed. As part of their work, chemists perform experiments and write reports. Textile chemists work for chemical companies, fiber manufacturers, textile mills, and private testing labs. They often do research in university laboratories.

Through research and development, chemists create manufactured fibers with particular characteristics. A textile chemist's work may join with other branches of science. Examples are the chemists who develop recyclable fibers and those who are trying to devise fabrics that deliver medications through the wearer's skin. Chemists sometimes serve as consultants, helping others solve problems.

Textile Converter —

Textile converters specialize in applying designs, textures, and other finishes to fabrics. As the "middlemen" of the textile industry, they buy unfinished fabric from textile mills and turn it into fabrics for apparel and home fashion manufacturers.

Most converters are small operators who work quickly to supply last-minute orders. They must stay up-to-date on the latest trends in colors, patterns, textures, and finishes. By understanding how the fashion industry operates, they are better able to anticipate demands. Because they fill smaller orders than large textile mills, they have a special role in the global marketplace.

Chemical Technician

Chemical technicians, also called process technicians, do much of the daily work in the research lab. They set up and run experiments. For example, they might test the damaging effects of heat and light on nylon. Technicians record results, interpret data, and may suggest conclusions. They keep careful notes on every step and each development.

Greater use of computers and robotics has changed the technician's job in recent years. The technician who skillfully uses the latest mass spectrometer may suggest and carry out better ways to use and care for this equipment.

A textile chemist might determine the best dyeing methods for a certain fiber.

Here, a quality control worker surveys a textile spinning operation.

Machine Operator

In a textile mill, trained machine operators create fibers, yarns, and fabrics by extruding, spinning, weaving, knitting, printing, and dyeing. Using a computer, each operator oversees multiple machines, such as padding machines, treating tanks, dye jigs, and vats. The operator prepares a specific set of machines for production and corrects or reports any problems during a run.

As an example, a loom operator checks and adjusts the timing on each machine. Then, using sophisticated computer programs, the operator quickly threads the harnesses with the yarns for the pattern. The operator keeps the machine supplied with yarn, stopping to repair any breaks. Machine operators on the production line show initiative as they work with others to solve problems and improve processes.

Environmental Engineer

Environmental engineers use knowledge of scientific and mathematical principles to prevent or solve environmental problems caused by building and running the plant. An engineer might redesign a textile mill's steam production system so it uses less water from a nearby river. Engineers have shown denim manufacturers how to recover and reuse indigo dye. Other engineers have found a way to capture and pipe methane gas from a landfill to fuel a mill's operations.

Environmental engineers are a textile company's link to outside groups and programs. An engineer might serve on one of the industry's environmental protection boards or present a plan to reduce the chemicals released in the factory's wastewater.

CAREER APPLICATIONS

1. **Internships.** Research internship opportunities in the textile production field. Find out how people can take advantage of these opportunities, what preparations must be made, and where they fit into a student's studies. Write a report of your findings.

2. **FCCLA.** Research the effects that education and training have on career options and advancement in the textile industry. Present your findings in an Illustrated Talk.

3. **Professionalism.** You're interviewing for an entry-level job in a textile mill. The interviewer asks you this question: "In our company we look for people who will carry out their work with a high level of professionalism. What qualities do you have that show you're that kind of person?" What qualities will you list for the interviewer and what reasons will you give for including them?

UNIT 5
Clothing Care

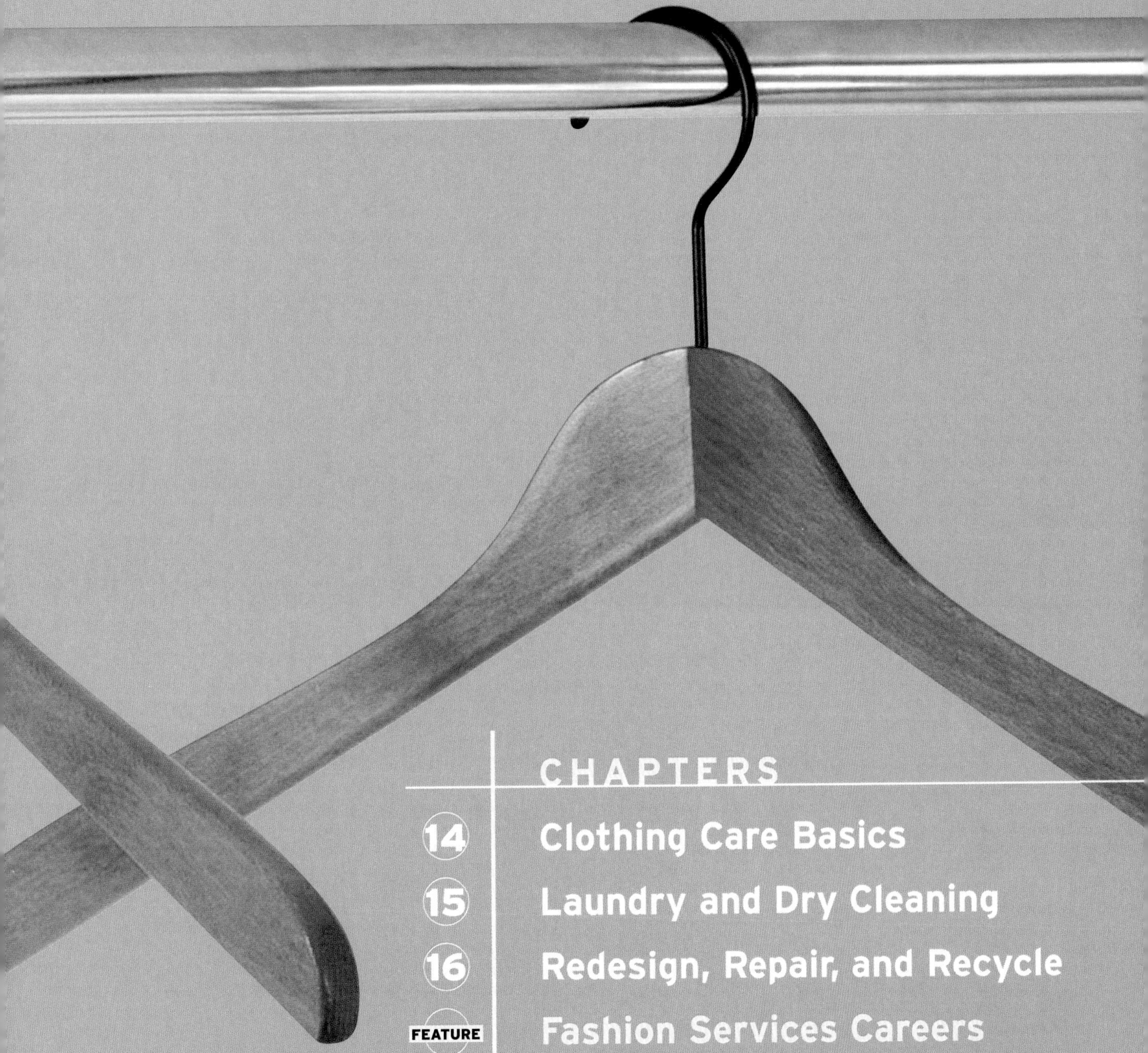

CHAPTERS

Clothing Care Basics

OBJECTIVES

- Explain how to care for clothing on a routine basis.
- Choose the best methods for removing specific stains.
- Give examples of the information on care labels.
- Describe how to store clothing effectively.

KEY TERMS

enzymes
fabric care symbols
pressing
pretreating

prewash soil-and-stain remover
tumble dry

EXAMINETHISISSUE

Learning to be organized. "I'm not an organized person; it's just not me," one teen explained. Many people feel the same way. They don't mind disorder and learn to live with it. Other people prefer order. They like the way it feels and believe they save time when their life and possessions are in order.

What do you think?

What role does order play in your life? As you read this chapter, you'll see suggestions for an organized approach to clothing care. Do you think most people can learn these habits?

YOU JUST WASHED YOUR SHIRT, but the stain is still there. You're getting ready to go out, but the pants you planned to wear have a ripped seam. You want your favorite sweater, but it's lost somewhere in a cluttered room. Do any of these situations sound familiar? If so, this chapter has some ideas that can help you.

ROUTINE CARE

Responsible clothing care brings several benefits. With a little knowledge and a few good habits, you can enjoy all the rewards that come with taking good care of your wardrobe. See *Fig. 14-1.*

One positive effect is feeling more confident. When people know their clothes are clean and presentable, interacting with others is often easier.

A daily clothing care routine also helps you make better use of time, while cutting down on frustration. If you're not doing so already, try setting aside specific times each week to launder, hand-wash, iron, and mend. When you do, your clothes are always in order. A last-minute decision to go somewhere won't send you scurrying to find something to wear. You might even gain a few extra minutes to sleep in the morning.

Clothing care can also save you money. With improper care, garments don't last as long. They may even be ruined. By following good care practices, you spend less money replacing clothes. Learning to remove spots and stains yourself saves on cleaning bills.

Examining Garments

To make routine care part of your daily schedule, take a few seconds to check your clothes

14-1 What are the benefits of making clothing care part of your daily routine?

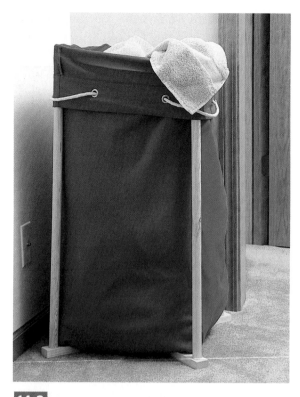

To remove dust, lint, or animal hair, gently brush the garment. You can use a special clothing brush, lint brush, or a specially designed roller with an adhesive surface. See *Fig. 14-3*.

If your shoes or boots are dirty, wipe away dust or mud before putting them away. Damp shoes should air-dry before going in a shoe bag or closet.

Stain Removal

If you find a stain when checking a garment, take care of it as soon as possible. The longer a stain remains on fabric, the harder it is to get out. Be sure to treat stains before laundering a garment. Hot water and heat can set a stain, making it difficult to remove later.

14-3 If you don't have a roller like this one, even a piece of masking tape can remove lint in an emergency. What techniques might be more economical than a roller that needs refills?

before putting them away. Does any garment need to be laundered or dry-cleaned? Soil and stains show clearly on light-colored fabrics, so you can evaluate them easily. Even though soil is harder to see on dark-colored clothes, those garments also need regular cleaning. If you allow fabrics to get too dirty, cleaning them is more difficult.

Clothes that need washing should be placed in a location set aside for storing dirty clothes, as shown in *Fig. 14-2*. Then the clothes won't be overlooked when laundry time comes. Clothes that are not washable should be taken to a dry cleaner as soon as possible.

Some garments can be worn again. If freshening is needed, hang a woven garment where the air can circulate around it. This helps remove odors picked up by the fabric. A knitted garment, such as a sweater, can be draped over a chair.

What takes out one stain won't necessarily work on another. Ask yourself what caused the stain and then choose an appropriate stain-removal procedure. Some techniques are described in *Fig. 14-4* on pages 254-255. For stubborn stains, a procedure may need to be repeated several times. Basic stain-removal methods are described below.

- **Rinsing.** You might get a fresh stain out of washable fabric by rinsing it immediately in cold water. See *Fig. 14-5*.
- **Soaking.** Many stains can be dissolved or loosened by soaking the fabric in cold water for up to 30 minutes. This works well for water-based stains, such as fruit juice and soft drinks. Adding laundry detergent to the water can aid stain removal. Protein-based stains, such as chocolate, blood, egg, grass, meat juice, milk, baby formula, and perspiration, are often more difficult to remove. Adding an enzyme presoak powder to the water works best for these types of stains. **Enzymes** are special proteins that control chemical activity. Some enzymes break down certain soils so they can be more readily removed during washing. Because these products dissolve protein-based soils, they also attack protein fibers, making them unsuitable for wool and silk.
- **Pretreating.** **Pretreating** is done just before laundering in order to give heavy dirt and stains extra attention. One method is to apply liquid laundry detergent or a paste of water and powder detergent to a stained or heavily soiled area, such as "ring-around-the-collar" on shirts and blouses. Lightly rub the detergent into the stain. Another method is to apply a **prewash soil-and-stain remover**, which is effective in dissolving oily, greasy, or heavily soiled stains. Wait one to five minutes before washing to allow the product to penetrate and break up the stain. See *Fig. 14-6*. Pretreating also helps remove any stains that remain after soaking. For heavy grease stains, blot with a paper towel to absorb the stain and prevent it from reentering the fabric.

14-5 An immediate cold rinsing removes many stains from washable fabrics. Why is the sooner, the better?

14-6 Some pretreatment products are sprayed on and others are rubbed on with a stain stick. Why should this be done before laundering the stained fabric?

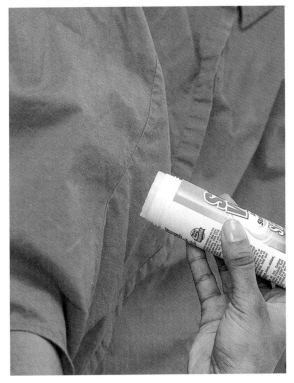

Stain
Removal Methods

BLOOD   Soak in cold water as soon as possible for 30 minutes or longer. Pretreat any remaining stain. Launder. For dried stains apply an enzyme presoak or rub detergent on stain. Wash, using bleach if safe for fabric.

CANDLE WAX   Harden by placing in freezer or rubbing with ice cube. Scrape off with dull knife or fingernail. Place between several layers of paper towels and press with warm iron. Sponge remaining stain with prewash stain remover or cleaning fluid. Launder.

CATSUP; TOMATO PRODUCTS   Scrape off excess with a dull knife. Soak in cold water. Pretreat remaining stain. Wash, using bleach if safe for fabric.

CHOCOLATE   Scrape off; then soak in cold water. Pretreat any remaining stain. Wash, using bleach if safe for fabric.

COFFEE; TEA   Use an enzyme presoak. Wash in hottest water safe for fabric.

COSMETICS   Rub detergent into area or use a prewash stain remover. If stain is stubborn, sponge with cleaning fluid. Launder.

DEODORANT; ANTIPERSPIRANT   Pretreat stain and wash in hottest water safe for fabric. Also see directions for perspiration stains.

FRUIT; FRUIT JUICE   Soak in cold water. Pretreat remaining stain. Wash, using bleach if safe for fabric.

GRASS   Rub detergent into area or use an enzyme presoak. Then wash, using bleach and hottest water that is safe for fabric.

GRAVY; MEAT JUICE   Scrape off excess with a dull knife. Soak in cold water. Pretreat remaining stain. Wash, using bleach if safe for fabric.

GREASE; OIL Scrape off or blot with paper towels. Use a prewash stain remover or rub detergent into area. Launder. If stain remains, sponge with cleaning fluid and rinse.

GUM Harden by placing in freezer or rubbing with ice cube. Scrape off with dull knife or fingernail. Pretreat remaining stain, and wash.

INK Spray with hair spray or sponge with rubbing alcohol. After a few minutes, blot with paper towels. Repeat if necessary. Rub detergent into stain, and wash. Alternative: use a prewash stain remover; then launder. (Some ballpoint, felt tip, and liquid inks may be impossible to remove.)

MAYONNAISE; MUSTARD; SALAD DRESSING Pretreat stain and wash in hottest water safe for fabric. Use chlorine bleach if safe for fabric. If grease stain remains, soak in warm water with a pretreat product, rinse thoroughly, and relaunder.

MILDEW Pretreat stain, and launder, using chlorine bleach if safe for fabric. Alternative: soak in an oxygen- or all-fabric bleach and hot water; then launder. (Heavily mildewed fabrics may be permanently damaged.)

MILK; ICE CREAM; BABY FORMULA Soak in warm water. Launder in hottest water safe for fabric; use appropriate bleach. If stain remains, soak in warm water with a pretreat product, rinse thoroughly, and relaunder.

NAIL POLISH Place stain face down on paper towels. Sponge with nail polish remover (do not use acetone on acetate fabrics). Rinse thoroughly and launder in hottest water safe for fabric. (Nail polish may be impossible to remove.)

PAINT Do not let paint dry. For latex paint, rinse in cool water and launder. For oil-based paint, sponge with turpentine or mineral spirits and rinse with water. Launder. (Once paint is dry, it cannot be removed.)

PERFUME Soak in cold water. Pretreat remaining stain. Wash, using bleach if safe for fabric.

PERSPIRATION Use a prewash stain remover or enzyme presoak, or sponge fresh stain with ammonia. For old stain, sponge with white vinegar and rinse. Rub detergent into stain and wash in hottest water safe for fabric.

RUST Wash with a rust remover, following manufacturer's directions. Do not use chlorine bleach, as it will intensify the stain.

SOFT DRINKS Sponge or soak in cold water. Pretreat any remaining stain. Launder.

UNKNOWN STAINS Pretreat stain and soak in cold water. Wash in cold water with detergent. If stain remains, rewash in warm water. If stain still is not removed, wash again in hot water.

- **Bleaching.** Some stains may come out when bleach is added to water for presoaking or laundering. Nonchlorine bleach may be used on all fabrics and colors. Chlorine bleach should not be used on wool, silk, leather, spandex, and noncolorfast fabrics. When using bleach, always follow the manufacturer's directions for amount, water temperature, and soaking time. See Chapter 15 for more information about bleach.
- **Using cleaning fluid.** Cleaning fluid can be used on some stubborn stains, but use it carefully and follow the manufacturer's directions. Rinse the fabric thoroughly before laundering.
- **Dry cleaning.** If you're worried about removing a stain from a special garment, the best solution may be the professional attention of a dry cleaner.

When using stain-removal products, caution is essential. Used incorrectly, some products can make the problem worse and even be dangerous. Never combine stain-removal products. Chlorine bleach and ammonia, for example, can produce noxious (harmful) fumes. Always read the manufacturer's directions on any stain-removal product before using it, and keep the products locked away from children.

Checking for Repairs

Has a seam ripped or a hem come loose? No matter how careful you are with clothes, small repairs can't be avoided. A quick repair keeps the rip from lengthening and the entire hem from falling out. Place garments that need mending where you won't forget about them. Then make the repairs when you have a few spare minutes. Otherwise, you may not have time to do a repair when you want to wear a garment. See *Fig. 14-7*.

Many repairs can be done quickly with hand sewing. Restitching a loose button, snap, or hook and eye takes only a few stitches. Re-anchoring a loose fastener is easier than replacing one that has fallen off. In Chapter 16 you'll learn how to make simple repairs. see→ p 530

Pressing

Suppose you're getting ready to go somewhere and the pants you want to wear are slightly wrinkled from hanging twisted in the closet. What can you do? You don't need to iron the whole garment since a touch-up pressing will work.

In **pressing** fabric, you raise and lower the iron from one area to the next. This technique quickly removes a few wrinkles and sharpens creases. The heat and steam smooth the fabric, so heavy pressure isn't needed. See *Fig. 14-8*.

Press on the wrong side of the fabric, whenever possible, to prevent a shiny mark on the right side of the fabric. If you must press on the right side, always press gently or use a press cloth. Be sure to use the correct temperature setting for the fabric and follow safety precautions. These are explained in the section on ironing in Chapter 15.
see→ p 511

14-7 Making simple repairs is easy. If you don't know how to make them, who might teach you?

14-8 A garment may need only a touch-up pressing to be wearable. What is the technique for pressing?

14-9 Wrinkles can be removed from many garments with steam. On what fibers and fabrics might steaming not work?

If a garment is lightly wrinkled, there are other ways besides pressing to make it look fresh. Hand-held steamers can eliminate wrinkles while the garment remains on the hanger. See *Fig. 14-9*. If you don't have this device, try hanging the garment in the bathroom when you take a steamy shower.

When you're in a big hurry, what can you do? Keep a can of wrinkle-remover in the cupboard. Just spray the garment and smooth out the wrinkles with your hands. This product works best on knits and natural fibers. Both steamers and spray products add moisture to the garment, so you'll have to wait a few minutes for the garment to dry before wearing.

Putting Clothes Away

One simple way to prevent wrinkles in clothes is to always put them away. See *Fig. 14-10*. By hanging clothes up and folding them neatly, you avoid extra pressing. You also know where clothes are when you want them. What if you spent just five minutes each day hunting for misplaced clothes? How much time would that cost in a year?

14-10 When clothes are put away each day, the pile doesn't grow to an unmanageable size.

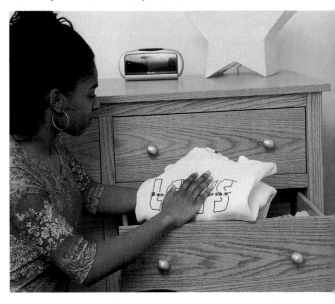

Most woven garments should be hung on hangers after emptying the pockets. Close the zipper or top button to keep the garment from twisting or falling from the hanger. For jackets and clothes that might be creased by a narrow metal hanger, use wider plastic or wooden hangers like those in *Fig. 14-11*. These support the shoulder area of the garment better. To keep the shape of stretchable and loosely knitted garments, such as sweaters, store them flat on a shelf or in a drawer.

UNDERSTANDING CARE LABELS

Look inside any garment and you'll find a permanently attached care label. It's usually stitched to the center back of the neckline or into a side seam and must remain readable for the life of the garment. See *Fig. 14-12*. The Care Labeling Rule of the Federal Trade Commission (FTC) regulates information on these labels. Only a few garments, such as socks and hosiery, are exceptions.

Care Labeling Information

The fiber, fabric construction, finish, color, interfacing, lining, and trims determine what care method is listed on a garment label. Although some manufacturers list more than one safe method of care, only one is required. Directions for either machine washing, hand washing, or dry cleaning must be supplied. Any methods listed on the label have been checked for safe use. The manufacturer doesn't have to mention any other safe method.

Labels must provide specific information. For example, the care label for a washable garment must include the following: washing method, safe water temperature, and method and safe temperature for drying. If chlorine bleach is not safe to use, a warning must be added. For garments that need ironing, the temperature for ironing must be included. If no warnings are given, you don't need to adjust the care methods listed on the label.

On care labels look for the general information described below. Some examples are shown in *Fig. 14-13* on page 260.

- **Washing.** "Machine wash" means you can wash and dry the garment by any method at any temperature—hot, warm, or cold.

14-12 Check the care label before you buy a garment and before you clean it. Why is this helpful in both of these situations?

Trends in TECHNOLOGY

>>COLOR LOSS IN FABRICS

Although the label on her new blue sweatshirt said, "Wash before wear," one teen wore it without washing. Later she found blue stains on the white shirt worn under the sweatshirt. What happened? Unstable fabric dyes can run, fade, or rub off, especially bright colors and dark colors, which have more dye. Here are some common dye problems and their prevention.

- **Color bleeding.** Some dyes bleed, or transfer to other fabrics, during laundering. After dissolving in the water, the dye is absorbed by the other fabrics. Hot water and a long soaking time increase the chance of color bleeding. Watch for care labels that say "wash separately" or "wash with like colors." Always wash dark or brightly colored clothing with similar colors.

- **Crocking.** Color from excess dye in new fabrics may rub off onto skin or other clothes when first worn. This occurs more where there is moisture, such as perspiration. Care labels that say "wash before wear" offer warning.

- **Fading.** Ultraviolet rays from light can change the chemical structure of dyes, which results in fading. Although blue, green, and lavender dyes are particularly light sensitive, most colors can fade. Even whites can turn yellow. Hang garments where they're protected from strong light.

- **Color loss.** Some dyes, especially the blues in cotton denim, come off where the fabric rubs against other things. This is why blue jeans often lose color along seam lines and garment edges. If jeans rub against the post inside the washing machine, streaks may appear where the color rubs off. Prevent by turning jeans inside out before washing.

- **Chemical damage.** Perspiration and alkaline substances in toiletries can damage dyes. Spills with lemon juice, bleach, and stain removal products can remove color. Protect from spills and follow bleaching directions carefully. Rinse immediately after a spill.

INVESTIGATION ACTIVITY

Describe a fabric dye mishap you or your family had. Find information on how the problem might have been avoided.

14-13 By reading the care label, you'll know what care will keep your garment in good condition. Why is it a good idea to leave the care label attached to a garment?

Otherwise the label indicates the appropriate wash cycle, such as delicate or gentle, and water temperature to use. If no temperature is mentioned, any temperature is safe. "Wash separately" means to wash alone or with like colors. "Hand wash" means to launder only by hand in lukewarm water.

- **Bleaching.** A label might not mention bleach, which means any bleach may be used when needed. If only chlorine bleach is harmful, the label states "no chlorine bleach." If all bleaches are harmful, the label must warn "no bleach."

- **Drying.** "Tumble dry" means the garment can be dried in a tumble dryer at the specified setting—high, medium, low, or no heat. Otherwise, the label indicates "line dry" or "dry flat."

- **Ironing.** If ironing is needed, even for a touch-up, the label must say so. If the hottest setting isn't safe, the label must indicate "warm iron" or "cool iron." A label that states "do not iron" means that even the coolest setting could be harmful to the fabric. "Iron damp" means to dampen the garment before ironing. If no

ironing instruction is given, ironing probably isn't needed.

- **Dry cleaning.** Some fabrics can't be washed. If the label says "dry-clean only," a garment may be dry-cleaned by any method, including a coin-operated machine. Any necessary warning about solvents or steaming must be supplied.

Fabric Care Symbols

How can different care methods be understood when garments are sold where different languages are spoken? In 1997 manufacturers solved this problem by putting **fabric care symbols** on care labels. The symbols show proper care in a visual way. As you can see in *Fig. 14-14*, the six basic symbols are wash, bleach, tumble dry, dry, iron, and dry-clean. Each symbol is tailored to provide specific information about temperatures, methods, and settings. Any warnings are indicated by a large X across the symbol.

STORING CLOTHES

Whether you have lots or little storage space, getting organized keeps your clothes neat and easy to find. See *Fig. 14-15*. The information here and the tips on page 262 provide ideas you can put to use.

14-15 Putting away clothes in an organized manner may seem time consuming, but it can save you time when it comes to finding what you want later.

What Do Fabric Care Symbols Mean?

WASH

Cool/Cold Temperature

Warm Temperature

Hot Temperature

Do Not Wring

Normal Cycle

Permanent Press Cycle

Delicate/ Gentle Cycle

Hand Wash

Do Not Wash

BLEACH

Bleach As Needed

Nonchlorine Bleach As Needed

Do Not Bleach

TUMBLE DRY

No Heat/ Air

Low Heat

Medium Heat

High Heat

Do Not Tumble Dry

Any Heat/ Normal Cycle

Permanent Press Cycle

Delicate/ Gentle Cycle

DRY

Line Dry

Drip Dry

Dry Flat

Dry in the Shade

Do Not Dry (Used With Do Not Wash)

IRON

Low Heat

Medium Heat

High Heat

Do Not Iron with Steam

Do Not Iron

DRY-CLEAN

Dry-Clean

Do Not Dry-Clean

How To... CREATE CLOTHING SPACE

Few people think they have enough storage space. How about you? If you'd like more space, a little creativity might be the answer. Try the ideas described here to get started.

- **Shoe bags.** Not just for shoes, these compartmented bags can hold rolled-up belts, scarves, socks, and underwear. They could also hold a clothes brush or roller, shoe polish supplies, garment hangtags, and extra buttons and yarns that come with clothes. Shoe bags can hang on the back of a door or on the wall. In a deep closet, they can go behind your clothes to store off-season shoes or special-occasion accessories.

- **Hooks and hangers.** Small hooks hold belts, necklaces, and chains. Larger ones hold caps, hats, tote bags, and backpacks. Some hooks have an adhesive back; others can be screwed into wood. Mount hooks on the inside of the door or closet, or screw several into a strip of wood that mounts on the wall. A tie rack is a special hanger that holds more than ties. Use it for such small items as belts, scarves, handbags, and jewelry.

- **Baskets, crates, and boxes.** In natural wicker, modern wire, or colorful plastic, these make attractive and functional storage additions for T-shirts, sweaters, jewelry, hats, and grooming supplies. Put them on a dresser or stack them on the floor. Vary the sizes and shapes—round, oval, or square—to suit your needs. Store out-of-season or seldom-worn clothes in low boxes under your bed.

Exploring Clothing Space

Evaluate the storage space that you have. What type of extra storage do you need? What would be the best way to create this storage? Write a description of your ideas.

An Organized Closet

Cartoonists have often drawn the infamous overstuffed closet with the door that just won't close. You can avoid this problem. First, make sure unneeded garments are sorted out. Chapter 16 can help with this task.

Then look for ways to arrange clothing efficiently. A shirt hidden between two jackets could be lost for weeks. By placing similar items together, they're easier to find. Hang garments of similar length together to create room for shelves or baskets under the short garments. You can even suspend a second, lower rod from the upper one to double the hanging space for short items.

Multiple shirt, pants, and skirt hangers also save space. You can put five or six garments on one hanger. Place folded clothes and accessories in plastic or cardboard boxes on the shelf or floor. Label the boxes for quick identification.

Drawers and Shelves

To get control of drawers, store similar items together. That is, have specific drawers for socks, underwear, and T-shirts. Some people place a tray on top of a chest or dresser to hold a watch, jewelry, and other small items.

Use shelves inside the closet or in the room for additional storage. For easy access, stack folded sweaters and sweatshirts. Line up hats, caps, and other accessories. Luggage and seldom-used items can be stored on hard-to-reach, top shelves.

Seasonal Storage

If you live in a seasonal climate, clothing can be stored when not in use, leaving space for the clothes you're using. See *Fig. 14-16*. Clothing and accessories should be clean before storing. Because some stains don't appear right away, an item may look clean when it isn't. Then during storage, the stain turns brown or yellow and becomes impossible to remove. Stained and soiled fabrics attract such insects as moths and silverfish, which eat holes in fabric. Moths are particularly fond of oil-based soils on wool clothing. Moth and insect repellents are available. If you use them, follow the manufacturer's directions carefully.

14-16 Sweaters can be stored off-season in plastic containers that slide under the bed.

Store items in large garment bags, boxes, or chests. For added protection, seal with tape before storing. Drape leather or fur items with a piece of fabric. Don't place them in plastic bags since they need air circulation.

Find a dry place to store clothing. Dampness causes mildew, which can stain or damage fabric and be difficult to remove. Careful attention to storage can preserve your clothes for added seasons of wear.

Fashion Facts

MOTH PROTECTION. Moths are unwelcome guests in any closet. Items in storage, especially those that are put away soiled, are particularly prone to moth attacks. Some experts caution against treating affected garments with moth balls or insecticide, since some toxic substances can damage garments as much as the moths themselves. Laundering, steam or dry cleaning, and even freezing clothes (for three days, sealed in a heavy plastic bag) are effective ways to kill moths and their larvae.

Review

CHAPTER SUMMARY

- Caring for garments properly has several benefits.

- Routine care includes removing stains, making small repairs, and storing correctly.

- Different types of stains require different stain-removal techniques.

- A garment's permanent care label tells you how to care for it.

- Symbols on permanent care labels are a guide to care.

- Organized clothing storage saves time and helps keep clothes looking good.

USING KEY TERMS

Write a short paragraph that explains the routine care of clothing. Include all Key Terms, used correctly. For a creative approach, describe the actions of a fictitious person. A possible opener might be: "Eric arrived home, starving and late as usual after basketball practice. He dropped a duffle bag stuffed with school clothes on the floor and..."

RECALLING THE FACTS

1. How does giving garments needed care benefit you?

2. What routine care do clothes need after wearing?

3. Why should stains be treated quickly?

4. When might freezing clothes be a recommended stain-removal treatment?

5. For what types of stains might an enzyme presoak be needed? Give examples.

6. Give some tips for using bleach on clothes.

7. How should you treat a stain if you're not sure what caused it?

8. Would mixing two stain-removal products bring better results? Explain.

9. What is the advantage of making small garment repairs right away?

10. Identify two ways to remove small wrinkles from garments.

11. What specific information must a permanent care label provide?

12. What are your laundering options for an item labeled "machine wash"?

13. Describe an organized closet.

14. Why should clothes be clean and dry before storing for a season?

and Activities

THINKING CRITICALLY

1. Some people use home remedies that don't involve chemicals to treat stains. Do you think this is a good idea? Explain your position.

2. Why do you think chemical products should be kept in their original containers instead of transferring them to other boxes and bottles for storage?

3. At one time, care labels were not required on garments. What do you think caused the laws to be changed?

APPLYING KNOWLEDGE

1. **Stain removal.** Working with a team, experiment with different methods of stain removal. Apply several different stains to various fabrics. Evaluate how well the methods work and why.

2. **Color bleeding.** Soak red fabric that isn't colorfast with white or light-colored fabrics. Once the red color bleeds, test whether washing, bleaching, or stain-removal products can restore the original color of the other fabrics.

3. **Fabric care symbols.** Conduct a survey to learn whether friends and family members can identify fabric care symbols. Do they use the symbols? Record their opinions along with the results of your survey.

4. **An ideal closet.** With a partner, design a closet arrangement that would appeal to teens. Use catalogs or store flyers to find helpful storage organizers. Make a floor plan and drawings to illustrate the arrangement. Present your design to the class.

5. **Closet organization.** Plan and carry out a closet reorganization. The closet could be yours or another one in your home, or you could team to work on a friend's closet. Take before and after photos. Write a summary of the plan and the results.

CREATIVE SOLUTIONS

While putting clothes away after laundering, you notice that a shirt with marker stains near the two top buttonholes was accidentally washed without pretreatment. Now they seem set. The marker is red, the shirt is yellow, and the stains are hard to miss.

Think Creatively

What can you try in order to salvage this shirt from the rag bag?

Laundry and Dry Cleaning

OBJECTIVES

- Explain the use of laundry products and equipment.
- Describe the steps involved in laundering clothes.
- Compare ways of drying clothes.
- Demonstrate how to iron clothes.
- Explain dry-cleaning processes.

KEY TERMS

agitator	ironing
detergents	laundering
dry cleaning	solvent

JUST A FEW GENERATIONS AGO, doing the laundry was nothing like what it is today. Imagine hand-feeding each garment through a wringer to squeeze out the water before hanging everything on lines to dry. Although methods have changed, there is still much to learn today about keeping clothes clean and in good condition.

The garment care label is your guide. It tells you whether to machine-wash, hand-wash, or dry-clean a garment. This chapter tells you how.

LAUNDRY PRODUCTS AND EQUIPMENT

In one family, everyone is convinced that the washing machine eats socks. In another family, turning white clothes pink or blue happens a little too often. You may know stories about shrinking garments, mysterious holes, or stubborn stains. Whatever the problem, a skillful approach to handling laundry can help. Begin by learning how to select and use laundry products and equipment.

Selecting Laundry Products

When confronted by a store aisle full of laundry products, choosing isn't easy. If you learn about products before you shop and then read labels, decisions are easier to make.

In using laundry products, be sure to follow label directions. You'll achieve better results and be safe in the process. Some products, such as bleach, are harmful if they come in contact with eyes and skin. Since swallowing can be hazardous, always keep laundry products locked away from children's reach. See *Fig. 15-1.*

15-1 Special locking devices on cabinets keep laundry products and other cleaning supplies safely away from children's exploration.

15-2 To use a detergent correctly, you'll need to read the information on the box. It will tell you how much to use based on the washer and load size.

Laundry Detergents

Detergents are cleansing agents that remove soil from fabric and prevent it from returning to the fabric. They are available as powders, liquids, and premeasured tablets.

Detergents have essentially replaced soaps for laundering because they work well in both hard and soft water. Soap reacts with minerals in hard water and in the soil on clothes to form a white, powdery curd that stiffens fabric. The soap's ability to clean decreases. Since hardness minerals have less effect on detergents, detergents make a better choice for laundry products.

You'll find several types of laundry detergents in stores, so you can choose according to your need.

- **All-purpose detergents.** These are suitable for all washable fabrics. Powder detergents are good for all types of laundry, from lightly soiled shirts to heavily soiled work clothes. Liquid detergents are also all-purpose but work especially well on greasy or oily stains.
- **Ultra detergents.** In general, both liquid and powder detergents come in this concentrated form. The packages are smaller, and you use less product.
- **Combination detergents.** Some detergents combine color-safe bleach or fabric softener with detergent. Adding bleach improves cleaning as well as stain removal. Adding a softener makes fabrics feel softer and reduces static electricity. These products are available in both powder and liquid forms.
- **Fragrance and dye-free detergents.** For people with certain allergies, these products are available.
- **Light-duty detergents.** These detergents work well for hand- or machine-washing delicate or lightly soiled fabrics, such as hosiery and lingerie.

Many detergents are low foaming in order to work well in the newer front-loading, high-efficiency washers, which create more suds. Too much suds can keep clothes from tumbling and getting clean.

When laundering clothes, use the detergent amount specified on the box or bottle. The manufacturer's recommendations are for an average load with average soil in water of average hardness. Use less detergent for small loads, lightly soiled clothes, low water levels, and soft water. Use more detergent for big loads, extremely dirty clothes, high water levels, and hard water. See *Fig. 15-2.*

Soil-and-Stain Removers

For removing stains and treating clothes that are particularly dirty, you can keep appropriate products on hand. Use the guidelines for stain removal in Chapter 14.

- **Prewash soil-and-stain removers.** These are applied to fabric before washing. They are available in spray, liquid, stick, gel, and aerosol forms.
- **Enzyme presoaks.** These come in a powder form and can be used prior to washing or added to the wash cycle along with detergent.

Laundry Bleaches

Bleaches remove stains, whiten and brighten fabrics, and destroy bacteria. See *Fig. 15-3.* If used too often or if highly concentrated in water, however, bleach can weaken fibers. There are two types of bleach, with and without chlorine.

- **Chlorine bleach.** Labeled "chlorine" or "hypochlorite," chlorine bleach is most effective for whitening, disinfecting, and deodorizing. It cannot be used, however, on wool, silk, leather, spandex, and nonfast colors.

- **Nonchlorine bleach.** Also called oxygen bleach, this product may be identified as "color safe" or "safe for all fabrics." Because it's mild, nonchlorine bleach can maintain the brightness of both whites and colors but cannot restore whiteness to gray and dingy fabrics.

Always add bleach to the water while the washing machine fills. Then add the clothes. This prevents fabric discolorations caused by splashing or pouring the bleach directly onto clothes. Some washing machines have a special bleach dispenser that automatically dilutes the bleach.

Other Laundry Products

For further help with laundering, other products are available.

- **Fabric softeners.** Fabrics feel softer, have less static electricity, and are fragrant with the use of fabric softeners. See *Fig. 15-4.* Liquid softeners are added to the water during the final rinse. Pouring directly on the clothes could cause stains. With some washing machines, the softener goes in a dispenser. Too

15-3 Bleach can turn dingy white clothing brighter and whiter. Suppose you have a stretchy white top that looks grayish around the neckline. Would you wash it in bleach?

15-4 Fabric softeners are available for use in the washer or the dryer, as shown here. What advantages might each method have?

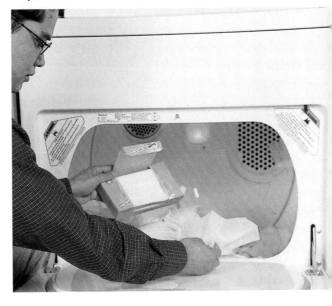

much fabric softener can make towels less absorbent, but you can remove the excess by washing the towels several times without any softener.

Fabric softeners in the form of nonwoven sheets can be placed in the dryer, either with the clothes or in a holder to avoid direct contact with fabrics. The heat of the dryer releases the fabric softener and scent, which adhere to the fabrics. Add only one sheet per load and don't reuse.

- **Starches.** These are a type of sizing that gives body to fabrics and makes ironing easier. Spray starch can be applied before ironing. Dry and liquid starches should be mixed with water before using.

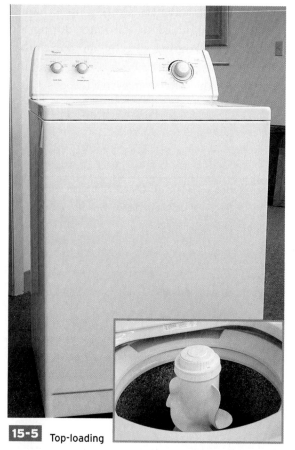

washing machines have been in use for many years. The motion of the agitator pulls the clothes through the water, which enables the detergent to work into the fabric.

- **Water softeners.** Mineral deposits that prevent thorough cleaning can be removed from hard water with water softeners. The powder form goes in either the wash or rinse cycle. The liquid form is added only to the rinse water. Some families have a water softening system installed at home to remove many of the minerals in water.
- **Disinfectants.** The germicides in these products destroy bacteria on fabric. Available in liquid form, they may be used when a family member is ill.

Using Laundry Equipment

What equipment do you need to do laundry? A washing machine, clothes dryer, iron, and ironing board are basic. Families who don't own a washer and dryer can use machines in self-service laundries. Many apartment buildings have laundry rooms with coin-operated machines for tenant use only.

Washers and Dryers

Of the two types of washing machines, the common top-loading machine has been around for years. It has a lid that lifts up and a center post, called an **agitator**, which jiggles clothes during the wash cycle to loosen dirt and get out soil. See *Fig. 15-5.*

Putting your hands inside an agitator washer that's running is dangerous. To prevent this, most machines stop agitating when the lid is raised. Some machines even have a safety lock to keep the door closed until the machine motion stops.

The second type of washing machine is front-loading, with a door on the face of the machine. No agitator is present. Instead, the washtub rotates clothes with a tumbling action similar to a clothes dryer. The newest models of these machines use less water and energy than agitator washers. See *Fig. 15-6.*

Washing machines often have a dispenser that automatically releases detergent, fabric softener, or bleach at the right time. With buttons or dials, you control such settings as water temperature, water level, length of washing time, and speed.

15-6 Some washing machines load from the front. The newer models use less energy and water than top-loading machines. How else are they different?

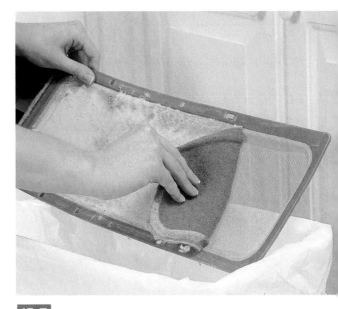

15-7 Even one load that has been dried in a dryer may produce considerable lint. The dryer operates more efficiently and dries clothing faster when you remove lint after each load. What fabrics do you think would produce the most lint?

Most washing machines offer at least three wash cycles: regular, wrinkle-free or permanent press, and gentle.

Clothes dryers have buttons or dials for controlling air temperature and drying time. The most common drying cycles are regular, wrinkle-free or permanent press (used for durable-press fabrics), and air fluff. Air fluff is a no-heat cycle for drying fabrics that can't handle heat, or for freshening pillows, bedspreads, and draperies. After each load, the dryer lint filter should be cleaned. Lint buildup can increase drying time by limiting airflow. See *Fig. 15-7*. To prevent a fire hazard, remove any gradual lint buildup in dryer pipes and vents at the rear of the dryer.

Irons and Ironing Boards

To remove wrinkles from garments, you'll need an iron and ironing board. Most irons have a dial or control button with temperature settings for different fibers. See *Fig. 15-8*. Cotton, linen, wool, and rayon are usually marked. Acetate, nylon, silk, and polyester might be too.

15-8 Some irons have more settings and features than others, which affects cost. You'll want different temperature settings and probably the ability to use steam. When choosing an iron to buy, also consider its weight and the design of the handle for comfortable use.

NO LAUNDRY DAYS. Washing clothes was of less concern to people in times past. In the Middle Ages, farmers, blacksmiths, and other laborers washed only their underclothes. Outer clothes apparently were deodorized by exposure to the scent and chemicals released in wood smoke, which was common in the days before the discovery of electricity. In the late 1500s, wealthier classes sometimes solved the problem of laundering by giving away their used clothing, often to poorer people or theater troupes.

Many irons can be used either dry or with steam. Steam helps take out stubborn wrinkles in fabrics. Some irons also have a spray button that provides extra moisture. Some steam irons can be filled with tap water; others take distilled water. Most should be emptied of all water before storing.

To avoid burning your hands, iron carefully. Keep your face away from the steam. Always rest the iron upright on its heel, not flat on its soleplate.

Some irons have an automatic shut-off feature. If the iron isn't used for a certain period of time, it turns off automatically. This is a safety feature, not a reason to leave a hot iron unattended. All irons should be turned off and unplugged when not in use.

A sturdy, level ironing board helps prevent the iron from falling. You'll be more comfortable using a board with an adjustable height. The board should have a pad and cover that provide a smooth, clean surface for ironing. Without them, the heat of the iron bounces back at you. Most covers have a silicone finish to prevent scorching and make them last longer. When the pad and cover become worn or damaged, they should be replaced.

LAUNDERING CLOTHES

Laundering may not seem like fun, but compared to a bucket and a washboard, it's not that bad. **Laundering** means washing fabric by hand or machine with a soil-removing product. You can keep your clothes in good condition longer by following the simple laundering guidelines in this section.

Sorting Clothes

Before laundering, resist the temptation to throw everything together in one load. Some clothes wash safely together, but others don't. Therefore, sort clothes before you begin. Read the care labels for recommended procedures. Then you can sort clothes by color, amount of soil, and fabric type. See *Fig. 15-9*.

First, separate the clothes by color. To prevent any bleeding of colored dyes, all dark colors should be washed together. Many white fabrics, especially those made from manufactured fibers, will pick up color, even from colorfast fabrics.

15-9 If you don't sort clothes before laundering, the color from one garment could ruin another. Minimally, your white and light-colored clothing will become dingier.

White fabrics may become dull and gray after repeated washings with colored garments, so wash them separately.

Next, consider the amount of soil on the garments. Heavily soiled work and play clothes should be washed separately. They need a longer wash cycle and can dull lightly soiled items that pick up extra soil from the wash water.

Finally, consider the fabrics in the laundry. Some fabrics, such as white cotton socks and underwear, require hot water and a long wash cycle. Washable wools and fabrics with dark colors need cold water and a short wash cycle to prevent fading or shrinking. Durable-press fabrics need special treatment to minimize wrinkling. Keep delicate fabrics separate so heavier items don't cause them to tangle and tear. Fabrics that create lint, such as terrycloth towels and fuzzy sweatshirts, shouldn't be washed with fabrics that might attract lint, such as corduroy, velveteen, and durable-press finishes. You can turn lint-producing fabrics inside out to keep other fabrics from picking up lint.

After sorting, you may have several stacks: dark colors, light colors, whites, and towels. Create a special pile for items to hand-wash.

Pretreating

While sorting clothes, set aside any garments with stains that need special attention. Refer to the stain removal chart on pages 254-255.

Pretreat heavy soil on collars and cuffs with a liquid detergent, a paste of powder detergent and water, or a prewash soil-and-stain remover. Rub into the stained area; then wait one to five minutes before laundering.

Soaking fabrics in water for up to 30 minutes helps to dissolve many stains and remove excess soil and mud. Adding an enzyme presoak or laundry detergent can aid stain removal. Use warm water for oily stains and cold water for such protein stains as blood, egg, and grass.

Machine Washing

If you simply throw dirty clothes into the machine, pick any water temperature, and dump the detergent on top, the outcome may be disappointing. There's actually more to laundering, but over time, the steps become automatic.

Loading the Machine

Before loading the machine, be sure all pockets are empty. Tissues, lipstick, crayons, and ballpoint pens can create lint or permanently stain fabrics. Close zippers and fasten hooks and eyes to prevent snagging clothes in the wash. Unfold sheets and towels. Small items can be placed in a zippered mesh bag to prevent tangling.

Add detergent according to the machine's manual and the directions on the box or bottle. If fabrics allow, you can add bleach and/or fabric softener.

Avoid overloading the machine. Items must move freely for good cleaning and rinsing action and to keep them from wrinkling. For best results, distribute the fabrics evenly around the agitator in machines that have one. See *Fig. 15-10.*

15-10 If items in a top-loading machine become unevenly placed, they can cause the machine to shake, rattle, and roll during the spin cycle. Open the lid and redistribute the items. Loading carefully can help prevent this from happening.

15-11 • Washing and Rinsing Temperatures

FABRIC	WASHING TEMPERATURE	RINSING TEMPERATURE
Most washable fabrics, including cottons and linens, but not durable press, wools, and delicates.	Cold or warm for presoaking. Cold for bright colors, darks, and lightly soiled fabrics. Warm for colors and moderately soiled fabrics. Hot for white and heavily soiled fabrics.	Cold or warm.
Durable-press fabrics.	Hot for whites and heavily soiled fabrics. Warm for everything else.	Cold.
Delicate fabrics, including lingerie, sheer and lacy fabrics, and loose knits.	Cold for bright colors. Warm for everything else.	Cold or warm.
Hand-washable fabrics, including wools and embroidery.	Cold or warm.	Cold or warm.

Mix small items with large items to provide good washing action as the garments rotate in the machine.

Water Temperature and Level

Depending on the fabric, water temperatures for washing range from varying levels of cold to hot. Follow the directions on the care label of the garments to select the proper water temperature. See *Fig. 15-11*.

Hot water (120°–140°F; 49°–60°C) cleans fabric the best and offers sanitizing benefits. Water that's too hot, however, can shrink some fabrics. Warm water (85°–105°F; 29°–41°C) is recommended for many fabrics, especially those with manufactured fibers and durable-press finishes. Cold water (65°–75°F; 18°–24°C) doesn't have much cleaning power, but it saves energy and can be used for delicate fabrics and lightly soiled clothes.

For most machines, you can adjust the water level according to the size of the wash load. If you're not washing a full load, select a lower level.

Wash Cycle

Before washing, choose the settings you want for the wash cycle. Basic machines have only a few settings, as shown in *Fig. 15-12*, but some machines have many.

- **Cycle type.** Wash cycles are programmed for different lengths of time, agitation speeds, and rinse temperatures. Use the normal (regular) cycle for sturdy fabrics, such as cottons and denims, and heavily soiled clothes. The gentle (delicate) cycle is shorter and has less motion. Use it for loosely knitted garments, sheer fabrics, and lingerie. The wrinkle-free (permanent-press) cycle has a cold rinse to minimize wrinkling.
- **Time.** Most wash cycles can be adjusted for length of wash time. From two to ten minutes is common.

15-12 When using a washing machine, you choose a water level, water temperature, and wash cycle. What are the advantages of making the correct choices?

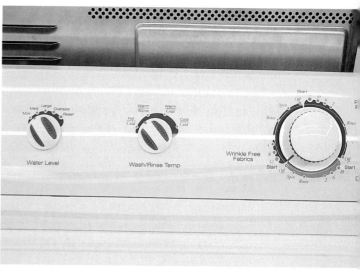

15-13 Hand washing is recommended for woolens, silks, and other delicate fabrics. Soak the garment, gently squeeze to clean, and rinse. What are the final steps?

- **Rinse temperature.** You may be able to choose a different rinse temperature, warm or cold. A cold rinse helps prevent wrinkles during spinning. This is useful for easy-care and wrinkle-free fabrics.

Hand Washing

Hand washing is recommended for many woolens, silks, and other delicate fabrics. Items that need separate handling might also be hand-washed. See *Fig. 15-13*. If possible, wash only one or two items together at a time. The care label tells the water temperature to use.

To begin, pretreat any spots and stains. Then add the laundry product to the water and swish until dissolved. Place the garment in the water and gently squeeze to clean. To remove stains, you can soak the item for 15 minutes or longer. Heavily soiled areas may need rubbing between your fingers to remove soil. Don't scrub or wring delicate fabrics.

To finish hand washing, rinse the garment in cool or cold water several times until the water is clear. Then roll it in an absorbent towel to remove as much water as possible.

DRYING CLOTHES

Some clothes can be dried by machine. Others should be hung up or laid flat to air dry. Always check the care label for drying instructions.

Machine Drying

Automatic dryers usually have temperature and cycle settings to select. Again, fabric determines what you choose. Manufactured fibers, which are more heat-sensitive, should be tumble-dried at a lower temperature than cotton or linen. Heavier fabrics, such as denim and terrycloth, take longer to dry than lightweight fabrics. The cool-down time at the end of the permanent-press cycle uses no heat, which reduces wrinkling of durable-press fabrics.

The air-fluff cycle dries without heat. Since vinyls, plastics, laminates, and some wools can't take heat, air fluff is a good choice for them.

Before putting damp clothes in the dryer, loosen them by shaking. Don't overload the dryer, because this slows down drying time, increases wrinkling, and decreases fluffiness. One washer load in the dryer at a time is best. Avoid tumble-drying fabrics that produce lint with other fabrics.

To prevent wrinkles and damage to fabric, try not to overdry garments. Fewer wrinkles occur if you fold clothes neatly or hang them on hangers when still warm. Remove and hang durable-press fabrics as soon as the dryer stops. See *Fig. 15-14* on page 276. Elastic bands in shorts and socks should feel slightly damp when first taken from the dryer. All clothes, however, should be completely dry before putting them away in a closet or drawer. This prevents mildew from forming.

Line Drying and Flat Drying

If a garment is labeled "line dry" or "dry flat," you shouldn't put it in the dryer. The fabric may shrink or stretch out of shape.

To line-dry clothes, hang them while still damp. First, shake out each item and smooth wrinkles by hand. On an outdoor clothesline, place clothespins where they won't leave marks on the garments. If you're drying clothes indoors,

The durable-press setting on a dryer often buzzes several times before the dryer stops. This gives you time to remove and hang garments, which prevents wrinkles and ironing.

Special racks for drying clothes flat can speed the drying time. These plastic screens are stretched onto a frame supported by short legs. Air circulates under and over the garment for faster drying.

IRONING CLOTHES

With heat, moisture, and slight pressure, **ironing** removes wrinkles from clothes. The iron moves back and forth in a gliding motion. To avoid stretching fabric, always iron in the lengthwise or crosswise direction of the fabric.
see→ p 511

How much ironing will you need to do? That depends on the fabrics in your wardrobe. Most knits and durable-press fabrics, such as polyester/cotton, need little or no ironing. Fabrics that wrinkle, such as linen, cotton, silk, and rayon, usually need ironing.

When ironing, select a temperature that matches the fiber content of your fabric. Cottons and linens can be pressed at higher temperatures than manufactured fibers. For blended fabrics, select the setting for the most heat-sensitive fiber in the blend. If you're not sure what setting to use,

hang them on plastic hangers, because wire hangers may leave rust marks. Hang clothes where the air can circulate around them. Many people use the bathroom shower rod. See *Fig. 15-15*. A portable drying rack is another convenient way to line-dry clothes indoors.

For garments that stretch out of shape when hung to dry, including sweaters and many knit garments, dry them flat. Remove as much moisture as possible. To do this, place the garment on top of a clean, dry towel and smooth it out. Roll the garment and towel together. Then press the roll with your hands to transfer moisture to the towel. Next, spread a clean, dry towel on a large, flat surface that can withstand moisture. Remove the garment from the roll and lay it on the dry towel, patting the garment into shape. Leave it there until thoroughly dry.

Plastic hangers placed on a bathroom shower curtain rod provide a good way to dry clothes that can't go in the dryer. Why do these garments need to hang without touching each other?

How To ... IRON A SHIRT

How easy is ironing a shirt? With a plan in mind, you can do the job without adding more wrinkles than you remove. The secret is to follow certain steps—in order.

1. **Collar.** Start with the collar. Iron both ends; then move toward the center of the collar. Smooth out creases and puckers as you iron.

2. **Yoke.** Place the back of one shoulder over the narrow end of the ironing board. Smooth flat and iron. Repeat for the other shoulder.

3. **Cuffs and sleeves.** Iron the inner side of one cuff, then the outer side, smoothing out any puckers. Lay the sleeve flat on the ironing board, with the sleeve seam at the edge of the sleeve. Press one side, turn the sleeve over, and press the other side. Repeat for the other cuff and sleeve.

4. **Placket.** Press the button and buttonhole areas, without ironing over the buttons. Most irons have an indentation on each side of the point. These allow the iron to go around the buttons as it smoothes the fabric underneath.

5. **Shirt body.** Place the right side of the shirtfront on the ironing board with the shoulder portion over the narrow end of the board. Smooth flat and iron. Move the shirt away from you to the next section to be ironed. Continue until the entire shirt is ironed.

6. **Inspection.** Hold the shirt up. How does it look? If needed, touch up any missed areas. Then place the shirt on a hanger and button the top button.

Exploring **Ironing**

Locate or create your own technique for ironing a pair of pants. Demonstrate this for the class and compare your method to those used by classmates.

start with a low temperature. Increase the temperature gradually to keep from damaging the fabric.

To avoid putting a shine on a fabric's right side, iron on the wrong side. If you must work on the right side, always press gently or use a press cloth.

To use moisture settings, choose dry (no steam) for fabrics that take a low iron temperature. These fabrics include the delicate ones, such as acetate, silk, and polyester. Choose the steam setting for fabrics that need a higher temperature to remove wrinkles. Linen, cotton, and wool are examples.

When ironing with steam, wait until the iron has reached the proper temperature. A light may indicate readiness. Don't overfill the water supply area. With too much water, the iron may spit and put spots on your clothes. If your iron has a spray button, push it when needed to add moisture to stubborn wrinkles. If your iron doesn't supply steam or spray, cover the fabric with a damp press cloth.

When ironing several items, start with those that take a lower temperature. On each garment, begin with small detail areas. Then iron the major parts of the garment. Work carefully, ironing small sections at a time, as shown on page 277.

DRY-CLEANING CLOTHES

The **dry-cleaning** process uses special liquids containing organic solvents to clean fabrics without water. A **solvent** is a substance that dissolves another substance. Dry cleaning can be done by a professional dry cleaner or in a coin-operated machine. To dry-clean at home with your own dryer, follow the guidelines on page 279.

Professional Dry Cleaning

Dry cleaners have special cleaning products for removing some stains that you can't. Always point out any stains—and their cause, if possible—to the dry cleaner. See *Fig. 15-16*. If you know a stained garment will be dry-cleaned, don't try to remove the stain yourself. You might use something that later reacts with the dry-cleaning solvents and permanently sets the stain.

Dry-cleaning solvents can damage some buttons and trims. Discuss this with the dry cleaner. If the cleaner decides to remove the items, they will be replaced after cleaning.

When clothing is professionally dry-cleaned, items are separated by light or dark colors and by delicacy of fabric. Separate loads are placed into machines that resemble an automatic washer. While the clothes rotate, the solvent releases and gradually removes the soil. Then the solvent is spun away, and the clothing is tumbled or air-dried until all traces of the solvent are gone.

Steam pressing takes out wrinkles, smoothes seams, and restores creases and pleats. Some garments are placed over form finishers, mannequin-like forms that allow steam from the inside to permeate the garment and remove wrinkles. Special hand irons and steam presses do other pressing.

Some professional dry cleaners do minor repairs and alterations. Learning to sew on but-

15-16 Knowing what caused a stain helps the dry cleaner decide what solvents to use for removal. Try to give that information if you can.

To save on dry-cleaning expenses, many people today buy dry-cleaning kits to use in home dryers. Each kit includes several premoistened cloths and a reusable bag that holds the clothes.

These kits will clean lightly soiled clothes and freshen and deodorize items. They work best on wool, rayon, silk, linen, and cotton knit fabrics and aren't recommended for leather, suede, acetate, and satin. In addition to clothes, they can be used on scarves, gloves, throw pillows, small blankets, and stuffed animals. Follow the instructions carefully at each step.

Before cleaning, visible stains must be completely removed. Stain removal materials come with the kit. Always test for colorfastness on a hidden area of the garment. For heavy stains and ground-in soil, professional dry cleaning is recommended.

So items can tumble freely, the bag should be only three-fourths full—no more than four garments. Fasten buttons and zippers. Garments with perspiration odors should be turned inside out. Place the premoistened cloth in the bag with the clothes. Then seal the bag and place it in the dryer. Tumble dry for 20 minutes on the low or permanent-press setting. For light freshening, tumble dry for 10 minutes.

As the bag tumbles, the heat-activated cloth releases biodegradable cleaning and freshening ingredients that permeate the fabrics. The controlled humidity within the bag helps prevent wrinkling.

While the garments are still warm, remove them from the dryer. Promptly shake them out and place on hangers. Pressing may be needed.

INVESTIGATION ACTIVITY

Survey three people who have used home dry-cleaning kits. Prepare a list of questions to ask about brands, costs, results, and suggestions. Present your conclusions to the class.

tons and alter hems yourself, however, saves the expense. see→ p 530, p 537

Coin-Operated Dry Cleaning

Coin-operated dry cleaning is faster and costs less than professional dry cleaning. Although the machines remove most soil, the clothes don't get special spot removal or pressing.

Some laundries offer a dry-cleaning service. After clothes are weighed, you pay by the pound. An attendant puts the clothes in the machine and hangs them up when done. If you point out stains, they will be treated before cleaning.

If clothes are put on hangers while still warm, many wrinkles fall out. Professional pressing, however, gives garments a crisper finish.

Review

CHAPTER SUMMARY

- Choosing the right laundry products helps make washing clothes easier and more effective.

- The fabrics, the type of stains, and washing machine you use determine which laundry product you need.

- Adjustable settings on washers, dryers, and other laundry equipment allow you to tailor their use to your needs.

- Clothes should be sorted for washing by color, amount of soil, and fabric.

- Clothes can also be washed by hand and dried on a line or rack.

- Dry cleaning may be the best option for some garments.

USING KEY TERMS

With a partner, take turns giving one fact about each Key Term.

RECALLING THE FACTS

1. Why are detergents better than soaps for laundering?

2. What are two advantages of using an ultra detergent?

3. Is a high-foaming detergent a better product? Explain.

4. Describe four other laundering products beside detergents.

5. Compare the two basic types of washing machines.

6. Why should lint be removed from a dryer's filter, pipe, and vents?

7. Explain how to use an iron safely.

8. What can happen if a white dress shirt is washed with a pair of jeans that was worn to weed the garden?

9. To prevent a laundering mishap, what should you do to a fleecy sweat jacket with pockets before washing?

10. In what ways can a wash cycle be adjusted for a particular load of laundry?

11. What steps can you take when machine drying to help clothes look their best?

12. How can you help garments keep their shape when drying flat?

13. How is an iron setting different for silk and cotton shirts?

14. How does dry cleaning remove stains without water?

and Activities

THINKING CRITICALLY

1. A friend believes that when it comes to laundry detergent, "If some is good, then more is better." What do you think of this reasoning?

2. How would you decide what laundering methods to use if a garment's care label is missing?

3. Suppose someone washes all clothes in cold water, regardless of care label recommendations, in order to save on energy bills. Is this person necessarily saving money? Why or why not?

APPLYING KNOWLEDGE

1. **Detergent ingredients.** Using empty laundry detergent containers, work with a few classmates to identify the purposes of listed ingredients and the meaning of such terms as antibacterial and phosphates. Use a dictionary, encyclopedia, science text, the Internet, and other references as needed. Report what you learn to the class.

2. **Environmental impact.** Locate a detergent designed to be environmentally safe. Analyze the ingredients. Why is the product considered "earth friendly"? Conduct an experiment to compare the cleaning ability of this detergent to a standard brand.

3. **Consumer research.** In a consumer magazine, find an article that compares different brands of laundry products or laundering equipment, such as washing machines, dryers, or irons. Study the researchers' methods and findings. Based on their results, which product or equipment brand do you think is the best buy? Why? Write a report of your conclusions.

4. **Laundry site.** Create a home page and several content pages for a Web site that contains information and tips on how to launder and dry clothes. Include specific facts on the content pages.

5. **Ironing and pressing.** Demonstrate the difference between ironing and pressing for the class. Include safety principles.

6. **Home dry cleaning.** Using a home dry-cleaning kit, demonstrate its use for the class.

CREATIVE SOLUTIONS

A cousin who is away at college uses the coin-operated washing machines in her dormitory. She usually launders all of her clothes in one load, though she knows that washing garments separately would give better results. She says: "If I sorted and washed everything the way I know I'm supposed to, I'd have three or four half-loads every week. I can't see spending the time and money and using all that energy."

Think Creatively

How can your cousin give her clothes the recommended care while avoiding the problems she mentions?

Redesign, Repair, and Recycle

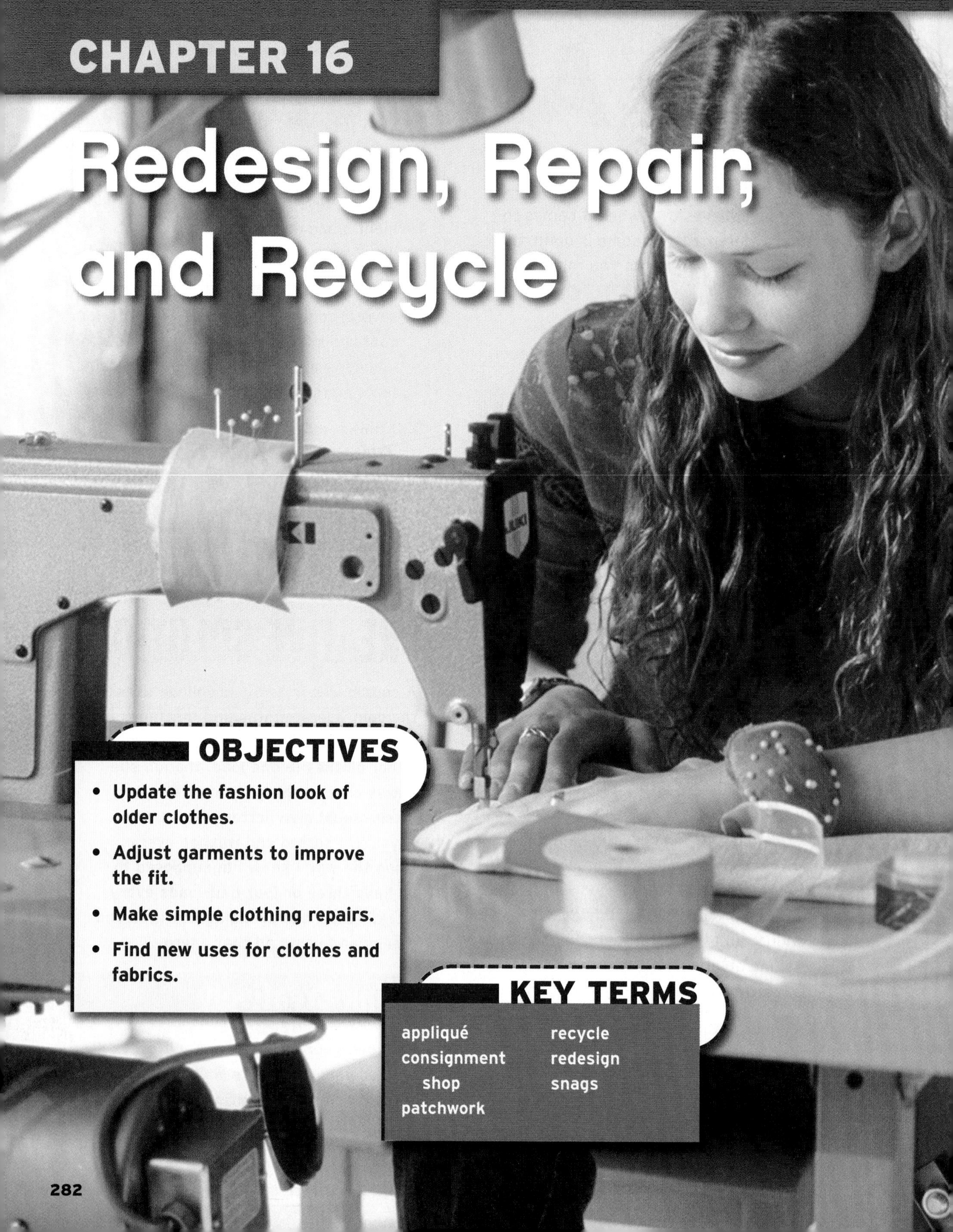

OBJECTIVES

- Update the fashion look of older clothes.
- Adjust garments to improve the fit.
- Make simple clothing repairs.
- Find new uses for clothes and fabrics.

KEY TERMS

appliqué
consignment shop
patchwork
recycle
redesign
snags

WHEN A CLASSMATE ADMIRED HER new skirt, one teen smiled and thought to herself, "It's not as new as you think." Actually, a family member gave her the slightly used skirt. The fabric was beautiful—and the style salvageable with a little creativity. The teen shortened the skirt, narrowed the flare, and added a short slit. With a little time—and no expense—she had a "new" skirt worth admiring.

In a society that's known for throwing too much away, extending the use of clothing can make a difference. While redesigning is one way to make clothing last, in this chapter you'll read about how to repair and recycle clothing as well. See *Fig. 16-1*.

16-1 What happens to clothing that becomes worn, outdated, or simply unwanted? In this chapter you'll learn about three ways to make the most of the garments in your closet.

REDESIGNING CLOTHES

To **redesign** is to change an existing garment to make it suitable for more wear. When redesigning, you can change a garment's style and fit as well as its color and trim. Thus, you may be able to achieve the current fashion look by making only minor changes to an outdated garment.

Redesigning is a practical way to get the most from what you already have. By using your time and skills, you can expand your wardrobe at little or no cost. You also have a chance to be creative. Wearing a one-of-a-kind garment that expresses your individuality can make you feel proud.

Changing the Style

From year to year, fashions change. When the change affects a garment's shape, redesigning can rescue the article from looking dated.

How can you redesign older clothes to update them? You can raise, and sometimes lower, a hemline. An oversized jacket can be taken in to look more fitted. Adding a belt at the waist or hips gives more control to a full-cut dress. Wide pant legs can be straightened and narrowed.

In seeking a new look for a garment, you may want a more significant change. If you like, you can change the entire style. Long pants can be turned into cropped pants or shorts by changing the hemline. See *Fig. 16-2*. A long-sleeved shirt can become a short-sleeved one. Removing the sleeves on a jacket can create a vest. Shortening a coat turns it into a jacket.

Before you begin any redesign project, work out the steps and solutions. Ask yourself these questions: Where should I cut off these pant legs to leave enough fabric for a hem or cuff? If I take out the sleeves of this jacket, how will I finish the armholes for a new vest? A well-thought-out plan brings better results.

Adjusting the Fit

No one likes to wear clothing that's uncomfortable or unflattering. Even a small problem, such as a binding waistband, can leave a garment hanging in the closet, unwanted and unused.

Minor corrections can often be made easily, with just some basic sewing skills. Maybe moving a hook or button on a tight waistband will give the added comfort you need. Major problems, however, are best left to a professional dressmaker or tailor, especially on certain garments. A prom dress, for example, might need the attention of an expert.

Length Adjustments

Most garments can be shortened; fewer can be lengthened. Plain hems are simply measured, refolded, and restitched. Cuffed garments take extra planning and construction steps.

To shorten a hem, mark the new hem length with pins or chalk. Remove the old stitching and fold up the fabric along the new hemline. See *Fig. 16-3*. You may need to trim the hem allowance.

16-2 If jeans become worn at the knees or below, they could be cut off and hemmed to make shorts.

Most hems should be no wider than 2 to 3 inches (5 to 7.5 cm). A wider hem can add bulk, looking uneven and obvious. If the fabric ravels, finish the edge of the hem allowance with zigzag stitching, pinking, or seam tape. Attach the hem to the garment by hand stitching, machine stitching, or fusing.

see→ p 537

Lengthening a hem is a little more involved. First, check that there is enough fabric to create the added length. If not, you may be able to add wide, hem-facing tape on the inside of the garment edge to complete the hem, as was done in *Fig. 16-4*. Unfortunately, the crease of the old hemline may be impossible to iron out. Check before you sew. One solution is to hide the original hemline with trim or several rows of machine stitching. This method, however, often looks like a cover-up rather than part of the garment design.

Width Adjustments

Altering the width of a garment is usually more complicated than changing the length. Minor width adjustments can usually be made at the side seams, with equal amounts taken in or let

16-3 When you shorten a hem, the crease from the old hem will be hidden inside the garment.

Shortening a hem

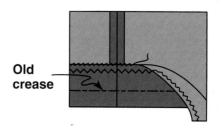

Old crease

Lengthening a hem

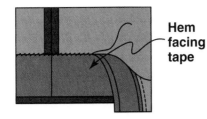

Hem facing tape

16-4 When you lengthen a hem, the crease from the old hem may show on the outside of the garment. What can you do?

Making a garment smaller

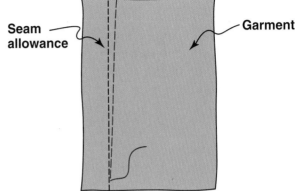

Seam allowance

Garment

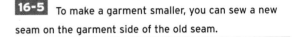

16-5 To make a garment smaller, you can sew a new seam on the garment side of the old seam.

out at each side. Be sure to gradually taper the new seam to meet the old one at an armhole or waistband.

To take in a garment, or make it smaller, you stitch the new seam within the garment itself. See *Fig. 16-5*. To let out a garment, or make it larger, you stitch the new seam in the seam allowance, outside the original seam line. See *Fig. 16-6*. Therefore, the seam allowances must be wide enough to allow for a new seam. For instance, the seams on some ready-to-wear garments are trimmed and finished to ¼ inch (6 mm). With such a narrow seam allowance, you wouldn't be able to make the garment wider.

Adding Accessories and Trims

If you're bored with an older garment, why not try a new accessory before discarding the item? A new belt, scarf, tie, or jewelry piece can produce a fresh look. Check fashion magazines for the latest trends. If the natural look is in style, a braided rope belt can add new appeal to multiple outfits. For other seasons, a shiny gold belt or a bright red one may be the important look. A gold or silver clasp adds a touch of sophistication to a colorful scarf. A tie in a dark, subdued print makes a casual shirt look more formal.

Changing buttons is an easy way to give a garment a new look. Many ready-to-wear outfits have inexpensive buttons that fade or discolor

Making a garment larger

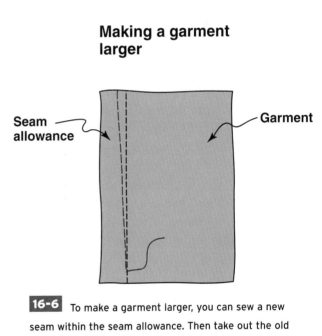

Seam allowance

Garment

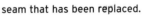

16-6 To make a garment larger, you can sew a new seam within the seam allowance. Then take out the old seam that has been replaced.

after repeated washings or cleanings. Replacing these buttons can improve a garment's appearance. To save money, you can even salvage nice buttons from a worn garment to sew on another.

Adding colorful trim is another way to change the look of a garment. For a romantic mood, you

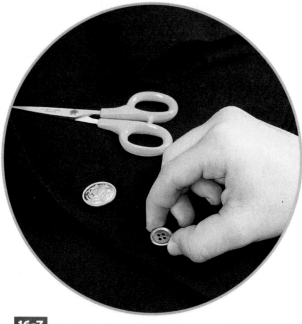

Replacing the buttons on a garment can create a new look. How would different button styles and colors affect the look of a garment?

could choose delicate lace. Brightly colored rick-rack can create a casual look. Braids and ribbons range from tailored to dressy. **Appliqués**, cutout pieces of fabric applied as a decoration, can be cartoon characters or intricate designs. Embroidery can be added as a simple monogram or as an elegant finish to a wedding gown. Many moods are possible.

Trim can also be rhythmic. You might add two or three rows of trim instead of one, or repeat the trim at the hem of a sleeve or bottom of a skirt. An appliqué on both patch pockets may look better than only on one pocket. Experiment by pinning trim in place before attaching it permanently. *Fig. 16-7* shows how to create a different effect on a garment with buttons.

Changing the Color

Suppose you need a green shirt to wear with your team at a fund-raising festival, but you don't have one and don't want to spend money on a new one. Turning an old shirt from white to green might be just the answer.

A color change may serve a practical need, but it can also be planned for other reasons. A change of color can give a garment a fashion update. Faded fabric could become brighter. Even a problem might be covered with the creative use of color.

Dyeing Fabric

You can change the entire color of a garment by dyeing the fabric. See *Fig. 16-8*. Fabric dyes come in liquid and powder forms.

Before you dye a garment, think carefully about the change you want to make. Check the fiber content of the fabric, since some fibers dye better than others. Consider the trims too. You can go from a light to a dark color easily, but you must first remove the original color before going from a dark to a light color. The garment should be stain-free, as stains will still show after dyeing. Will your fabric shrink? If so, you will need a cold-water dye.

By planning your project carefully, you'll save disappointment. Read the instructions on the package carefully and follow them exactly, step by step. Otherwise the dye may not be permanent, and the color may fade or bleed when you wash the garment.

When dyeing fabric, wear gloves. You'll also want to protect your clothing and any surrounding surface area from splatters.

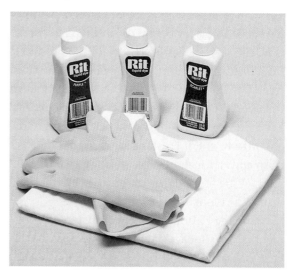

Painting Fabric

With fabric paints, you can create colorful designs on clothing and accessories. See *Fig. 16-9.* A shirt, jacket, jeans, sweatshirt, bag, or child's outfit can become a canvas for your creativity. Even shoes can be decorated.

Some fabric paints come in ready-to-use tubes. Others are applied with a brush or marker. The paints have a wide range of colors, including metallic. Some even create a raised design. Be sure to choose washable paints.

REPAIRING CLOTHES

According to an old saying, "A stitch in time saves nine." In other words, a repair made early prevents a bigger repair job later. By making simple repairs as soon as possible, you can keep your clothes in good shape and always ready to wear.

When several garments need small repairs, why not set aside a little time to fix them all? Good management means using time effectively. As long as you have the tools and notions out, doing several repairs at once makes efficient use of time.

Restitching Seams

When stitches break, seams rip open and the garment may become unwearable. Broken stitches are common, but easily repaired. You can fix a seam with machine or small hand stitches, as

16-10 A hem that is falling out needs repair before it becomes worse. What tips would you suggest so that the repair work doesn't show?

16-9 You can use fabric paints to make colorful designs on clothing, accessories, and gift items.

shown on page 288. For seams in areas that receive extra stress, such as the underarm of a shirt or the crotch seam of pants, sew a double row of stitching $\frac{1}{8}$ inch (3 mm) apart for added reinforcement. ▌see→ p 519

Restitching Hems

A hem will sag if the stitches come loose or catch on an object. See *Fig. 16-10.* Many ready-to-wear garments have hems sewn with a chain stitch that can easily pull out around the entire garment if a stitch is broken. It only takes a few minutes to restitch an opened hem, as shown on page 288. ▌see→ p 537

Sometimes the hem in a new garment puckers or pulls, creating a rumpled look. To smooth the area, remove the old stitches and restitch the hem.

Replacing Fasteners

Many homes have a button jar like the one in *Fig. 16-11* on page 289 for saving extra buttons that come with ready-to-wear garments. It makes replacing a lost button easier. If an identical button is not available, you may have to replace it with one that's similar. If possible, attach the mis-

MAKE SIMPLE REPAIRS

Repairing a Hem

Pin the loose hem in place. Using a single thread, stitch along the upper edge with a hemming stitch, blindstitch, or catchstitch. See page 539 for specific directions. Extend the new stitching so it overlaps with the old. Keep the stitches slightly loose so the fabric doesn't pucker. Be sure the stitches don't show on the outside of the garment.

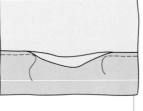

Reattaching a Button

A loose or missing button can be reattached with a few simple stitches. Use a double strand of thread and tie a small knot at the end.

- **Shank button.** Make four or five small stitches through the shank and the fabric. Fasten the thread securely under the button with tiny stitches or a knot.

- **Sew-through button.** Place a toothpick, match, or heavy pin on top of the button. Stitch up through one hole, over the object, and down through the second hole; repeat four or five times. Remove the object and pull the button to the top of the thread loops. Wind the thread tightly around the stitches under the button and secure.

Restitching a Seam

To restitch a seam, turn the garment inside out, align the two sides of the seam, and pin. If possible, knot the ends of the broken seam so more stitches won't pull out. Using a double strand of thread for extra strength, make short backstitches along the original seam line. Extend the new stitches beyond the actual opening so they overlap the original stitching at both ends.

If you are unable to repair the seam from the inside, use a slip stitch to attach one folded edge, such as a patch pocket, to the garment. To make a backstitch and slip stitch, see page 507.

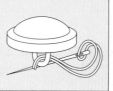
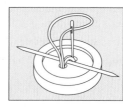

Exploring **Repairs**

Look through your clothes to find garments that need simple repairs. Make two different types of repairs. Ask family members for something you might repair if you need additional items.

matched button where it will be less noticeable, as on the bottom of a shirt. If a button is already there, you can move it to the more visible location. When a match is essential, you may have to buy a new set of buttons for the garment.

Sometimes buttons, snaps, and hooks and eyes on ready-to-wear clothes are loosely attached. A quick restitching by hand holds them fast. See page 288. You can also add these fasteners at a neckline, front closing, or waistband to help hold the fabric together more securely or smoothly.

see→ p 530

Fixing Snags

Knitted or loosely woven fabrics often get **snags**, loops of fabric that pull out. If ignored, a hole can form and grow. Use a small crochet hook, snag fixer, or needle threader to repair the snag. Insert the hook through the fabric directly under the snag. Grasp the snag with the hook and pull it to the underside of the fabric. See *Fig. 16-12*. Smooth any puckers by gently stretching the fabric in the direction of the pulled thread.

Mending Tears

When a small tear or rip occurs in fabric, a quick repair can prevent it from becoming larger. Try to repair the tear before the garment is laundered to prevent more tearing. A straight tear can

16-11 Where can so many buttons come from?

be mended with machine zigzag stitching to hold the torn edges together. See *Fig. 16-13*. Begin and end the stitches about ¼ inch (6 mm) beyond the tear. Because the stitching shows on the outside of the garment, this method is suitable only for casual or work clothes. For a more hidden repair, fuse a patch underneath the torn fabric.

Patching Holes

A patch can be applied with hand or machine stitching, as shown in *Fig. 16-14*. Trim away any frayed threads from around the hole. Cut a patch of fabric slightly larger than the hole, and pin to the inside of the garment. Fold in the edges of the patch and stitch in place. On the outside of the garment, turn the edges of the hole under and slip-stitch to the patch. For added strength, top-

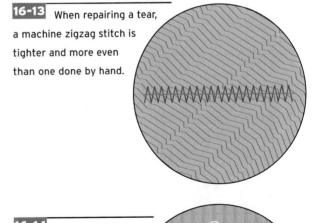

16-13 When repairing a tear, a machine zigzag stitch is tighter and more even than one done by hand.

16-12 Most snags are no longer visible when carefully pulled to the inside of the garment.

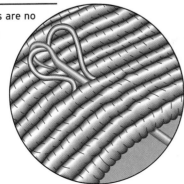

16-14 When patching, you may need to trim the hole to give it a better shape and edge—even if this enlarges the hole just a little.

stitch around the patch on the outside of the garment.

Fusing is another method of patching a hole. Cut a patch of fabric the exact size of the hole. Position the garment wrong side up on an ironing board. Place the patch, wrong side up, over the hole. Cover the area with a piece of fusible web and then a piece of firmly woven fabric. Press from the wrong side to fuse the patch in place.

Iron-on patches or mending tape may also be used. Press the patch to the fabric according to package directions.

Covering Worn Areas

Sometimes just one area of a garment becomes worn, while the rest stays in good condition. You've probably seen this happen on the elbows of a sweater, jacket, or heavy shirt. Oval patches are attractive coverings for these areas. See *Fig. 16-15*. Topstitch or fuse the patch, using such contrasting fabric as leather, suede, corduroy, or flannel.

On sleeves and pant legs, the edges are also subject to extra wear. To hide frayed spots, apply a row of trim, fold-over braid, or bias binding to the worn edge. Patches, pressed or stitched to the

16-15 A patch can match the fabric of the garment or be in contrast. You can prolong the usefulness of a garment by applying patches to worn areas.

inside or outside of a pant leg, can reinforce knees or cover a hole. Stubborn stains that resist removal can be hidden under an appliqué or trim.

Making Emergency Repairs

If you're away from home when you discover a needed repair, double-face tape or safety pins can come to your rescue. Just be sure to make the repair as soon as possible—before it becomes a major one.

RECYCLING CLOTHES

To **recycle** means to reclaim items for another use. Just as people recycle aluminum, glass, and plastic items, clothing can be recycled too. When you recycle clothing, you find continued use for garments you no longer want. Whether aluminum cans or clothing, recycling can be a family project.

Recycling saves money. A family member's wardrobe expands at no cost when garments are passed to others who can use them. One teen, who managed her own clothing budget, was happy to inherit a nice sweater from her sister. After buying a skirt, she had a new two-piece outfit for the cost of only one item.

On a larger scale, recycling shows concern for the environment. First, it helps preserve natural resources. Fabrics are made from either natural or manufactured fibers. Recycling helps conserve the sources of these fibers as well as the energy used at every step of the manufacturing process. It also reduces waste by extending the life of a garment or fabric. The longer you keep a garment in use, the longer you keep it out of a landfill.

In what ways can you recycle clothing? You might be surprised by the possibilities.

Passing It On

Sometimes a garment that you no longer need is just what someone else is looking for. Offer your unwanted clothing at garage or tag sales, bazaars, flea markets, and consignment shops. A **consignment shop** pays the seller a percentage of the selling price after the item is sold. These shops typically want clothing that's in good condition.

PROTECTING THE ENVIRONMENT.
Many people recycle clothing and other materials out of respect for the environment. Protecting natural resources is a major concern of some clothing makers as well. These companies strive to produce garments in an environmentally responsible way at each step of manufacture. They use only natural fibers that are organically grown—that is, without pesticides, herbicides, or synthetic fertilizers. Designs are printed with non-toxic, water-based inks.

16-16 Passing garments along to a younger sister or brother is an easy way to recycle clothing that you no longer wear. How would you make this a positive experience for a younger sibling?

You can also buy clothing at these outlets for much less than you would pay for new clothing.

Selling is just one way to find a new owner for underused clothing. Suppose a friend has always admired a sweater that you seldom wear anymore. You might exchange it for a jacket that your friend no longer wears. You've each added to your wardrobe without spending anything.

Outgrown, wearable items may be passed along to a younger brother, sister, cousin, or neighbor. Be sensitive to feelings when you do this. Younger siblings sometimes resent having to accept used garments, especially when older siblings get the new ones. See *Fig. 16-16.*

Unwanted but usable clothing can also be donated, through charitable groups, to someone in greater need. Learn what religious groups or service agencies in your area accept used clothing. Your clothing contribution could bring comfort to a family that has lost its belongings in a fire, flood, or other disaster.

Finding Other Uses

Even when a garment can't be worn in its current form, its useful life may not be over. Give it a second start with a new purpose, ranging from accessories, to dress-up clothes, to cleaning cloths.

Accessories

Be imaginative. What accessories could you make from an old pair of jeans? How about a sturdy belt pack made from one of the legs, and a clutch purse from the other? Don't forget nonclothing accessories, such as a throw pillow for your bed or a shoe bag to hang on your closet door.

Turn your creative eye to other fabrics in your home as well. A badly stained tablecloth might be cut and finished as a set of placemats. Transform a colorful old beach towel into a beach carryall.

Children's Clothes

Many garments that are in good condition can be "downsized" to make children's clothes. In fact, children often like the feel of used fabrics, which are often softer and more comfortable than new clothes. It's the same reason that some people pay

Could a garment you wear have once been a plastic bottle? It's possible. Discarded items that once crowded landfills are now being converted into fashion apparel. For example, 27 recycled water bottles can make enough fabric for a new sweater.

- **EcoSpun®.** When plastic bottles are recycled, they can be turned into the fiber EcoSpun. First, the bottles are crushed in a process called densifying. Then they are ground, washed, and melted into a gooey substance. The polyfibers extracted from this substance can be woven into fabrics resembling everything from wool, to cotton, to fleece. The fibers can also be blended with other natural or manufactured fibers.

- **Reused Denim®.** This is the trade name for fabric made from 50 percent new cotton fibers and 50 percent reclaimed cotton denim. The reclaimed denim comes from scraps remaining after new denim fabric is made into jeans and other apparel.

- **Recycled wool.** Wool fibers from wool products can be shredded back into a fibrous state for recycling. A wool product containing the used fibers must be labeled as recycled wool. A fabric of 100 percent recycled wool can be as strong and soft as a comparable product of 100 percent virgin wool. The use of recycled wool is relatively small because the wide use of wool blends makes it difficult to separate the wool from the nylon or polyester fibers.

- **Boots and shoes.** Some manufacturers make sturdy hiking boots and canvas shoes from 17 to 75 percent recycled materials. Such materials as tires, plastic bottles, coffee filters, polystyrene cups, and diapers may be used in the process.

INVESTIGATION ACTIVITY

On the Internet find more information about EcoSpun. What garments are made from this fiber? What qualities do they have?

a premium price for prewashed jeans. A corduroy skirt may have enough material for a child's jumper. You can fashion a small quilted robe from pieces of a larger one.

As *Fig. 16-17* shows, old clothing can be a treasure for children who like to play dress-up. A child's imagination takes flight when inspired by grown-up clothes and props. Old clothes are also an excellent source of creative costumes for parties and class plays at school.

16-17 Young children love to dress up in old clothes, hats, jewelry, and shoes. When kept in a large box or trunk, they are readily available for creative play.

Patchwork Projects

Have you ever admired a century-old quilt, meticulously pieced together by hand? That craft is known as **patchwork**, sewing together small fabric shapes to create a new, decorative piece of fabric. See *Fig. 16-18*.

Patchwork quilts are still made today, although many other uses for the technique have been found. A wall hanging could display T-shirt emblems from high school

16-18 Patchwork is a technique you can use in many creative ways.

sports competitions. You can also make patchwork pillows, placemats, tote bags, and stuffed toys.

Garments and accessories can be created from patchwork designs. Craft books and magazines suggest ideas for planning such clothing projects as vests, jackets, belts, and aprons. You can preserve an item with sentimental attachment or make an item with special meaning. For example, imagine a vest made from old neckties or a grandmother's apron made with fabrics donated by each grandchild.

Combining available fabrics in a patchwork design offers a challenge in creativity and resourcefulness. What kind of pattern could you devise with colors and prints that blend or contrast? A few restrictions do limit your creativity. Since the pieces of fabric will be stitched together, select fabrics that are firmly woven and require similar care. Blue denim and a delicate silk print might look striking in a jacket, but how would the fabrics wear and launder?

Household Cleaning

Clothing that has exhausted every other use may have one final destination: the bag of cleaning cloths. Every household needs fabric pieces for dusting and wiping. Larger pieces—old towels, sheets, and tablecloths—can cover the floor when painting, sanding, or staining. Flannel is good for polishing silver and brass.

For cleaning, save absorbent fabrics, such as 100 percent cotton or cotton blends. Be sure to remove all buttons and other fasteners, which could scratch surfaces as you clean. Save these to use on future sewing projects. You may want to cut off trims, pockets, and bulky seams to make the cleaning cloth easier to handle.

Finally, fibers can be recycled for use in padding and paper. Some organizations collect old clothing and fabrics for this purpose. Who knows? This very book may contain traces of what was once a cotton shirt. As you can see, recycling can send the garments you once wore to useful, and sometimes surprising, destinations.

Review

CHAPTER SUMMARY

- You can redesign an outfit in a number of ways.

- Redesigning a garment takes some time but extends the life of the garment.

- Simple repairs can make a garment last longer.

- It takes only a few minutes to restitch hems and seams, change buttons, add snaps or hooks and eyes, and mend small holes.

- Recycling reclaims items for other purposes.

- Just as people recycle cans and bottles, they can recycle clothing too.

- You can recycle clothing when it's wearable and when it's not.

USING KEY TERMS

One of the Key Terms in this chapter is "patchwork." Pioneer women created patchwork designs for quilts that are famous as a uniquely American craft. Research the history of various patchwork designs, such as Log Cabin, Lone Star, and Dresden Plate. Report your findings to the class.

RECYCLE CLOTHING HERE

RECALLING THE FACTS

1. What are three benefits of redesigning clothes?

2. When redesigning garments, what are three possible changes to make?

3. Why should a redesign project be well planned?

4. What must you check about the fabric before lengthening a hem or letting out a seam?

5. Why might a person decide to change the color of a garment?

6. What are two things you need to know about a fabric before dyeing it?

7. How could you use trim to create rhythm in a design?

8. Why should the broken stitches in a seam be repaired as soon as possible?

9. How would you fix a snag in a sweater?

10. Would you repair a tear and a hole with the same method? Explain.

11. What can you do to hide a worn or frayed area of a garment?

12. What are three benefits of recycling clothes?

13. What could you do with wearable clothing that you no longer want?

and Activities

THINKING CRITICALLY

1. Do you think attitudes toward wearing used clothing are changing? If so, how are they changing and why?

2. Explain the points of view a parent, older sibling, and younger sibling might have when clothes are handed down.

3. According to an old saying, "You can't get something for nothing." Explain whether this chapter supports that comment.

APPLYING KNOWLEDGE

1. **Redesign project.** Choose one item from your wardrobe to redesign for yourself or for another family member. Explain what steps or techniques you would use.

2. **Creative designing.** Create a new look for an old-but-nice T-shirt by tie-dyeing the fabric, using fabric paints, or adding decorative trims.

3. **Simple repairs.** Practice making the following simple repairs on fabric: restitch a seam; sew a button; repair a hem; sew snaps; mend a small tear; sew a hook and eye; and patch a hole.

4. **Management process.** Utilize the management process described on page 54 to carry out a clothing repair project. To plan the project, first locate personal or family apparel in need of repairs. Gather the garments and organize them by sorting according to the repairs needed. Plan a schedule for completing the repair tasks at home. Evaluate the success of your plan and your workmanship.

5. **Recycling programs.** Contact charitable groups in your areas to learn whether they recycle clothing. Ask their policies for collecting and distributing the clothing. Share your findings with the class.

6. **Clothing collection.** Collect old clothing, accessories, and jewelry for a dress-up box. Donate it to a child-care center, nursery school, or preschool program.

7. **New uses.** Find an old garment that could be recycled into something usable. Could an old sweater become a pillow? Could you dress a doll for a child, using old fabrics? Carry out your project.

CREATIVE SOLUTIONS

While looking through an old trunk, one teen found a dozen samples of crocheting that her great-aunt made years ago. The pieces ranged in size from about four to six inches. Some were round and some square, and all had been well preserved. Individually they weren't very useful, but the teen wanted to show off the fine handiwork.

Think Creatively

How might the crocheted pieces be put to use?

Careers

Fashion Services

Wherever there are busy people, services are welcomed. Limited time for baking and cooking sends people to bakeries and restaurants. When people can't get the lawn mowed or the leaves raked, someone can supply these services. Service providers can clean the house, paint the kitchen, and even walk the dog.

The fashion industry is no exception when it comes to offering services. In the clothing care area, businesses launder and dry-clean clothing. The person who doesn't have the time or skills needed to shorten a pair of pants or take in a skirt can find people who will make the alterations. Such services have become routinely used over the years.

People who are particularly concerned about image in the business world turn to services that can help them. Wearing the "right" suit can make the difference between impressing clients and losing them. Some people make it their job to give advice on choosing clothes and even do the shopping as part of their service.

Work in the service field is varied. Opportunities are greater in some specialties than in others. Depending on the service provided, income potential varies. If you're looking for something a little different, however, you might find it here.

IS THIS FIELD FOR YOU?

As with any service career, personality affects success in the fashion services area. Training and skills vary, but you have an advantage if you fit these personal traits.

- I'm self-motivated.
- I'm a good listener.
- I genuinely enjoy helping people.
- I'm sensitive to people's needs and circumstances.
- I have confidence in my own judgment.
- My reputation is very important to me.

Some tailors are self-employed. Others work for stores that sell garments and alter them for customers.

Education and Training

Jobs in fashion services are many and varied, so the education and training needed is too. Preparation may come on the job, through a combination of work experience and technical training, or from another field entirely.

A solid grounding in fabrics or fashion is recommended. Such knowledge might be gained through formal education or through independent study.

Depending on the job, a person may choose an education that stresses either the technical or "artistic" aspect of clothing. College degrees are not required for many of the positions, but education positions people to explore different fields in the future.

Possible Career Paths

As with other fields, training and experience are keys to traveling a career path in fashion services. For some jobs, the way is less defined than in production or merchandising. A college degree is not required to be a personal shopper. You don't start as an assistant and work your way up. In this type of career, your talents and interests determine your success and satisfaction.

Many service jobs lend themselves to self-employment. A large percentage of dry-cleaning businesses, for example, are family or individually owned. For that reason, the field appeals to people who want to be their own boss. Running your own business also requires qualities that have more to do with personality than with formal education.

THE SKILLS YOU NEED

If you're thinking about a fashion service career, check the following list of useful skills:

- Communication
- Organization
- Management
- Self-discipline
- Knowledge of fibers and fabrics
- Sewing skills
- Fashion sense

A color consultant offers expert advice and information about color choices. The consultant might help a client find colors that exactly match historic costumes or predict what colors might be in during an upcoming season.

Choosing a Fashion Services Career

ALTERATIONIST | *CLOTHIER* | COLOR CONSULTANT | *DRY CLEANER* | LAUNDRY WORKER | *PERSONAL SHOPPER* | SPECIALIST IN HOME DECORATIONS | *STYLIST* | TEXTILE RESTORER | UPHOLSTERER | *WARDROBE CONSULTANT*

Dry Cleaner

Dry cleaners need special knowledge for their work. They type garments according to fabric, construction, and stain, then choose pretreatments. Besides using varied machines for cleaning, they work with spotting guns to remove stains. They press and shape garments on finishing forms and tables. Some also store and preserve clothes.

Although routine skills may be learned on the job, continuing education and training is helpful. After self-study courses in dry cleaning, a person can earn certification by passing a follow-up exam.

Wardrobe Consultant

Public figures, including television personalities and politicians, turn to wardrobe consultants for help in projecting a desired image. Working with a client, a consultant analyzes the person's style and body type and helps assemble a wardrobe. Teaching basic clothes-buying strategies, such as mixing and matching and accessorizing, is part of the service.

Businesses hire wardrobe consultants to give seminars for employees. These cover dress-code and casual-day policies, the messages clothing sends to customers and superiors, and the economic value of appropriate dress in business.

Stylist

Like wardrobe consultants, stylists enhance images. They choose clothes and accessories for magazine spreads and fashion shows, music videos and television ads, and celebrities. Besides knowing fashion trends, stylists can relate garments to a mood. For example, they choose just the right garments to match a soft, romantic scene.

Stylists need skills of persuasion. They might have to convince a photographer that they can carry out the proposed scene or convince a publicist that their ideas will advance a client's career. Top stylists have hectic schedules, filled with long, tiring hours, but they are typically well paid.

Some stylists persuade fashion designers to loan clothes for a celebrity's appearance. Here, a stylist prepares clothing for a photo shoot.

Interior decorators help people plan room décors. Using expert knowledge of fabrics and an understanding of their clients, they choose suitable upholstery and drapery fabrics.

Personal Shopper

Personal shoppers are paid to shop. Some upscale department stores employ personal shoppers as a service to customers. Shoppers find what customers need and arrange to show the garments. Since they work on commission, personal shoppers must be familiar with the store's inventory.

When self-employed, personal shoppers assess a client's style, needs, wardrobe, and budget before buying appropriate clothing and accessories. Some personal shoppers give seminars and sell videotapes that explain their methods. With a background in fashion merchandising, personal shoppers anticipate trends and know where to find upcoming styles. A basic knowledge of business and a pleasing personality are assets.

Clothier

A clothier (CLOTHE-yur) is a dressmaker or tailor who designs original garments, sews from existing patterns, and does alterations and repairs. Some specialize, as in wedding gowns or costumes. When working with a client, clothiers help choose a style and fabric according to taste, budget, body type, coloring, and occasion.

Clothiers need an eye for design elements and illusions. Many use computer-aided design (CAD) programs for grading, detailing, and printing out patterns. They work tactfully and patiently with clients. Some clothiers are self-employed. Some develop and sell their own CAD software. Others work for department stores and dry-cleaning businesses.

CAREER APPLICATIONS

1. **Providing a service.** Think of a clothing service you could provide. What about a lunch-hour, small repair service for sewing on buttons or fixing hems, or a color-analysis service? Write a plan for carrying out the service.

2. **FCCLA.** Along with a team, plan an Interpersonal Communications Project. Identify typical communication problems that a clothing service provider might experience. An example is a dry cleaner dealing with a customer whose garment has been lost. Plan skits that demonstrate the problems and how to react with skillful communication.

3. **Professionalism.** You're a clothier whose client requests an outfit in a style that you know won't suit the person's appearance and a fabric that doesn't complement the style. You're afraid the client won't like the garment. As you steer the client toward something more suitable, the person becomes angry. The project is complicated and will pay well. How will you handle the situation professionally?

UNIT 6

Clothing Selection

CHAPTERS

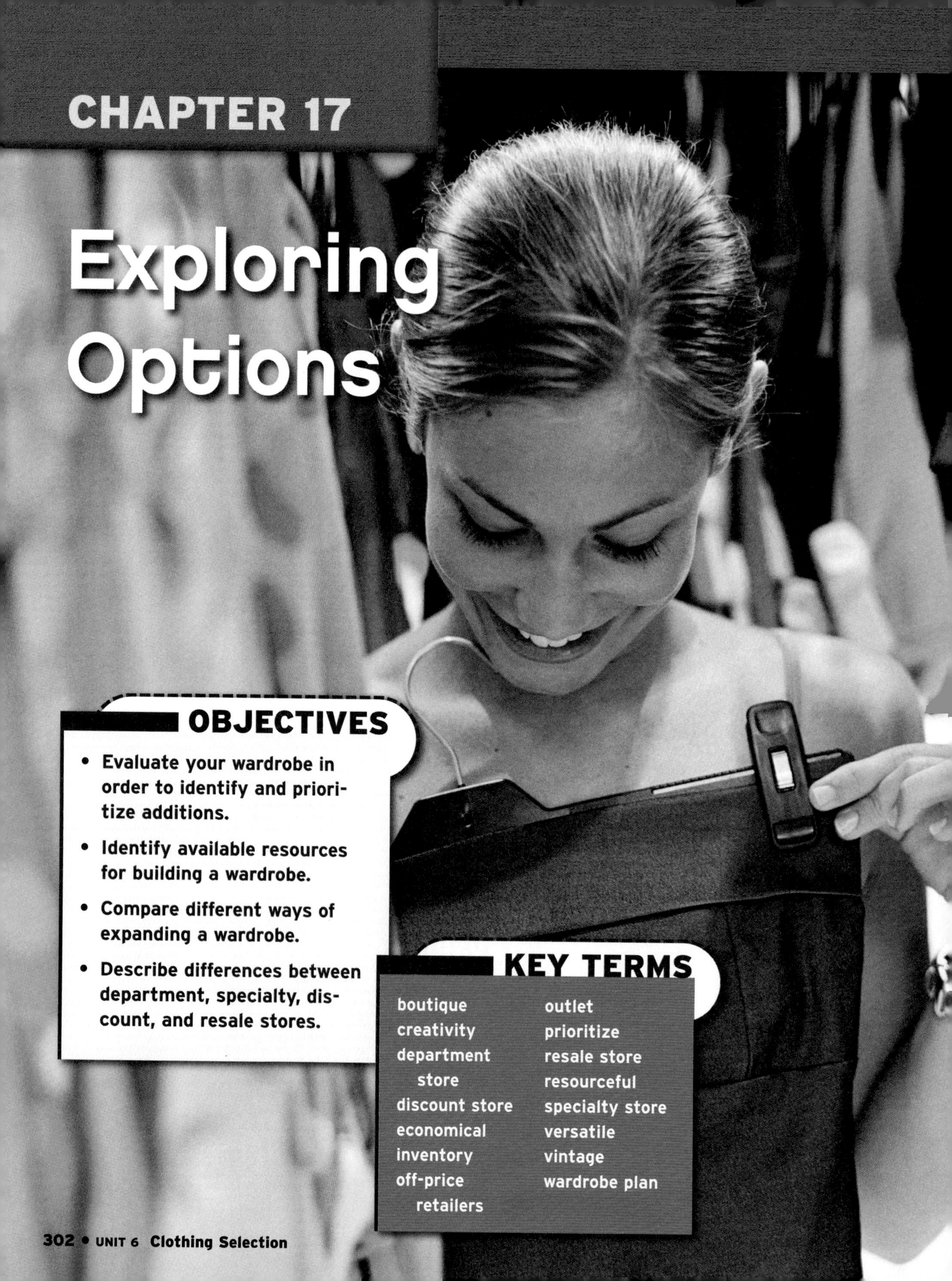

Exploring Options

OBJECTIVES

- Evaluate your wardrobe in order to identify and prioritize additions.

- Identify available resources for building a wardrobe.

- Compare different ways of expanding a wardrobe.

- Describe differences between department, specialty, discount, and resale stores.

KEY TERMS

boutique
creativity
department
  store
discount store
economical
inventory
off-price
  retailers

outlet
prioritize
resale store
resourceful
specialty store
versatile
vintage
wardrobe plan

I N A WELL-KNOWN FAIRY TALE, *Cinderella* attends the ball because her fairy godmother and a host of industrious mice make her wardrobe dreams come true. In real life, no such magic exists.

Putting a wardrobe together can be both exciting and challenging. Fortunately, you can create your own wardrobe magic by using resources effectively. Take some time to evaluate your wardrobe and look at all your options before dashing out to shop.

EVALUATING YOUR WARDROBE

With just five basic steps, you can evaluate your wardrobe and develop a plan for building the wardrobe you want. The steps are listed in *Fig. 17-1.* Here's how to accomplish each step.

Step 1: Take Inventory

Do you know what clothes you own? Are there some hidden in the back of your closet or deep in drawers? Just as retailers identify the merchandise in their stores before reordering, you can take a clothing inventory before deciding what to replace in your wardrobe.

An **inventory** is a list of items on hand. To take inventory of the clothes and accessories you own, you'll need a place to list everything. A wardrobe chart like the one on page 304 is a handy tool. With it, you can collect and organize information while examining your wardrobe. Begin your chart by listing the items you own in the first column and entering a short description of each one in the second column.

Step 2: Evaluate Items

As you list items while taking inventory, evaluate their usefulness and condition. Ask yourself how often you wear or use each item. Like most people, you probably have garments that you wear often and some that you seldom wear. To check condition, note how worn the item is and what repairs could be made. Write this information in the third column of your wardrobe chart.

Step 3: Develop an Action Plan

As you evaluate each item, decide what to do with it and enter that information in the fourth column of the chart. You might choose to keep,

17-1 By following these steps, you can evaluate your wardrobe and plan for future additions.

Steps in Wardrobe Planning

Step 1: Take inventory of clothes and accessories.

Step 2: Evaluate the condition and usefulness of each item.

Step 3: Develop an action plan of what to do with each item.

Step 4: Consider what new items to add.

Step 5: Set priorities for a wardrobe plan.

How To ...

MAKE A WARDROBE CHART

A wardrobe chart provides a handy tool for evaluating the clothing you own and planning wardrobe additions. The sample shown here is part of one teen's chart. Other categories might include dresses, skirts, pants suits, athletic wear, shorts, T-shirts, sleepwear, underwear, socks/hosiery, belts, scarves/ties, hats, and jewelry.

Sample Wardrobe Chart

CLOTHING	DESCRIPTION OF ITEM	EVALUATION OF CONDITION AND USEFULNESS	ACTION PLAN	PRIORITY OF ITEMS TO BUY OR REPLACE
Coats/Jackets				
Dress coat	Full length; black	Good	Keep	
Winter jacket	Short length; beige	Old; very worn	Need to replace	2
Pants/Slacks				
Chinos	Long; beige	New	Keep	
Jeans	Blue denim	Old but usable	Keep	
Cropped pants	Black twill	————	New purchase; want to have	5
Shirts/Blouses				
Blue denim	Long sleeves	Worn but like it	Keep	
Sport shirt	Green plaid; short sleeves	Two buttons missing	Repair and use	
Sweaters				
Vest	Plaid	Never wear; out of date	Donate; don't replace	
Cardigan	Red; long sleeves	Shrunk; sleeves too short	Give away; want to replace with green one	4
Shoes/Boots				
Loafers	Brown	Scuffed; soles very thin	Need to replace	3
Athletic shoes	Black	————	New purchase; need for basketball	1

Exploring Wardrobe Charts

Create your own wardrobe chart on paper or computer. With a computerized chart, you can easily review and update your wardrobe plan. You could use a word-processing table or a spreadsheet.

17-2 Deciding what to do with clothes can be difficult. Some people can't part with anything, yet others like to streamline their closet, keeping only what they wear. Which type are you?

repair, give away, discard, or replace items. See *Fig. 17-2*. The following questions will help you decide which action is best:

- **Do you like the item's style and condition?** If so, it remains in your wardrobe. Mark it as a "keeper" in the chart.

- **Do you seldom or never wear the item?** Some experts say if you haven't worn a garment for over a year, you probably don't need it. Special-occasion garments might be an exception. Before you enter "discard" by an item, however, think of possible alternatives. If you just dislike a garment, you might improve the fit with a simple alteration or change the style for a new look. To avoid repeating mistakes when you buy new clothes, always think about why you don't wear a garment.

- **Can you make any needed repairs?** Replacing a missing button or fixing a ripped seam or loose hem could make a garment wearable. A trip to the shoe repair shop might save the cost of new shoes. Make note of what you plan to do. see→ p 530

- **Is the item outgrown or too worn for wear?** If you need the item, note in your chart that it needs to be replaced. Outgrown or unwanted garments can be passed along to others. Perhaps the fabric can be recycled.

Step 4: Consider New Additions

In your wardrobe chart, the plan for each item stands out clearly, but you may notice something else. Your wardrobe may have some gaps. Would a new pair of wool slacks allow you to make better use of a sweater you already own? Could you make several different outfits if you had a new black blazer? To help you decide whether an additional garment would improve your wardrobe, think about your needs and wants.

Distinguishing Needs and Wants

To young children, needs and wants are the same. They "need" a cupcake the same way they need pencils for school. Teens can distinguish between needs and wants more clearly. One teen decided he *needed* a sturdy pair of shoes for school and a dressy pair for special occasions because these were essential. Since a certain brand of cross-trainers and a stylish pair of suede boots weren't essential, he realized that he only *wanted* them.

As a student, your clothing needs are influenced by what's acceptable in school. Many school dress codes are flexible. Jeans, T-shirts, pants, skirts, and sweaters are all options. Other schools have dress codes that prohibit specific clothing styles and accessories. Some schools require students to wear uniforms.

17-3 A clothing need is something essential that you must have. A special garment or uniform for a part-time job fits this description.

Students who work part-time may need appropriate garments. A restaurant, for example, might provide a uniform or ask that employees wear shirts or blouses of a certain style and color. See *Fig. 17-3*.

Wants arise more from emotions than necessity. A desire to impress others or fit in with peers can make a person want a particular garment. Wearing a special garment makes some people feel attractive, confident, slimmer, taller, or shorter. As a status symbol, a garment makes some people feel important. One teen may want to wear something that shows conformity, yet another wants something that expresses individuality. What other reasons might inspire wants?

Deciding What to Add

Wardrobe additions rarely fulfill needs and wants equally. Buying a new pair of jeans meets a need if you've outgrown the ones you wear all the time. If you choose the same style that your friends are wearing, you're also fulfilling a want.

Values help you decide what's more important. Should you spend more for designer jeans or buy a pair of regular jeans on sale and use the savings for something else?

To help you decide whether to buy something new, think about the questions below. If you decide to make an addition, add the item to your chart.

- **How often would you wear the item?** Some people are more willing to spend money on a down coat to wear all winter than on a velvet jacket to wear only a few times.
- **Can the item be worn for different occasions?** Garments are **versatile** when they can be worn for more than one activity, perhaps to school as well as parties. See *Fig. 17-4*.
- **Will the item go with other clothes in your wardrobe?** A teen who owns a blue blazer, khaki pants, red sweater, and a plaid skirt might buy a shirt in a solid color that goes with all of them. The result is more than one new outfit. Such items make a wardrobe seem larger.
- **Is the item a need or a want?** A wardrobe can include items you want because they're fun, unique, or up-to-date. Meeting clothing needs first, however, is the higher priority. The best additions to a wardrobe are clothes and accessories that satisfy both needs and wants.

17-4 A versatile school outfit like this one might be worn for other occasions as well.

Step 5: Set Priorities

The final step in your wardrobe evaluation is to **prioritize**, or rank, items so you know which ones to replace or add first. Scan the chart, looking at the new items you've listed and the items marked for replacement. Those you need the most should be given the highest priority. Garments that you can get by without for a while are lower priority. Those that are least essential get the lowest priority ranking. Numbers can be used to indicate priority in the last column of your chart.

With your chart completed, you have a **wardrobe plan** in place. This is a guide for making future additions to your wardrobe. By reviewing the plan every few months, you can make adjustments as your needs and wants change.

IDENTIFYING YOUR RESOURCES

How can you build the wardrobe you want? Many people think only of money as a resource, but there are others as well. **Resourceful** people identify all the means and methods they have for accomplishing goals.

- **Money.** A wardrobe plan shows what you need and want, but your budget affects what you can do. When money is limited, you may need to adjust your wardrobe plan. You could take the lowest-priority items out of the plan. You might want two new shirts, but one will do. You could earn money for clothes from an after-school, weekend, or summer job. See *Fig. 17-5*. You can also turn to other resources to put your plan into action.

- **Skills.** Your skills and abilities can help your money go further. Using good consumer skills, you recognize bargains when you see them. Buying clothes on sale or at discount stores can bring added savings. By developing sewing skills, you can make simple repairs, update garments, and expand your wardrobe with new clothes and accessories. You might even earn money by sewing or altering clothes for others. see→ **p 530**

- **Creativity.** Taking a creative look inside your closet might have interesting results. **Creativity** is the ability to use your imagination to come up with an original idea or prod-

17-5 Some teens find ways to earn money in order to buy new clothes. What other resources can a person use to build a wardrobe?

uct. In the last chapter, you learned a number of ways to redesign garments. These ideas help expand a wardrobe. You'll find other ways to use your creativity for the same purpose later in this chapter.

- **Time.** How can time help you with your wardrobe plan? If you have extra time, you can shop for bargains, develop sewing skills, or be creative. If time is limited due to school, work, or other activities, use your time wisely. When shopping, decide what you need and where to find it, instead of traveling from store to store. If you like to sew, set aside some time during school vacations to make new outfits. Save time by choosing easy-to-sew patterns.

- **Other People.** As you consider resources, don't overlook people. Siblings, cousins, and friends may pass along garments. Coats, jackets, and prom dresses often go this route. Do you have relatives who like to knit or sew? Perhaps they would knit a sweater, make curtains for your room, or teach you to knit or sew. A clothing teacher might give advice about restyling a garment. All of these can be valuable resources for expanding your wardrobe.

WAYS TO EXPAND YOUR WARDROBE

With your resources in mind, your wardrobe goals may be closer than you think. How can you put your money and time to good use? How can your skills and creativity help expand your wardrobe? Can you find ways for people to help you, and perhaps for you to help them in return? You might be surprised at the number of ways you can put your resources to work in order to build the wardrobe you want.

Using What You Have

A gifted chef can open the refrigerator and make a delicious meal out of whatever's inside. This approach also works in expanding your wardrobe. Sometimes what you need is right there in the closet or dresser.

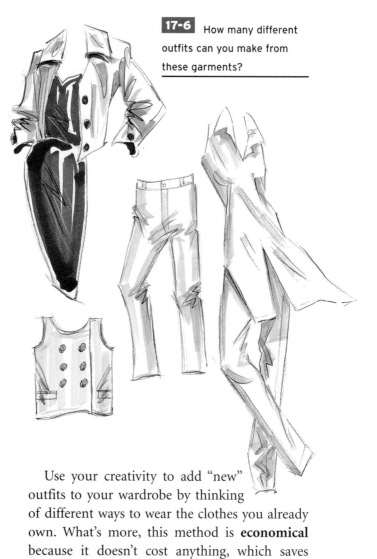

17-6 How many different outfits can you make from these garments?

Use your creativity to add "new" outfits to your wardrobe by thinking of different ways to wear the clothes you already own. What's more, this method is **economical** because it doesn't cost anything, which saves money for other uses.

Creating New Combinations

Sometimes a clothing combination seems so right that you never separate the pieces. Why not try pairing each item with a different garment? Can you mix and match the garments in two outfits? A matching skirt and top, or pants and jacket, don't always have to be worn together. See *Fig. 17-6.*

Experiment with new color mixes as well. During some seasons, unusual combinations, such as purple and red, are very fashionable. Black pants look good with a bright red sweater, but how would they look with a dark green or pale beige sweater, or topped by a gray-and-white tweed blazer?

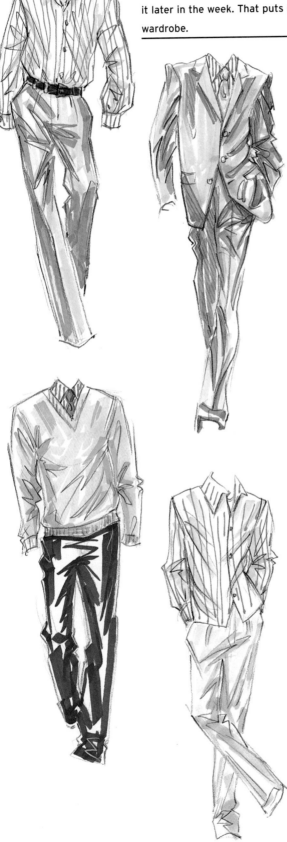

17-7 With a little creativity, you can make a garment you wear on Monday look quite different when you wear it later in the week. That puts some "stretch" in your wardrobe.

Different fabric combinations also give clothes a new look. Compare the effects of pairing a corduroy jacket with denim jeans and the same jacket with wool slacks. In some seasons, combining more than one print in an outfit is the fashion. Checks might be worn with stripes, and prints with plaids. Patterns and colors must be carefully matched, however, to create an outfit that pleases the eye and looks fashionable.

Finding New Uses

When is a tie not a tie? When it's used as a belt. Likewise, a denim shirt can become a lightweight jacket when worn over a T-shirt. With a little experimentation, you may find new ways to wear clothes you already own. See *Fig. 17-7*.

Clothing can be surprisingly versatile. A raincoat with a zip-out lining might be worn year-round. A turtleneck typically worn with blue jeans could also be worn with pants and a sweater for a dressier look. A vest worn most often under a jacket might be worn over a dress or shirt. A sundress might double as a jumper. A change of accessories could transform an outfit from casual to dressy.

One simple technique is changing the way you wear a particular garment. You could tuck pants into boots, belt a loose-fitting jacket, and layer tops in a different order. Many up-to-date ideas can be found in fashion magazines.

Designing New Looks

One teen noticed her sister's denim jacket in the garage sale box. It was still in good shape, so she offered her sister two dollars for it. After the teen trimmed it with rhinestones, her sister said, "That looks great. Why didn't I think of that?"

Two dollars is a small investment for a "new" denim jacket. With a little creativity, you can come up with other ideas. Why not decorate gar-

17-8 By sharing or trading garments, you can expand your wardrobe and save money at the same time. What items would be good possibilities for sharing?

works especially well with special-occasion items. One mother and daughter shared a small evening bag rather than each owning one. If you share an item, take good care of it in order to keep the relationship strong.

Trading clothes with a family member or friend gives each person's wardrobe a new addition at no cost. Be sure you can part with a garment, however, before letting it go.

Sewing

Sewing can show off your creativity, as well as save money. See *Fig. 17-9.* Anyone can learn to sew. To begin, learn simple skills, such as sewing buttons or stitching a hem. You'll save money by making simple repairs that extend the life of garments you already own. By updating garments

17-9 Sewing skills are useful, whether you make something new or repair a garment in order to wear it again. In what other ways can sewing skills be a good resource?

ments with fabric paint or trims? You could paint or appliqué a design on a T-shirt or add sequins to a top. Trim the hem of jeans with fringe or ribbon. As you read fashion ads and shop for clothes, look for details that you can duplicate on less expensive garments. see→ p 581

Adding accessories to create new looks is another idea. Flea markets and second-hand stores are good sources for inexpensive accessories. You can also make them. Braid leather or decorative cord to make a belt, or sew a canvas bag instead of buying one. Make hair ornaments from fabric, ribbons, or braid left over from other projects. Attractive jewelry can be created from beads and even modeling clay. Check out the craft area in a bookstore or library for ideas. Some craft stores provide free instructions and offer classes.

Sharing and Trading

Friends and relatives are good resources for sharing and trading items. See *Fig. 17-8.* Sharing you no longer wear, you can expand your wardrobe with little expense. Shortening a hem or taking in a seam can make a garment fit perfectly. Adding trims, embroidery, or monograms gives a new look to an old garment. see→ p 437

As your skills build, you can try easy-to-sew projects, such as a T-shirt or shorts. Eventually, you might make a shirt, jacket, or backpack. Home sewers can make clothes in just the size, color, and style they want.

Besides sewing clothes, how about giving rooms in your home a new look? You can find many patterns for curtains, pillows, slipcovers, bedspreads, and table linens. The cost savings can be huge compared to buying these items ready-made.

As one more use for your sewing skills, you could make gifts for family and friends. People appreciate the time and effort that goes into a one-of-a-kind gift.

Renting

People often think of renting a car, but what about clothes? Clothes for special occasions are routinely rented to save the expense of purchasing. Caps and gowns are rented for graduation. Tuxedos can be rented for school dances, weddings, and other formal events. In some cities, shops rent formal clothing for females as well as males. Uniforms and costumes can also be rented.

If an item, such as a tuxedo, will be worn several times, figure the total cost for rentals. Purchasing the garment on sale or at a resale store might be more economical.

Buying

Shopping options are everywhere today. See *Fig. 17-10*. If you like hands-on buying, you can visit a store, mall, or craft fair. For shopping ease, you can stay at home and order from catalogs, television, or the Internet. Although buying to build a wardrobe can be costly, some of the most inexpensive "finds" are discovered at resale stores, flea markets, and tag sales. Each option has advantages and disadvantages.

Stores

Buying in a store gives you a firsthand look at the merchandise. You can try on clothes to see how they look. Evaluating the style, quality, and fit is easier than when buying from only a picture and description.

Stores vary in type of merchandise, special services, and prices. See *Fig. 17-11* on pages 312-313. Some specialize in certain price ranges—low, medium, or high. Others offer a range of prices within each category.

If you've shopped in different cities, you know that the same stores can be in many places. Known as chain stores, these are part of a large retail company that operates stores in many cities and towns all over the country. Department stores, specialty stores, and discount stores can all be chains. The headquarters or home office is where all merchandising decisions are made. Because chains have so many stores, the same styles may not be carried in each one. Instead, chains may buy different merchandise for stores in certain regions.

17-10 Stores are filled with so much clothing that narrowing your decision down to only a few items can be difficult. What can you do to prepare yourself for these shopping decisions?

CATEGORIES *of*
Retail

DEPARTMENT STORES are large stores

with merchandise grouped into areas according to specialty—for example, clothing, cosmetics, accessories, luggage, housewares, and sometimes appliances, electronic equipment, and furniture. Services may include gift wrapping, delivery, alterations, bridal registry, a beauty salon, repairs, interior decoration, and fashion consultation.

Clothing departments are organized by size and gender (petites, menswear); by fashion and price categories (designer, budget); and sometimes by designer collection (DKNY, Ralph Lauren, Liz Claiborne, Tommy Hilfiger).

Most department stores have one main store, usually in a city's downtown area. This flagship store oversees one or more branch stores that operate separately in nearby suburbs or faraway states. Most branches serve as an anchor in a shopping mall, helping to attract mall customers.

In addition to brand-name items, many department stores sell products with their own private label. Store ads are published almost daily in newspapers; catalogs are mailed to customers throughout the year.

Examples of major department stores are Macy's, Bloomingdale's, Lord & Taylor, Marshall Field, Dillard's, Belk, Rich's, Burdines, and May Company. Two department store chains are JCPenney and Sears.

Macy's began as one small storefront in the 1800s. Today it is a major department store, with locations across the country.

SPECIALTY STORES carry a limited line of

merchandise, such as clothing, accessories, or fabrics. Some focus on a particular group—children, petites, or large sizes. Others sell a specific category—lingerie, swimwear, bridal gowns, jewelry, or shoes.

Small specialty stores are typically owned by one or more people. These provide personalized service, often with the owner as manager, buyer, and sales associate. A specialty store that features very fashionable or unique designs is called a **boutique**. Although prices are usually higher, boutiques appeal to customers looking for fashion-forward styles or a special look.

Specialty chain stores carry similar items with similar prices and look very much alike. Some sell only their own brand of merchandise. The Limited, Gap, Old Navy, Ann Taylor, Banana Republic, Victoria's Secret, and Payless Shoes are examples. The newest category is the subspecialty store, which carries only one type of merchandise, such as ties, socks, or athletic shoes.

Stores

DISCOUNT STORES sell merchandise at less than full retail price and usually lower than in department and specialty stores. Once located in plain buildings with few services, most discount stores now have fashion displays and dressing rooms. Relying on self-service and checkout counters, they have few sales personnel. Some are chains that carry brand-name items, as well as little-known or private label brands.

Discount stores are not all the same. Stores described as mass merchandise discounters obtain lower prices from manufacturers due to their high sales volume. Examples are Wal-Mart and Target. Although they sell other products, these stores have created a role as fashion merchandisers, emphasizing price and value.

Off-price retailers sell brand-name and designer merchandise at reduced prices. They buy late in the fashion season when manufacturers are eager to sell at low prices. Designer labels can be found at T.J. Maxx, Marshall's, Dress Barn, Syms, and Burlington Coat Factory. Some retailers operate their own off-price stores, such as Filene's Basement, Saks Off Fifth, and Nordstrom Rack.

Outlets sell only the brands produced by the designer, manufacturer, or factory that owns the store. Some outlets are located next to the factory; others are located in malls that consist solely of outlet stores. The garments are overstocks, cancelled orders, or last season's designs. Some may have imperfections or flaws.

RESALE STORES specialize in used or second-hand clothing. Prices are less than similar new items, and all purchases are final. Items can't be exchanged or returned. Some stores sell garments that are almost new, particularly party clothes and one-of-a-kind items.

Thrift stores are resale stores owned by such organizations as a church group or charity. Clothing is inexpensive and may be in less-than-perfect condition. Most consignment stores offer clothes that are in very good condition. Although higher priced than in thrift shops, these clothes cost less than new ones.

Some resale stores specialize in **vintage** fashions from earlier decades—the 1930s to the 1980s and even the Victorian era. Depending on age, condition, and rarity, vintage clothing can be reasonably priced or very expensive.

Discount stores like Target (below) sell enough merchandise to offer lower prices. In a thrift store (right), you might find unusual items.

Buying has never been easier. With an on-line computer service, consumers can now go e-shopping. Using electronic shopping areas, they learn about products and also buy merchandise and services.

When you access a retailer's Web site, you may find an on-line catalog. A symbol or message indicates the site is secure. To order a product, enter the requested information. Specify size and color, if needed, and enter your credit card number and shipping address. This data travels electronically to the retailer's computer, and a return e-mail confirms your order. The retailer ships the merchandise to you by mail or delivery service. Once you have purchased something through a Web site, you may receive e-mails notifying you of new products and special offers.

Many manufacturers have Web sites that describe their products. If you can't order directly from these sites, a list of stores or links to other purchasing sites may be provided.

A search engine is useful when you don't know a Web address. On the search engine site, you enter a word or phrase that indicates what you want to find. An electronic hunt ends with a displayed list of possible sites. Two popular search engines are Yahoo and Excite, but there are many more. Since they handle information differently, you may need to try several search engines and different key words before finding what you want.

INVESTIGATION ACTIVITY

Using more than one on-line search engine, locate information on a product. Try different key words to find the same product. What tips do you have for streamlining an on-line search?

Some stores, usually smaller, are individually owned by one or more people. The atmosphere and service may be more personalized than in larger stores. Often the sales associate is the owner or manager.

Catalogs

Catalog shopping is a popular alternative to buying in a store. Many people like the convenience of ordering from store and mail-order catalogs. See page 324 for information on placing catalog orders.

Catalog shopping has advantages. You can shop at home at any time of day or night with just a telephone, a toll-free number, and a credit card. No time and money are spent on transportation to stores. Orders can also be placed by mail, along with a check or money order. Catalogs picture the items and describe them in detail, including styles, fabrics, colors, sizes, and prices. The selection of products may be greater than in stores and may include items unavailable locally. When ordering, if you don't receive what you expected, most items can be returned with no questions asked.

Among the disadvantages to catalog shopping is not being able to examine the actual article. Colors and details may not be clear. Getting the proper fit is harder when you can't try on a garment. The wait for delivery can take from several days to several weeks. Other disadvantages involve extra costs. Shipping and handling costs are usually added. If the catalog doesn't have a toll-free number, you pay for a long distance call. Finally, to return or exchange an item, you have to repackage and mail it. Often you pay the return shipping cost. Catalog retailers that have stores may permit customers to return items to a local store.

Internet

The advantages and disadvantages of Internet shopping are generally the same as for catalog shopping. One important difference is that a credit card is usually necessary. Checks and money orders aren't generally accepted, although a few sites bill by mail. For more information, see page 314.

Television

Certain television channels have 24-hour, home shopping programs that take orders for merchandise, including jewelry and designer apparel. Home Shopping Network (HSN) and QVC are the largest of these services.

After merchandise is shown and described, a host usually urges viewers to order by calling a toll-free number. Customers pay for the items with a credit card, and the merchandise is sent within a day or two.

Television shopping can be easy and convenient, but the shows do promote impulse buying. If you evaluate your wardrobe needs and budget before ordering, you'll avoid buying regrets.

At-Home Selling

At-home retailers sell merchandise to individuals or groups in customers' homes. Often the event is designed as a "party" for the hostess and friends. A sales representative displays or demonstrates such items as clothing, lingerie, jewelry, or cosmetics. Orders are taken and the items are delivered later.

Merchandise offered through at-home selling is usually high quality. It may be higher priced, however, than similar items in stores. Sometimes customers feel pressured to order items they may not need because of the host's hospitality and the party atmosphere. If you're invited to a party event, set a spending limit before attending.

Fairs and Flea Markets

At indoor and outdoor fairs and flea markets, people rent booths in a parking lot, field, school, shopping mall, church, or club. Craft fairs usually feature handmade clothing and accessories. Bazaars and flea markets sell used clothing and accessories or new items that have been purchased directly from a manufacturer.

One or more families may hold a garage sale or tag sale. See *Fig. 17-12*. Just because something is sold at a low price doesn't make it a bargain. Take time to inspect any item before purchasing.

17-12 Cash is usually expected at garage sales, and you can't return what you buy. The price, however, may be worthwhile.

Review

CHAPTER SUMMARY

- The first step to building a wardrobe is to evaluate the usefulness of clothes you currently own.

- Prioritize clothing needs and wants when adding garments to your wardrobe.

- Consider all your resources to make the most of your current wardrobe and of any items you add to it.

- A wardrobe can be expanded in more ways than just by buying new clothes.

- You have many options for buying clothes. Each has advantages and disadvantages.

USING KEY TERMS

Create a quiz, based on at least ten of the Key Terms in this chapter. Exchange quizzes with a partner and complete the quiz written by the other person. Return the quizzes. After checking the answers, discuss any problems you each had in answering the questions.

RECALLING THE FACTS

1. Why is an inventory part of wardrobe evaluation?

2. What do you need to know about a garment in order to develop an action plan for your wardrobe?

3. How can comparing needs and wants help you decide whether to add a garment to your wardrobe?

4. How do you prioritize when making a wardrobe chart?

5. Why are sewing skills a valuable resource?

6. In what ways can other people be resources for meeting clothing needs?

7. How might clothing that a person already owns be used to expand a wardrobe?

8. When might renting a garment be more reasonable than buying?

9. What are some advantages of buying clothes from a store rather than a catalog?

10. What conveniences do catalogs offer?

11. Describe advantages and disadvantages of shopping at craft fairs and bazaars.

12. Give two reasons why clothing tends to be more expensive at a boutique than at a mass merchandise discounter.

13. How are thrift stores and consignment stores similar and different?

and Activities

THINKING CRITICALLY

1. Which do you like to acquire more, clothes that you need or clothes that you want? Why?

2. Trading or sharing clothes doesn't work for everyone. Why do you think that's true?

3. Of the different methods available for buying clothes, which do you think is most likely to lead to overspending? Why?

APPLYING KNOWLEDGE

1. **Need or want?** Make a quick list of five to ten clothing items that you've thought about owning. Then determine whether each is a need or a want. What conclusions can you reach about yourself?

2. **Advising a friend.** Suppose a friend says that he or she just can't let go of old clothes. Everything stays in the closet year after year whether it's worn or not. What would your advice be? What reasons can you give to your friend in order to be convincing?

3. **Wardrobe chart.** Make your own wardrobe chart, using the steps described in the chapter.

4. **Creating uses.** List five garments in your wardrobe. Describe two new ways to wear each one.

5. **On-line shopping.** Research the technology used in creating a secure Web site for purchasing merchandise on-line. How do such sites compare to those that are not secure?

6. **Rental costs.** Research the costs of tuxedo rentals at different shops in your area. Compare these costs to the cost of buying a new or used tuxedo.

CREATIVE SOLUTIONS

Suppose a fire recently damaged the home of someone in your class at school. Although no one was injured, flames and smoke caused major losses, including to clothes. Your classmate has lost most of her wardrobe, and you and your friends want to help her rebuild.

Think Creatively

What resources described in the chapter could you all use to help your classmate? What actions would you take to put these resources to work?

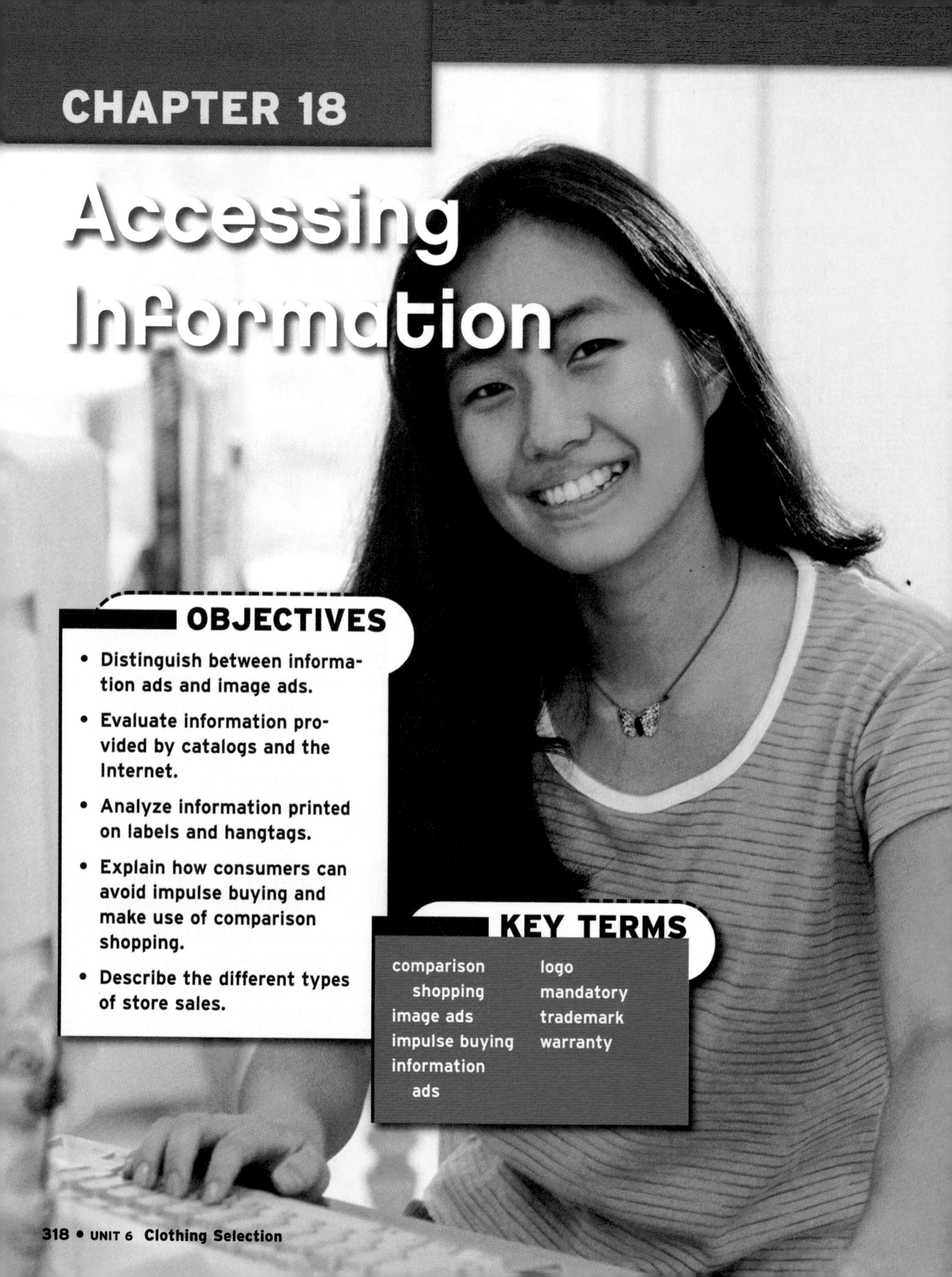

Accessing Information

OBJECTIVES

- Distinguish between information ads and image ads.

- Evaluate information provided by catalogs and the Internet.

- Analyze information printed on labels and hangtags.

- Explain how consumers can avoid impulse buying and make use of comparison shopping.

- Describe the different types of store sales.

KEY TERMS

comparison shopping

image ads

impulse buying

information ads

logo

mandatory

trademark

warranty

WHILE BROWSING AT A STORE'S SHOE display, one teen noticed a style that she had seen a well-known singer wear. After buying the shoes, she later wished she had spent her money on something else.

What information do you use when making purchases? It pays to gather data about products and services before you buy. You're more likely to choose clothing you need and want and build a wardrobe that looks good. What's more, you'll get better value for the money you have to spend. See *Fig. 18-1.*

SOURCES OF INFORMATION

People often talk about information overload. That's because information is everywhere in today's world. When you buy clothing and accessories, the primary sources of information available are advertising, catalogs, the Internet, and labels and hangtags. You'll need to sort through the information to make careful purchasing decisions.

Advertising

The purpose of advertising is to sell something. It might be a product, a service, or an idea. If you buy, the advertising was successful for the seller. To use advertising to your own advantage, be sure you understand its intent.

Information or Image?

Advertisements fall into one of two general categories: those that provide information and those that promote an image.

- **Information ads.** When you observe an advertisement, ask yourself what you learned. An **information ad** includes many details about a product. For a shirt, the style and fabric might be described, as well as the sizes, price, fiber content, care, and brand name. The ad might tell you where the shirt is sold. By reading several such ads, you can decide what to buy without going from store to store. The more facts supplied, the more useful the ad. Specifying a fabric as "50-percent cotton/50-percent polyester" is more informative than listing it as just a "cotton blend."

18-1 Gathering information about products before you buy helps you make better purchasing decisions.

18-2 If certain sunglasses make the model or celebrity in an image ad look good, you might feel like trying them yourself. This is how some ads capture your interest—and your money.

• **Image ads.** An effective **image ad** can make a pair of new white socks seem like a dream come true. While this is an exaggeration, that's the basic aim. Image ads tempt you to buy items by making you want them. They do this in many ways: by appealing to emotions and fantasies; by suggesting a sense of approval; by encouraging you to have the "very latest" items; and by arousing a desire for adventure or individuality. See *Fig. 18-2*. Some ads make a fashion statement or promote a designer or manufacturer. As the name suggests, image ads are usually very visual, with most space devoted to drawings or photographs. Although the ads are typically short on product information, they may have ideas for styles, colors, and fabrics to add to your wardrobe. Some ads

create a mood to associate with the product. Fragrance and cosmetic manufacturers frequently use such ads to stir your interest.

Advertising Medias

To spread their message to as many people as possible, advertisers use different forms of mass communication. The print medias, including magazines, newspapers, and billboards, have been around for a long time. See *Fig. 18-3*. Other forms are electronic: radio, television, and, most recently, the Internet.

Each media has its own format and limitations. Because of this, the same product may be advertised differently in different medias.

• **Magazines.** Some advertisers choose the full-page, glossy format offered by magazines. Ads usually combine information with a large photograph or illustration to create an image for the product or brand. Ads that appear in national or regional publications may not supply the product's price or where to buy it.

18-3 Magazines and newspapers charge fees for advertisements. If enough people buy because of an ad, the cost of that ad is worthwhile to the advertiser.

- **Newspapers.** Except for the special ads in large Sunday editions, these ads are usually black-and-white photos or drawings. Lacking the "flair" of magazines, they also tend to be more informative. Since many newspapers are sold locally, their ads tell where products can be found and what they cost.

- **Promotional articles.** Promotional articles often appear in newspapers and magazines. An article on organizing your closet may suggest using the shoe bag mentioned in a store ad on the same page. Although accurate, the information may also be slanted and incomplete.

- **Advertorials.** *Adv*ertisement edi*torials* are designed to look like articles but are really paid ads. If you look carefully, you'll see the word "advertisement" printed above or below the article.

- **Billboards.** Because they're found along roads and highways, on buildings, and on the sides of buses, these ads are seen for only a short time. The messages are brief and bold.

- **Radio and television.** Ads on radio and television, called commercials, are typically 30 or 60 seconds long. Some are as brief as 15 seconds. These ads are short and splashy, designed to capture your attention and fix the product's name in your mind. Most are image ads that give little information.

- **Movies.** When you rent a movie or see it in a theater, ads may appear on the screen before the feature begins. Manufacturers also pay fees to have their products used—and subtly noticed—in a movie or television show. This form of advertising is called product placement. See *Fig. 18-4.*

- **Infomercials.** *Info*rmation com*mercials* are lengthy television presentations about a product. Some follow a talk-show format, complete with a celebrity host and an "expert guest" who models or demonstrates the item's use. Designed to look like a 30-minute television show, they are really advertisements. These shows provide a toll-free number for convenient ordering.

- **The Internet.** This media brings advertising into the twenty-first century. Eye-catching ads use the latest visual technology to appeal to computer-wise people. Animated figures appear on the top of a Web page; pop-up windows intrude over it. These quickly link you to the seller's Web site, where you may find a complete catalog of products.

- **Sales promotions.** These subtle forms of advertising let consumers see products in use. Fashion shows and demonstrations, such as how to accessorize with scarves, are two popular examples from the fashion industry. At

18-4 Even when you go to a movie, advertising may reach you. Can you explain how?

18-5 Fashion shows, whether on high-fashion runways or at shopping malls and department stores, entice people to buy. Experts in fashion present the latest looks in this entertaining format.

these events, fashion models and special lighting help make the garments attractive and appealing. See *Fig. 18-5.*

- **Point-of-sale advertising.** Advertising that appears in the store may be right next to the merchandise or in the same department. Some fashion designers produce videos of their collections, inspiring customers to buy multiple garments from the designer's line. Posters are another point-of-sale advertising method.

Advertising in Perspective

Because fashion is an industry, its main purpose is to stay in business by selling more clothes and accessories. To do this, fashions must change constantly. Every season ads describe the newest and the latest.

A new style may be introduced, last for several years, and then fade away. The best shopping strategy is to purchase a style that is near the beginning of its fashion life, rather than at the end.

Read, look, and listen carefully to what is said about new fashions. You'll soon be able to tell the difference between a fashion that will last and a fad that will quickly fade from popularity. Look for the key words used to describe a new style. If you notice "latest," "newest," "hottest," or "the big news is . . .," the style may not be fashionable for long. If words like "classic," "traditional," or "always in fashion" are used, the style probably isn't a fad.

Buying an item that is a fad or status symbol isn't wrong. You should know what you're buying, however, and base your decision on your own thinking rather than the lure of an advertisement.

Catalogs

As you read in Chapter 17, catalogs are a buying option that many people like. Catalogs can also be a useful information resource, even when you're not ready to make a purchase. See *Fig. 18-6.* You can use them to gather ideas about new styles and colors. Since stores and manufacturers try to include all relevant facts about a product in their catalogs, you'll find details about styles, colors, and sizes, usually accompanied by color photos. Ideas about cost will help you plan around a budget. Recognizing bargains will be easier when you do shop.

18-6 You can use catalogs even when you don't plan to place an order. They have ideas for combining ties and shirts, choosing shoes to go with outfits, and putting colors together. How else might they help?

When you do decide to buy a product, you can order it by mail, by phone, or through the company's Web site. More about catalog shopping can be found on page 324.

The Internet

Like catalogs, the Internet is another information source to use before you shop. On-line catalogs, found on the Web sites of many companies, provide the same information that mail-order catalogs have. You can research details about styles, colors, sizes, and prices before you shop.

Internet information is useful in other ways too. For one thing, you can check availability. With on-line access to sellers, you usually know immediately whether an item is available in the style, size, and color you want. In addition, many on-line catalogs have special sections that adver-

Trends in TECHNOLOGY

≫BUYING SEWING PATTERNS ON-LINE

Technology has made finding a sewing pattern simpler than ever today. All major pattern companies have Web sites where you can view their catalogs and purchase patterns on-line. Without entering a store, you can find a pattern for anything from sportswear to a prom dress or pillow.

Small pattern businesses also sell patterns and directions on the Internet. Some fill a special niche, offering modern garments based on vintage styles, historically accurate clothing, square dancing outfits, skating costumes, Western wear, lingerie, or special sizes. Web sites are usually listed in sewing magazine ads. If you're not sure where to go on the Internet, start with a search engine.

Typing in such phrases as "sewing patterns," "fashion sewing patterns," or "costume sewing patterns" should bring results.

While browsing on the Internet, you may discover an unfamiliar company. Since you can't examine the actual pattern and you're not familiar with the way the company's designs fit, what can you do? You could participate in an on-line sewing group. First, find a group that suits you. While some groups are for sewers of all skill levels, others focus on advanced skills. Some groups are for people who use specific sewing machine brands. Others are for people with special interests, such as computerized embroidery, heirloom sewing, or costume design. When you post a question, other sewers share their experiences with you. To locate lists of sewing groups, access a search engine and type in "sewing forums," "sewing digests," or "sewing bulletin boards."

INVESTIGATION ACTIVITY

Do you have a sewing question or problem? Try linking with a sewing group on-line to get an answer.

How To... ORDER FROM CATALOGS

Catalog shopping by phone is easy and convenient. Follow these steps:

1. Find the merchandise you want to order in the catalog. Mark the item number, size, and color in the catalog or write it on a separate paper. Have your credit card ready.

2. Call the order number provided. Many are toll-free. Ask any questions you have about size, color, fabric, shipping date, and special services.

3. Provide the credit card number and expiration date printed on the card.

4. Keep a record of your order, including confirmation number, total cost, and order and ship dates. If not shipped within 30 days, you can cancel the order and obtain a refund.

Catalog Shopping Tips

- Look for easy-fitting styles and P-S-M-L-XL size ranges. Numbered sizes require a more accurate fit. Many catalogs have detailed sizing information.

- Consider shipping charges as part of the cost when you order. These can vary widely among companies. Taxes may be added, depending on the state where you live.

- Read return policies. Most companies accept returns for refund or credit, but don't refund shipping charges.

- If ordering by mail, send a check or money order. Never send cash because you have no proof of lost or stolen money.

Exploring Catalog Shopping

With a partner, practice placing a catalog order, using a real catalog. One person should act as the customer and the other as the order taker. Repeat with roles reversed.

tise sale items. If you can't find something in the stores, you might find it on the Internet. For example, if a store doesn't have an athletic shoe in an unusual size, you might be able to order them directly through the manufacturer's Web site. To review information on e-shopping, see page 314.

Labels and Hangtags

Each garment comes with a miniature owner's manual, the labels and hangtags attached for easy access. These sources of information easily go unnoticed unless you realize their usefulness.

Clothing labels are a relatively recent development. At one time, all clothes were made from natural fibers. People knew what to expect from these materials and how to care for them. With advances in textile chemistry in the 1940s came new fibers, including names like nylon, polyester, acrylic, and spandex. People weren't familiar with these fabrics or their care. Clothes were marked and advertised in a way that led many consumers to believe they were buying one thing, when they were actually getting something quite different.

In 1958, Congress approved the Textile Fiber Products Identification Act (TFPI). This law protects consumers against misinformation on the fiber content of textile goods. Similar laws have been enacted by Congress to cover fur and wool products.

Mandatory Information

Thanks to the TFPI, every garment sold must have one or more labels that give the consumer

18-7 When you know where the labels are, you're more likely to check them for information. What information is on this label?

specified information. This information is **mandatory**, or required by law. The law states that labels must be attached to garments where they are easy to find. This is usually the center back of a garment at the neck or waist, although you may see labels in the inside, lower-front seam of a jacket or the side seams of lingerie. See *Fig. 18-7*.

Labels must be attached so they won't come off unless removed by the purchaser. They can be glued, sewn, printed, or stamped on the fabric, or attached to the outside of the garment. If the garment is sold in a package, the fiber content label can be affixed to the package only.

A further aid to consumers is the Permanent Care Labeling Rule of 1972. This law states that all textile garments sold in the United States must carry permanent labels that fully describe the item's regular care needs.

Today, the following five pieces of mandatory information must appear on all garment labels:

- **Fiber content.** The fibers must be identified by their generic names, not their trade names.
- **Percentage of fiber content by weight.**

Fashion

OUCH! Have you noticed any garment labels scratching the skin on the back of your neck? If so, you're like many others, and there's a reason. As a cost-cutting measure today, some manufacturers are using label materials that aren't as soft and pliable as they used to be. The labels are also sliced to size, leaving the edges sharp. As consumers call more attention to this problem, changes may be made.

- **Identification of manufacturer.** Either the manufacturer's name or RN, a registered number assigned by the Federal Trade Commission, must be identified.
- **Country of origin.** If parts of the garment were manufactured in another country, or if the garment was assembled in another country, the label must state this. If the fabric or yarn is from another country, this information must also be included.
- **Care instructions.** One method of safe care must be listed.

Voluntary Information

Apparel manufacturers may show other information on a garment's permanent label or on hangtags that are attached with a strip of plastic, string, or safety pin. See *Fig. 18-8*. This voluntary information may include the following:

- **Size.** The size may be part of the garment's permanent label, printed on a small separate label, or printed on a hangtag. While this information isn't required, consumers and retailers expect it.
- **Brand names or trademarks.** Tags and labels can serve as mini-advertisements for a brand name or trademark. A **trademark** is an identifying mark used by a manufacturer or retailer to distinguish its products from those of the competition. The trademark may be a word, design, letter, or **logo**, an identifying symbol. Not only manufacturers but also fibers and finishes may be identified by trademark. Whoever legally registers a trademark has exclusive rights to its use.
- **Warranty or guarantee.** A **warranty** is a pledge or assurance about a product's quality or performance. Clothing warranties typically offer a refund or replacement garment if the original doesn't provide normal wear for a specific period of time. A few organizations, such as the International Fabricare Institute, maintain test laboratories that issue warranties or seals of approval. These pledges guarantee that the product will live up to the standards set by that particular laboratory. Some manufacturers provide additional warranties of their own.
- **Union label.** Garments made by union workers in the United States bear the label of the Union of Needletrades, Industrial, and Textile Employees (UNITE). This organization was created in 1995 by the merger of the International Ladies' Garment Workers' Union (ILGWU) and the Amalgamated Clothing Workers of America (ACWA). See *Fig. 18-9*.
- **Inventory control.** Retailers maintain inventory records by using special codes printed on hangtags. When an item is sold, a scanner "reads" the information on the tag or the sales associate enters the code in the register. This information goes to the computer, which records the style, color, size, price, and manufacturer and tracks how many are sold.

18-8 While you can leave a label in a garment for occasional reference, a hangtag is removed before wearing. Some hangtags even have an extra button or length of yarn attached for repairs. Where are hangtags often located on garments?

UNION OF NEEDLETRADES, INDUSTRIAL AND TEXTILE EMPLOYEES, AFL-CIO, CLC

18-9 If you see this on a garment label, what does it mean?

USING INFORMATION EFFECTIVELY

Information about products and services is of little value if you don't take advantage of it. Some people simply forget to use available information. Others don't know how to use it. Both of these situations can be overcome.

Impulse Buying

One teen tries to shop with a plan. He goes to the store to get one or two specific items and comes home with several extras. "What am I doing?" he wonders. "My budget can't handle this."

Shopping often leads to **impulse buying**, making unplanned purchases. See *Fig. 18-10.* Store displays are designed to catch attention. An entire outfit displayed with accessories tempts you to buy the whole outfit instead of buying just one item to coordinate with clothes you already own. Impulse buying is one reason why some closets are filled with garments that are rarely worn.

Becoming an educated shopper makes it easier to resist impulse buying. Knowledge tells you what's worth owning. It also helps you identify why you want to buy. If you learn to recognize impulsive instincts, you can manage them better.

Buying something because it makes you feel good won't be a problem as long as it's only occasional. Most people enjoy a treat now and then. You might restrict unplanned purchases to small, inexpensive items, such as a scarf, belt, lipstick, or pair of socks, but be careful since these costs can add up too. When impulsive buying is under control, you can mean it when you tell the sales associate, "I'm just looking."

Comparison Shopping

How do you know whether something is a good buy? With **comparison shopping**, you look at the quality, price, and usefulness of similar items to find the best value for your money. You're less likely to buy impulsively if you develop the habit of examining competitive products first.

Comparison shopping begins at home. Read, watch, and listen to ads. Study mail-order catalogs. If you have access to the Internet, do a little research. Later, when you're in the store, you can compare the information you've acquired to the merchandise you find. Do you want to pay dry-cleaning bills? Do you like some fibers more than others? Reading labels and hangtags will help you decide which garment is the best buy for you.

Buying at Sales

Some people say, "I try not to buy anything unless it's on sale." These people see a sale as more

18-10 Impulse buying can be a problem if it happens too often. Leaving credit cards at home and taking only the amount of money needed when shopping can help.

18-11 Typically, when the number of potential buyers is lowest, you're likely to find better prices. A pre-season sale price may be offered, for example, to lure shoppers. As more shoppers want and need the season's fashions, the prices may go up.

than just a way to expand a wardrobe. It's a challenge they enjoy. After planning their purchases, then waiting for sales, they set out to find the best values. With sales of many types going on all the time, these shoppers have many chances to sharpen their sales-hunting skills.

Types of Sales

Items go on sale for many reasons. Have you found bargains at any of these?

- **Pre-season sales.** These sales feature merchandise for upcoming seasons well ahead of time. Back-to-school sales are held in July. Although the Christmas season traditionally starts the day after Thanksgiving, the sales season begins just after Halloween. Spring fashions often compete with winter clothes for display space in January. See *Fig. 18-11*.
- **Coupon sales.** With coupon sales, customers redeem coupons for special discounts. These coupons are usually mailed to the people on the store's mailing list. Some coupons are printed in newspapers.

- **Preferred customer sales.** People who have charge accounts at a store or who are on a special mailing list are alerted to special sales. Department stores have these sales several times a year.
- **Holiday sales.** A tradition for many stores and shoppers, these sales are held on legal holidays, such as Presidents' Day. They offer a way for some people to spend a day away from work or school. A store may use a sale to "celebrate" a special day of its own, such as the founder's birthday.
- **Clearance sales.** With clearance sales, stores move out items that didn't sell during the season, making room for incoming merchandise. See *Fig. 18-12*. Merchandise that a store decides not to carry anymore may be offered in a "clear out" sale.
- **Inventory sales.** These occur once a year when a store takes inventory. Selling merchandise before taking inventory leaves fewer items to be counted. Many stores hold inventory sales in January, when stock is already low after Christmas. Stores may also hold the sale after taking inventory, to reduce an oversupply or move the last of a merchandise line.

18-12 Planning ahead can be a real money saver. If you can wait until the end of a season to buy, prices are usually lower. What happens to the selection?

18-13 Check for flaws before you buy a garment. A zipper, for example, might look fine even though it's defective. A quick test will tell you whether it operates smoothly and remains closed as needed.

- **Going-out-of business sales.** When stores have lost their lease or gone bankrupt, they may have a going-out-of-business sale. Usually all merchandise in the store must be sold.

Check Merchandise

Just because merchandise is on sale doesn't necessarily mean it's a bargain. Understanding what items make it to the sale racks can help you find a good buy. Clothing sold at a discount price is usually one of the following three types:

- **Overruns.** Excess merchandise results when manufacturers produce more than they can sell to stores. The merchandise is usually "first quality," or considered perfect. You'll frequently find overruns in discount stores, especially off-price retailers and factory outlets.
- **Irregulars.** Garments that don't pass inspection due to small imperfections are called irregulars. A pull in the fabric, an uneven color, or a mislabeled size might be the cause. These flaws won't affect the wear of the garment. Discount and outlet stores sell this merchandise; department stores may offer irregulars as part of a special sale.
- **Seconds.** Garments with more serious flaws are seconds. One sleeve may be longer than the other, or the buttonholes may be sewn in the wrong place. It may take some skillful sewing to repair these garments.

Garments that are known to have flaws may be sold "as is." This notation on the label means that you can't return the garment if you find a flaw after purchasing. "As is" items may be garments that were perfect when the store received them but were damaged while for sale. Before you buy, look for such problems as a ripped hem, a missing button, or a makeup stain.

To be on the safe side, check all merchandise for flaws, whether sale- or regular-priced. See *Fig.*

18-13. If you find a flaw, can it be mended easily? Is it minor enough to go unnoticed? The size of the flaw will determine whether you think the garment is still a bargain.

Evaluating Sales

If you hate orange, is an orange sweater a bargain at 50 percent off? Probably not, but for someone who likes orange, it might be. The appeal of saving money makes some people forget to evaluate carefully. If an item wouldn't interest you at full price, it isn't a good buy on sale.

Before you buy, compare the sale price to the item's regular price. Also try to check other sale prices. Some stores may have better bargains.

Many sales are final. Merchandise marked "final sale" cannot be returned or exchanged. The store's return policy should be posted on a sign by the checkout area or printed on the sales receipt. Stores have time limits on how long you can keep an item before returning it. Some stores will refund your money, yet others give only store credit. Always check the policy before you buy.

One last thought to keep in mind when you shop the sales is that a bargain isn't a bargain if it's beyond your budget. You'll be much happier if you save for your purchases and then stretch those dollars during a good sale.

Review

CHAPTER SUMMARY

- Advertisements appear in many different medias. Some provide information about a product. Others focus on promoting an image for the product.

- Catalogs and Internet sites are useful for locating items and comparison shopping.

- Mandatory information on labels tells you the garment's fiber content and care.

- Voluntary information appears on labels and hangtags.

- Gathering information about garments helps you avoid impulse buying and compare before shopping.

- Learning to evaluate sales can help you save money on quality merchandise.

USING KEY TERMS

Using all the Key Terms, arrange them in pairs. Each pair should share a common link. Explain what links the terms in each pair. Does one pair have only a weak link at best? Which pair is that?

RECALLING THE FACTS

1. How do an information ad and an image ad differ?

2. If you were a clothing retailer, what five advertising medias would you choose for your ads? Why?

3. How can a promotional article be a form of advertisement?

4. Describe similarities between billboard and radio ads.

5. Why do infomercials sometimes surprise people?

6. Describe a wise approach when using ads to get fashion information.

7. How can the Internet be a source of useful information?

8. Describe five pieces of mandatory information on clothing labels.

9. Describe five pieces of voluntary information on clothing labels and hangtags.

10. How does information help prevent impulsive buying?

11. What is meant by the statement, "Comparison shopping begins at home"?

12. What are four situations a store might use as a reason to have a sale?

13. Does a discounted price mean a garment is a bargain? Explain.

14. In what way can garment irregulars be an economical buy?

15. Give suggestions for using sales wisely.

and Activities

THINKING CRITICALLY

1. Why do you think image ads might be especially effective in selling clothes?

2. How might some people try to meet emotional needs through impulse buying?

3. What impact do you think friends have on impulse buying? Where does the final responsibility lie? Why?

APPLYING KNOWLEDGE

1. **Analyzing ads.** Locate five ads in magazines. Classify each ad as either information or image. What elements led to your conclusion?

2. **Labels and hangtags.** Examine labels and hangtags on clothing in a store to see how information is listed. Using what you've learned, design a label and hangtag of your own for a garment. Include both mandatory and voluntary information.

3. **Textile Fiber Products Identification Act.** Using the Internet or other sources, locate a copy of the Textile Fiber Products Identification Act. One source is the Web site of the Federal Trade Commission, www.ftc.gov. Read and report on one or two sections pertaining to garment labels.

4. **Store methods.** As you walk through a store, notice methods used to encourage impulse buying. List these and explain why they work.

5. **Comparison shopping.** Using three or more product resources, including catalogs or the Internet, find information on an item of clothing or an accessory that you would like to buy. Make a chart that compares design, quality, and price.

6. **Shopping list.** Working with a partner, compile a list called "Top Ten Shopping Do's and Don'ts," giving tips on shopping for clothes. Use information from the chapter.

CREATIVE SOLUTIONS

An older cousin of yours is a newlywed. While you're shopping with her one Saturday afternoon, she starts talking about what a money saver her husband is. "He won't spend a dime," she says. "Now me, I love to shop." A couple hours later, the two of you are headed home. Your cousin looks at all her bags, saying, "Oh-oh, why did I buy this much?"

Think Creatively

Why do you think your cousin is in this situation? What problems may be ahead for her? If you have the opportunity, what suggestions can you give her?

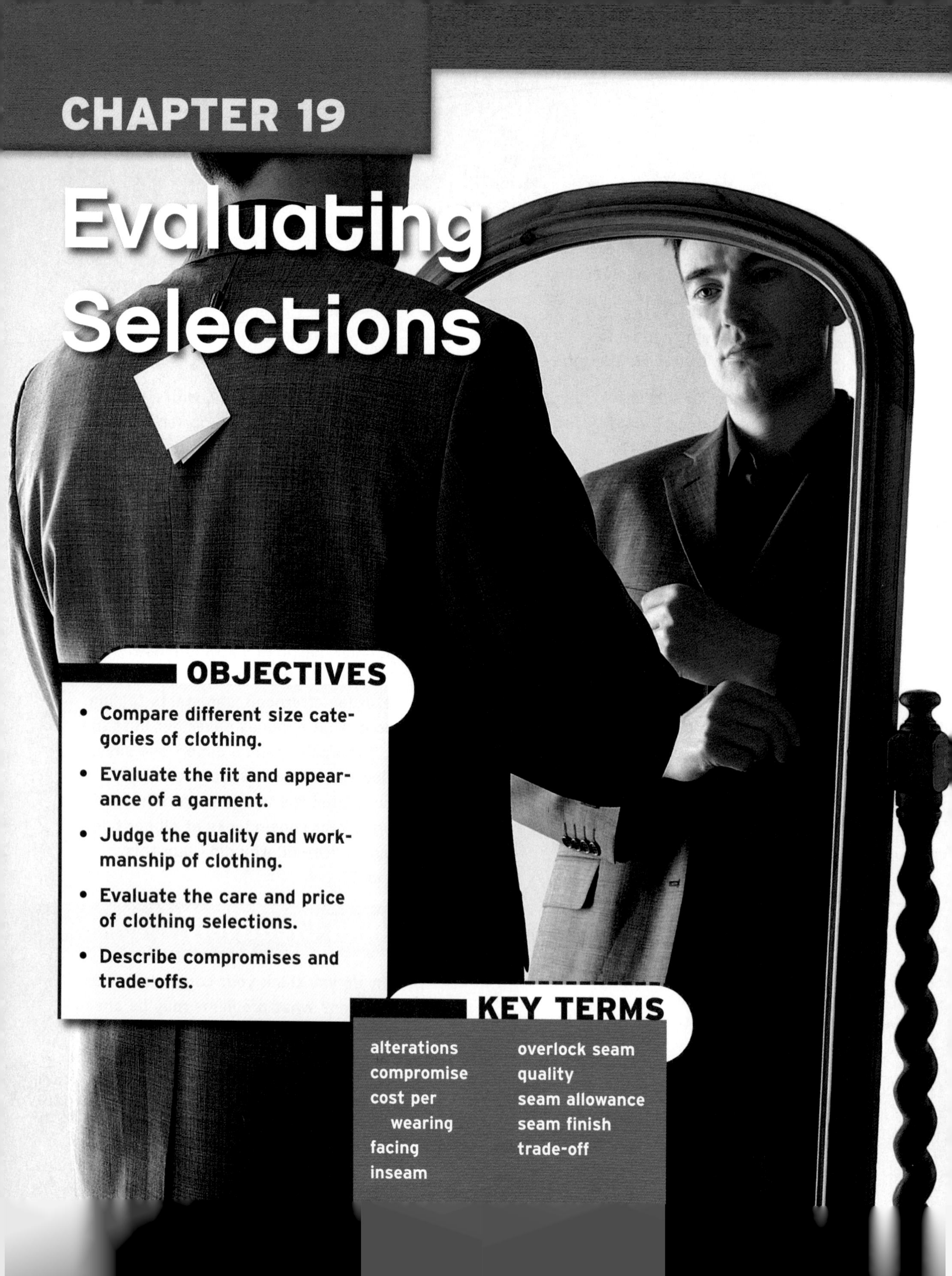

Evaluating Selections

OBJECTIVES

- Compare different size categories of clothing.
- Evaluate the fit and appearance of a garment.
- Judge the quality and workmanship of clothing.
- Evaluate the care and price of clothing selections.
- Describe compromises and trade-offs.

KEY TERMS

alterations
compromise
cost per
   wearing
facing
inseam

overlock seam
quality
seam allowance
seam finish
trade-off

W HILE SHOPPING FOR CLOTHES, one teen said to another, "You like it, don't you? Then why don't you buy it?"

"I do like it," was the reply, "but I can't just buy something because I like it. I've got to think about other things too."

A garment that catches your eye in the store may seem like a good choice at first glance. Unless you consider size, fit, quality, care, and cost, however, you won't know for sure.

FINDING THE CORRECT SIZE

When buying clothes, finding the correct size is sometimes a challenge. Clothing sizes can look like parts of an algebra problem. You'll see 6P, 18H, XS, and XXL, to name a few. Unlike math, however, one size 12 isn't always equal to another size 12. The same size may differ among brands. Even within the same brand, sizes aren't always consistent. Why does this happen?

Why Size Can Differ

Suppose you find a shirt you like in a store. You're not familiar with the brand, but the price is lower than you would normally pay and the shirt comes in your size. Then you try it on, but the sleeves barely reach your wrists. Have you gone on an overnight growth spurt? Was the garment mismarked? Most likely, neither of these is what happened.

Each ready-to-wear manufacturer has its own standard size measurements, influenced by production costs among other factors. By cutting a size-10 garment just a little smaller, the manufacturer reduces production costs. Just a 1-inch (2.5-cm) savings per garment can save hundreds of fabric yards and hundreds of dollars. The manufacturer can sell the garment at a lower price. This explains why you may wear a larger size in less expensive clothes.

Even if you already own several items from a manufacturer and are satisfied with the way they fit, size consistency isn't guaranteed. One teen ordered a pair of pants from a catalog. The size was perfect, so she ordered a second pair of the same style in a different fabric, but that pair did not fit well at all. When the teen returned the

VIRTUAL DRESSING ROOMS. On-line apparel sales are growing and expected to grow rapidly in the future. One of the problems for consumers, however, has been choosing the right style and size when ordering. New software allows buyers to mix and match items on the screen, even rotating outfits for a 360-degree view. On some Web sites buyers can see how garments look on models that duplicate their own measurements. As these techniques improve, merchandisers hope the number of returns will go down.

19-1 • Size Categories for Females

CATEGORIES	SIZES*	PROPORTIONS
Teen girls	7 to 14	For girls whose figures are beginning to mature
Juniors	3 to 15	For females with a slender, shorter-waisted figure
Misses	4 to 18	For females with a developed figure and average proportions; 5'5" to 5'9"
Women's	14 to 26 1X to 4X	For females with large proportions
Petites	2P to 16P	For females under 5'4" with a small body structure
Tall	8T to 18T	For females over 5'9"
Extra-Small (XS) or Petite (P)	2 to 4	
Small (S)	6 to 8	
Medium (M)	10 to 12	
Large (L)	14 to 16	
Extra-Large (XL)	18 to 20	

* Sizes may vary among manufacturers.

pants, the sales associate noted that variations can occur during production. A seam might be sewn slightly wider than usual, for example. Fabric can make a difference too. A style made with a crisp fabric might fit differently when made with a softer fabric.

For all of these reasons, trying on a garment before buying is an advantage. You can save the time it takes to return the item and find a replacement.

Size Categories for Females

When you understand how sizes are categorized, you can choose the right one for you. The sizes for female clothing represent a combination of body measurements, proportions, and height. See *Fig. 19-1.* Adult size categories include misses (even numbered sizes), juniors (odd numbered), petites, and women's. Tall sizes are also available. Special teen departments carry sizes for the developing preteen and teen figure. Girls' sizes fit preteens who have not begun to mature.

Skirts and pants are sold by size or by the waist measurement. Size 25 pants measure 25 inches (65 cm) at the waist. Sweaters, T-shirts, and other loose-fitting garments may be sold in these sizes: petite or extra small, small, medium, large, and extra large.

Size Categories for Males

Men's sizes for tailored suits, sport jackets, and coats include regular, short, and long. These are based on chest measurement and length. A size-38 jacket fits a man with a 38-inch (96.5-cm) chest. A jacket marked 38-short is 2 inches (5 cm) shorter than the regular size 38. A 38-long is for a taller man with longer arms. Some manufacturers also offer extra long, portly, and large sizes. For young males, sizes include teen boys and boys, along with special husky and slim. See *Fig. 19-2.*

Pants are sized at the waist and inseam. The **inseam** is the inside leg measurement, from the crotch to the hemmed edge of the pants. Pants labeled 28/31 have a 28-inch (71-cm) waist and a 31-inch (79-cm) inseam. (In some catalogs women's pants are also sold by inseam.)

Shirt sizes are based on the measurement around the collar and the sleeve length, such as 14/32 (36/82 cm). To find collar size, measure around the neck and add ½ inch (1.3 cm). Sleeve length is the distance from the base of the neck at the center back, across the shoulder, around the outside of a slightly bent elbow, to the wrist bone.

see→ p 443

Many shirts, sweaters, and casual jackets are available in small, medium, large, and extra-large sizes. Tops and jackets described as having a "relaxed fit" are larger through the chest and have

19-2 • Size Categories for Males		
CATEGORIES	**SIZES**	**PROPORTIONS**
Teen boys	14 to 20	For boys of average build
Slim Teen Boys	14S to 20S	For boys of slender build
Husky Teen Boys	14H to 20H	For boys of heavier build
Men's Regular	34 to 48	For males, proportionally built, 5'8" to 5'11"
Men's Short	34S to 48S	For males under 5'8"
Men's Long	38L to 48L	For males 6' to 6'3"
Men's Extra Long	38XL to 50XL	For males 6'4" and over
Men's Portly	36 to 48	For males with thicker waistlines
Men's Large	46 to 50+	For larger size males
Small (S)	34 to 36	
Medium (M)	38 to 40	
Large (L)	42 to 44	
Extra-Large (XL)	46 to 48	
Extra-Extra-Large (XXL)	50+	

wider armholes. In pants, the term means more room in the thigh and seat areas.

EVALUATING FIT

No matter what size is marked on the label, what really counts is how the garment fits. When trying on clothes, look in a full-length mirror, observing from both the front and back. Check for wrinkles and bulges that indicate a poor fit.

Many people buy clothes a bit snug, thinking this provides a slimming effect. Actually, the opposite is true. Clothing that is too tight draws attention to that fact and can add pounds to a person's appearance.

Testing the Fit

Doctors give patients a fitness test to learn whether they're physically fit. You can give clothes a "fitness" test to see how they fit physically. High marks on this test indicate the garment fits well and will be comfortable to wear. Use the suggestions below and the information on page 336 to judge the fit of a garment. see→ p 543

1. **Standing straight, check the overall appearance.** Note where and how the seams, hem, and special design features fall.

2. **Bend your arms in front of you at shoulder height.** Shirts, jackets, dresses, and blouses should be roomy enough to permit this without any strain across the shoulder blades. Sleeves should not ride up or feel uncomfortably short.

3. **Raise your arms straight up over your head.** The armholes should not bind. Jackets and coats should not feel tight in the shoulders. Blouses, shirts, and sweaters should stay tucked in. When you lower your arms, a dress should fall back in place comfortably, needing little pulling or tugging to straighten.

4. **Sit down.** Notice any strain or pull at the hip, stomach, and thigh areas. Pay attention to the waistline of pants and skirts. It should remain comfortably loose, without gapping at the center back.

5. **Stand up and bend over as if to touch your toes.** You may not plan on doing aerobics in your clothes, but you might have to lean over to pick up a napkin or tie your shoes. Even formal party clothes may need to hold up to active dance moves.

Alterations

When choosing a garment, you might take your second color choice, but you shouldn't lower the standards on fit. Sometimes a garment needs only simple alterations to make it fit properly. **Alterations** modify or change a garment in some

CHECK A GARMENT'S FIT

A garment that fits well is more likely to be worn—and it's more comfortable too. When you know what to look for, checking the fit of a garment can be easy. Here are some basic points to remember.

Collar or neckline fits close to the neck, without binding or gripping.

Armhole seams lie at the edge of shoulder unless designed otherwise.

Chest and back fit smoothly, with room for movement. Closing doesn't pull or gap.

Sleeves are loose enough to raise arm and long enough to cover wrist bone when arm is bent.

Buttons and buttonholes don't pull or strain as you move.

Jacket or coat fits comfortably over other garments.

Waistline or waistband feels comfortable, doesn't pull or bind, and allows tops to be tucked in.

Hip area skims body smoothly, without pulling or forming extra folds. Crotch doesn't wrinkle or bind.

Zipper opens and closes smoothly.

Pleats and gathers hang vertically and unbroken.

Pant legs fall straight from hipline, without wrinkles.

Hemlines are parallel to the floor, meet evenly at openings, and are the right length for body proportions and current fashion.

Exploring **Garment Fit**

With a partner, plan a class demonstration on garments that do and don't fit well. Model garments that match the points to be made. You might have one person act as the model while the other describes the fit.

At one time, the only way to have a garment made to your measurements was to make it yourself or have it made for you. Today, computers provide technology for custom sewing, called mass customization. A garment can be modified at the factory to match a customer's measurements.

First, the customer picks a garment style. Following computer instructions, the sales associate measures the customer with a tape measure or uses a

three-dimensional computerized body imaging to "scan" the customer's body dimensions. The measurements are entered into the computer, and the customer can make changes in the fit, fabric, or color.

Next, the computer sends the information to a computerized fabric-cutting machine at the factory. As the garment is cut out, special bar codes are attached to fabric pieces to track them during production. The customized garment is completed along with other individualized and mass-produced garments. The process takes several weeks. When finished, the customized garment is shipped to the store or directly to the customer.

Mass-customized garments are more expensive than mass-produced ones. For people who don't fit standard sizes or those who want a perfect fit, however, the benefits of this new technology are worthwhile.

INVESTIGATION ACTIVITY

Do any stores in your area offer mass-customization technology? If possible, arrange for a demonstration.

way. Changing the hem length, taking in a seam, shortening sleeves, or moving a button can make a big difference in a garment's appearance and comfort.

Shortening a garment is usually possible. If the item needs lengthening, however, make sure the current hem has enough fabric to let the hem down. If the garment needs to be wider, be sure the seam allowance is wide enough to accomplish this. The **seam allowance** is the extra fabric on the inside of the garment between the seam line and the fabric edge.

Alterations in tailored garments, such as suits and trousers, can be more complicated. Jackets may need adjustments in the outer fabric, shoulder pads, and lining. Tailored trousers may need adjustments in the waistband and the seat area. Usually a skilled clothier does these alterations best.

If the garment requires more than a simple alteration, it may not be a good buy. Major alterations can be expensive and may not achieve the look you want.

EVALUATING QUALITY

What does "quality" mean in clothing? Is it a high price? A designer label? Neither of these guarantees **quality**, or superior characteristics. In a garment, quality means two things: good fabric and good workmanship.

Judging Fabric

From your study of fabrics, you know they can be evaluated by more than just look and feel. A fabric has many other qualities besides an appealing pattern or a silky hand. To judge a fabric's quality, try the following tests:

- **Examine the fabric for flaws.** Is the color even throughout the garment? If the fabric is a print, do design elements and colors appear in the right place? Check for snags or pulls in the fabric, as well as stains.
- **Test wrinkle resistance.** Crush a corner of the garment in your hand. If the fabric wrinkles easily, the garment will crease easily during wear.
- **Test stretchability.** If the fabric is a stretchable weave or knit, pull to see how much it gives. Does the original shape return?
- **Be sure the fabric is "on grain."** This means the crosswise and lengthwise yarns meet at right angles. When fabric is finished on-grain and cut on-grain, the garment looks better and wears longer. Seams hang straight, without twisting to one side. The hemline hangs evenly. If a garment is cut off-grain or the fabric printed off-grain, the lines of a plaid or a striped design won't match.
- **Evaluate the fabric's suitability for use.** A delicate lace or chiffon would be a poor choice for a shirt that you plan to wear on hiking trips. Why would poplin or denim be a much better choice?

Judging Workmanship

Another test of quality is workmanship, marked by careful sewing and appropriate techniques. If fabric is loosely woven and frays easily, for example, the garment should be lined or the seams should be finished. In garments with quality workmanship, you'll notice the following:

- **Secure and even stitching.** Straight, unbroken stitching means the seams lie flat and smooth. Thread color should match fabric color, unless designed to be contrasting. Avoid garments sewn with clear nylon thread, which melts easily when ironed.
- **Matching plaids and stripes.** Check for design continuity. Plaids and stripes should match at the garment's center and side seams, and even in smaller areas—the collar, pockets, and bands.
- **Smooth, flat, unpuckered seams.** No ridges should show on the outside.
- **Properly finished seam allowances.** Check seam allowances for seam finish, if needed. A **seam finish** is any method that stitches or trims seam allowances to prevent fraying. Many ready-to-wear garments have a narrow **overlock seam**, a special combination of stitches that join the fabric and finish the seam edges in one operation. This creates a very narrow seam allowance. See *Fig. 19-3.*

see→ p 465

19-3 The seam finish can mean the difference between a seam that unravels and one that doesn't. Why is this seam likely to remain intact? Does the type of fabric affect whether a seam needs to be finished?

- **Neatly constructed darts.** Darts should be pressed smooth and flat, with no puckers and no "dimple" at the tip. They should point to the fullest part of the body. see→ p 514
- **Smooth, flat facings.** A *facing* is fabric that finishes a raw edge, such as a neckline or armhole. It is turned to the inside of the garment and shouldn't show on the outside. see→ p 524
- **Smooth collar curves and sharp corners.** A collar should cover the neckline seam, with edges lying flat to hide the under collar. The area should be finished neatly on the inside so you can wear the collar open. see→ p 556
- **Properly placed and securely stitched fasteners.** Buttons, snaps, and hooks and eyes should be firmly attached, with no loose threads. See *Fig. 19-4.* Buttonholes should be sewn with tight, even stitches. The button should slip through easily without popping back out unexpectedly. Make sure the zipper opens and closes smoothly, and stitching is straight and unbroken. see→ p 530
- **Secure and even trims.** Check for missing beads or sequins. see→ p 581
- **Straight and even hem.** The stitches of the hem shouldn't pull or pucker the fabric. In fact, they should be invisible from the right side of the garment, unless the hem is topstitched. Inspect the hem allowance on the inside of the garment. It should be an even width and finished along the edge if the fabric ravels. see→ p 537

EVALUATING CARE

For a person who hates to iron, a shirt that doesn't need pressing is probably a better choice than one that wrinkles easily. The routine care needs of a garment should be considered when evaluating what to buy. Some fabrics need more time, work, and money to keep them looking good.

Specific directions about washing, bleaching, drying, ironing, and dry cleaning are included on the care label attached to every garment. You can check the garment hangtag for any fabric finishes

19-4 If a garment is missing a button, you might not want to buy it. Finding an exact match as a replacement may not be easy. Loose buttons on a new garment that you buy should be reinforced to prevent them from falling off.

that affect care. See *Fig. 19-5* on page 340. Use the following questions to become informed about garment care needs:

- **Washability.** How often will the fabric need washing? Some fabrics, especially light-colored ones, show soil more easily than darker ones. Can the garment be washed by machine or must it be done by hand? Not all people have easy access to a washing machine. Hand washing is simple, but it takes time and space. Will you take time to hand-wash a sweater? Do you have the space to dry several items at once?
- **Dry cleaning.** Must the garment be dry-cleaned? Over a long time, dry-cleaning expenses can add up to more than the garment's cost.
- **Stain and spot resistance.** Will the fabric resist stains and spots? Some fibers absorb stains more easily than others. Special fabric finishes that help repel stains or release them in the wash make care easier. Coats, jackets, and children's clothing often have these treatments.
- **Wrinkle resistance.** Will you have to press or iron the garment to remove wrinkles? Fibers have different characteristics that affect wrinkling. Polyester is very wrinkle-resistant, but

cotton and rayon wrinkle easily. Fabric construction also affects wrinkling. A knitted cotton shirt, for example, may emerge unwrinkled from the dryer, while a woven, cotton shirt needs ironing. Special finishes, such as durable press, can improve the wrinkle resistance of many fabrics.

EVALUATING PRICE

Have you heard the expression "penny wise and pound foolish"? It means that scrimping on details or small expenses can cost more than it saves in the long run. For example, the cheapest CD player in the store can be quite costly if it ruins your CDs. The same applies to clothing when you compare cost and quality.

Cost Versus Quality

If the cost fits your budget, you might be willing to pay more for a quality garment. When a manufacturer uses fine fabric to create a well-made garment, the costs are passed along to the consumer. The price is typically higher than for a garment made of cheaper materials and inferior workmanship.

Assuming that a high price means quality, however, can be a mistake. Prices can be higher for other reasons. Adding extra trim, for example, could increase price but have no effect on quality. A designer garment might cost more than a similar one made by another manufacturer. Two garments made in different locations could have the same quality but different prices if production costs weren't the same.

To further complicate the picture, a high-priced garment could be poor quality, while a low-priced garment has high quality. Think about why. A manufacturer who buys fabric in great quantity might be able to pass along the savings. A retailer might mark up the price to get a greater profit.

What this means is that you need to judge quality carefully and knowledgeably to get the best for your money.

Cost of Care

Your financial investment in a garment goes beyond purchase price. It includes the cost of care as well. Care costs depend on how often the garment must be cleaned and the cost of the cleaning in terms of time and money.

Dry-cleaning costs are generally much higher than laundry costs. One blouse might be machine- or hand-washed for a few cents, yet another blouse costs a few dollars to dry-clean.

Money isn't the only care cost. Time and skills count too. A durable-press finish may increase a garment's price, for example, but save you time in ironing.

Which method of care do you prefer? Your choice depends on available resources and how you prioritize them. Some people prefer only machine-washable items. For others, hand washing is easy and convenient. If time is scarce or laundry equipment is unavailable, then dry cleaning may be preferred despite the cost.

Cost Per Wearing

Here's something you might not have thought about before. Increasing the number of times you wear a garment reduces the **cost per wearing**. This cost is the sum of a garment's purchase price plus the cleaning costs, divided by the number of wearings. As *Fig. 19-6* shows, this handy formula gives you another way to compare garments when making selections.

MAKING A FINAL DECISION

If you've evaluated a garment carefully, you're ready to decide whether to buy it. You've studied the fit, quality, care, and cost. Recalling earlier ideas in this unit, ask other questions. Does the garment fit your wardrobe plan? Have you gathered enough information to make a sound decision? Do you need to compare other prices and garments? With your mental checklist complete, you can make a decision.

Compromises and Trade-Offs

"After thinking about it, I knew I shouldn't buy that outfit, but I still wanted it. I felt bad about putting it back on the rack." This teen's lament is common but wise. Sometimes a purchase isn't a good idea. Listening to your sense of reasoning and logic can save you from buying something that is too costly or isn't right for you. To look on the bright side, you might try a compromise or trade-off.

A **compromise** is a settlement that comes when you give up something in favor of another option. Could you settle for lower quality and make improvements? A simple change, such as nicer buttons, might improve the appearance of a less-expensive garment. Could you make do with what you have for a while in order to wait for a sale? Back-to-school clothes might be less expensive in late fall.

A **trade-off** exchanges one thing for another. Could you trade quantity for quality? You might purchase one well-made jacket rather than two that cost less and are not as well made. You could look for shoes that can be worn with many outfits instead of special ones for every outfit. Could you make a garment instead of buying one? By sewing, you could make a garment in the exact style and color you want and save money at the same time.

19-6 Calculating the cost per wearing helps you decide what garment to buy. In comparing the jackets, will the jacket with the highest purchase price be the most costly to wear? Why? What other factors would you weigh in choosing one of the jackets to buy?

	PURCHASE PRICE	CARE NEEDED	ESTIMATED COST OF CARE	ESTIMATED NUMER OF WEARINGS	TOTAL COST	COST PER WEARING
Calculating Cost per Wearing for One Year						
Formula: Purchase Price + Cost of Care ÷ Number of Wearings = Cost Per Wearing						
Jacket A	$40	Wash	All washings = $1	40	$41	$1.03
Jacket B	$40	Dry Clean	$8 × 2 cleanings = $16	40	$56	$1.40
Jacket C	$50	Wash	All washings = $1	40	$51	$1.28
Jacket D	$60	Dry Clean	$8 × 2 cleanings = $16	40	$76	$1.90
Jacket E	$70	Wash	All washings = $1	40	$71	$1.78

Review

CHAPTER SUMMARY

- Garment size is determined by style, manufacturer, and quality, as well as the age and gender of the intended wearer.

- Examining and trying on clothes before buying can help you evaluate the fit.

- Quality clothing consists of suitable fabrics assembled with skillful workmanship.

- Considering a garment's care needs can help you decide whether it will be a good buy for you.

- When judging price, consider the garment's quality, usefulness, and cost of care.

- Making satisfactory clothing buys often means making acceptable compromises and trade-offs.

USING KEY TERMS

For each of the following Key Terms, write a tip that would help someone when deciding whether to buy a garment: cost per wearing; facing; inseam; seam allowance; and seam finish.

RECALLING THE FACTS

1. Give two reasons why garments of the same size may fit differently.

2. Two females who are obviously different in size each buy a size-10 dress. How is that possible?

3. What measurements are used to size men's pants and shirts?

4. What signs might tell you that a jacket doesn't fit you well?

5. When might it be reasonable to buy a garment that needs altering in order to fit well?

6. Describe a quality fabric.

7. In buying a shirt, what are six construction features that show quality workmanship?

8. Why should you consider care needs before buying a garment?

9. What four care considerations should be made before buying a garment?

10. Is price a reliable indicator of quality in clothing? Explain.

11. If you can't afford the garment you want, how might a compromise or trade-off help?

and Activities

THINKING CRITICALLY

1. Do you think sizes should be standardized throughout the clothing industry? For example, all size 12 garments would be the same. Would this be possible? Why or why not?

2. Why do you think pants for males often include an inseam measurement, but pants for females seldom do?

3. What are some advantages of wearing a garment that fits well?

APPLYING KNOWLEDGE

1. **Comparing sizes.** Using garment catalogs, compare sizing charts. What similarities and differences do you find?

2. **Examples of fit.** Look for magazine photos that illustrate how garments fit. Create a poster that shows at least six points made in the chapter about good fit.

3. **Fit versus cost.** You're trying on shirts in a store. One shirt, priced at $30, fits very well. Another shirt also fits well, except the sleeves are a couple inches too long. It costs $21. Which shirt would you buy? Why?

4. **Evaluating quality.** Look at several garments in different price ranges in a store. Evaluate the fabric and workmanship on each. What differences do you see? Are the best fabrics and workmanship always on the more expensive garments? Report your findings.

5. **Evaluating care.** Survey the class to find out how many students read care labels before buying a garment. Why would this be a good habit to start?

6. **Cost per wearing.** Choose three similar garments from a catalog or advertisement, including at least one that requires dry cleaning and one that doesn't. Use these items to create a cost-per-wearing chart similar to the one on page 341. Estimate care costs and the number of wearings per year. Which garment do you think is the best buy? Why?

CREATIVE SOLUTIONS

In a catalog you've found a garment that you think you want to buy. Your only question is whether its quality is worth the price. You wish you could examine the garment itself, but all you have is a small picture and description in the catalog.

Think Creatively

How can you determine whether the garment has the quality you want?

Consumer Responsibilities

OBJECTIVES

- Explain the consumer's responsibilities when shopping.

- Compare various ways to pay for items.

- Describe how to make exchanges and returns.

- Identify consumer protection laws, regulations, agencies, and organizations.

KEY TERMS

arbitration	mediation
credit card	money order
debit card	recalled
finance charge	standards
hidden costs	toxic

S UPPOSE YOU'RE DRIVING A CAR, waiting to make a left-hand turn against a long line of oncoming traffic. A driver in the line sees your plight, stops, and motions you through. You wave your thanks and travel on your way.

The marketplace works on a similar basis of lawfulness, fair play, and courtesy. Buyers and sellers alike rely on rules to keep the process moving and on the kindness of others to make it run smoothly.

THE RESPONSIBLE CONSUMER

If you see an outfit on a clearance rack because someone returned it without the belt, is that a good deal? The money you save on the outfit may not be worth the time and effort it takes to find a new belt. Meanwhile, the retailer raises other prices to make up for the loss.

One consumer's neglect affects many others. Who pays to clean and repair clothes damaged by careless shoppers? Who pays for items stolen by shoplifters and for the higher insurance premi-

ums that can result? Who pays for the extra workers' hours spent handling returns and exchanges? Who makes up the difference if these goods are sold at a loss?

The expenses for customer carelessness, theft, and returns are included in an item's **hidden costs**. See *Fig. 20-1*. Storeowners absorb some of these costs, denying them a fair profit. Others are passed on to buyers in the form of higher prices. If items are priced beyond your budget, then the hidden costs limit your choices. If losses drive a retailer out of business, the costs are very high indeed.

Since this problem is caused one customer at a time, it can be solved the same way. Through consideration, honesty, and an understanding of store policies, each shopper helps reduce hidden costs.

Show Consideration

Consideration of others is easy when you're having a good time shopping with a friend at the mall. On the other hand, if you're tired and frustrated because you can't find what you want, you may be tempted to complain too loudly or slip ahead of others in line. Treating people rudely, however, never solves a problem.

To do what's right, put yourself in the other person's place. Remember that the sales associate doesn't set prices or control inventory. With a

20-1 Damage to merchandise costs the retailer and eventually the buyer.

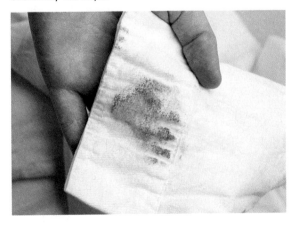

smile and pleasant, polite attitude, you're likely to get better service. You might even make a positive difference for someone who's having a difficult day. Remember, too, that other shoppers dislike long lines as much as you do and want to shop without aggravation. People will appreciate your willingness to wait your turn in line to pay or for a dressing room, to not block aisles, and to keep talk and laughter at a reasonable volume. A considerate shopper understands other points of view and reacts thoughtfully.

Handle Merchandise Carefully

Handling clothes and other items with care is another form of consideration. A footprint or a lipstick stain, left while trying on a garment, shows careless disregard for the store. Following a few guidelines helps prevent accidental damage when trying on clothes.

- Try on only what fits. Broken zippers, lost buttons, and ripped seams result from trying to squeeze into garments that are too small.

Trends in
TECHNOLOGY

››PREVENTING SHOPLIFTING AND THEFT

Shoplifting and employee theft are costly crimes for everyone. Storeowners must raise prices to cover the costs of goods that "disappear" from their stores. Experts estimate that every consumer in America pays hundreds of dollars per year to make up for these losses. Security guards are part of the solution. Also, many new devices help control shoplifting and employee theft.

- **Electronic article surveillance.** These heavy, plastic, security tags are attached to garments and other merchandise. If the tag isn't removed with special equipment at the cashier's desk when the item is sold, special sensors at the store's exits set off an alarm. With some versions of the tag, a nonwashable ink spreads over the garment when the tag is improperly removed. Another type beeps and sets off an alarm if tampering occurs. Some garments have smaller tags hidden in a pocket or seam allowance and must be deactivated.

- **Weight sensor devices.** These electronic surveillance devices sound an alarm or recording that other shoppers can hear when an item is removed or added to a shelf or rack. Some of the devices also send an electronic alarm to the nearest sales associate.

- **Closed circuit cameras.** These cameras hang from the ceiling, fit into rack lighting, and hide behind wall panels. A special mannequin has a camera hidden behind her glass eyes and a hidden microphone that allows security personnel to hear conversations.

INVESTIGATION ACTIVITY
Find out what the penalties are for shoplifting. Report your findings.

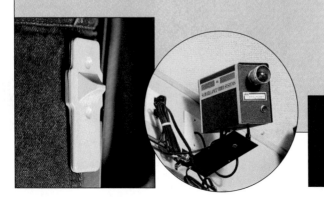

- Pull garments over your head carefully to prevent makeup stains.
- Take off shoes before stepping into a garment. The fabric stays clean, and you won't catch your shoe in the hem.
- Remove any jewelry that might snag fabric.
- Leave all labels, hangtags, and price tags on garments. Replacing them costs the store time and money.
- Keep garments and accessories on hangers before and after trying them on. They might get wrinkled or dirty on the fitting room floor.
- Return unwanted items to the sales associate or checker.

Be Honest

Shoplifters cost retailers in North America over $10 million in merchandise every day. Some of these costs are passed on to consumers as higher prices. Shoplifting and employee theft are crimes that can result in stiff fines, legal supervision, a jail sentence, and a lifetime police record.

Many stores are taking greater steps to combat these crimes, whether committed by customers or by employees. Some methods are described on page 346.

Understand Store Policies

A retailer doesn't typically sell long-sleeved shirts just as warm weather sets in, yet a store-owner may have little choice when customers take weeks to return items. The markdown on these "leftovers" is another hidden cost caused by inconsiderate shoppers.

Before buying, learn the store's policies, usually posted in the store. If you can't find them, ask these questions: Can you return the item? How long after you have bought it? Will you get cash or store credit?

If you're not paying with cash, check store policy for other acceptable payment methods. Although some stores accept credit and debit cards, others don't. Some accept personal checks.

To help avoid exchanges and returns, check the fit and quality of an item before you buy. Save the sales receipt, hangtags, and any warranties that come with your purchase. See *Fig. 20-2*. The sales slip proves where you bought the merchandise and how much was paid. If you must return the item for any reason, you'll need to show the sales slip. The warranties and hangtags give valuable information about the performance of your purchase.

PAYING FOR PURCHASES

When you buy something, the methods for payment allow you to pay now with cash, or later with credit. The various methods for each have both advantages and disadvantages.

Making Cash Transactions

Although the word *cash* usually means paper money or coins, any payment made at the time of sale can be called a cash transaction. Paying right away makes controlling expenditures easier because you can't spend more than you have.

Instead of using actual cash, immediate payment can also be made with a check, debit card, or money order. Layaway plans are another option. C.O.D., which stands for cash on delivery, is seldom used anymore. With this method, people pay the delivery person when merchandise arrives. Many stores and companies no longer ship C.O.D. because often no one is home to make the payment.

Cash

Since all stores take hard currency, or cash, this is usually the quickest and simplest means of pay-

20-2 If you save store sales receipts, you can exchange merchandise when necessary.

ment. No extra costs are involved, such as the financing charge on a credit transaction.

With cash, you can spend only as much money as you're carrying. As some say, "once it's gone, it's gone." Unfortunately, the same expression applies to cash that disappears. When carrying sums of money, you risk loss and theft.

Check

A check authorizes a store to withdraw a specified amount of money from your bank account. Before accepting your check, most stores ask for proof of who you are. A driver's license or a credit card can be used for identification.

When writing a check, write clearly in ink, as shown in *Fig. 20-3*. Be sure to record the check number, the date of purchase, the name of the store, and the amount in the check register.

A new twist on writing checks is point-of-purchase check conversion. The cashier runs a blank check through an electronic reader. The reader records the check number and account information, which is used to deduct the purchase amount from the account. The cashier returns the check, stamped "void," along with a copy of the sale and a receipt to sign, which authorizes the electronic debit, a subtracted amount. This deduction appears on your monthly bank statement.

20-3 To write a check, fill in items B, C, E, F, and G. H can be entered as a personal reminder. A is already printed on the check and should not include such personal information as a social security number.

Writing a Check

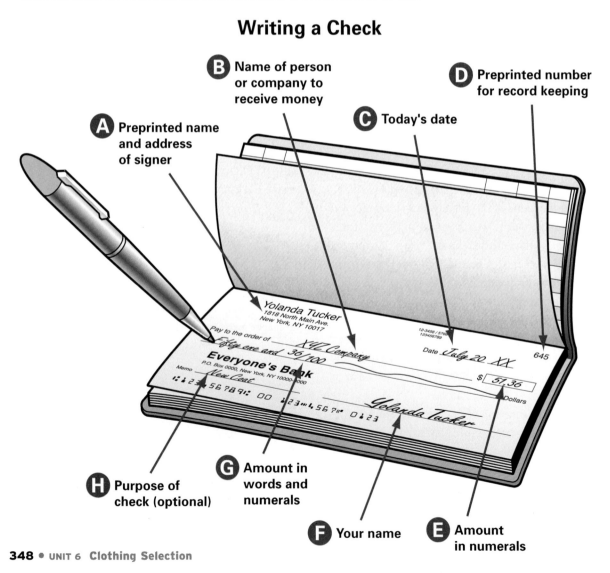

B Name of person or company to receive money

D Preprinted number for record keeping

C Today's date

A Preprinted name and address of signer

H Purpose of check (optional)

G Amount in words and numerals

F Your name

E Amount in numerals

Paying by check reduces the need to carry cash. Extra time might be necessary, however, especially when a store manager must verify all forms of identification. Some stores won't accept checks.

Checks can also be used to order merchandise from catalogs. They are much safer than sending cash through the mail.

Debit Card

When you pay by **debit card**, money is transferred electronically from your checking account to the store's account via computer. See *Fig. 20-4*. The amount is immediately debited from your account. You receive a printed record of each deduction so you can make sure the bank records of your account are accurate.

Debit cards offer the convenience of credit cards without the added fees, but also without the safeguards. If your credit card is stolen, for example, you're responsible for no more than $50 of

20-4 Debit cards, also known as check cards, look like credit and ATM cards. When you use a debit card, your money is quickly deducted from your bank account. Some banks issue ATM cards that function as debit cards too.

unauthorized charges. With a debit card, you may be responsible for all charges up to $500 if you fail to immediately notify the company that issued the card.

Money Order

Like a check, a **money order** is a document stating that money is to be paid to a particular person or store named on the form. Unlike checks, money orders are bought individually from a post office or private company, such as a bank. You pay the face amount plus a service charge. Money orders are useful if you want to make a payment by mail but don't have a checking account.

Layaway

With a layaway plan, you give the store a small down payment to hold an item for you. Then you pay a certain amount of money each week or month until the total amount is paid, plus a service charge. After the store has received the full payment, you receive the garment purchased. This is a useful way to buy an expensive item that you don't need immediately, such as a winter coat on sale in August. On the other hand, the store has the use of your money while you pay for the garment.

Using Credit

Instead of cash, purchases can also be made with the credit method. A **credit card** allows the cardholder to buy and receive merchandise, but pay for it later. In effect, you're renting the money for a certain amount of time and paying a fee for the service. When you buy on credit, the financial institution or company that issued the credit card pays the price to the store for you. Then each month you pay back some or all of the debt to the card issuer.

While credit card offers appear many places these days, getting a card depends on information collected about an applicant. Some is on the application form. Income, existing bank accounts, and credit history indicate a person's credit risk. You must be age eighteen or older to get credit in your own name, but some issuers let

20-5 When you make a purchase with a credit card, the sales associate swipes your card through a reading device. A telephone number may be entered for verification.

younger teens use a parent's card with parental permission. Parents can also buy special cards for teens, with a spending limit set by the parents.

Types of Credit Cards

The three basic types of credit cards are determined by who issues them. All can be used in the same way, although not every store accepts all cards. See *Fig. 20-5*. Many credit cards can be used to obtain cash advances from an automated teller machine, or ATM.

- **Bank cards.** These are issued by financial institutions and processed through Mastercard®, Visa®, or Novus® (Discover) networks.
- **Company cards.** A store or a catalog may issue its own card, which can only be used for purchases at that company.
- **Travel and entertainment cards.** These are issued by such companies as American Express® and Diner's Club®.

Monthly Statement

A credit card bill comes in a monthly statement, a status report of your account. The statement shows the amount of your last bill, any payments made, and any credits or returns. It lists each purchase charged to the account since the last statement, any additional fees, and the total amount owed. See *Fig. 20-6*.

The statement shows the minimum payment amount to make for the month, usually ten percent of the total. This amount must be received by a specific date to be on time. The statement also includes the available line of credit. This is the maximum amount of money that can be charged by the cardholder.

To catch possible errors, save receipts and compare them to each monthly statement. If you discover an error, you must follow the specific procedures outlined by the credit card issuer. Look on the credit card or monthly statement for a toll-free number to call for billing inquiries and customer service.

Finance Charges

A **finance charge** is a fee added for the use of credit. If you make only a partial payment rather than the full amount owed, a finance charge is added to the next monthly statement.

A finance charge is figured as a percentage of the monthly bill, typically around 1.5 percent. This is an annual percentage rate (APR) of 18

20-6 A monthly statement shows what has been billed to an account and what is owed. What other information does it contain?

| | | | | | C-031460 | A |
| | | | | | | (309) 682-2600 |

Famous-Barr Account Summary BILLING QUESTIONS?

To avoid incurring additional finance charges ▼ you may remit your new balance in full within 25 days of the billing date shown below

PREVIOUS BALANCE	+PURCHASES	+FINANCE CHARGE	-PAYMENTS	-CREDITS	=NEW BALANCE
.00	58.86	.00	.00	5.87	52.99

ANNUAL PERCENTAGE RATE	MONTHLY PERIODIC RATE	AVERAGE DAILY BAL.		PAST DUE AMOUNT	PAYMENT NOW DUE
21.60	1.800				20.00

ACCOUNT TYPE			BILLING DATE	PLEASE MAIL B
FLEX			08/24/01	09/17/01

This bill contains transactions through ▼

NOTICE: See reverse side for important information.

percent per year. According to the Truth-in-Lending Law, the credit card issuer must provide the annual percentage rate in writing. State law controls the maximum rate.

Although you could pay as little as ten dollars on some bills each month, paying the full amount means no finance charge will be added. When a balance is carried over from month to month, finance charges can add up quickly.

Weighing Advantages and Disadvantages

Credit represents the "buy now, pay later" idea of budgeting. Unfortunately, "pay later" often means "pay more." Used wisely, credit has a number of advantages, but as *Fig. 20-7* shows, it also has disadvantages. Before using credit, weigh the pros and cons carefully. Credit is best used only when you know you have the resources to pay the debt before it comes due.

If you choose to use a credit card, remember that your card and account represent real money, just like cash. Guard the card well. Be sure your card is returned each time you use it. Keep a record of your credit card number in a safe place. If your card is lost or stolen, notify the issuer immediately.

EXCHANGES AND RETURNS

If something is wrong with a clothing purchase, you can return it promptly to the store for exchange, credit, or refund. Any item you buy should perform properly.

Acting in Good Faith

Responsible consumers act in "good faith" by exchanging or returning merchandise only for legitimate reasons. For example, a water-repellent raincoat shouldn't leak in a light drizzle; the heel shouldn't come off a shoe during the first wearing; and a shirt shouldn't fade after one washing. Receiving a gift that's the wrong size isn't the seller's fault, but this, too, is a legitimate reason for a return.

A store shouldn't be expected to exchange or refund merchandise that has been mishandled. Did the shirt fade because it was washed in hot water rather than cold, as the label instructed? If a sweater labeled "dry-clean only" shrinks when washed, this isn't the store's fault. Consumers must accept responsibility for problems they cause themselves.

Expectations about the wear and performance of a garment should also be reasonable. If a new bathing suit fades after two wearings, returning is reasonable. If it fades after two months of frequent wear, returning isn't appropriate.

20-7 • Advantages and Disadvantages of Using Credit	
ADVANTAGES	**DISADVANTAGES**
Customer can enjoy merchandise, including more expensive items, while making payments.	People are more likely to buy on impulse, resulting in unneeded items and bills that are hard to repay.
Making returns is simplified since the amount is credited to the account electronically.	Finance charges increase the cost of items and add up quickly.
Customer can pay for all purchases on the monthly statement with one check or money order.	Extra fees may be added for late payments.
When ordering by telephone, using a credit card is more convenient than mailing a check or money order.	Some credit cards have an annual fee or membership fee of $25 or more.
Customer can shop with little or no cash.	Credit card or account numbers can be stolen and used by others.
Emergency expenses can be covered.	Late or missed payments can result in a poor credit rating, damaging a person's ability to get credit in the future.

Complaining Effectively

According to the saying, "you catch more flies with honey than with vinegar." Let this be your guide when you have reason to complain about an item or service. People are motivated more by kind words than harsh ones.

Try to make it easier for people to help you. First, go to the right place. Start with the department where you purchased the merchandise and talk to a sales associate or department manager. Some stores have a customer service department that handles all complaints. If the problem isn't solved, ask to see the store manager or owner. Proceed up the chain of command as far as you feel the problem merits. See page 354 for more information on making effective complaints.

If you are persistent and act in good faith, your problem will usually be resolved. Most stores and manufacturers want satisfied customers who will continue to purchase merchandise and services.

CONSUMER PROTECTION

You may have heard that rights and responsibilities go hand in hand. They certainly do in the marketplace. A consumer's responsibilities are balanced by legally protected rights.

Consumer Bill of Rights

In the past, consumer protection was a personal matter—you looked out for yourself. Few laws protected consumers from unfair business practices, before or after a sale.

In 1962 in a special address to Congress, President John F. Kennedy introduced the landmark Consumer Bill of Rights. It was created because of mounting problems that consumers were having with goods and services. More legislation, backed by Presidents Richard Nixon and Gerald Ford, added other consumer rights. Six basic rights are now written into law. They are as follows:

- **Right to safety.** Protects against manufacturing and selling goods that are hazardous to health or property.
- **Right to be informed.** Requires sellers to disclose relevant facts and to advertise and label products truthfully.
- **Right to choose.** Gives consumers a variety of reasonably priced goods and services by barring businesses from unfairly limiting competition or controlling prices.
- **Right to be heard.** Gives consumers a voice in legislation and decisions that affect them.
- **Right to redress.** Entitles consumers to have problems corrected or receive compensation for damages. See *Fig. 20-8.*
- **Right to consumer education.** Provides for ready access to facts needed to make a good choice, such as safety, pricing, and buying guidelines.

Consumer Agencies and Organizations

Consumers are responsible for knowing and acting on their rights. They also have help from government and private groups. Some government agencies are responsible for enforcing laws that affect consumers. Private organizations usually focus on certain consumer issues of interest to their membership.

- **Federal Trade Commission (FTC).** This federal agency is the marketplace "police." Its

20-8 Because the Consumer Bill of Rights provides the right to redress, you can return an unsatisfactory item to the store. What determines whether you exchange the item or get your money back?

mission is to eliminate unfair or deceptive business practices and remove threats to informed choice. The FTC enforces consumer protection laws and promotes consumer awareness. It is responsible for the fiber identification and care labeling laws.

- **Consumer Product Safety Commission (CPSC).** Also a federal agency, the CPSC guards the public against physical harm related to consumer goods, such as flammable fabrics and hazardous substances. It helps industries develop voluntary **standards**, specific models of quality or performance against which products are judged, and enforces mandatory safety standards of its own. The agency also educates consumers on product safety issues.
- **Better Business Bureau (BBB).** This is a private, nonprofit, voluntary alliance of businesses. Members agree to follow standards of ethical behavior to promote public confidence in the marketplace. The BBB helps consumers settle complaints against member businesses through **mediation**, settling a dispute with the help of a neutral third party. Some cases move

on to **arbitration**, the settlement of a dispute by a person or panel that hears each party and issues a decision. The BBB also provides consumers with a member's history regarding complaints and resolutions. See *Fig. 20-9.*

Government Regulations

Basic consumer rights are enforced through volumes of federal, state, and local regulations. Some laws specifically relate to the textile and apparel industries. Others apply to consumer transactions, such as credit use.

- **Textile Fiber Products Identification Act (TFPIA).** This legislation specifies that the generic name of every fiber (unless under 5 percent of total fiber weight), percentage of each fiber, name or identification of the manufacturer, and country of origin must appear on the labels of textile products.
- **Care Labeling Rule.** This ruling regulates the care information that must appear on the permanent care labels attached to garments and other textile products. The latest revision, in 1997, authorizes the use of certain symbols in place of words.
- **Wool Products Labeling Act.** This law requires manufacturers to identify the type

20-9 Before you do business with an unfamiliar company, you can call the Better Business Bureau to find out whether any complaints have been filed against it.

How To...

COMPLAIN EFFECTIVELY

When you have a problem with something you've bought, you may need to take action. The procedure described here should bring results. If any step isn't successful, go on to the next.

1. Take the item and sales receipt to the place of purchase. Explain the problem politely and calmly to the sales associate, manager, or customer service representative.

2. Write a letter to the store, addressing the owner, president, or head of customer service. Describe the item or service, the problem, and how and when it occurred. State what you would like done, and include your name and address. Enclose a copy of the sales receipt, not the original.

3. Write to the manufacturer's Customer Relations Department. Enclose a copy of your letter to the store and a copy of the sales receipt. You can obtain a company's address from the Internet or library reference books. If the response is unsatisfactory, write directly to the company president.

4. Notify the store or manufacturer of your intent to contact the Better Business Bureau. Most stores and manufacturers don't want a negative reputation and may deal with your complaint at this point. If that doesn't happen, contact the Bureau for help. Other resources are the consumer reporter at a local newspaper or television station.

5. For serious problems, contact a lawyer or legal service for assistance. Less serious complaints can be settled in a small claims court where you present your own case before a judge.

Exploring Complaining Effectively

Learn more about how the Better Business Bureau helps consumers by visiting its Web site on the Internet.

and amount of wool used in a garment, its country of origin, and whether it's new or recycled.

- **Fur Products Labeling Act.** By law, apparel manufacturers must indicate the fur used in a garment, the country of origin, and whether the fur has been dyed.
- **Flammable Fabrics Act.** This legislation, revised in 1971, is still the standard for fabric safety. It bans the sale of dangerously flammable fabrics and apparel. The law helped develop the standards for children's flame-retardant sleepwear. See *Fig. 20-10.* Mattresses, rugs, carpets, and some upholstery fabrics also have flammability standards.
- **Federal Hazardous Substance Act.** This act requires that potential choking hazards, such as buttons and other decorations on children's clothing, pass use and abuse tests. It also prohibits the use of lead paint on children's items, including clothing and buttons. Lead is particularly **toxic**, or poisonous, to young children, who tend to put many things in their mouth.
- **Consumer Credit Protection Act.** This requires creditors to explain all terms of the credit agreement clearly. It includes the Truth-in-Lending Law, by which creditors must disclose, in writing, the interest charged on the balance, both as a monthly percentage and an annual percentage rate (APR). This makes it easier to shop for credit. Truth in Lending also limits your liability for charges made if your credit card is stolen.
- **Fair Credit Billing Act.** If you have a problem with a charge on your statement or with an item purchased, this provides recourse. You must notify the creditor of the problem in writing within 60 days. The creditor has 30 days to respond and 90 days to resolve the situation. You don't have to pay the disputed amount until the question is settled.

Protecting Yourself

Government regulations and voluntary standards are valuable protections in the marketplace. Responsibility for getting a fair deal, however, rests with consumers themselves.

Investigating products and companies before you buy is part of your right to consumer education. Disclosure laws, such as Truth in Lending, and modern communications technology make exercising this right easier than ever. At the same time, they demand a more critical approach from you. For example, how do you know whether an Internet source is reliable? Is the "whitening" power claimed for a laundry detergent found only in that product?

Regulations have cut down on abuses, but a clever marketer can find ways around the law. You may need input from a variety of sources. *Consumer Reports* magazine has a reputation for testing products thoroughly. The FTC Web site lists defective products that have been **recalled**, or ordered returned to the manufacturer for repair or replacement. A neighbor might give good advice from personal experience.

As a consumer, you have both rights and responsibilities. If you use them wisely, you can enjoy what the marketplace has to offer.

20-10 This label shows that these pajamas for a child are flame-resistant. Thousands of serious burn injuries have been prevented since laws were established to ban flammable fabrics in children's sleepwear.

CHAPTER SUMMARY

- Shoppers have a responsibility to show consideration, honesty, and respect for store policies.

- Purchases may be made with different types of cash and credit payments. Each method has advantages and disadvantages.

- When handled correctly, exchanges and returns can go smoothly for consumers and businesses.

- Consumers have certain rights that are protected by government and private agencies and are written into law.

- By learning and exercising both their responsibilities and rights, consumers help ensure a good shopping experience for themselves and others.

USING KEY TERMS

Most people are familiar with the Key Term credit card. Debit cards and money orders, however, may be less familiar. Research how these work and plan a demonstration for the class.

RECALLING THE FACTS

1. Explain how responsible consumers affect clothing prices.

2. Describe five actions that show care when trying on clothes.

3. Describe three methods businesses use to deal with theft.

4. Compare the advantages of using cash with those of using checks.

5. How does layaway differ from credit?

6. What information about a credit account can you learn by reading a monthly statement?

7. What are three advantages and three disadvantages of using credit?

8. Give three tips for using credit wisely.

9. How does acting in good faith relate to consumer responsibilities?

10. List the six basic rights guaranteed by law in the Consumer Bill of Rights.

11. Name and describe three private and government agencies that help protect consumers.

12. Why are the Flammable Fabrics Act and the Federal Hazardous Substance Act especially valuable to parents of small children?

13. How does the Truth-in-Lending Law protect consumers?

14. Describe ways that consumers can help protect themselves in the marketplace.

and Activities

THINKING CRITICALLY

1. A shoplifter says, "But I only took one little item." Why is this reasoning flawed?

2. Do you think consumer protection is more necessary in today's world than it was in the past? What about protection for businesses? Explain.

APPLYING KNOWLEDGE

1. **Customer reactions.** Write a description of a reasonable response in each of these situations: you've been waiting in line and the busy sales associate starts to wait on a person who just walked up; while waiting on you, the sales associate takes a phone call that lasts several minutes; after leaving a store, you notice that the sales associate charged you full price rather than the sale price. Compare responses with class members.

2. **Role reversal.** Imagine that you have a part-time job as a sales associate. Describe ways to show courtesy and appreciation for customers.

3. **Credit terms.** Bring and compare informational literature from credit card applications. Identify the APR and other terms and charges. Which offers are the best?

4. **Return policies.** Visit the Web sites of two national or regional clothing retailers to learn each store's return and exchange policy. How are store policies similar? What might explain any differences?

5. **Letter of complaint.** When shopping for shoes, you find a sale that allows you to buy a second pair at half price. The store doesn't have your size for the second pair, so the sales associate tells you to buy the wrong size and exchange the shoes later. When you return to exchange the shoes, a different associate expects you to pay the difference in price on the shoes and won't make the exchange unless you pay. Write a letter of complaint to the company.

6. **Product research.** Choose an item you would like to buy. Use consumer magazines, catalogs, the Internet, and store visits to research the item. Which brand and model would you buy? Why?

CREATIVE SOLUTIONS

You are shopping for clothes with a friend. Your friend takes three shirts into the fitting room but comes out with only two. When you ask, "Did you forget one?" your friend says, "No, I just had the two." You suspect your friend is trying to shoplift. You don't want to make accusations, but you know that getting caught will mean embarrassment and worse consequences for your friend.

Think Creatively

How do you handle this possible shoplifting situation with your friend?

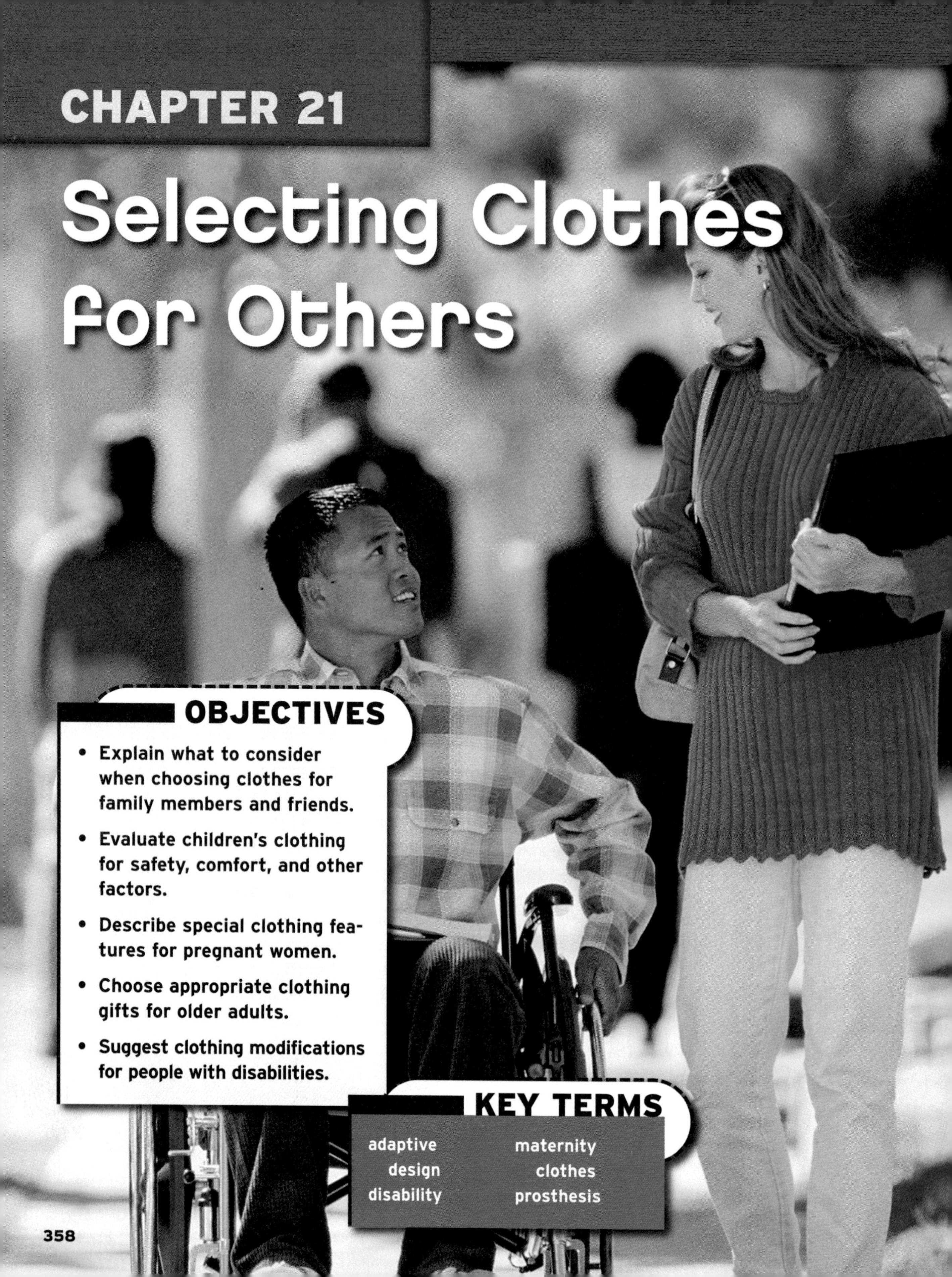

Selecting Clothes for Others

OBJECTIVES

- Explain what to consider when choosing clothes for family members and friends.

- Evaluate children's clothing for safety, comfort, and other factors.

- Describe special clothing features for pregnant women.

- Choose appropriate clothing gifts for older adults.

- Suggest clothing modifications for people with disabilities.

KEY TERMS

adaptive
design
disability

maternity
clothes
prosthesis

HAS THIS EVER HAPPENED TO YOU? You give a gift to someone—perhaps a sweater or scarf that you like enough to wear yourself—but you never see the person wear it. Why did that happen? Maybe the gift was better suited for you than the receiver.

Shopping for someone else often means putting aside your own tastes and seeing with the eyes of the other person. To choose well, you not only think about size but also about the person's individual characteristics.

SHOPPING FOR FAMILY AND FRIENDS

A grandmother's birthday, a new baby in the family, a friend leaving for college—these are just a few occasions when a gift of clothing might be appreciated. Buying a gift certificate is easy, but taking the time to choose something special is as much a gift as the garment itself. See *Fig. 21-1.*

When you choose a gift for someone who has little time or opportunity to shop, you're doing a special favor for the person. New mothers, for example, are often too busy and too tired to spend time shopping. You might enjoy the experience, however, if you know what to look for. With some basic information in mind, you can choose clothing gifts that you'll be glad to give, and your friends and family will be pleased to receive.

Consider the Needs of Others

Before shopping for a friend or relative, listen for clues about the person's needs and wants. The remark, "This old belt has about had it," gives an obvious gift idea. Listen for such comments as these: "I wonder where Paul got that sweater; I really like it" or "I need a new denim shirt to replace my old one." If you write down gift ideas as you observe them, you'll have a reference list when gift-giving occasions come along. Some people keep such information on index cards, either filed at home or in their purse or wallet.

21-1 A gift is special when you've chosen it carefully.

Interests and Activities

If you don't get any clues about possible gifts, focus on a person's interests. A teen who likes fashion, for example, might want the latest fad. Consider hobbies. How about special garden gloves or a wide-brimmed sun hat for an avid gardener? An amateur baker or potter might like a sturdy, washable apron. A sports enthusiast might need running shorts, a warm-up suit, or athletic socks.

If you know what activities a person likes, you might think of a compatible gift. What gifts might be good for people who spend time outdoors, traveling, or at formal events? Think about occupation too. An employed person might need something to wear to work. A stay-at-home parent might like casual wear.

21-2 If you consider a person's hobbies and interests, you might think of suitable gift ideas. What gifts might be enjoyed by someone who likes to garden?

Gifts that match a person's interests and activities are usually the best. Choosing them takes thought, but the time is well spent. See *Fig. 21-2.*

Styles and Colors

Tastes in clothing are like tastes in pizza. A group of friends may agree to order a pizza, but what kind? Sausage, pepperoni, or meatless? Onion, green pepper, or black olives? Likewise, choices in clothing differ, even among close friends. While some people like the latest fashions, others prefer more traditional styles, and some create styles of their own. Before choosing gifts for friends and family, take note of their personal style preferences.

Your favorite color may not be the best choice for someone else. Does the person you're buying for wear bright colors and geometric designs or subdued prints and solids? On your index card of gift ideas for individuals, add the colors of their favorite garments. If you choose something that coordinates with a person's existing wardrobe, it's like giving several gifts in one. A plaid scarf might go with both a blazer and sweater. A pale yellow shirt could go with a skirt and pants.

On the other hand, a gift that's just a bit different can be fun. If you see another side to a friend's personality, you can help bring it out with the right gift.

Size

Often the first question asked by a sales associate is this: "What size do you need?" In clothing, a good fit is basic to a good buy. The sizes that friends and family take are something else to add to your index cards of gift information. Update this information periodically.

Since sizes may vary among manufacturers, developing an eye for size is helpful. Note how a medium in one clothing line compares to another, and how both relate to the size of the person you're buying for. Save receipts in case you choose the wrong size. Many stores supply gift receipts that can be wrapped with the gift so the person can exchange for another size or return the item if there's a problem. The price doesn't appear on the receipt. See *Fig. 21-3.*

21-3 If you enclose a gift receipt when you give a gift, the receiver can easily make an exchange. Some stores tape gift receipts inside the box.

If you're not sure of a person's size, look at accessories. Scarves, ties, hats, bags, and jewelry are popular gifts because "one size fits all."

Consider Your Resources

"Why do I always want to spend too much for gifts?" one teen wondered. It's common for the heart to say that no gift is too expensive, while the bank account says otherwise. Fortunately, reasonable people don't expect you to spend more than the budget allows. Extravagant gifts are even apt to make others feel uncomfortable.

Making or sewing a gift instead of buying one is a good option. A handcrafted item can be designed to the person's specific tastes or interests. Even a gift that's less than professional earns appreciation for the time and effort—two invaluable resources—used to create it.

CHOOSING CLOTHES FOR CHILDREN

Anyone who browses thrift shops and garage sales knows that they offer many secondhand clothes for infants and children. Physical growth, not fashion, makes parents quickly discard youngsters' clothes. In the first year of life, the human body grows faster than at any other time.

Toddlers, from ages one to three, also have a fast rate of physical development. The twelve-month-old child tottering on two feet is soon running, climbing, tossing balls, and pedaling a tricycle.

At any age or stage of development, children have certain clothing needs. See *Fig. 21-4*. The most adorable outfit in the store is a poor choice unless it is the right size and meets standards for safety, comfort, durability, practicality, ease of dressing, color, and texture.

Children's Sizes

Clothing sizes for young children are based on weight, height, and body proportions in different age groups. The three size categories are shown in *Fig. 21-5* on page 362. Note that toddlers' sizes include extra room to allow for diapers. Children's sizes are designed for young children who are taller and more slender than toddlers, and no "diaper allowance" is included.

Choosing the right size for a child can be confusing. Don't go by the child's age. Most children fit best in sizes that are larger than their actual

21-4 Around age four many children develop an interest in their clothes. When buying for them, you might first try to find out what they like.

21-5 • Size Categories for Children		
CATEGORY	**AGE RANGE**	**SIZES**
Infants	Newborn to one year	Months: 0-3, 6, 9, 12, 18, and 24* Other sizes: newborn, small, medium, large, extra-large (weight ranges usually on hangtag)
Toddlers	One to three years	2T, 3T, and 4T
Children	Three to six years	Females: 3, 4, 5, 6, and 6X Males: 3, 4, 5, 6, and 7

* Infants typically wear a size that is larger than their actual age.

age. For example, on a baby's first birthday, the child may wear an eighteen-month or twenty-four-month size. A two-year-old toddler might wear a size 3T or even 4T.

Infants outgrow a size very quickly, so most people try to buy sizes they can grow into. You'll need to think about the season when the garment will be worn in order to choose a suitable style and fabric.

Safety

Safety first is the rule for children's clothing. A proper fit is basic to safety. Poorly fitting clothes that hinder movement, such as pants that are too long and dangling shoelaces, can cause stumbles and falls. Shoes that have Velcro™ fasteners and nonslip soles are safer. If long drawstrings on hoods and flowing scarves catch in strollers, play equipment, or school-bus doors, they can cause strangulation. Remove or replace these details before giving the item as a gift.

Children learn by doing and testing. No inborn sense tells them not to put loose buttons or trims in their mouth. Therefore, avoid buttons, beads, sequins, and other decorations that are easily pulled off and swallowed. Adults must eliminate such potential choking hazards from the start.

Another essential safety feature is flame-retardant fabrics for children's sleepwear. The Flammable Fabrics Act requires that sleepwear, size twelve months and larger, be treated to prevent the fabric from burning quickly if acciden-

tally ignited. Note that these garments are not fireproof. Be sure to follow care label instructions for laundering to retain the flame-retardant properties.

Children also need more protection from weather than adults do. Small hats, mittens, and sunglasses make practical gifts. Hats may be a safer alternative to large hoods that can block a child's view. See *Fig. 21-6*. Talented knitters can make some of these items themselves.

Comfort

Comfortable clothes encourage a child to move, play, and explore. Clothing should fit well, yet allow free movement. Popular choices for infants

21-6 A child's hat protects sensitive skin while keeping sunshine out of the eyes.

and toddlers are one-piece playsuits and overalls that fit easily over diapers. Simple dress styles that hang from the shoulders are also popular.

Look for features that hold clothing in place. Straps that cross in the back, for example, are less likely to fall from the shoulders. Shoulder tabs on shirts also hold straps.

With their sensitive skin, babies, especially, need soft clothing. Cotton fabrics, which breathe well, help keep infants dry and comfortable. Stretchy knits provide freedom of movement without restriction.

Durability and Practicality

Young children need well-made clothing suited for active lives. Firmly knitted or tightly woven fabrics, such as broadcloth, denim, and corduroy, are sturdy yet comfortable. Reinforcement at seams, knees of pants, and other points of wear help extend a garment's life.

For children, an active life is often messy. Their clothes encounter dirt, grass, food, formula, and colored markers. Many children become attached to a favorite piece of clothing. Everyone is happier when the item can be easily cleaned and quickly returned to the child.

When buying a child's garment, check hangtags and labels for fabric and care information. Note sturdy construction that helps clothes stand up to repeated washings. If you're sewing a garment, read the label on the end of the fabric bolt to find such words as "permanent press," "soil retardant," "stain repellent," and "shrink resistant."

For economy, clothing that "grows" with the child is best. Open necks and waists accommodate a child's expanding measurements, plus they're more comfortable. Adjustable straps and deep hem allowances are other features that lengthen an item's useful life.

Ease of Dressing

Parents like clothing that's easy to put on and take off, especially when changing a diaper. Helpful features include the following:
- One-piece designs in stretchy knits.

- Snaps or buttons on the shoulder or front of shirts and sweaters.
- Gripper snaps on the inside leg seams of infants' and toddlers' pants.

Older toddlers and preschoolers take pride in dressing themselves and caring for personal needs. To promote self-dressing, choose garments with these features:
- Elastic waistbands.
- Large neck and armhole openings.
- Easy-to-handle closures, such as large buttons and snaps, zippers with oversized pull tabs, and Velcro™ fasteners.
- Openings and fasteners in front, rather than in back.
- Design features that help identify the front from the back, such as a pocket, decorative stitching, or appliqué.
- Shoes and sneakers with Velcro™ fasteners.

Color and Texture

Red and yellow are the first two colors a baby recognizes. This interest in bright colors, especially primary colors, carries over to a child's clothing preferences. Bright, bold colors are stimulating. They also hide dirt better. A grape juice spill is less obvious on a purple sweatshirt than on a pale, lavender one.

Fashion Facts

CHILDREN'S CLOTHES IN HISTORY. Children's clothing needs weren't always recognized as they are today. Before the 1900s, children were dressed like miniature adults. Garments were simply scaled-down versions of adult clothing. Clothing of this time didn't emphasize gender differences in children; both males and females wore dresses until about age three. Today, the children's market is a vast, economically important segment of the garment industry. Some designers have created entire fashion lines for infants.

Why do you think young children are so fond of stuffed animals like teddy bears? These toys are warm and comforting to cuddle and touch. The same is true of some clothing. Soft knits, flannel, corduroy, velveteen, fleece, and terrycloth are all fabrics that feel pleasant to a child's touch.

Since children eventually like to choose their own outfits, look for items that can be worn with what they already own. They're more likely to put coordinating outfits together, which parents will appreciate.

SELECTING MATERNITY WEAR

When golfer Brenda Corrie Keuhn, eight months pregnant, played in the 2001 U.S. Women's Open, she couldn't find clothing suitable for her condition. Her most workable option, wearing men's golf shirts, wasn't very satisfying. As Brenda described the results, "I will not be making a fashion statement."

Trends in TECHNOLOGY

>>LICENSED CHILDREN'S WEAR

Although children's wear has always been designed with comfort, function, and practicality in mind, the latest trends in colors, fabrics, and styles used to get less attention. That's different today. Children's garments now reflect teen fads and carry designer labels. Through licensing, many items are adorned with popular images that children love to wear. These appear on T-shirts, sweatshirts, pajamas, bed linens, lunch boxes, and many other items.

Some of the most popular character licenses include Mickey Mouse, Bugs Bunny, Snoopy, Winnie the Pooh, Barney, and the *Sesame Street* characters. Superman, Batman, and Barbie are other favorites. Children's books featuring Harry Potter, Dr. Seuss's creatures, and Beatrice Potter's animals are other sources of character licenses.

Sports figures and teams also enjoy instant recognition with children. Professional football, baseball, basketball, and hockey teams license their names, as do many colleges and universities. Famous athletes, such as Michael Jordan and Tiger Woods, have licensing arrangements too.

Some characters, especially those associated with feature-length movies, are short lived. The challenge for manufacturers and retailers is to forecast which of the newest characters and real-life stars will stay popular and profitable in children's wear.

INVESTIGATION ACTIVITY

What characters are the current favorites on children's clothes? How do manufacturers of nonclothing products benefit as well?

21-7 At least a few maternity outfits need to be roomy enough to fit during the last stage of pregnancy. Not all maternity garments on the market are made to fit for the entire pregnancy.

While most expectant mothers won't be in Keuhn's position, they have similar needs in **maternity clothes**, those designed for wear by pregnant women. They want garments that are comfortable, functional, and fashionable.

Maternity Wear Features

Nonrestrictive clothing is important throughout pregnancy. By allowing good blood circulation for the woman and the developing child, clothing promotes health as well as comfort. For the first half of pregnancy, a woman can often get by in any loose-fitting garment. Oversized shirts and sweaters, wrap skirts, stretch pants, and box jackets may combine the needed adjustability and comfort with the desired style.

As pregnancy progresses, the advantages of specially designed maternity wear are appreciated. See *Fig. 21-7*. Maternity clothes are similar to regular women's apparel but have features that accommodate the body's changing shape. A woman takes the same size in both types of clothing. Maternity tops and dresses have pleats, gathers, or extra fullness in the front. Pants, shorts, and skirts have an elasticized panel across the front, along with an expandable waistband. Maternity clothes have lower hems in front so garments will hang evenly on the expanding body.

Current fashions influence maternity designs. Many try to minimize a woman's expanding shape. Straight lines, as in tunic tops and leggings, give a slimming effect. Tops and dresses fit at the shoulder. Other designs emphasize the pregnancy with stretch fabrics and fitted bands beneath the abdomen.

When buying maternity wear, remember that it will be needed for only four or five months during the second half of pregnancy. Look for styles and colors to fit the seasons that the garment will be worn—fall into winter, for example, or spring into summer.

Economical Choices

For those who choose to spend the money, the options for maternity clothing are as varied as for regular styles. Catalogs offer jumpers and pantsuits as work attire. Maternity athletic wear includes biking shorts, tennis dresses, and swimsuits.

The high cost of new maternity clothes compared to their limited use bothers many pregnant women. Some find quality used garments in thrift or consignment shops. Others borrow clothes from relatives or friends. Sewers can find patterns for maternity fashions in both dressy and casual designs.

For added economy, look for maternity clothes that can be restyled after the baby is born. Dresses that are worn loose during pregnancy might be belted to create a new look.

CHOOSING CLOTHES FOR OLDER ADULTS

Think of the best-known people in the world: political figures, religious leaders, famous authors, and scientists. Many of these active, vigorous people are in their sixties or beyond. Even in retirement, people take new jobs and become involved in different activities.

The economic circumstances of older adults are quite varied. Those who are financially comfortable may be better able to buy what they need than they used to be. They may also have fewer needs. Those who live on fixed incomes, however, may have basic needs to be met. When buying gifts, think about specific situations.

21-8 A new interest can generate new clothing needs. For the retired traveler or jogger, an office wardrobe may be abandoned for more casual clothes.

Interests and Hobbies

Older adults who maintain their health and a positive outlook may want clothes for new activities. Emerging interests in sports, travel, and volunteer work might suggest gift ideas for apparel they never needed before. See *Fig. 21-8*. A shirt or apron with a berry print would be fitting for a home canner. A traveler might appreciate a tie with an old-world-map design or a vest with extra pockets. Museum shops, specialty stores, and craft fairs often have gift ideas.

Tastes and Values

Would you wear a garment designed for a ten-year-old, even if it fit? Like you, older adults typically want clothes that match their tastes and values. You can tell what they like by what they wear, so choosing similar styles and colors should be pleasing. Avoiding fads is best unless you're aware of a special request. When in doubt, choose an accessory, such as a simple lapel pin or scarf that complements an existing outfit.

Older adults especially value a handmade gift. Such gifts clearly show your regard for the person, which is often more meaningful to an older adult than to someone younger.

Physical Changes

Aging brings continual change as people move from the middle years and on into their seventies, eighties and nineties. See *Fig. 21-9*. Physical changes gradually appear. Did you ever notice an elderly person wearing a sweater on a warm day? Some people develop circulatory problems as they grow older. For this reason, lightweight garments that can be layered make good gifts. A flannel shirt or cardigan sweater made of an acrylic blend, for instance, adds warmth with little weight. Warm slippers are also a good choice.

With changes in personal coloring come new possibilities in clothing colors. The bright red that clashed with strawberry blond hair may complement silver hair. Clear colors and pastels brighten older skin, while brown and yellow shades tend to exaggerate any skin discoloration.

21-9 Finding clothes that fit well can become more difficult as people age. Standard sizes and styles don't always accommodate the physical changes that occur.

Some elderly people have a rounded back, thinner arms and legs, or larger waist and hips than when they were younger. Purchased garments should be chosen with dimensions in mind and may need alterations for the best fit. If you're sewing a garment for an elderly person, you may need to adjust some pattern dimensions.

SELECTING CLOTHES FOR PEOPLE WITH DISABILITIES

Could you dress yourself with a broken arm or leg? Would your clothes fit over the cast? When buying clothes, people with disabilities deal with similar questions. A **disability** is a condition that hinders full functioning. A disability may be present at birth or acquired through illness or accident. Some older adults become disabled due to declining health.

A physical disability restricts the movement or function of some part of the body. Such conditions as arthritis weaken the physical abilities of some older people. Slipping on and buttoning a shirt can be a painful, or even impossible, task.

People with disabilities might use a wheelchair, walker, or crutches. See *Fig. 21-10.* They may wear a cast or brace. A lost arm or leg may be replaced by a **prosthesis** (prahs-THEE-sus), an artificial device used to replace a limb.

Comfort and Appearance

People with disabilities appreciate clothing features that add to comfort and appearance. Clothing styles and fabrics make a difference.

For wheelchair users, an elasticized waistline, or none at all, is preferable. A higher rise in the back of shorts and slacks keeps the waistline in place. A lower rise in front prevents the fabric from bunching up and creating a bulky look.

Lightweight fabrics are preferable to heavy ones for wear in a wheelchair. These fabrics reduce bulk and can be layered if needed for warmth. Stretch and knitted fabrics offer added comfort, but clingy fabrics tend to emphasize braces and prostheses. Scratchy fabrics that irritate the skin are particularly troublesome to wheelchair users.

21-10 A disability can make getting dressed difficult. What clothing features would be best for someone who uses a walker?

Use of a walker or crutches makes it difficult to keep a blouse or shirt tucked in. Long shirttails are one solution. To eliminate the problem entirely, choose tunics, overblouses, sweaters, and other tops that look stylish over pants. When buying skirts and dresses, look for hems that are specially weighted to keep them from catching in a brace or prosthesis. This feature is also found in capes and ponchos, which are convenient styles of outerwear for wheelchair users.

Ease of Use

Like all people, those managing with disabilities want to be self-sufficient. Clothes with appropriate fabrics are one answer. For minimal care, choose washable fabrics that require little or no ironing. Since doing laundry can be challenging, clothes made with bright, colorful prints that don't show stains as easily as solids are a good choice. Because crutches and braces often rub against a garment, the fabric should be sturdy enough to handle the strain. Wheelchair users put continual stress on the knees and seat of pants. These areas should be of sturdy construction.

Clothing that is easy to put on and take off also promotes self-sufficiency. See *Fig. 21-11*. Look for styles that fasten in front, not in back. Raglan sleeves, wrap skirts, and pants with an elastic waistline are good choices. Clothes that are one size larger can provide added comfort and ease of dressing.

Manufacturers are beginning to respond to a growing market among people with disabilities. Some have created clothing lines that use **adaptive design**, which reduces the effort needed to put on and take off garments and promotes independence. Adaptive features include the following:
- Velcro™ closures "camouflaged" by buttons that have been sewn onto buttonholes.
- Pockets on shirtsleeves or at the knees, rather than the hips or seat of pants.
- Lower and larger armholes.
- Velcro™ tabs that adjust garments.
- Pleats in armhole seams for freer arm motion.
- Long zippers in legs so pants fit over a brace or cast.

- Pre-tied neckties, belts with Velcro™ fasteners, and slip-on shoes.

Customizing Garments

Since not all garments are "user friendly," a person with sewing skills can adapt ready-to-wear clothes. Sometimes a simple alteration is all that's needed. You could reinforce an area of strain by adding a fabric patch. Other customizing ideas are on page 369.

For people who are visually impaired, textural cues can identify and match garments. You might mark a green sports shirt by replacing the plastic buttons with wooden ones. Initials embroidered on a pocket distinguish a blue dress shirt. Small thread knots stitched to the inside of garments identify colors. One knot could mean red, two knots blue, and so on.

21-11 What types of garments would be easiest to put on and take off while seated in a wheelchair?

CUSTOMIZE GARMENTS

Simple clothing alterations can provide comfort and self-sufficiency for people with disabilities.

- **Hook-and-loop tape.** One strip of this tape is covered with tiny hooks and the other with tiny loops. Velcro™ is a well-known brand. Although the tapes hold when pressed together, they pull apart easily. Use small pieces to replace snaps or buttons. Use in longer strips to replace a zipper or provide an adjustable closing. By opening the seam on pants or a sleeve and applying the tape, dressing over a cast or brace is easier. see→ p 530

- **Elastic.** Insert elastic at waistlines to help keep garments in place. Replace the waistband of a skirt or pants with a casing; insert a drawstring or elastic for added comfort. Replace shoelaces with elastic to eliminate tying. see→ p 527

- **Buttons.** Replace small buttons with large, flat buttons and enlarge the buttonholes. Use elastic thread to sew on buttons at cuffs and other openings and eliminate unbuttoning.

- **Large hooks.** Replace small hooks and eyes with large metal hooks and bars. For an adjustable waistline, sew on two bars to accommodate weight changes or provide added comfort.

- **Zippers.** Fasten a large ring or a ribbon loop to the zipper pull to make it easier to grasp and pull up or down. Replace a conventional zipper with a two-way one, so the garment can be opened from the top, bottom, or both. see→ p 535

Exploring Customization

Using an old garment, practice one of the customizations described, or adapt a garment for actual use if possible.

Review

CHAPTER SUMMARY

- Gifts of clothing are most appreciated when they reflect the recipient's needs and tastes.

- Clothes for children should be safe, comfortable, durable, and brightly colored. They should also promote self-dressing.

- Maternity wear should be flattering, while accommodating a woman's changing shape.

- Older adults have a wide range of needs, interests, and abilities. Clothing should be carefully chosen for each person's situation.

- Self-sufficiency, as well as comfort and appearance, are important factors when choosing or customizing clothes for someone with a disability.

USING KEY TERMS

One of the Key Terms, adaptive design, is discussed in relation to disabilities. Clothing for elderly people could also have adaptive designs. Think of specific problems with mobility that an elderly adult might have. Then draw an adaptive design of your own that would suitably address these problems.

RECALLING THE FACTS

1. How can you get ideas for clothing gifts for a particular person?

2. Must a clothing gift be expensive to be appreciated? Explain.

3. Why is buying the correct size for an infant or child often difficult?

4. Identify general features that promote safety in young children's clothes.

5. Why is ease of cleaning particularly important in children's clothing?

6. Name four design features that help promote self-dressing in preschoolers.

7. How do maternity clothes accommodate a woman's expanding middle?

8. Suggest economical options for clothing gifts for a pregnant woman.

9. What changes might an older person experience that would affect his or her clothing needs?

10. Describe clothing features that would be especially appreciated by someone who uses a wheelchair.

11. What special features would you look for when choosing clothes for a person who uses a walker or braces?

12. List five examples of adaptive design.

13. What simple customization can help a visually impaired person identify clothing?

and Activities

THINKING CRITICALLY

1. In some families, people make lists of gifts they would like to have, and then share these at gift-giving times. Some people think the giver should make the choice and surprise the recipient. Explain your point of view.

2. How could a pregnant woman extend the time for wearing her regular clothes in the early months of pregnancy? Give specific examples.

3. Do you think an elderly person can comfortably wear the same clothing designs that people twenty or more years younger wear? Why or why not?

APPLYING KNOWLEDGE

1. **Gifts.** List gifts that you could buy or make for a friend or relative, using suggestions from the chapter. Ask that person to evaluate your choices.

2. **Cost comparison.** Calculate the cost of an article of clothing or an accessory that you could make as a gift for someone, and compare that to the cost of buying something similar. After factoring in the time and effort needed to finish the project, which choice makes better sense to you? Why?

3. **Reference cards.** Fill out index cards with information about family members and friends. Include sizes, interests, and personal needs and tastes. Update these with gift ideas as they come to mind. Keep your file as a reference when buying gifts.

4. **Children's clothes.** Using catalogs and magazines, analyze children's clothing for ease of dressing, safety, comfort, wearability, and care.

5. **Maternity wardrobe.** Using catalogs, magazines, or other resources, put together a basic maternity wardrobe for a woman who lives in the Midwest, has a limited budget, and will be pregnant from January through September. What must be considered when developing this wardrobe?

6. **Adaptive designs.** Use the Internet to research adaptive designs in clothing for people with disabilities. Where are such garments found? What are their costs?

CREATIVE SOLUTIONS

Your fourteen-year-old cousin is going to wear a back brace for a year after surgery to correct a spinal problem. Some of the contours of the brace can be seen beneath her clothing, making her feel self-conscious. She worries that it will be even more noticeable under the tank tops and stretchy knits she likes to wear in the summer.

Think Creatively

What clothing strategies might help ease your cousin's concerns?

Careers

Fashion Merchandising

ALKING BETWEEN THE RACKS OF dresses, a stylish-looking woman glances at each one, her eyes darting quickly over the garments. She stops to examine the fabric of a colorful, patterned dress. "Why do you think this one isn't selling?" she asks the sales associate. Because the woman is the buyer for the department, the answer is important to her. Like other professionals in the fashion merchandising field, she pays close attention to what the store's customers buy. She knows that retailing is a very competitive field.

Fashion merchandising is part of the huge retail industry that sells goods to consumers. Fashions are sold in stores, as well as through catalogs and the Internet.

Careers in fashion merchandising are varied. People must plan what to sell, buy the merchandise, and then do the selling. Those in management positions oversee others and make high-level decisions. In a small store, one person might have varied responsibilities. In a large store or a chain, careers tend to be specialized. Because many stores are open at night and on weekends, hours can be flexible. Technology is part of most positions. People use scanners to track inventory, software to plan shelf space, and information systems to run Web sites. Fashion merchandising offers career possibilities for people with wide-ranging interests and talents.

IS THIS FIELD FOR YOU?

Merchandising jobs are people-oriented. They are also high-pressure and often stress-filled. People who excel in the field generally identify with the statements below.

- I'm very interested in fashion.
- I tend to lead rather than follow.
- I can "roll with the punches."
- I enjoy learning different skills.
- I'm interested in working with others.
- I see new technology as an asset.

Outstanding sales associates, who help customers choose and buy merchandise, are valued in business. What do you think it takes for a sales associate to be helpful but not pushy?

Education and Training

A job as a sales associate or stock clerk is a good start to a career in retailing. Hours can be flexible and part-time, which works well for those still in school. As entry-level positions, these jobs reveal how a store operates "from the ground up."

Education after high school makes promotion more likely. A two- or four-year degree from a college or business school is advisable, with course work in communication, finance, marketing, merchandising, and information systems. For a career in management, a university degree—perhaps in retailing—plus business administration courses is a good plan.

Getting a degree may make a person eligible for an executive training program, offered by many large retailers. A person gains experience in all areas of a retailer's operation, qualifying for a little higher position on the career ladder. Starting as a retail management trainee rather than a sales associate or as an assistant buyer instead of a stock clerk is possible.

Possible Career Paths

Although few people rise from stock clerk to company president, advancement is encouraged. Most companies find that promoting from within is more effective, less expensive, and increases employees' incentive to succeed.

THE SKILLS YOU NEED

People in fashion merchandising do well when they have the skills below.
- Interpersonal communication
- Organization
- Management
- Decision making and problem solving
- Mathematical ability
- Analytical thinking
- Mental and physical stamina

Merchandising careers tend to follow either a fashion or business path. An assistant buyer learns the job from a head buyer and can advance to that position when the head buyer is promoted to merchandise manager. Likewise, after designing window and in-store displays for a few years, a display artist may join the fashion office staff and eventually become fashion director for the entire store. Of course, crossing career lines is not uncommon. A display artist may grow interested in sales promotion, someday becoming a vice president in that division.

Imagine being the buyer for a large department store. The jewelry you like best might not be right for the store. How would you choose jewelry and other items that customers will like?

Choosing a Fashion Merchandising *Career*

BUYER | CUSTOMER SERVICE REPRESENTATIVE | DEPARTMENT MANAGER | FASHION COORDINATOR | MERCHANDISE MANAGER | PRODUCT DEVELOPER | SALES ASSOCIATE | STOCK CLERK | STORE MANAGER

Stock Clerk

Stock clerks manage the merchandise in stock rooms and on sales floors. In this entry-level position, they support the sales staff by restocking the shelves, tables, and racks with merchandise. Stock clerks may gather clothes from fitting rooms and return them to the sales area. They may attach security tags to expensive items.

In larger stores, as well as mail-order and Internet businesses, stock clerks may be inventory clerks or merchandise distributors. Behind the scenes, they help the shipping clerk unpack and inspect merchandise when it arrives. They set aside damaged goods for the store's buyer to examine. Although conveyor belts and automatically guided vehicles are increasingly used, this work can be physically demanding.

Buyer

A store's success depends heavily on the buyer's fashion foresight. This is the person who selects and purchases what the retailer sells. While you're looking at what's trendy now, the buyer is trying to predict what will be popular next season.

To make predictions, buyers do research. They review industry publications and Web sites and keep a lookout for trends in the making. Another prediction tool is sales analysis. Careful interpretations can indicate where changes are happening. Buyers travel regularly to market weeks in New York City, Paris, and other major cities to visit the showrooms of designers and manufacturers. There they can see what's new and place orders for future deliveries.

Sales Associate

Sales associates and sales specialists ring up sales, rehang clothes, and assist customers. A good sales associate is familiar enough with the store's merchandise to help customers find what they want and make choices.

Shoppers can be pleasant or unpleasant, but a good sales associate remains polite and helpful. Those who work on commission, earning a percentage of the clothing's price, benefit by a positive attitude. Since the retail business is very competitive, a likable, competent sales staff is needed to help a store build loyal customers.

Fashion coordinators stay up-to-date on fashion. These professionals work with different departments so that decisions about buying, advertising, display, and promotion are "coordinated."

Fashion Coordinator

Each retailer has a fashion personality, an image to present to the public. Compare the personalities of a trendy boutique and family-oriented department store, for example. Upholding this image is the task of the fashion office, and especially its head, an upper-level executive called the fashion coordinator.

The fashion coordinator travels to designers' showings and textile mills, reads trade publications, and taps other sources to learn about the latest fashion trends. This information is shared with the buyers, department managers, merchandise managers, and advertising and display departments. The result is a common theme or image that unites every department of the store.

Orchestrating fashion shows is another responsibility of coordinators. A fashion coordinator's work is demanding but very appealing to many.

In working with a buyer, the merchandise manager guides decisions about what items the store will sell.

Merchandise Manager

Merchandise managers focus on the sales performance of one or more departments. In this role, they oversee and approve the decisions of buyers who report to them.

Merchandise managers must understand market trends, sales projections, and the retailer's fashion image. Competition demands that these managers be creative in coming up with new merchandise and promotions that will increase sales. They often travel with buyers to markets and always authorize their budget. This career has a high level of responsibility, but the financial rewards can be good for someone who is well organized and energetic.

CAREER APPLICATIONS

1. **Pros and cons.** Before choosing a career, think about the pros and cons. What would the positive and negative sides of a career in sales be? List points under each. Then explain why that would or would not be a suitable career field for you.

2. **FCCLA.** Plan a Chapter Service Project on balancing work and family life. Through interviews and library research, study merchandising company policies on personal days and child care. Talk to families about how they handle time demands. Compile your findings on the problems, solutions, and resources.

3. **Professionalism.** Choose one of the careers described here. Then give examples of how people in that career might demonstrate the following qualities: honesty, reliability, fairness, cooperation, self-discipline, and loyalty.

UNIT 7
The Workplace

Career Preparation

OBJECTIVES

- Evaluate your interests and skills.
- Research career paths.
- Compare sources of information about jobs.
- Describe the steps in applying for a job.

KEY TERMS

application form	interview
aptitude	networking
career path	portfolio
cover letter	references
entry-level job	résumé
	shadowing

A S YOUR HIGH SCHOOL YEARS DRAW closer to an end, the future becomes more of a reality. Are your career plans coming together? If you're not sure what career is ahead for you, now is a good time to explore. Some careers, including many in the fashion field, may not have occurred to you as options. Would you like to design clothing, own a fabric store, or be a store buyer? Taking action now can help you find a career and get your future off to a good start.

KNOWING YOURSELF

Have you ever heard a person say, "I always knew what I wanted to be"? Most people are more likely to know what they like to do and choose a career based on those interests. What do you like to do? What do you do well? Simple awareness of **aptitude**, or natural talent and capacity for learning particular skills, is a good place to begin when searching for the right career.

Identifying Interests and Skills

To identify your interests and skills, look closely at yourself for answers. In school, the classes you like best indicate interests. A future fashion writer might enjoy language arts more than science, whereas a love of science might lead to a career as a textile chemist. See *Fig. 22-1.*

Leisure activities also offer clues to interests. Someone who likes to update a home Web site might choose a career maintaining a catalog company's Web site. A love of sewing or other crafts could lead to a career in designing, manufacturing, or merchandising. Another clue is a preference for solitary or group activities. Some career fields, such as research and graphic arts, involve lots of independent work. Sales and marketing careers require much more interaction with customers and coworkers.

To identify skills, look at school accomplishments. Getting good grades in math, for example, takes more than memorizing formulas. Students must organize information, see relationships, and apply principles. Success with writing and art shows creativity. Students who do well in science classes enjoy experiments, evaluations, and analyses. When students succeed in clothing, fabrics, and construction courses, they show sewing skills and knowledge of design and fashion. Career success is more likely when personal skills relate to the work.

22-1 Your interests and skills reveal much about you. Why would it be a good idea to match them to your career?

Accomplishments outside of school also point to skills. What achievements have made you proud? One teen redecorated her bedroom with a unique look. Another received compliments about his photography. Accomplishments like these show skills that give career ideas.

Even when you don't recognize your own skills, someone else might. Turn to people you respect and who know you well. A teen might be good at telling amusing stories, but not realize that talent as a communicator until a friend mentions it.

To identify your skills, think positive. Remember that no one is "average" in everything. When you look closely, you can always find things that you like to do and that you do well.

Interest Surveys

When interests and skills aren't clearly apparent, special tools can help. Special surveys identify interests and skills through a person's responses to carefully constructed questions. They might confirm what you already know about yourself or suggest something new. The results are then related to certain jobs. Interest surveys aren't foolproof, but they give a better idea of what your abilities are and where they might take you.

Such surveys are among the resources available from career counselors. These professionals guide people in exploring interests and skills and choosing a line of work. High school guidance counselors also administer and interpret surveys. Some schools have interactive software programs to help students discover their interests, preferences, and skills.

Developing Skills

With a clear picture of your interests and skills, you can refine and develop them. If art and clothing courses awaken an interest in fashion and

22-2 Employers want these skills in an employee. In what high school classes are you learning them? Where else can you develop them?

SCHOOL-TO-CAREER SKILLS

SCIENCE APPLICATIONS

DECISION MAKING

READING AND WRITING

LEADERSHIP

TECHNOLOGY

MATH APPLICATIONS

LISTENING AND SPEAKING

GOAL SETTING

MANAGEMENT

PROBLEM SOLVING

TEAMWORK

CRITICAL THINKING

Career Clusters		
1. Agribusiness and natural resources	6. Environment	11. Marine science
2. Business and office	7. Fine arts and humanities	12. Marketing and distribution
3. Communications and media	8. Health	13. Personal service
4. Construction	9. Hospitality and recreation	14. Public service
5. Family and consumer services	10. Manufacturing	15. Transportation

22-3 The U.S. Office of Education has grouped careers into 15 clusters based on similar job characteristics. Which areas appeal to you?

drawing, signing up for more classes makes good sense. A search of community resources might reveal added opportunities—exhibits at an art museum, a selection of useful books at the library, or a part-time job at a clothing store.

School activities help a teen learn and grow. A budding fashion writer gains insight by working on the school paper and learning about deadlines and editorial decisions. Joining the debate club builds confidence in public speaking, a real asset to a fashion designer who presents a new collection to a manufacturer.

Academics should never be overlooked. Skills developed in math, science, and language arts classes affect performance on any job. Helping a customer find just the right item may take analytical skills gained in science, problem-solving techniques learned in math, and communication skills acquired in language arts. Computer experience—in word processing, databases, spreadsheets, desktop publishing, and Internet research—is valuable in every field. *Fig. 22-2* lists a number of skills that are learned in school and valued by employers.

RESEARCHING CAREER PATHS

Once you've pinpointed your interests and skills, look for careers that match. Focusing on one or two career clusters narrows your search more quickly. Each cluster is a group of careers with similar characteristics. See *Fig. 22-3*.

By studying a cluster, you can learn where to begin a **career path** that links a series of related jobs within a field of work. You can find out what experience, education, and training it takes to move from one job to another toward your ultimate goal.

The Internet can start your career research. Using a search engine, type in a job title to obtain a list of sources. More information on Internet job searches occurs later in this chapter. School guidance counselors are another resource for information about the job market and the education and training needed for careers.

Learning About Training and Education

Can you name a job that doesn't require some type of specialized knowledge? Doing a job well takes certain skills, whether it's moving cartons without hurting your back or developing a new fiber.

Some jobs are **entry-level**—little or no special training or experience is needed. Learning on the job is typical. For many other positions, you'll need training or education, as shown in *Fig. 22-4* on page 382. The farther you travel along a career path, the more education or training you'll need.

In researching education and training, you'll want answers to such questions as these: What schools offer a program for the career that interests you? How long does the program last? What is the cost and is financial assistance available?

Your counselor can help you find information on schools. If you wish, contact a college or university directly to get brochures and catalogs about programs and admission requirements. If

22-4 • Training and Education Needed for Careers		
TRAINING OR EDUCATION	**DESCRIPTION**	**CAREER EXAMPLES**
High school education	Four years of high school.	Sales associate; assembly-line worker; entry-level positions.
Technical training	Provided at community college, technical or vocational school; courses last few months to several years.	Pattern maker; textile machine technician; dry cleaner.
University degree: bachelor's	Four years of course work at college or university; may need specialization in a certain subject.	Retail buyer, public relations specialist, market analyst; family and consumer sciences teacher.
University degree: master's and beyond	Additional years beyond bachelor's degree; course work at college or university.	Textile chemist; environmental engineer.

you want training, contact a counselor at a technical school or community college that offers a program of interest. Ask where some of their graduates are employed. What type of career placement, or help in finding jobs, do they offer?

Many states have tech-prep programs that link high school and community college courses. The programs have also formed partnerships with community businesses and industries. Courses are coordinated to help students move from high school, to community colleges, to highly skilled careers.

Talking to Others

For a real-life look at a job, experienced people are a good resource. If approached politely and at their convenience, many people are happy to talk about their work. Ask about typical daily tasks. Do they work a standard eight-hour day, or are weekends, evenings, and overtime included? Does the job require travel? Are the trips long or short, frequent or occasional, in the United States or abroad? What school subjects are most useful in the job? What career paths do they suggest? Where will you find opportunities in the field?

If possible, arrange to spend a few hours or a whole day **shadowing** a worker, accompanying the person to learn about job responsibilities. This experience can help you see firsthand whether the career suits you.

Getting Part-Time Experience

Working part-time teaches you about a career "from the inside out." Many part-time jobs for teens are opportunities for career exploration. A sales associate in a clothing store, for example, learns about retailing: how buying decisions are made; the costs of operating a business; the concerns of management. Working in a large department store gives one view of the industry; working in a small shoe store offers another. The experienced people you work with can advise and teach you. They might even be sources for job information later. Equally important, you can learn whether a job is not for you before investing time, effort, and expense.

Volunteer work is another valuable experience. What might you learn as a guide at an art museum? What skills do you gain by teaching young children to sew or helping a charity with its benefit fashion show? For many people, volunteer work has been the first step on their career path.

LOOKING FOR A JOB

To learn what hunting for a job is like, ask people who've done it. Each story is likely to be different. Most people agree, however, that you need to be resourceful and patient and to keep trying. Whether you're looking for a part-time job or a career position, job-hunting techniques are similar.

Many job ideas come through **networking**, talking to people to gather information and advice. Word of mouth can be a swift and efficient messenger. Tell family, neighbors, teachers, counselors, friends, parents of friends, and friends of parents that you're looking.

Check the classified ads in the newspaper, looking for job listings. The Sunday edition usually carries an expanded section. Small businesses often advertise openings in weekly community newspapers. Part-time jobs may be listed under a separate heading or scattered throughout the listings. Keep your eyes open for "Help Wanted" signs at businesses or on community bulletin boards.

You can search the Internet for jobs in all career areas. The information below explains how.

Read all print and on-line ads carefully, watching for words and phrases that identify entry-level jobs. "Trainee," "growth opportunity," and "must have desire to learn" are clues. Also, compare names, addresses, and phone numbers to make sure you're not looking at differently worded ads for the same position.

If you're interested in working for a particular employer, find the name of a contact person. With large companies you may be told to call or write to their human resources department. Let

Trends in TECHNOLOGY

≫JOB SEARCH VIA THE INTERNET

Using the Internet, you can view job listings, research career opportunities, and even send your résumé electronically. Internet career services include Web sites, newsgroups, and bulletin boards, most sponsored by trade associations, professional organizations, large companies, and the U.S. Department of Labor.

To locate job listings, log onto the Internet. Use a search engine and such key words as *employment opportunities, job listings, job banks, job postings,* and *careers.* You'll find many job-related sites. Company listings usually include a description of the jobs available and an e-mail address or phone number. In addition, many newspapers post "Help Wanted" sections and other job advertisements on their own Web sites.

If you want information about a particular company, enter the company's Web address or go to a search engine and enter the company's name. If you can't locate the site this way, try the search words *company profiles.* You'll be directed to Web sites that store information on hundreds, even thousands, of companies. Most on-line job listings include an e-mail address for submitting a résumé electronically.

INVESTIGATION ACTIVITY
Choose a career that interests you. Using the Internet, research job opportunities.

Fashion Facts

CAREERS OF YESTERDAY.

As a young woman looking for work in the early 1800s, you could apply at a New England fabric mill in America. Your coworkers would have been girls and women, ages twelve to twenty-five. One mill built boardinghouses shared by the female labor force. With about twenty-five people in each house, the young women worked, ate, and spent leisure time together. As wages decreased for long hours of work, discontent grew, leading to unionization and strikes in the 1830s and 1840s.

your interest be known, even if the company isn't currently hiring.

If you're looking for summer work, you might register with an agency that specializes in temporary jobs. In this increasingly popular arrangement, you work for the agency, which sends you to different employers. One month you might be a typist at a company; later you're a mailroom clerk at another. The company pays the agency, and the agency pays you.

Employment agencies are an option for those who want full-time jobs. Some agencies charge a fee or a percentage of your salary if they find you a job. Sometimes you're responsible for paying the fee, sometimes the employer, and sometimes each party pays half. Be sure you understand all the terms before signing a contract with an agency.

APPLYING FOR A JOB

Applying for a job may be your first taste of workplace competition. Even when workers are in short supply, employers won't take "just anybody." Filling out a job application and going for an interview are opportunities to demonstrate that you're the best person for the job.

Completing an Application

A company's job **application form** is the information document filled out by a job applicant. See *Fig. 22-5*. The form may ask for facts about you, your education, your work experience, and special skills, such as computer use. It cannot legally require such personal information as race, religion, or marital status.

Before you start to fill out an application, read it carefully. Be sure you understand the directions and what information is requested. Ask for help if you're unsure. Print or type your responses in blue or black ink. You may want to ask for two application forms—one for practice, the other to turn in.

Since past work experience is part of most job applications, you may need to bring a list of addresses, starting dates, and ending dates for previous jobs. You'll also need the names, addresses, and telephone numbers of two or three **references**. These are people who will speak well of your personal character and qualifications. A school official, previous employer, clergy member, or long-time adult friend may be a good reference. Avoid listing relatives or friends your own age. Be sure to ask permission from people before using their names.

22-5 A job application form should be filled out neatly. To avoid mistakes, look over the form carefully before writing. How would you mark out something that you didn't intend to write?

Preparing a Résumé

To apply for some part-time jobs and many full-time positions, you may need to send or bring in a **résumé** (REH-zuh-may). This is a detailed summary of your education, work experience, and job-related activities. See *Fig. 22-6.*

Since your résumé represents you when you aren't there to speak for yourself, a professional look is a must. Keyboard the information with single-spacing on one piece of plain white, 8-by-11-inch paper. If keyboarding isn't one of your skills, ask someone to keyboard it for you. Computer programs that enable you to insert personal information into an outline format are available. Proofread your résumé for spelling and grammatical errors and ask someone else to read it too.

Résumés can be organized in different ways. One way is to list work experiences chronologically, starting with the most recent. Another way is to organize by skills, such as computer and communication. The skills format has become popular because many companies scan and save résumés electronically. When they have a job opening, they search their résumé database with keywords for specific skills.

22-6 Most employers don't have time to read long résumés. That's why one page is best. You can buy résumé-writing guidebooks that show many different résumé styles to create on the computer.

What can you put on a résumé if you haven't much work experience? Employers are interested in any achievement or position that shows you have the skills needed for the job. You could list hobbies and activities that show your skills. If you're applying for a job as a sales associate, two summers spent tutoring children may carry more weight than two years repairing lawn mowers.

Writing a Cover Letter

Every résumé sent should include a **cover letter**. This introductory letter requests a meeting or interview and shows your written communication skills, as well as a bit of your personality. Make it brief, but not necessarily dry. You might mention why you want to work for the company. Definitely mention any skills or experiences that would make you a particularly valuable employee, even when included in your résumé.

A cover letter should be keyboarded and, if possible, addressed to the person who handles job applications at the company. If you can't find a name, send your letter to the human resources director. For small businesses, send it to the owner or manager.

Interviewing for a Job

After reading your application form or résumé, the owner, manager, or human resources person may want to interview you. A job **interview** is a meeting to discuss the details of the job and the qualifications of the applicant. For jobs that require artistic and creative skills, bring along a **portfolio** of your work. This can include drawings, photos, written articles, and samples.

Making a Positive Impression

Even seasoned workers may feel nervous about an interview. It's easy to think of the interview as a test to pass. Seeing the meeting as a chance for you and a potential employer to get acquainted and learn whether you'd make a good match is more helpful. Other tips to help ease the job interview jitters include the following:

- **Research the business beforehand.** Scan the business section of the paper for current

How To... DRESS FOR A JOB INTERVIEW

During a job interview, a potential employer notices what you're wearing first. When the interview is over, however, your attitude and skills should be remembered, not your clothes. The following tips can help you present yourself well:

- Wear an appropriate outfit. A nice, casual outfit is fine for many interviews, but a suit is a better choice for more formal workplaces. Flattering colors and styles build confidence. Blue jeans, T-shirts, athletic shoes, and unconventional garments are not appropriate.

- Choose a comfortable outfit that fits well so you can concentrate on the interview, not what you're wearing. Try it on a few days early, checking in a full-length mirror. Females should choose a modest outfit that isn't too dressy, too tight, too low, or too short.

- On the day before the interview, make sure the outfit is clean and pressed. Clean or shine your shoes, if necessary.

- Select complementary jewelry and accessories. Avoid flashy jewelry and too many accessories.

- Follow good grooming practices. Shower, shave, and use deodorant. Hair should be clean and combed, and nails neatly trimmed. Avoid heavy make-up and strong perfume or after-shave.

- Double-check your appearance before arriving at the interview. With confidence, you can relax and focus on your conversation with the interviewer.

Exploring Outfits for an Interview

Using a catalog or clothing advertisements, find outfits that are suitable for a job interview. Present your examples to the class and explain why you chose them.

news. Ask a reference librarian where to find background information, or search the Internet. If the business is a store, check their merchandise selection. Knowing something about the employer shows your interest. You'll be better prepared to respond if an interviewer asks, "Why do you want to work here?"

- **Dress appropriately.** Appearance counts. Use the ideas on page 386 to dress for an interview.
- **Arrive on time.** Allow plenty of time to prepare and get to the interview. Learn exactly where you should be; make a trial run if needed.
- **Show up alone.** If you bring relatives or friends for moral support, have them wait outside.

Strive to create a winning impression during the interview. Remember the following ideas:

- **Greet the interviewer in a friendly manner.** If a handshake is offered, accept with a firm grasp. Sit down only when invited. Any items brought with you should be placed on the floor, not on the interviewer's desk.

22-7 When your job interview ends, thank the interviewer for spending time with you. Make eye contact and smile. A firm handshake often signals that the interview is over.

- **Speak clearly.** Look directly at the interviewer when talking. Avoid slang expressions.
- **Sit comfortably but correctly.** Avoid slumping in the chair and fidgeting with your hands or hair. Clasp your hands loosely on your lap. Try to relax.
- **Answer questions with more than a yes or no.** Try to include something about yourself. After pointing out membership in the debate club, an applicant can add, "It's taught me a lot about quick thinking and teamwork."
- **Give honest answers, even if they include negative facts about you.** Explain how you've learned from past mistakes and poor experiences, but don't dwell on this information. Avoid blaming or criticizing former employers.
- **Ask questions about the position.** This shows your interest. You might ask about specific duties and opportunities for advancement.
- **Express enthusiasm.** Have a positive attitude about work opportunities.
- **Thank the interviewer as the meeting ends.** Express appreciation for the time spent with you. See *Fig. 22-7.*

Following Up

When you get home, type or neatly write a letter to the interviewer. Repeat your thanks and interest in working for the company. Mention again the particular skills that you hope to bring to the job. Sometimes little extras like these make the difference in getting the job.

Responding to Rejection

Not every job search ends with the welcome words, "When can you start?" Not getting a job can be disappointing and feel like personal rejection. If you're not offered the job, ask yourself why. You can also ask for feedback from the interviewer. Were you too quiet at the interview? Learn to speak out more. Was your résumé lacking? Add to your résumé with more school activities or community involvement. Work at improvement and the next job may be yours.

Review

CHAPTER SUMMARY

- Consider your own interests and skills when deciding on a career.

- By researching career paths, you can identify the education, training, and skills needed for various careers.

- You can learn about careers through part-time jobs and talking to others.

- When looking for a job, use many different resources.

- A carefully completed application form and a thoughtfully written résumé and cover letter increase your chances of getting an interview.

- At the interview, strive to present yourself as confident, qualified, and eager to learn.

USING KEY TERMS

Work with a partner, taking turns telling one fact about each Key Term. Repeat until you've covered the related facts discussed in the chapter.

RECALLING THE FACTS

1. Explain how a close self-evaluation can help identify aptitudes.

2. Why are school experiences important to career success, even when they don't seem related?

3. How can a high school counselor's office help you choose a career?

4. If you were a sales associate at a clothing store, what additional training would you need to become the store's retail buyer?

5. Identify ways to learn about the training required for a certain career.

6. What are three ways to learn what a job or career is like?

7. How can working at a part-time job help you choose a career?

8. List sources for learning about job openings.

9. Give three tips for filling out an application form.

10. Describe the qualities of a professional-looking résumé.

11. What are five tips for communicating well during an interview?

12. Should you wear your most formal outfit to a job interview? Why or why not?

13. If you don't get the job you're after, how can that be a learning experience?

and Activities

THINKING CRITICALLY

1. Should a naturally quiet person choose a career that demands an outgoing personality in order to become more outgoing? Explain.

2. Why are friends and relatives not recommended as references?

3. Why is giving dishonest answers during an interview a mistake?

APPLYING KNOWLEDGE

1. **Interests and skills.** Take an interest survey that helps you identify your interests and skills.

2. **Job market.** Create a display of newspaper job listings in clothing-related fields. Highlight job responsibilities in one color, and the education, training, or experience required in another.

3. **Mapping a path.** Research a fashion career. Identify "stepping stone" positions for advancing to different job levels. Use your findings to develop a personal career path toward a specific goal.

4. **Education and income.** Compare salary levels of jobs requiring only a high school education with those requiring additional education.

5. **Personal résumé.** Write two versions of your personal résumé, one based on your current education and experiences and a second that reflects the achievements you hope to make in five years. What steps can you take to make your hoped-for résumé a reality?

6. **Cover letter.** Write a cover letter that could be sent with your résumé when applying for a fashion industry career.

7. **Interview attire.** Find magazine illustrations of people in various styles of dress. Explain whether each outfit would be appropriate for a job interview.

8. **Interview clinic.** Working in pairs, write questions that might be asked during a job interview. Take turns interviewing each other. Discuss ways to improve your skills.

CREATIVE SOLUTIONS

Your older cousin has an interview for a job that he wants very much. He is applying for a position as an assistant display designer for a large department store located in another city. He has never been to this store and believes a number of candidates will be interviewed before a decision is made. A week before the interview, he tells you, "I'm a nervous wreck. I want everything to go right. I don't want to do anything that will hurt my chances."

Think Creatively

What help can you give to try to improve your cousin's confidence and chances of getting the job?

Success on the Job

OBJECTIVES

- Relate personal qualities to on-the-job success.
- Demonstrate productive ways to work with those in authority.
- Describe ways to advance or change jobs.
- Give practical advice on balancing work and personal life.

KEY TERMS

ethics	parliamentary
flexibility	procedure
initiative	procrastinate
leadership	punctuality
mentor	teamwork

EXAMINE THIS ISSUE

Worker status. One trend in many industries is the increased use of part-time and project workers, those hired only to work on a specific assignment. The company can pay for help as needed without having to provide full benefits. Some employees like the flexibility this type of work offers. Others are unhappy if they do similar work to full-time employees who receive benefits and possibly higher pay.

What do you think?

What are possible consequences of this practice?

C AN YOU IDENTIFY SOMEONE WHO HAS had a successful career? The person you choose says something about how you view success. Success can be measured in many ways. Some people point to money, prestige, and power. Others say making a contribution to society is a sign of success. Gaining respect for a job well done can mean success. So can achieving career goals. Often success is viewed as gaining a feeling of self-fulfillment through enjoyable work. Whatever the mark of success may be to any individual, certain qualities make getting there easier. See *Fig. 23-1.*

INGREDIENTS FOR SUCCESS

To move ahead in today's work world, you need a combination of attributes. See *Fig. 23-2.* High on the list is the ability to adapt to a changing technological workplace. The skills described on page 392 are just a few that you may need. Specific jobs take many other kinds of technological know-how.

In addition to specific skills, employers want people who can think critically, make decisions, and solve problems. In addition, people who demonstrate the positive personal qualities of a responsible employee are valued no matter what the job title may be.

23-2 Some people have qualities that point them toward success even before they begin a job. Are any qualities for success apparent here?

23-1 A job well done can bring feelings of success. What does success on the job mean to you?

»TECHNOLOGY SKILLS IN THE WORKPLACE

Today's employees use many technology skills for on-the-job success. The ability to use the following technology makes an employee more valuable:

- **Word processing.** This software creates text-based documents. You can easily insert, move, and delete text with just a few keystrokes.

- **Databases.** With this software, you store data, then search and recombine it in new ways. A retail store, for example, might record daily sales and keep inventory records up-to-date. Recombined data produces daily, weekly, monthly, or yearly sales reports. One data sort might show which items are fast and slow sellers.

- **Spreadsheets.** On spreadsheets, data is arranged in rows and columns. Spreadsheets can also perform math calculations. In business, they keep accounts payable records and predict sales and expenses.

- **Desktop publishing.** Using a computer, printer, and desktop publishing software, companies design and print their own brochures, newsletters, reports, invitations, business cards, calendars, and greeting cards.

- **Teleconferencing.** Holding a discussion or conference with people in different locations is possible with telecommunications equipment, such as closed-circuit television.

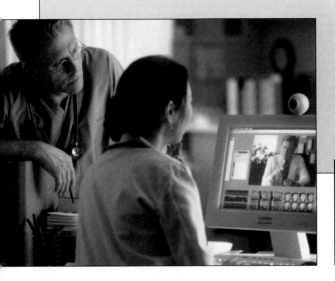

INVESTIGATION ACTIVITY
Choose one of the technologies mentioned to explore and demonstrate for the class.

Qualities of a Responsible Employee

Suppose you were an employer. What qualities would you look for in an employee you trust to help you keep your business running? Several qualities are described here, but you may be able to add more to the list.

Reliability

If you have a family car that gets you to school even on the coldest morning, you can appreciate reliability. Your own reliability is no less important. An employer counts on you to work conscientiously, without constant supervision, carrying out even tedious jobs to the best of your ability.

Punctuality, or arriving on time, is a sign of reliability. As a punctual employee, you're at work and ready to start when your shift begins. You keep working until it's over, even staying a while longer to finish a task. You take only the time allotted for meals and breaks. You might socialize with coworkers, but not at the expense of work that needs to be done. Time is money to an employer. Like nickels and dimes, the few extra minutes taken when someone is late, unprepared, or unproductive add up.

Working Well with Others

Most jobs involve interaction with other people, and all people deserve respect. You show respect when you're patient with customers, helpful to coworkers, and cooperative with your supervisor. You make allowances for other people's mistakes, bad moods, and personal problems, knowing that others have done the same for you. Your overall manner is one of courtesy and consideration.

23-3 Success in almost every job relies heavily on communication skills. Giving and understanding instructions is just one example.

Other valuable interpersonal skills include recognizing and showing appreciation for the skills and contributions of coworkers. If you accept criticism positively, it can help you improve. A defensive attitude isn't productive. In turn, offer only constructive criticism to others. Keeping a sense of humor helps relieve tension and stress in the workplace.

Good Communication Skills

Because people communicate daily, many assume they do it well. Practice doesn't make perfect, however, if you repeat poor habits. As a student, you have many opportunities to practice reading, writing, listening, and speaking effectively. If you take advantage of them, you'll be repaid on the job when you write well-organized reports, help customers choose flattering styles, and follow directions for using equipment. See *Fig. 23-3*.

Good communication skills are also needed when talking on the telephone and sending messages by fax or e-mail. See page 407 for ideas about using e-mail. For written messages, good grammar and spelling make your words more credible. Be aware of the tone of your voice or your writing. You want to convey the message clearly, pleasantly, and politely. Good communication skills will help you share information, propose new ideas, and persuade others to follow your advice.

A Positive Attitude

A positive attitude looks at the pluses, not the minuses. When a problem arises, positive thinking focuses on advantages and resources, making a solution easier to find. Other people enjoy interacting far more with someone who remains positive when faced with a disappointment or problems than with someone who always complains, criticizes, and blames others.

Willingness to Learn

When you're new on the job, it's easier to accept that you don't know everything and need to learn workplace routines and methods. Gaining experience and confidence in your skills shouldn't change this openness to learning. If you let a coworker or supervisor show you a more efficient or safer way to do your job, you increase your own value as an employee.

Continued learning takes **flexibility**, a willingness to adapt to new opportunities and situations. Accept new assignments as a chance to learn more about the business and as a sign of your employer's trust. Volunteer for new responsibilities. Look for opportunities to get more training or education. Some employers pay for training sessions, workshops, or college courses for their employees. These, in turn, make your job more interesting and provide valuable experience for future jobs. See *Fig. 23-4.*

Initiative

Suppose you work for a small business owner who mentions the need for a better way to keep track of clients' accounts. If you offer to work out a system, you're showing **initiative**, the desire and willingness to plan and carry out a task.

Employers appreciate initiative, within the limits of a worker's duties. If you have a terrific idea and wonder, "Why don't they do this already?" always ask permission before taking on a project. There may be good reasons why certain methods are followed. On the other hand, your idea may be the perfect solution to a business problem.

Teamwork

Have you ever played a team sport? Just as in sports, businesses emphasize teamwork to get a job done. **Teamwork** is work done cooperatively, rather than individually, by several associates. By sharing abilities and skills, team members can be more efficient in reaching a common goal. They share both the responsibilities and rewards of their efforts. To be an effective team member, use the ideas on page 395.

Teamwork is generally more productive than having the same number of employees work separately. Workers have greater job satisfaction because they help make decisions and solve problems. They may rotate tasks and develop new skills. Because team members must communicate

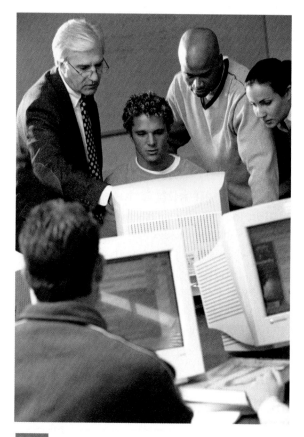

23-4 Some companies provide training sessions. If they don't have what you need, reimbursement for the cost of outside workshops and courses might be possible.

with each other, they get to know their coworkers better. Greater productivity also means increased profits for the company.

Leadership

All workers can show leadership skills, not just people in high-level positions. Anytime you guide or influence others, you're practicing **leadership**. Helping coworkers resolve a dispute and accepting a coworker's ideas for a window display both show leadership. Modeling good workplace habits is a subtle but powerful form of leadership that anyone can demonstrate.

Leaders develop a number of skills. They know how to communicate, set goals, make decisions, solve problems, and manage resources. They promote teamwork and organize group tasks. Conducting a meeting properly is a leadership

How To... **BE A TEAM MEMBER**

Teamwork is the glue that holds many business situations together. Have you heard that "two heads are better than one"? Well, often several people can be more productive as a team than if they work separately. What qualities do you think team members need? What techniques make them successful? Here are some that work just as well in school as on the job.

- **Understand the group's overall goal. Then set short-, medium-, and long-term goals for each project, along with specific dates for completing each task.**

- **Listen actively and offer suggestions during meetings. Communicate with other team members throughout the project.**

- **Understand your assigned role and duties. If you have questions, ask the group leader or facilitator.**

- **Complete assigned tasks on time and follow through on any other duties.**

- **Evaluate progress on a daily or weekly basis.**

- **Help solve problems and resolve conflicts before they become major.**

- **Respect other team members. Avoid becoming competitive or resentful of others.**

Exploring **Teamwork**

Write a description of someone you would like as a teammate on an important assignment. Explain your reasoning.

responsibility. After learning the rules of **parliamentary procedure**, they lead group discussions in an orderly way. Some leaders keep a group on task by acting as a moderator.

Like other skills, leadership can be learned and developed. Students can join organizations that promote leadership. *Fig. 23-5* describes two organizations that offer many opportunities. You can learn more about them by accessing their Web sites on the Internet.

Ethical Behavior

Ethics are the moral principles and values that guide a person's actions. In an ethical workplace, both employers and employees follow high standards that build trust and respect.

Employees demonstrate a strong work ethic by working hard and doing their best work. Honesty is expected. See *Fig. 23-6*. Stealing money or property from an employer or coworkers is dishonest. So are more subtle acts, such as taking office supplies or copying software for personal use. All communications should be honest. Lying to customers or in expense reports is an unethical act that seldom goes unnoticed. In addition to destroying your reputation and chances for advancement, such behavior can result in job termination and legal charges.

Employees are expected to keep information about new products, promotions, and business plans confidential. Telling others, especially competitors, could harm the business. Negative gossip about the company and its management can result in lost business as well as lost jobs.

Employees should also respect coworkers' privacy. Listening to private conversations and

23-5 • Student Organizations			
DESCRIPTION	**MEMBERSHIP**	**BENEFITS TO STUDENTS**	**PROGRAM HIGHLIGHTS**
FAMILY, CAREER AND COMMUNITY LEADERS OF AMERICA (FCCLA)			
National student organization that helps young men and women become leaders and address important personal, family, work, and societal issues through family and consumer sciences education.	Students who are currently taking or have taken family and consumer sciences courses through grade 12.	• Develop such leadership skills as positive relationships, conflict management, and teamwork. • Build skills for life needed in the home and workplace, including planning, goal setting, problem solving, decision making, and communication. • Explore careers, including how to be successful on the job.	• **Leaders at Work.** Career-related projects, including the area of textiles and apparel. • **STAR Events.** Competitions that include career investigation. • **Career Connection.** Activities focused on career development. • **Dynamic Leadership.** Information, activities, and projects that develop leadership skills.
DISTRIBUTIVE EDUCATION CLUBS OF AMERICA (DECA)			
National student organization that develops future leaders in marketing, management, and entrepreneurship. Business partnerships help support activities.	High school students enrolled in marketing education and management courses.	• Develop understanding of the business world and career opportunities. • Train for leadership, while building confidence and communication skills. • Develop business skills, including ethics, a healthy competitive spirit, business etiquette, and citizenship. • Explore opportunities for scholarships and financial awards.	• **Competitive Events.** Events in such areas as apparel and accessories marketing, retail merchandising, and fashion merchandising. • **Leadership Development.** Conferences that focus on leadership skills. • **Conferences and Meetings.** Includes an annual apparel and accessories mini-conference in New York City.

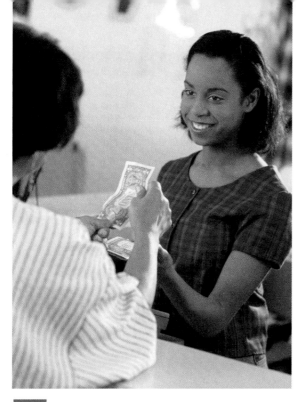

23-6 Handling money on the job is a big responsibility. An employee who is accurate and honest builds a reputation that can be carried to future jobs.

board of directors. For this reason, knowing how to work well with people in authority is a must for everyone.

Practicing positive work habits helps you establish a reputation as a solid, responsible worker. It paves the way for a smooth relationship with supervisors and managers. Disagreements can still arise, of course, especially when misunderstandings occur. You might not see the reason for a certain safety rule until you learn that claims paid for worker's compensation raise your employer's insurance premiums. Your supervisor might be bothered when you arrive a little late, not knowing that your last class ends only twenty minutes earlier.

How do you prevent misunderstandings? Clear communication saves many situations. See *Fig. 23-7*. Make it a point to keep your supervisor up-to-date on your progress, problems, and activities. If you have concerns, discuss them calmly in order to settle them. Try to understand

phone calls is unethical. E-mails, faxes, and voice mail deserve the same privacy as regular mail. Never go through the desk drawers, file cabinets, or lockers of coworkers without proper authority.

Sometimes employees are faced with ethical decisions about what is right and wrong. What should you do if you observe unethical behavior in the workplace? First, consider whether the incident is isolated or an ongoing practice. If dealing with an unfair coworker, try to resolve the situation before talking to a supervisor. If dealing with an abusive customer, stay calm and refer the problem to a manager. If an employer is unethical, you protect yourself and others by reporting the situation to authorities. Record your observations and collect evidence. No employee has to do anything that is illegal or unethical. It is better to resign and find another job.

Working Well with Supervisors

Most employees report to someone; even the chair of a large corporation is accountable to a

23-7 Good communication is a two-way street. What can both an employee and a supervisor do to communicate well?

23-8 • Aspects of Industry	
ASPECT	**RELATED TASKS IN INDUSTRY**
Planning	Deciding what to produce or what services to provide; setting goals; developing general policies and procedures.
Management	Choosing a structure for employees who oversee the work of others; implementing methods for operating the business.
Finance	Handling money decisions and procedures; choosing and carrying out accounting methods.
Technical and Production Skills	Developing skills needed by employees on the job, such as computer skills, machine operation, and teamwork.
Underlying Principles of Technology	Understanding how technology is used in a specific industry; identifying the impact of changing technology on the business; taking steps to stay current; analyzing new equipment.
Labor and Personnel Issues	Identifying worker rights and responsibilities; developing policies that involve labor organizations, cultural sensitivity, and employee concerns.
Community Issues	Developing a positive relationship with the community; providing community support.
Health, Safety, and Environmental Issues	Avoiding job-specific health threats; developing employer and employee responsibility for a safe workplace; respecting and protecting the environment.

your supervisor's point of view. Learning more about the business, including people's responsibilities and the costs of operation, may help. Lastly, recognize that supervisors have strengths and limitations, like everyone else. If you do, your outlook will be more realistic.

Understanding Industry

Positive qualities are your first links to success on the job. What else contributes? An understanding of the work world can give you a head start.

Whether you choose a career in fashion or another field, you're likely to be part of a large business or industry. All industries share certain common functions and concerns that are summarized in Fig. 23-8. Understanding these can benefit you as well as your employer, but how?

A guard on a basketball team wouldn't do very well without knowing what the forward does. Similarly, employees who understand the workings of industry see how their role fits into the "big picture." They know the "why" behind expectations. They see how personal development can lead to new opportunities. They appreciate the challenges that industries face. Sharing

company goals is easier when people recognize and respect the wide range of contributions that keep a company going.

TRAVELING THE CAREER PATH

If you're like most people, your first job won't be the only one you ever have. With more education and clearer goals, change is likely. Outgrowing one job can mean moving into another that offers new challenges.

Today's flexible workplace may impact your career choices. Technology allows some people to work from home and other locations distant from the office. To stay competitive in a global marketplace, companies often turn to less traditional work arrangements. Hiring project workers, who are not full-time employees, provides flexibility for both employer and worker.

Advancing on the Job

During your first days on a job, your main concern is to learn your duties well. Eventually you may want to take on more responsibility, especially in a position with career potential. As you look ahead to a career path, find out what's available. If other jobs interest you, what training and experience are needed? Do you have these skills? If not, how can you develop them?

Since promoting from within the company is generally easier and less expensive, employers want employees to develop skills. Some offer on-the-job training. After demonstrating your ability as a sales associate, for example, you might gradually assume the responsibilities of an assistant manager.

If an employee needs more education, the company may pay all or part of the costs. An assistant manager might get a tuition refund for business school classes needed to advance to manager.

To work toward career goals, you may find an ally in a **mentor**, someone who serves as a role model and advisor. See *Fig. 23-9*. While some companies have formal mentoring programs, a friendship with a more experienced coworker can bring the same rewards. Under a mentor's guid-ance, you can meet other people in the field and form mutually helpful relationships, a practice called networking.

Leaving a Job

Ideally, you leave one job for another that takes you closer to your career goals. Finding a new position before quitting the one you have typically makes a better impression on potential employers.

Maintaining good relations with employers and coworkers is worthwhile. They might become part of your professional network and references for your next job. To leave in good standing, give reasonable notice before you resign. Two weeks is standard. If possible, also help train your replacement.

Leaving a job under less than ideal circumstances is awkward. Although being fired or asked to resign doesn't reflect well, such events need not derail career plans. After all, people who were fired *do* get hired again. Learning from negative experiences shows growth.

What can be said at future interviews after a forced job loss? The best strategy is to acknowledge the problem. Certain workplace policies may have been troubling. Differences with a supervisor may have caused tension. Words should be chosen carefully when describing the situation. One interviewee said, "I felt that some of my supervisor's practices were unfair. I could

23-9 People who have been on the job for many years often have knowledge and insights to share with someone new. What term identifies these experienced people?

23-10 The more responsibilities a person has, the more difficult it can be to balance work and personal life. Do you think part-time work is manageable for teens?

either accept them or leave." This statement shows an objective view of the situation and takes responsibility for actions. If the person had said, "My boss always thought she was right," what would that have reflected?

Even if you feel pressure to leave a job, consider the long-term consequences carefully. Think of each job as a stepping-stone to your career goal. Evaluate a move in terms of how it can take you where you want to go in the world of work.

BALANCING WORK AND PERSONAL LIFE

Have you ever had to choose between spending time with a friend and finishing a school assignment? If so, you already know about the demands of balancing school and personal life. Adding a job to this mix adds to the challenge. See *Fig. 23-10.*

At one time, people were advised to leave work problems at work. Work situations shouldn't affect relationships at home, and vice versa. Were it possible, this approach might solve a lot of difficulties. If a teen could shut away problems at school like books in a locker, being a cheerful friend and family member might be easier. A teen

might be a better student if not distracted by problems at home.

Such a neat separation isn't possible in today's world. It's not even desirable. Wouldn't it help to know that a family member is worried about something at work or that a coworker has a problem at home? The relationship between work and personal life has a strong impact on happiness, health, and personal satisfaction.

Coping with Demands

You can learn to balance your time and energy so that obligations and expectations don't become overwhelming. The following techniques can help you better manage your work, family, and community life:

- **Make a list.** This basic step applies to many situations. Whether for shopping, school assignments, or job responsibilities, writing your obligations down helps with memory and organization.
- **Set priorities.** After making a list, rank items in order of importance. Managing your time, energy, and money will be easier. By prioritizing according to your values, you make the most satisfying use of resources.
- **Break down large tasks.** Look for the small steps that make up a long-term project. For example, what manageable steps might be part of a bedroom redecoration project? You're less likely to **procrastinate**, or put off a project, if you tackle only one part at a time. The stress that comes when an entire project must be done at the last minute can be avoided.
- **Set up a weekly schedule.** Plan and organize by writing down what you want to accomplish on each day of the week. If you don't, you may have too much to do at week's end. A planning book can be purchased to help you stay organized.
- **Dovetail activities.** Some tasks don't require undivided attention. While walking the dog, you could think about a term paper topic. You could exercise while watching TV or mend a hem while talking on the phone.

23-11 Time for fun should be part of every person's schedule. What might happen if time spent on recreational activities is either too much or too little?

- **Plan for fun.** Everyone needs recreation. Even an hour in the evening to read, listen to music, jog, or work on a hobby can be relaxing and fun. Reserve that hour, just as you would schedule an appointment. See *Fig. 23-11*.
- **Manage stress.** The pressure of multiple roles can create stress. Learn effective ways to manage stress—relax, exercise, and plan ahead—so you don't feel overwhelmed.
- **Have realistic expectations.** The media show images of perfection: fashion models have perfect looks; magazines feature perfect homes; and recipes produce perfect meals. Real life is never perfect. Take pride and pleasure in all that you do accomplish and avoid worrying about achieving perfection.

Developing a Support System

Even the best personal management system needs support. In times of crisis, people turn to others for help as normal routines change and stress increases. See *Fig. 23-12*. Relatives and friends may provide child care, transportation, or meals for working parents. Sometimes coworkers take on extra work responsibilities. Supervisors might offer flexible hours or work-at-home arrangements. Community and professional services can also be part of a support system by providing counseling, health care, and financial assistance.

When people use good management strategies and have ready support, work and personal life balance well. Success in life and on the job depends on the right balance.

23-12 Support systems are a combination of give and take. A teen can help make a busy parent's life easier, just as people help each other on the job.

Review

CHAPTER SUMMARY

- Career success depends on developing technical skills and personal qualities that will make you an asset to an employer now and in the future.

- Valued employees balance teamwork skills, such as communicating and working with others, with personal reliability, initiative, and a willingness to learn.

- Ethical behavior is a quality desired in all positions.

- Maintaining good relationships with those in authority and learning other aspects of business can add to your effectiveness and satisfaction at work.

- Developing useful skills and a range of relationships can help you change jobs and advance in a career.

- Learning to manage time and energy helps you balance and enjoy work and family relationships.

USING KEY TERMS

Create a crossword or other word puzzle, using as many of the Key Terms as possible. Exchange your puzzle with a classmate for solving.

RECALLING THE FACTS

1. How can employees who are skilled in desktop publishing help save an employer time and money?

2. Describe an employee who works well with others.

3. How can you make written and spoken messages most effective?

4. What are the advantages of maintaining a positive attitude at work?

5. List ways to show openness to continued learning.

6. What benefits come when coworkers show teamwork?

7. How do people show a strong work ethic?

8. Describe positive ways to deal with unethical workplace behavior.

9. How can you promote good relationships with managers and supervisors?

10. In industry why is it helpful for each person to know something about what is going on in other areas of the company?

11. How can a mentor help you in your career?

12. What is the proper way to leave a job in good standing?

13. When interviewing for a new job, how should a person handle the subject of a forced job loss?

14. List five techniques that can help you balance work and family life.

and Activities

THINKING CRITICALLY

1. Do you think it's easier to be a supervisor or an employee? Why?

2. Should people be required to work on a team with ineffective people? Explain.

3. What might an employer assume about an applicant who changes jobs frequently? How accurate might these assumptions be?

APPLYING KNOWLEDGE

1. **Applying qualities.** Choose a career that interests you. Give specific examples of how each quality described in the chapter might be needed in that job.

2. **Teamwork and leadership.** Suppose you're working on a project with two other people. You're the leader. Person *A* starts working ahead without consulting the team. Person *B* seems happy to let *A* do the work. How will you handle this situation?

3. **Getting along.** How would you handle these work situations effectively: (a) your supervisor often asks you to do something at the last minute; (b) your supervisor points out improvements needed in your work, but you disagree; (c) your supervisor often asks you to do something boring and gives the interesting work to someone else.

4. **Examining ethics.** Sometimes people use the unethical behavior they notice in others to justify what they do. They might say something like this to themselves, "Well, everybody else takes paperclips, so why shouldn't I?" Evaluate this reasoning.

5. **Setting priorities.** List and prioritize what you need to accomplish in the coming month. Create a plan for accomplishing these tasks. Then carry it out.

6. **Stress and health.** Research the relationship between emotional stress and physical illness. How might problems in balancing work and personal life affect a person's health?

CREATIVE SOLUTIONS

A friend is disappointed in her job as a sales associate. She took the job because the outlet sells athletic wear licensed by professional sports teams. She thought this job would be a good way to learn more about careers in fashion merchandising. Although your friend has told her supervisors of her interest, they seem reluctant to help when she asks about opportunities in the field and about the pros and cons of a merchandising career. Your friend is frustrated and thinking about quitting and giving up her idea for the future.

Think Creatively

What advice do you give your friend?

Fashion Entrepreneurs

OBJECTIVES

- Relate personal qualities to success as an entrepreneur.
- Compare different business opportunities for self-employment.
- Describe major responsibilities of entrepreneurs.
- Explain the importance of all parts of a business plan.

KEY TERMS

entrepreneur	self-motivated
franchise	target
freelance	audience
profit	

MANY PEOPLE MAKE A LIFE-LONG dream come true when they become an **entrepreneur** (AHN-truh-pruh-NUR), someone who organizes and manages his or her own business. After renting a location, some entrepreneurs sell fashion items or offer a service, such as dry cleaning. They might sell merchandise supplied by manufacturers or even market their own jewelry line. Other entrepreneurs offer clothing, accessories, or home fashions through catalogs or the Internet. Still others use their talents to write, draw, or consult with clients at home or at the client's site. See *Fig. 24-1*.

Owning and managing your own business can be exciting. Before taking on the challenges, however, a potential entrepreneur weighs the benefits against the risks.

QUALITIES OF THE SUCCESSFUL ENTREPRENEUR

If you've earned money by taking care of children or mowing lawns, you've already had a taste of self-employment. A world of difference, however, separates those experiences from a career as a business owner. Not everyone who takes care of children could successfully run a child care center. To be successful and satisfied, an entrepreneur needs certain personal traits, including these:

- **Self-motivation.** When you own a business, you're the leader. You make decisions about the product or service, the workplace, and how to do financing and marketing. You can't wait for someone else to give directions and do the work. That means entrepreneurs must be **self-motivated**, able to set goals and work independently. People who are self-motivated take action without prodding from others. As they gain satisfaction from accomplishments, their motivation grows.

- **Organization and management skills.** Suppose you're hired to knit a sweater. Before starting, you need to know the sweater size and

24-1 Some people turn a personal interest into a business. A love for knitting, for example, could be transformed into owning a shop that offers lessons and supplies for people who like to knit, embroider, or do needlepoint.

color, yarn type and cost, how long the project will take, and how much to charge for your work. Entrepreneurs make the same decisions. They also keep records, pay bills, produce or order merchandise, and stay current on laws and economic trends that affect their business. They may hire and direct employees. To these, add obligations to family, friends, and community, and you start to appreciate the entrepreneur's need to be organized as they manage time, money, and other resources.

- **Willingness to take risks.** Statistics show that nine out of ten small businesses begun in a given year will fail. Although people who start businesses know that success isn't guaranteed, they willingly risk financial and career security. Successful entrepreneurs know what hazards new businesses face, yet their confidence in themselves and their product or service outweighs this knowledge. They balance risk with good planning and foresight. Even when everything goes well, they risk change to increase productivity. See *Fig. 24-2*.
- **Physical stamina.** Regular nine-to-five business hours don't apply to most small busi-

ness owners. Entrepreneurs are typically involved in every aspect of running the business, especially at the start. After business hours, the owner may have to print employee schedules or wash windows. After completing a job, the self-employed worker may send out customer satisfaction surveys or design flyers. To meet such demands, a budding entrepreneur needs plenty of energy and stamina.

- **Ability to handle stress.** As you can imagine, handling so many responsibilities can take an emotional toll. People who are not easily upset or discouraged by problems and who can make decisions, often under pressure, have the temperament to cope with the stress of running a business. They keep a sense of perspective and a sense of humor about their work. They are anchored by a clear set of values and priorities.
- **Ability to get along with others.** Owning your own business means selling your product or service to others. Good communication skills—listening, speaking, writing, and electronic—make interactions with customers and suppliers go smoothly. As a business grows, an entrepreneur might hire production workers or sales associates. With effective leadership skills, small business owners can train, manage, and motivate these employees.

OPPORTUNITIES FOR ENTREPRENEURS

Looking at entrepreneurs in action, people sometimes wonder why they didn't start a similar business themselves. Why didn't they? They might not have had the courage to take risks or the drive to figure out how to start a business—or they might not have had an inspiring idea in the first place. In the fashion field, ideas for entrepreneurship are plentiful. Choosing the right idea and implementing it, however, takes some thought.

Buying a Business

One way to become an entrepreneur is to buy an existing business. While growing up, one

24-2 As owners of their own business, this couple believe the risks are worth the satisfaction of ownership. They enjoy the challenges and rewards of designing, producing, and selling their own clothing line.

How To... USE E-MAIL

Just as the microwave oven has streamlined cooking, e-mail is doing the same for communication. Electronic mail carries both business and personal communication at an increasing rate. An e-mail message represents you in the same way that any other communication does. Although teens tend to be informal when they communicate with peers, developing good e-mail habits now will help you when you use this communication method as part of your job.

- **When you send an e-mail message, fill in the subject line with a few words that identify the message content. Some people won't open an e-mail that lacks a subject line. Locating a stored message at a later date is easier when this information is included.**

- **Keep e-mail messages short. Long messages and reports can be attachments.**

- **Check spelling, grammar, and punctuation with the spell-check feature. Friends may understand phrases like "g2g" (got to go), "lol" (laughing out loud), and "oic" (oh, I see), but coworkers may not.**

- **Treat e-mail to coworkers the same as personal mail or files. Don't read messages unless they are addressed to you.**

- **When forwarding a message to other people, send a copy to the original sender to let him or her know you're doing so.**

- **Remember that employers have the right to set rules regarding the use of company e-mail. They also have the right to read all messages.**

Exploring E-mail

Suppose you own a fabric store and a shipment of fabric is late. You have already asked once about the shipment and received no response. Write an e-mail that expresses your second inquiry.

24-3 Buying an existing business takes careful research to be confident that the business will make a profit.

young man had a favorite sporting goods store. Eventually, he owned one of his own. See *Fig. 24-3*.

Buying a business is something like buying a home. You inherit all the advantages and disadvantages in location, condition, and reputation. Like a homebuyer, a business buyer needs to ask why the owner is selling. Is the owner retiring or moving on to a bigger venture, or is the business failing or product demand decreasing?

To reduce unknown risks, a franchise business may be the answer. A **franchise** is the right to sell a company's goods and services in a given area. Franchise owners first pay the parent company a set sum to purchase the franchise, then pay royalties on all goods or services sold. In return, they receive an established name and product, training, and advertising. They are responsible for daily decisions but have less control over the business's long-term direction.

While usually associated with fast-food restaurants, franchises are rapidly growing for clothing, accessories, home furnishings, and fabric stores. The Athlete's Foot (athletic shoes and activewear), Gymboree (children's wear), and Lady Madonna (maternity) are manufacturer-franchise stores.

Such designers as Ralph Lauren, Yves Saint Laurent, Donna Karan, and Calvin Klein have designer-franchised shops in major cities.

Starting a New Business

For many would-be entrepreneurs, starting a new business is appealing. Self-starters have confidence in an idea and also in their personal abilities. They feel positive about future success. To take action, decisions must be made about how much money, time, and energy to commit, based on available resources. Other major decisions include the following:

- **Will a product be sold?** Merchandise can be purchased from manufacturers or craftspeople to sell to customers. A budding entrepreneur might sell personally produced products. Examples are hand-knitted sweaters, decorative pillows, and children's clothes. Some entrepreneurs have turned off-the-rack items into unique, personalized clothing. By embroidering a name, painting a sunflower, or adding a colorful appliqué, they create one-of-a-kind designs. See *Fig. 24-4*.
- **Will a service be sold?** In many communities, the most visible service jobs are dry clean-

24-4 Adding designs to sweatshirts is a small business that can be successful when managed well.

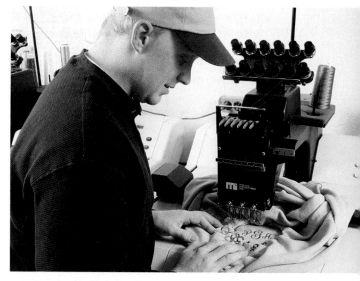

ers and alteration specialists. Opportunities exist behind the scene as well. Copywriters, illustrators, and photographers sell their work to retailers, newspapers, magazines, catalogs, and advertising agencies. Wardrobe consultants advise clients on their appearance and image. Dressmakers create custom bridal gowns and veils. Many writers, artists, and consultants in fashion services are freelancers. To **freelance** is to sell work or services without earning a regular salary from any one employer. Freelancers charge by the job or the hour.

- **Where will the business be located?** Many entrepreneurships begin as an in-home business. Business growth can lead the owner to a separate office, workroom, or factory. Businesses that sell goods made by others are usually located in a store. An office might be needed for a service that employs several people, such as a design office or a mail-order business.

Trends in TECHNOLOGY

>>ERGONOMICS

Ergonomics means designing and arranging physical surroundings and tools so that a person is more comfortable when working. Work can be done more quickly and with fewer mistakes. A quilter cuts out many small fabric shapes, which can cause cramped hands and sore fingers. With an ergonomically designed rotary cutter, the handle fits the human hand, making the process easier.

Because computers are used for so many tasks, chairs are often the focus of ergonomic concern. Over an extended period of time, all sitting positions strain the body. The body needs movement and circulation to work efficiently and stay healthy.

An ergonomically designed chair allows a person to spend many hours at the computer without straining the back or putting stress on other parts of the body. Some chairs adjust so the position can be changed to suit individual body proportions and tasks. Others are designed for a specific task or situation. An orthopedist's office, for example, accommodates people with crutches, walkers, and canes. The design for waiting room chairs is different from those in a dentist's office.

Even when using an ergonomic chair, a person should get up and move about for at least five minutes each hour. These mini-breaks increase the body's blood flow and help reduce fatigue.

INVESTIGATION ACTIVITY
Choose one of these topics to investigate: a career as an ergonomist; ergonomic products; the history of ergonomics; or other uses of ergonomics besides at work.

- **How will customers be reached?** If offering a service, will customers come to a home, store, or office, or will clients be met at their own site? If offering a product, will the entrepreneur sell it in a store, through a catalog, or on-line? Another option is to sell on consignment. With this method, a handmade item could be displayed in a craft shop. The maker receives a percentage of the price after the item is sold. Since the shop provides the "showroom" for the product, the craftperson's overhead expenses are limited.

In-Home Business

Up to 20 percent of all new businesses operate from the owner's home. An office or workroom can be set up in a den, basement, or spare bedroom. A copywriter or graphic artist needs a computer and desk for workspace. An alterations specialist needs a sewing machine and pressing equipment, plus a place for customers to try on garments.

With an in-home business, space is not an extra expense. If the business fails, no money is lost on unused property or an unneeded lease. The arrangement, however, has drawbacks. Young children, playful pets, and telephone callers can be daily disruptions. The entrepreneur may need to set strict rules about when family

and neighbors are free to interrupt. Operating an in-home business can affect the homeowner's insurance policy, as additional coverage may be needed. See *Fig. 24-5*.

Store or Shop

Have you heard anyone describe the "three" most important concerns when buying a home? They are "location, location, and location." The point made is certainly also true of a store, whether a boutique, a fabric store, or a yarn and needlework shop. The right location can make the difference between success and failure. A highly visible site is not only easy for customers to find, but it also encourages passers-by to window-shop. In this sense, a good location is like free advertising.

A new store usually requires constant attention from the owner. Finding a trustworthy store manager to share responsibility can be challenging, and training the person often takes time.

Mail Order

A mailbox stuffed with catalogs may annoy many consumers, but catalogs are critical to mail-order businesses. See *Fig. 24-6*. Those who develop mail-order businesses take orders for merchandise and ship it to customers. They avoid the cost of buying or leasing space to display their merchandise. They have other expenses, however, including advertising, packing, and shipping costs.

Mail-order businesses can start small. Suppose a person makes beautiful baby blankets and quilts. Showing them at craft fairs, along with a business card, might get sales started. Finding places that allow flyers and photos to be displayed is another idea. As sales pick up, the entrepreneur may be able to afford advertising in a newspaper

24-5 In-home businesses are common today, especially those that can be conducted via computer. What are some examples?

or magazine. Since items can be made as orders are received, only a small product inventory is usually needed at first. As the business grows, additional space may be needed for production, storage, and shipping.

Web Sites

As on-line shopping increases, many entrepreneurs set up Web sites to do business. With just a few clicks of a mouse, customers from all over the world can view merchandise and order on-line. Running an on-line business has similar advantages and disadvantages to a mail-order business.

Small business owners may set up a site themselves or hire a Web-site designer to produce the pages, containing text, graphics, and possibly sound. All Web sites must have a registered domain name, paid with an annual fee. Space for the site must be obtained from an Internet provider, who sometimes supplies this as part of the service. The size of the site determines whether customers will be able to actually order on-line or must call the telephone number shown on the site. When the site is set up, key words that people might use when searching the Internet are placed in a special location for access by the search engines.

RESPONSIBILITIES OF ENTREPRENEURS

When you are your own boss—and possibly someone else's too—you can't sit back and wait for things to happen. You have to take charge right from the start. Before launching a business, entrepreneurs make plans and do research. Long-term success hinges on recognizing all responsibilities and meeting them.

Market Research

Market research provides information needed to start and maintain a business. After hearing people say they couldn't find anyone to make wedding and prom gowns, one person with excellent sewing skills decided to investigate. She found that no one was providing this service in her area. After verifying that the need existed, she launched a dressmaking business of her own.

Fashion Facts

READY OR NOT? Two economics researchers report that entrepreneurs are becoming an increasingly important segment of the American economy. The authors state that schools in the United States should teach and encourage teens to become entrepreneurs. Without understanding the basics of owning a business, teens may not be ready for the workplace. The report also states that the entrepreneurial spirit of self-confidence, problem solving, and taking chances is valuable to success in personal life, as well as to career success.

24-7 Before starting a business, an entrepreneur needs to know whether a product or service is marketable. Computer research can provide some of this information.

Financing

Almost every business needs funds to cover start-up costs. A specialist in making slipcovers and draperies, for example, needs a good sewing machine and varied equipment to start. The cost of rented space must be figured. To make the business grow, advertising money is needed. Without adequate funding, a business might not be able to survive the growth period that every new business faces. A bigger undertaking requires a bigger investment.

Some new entrepreneurs pay costs from their own savings. Investing their own money shows they have confidence in the venture, which is helpful if a loan is also needed. Family and friends may provide sums of money, but this can put people in an awkward position if the loan can't be repaid.

Many entrepreneurs prefer to apply for a loan at a bank or credit union. See *Fig. 24-8*. Another possibility is the government-funded Small

Identifying whether a service or product is in demand is a basic part of market research.

Market research also predicts which people will buy, how often, under what conditions, and at what price. This information helps identify a **target audience**, a specific group of potential customers. See *Fig. 24-7*.

Large corporations spend huge sums on market research. They check the competition very carefully, as any entrepreneur must. To sell a product yourself, you would need to check the competition. You could visit stores to see whether something similar is sold and for what price. Advertisements and an Internet search might yield more information. Before marketing a handcrafted product, you could browse craft fairs. Your product would need to stand out from the rest. When offering a service, you must decide how to make it better than the competition.

24-8 Financial support is needed to get many businesses started. What resources do people have?

24-9 An attorney can help sort through the different regulations an entrepreneur must consider when starting a new business.

Business Administration. This organization provides financial aid and advice to independently owned businesses that have a limited number of employees, assets, and sales and do not dominate their field.

Regardless of the lender, aspiring entrepreneurs must make a strong case for themselves. They'll be asked about their education, business experience, and personal finances. A lender needs to know about the business itself: its size and location; the expected start-up costs; the goods or services offered; and the competition. The larger the loan, the more information the lender wants.

Regulations

Is a mail-order company that runs out of a spare bedroom a business? In the eyes of the law, it may be, and a wise entrepreneur checks and meets legal requirements—federal, state, and local.

Learning about regulations should begin early, since such processes as those involving licensing and inspections can take time. The chamber of commerce, the secretary of state's office, and the Small Business Administration are excellent sources of information. Hiring an attorney who specializes in business law is often money well invested. See *Fig. 24-9*.

A business may have to satisfy laws and ordinances related to the following:

- **Zoning.** Most communities limit business operations in residential areas. Health and safety codes dictate certain features of commercial property, such as number and placement of exits.
- **Permits and licenses.** Most businesses need some type of operating permit. Depending on its type, a business may also need to register with a number of government regulatory groups. For taxation purposes, for instance, a business needs a tax identification number. It may need a city occupational license. Special licenses are needed to manufacture some items, such as stuffed toys and quilts.
- **Name registration.** One point of pride in starting a business is choosing a distinctive name. For identification and to prevent duplication, this name must be registered with the state.

Setting Prices

According to one saying, "The fool knows the price of everything and the value of nothing." The entrepreneur, on the other hand, must know the value of many things to set a fair price for a product. What should an entrepreneur consider when deciding how much to charge?

- **Cost of goods or supplies.** Obviously, the price has to cover what is spent for ready-made goods or the supplies to make items.
- **Operating expenses.** Rent, utilities, advertising, salaries, and other costs of doing business add to the markup, or increase in price. Entrepreneurs should include their own salary as an operating cost.

Fabric Store Yearly Income and Expenses

INCOME FROM SALES		
Sales	$248,150	
Cost of goods	126,795	
Gross Profit		**$121,355**
OPERATING EXPENSES		
Salaries	$ 27,392	
Rent	18,000	
Utilities	6,785	
Advertising	3,274	
Total Operating Expenses		**$ 55,451**
Net Profit (Before Taxes)		**$ 65,904**

24-10 No business can survive for very long without a profit. What determines the amount of profit a business makes?

Keeping Records

In even the smallest business, accurate records are vital to success. An inventory record, for example, reveals whether an item is selling or just taking up space. This influences decisions about buying supplies and setting prices. Recording income and expenses is essential to figuring profit or loss, and also when paying taxes. Spreadsheet software for financial planning simplifies record keeping for businesses of every size. See *Fig. 24-11.*

Advertising and Promotion

The most outstanding products and services are of no use if people are unaware of them. Entrepreneurs can plan advertising to

- **Consumer demand.** Sometimes prices can be higher when demand is high, partly to make up for slow sales when demand drops.
- **Competitors' prices.** The price of a product must be on a par with what the competition charges, given the relative quality of the products. Service providers likewise need to know how their service compares to that of others, and whether to ask more or less than the going rate.
- **Profit.** The goal of every business is to make a **profit**. This is the amount of money remaining after subtracting the cost of goods or supplies and operating expenses from income. If costs exceed the income from sales, then the business has lost money. See *Fig. 24-10.*

24-11 A growing business requires careful record keeping, inventory control, and cost analysis. Such records can be maintained with computer software.

Business Plan

Description of the Business	Marketing Plan	Management Plan	Financial Management Plan
• Type of business • Product or service • Location • Goals	• Potential customers • Competition • Pricing • Advertising and public relations	• Personal skills • Personnel needs • Responsibilities of self and employees • Special needs of employees	• Start-up money • Operating budget • Loans needed • Accounting and inventory-control systems

24-12 A business plan should be thoroughly prepared. These are the main components, but many details go into the finalized plan.

reach potential customers most effectively if they research their target audience. Suppose you had a business personalizing T-shirts and caps with sports symbols. You might advertise in the sports section of the local newspaper, leave business cards at a sporting goods store, and hand out flyers at sports events.

Promotion, which is advertising that isn't paid for, is especially valuable to a new entrepreneur. For example, an article in a local paper and referrals by related businesses inform potential customers at no cost. Word of mouth spread by satisfied customers is worth more than many paid ads.

DEVELOPING A BUSINESS PLAN

What would you think if you heard a homebuilder say, "Oh, we don't need blueprints. We'll just lay a floor until the floorboards are gone and then start building the walls. Once we run out of drywall, we'll know whether we have enough shingles for a roof." Would you expect good results?

Despite all the time, energy, and money invested, many entrepreneurs treat their business in a similar way. They're excited about owning a business and perhaps encouraged by early success. They forget a well-known warning among established business owners: poor planning, and not a poor product, is the main reason that businesses fail.

A business plan is like a blueprint. It organizes, in outline form, all the information an aspiring entrepreneur needs to gather before taking action. It details the topics to research and analyzes competition. It includes documents and forms, such as loan applications, equipment and supply lists, and projected earnings statements. See *Fig. 24-12*.

A thorough business plan is worth the effort. The plan identifies potential problems, allowing the owner to budget more resources where needed. Equally important, a business plan is a tool for goal setting. By defining the business in all of its particulars, the plan promotes a sense of direction and confidence in the future.

Review

CHAPTER SUMMARY

- Entrepreneurs must be self-motivated people who are willing to assume all risks and responsibilities for managing a business.

- An entrepreneur may buy an existing business. Starting a new business requires making decisions about what to sell and where to locate.

- A small business may be run from the owner's home, a rented location, by mail order, or over the Internet.

- A would-be business owner needs to investigate markets, financing, and regulations.

- An entrepreneur must figure the costs of business to set a price for goods or services provided.

- A good business plan helps an entrepreneur get off to an effective start by organizing important information in four main categories.

USING KEY TERMS

For each Key Term, write a question that can be answered by that term on a separate slip of paper. Have one person read the questions while classmates take turns providing the answers.

RECALLING THE FACTS

1. Why is self-motivation an important trait for entrepreneurs?

2. Why do entrepreneurs need good physical and emotional health?

3. What are some advantages and disadvantages of buying a franchise?

4. What questions about the product to be sold must an entrepreneur ask?

5. What options does an entrepreneur have for reaching customers?

6. What factors should an entrepreneur consider before opening an in-home business?

7. Describe the expense concerns of running a mail-order business.

8. What decisions does an entrepreneur have to make when setting up a Web site?

9. What valuable information can be revealed by market research?

10. How might an entrepreneur finance a business?

11. Name and describe two types of regulations that a business owner needs to comply with.

12. What factors must be considered when deciding what to charge for an item?

13. Compare advertising and promotion.

14. What is the value of a good business plan?

and Activities

THINKING CRITICALLY

1. Henry Ford said, "A setback is the opportunity to begin again more intelligently." Why is this a useful motto for an entrepreneur?

2. In a small clothing shop, what training is needed by sales associates who fill in for the owner? Is use of equipment enough? Explain.

3. The number of hits on the Web site of a new Internet company that sells a product has high impact on the owner and business. Why?

APPLYING KNOWLEDGE

1. **Self-analysis.** Using a scale of 1-10, rate yourself on each of the six personal qualities needed for success as an entrepreneur. Ten should show a high degree of that quality. Total the numbers and compare with classmates.

2. **Setting prices.** Working in small groups, select a textile product that could be made and sold at your school. Using the guidelines found in the chapter, determine a selling price for the item.

3. **Market research.** Think of a product or service that you could provide. Research the market potential for this idea. How can you determine the demand and assess the competition? How could you set your product or service apart from others? Share your research with the class.

4. **Business software.** Practice using a computer software program designed for business. For example, you might use a database to record inventory for an imaginary business or a spreadsheet to compute pay for several employees.

5. **Business brainstorm.** Think of a service that teens could provide in your community. Create a flyer promoting the new business.

6. **SBA research.** Visit the Small Business Administration Web site (www.sba.gov) to learn more about the services this group offers. Report on how a small business owner can benefit by contacting the SBA.

CREATIVE SOLUTIONS

After enjoying success as a wedding photographer, a family friend has decided to try earning his living as a fashion photographer. Another photographer who is retiring has offered to sell her studio to your friend. After applying for loans at several banks, however, your friend has found that he can barely afford a down payment on the site. He isn't sure that he'll do enough business to make the monthly payments, especially while just starting out.

Think Creatively

How can your friend realize his career goals, given his limited finances?

Global Marketplace

OBJECTIVES

- Compare the pros and cons of off-shore production.

- Describe unethical practices associated with sweatshops and counterfeiting.

- Identify laws and regulations affecting trade.

- Describe current trends in the textile and apparel industries.

KEY TERMS

balance of trade	imports
counterfeit	off-shore production
domestic	OSHA
exports	quota
free trade	sourcing
global sourcing	tariff

shirts for an apparel company based in the U.S. The apparel company sells the shirts to U.S. retailers, as well as to stores in Europe and Japan.

Decisions about **sourcing**, or choosing where to manufacture or purchase goods, impact a company's competitive edge and profitability. Many textile and apparel manufacturers, as well as retailers, have turned to **global sourcing**. By producing or buying goods in other countries at lower costs, U.S. companies can compete more successfully in the global marketplace. Global sourcing, however, raises issues about imports and exports, the balance of trade, market shares, foreign competition, and international laws and regulations.

Imports and Exports

Goods that travel between countries are imports and exports. **Imports** come into a country from foreign countries. **Exports** are sent out from one country to others. The **balance of trade** compares the values of a country's imports and exports.

I F YOU EXAMINE THE GARMENT LABELS IN your clothing, you may be surprised. In addition to "Made in the U.S.A.," you'll find many other countries listed as the fabric source or the place where the garment was made. This list could include Sri Lanka, India, China, Taiwan, Egypt, Jamaica, Malaysia, Macao, Turkey, Israel, Brunei, Hong Kong, and the Philippines. Your closet represents the global marketplace. See *Fig. 25-1.*

GLOBAL ISSUES

In today's world, raw materials and finished products flow back and forth among countries all over the globe. Bales of cotton grown in the United States, for example, could be shipped overseas to Turkey, where the fibers are processed and woven into fabric. The fabric then ships from Turkey to Taiwan, where it's cut and sewn into

25-1 Labels show that many garments and other items, including fibers and fabrics, come from a long list of different countries.

25-2 Many products come to the United States from countries where production costs are cheaper. What explains the lower costs?

The term domestic is often used when talking about international trade. For any country, the products that originate there and the companies that reside there are known as **domestic**. In the United States, domestic companies produce huge amounts of fiber, fabric, and apparel goods. At the same time, the U.S. imports vast quantities of these from all over the world. In fact, the U.S. imports three times the amount of textile and apparel products that it exports. Thus, the value of exported goods is lower than the value of imported goods. This deficit in the balance of trade concerns the textile and apparel industries.

To increase their share of global markets, many fabric producers acquire or establish mills abroad, usually near fiber sources. The mills may be wholly owned by a U.S. firm or jointly owned with a partner from another country. By producing some goods abroad, domestic manufacturers are better able to defend against the competition of foreign-made fabrics. This also puts domestic manufacturers in a more favorable position to sell in countries that limit U.S. imports.

The apparel industry also faces tough competitive challenges as the global clothing market grows. Production costs are cheaper in many other countries. Standards of living are lower. People are paid much lower wages. Employers in

many foreign countries don't provide healthcare benefits, contribute to retirement plans, or offer many of the other benefits that U.S. workers have. This means that apparel from foreign sources can be sold at lower prices than clothing manufactured in the U.S. See *Fig. 25-2*.

Imports also affect the accessories field. Today, most higher-priced leather shoes come from Italian manufacturers. For less expensive leather shoes, the bulk is imported from China, Brazil, and Spain. Very little footwear is still manufactured in the U.S.

To help increase exports, U.S. companies are promoting the "Made in the U.S.A." label, which has prestige in other countries. Because the apparel industry has a reputation for quality goods and trend-setting styles, foreign consumers eagerly seek many U.S. brands. Individual American designers also have strong followings in such countries as Canada and Japan.

Sourcing and Off-Shore Production

Sourcing decisions are important to textile and apparel manufacturers, as well as retailers. Some companies are very committed to domestic production and want to label their products "Made in the U.S.A." See *Fig. 25- 3*. Other companies are concerned about producing their goods at the best possible price, regardless of manufacturing location.

25-3 Some labels are evidence of domestic production in the U.S. Why are these labels significant to American labor?

SMALL BEGINNINGS.

Because sewing clothes requires little equipment, it's a popular way for women in developing countries to make money. Some international aid groups help women increase their income by funding small banks, which loan the money needed to buy fabric and sewing machines. The women pay back the loans from their earnings and often take out larger loans as their business expands. Some women pool their resources to form a cooperative business, one that is jointly owned. These programs allow women to lift themselves and their families out of poverty.

With **off-shore production**, domestic companies manufacture merchandise in foreign countries. They can lower costs and compete more effectively with low-cost imports. Some people see this as a threat to American labor; others believe it's the only way for U.S. manufacturers to remain competitive.

Because apparel production is labor intensive, labor costs are an issue in sourcing decisions. Many U.S. apparel makers have moved some or all of their production off shore, where wages are much lower. Off-shore production is found in such developing countries as Costa Rica, Guatemala, and China and in such newly industrialized countries as Mexico, Brazil, Hong Kong, South Korea, and Taiwan. Even long-industrialized countries—Canada, Japan, and those in Western Europe—produce goods for U.S. manufacturers.

Fabrics are also produced off shore, in such countries as Korea and China. As a result, most domestic textile companies now produce fewer textiles for apparel and more for industrial and household goods. Over 60 percent of fabrics made and sold in the U.S. are for the nonapparel market.

Some domestic companies own or lease their own facilities overseas. They believe producing products in their own plants provides greater quality control. Others companies use contractors, which usually gives greater flexibility. The companies are free to move production to another plant or another country to obtain a better price or better quality.

For a retailer, buying foreign-made clothing has limitations. Purchasing decisions must be made very early—at least eight to nine months before the merchandise arrives in the store. If a particular style turns out to be a best seller, there is no opportunity for reorders.

Sweatshops

Sweatshops got their name from working conditions in the nineteenth century. Clothing manufacturers profited by paying their employees very low wages for working excessive hours under unsanitary conditions. Profits were said to be "sweated" out of the workers.

Today, many national and international laws prohibit sweatshops. Most manufacturers follow safe and fair employment practices. See *Fig. 25-4* on page 422. Unfortunately, sweatshops still exist, both in the U.S. and in other countries. Unethical owners and operators pay their employees less than minimum wage, don't pay overtime, and follow other illegal practices, such as evading taxes and violating fire and building codes. They often seek and exploit undocumented immigrants, who suffer long hours, low pay, and miserable working conditions just to have a job. Such employers take advantage of immigrants who are not fluent in English and who fear deportation if they report the poor working conditions.

One reason sweatshops still exist is the pressure to produce goods at low cost. As companies have shifted from owning their own factories to using contractors and subcontractors to handle the assembly part of production, many specialized facilities have appeared. These small operators are more difficult for federal and state agencies to monitor and inspect.

25-4 Since working conditions are regulated, most clothing production takes place in environments that are safe and fair.

In the U.S., government inspectors have found people working under horrid conditions, for far less than minimum wage (as little as 65 cents per hour), for long hours (16 to 18 hours a day), and with children working and playing alongside their mothers in factories. In other countries where government officials aren't interested in supporting human rights, conditions may be even worse. In Bangladesh, apparel workers earn as little as 20 cents per hour; in parts of El Salvador, they earn 56 cents an hour.

U.S. government agencies have asked manufacturers and retailers to take greater responsibility for the working conditions of their contractors and subcontractors, both domestically and off shore. Many large retailers and mass manufacturers have adopted sourcing guidelines. They regularly inspect foreign contractors to ensure that workers are not exploited. Other groups, including labor, human rights, and religious groups, have put pressure on apparel manufacturers and retailers not to use foreign suppliers and contractors who violate human rights. In many cases, the best response isn't easy to identify. The need to protect children is pressing, yet many families in developing countries rely on children's contributions to family income. A recent task force set the international minimum age for hiring at fifteen. This was reduced to age fourteen only in countries that allow employment of factory workers younger than age fifteen.

Industrial Piracy

As you're aware, well-known labels and logos on apparel and accessories attract consumers. Demand for these items has led to such unethical practices as trademark infringements and counterfeit goods. **Counterfeit** items are made with unauthorized use of registered trade names or trademarks. Typically, counterfeit goods are of much lower quality and sold at a far lower price than the authentic merchandise. Counterfeiting operations take many forms, from large-scale pirates, who reproduce thousands of items, to small-time operators. See *Fig. 25-5.*

Another unethical and illegal practice is making black market or bootleg goods. The same manufacturers that make the legitimate item also make these. The goods end up on the "black market," selling on the street for less than half the retail price.

25-5 Copied labels and logos can make counterfeit items look real, although prices and quality are lower. What would you think if you were offered a designer item by a salesperson on the street?

25-6 Many products enter and leave the country at shipping docks. Quotas control imported amounts.

The Trademark Counterfeiting Act of 1984 created criminal sanctions against domestic manufacturing of counterfeit goods. This covers everything from fake Levi jeans, to fake Rolex watches, to fake Kate Spade bags. Retailers who knowingly sell such goods can also be charged with breaking the law. Companies protect their trademark by monitoring production of their goods, using coded labels to distinguish real goods from imitations, and working with the U.S. Customs Service to catch imported counterfeit items.

Laws and Regulations

As the fashion industry becomes global, many U.S. producers and manufacturers deal with companies in other countries. As a result, U.S. businesses are affected by government regulations enacted to ensure that imported goods won't provide unfair competition for goods produced at home.

Regulation of Imports

One way the Federal government protects U.S. manufacturers from unfair competition is with quotas. A **quota** is the set amount of specific merchandise that a country's government allows to be imported. In general, quotas are expressed as numbers of units rather than dollar amounts. Because silk is not produced in the U.S., silk doesn't have quotas. On the other hand, cotton is produced in the U.S., so the amount of cotton that can be imported from other parts of the world is limited. Quotas on cotton are varied. For example, different quotas are set for fibers of different staple lengths. See *Fig. 25-6.*

Tariffs are another way to protect U.S. manufacturers. A **tariff** is a tax on imported items. The amount is usually a percentage of the item's appraised value. The tax rate varies according to the individual item and its country of origin.

Trade Agreements

International agreements affect how the U.S. trades with other countries. There are three major trade agreements.

- **Most-Favored Nation status (MFN).** For political and diplomatic reasons, certain countries are granted lower tariff rates. Some developing countries can ship goods to the U.S. duty-free (no tax) to help improve their economic situation.

- **North American Free Trade Agreement (NAFTA).** Approved in 1994, this agreement created **free trade**, or the movement of goods not restricted by tariffs or quotas, between the U.S., Canada, and Mexico. The aim is to create economic growth in all three nations. Labor unions fear, however, that U.S. employment will suffer because of lower wages in Mexico.

- **Caribbean Basin Initiative (CBI).** This program offers trade protection to U.S. manufacturers, while encouraging growth of apparel industries in Latin America. Because these countries have low labor costs, they have become important producers of fashion products. Special tariff schedules are permitted for products made of U.S. fabrics but assembled or sewn in CBI countries.

International Trade Laws

Federal laws regulate the international trade of products, including textiles and apparel. The primary objective of these laws is to establish fair trade among countries. Any U.S. textile or apparel company that imports or exports goods is affected by these laws, which are administered by the U.S. Customs Service.

- **General Agreement on Tariffs and Trade (GATT).** This multinational agreement on global trade policies permits the use of tariffs to protect domestic industries. It also permits import quotas on certain textile and apparel merchandise from specified countries. More than 100 countries, including the U.S., are members of GATT. By 2005, GATT will reduce tariffs and eliminate quotas in most countries.
- **World Trade Organization (WTO).** One agreement established by this organization provides for the phased liberalization and elimination of quotas on textiles and apparel imported from WTO member countries by 2005.

FASHION INDUSTRY TRENDS

New technologies and new ways of doing business have helped make the fashion industry more profitable. They have also made it easier to produce and sell textile and apparel products almost anywhere in the world.

Advanced Technologies

Advanced technologies have revolutionized every segment of the fashion industry, from the production of raw materials to the final distribution to consumers. Their chief advantages are saving time and reducing costs.

- **CAD (computer-aided design).** Businesses that employ CAD systems for textile and garment designs are able to produce designs faster, more accurately, and with fewer people. CAD also provides flexibility, making it easier to react to changes in market demand.
- **CAM (computer-aided manufacturing).** These computer systems control the production steps in textile and apparel manufacturing. Programmable pattern-making machines, cutting machines, and sewing machines speed up production. See *Fig. 25-7.*
- **CIM (computer-integrated manufacturing).** This system links computers to direct the entire production process, from design to finished garments. Both CAD and CAM systems are linked into CIM. Computers interface with each other, prepare specification sheets, and report costs. A CIM system eliminates repetitious data entries, reduces errors, and offers great cost savings.
- **Quick Response (QR).** This technology, described on page 141, covers management systems and business strategies that reduce the time between fiber production and the sale of finished products to consumers. Benefits include increased efficiency, a shorter timeline for production and distribution, and increased profitability.

25-7 Through specialized technology, such as this cutting machine, production in the fashion industry is streamlined.

Business Growth

Businesses are constantly seeking new methods to make themselves more efficient and competitive in the global marketplace. Some common strategies include the following:

- **Mergers and acquisitions.** Companies merge or purchase (acquire) other companies to form a larger corporate organization. The goal is to increase sales, reduce operating costs, and obtain financial resources. At the retail level, Federated Department Stores has acquired a number of stores, including Macy's, Bloomingdale's, Burdines, Rich's, Lazarus, and Broadway. The GAP, Inc., also owns Banana Republic and Old Navy. The Limited, Inc., owns many specialty stores and direct-mail companies, including Abercrombie & Fitch, Bath and Body Works, Cacique, Express, Lane Bryant, and Victoria's Secret.

- **Brand extension.** Many apparel companies use a successful brand name to diversify their product line by moving into a related apparel category. For example, men's suits can extend into coats, children's wear can expand into

Trends in TECHNOLOGY

»ELECTRONIC DATA INTERCHANGE

EDI, or electronic data interchange, is the technology that allows computers at two companies to "talk" to each other. The two computer systems may communicate directly or through a third party's computer system, called a VAN, or value-added network.

Large manufacturers and large retailers use EDI technology to eliminate paperwork between the two companies. Such forms as purchase orders, invoices, packing slips, inventory forms, and shipping documents are no longer needed. EDI saves clerical time, paper, and postage.

For retailers, one major advantage of EDI is that cross-dockable goods are received at their warehouse. Cross-dockable means that manufacturers ship goods as "floor ready" merchandise. These goods arrive at the retailer's warehouse on hangers with sales tags, including retail price and UPC code, already attached. With EDI technology, the manufacturer knows exactly what to print on the sales tags for each retailer.

EDI technology also gives the retailer's warehouse advance notice that goods are on the way. The warehouse can be ready to receive them and forward the proper quantities to individual stores. All of this is done electronically, without any need for phone calls, faxes, or mail correspondence.

INVESTIGATION ACTIVITY
What has been the textile industry's response to EDI? Use the Internet to make your assessment.

25-8 Even children wear designer clothes.

infants' garments, and shoe manufacturers can offer belts and handbags. Famous designers have expanded their businesses by designing for both genders, for children, and for different price levels. Tommy Hilfiger and Ralph Lauren, for example, design apparel for men, women, and children. See *Fig. 25-8*. Donna Karan designs a high-priced signature collection as well as DKNY, a lower-priced line.

- **Crossover merchandising.** Some companies try to extend their brand into a nonapparel category. The most successful crossovers have been from apparel to fragrances and cosmetics. Many designer brands have crossed over into accessories, such as scarves, ties, jewelry, watches, shoes, belts, handbags, hosiery, and socks. A few designers, including Bill Blass, Ralph Lauren, Liz Claiborne, and Calvin Klein, have expanded into such home furnishings as sheets, towels, and table linens. Brand crossovers are often accomplished through licensing agreements.

- **Licensing.** Some merchandise is identified with a highly recognizable name and is often considered a status symbol. As noted in Chapter 7, many well-known designers license the use of their original designs or just their names to manufacturers of a wide variety of goods. In addition to designers, other "names" have had licensing successes. For example, manufacturers of athletic shoes, such as Nike, Reebok, and Adidas, have licensed their names and logos to producers of active sportswear.

- **Private labels.** This merchandise carries a store's name or a brand name developed exclu- sively for a store. For example, one of JCPenney's private labels is Arizona®; Macy's has its Charter Club®. Private label merchandise can account for 20 to 45 percent of a manufacturer's output. Either the manufacturer or retailer designs the product line and specifications. If design is done by the manufacturer, separate design teams help maintain different images for the manufacturer's national brand and the retailer's private label brand.

- **Franchises.** Of all retail sales in the U.S., one-third is generated by franchises. Many established clothing retailers and designer stores offer franchises in order to expand their business. See *Fig. 25-9*.

Safer Working Conditions

Safety in the workplace is a two-way responsibility. Employers are obligated to provide a work environment free from recognized health and accident hazards. This environment must include equipment and materials needed to do the work safely. Employees must be instructed in their use. If certain conditions or materials are hazardous, the employer must notify workers. In addition, employers must keep records of all job-related illnesses and injuries.

25-9 Because of franchises, you can find the same stores in many locations throughout the country.

25-10 Employees must know how to operate equipment safely and report any unsafe conditions or practices.

In turn, employees must learn to perform the job safely. See *Fig. 25-10*. Workers and employees alike are responsible for following environmental protection laws.

To help ensure safety in the workplace, laws regulate work hours, set standards for safe working conditions, and limit child labor. All companies are regulated by the following laws:

- **Fair Labor Standards Act.** This act established a minimum wage and a maximum 40-hour workweek. The child labor provisions set the minimum age of fourteen for most jobs and limit the number of hours that fourteen- and fifteen-year-olds can work. They forbid the employment of children under sixteen in many jobs. Those under seventeen are limited from hazardous jobs, such as operating motor vehicles or power-driven machinery; handling explosives or nuclear materials; and working in the construction, demolition, and meat processing fields. Children of any age can deliver newspapers, work for parents in a nonfarm business, and perform in radio, television, movies, and other theatrical productions.

- **Occupational Safety and Health Act.** This act set standards for safe and healthful working conditions. As a result, the Occupational Safety and Health Administration, commonly known as **OSHA**, was formed. Operating under the Department of Labor, OSHA establishes, revises, and enforces job safety and health standards. It also requires employers to prepare and maintain records of occupational injuries and illnesses.

Environmental Efforts

Federal environmental laws regulate business practices related to pollution. The goal is to protect the environment from toxic pollutants. In the fashion industry, these laws primarily affect chemical companies that produce manufactured fibers. Current laws include the Clean Water Act, Clean Air Act, Resource Conservation and Recovery Act, and Toxic Substances Control Act.

The textile industry has invested over a billion dollars in environmental controls since the mid-1980s. Companies have taken time and money to develop cleaner dyeing and finishing processes. They use fewer toxic materials and less water.

In 1992, the American Textile Manufacturers Institute (ATMI) launched its Encouraging Environmental Excellence (E3) program. It calls for textile companies to implement a 10-point plan that includes environmental policies, audits, recycling, education, and community awareness. Companies must submit written information to ATMI that documents their compliance with the program. See *Fig. 25-11* on page 428.

Consumer concerns have helped prompt the development of environmentally friendly products. Many companies manufacture products that include organic or recycled materials. For

25-11 Companies can advertise their commitment to environmental excellence by placing this logo on product hangtags.

example, organically grown cotton is produced without synthetic chemical fertilizers or pesticides. Naturally colored cotton, such as Foxfibre® cotton, in shades of green and brown eliminates the need for dyes. Wool can be obtained from humanely sheared, free-range sheep.

The call to recycle has led to some interesting new products. See *Fig. 25-12*. Tencel® is cellulosic fiber made from harvested wood pulp that is processed with recycled chemicals. In production, virtually all the dissolving agent is recycled. The resulting fiber is machine washable, stronger than cotton or wool, and has a silkier touch. Plastic water and soda bottles take on new life as textile products. The bottles are sorted by color, chopped into pieces, and washed and dried. These pieces are heated, purified, and formed into pellets. From the pellets, the polyester is extruded as fine fibers for spinning.

Some apparel manufacturers support environmental awareness campaigns. These include sponsorship of beach cleanups, cooperative programs with environmental groups, and advertising campaigns that explain the company's stance on environmental issues.

Environmental awareness has affected other textile-related industries. In the home furnishings industry, manufacturers have eliminated toxic vapors emitted during production or product use, such as formaldehyde on fabric wall coverings. Recycled fibers are used for carpets, and recycled fiberfill for pillows and comforters. The floor covering industry collects used carpets for recycling. This industry has worked to eliminate certain chemicals in the glue used on carpet backings. These chemicals were suspected of causing cancer. Even mattress retailers offer convenient recycling programs. When a new mattress is delivered, the store will pick up the old mattress and recycle it.

While these developments are exciting, some parts of the consumer market resist due to cost. Organic and recycled textile products are usually higher priced. Not everyone is willing to pay the price for the benefits. Such issues facing the fashion industry involve the global marketplace today.

25-12 Recycled materials are made into ordinary garments—and some that are not so ordinary.

How To... PACK FOR TRAVEL

Travel, whether globally or short distances from home, is easier when you know how to pack. The number one rule is to pack lightly. Some travel experts recommend laying out everything you plan to bring on a trip—and then packing only half of it!

- **Make a list a few days before packing. Review to be sure nothing is forgotten.**

- **Choose basic outfits that mix and match for various occasions.**

- **Select accessories that will change the look of basic outfits.**

- **When packing, put heavy or bulky items, including shoes, on the bottom.**

- **Stuff shoes with rolled-up socks, hosiery, or other small, nonbreakable items.**

- **Roll items that don't wrinkle, such as T-shirts, sweaters, and jeans, into tight cylinders to take up less space. Use them to keep other items from sliding around.**

- **To prevent wrinkling, place tissue paper between the folds of clothes. Another technique is to cover a garment on a hanger with a plastic bag. Then slip out the hanger and place the bag and garment on a flat surface. Fold and press gently to remove air before packing.**

- **Place such items as tops and underwear in small plastic bags.**

- **Purchase travel-size toiletries, such as shampoo, deodorant, and toothpaste.**

- **If staying at a hotel, call the toll-free number to ask whether an alarm clock, hair dryer, and iron are available for guests.**

- **If traveling by plane, contact the airline about carry-on luggage rules. Any carry-on item considered a security risk will be confiscated at the security checkpoint. Depending on airline policy, it may or may not be returned.**

Exploring **Packing**

Demonstrate for the class the proper way to pack a suitcase.

Review

CHAPTER SUMMARY

- Increased global sourcing has raised issues related to fair trade and human rights.

- Off-shore production brings benefits to manufacturers but raises concerns about fair wages and domestic jobs.

- Manufacturers and governments have taken steps to discourage industrial piracy.

- International agreements promote fair and open trade.

- New technologies and business growth have increased the pace of clothing distribution and availability.

- Working conditions and the environment are continuing concerns.

USING KEY TERMS

Choose at least five Key Terms and assume you must teach them to junior high students. Develop a visual that makes each term easy to understand. Some possibilities are cartoon drawings, diagrams, and simple posters. Computer graphics might be used if available. You might even plan a skit, with students representing different countries and manufacturers.

RECALLING THE FACTS

1. Why might imported denim jeans cost less than a pair made domestically?

2. Summarize arguments for and against off-shore production of goods by U.S. manufacturers.

3. Describe the working situation of someone who works in a sweatshop.

4. Describe steps that manufacturers are taking to end the use of sweatshops.

5. What is the difference between counterfeiting and bootlegging?

6. How do tariffs and quotas aim to help a country's textile industry?

7. What is the purpose of NAFTA?

8. What is the main purpose of international trade laws?

9. How do CAD and CAM reduce costs for clothing manufacturers?

10. Describe two ways that EDI streamlines garment distribution.

11. What is the difference between brand extension and crossover merchandising?

12. Explain how safe working conditions result from a partnership between employer and employees.

13. What protections are provided by the Fair Labor Standards Act?

14. List two general ways that the fashion industry has responded to concerns about its effect on the environment.

and Activities

THINKING CRITICALLY

1. Some fabrics may be lower quality when produced in countries where looms and other equipment are old and not well maintained. Should such fabric be imported? What are possible consequences if they are imported? If they aren't?

2. Should young children in developing countries be allowed to work when their families need the income? Explain your reasoning.

APPLYING KNOWLEDGE

1. **Ending sweatshops.** Visit the Web site of a group that works to abolish sweatshops. What other social conditions are associated with sweatshop labor? What actions does the group urge to end sweatshop conditions around the world?

2. **Trade treaties.** Locate a newspaper or magazine article that deals with one of the trade agreements discussed in the chapter. Read and summarize the article. Compare findings with those of classmates to get an overview of the implications of these agreements.

3. **Eco-wear.** Visit the Web site of a vendor of clothing made through ecologically friendly or socially responsible practices. Note the items offered, their prices, and any information the company gives on itself and its standards for selecting merchandise. Report your findings. In class, discuss the issues raised by the sellers and how their merchandise responds to these concerns.

4. **Seeking accord.** Working with a small group, imagine you represent the interests of one of the following: consumers, workers, clothing makers, or environmentalists. In writing, describe your position and concerns regarding each of these issues: offshore production; free-trade agreements; and new production and distribution technologies. Compare your views with those of the other groups. Are there more points of agreement or disagreement?

CREATIVE SOLUTIONS

Your pen pal in another state has heard that the company that makes her school's jackets and athletic team uniforms uses cheap labor in a country where sweatshops are common. She's concerned about this possibility, and she thinks that other students in her school would be too if this situation is true. Her feelings are growing stronger about this issue.

Think Creatively

How can your pen pal get the information she needs? What would you suggest she do if the company does buy goods made in sweatshops?

Careers

Communication and Education

A MODEL ENTERS THE PHOTOGRAPHY studio. "Beautiful!" the photographer exclaims, admiring the fashion look she presents. He continues to chat amiably with her while readying the set. As the shoot begins, the model moves gracefully from one pose to another while the photographer continually offers verbal suggestions and encouragement. The camera flashes constantly. This scene is common in the world of fashion photography, which is just one career in the interesting areas of fashion communication and education.

The communication field is a good place for people who enjoy working with words. As they combine words with images, fashion writers, editors, illustrators, and photographers communicate fashion.

In the area of education, many opportunities exist. Teachers provide instruction in high schools, vocational schools, and colleges. County extension agents put on community programs through the U.S. Department of Agriculture. Consumer education specialists promote products of the companies that employ them. Anytime people help others learn, they are a part of education.

IS THIS FIELD FOR YOU?

Obviously, good communication skills count in communication and education careers. Some related abilities that are needed are represented in the statements below.

- I'm curious about how and why things happen.
- I like a fair amount of independence in my work.
- To me, a deadline is a tool for time management.
- I enjoy learning as much as teaching and doing.
- I can use constructive criticism to my benefit.
- Seeing the results of my work is more rewarding than money.

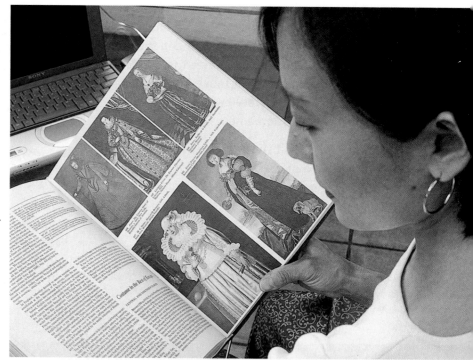

Historical researchers gather information about clothing of the past. A museum might need this information in order to prepare a display or to write an art commentary for museum guides.

Education and Training

In the fields of communication and education, a college degree is usually a necessity. The exact education needed varies with the career. Illustrators study color and design and art history, leading to a bachelor-of-fine-arts degree. A costume historian needs a background in textile restoration, visual culture, and textile and design history.

Being an intern, assistant, or volunteer during college is almost a requirement, especially in the most competitive fields. This is where a person starts to learn the skills of the trade. Setting up the backdrop for a photo shoot, for instance, a photographer's assistant notices techniques that make the staging effective. Equally important, a network of connections for the job search after graduation can be built.

To remain an expert takes continuing education. Courses in digital imaging allow a commercial photographer to take advantage of new opportunities. Teachers attend seminars and workshops on teaching strategies and issues in education. For jobs involving the Internet, staying current on software is essential.

Possible Career Paths

In fashion communication and education some careers follow a traditional path. New graduates begin as assistants. Those who show the desire and ability move up. A journalist may start as a proofreader, then advance to researcher before earning a chance to write.

Rapidly changing technology and other employment trends encourage cross-career moves. For example, a clothing writer might teach a high school clothing class and then go on to become fully certified. Likewise, some information technology (IT) jobs are so new that few colleges and universities have developed a specific curriculum. Thus, people enter one field from another.

Some Web-site designers create and maintain sites for clothing company catalogs. On many sites, Internet users can make catalog purchases on-line.

THE SKILLS YOU NEED

To be successful in the fields of communication and education, you'll need skills that include the following:

- Communication
- Management
- Organization
- Creativity
- Flexibility
- Self-discipline
- Self-confidence

Choosing a Communication or Education *Career*

CONSUMER EDUCATION SPECIALIST | **COOPERATIVE EXTENSION AGENT** | **COSTUME DESIGNER** | *COSTUME HISTORIAN* | **FASHION EDITOR** | *FASHION PHOTOGRAPHER* | *FASHION WRITER* | *FCS TEACHER* | *WEB-SITE DESIGNER*

Fashion Writer —

Fashion writers are journalists whose articles and columns appear in fashion magazines, newspapers, press releases, and even on the computer screen. Writers do research and conduct interviews, often traveling to wherever news happens. Although the effort is time-consuming, writers revise drafts of articles to make improvements.

Some writers work from home as freelancers. They must satisfy editors, who decide a publication's content and focus. Suggesting story ideas and keeping track of submissions, deadlines, and payments are part of the job.

FCS Teacher —

Many family and consumer sciences (FCS) educators teach courses in fashion and clothing construction. A teacher's workday typically involves preparing lessons, gathering materials, teaching, evaluating work, and record keeping.

Effective teachers manage demonstrations, discussions, and group work in the classroom. Through continuing education, they update their own skills and knowledge. Teachers must be licensed by a state board of education.

Web-Site Designer

Web-site designers produce Internet sites with visual appeal and navigation ease. Fashion manufacturers, magazines, and many others need sites to provide information and promote their products. After creating sites, designers keep them up-to-date and fresh by adding the most current visual and audio effects.

All of this takes technical as well as artistic skills with color, line, and other design elements. The designer must know how to use numerous computer programs for defining colors, spacing, and lettering.

Photographic skill involves more than just taking a picture. Knowledge of lighting, composition, and equipment is essential for the work.

Costume Historian

Costume historians are experts in the clothing of eras past. They are researchers who use documents and archives from museums, libraries, and historical societies. They describe what people wore and explain how these garments reflect a period of history.

While some costume historians design costumes, most work in research and consulting. Costume historians may be asked to authenticate garments for an auction house or private collector. They might date and restore antique clothes given to a museum or help members of a historical preservation society reproduce period costumes, as in Colonial Williamsburg. When fashion houses want to display styles by past designers, they may hire costume historians to organize and maintain the collection.

Educators work in many areas related to fashion. A family and consumer sciences teacher might work at the high school or college level. Teaching in a cooperative extension program is also possible.

Photographer

In the fashion industry top photographers are as well known and well paid as top models and designers. Most photographers, however, earn a more modest income and are not known by name.

Fashion photographers work as salaried employees and freelancers. They are associated with catalogs, newspapers, fashion magazines, advertising agencies, and large stores. Some own their own studio and sell their photos to publications. Independent photographers may market their photos to stock agencies that supply illustrations to go with printed material. The photographers earn a fee each time a photo is used.

Photographers work with models, striving for moods in their photos. Successful photographers are also artists. Richard Avedon, a renowned professional photographer for over fifty years, turned from fashions to portraits. His work is so distinctive that it is recognizable even when unsigned.

CAREER APPLICATIONS

1. **Fashion writing.** Assuming the role of a fashion writer, write a magazine article that reports on the fashions worn at an imaginary event of your choosing. Include information that shows your knowledge of fashion styles and designs.

2. **FCCLA.** As an Applied Technology Project, design a home page and follow-up pages for a Web site with a fashion focus. Choose and arrange colors, visuals, and text. Carry out your design in the most effective medium, including computer graphics software.

3. **Professionalism.** Choose a fashion communication or education career. Find out how professionalism is promoted in that career. Is there a professional society that people can join? Is there a code of ethics? Report your findings to the class.

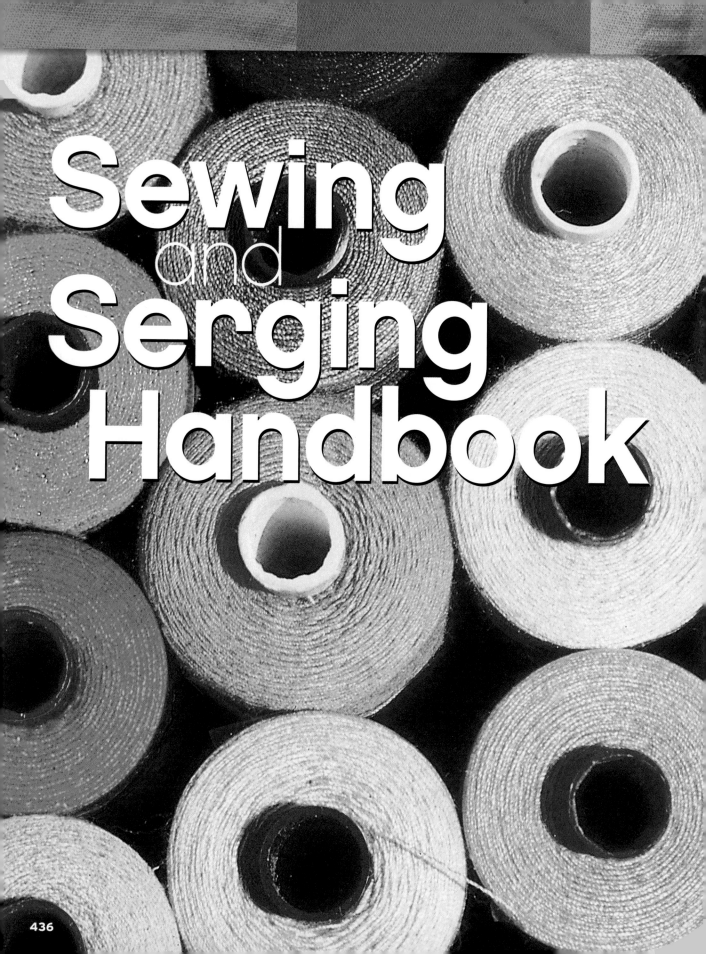

Sewing and Serging Handbook

Patterns, Fabrics, and Notions

Selecting a Pattern

WHEN YOU GET READY to sew, you'll need to make several decisions. Before you pick a pattern, think about the following questions.

- **What is your experience level?** Experience makes a difference. If you haven't sewn before, a simple project is best. Then, with each future project, you can build skills by choosing something more complicated.
- **How much time do you have?** With limited time, you're more likely to complete a project that has less detail. Ask for help in choosing a project if you're not sure what's involved.
- **Where will you sew?** If you don't have a sewing machine, you might be able to work at the home of a family member or friend. In some schools you can get permission to sew during study halls or after school.
- **What will you sew?** Many people like to sew for themselves, perhaps clothing or something for the home, such as a pillow or placemats. Making a gift for someone is another idea.

THE PATTERN CATALOG

Once these early decisions are made, you're ready to begin—with a pattern. A **pattern** is a set of tissue pattern pieces and instructions for creating an item from fabric. Most sewers use a pattern to guide them, but how do you choose one? Start by looking through pattern catalogs. Each company that manufactures patterns produces its own catalog. See *Fig. 1-1*. You may have some copies of catalogs in your classroom.

Catalogs are divided into sections that make choosing easy. For example, tabbed sections are marked for dresses, sportswear, and easy-to-sew styles. Special categories include larger sizes, children and toddlers, men and boys, home decorating, crafts, gifts, and accessories.

Garments are sketched in the catalog and often actual photographs are included. A close look at these gives you a good idea of what the garment will look like when done. You may even get ideas for accessories.

One pattern usually shows more than one view, identified by letter. View A might show a shirt with long sleeves, while view B is the same shirt with short sleeves.

1-1 Pattern catalogs provide information about the style, fit, design details, and sewing difficulty of patterns.

Customizing. If the pattern measurements and style aren't quite right for you, remember that you can customize a pattern. Lengthening and shortening are possible. You can also make the garment a little looser or more fitted in specific places. With careful planning, the pattern can be adapted to produce a garment that fits you well.

Stores that sell patterns have pattern catalogs. After browsing through a catalog, note the number of the pattern you want. Then find the cabinet drawer that contains that number. Most stores allow you to remove the pattern from the cabinet yourself so you can carry it with you while choosing fabric and supplies. Store displays also feature patterns that you can take from racks.

Several times a year most pattern companies publish a magazine that features a selected group of patterns. You can subscribe to these magazines or buy them at the newsstand. In addition, most pattern companies have Web sites where you can preview and order patterns.

SELECTING THE RIGHT STYLE

How can you tell from the drawing on a catalog page what the finished garment will look like on you? One way is to pay careful attention to the styles of items you already own. Which ones are flattering and enjoyable to wear? You might choose patterns with similar designs. Trying on ready-to-wear garments in a store is another way to determine whether a style is right for you.

As you study styles, remember all you've learned about design. Whether sewing or buying clothes, the design elements and principles can be helpful.

Clues on the Pattern Envelope

The pattern envelope shows you how the finished garment should look. Carefully examine the illustrations on the front of the envelope, shown in *Fig. 1-2*. Note the fit across the shoulders, waist, and hips. Is the garment fitted to the shape of the body, or is it full and loose? Also note

1-2 What information is provided on the front of this pattern envelope?

the type of fabric pictured. Is it a heavyweight or lightweight fabric? Is it a solid color, print, plaid, or stripe? These clues will help you choose fabric.

The back of the pattern envelope contains small line drawings that show the garment back. You'll also find other information, as shown in *Fig. 1-3* on page 442. The finished garment measurements, including "width at lower edge" and "finished back length," give an idea of the proportions of the finished garment.

Skill Level

For clues about sewing difficulty, read the description in the catalog or on the pattern envelope. Most pattern companies have easy-to-sew patterns, identified by such brand names as "Easy," "Fast & Easy," "Quick & Easy," and "6 Made Easy."

These patterns usually have fewer pattern pieces, simple-to-follow layouts, and easier construction techniques. Some easy-to-sew patterns

SEWING TIP

Measurements. The clothes in your closet can help you interpret the measurements on a pattern envelope. Measure the lengths of a few jackets, dresses, or pants that you wear. Also measure the bottom circumference, or distance around, of pants and skirts in different styles. Compare these measurements to those on a pattern you like. Then you'll know, for example, whether pant legs described as 20 inches (51 cm) at the lower edge are slimmer or fuller than those you already own.

are even marked with a sewing time that helps you estimate how long it will take to make the item.

SELECTING THE CORRECT SIZE

To determine the correct pattern size for you, first take your body measurements. Ideally you should take measurements over undergarments, not over clothes. If necessary, you can take them over snug-fitting clothes. Remove sweaters, belts, jackets, and other bulky items.

Use a flexible, 60-inch (150-cm), plastic-coated measuring tape. The tape measure should be held snugly, but not tightly, around the body. For width measurements, be sure the tape measure is parallel to the floor. For accuracy, have someone help you, writing down each measurement after it is taken.

As you record height and circumference measurements, include bust or chest, waist, and hips. Females need to take a back waist measurement. Males should take neck and sleeve measurements. For pants, the waist and inseam measurements are needed. These measurements are explained in *Fig. 1-4* on page 443.

Figure Type

Figure types, such as juniors and misses, are size categories determined by height and body proportions. In order to determine your figure type, you need to look at three pieces of information: your height, your back waist length (for females), and your body proportions. Then compare this information with the charts that appear in the back of the pattern catalogs to choose the figure type for you. See *Fig. 1-5* on page 444.

Pattern Size

After you have determined your figure type, the next step is to find your pattern size. Compare your measurements with those listed in the chart on the pattern envelope back. Make sure you are

The back of a pattern envelope gives more information per square inch than any other part of the pattern. Use it to choose fabric, notions, and sewing supplies for a project.

- **Identification information.** General information including pattern number; basic size category; style, such as "Misses' Pants"; number of pattern pieces (usually having fewer pieces means easier to make); and whether French and Spanish translations are included.

- **Back views.** Drawings that show all seams, darts, and design details on the garment back.

- **Body measurements.** All sizes for which the pattern was designed; actual pattern pieces are larger to allow for movement and comfort.

- **Yardage chart.** Amount of fabric needed for different views, sizes, and fabric widths. The terms "with nap" and "without nap" appear after fabric widths. "With nap" means fabric has a nap, pile, or one-way design, so all pattern pieces must be placed in one direction on the fabric. "With-nap" layouts sometimes take extra fabric.

- **Finished garment measurements.** Length and circumference measurements on completed garment. For example, "skirt width" and "side length" describe the fullness and length of the design.

- **Suggested fabrics.** Recommended fabrics for the garment; tells whether extra fabric is needed to match plaids and stripes and whether stretch fabric must be used; notes suitability of stripes, plaids, and diagonal designs.

- **Notions.** Quantity and recommended sizes of such sewing supplies as thread, buttons, tapes, and zippers.

1-4 • Taking Your Measurements

- **Height.** Stand against a wall in bare feet. Have another person make a mark that is level with the top of your head. Measure from this point to the floor. For pants and skirt measurements, it is best to wear shoes.
- **Bust/chest.** The tape measure should be straight across the back and over the fullest part of the bust or chest.
- **Waist.** Tie a length of string around the smallest part of the waistline. It will roll into the natural waistline position. Measure the waistline exactly where the string settles.
- **Hips or seat.** Measure over the fullest part of the hips in a straight line around the body. For most females, measure 7 to 9 inches (18 to 23 cm) below the waist. For most men, measure 8 inches (20.5 cm) below the waist; for teen males, measure 7 inches (18 cm) below the waist.
- **Neck (for males only).** Measure around the base of the neck. This measurement plus ½ inch (1.3 cm) is neck size.
- **Back waist length (for females only).** Bend the head forward to locate the prominent bone at the base of the neck. Measure from this bone down the center back to the waistline string.
- **In-seam.** Place pants that are the correct length on a flat surface. Measure along inner seam from the bottom of one leg to where the two legs meet.
- **Out-seam.** Measure from the waist to the point where the pants bottom breaks slightly on the shoe.
- **Sleeve.** Bend the arm up for men. Measure from the base of the neck across the center back to the elbow, across the elbow crook, and up over the wrist bone. For women, measure from the top of the shoulder over the bent elbow to the wrist.

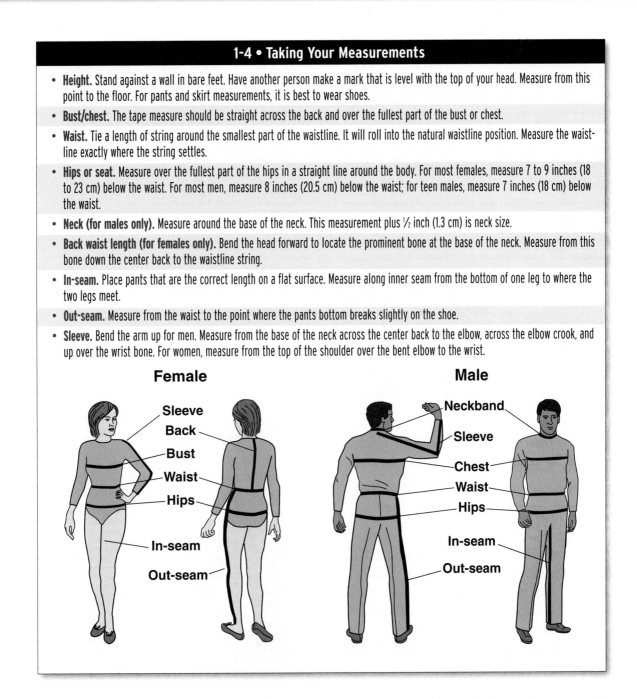

Female

- Sleeve
- Back
- Bust
- Waist
- Hips
- In-seam
- Out-seam

Male

- Neckband
- Sleeve
- Chest
- Waist
- Hips
- In-seam
- Out-seam

looking only at the measurements within your figure type category. Find the measurements that come closest to yours. That will identify your pattern size. Be sure you choose the size by actual measurements, not by the size you buy in ready-to-wear clothes. They may not be the same, and you might not be able to return the pattern. Even worse, you might spend time and money making a garment that doesn't fit.

Since few people are a perfect size, your measurements might not exactly match the sizes shown. If your measurements fall between two sizes, base your choice on the design. Select the smaller size if the design is full or loose fitting. Select the larger size if the design is closely fitted.

Simplicity's SIMPLIFIED

The Best Guide to Fit!

- **To Select your pattern size**, use your BODY MEASUREMENTS, not Ready-To-Wear size.
- **All Simplicity patterns are Multi-Sized** to help you get a Custom Fit.
- **Finished Garment Measurements** are printed on the pattern tissue and on the back of many pattern envelopes. Compare these against the Body Measurement Chart for your size. The difference is the amount of ease allowed.
- **To Take Accurate Body Measurements:** Follow the How To Measure steps below. Periodically check your measurements for changes.
- **Find your figure type:** Use height and back waist length measurements and descriptions in Measurement Charts to determine figure type.

Garment	Use this MEASUREMENT for correct size
Dresses, Tops Jackets and Separates	BUST, (if you have more than 2 1/2" (6.3cm) difference between Bust and High Bust, select your pattern size by HIGH BUST* measurement)
Skirts & Pants	WAIST measurement, (if your hips are two sizes or more larger than your waist, use HIP measurement.)
Maternity	SAME PATTERN SIZE you used before pregnancy
Between Two Sizes	SMALLER SIZE for a closer fit, or if you are small-boned. LARGER SIZE for a looser fit, or if you are large-boned.

(* Misses patterns are made for a B cup with 2 1/2" (6.3cm) difference between Bust and High Bust measurement)

How to Measure:

Measure over the undergarments you normally wear. Hold the tape measure comfortably snug, but not tight.

1. **Height:** Standing against a flat wall without shoes, from floor to top of your head.
2. **Bust:** around the fullest part of the bust and straight across the back.
3. **High Bust:** directly under the arms, straight across the back and above the bust.
4. **Waist:** Tie a narrow elastic around waist and let it settle naturally at your waistline. Measure over the elastic. Keep the elastic in place for the next measurement.
5. **Back Waist Length:** from the most prominent bone at the base of neck to the natural waistline.
6. **Hip:** around body at fullest part, usually 7"-9" (18-23cm) below waist.

For help:
Consumer Information Department,
Simplicity Pattern Co. Inc.
901 Wayne Street, Niles, MI 49121
1-800-334-3150

Body Measurements

(Detailed multi-sized body measurement charts for Babies, Toddlers, Child's, Girls/Girls' Plus, Misses/Miss Petite, Women's/Women's Petite, Unisex, Boys'/Teen Boys', and Men's sizes.)

1-5 Pattern catalogs provide measurement charts to help you decide what pattern size to buy.

If you're choosing a pattern for pants or a skirt, select the pattern size by waist measurement. If your hips are large in proportion to your waist, however, choose the pattern by hip measurement.

Almost all patterns are **multisized**, which means the pattern is printed with several sizes on each pattern piece. This is particularly helpful for people who are one size on top and another on the bottom. Each size range is identified by a letter code printed on the catalog page and on the pattern envelope. Be sure you select the size range that includes your pattern size.

Pattern Ease

All patterns have a certain amount of built-in "ease." In other words, the garment is larger than your body to give you the space to sit down and bend over in your clothes. This extra space, known as **wearing ease**, is the amount of fullness needed for movement and comfort. The only garments that do not have wearing ease are items made of stretch fabrics, such as bathing suits, body suits, and exercise wear.

A second kind of ease built into a garment is called **design ease**. This is the extra fullness a designer adds to create a particular style or silhouette. See *Fig. 1-6.* Some designers want garments to have a very loose-fitting silhouette. Others want garments to fit snugly against the body. The picture and the description on the pattern envelope give clues about the amount of ease.

1-6 Wearing ease allows you enough room for comfortable motion while wearing a garment. How is this different from design ease?

Selecting Fabric

AFTER CHOOSING A PATTERN, you can pick out fabric. Fabric is sold in rolls called **bolts**. To purchase fabric, first select one that suits the pattern style and your sewing skills. Then take the bolt to a cutting table where a clerk will remove the amount you want.

CHECKING THE PATTERN

How do you know which fabrics would be best for a garment? Look at the back of the pattern envelope to find suggestions. If denim, poplin, or corduroy is listed, choose one of these or another fabric that is equally firm. If jersey, tricot, or crepe is suggested, choose one of these or a similar soft and drapable fabric.

The pattern also tells what fabrics are not suitable. For example, stripes, plaids, and obvious diagonal prints can look unattractive in certain styles.

Sometimes a pattern is designed only for knit fabrics, which have some stretch. Make sure the knit you consider has the right amount of stretch for the pattern. All "knits only" patterns have a **stretch gauge** on the pattern envelope. The gauge shows how much the knit must be able to stretch. Pull the crosswise grain of the fabric with your fingers and compare the amount of stretch to what the pattern specifies. See *Fig. 2-1.*

If the pattern has gathers, grasp the fabric in your hand to see how it drapes. If the pattern has pleats, crease a small section of the fabric between your fingernails to see whether it will hold a pleat. Check the fabric for any flaws. The color should be even, with no streaks or spots. Any pattern design should be printed on grain. Check for wrinkle resistance by squeezing the fabric in your hand to see whether it wrinkles easily and holds the wrinkles. Read the end of the fabric bolt for information about fibers, finishes, and care requirements.

CONSIDERING SEWING SKILLS

The fabric you choose depends on your sewing expertise. If you're a beginning sewer, choose a fabric that's easy to sew. A medium-weight, firmly woven, or knitted fabric is a good choice. A small, all-over print helps hide small sewing mistakes.

Certain fabrics require special sewing techniques. The following fabrics are not good choices for beginners:

- **Slippery fabrics.** Hard to handle as you cut and stitch.

2-1 To use the stretch gauge on a pattern, hold a small part of the crosswise grain of the fabric between your hands. Place the left side at the beginning of the gauge and then stretch the fabric toward the right. As long as the fabric will stretch that far, it is usable with the pattern.

PICK-A-KNIT® RULE   FOR THIS PATTERN—4" (10cm) OF KNIT FABRIC MUST STRETCH CROSSWISE FROM HERE ➡   TO HERE ➡
POUR CE PATRON—4" (10cm) DE TRICOT DOIVENT S'ETIRER ENTRAVERS D'ICI   JUSQU'ICI

0

MISSES' SET OF KNIT TOPS: Pullover tops are sized for stretch knits only. Long sleeved A and D, Short sleeved B and E and sleeveless C have round neckline. Long sleeved F has scoop neckline. D and E are cropped. Suitable for Overlock/Serger.

SERIE DE HAUTS EN JERSEY POUR JEUNE FEMME: Hauts en jerseys extensibles seule D à manches longues. B et E à manches courtes et C sans manches avec enc à manches longues avec décolleté arrondi. D et E courts. Ces modèles Overlock/Surjeteuse.

Fabrics: Stretch knits only such as Cotton Interlock, Jerseys, Cotton/Lycra Blends. See Pick A Knit® Rule. Not suitable for obvious diagonals. Extra fabric needed to match plaids, stripes or one-way design fabrics. For pile, shaded or one-way design fabrics, use with nap yardages/layouts.

Tissus: Jerseys extensibles seulement tels que cotons interlock, jersey Voyez la Règle Choisissez-un Jersey. Les tissus à diagonales apparer ce patron. Prévoyez davantage de tissu pour raccorder les éco unidirectionnels. Pour les tissus à long poil, de différents tons ou utilisez métrages et plans de coupe "avec sens."

Notions: Thread, one pkg. straight seam binding. Look for Simplicity notions.

Mercerie: Fil; un paquet d'extra-fort rectiligne. Demandez la mercerie

- **Loosely woven fabrics.** Ravel easily and require special seam finishes.
- **Sheer or thick, bulky fabrics.** Hard to pin, sew, and press.
- **Fabrics with a one-way design.** Must have all pattern pieces laid out in the same direction.
- **Pile fabrics.** Require special pattern layouts and pressing techniques; include velvet and corduroy.
- **Stripes and plaids.** Must be matched at all seam lines and design points, such as collars, cuffs, and pockets.

CHOOSING FABRIC FOR YOU

A fabric should be right for your appearance and activities. Pick a color and texture that flatter your coloring and body shape. Coordinate the planned garment with items you already own. See *Fig. 2-2.*

Choose a fabric that fits your wearing plans. For example, suppose a pattern envelope suggests making a dress or shirt in denim. If you're making the garment for a formal event, denim probably won't be a good choice.

HOW MUCH TO BUY

The label or hangtag at the end of the fabric bolt tells you the width of the fabric. Most fabrics are 45 inches (115 cm) or 60 inches (150 cm) wide. A few are 36 inches (91.5 cm) wide. The yardage chart on the pattern envelope lists how much fabric you'll need for your size and the view you plan to make.

Don't buy a fabric that is narrower than the ones listed on your pattern envelope. For example, if the chart lists only 45-inch (115-cm) or 60-inch (150-cm) fabric, you don't want a smaller width. Some of the pattern pieces for that style are probably too large to fit on a narrower piece of fabric.

The yardage chart may indicate that fabrics with a nap, pile, shading, or one-way design take extra yardage. Corduroy and velveteen fabrics have a pile, and many knits have shading. With such fabrics, all pattern pieces must be cut so the pile or design runs in the same direction, using a one-way layout. Otherwise the finished garment looks as though it was cut from two different shades of fabric, or part of the fabric's design is upside-down. Stripes, plaids, and other designs may need additional fabric in order to match the fabric design at the seams.

2-2 The pattern envelope suggests fabrics that would be suitable for your project. What other suggestions do you have for choosing a fabric?

Selecting Notions

TO COMPLETE YOUR sewing project, you'll need thread, fasteners, and maybe more. The small items that become a permanent part of a garment are called notions. All notions are listed on the back of the pattern envelope.

Sitting down to sew and discovering you don't have what you need is frustrating. If you select notions when you buy the fabric, this is less likely to happen.

Lining, interfacing, trim, and elastic are some of the notions purchased by the yard or meter. Because the amount to buy may depend on pattern size, these notions are listed in the yardage chart.

Choose notions carefully, making sure the colors look good with the fabric. Also, choose buttons, tapes, trims, and interfacings that require the same care as the fabric. For example, a cotton shirt can't be washed if its trim can only be dry-cleaned.

After purchasing the notions for your project, keep them together in a safe place. A shoebox or zip-top bag makes a good storage container. When working at school, mark any notion packages with your name for easy identification.

CHOOSING THREAD

Thread, which comes in many types and colors, should be the same color as the fabric. See *Fig. 3-1.* If you can't find the exact color, choose a shade darker. Thread looks lighter after stitching. A good quality thread is strong and smooth, has even thickness, and resists tangling. As noted below, fabric type determines the thread you select.

- **Polyester or polyester/cotton thread.** This all-purpose thread can be used for sewing most fabrics. Strong and flexible, it shrinks less than other threads. Because the thread stretches slightly, it is recommended for knits and

3-1 Thread color should match the fabric as closely as possible. How would you choose thread for a plaid fabric?

SEWING TIP

Thread color. Try to match thread color as closely as possible to the fabric, especially when the fabric is a solid color. When matching a print or a plaid, select the background or dominant color for the thread. A single strand of thread will appear slightly lighter in color than it does when wound on the spool. If a small strand of thread is loose on the spool, hold that against the fabric.

3-2 In what types of garments would you find these zippers?

Conventional   Invisible   Separating   Two-way   Trouser   Decorative

stretch fabrics. Seams are less likely to break as the garment is worn.

- **Mercerized cotton thread.** This thread can be used to sew woven fabrics of natural fibers, such as 100 percent cotton or silk. Cotton thread is used mostly for quilting and crafts.
- **Silk thread.** Used on silk or wool fabrics, this thread is excellent for basting delicate fabrics.
- **Heavy-duty thread.** Use this strong and durable thread to sew heavy fabrics, such as those for slipcovers.
- **Buttonhole twist thread.** A thicker thread than most, this one is used for decorative top-stitching and hand-worked buttonholes.

Special threads are available for certain sewing and craft projects. These include serger thread, basting thread, quilting thread, rayon machine embroidery thread, and carpet thread.

CHOOSING FASTENERS

Fasteners are used to close a garment. They include zippers, buttons, snaps, hooks and eyes, buckles, and hook-and-loop tape.

Zippers

Zippers come in different colors and lengths and have metal or polyester coils. A lightweight, polyester, coil zipper works well with lightweight fabric. Zipper recommendations are listed on the back of the pattern envelope. Choose the right one for the job. See *Fig. 3-2*.

- **Conventional zipper.** Opens at the top and has a stop at the bottom; the most common zipper.
- **Invisible zipper.** Disappears into the seam when closed, so all you see is the tab at the top of the zipper.
- **Separating zipper.** Comes apart at the bottom for use in jackets and coats.
- **Two-way zipper.** Has sliders at the top and bottom, so can be opened from either end.
- **Trouser zipper.** Usually has metal teeth and wider tape.
- **Decorative zipper.** Has large teeth and a pull ring.

Buttons

The pattern envelope gives the size and number of buttons needed for a project. A button's size is measured across its diameter and stated in fractions of an inch. There are two basic button types. See *Fig. 3-3*.

Sew-through button

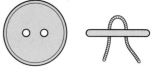

Shank button

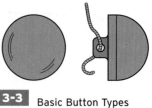

3-3 Basic Button Types

- **Sew-through buttons.** These have two to four holes on the face of the button for attaching with thread.
- **Shank buttons.** These have a metal, plastic, or fabric loop, called the shank, behind the button. Thread is stitched through the shank to attach the button. A shank allows room for the buttonhole to lie smoothly between the button and the fabric that holds it. Heavy fabrics may require shank buttons.

Snaps

Snaps range in size from 0000 or 4/0 (small) to size 4 (large). Snaps and other fasteners are shown in *Fig. 3-4.* Smaller snap sizes hold edges together where the strain or pull is minimal. Larger sizes are good for heavy-duty use. Large covered snaps are available for coats and suits. Snaps pre-attached to fabric tapes are ideal for sportswear and children's wear.

Hooks and Eyes

Hooks and eyes range in size from 0 (small) to 3 (large). They are packaged with two types of eyes.
- **Curved eye.** Used on edges that just meet, such as the edge of a collar or neckline.
- **Straight eye.** Used on lapped edges, such as a waistband or cuff.

Large covered hooks and eyes are available for coats and jackets. Specialty waistband fasteners have a large, flat, hook-and-bar closure.

Buckles

Buckles of many shapes, sizes, and materials can be purchased separately or in belt kits. There are two basic types.
- **Buckle with a prong.** These buckles must be used with eyelets. Ready-made metal eyelets can be applied to the belt with special pliers or an attaching tool. Eyelets can also be hand-sewn with a buttonhole stitch.
- **Buckle without a prong.** These can simply be stitched to the belt end; no eyelets are needed.

Hook-and-Loop Tape

This fastener consists of two nylon strips, one with tiny hooks and one with looped pile. The hooks and pile intermesh when pressed together. Such tape is often used on jackets, sportswear, and children's clothes. Available by the yard or in precut shapes, it can be stitched by hand or machine.

CHOOSING TAPES AND TRIMS

Tapes and trims can be functional or decorative. See *Fig. 3-5.* They reinforce a seam, cover a

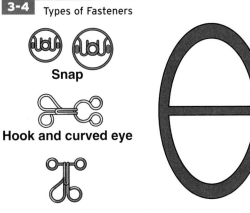

3-4 Types of Fasteners

Snap

Hook and curved eye

Hook and straight eye   Buckle without prong   Buckle with prong   Hook-and-loop tape

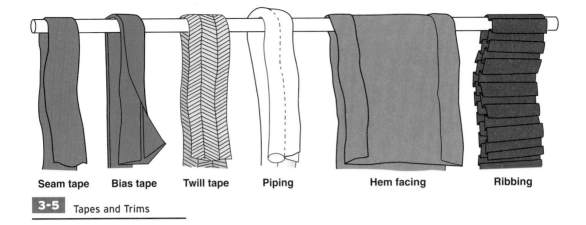

| Seam tape | Bias tape | Twill tape | Piping | Hem facing | Ribbing |

3-5 Tapes and Trims

fabric edge, or create a special design on the outside of a garment. You'll find many types, widths, and colors. They may be woven, knitted, braided, or made of lace. If you can't match trim color to fabric exactly, select a contrasting color instead.

Purpose determines which tape or trim to choose. To prevent fabric from stretching, select a firm, non-stretchable tape or trim. For areas that should stretch during wear, such as a knitted cuff, choose a stretchable tape or trim.

Some of the common tapes and trims include the following:

- **Seam tape.** Woven tape or lace used to finish hem and facing edges.
- **Bias tape.** Single-fold or double-fold tape for binding curved or straight edges; also used for casings, ties, and trims.
- **Hem facing.** Wide bias tape or lace for facing hems and binding edges.
- **Fold-over braid.** Knitted braid folded in half and used for binding and trimming edges.
- **Ribbing.** Stretchable knitted band used to finish a neckline, armhole, sleeve, pant leg, or lower edge.
- **Twill tape.** Firmly woven tape for reinforcing seams.
- **Piping.** Narrow, corded, bias strip of fabric inserted into a seam for a decorative trim.
- **Cable cord.** Filler for piping, cording, and tubing.

- **Belting.** Very stiff band used to reinforce belts and waistbands.

CHOOSING ELASTICS

Since elastic comes in several types and widths, your choice depends on whether it will be used in a casing or stitched directly to a garment. Read the label when purchasing elastic to be sure it will serve the correct purpose. See *Fig. 3-6*.

- **Woven elastic.** Stays the same width when stretched, so it can be stitched directly to a garment or used in a casing.
- **Braided elastic.** Recommended only for casings because it narrows when stretched.
- **Clear elastic.** Very stretchy elastic that is stitched directly to the fabric; particularly suitable for swimwear and lingerie.
- **Special-purpose elastics.** Available for lingerie, swimwear, and activewear.

CHOOSING INTERFACINGS AND LININGS

Interfacings and linings are fabrics used on the inside of a garment. They should not be seen through a garment. Both must be able to receive the same care as the outer fabric.

Interfacings

Fabric **interfacing** is placed between the outer fabric and the facing to prevent stretching of

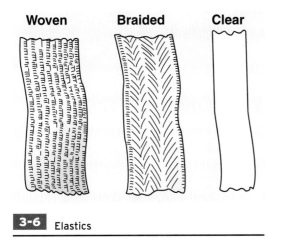

Woven Braided Clear

3-6 Elastics

necklines, front closings, and buttonholes. It adds shape to collars, cuffs, pockets, and hems. Interfacing can also add crispness and stability to waistbands and belts. Each of the basic interfacings has a different application method.

- **Sew-in interfacing.** Must be stitched by machine or hand to the garment; available in either woven or nonwoven fabrics.
- **Fusible interfacing.** Has a resin coating on the back of either woven or nonwoven fabric; fuses or bonds to fabric when pressed.
- **Combination fusible/sew-in interfacing.** Temporarily fuses to fabric with a cool iron so that it acts like a fusible during the sewing

SEWING TIP

Lining and interfacing. To check the final effect of lining and interfacing, drape a piece of fabric over them while you're in the store. Examine how they look and feel together. Remember that even though fusible and sew-in interfacing feel the same, fusible will give crisper results. Always test fusible interfacing on a fabric scrap.

process; when the finished garment is washed or dry-cleaned, the interfacing loses its bond and becomes a sew-in.

Interfacing weights range from very lightweight to heavyweight. Choose an interfacing that is the same weight or lighter than your fabric. Heavyweight interfacings are recommended only for accessories and crafts.

Linings

A **lining** is a fabric used to finish the inside of a jacket, coat, skirt, dress, or pants. A lining helps prevent the garment from stretching and reduces wrinkling. Select lining fabric that is firmly woven, slippery, and static-free. The color of a jacket lining can either match or contrast with the outer fabric.

A lining is constructed separately and then inserted into the garment. For skirts and pants, the lining is attached along the waistband and zipper. For coats, jackets, vests, and dresses, the lining is stitched around the facing edges. The hem of a lining can be sewn to the garment hem or hemmed separately. Jacket hems are usually sewn to the garment; coat and skirt hems are hemmed separately.

CHOOSING FUSIBLE WEBS

Fusible webs hold two layers of fabric together. The webs are a network of bondable fibers. See *Fig. 3-7*. When heat and/or steam is applied, the web melts and fuses the fabric layers. Fusible webs can be used to hem, apply trims, and hold facing edges in place.

Narrow- and wide-width fusible webs are sold by the yard. Some have a peel-off paper backing for easier cutting and use. Before applying, read instructions and test on scrap fabric.

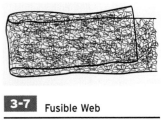

3-7 Fusible Web

Review

SUMMARY

- Choosing a pattern that is the right style and size for you and that matches your skill level will help you achieve better sewing results. (Lesson 1)

- Both the pattern catalog and pattern envelope have information about the style and fit of a pattern. (Lesson 1)

- To determine your correct pattern size, compare your measurements with the pattern charts. (Lesson 1)

- Certain fabrics require special sewing techniques and are not good choices for beginning sewers. (Lesson 2)

- Purchase all the notions for a project when you buy the fabric. (Lesson 3)

- Choose notions with care so that they are suitable for the fabric you've selected. (Lesson 3)

RECALLING THE FACTS

1. What can you learn from the front of a pattern envelope? (Lesson 1)

2. What information is listed on the back of a pattern envelope? (Lesson 1)

3. Name three characteristics of easy-to-sew patterns. (Lesson 1)

4. How are accurate body measurements taken? (Lesson 1)

5. How do you determine your figure type? (Lesson 1)

6. If body measurements differ from a pattern size, what should you do? (Lesson 1)

7. If two people are different sizes, could they share the same pattern? Explain. (Lesson 1)

8. What is the difference between wearing ease and design ease? (Lesson 1)

and Activities

9. Do you have to use the fabrics suggested on a pattern envelope? Explain. (Lesson 2)

10. List at least five fabrics that a beginning sewer should avoid. (Lesson 2)

11. How do you decide how much fabric to buy? (Lesson 2)

12. Why is extra yardage needed for some fabrics? (Lesson 2)

13. Why should notions be purchased at the same time as your fabric? (Lesson 3)

14. Why do some buttons come with a shank? (Lesson 3)

15. Why is interfacing used? (Lesson 3)

APPLYING KNOWLEDGE

1. **Easy-to-sew patterns.** Look through a pattern catalog and select patterns that beginning sewers might use. Identify which features make each pattern easy to sew.

2. **Pattern size.** Take your measurements. Then determine the pattern size that would be right for you.

3. **Notions.** Visit the notions department in a store. Research the types and prices of thread, zippers, buttons, snaps, hooks and eyes, tapes, trims, and elastics. Put the results in chart form.

4. **Cost.** Select a pattern you like. List the fabric yardage and notions needed. Compute how much the pattern, fabric, and notions for the garment would cost.

CREATIVE SOLUTIONS

A teen was selecting the notions needed for a garment she planned to make. The pattern called for six, $5/8$-inch (1.5-cm) buttons. The buttons she liked had to be purchased on cards of four, with each card costing $6. The teen was dismayed at the thought of adding $12 to the cost of her garment.

Think Creatively

Often people can find creative ways to keep the cost of a garment down. What ideas might this teen try?

5. **Project planning.** The management process begins with planning, as described on page 54. Plan a sewing project, utilizing the following planning steps:
   a. **Assess the situation:** Decide what to make, based on your teacher's recommendations, your needs and skills, and the costs of fabric and notions.
   b. **Develop a list of tasks:** List what you will do to complete the project. For example, include determining pattern size and buying fabric.
   c. **Identify resources:** List the resources you need to complete the project. For example, how will you use time, money, skills, and help from other people to complete your project?
   d. **Set priorities:** Determine the order of the tasks you have identified.

Using a Sewing Machine

THE MOST IMPORTANT and expensive pieces of sewing equipment are the sewing machine and serger. In this lesson you'll learn about conventional sewing machines. *Fig. 4-1* on pages 456-457 shows the parts of a sewing machine. You can work safely and more effectively when you are familiar with this information.

All sewing machines operate similarly, but some makes and models have differences. To learn how each part functions on the machine you use, study the instruction manual that comes with the machine. You'll find directions for operating the machine and any accessories. Machine care is also covered. Always refer to the instruction manual when you have a specific question or problem.

CHOOSING NEEDLE AND THREAD

Needles, which hold the upper thread on a sewing machine, come in many types and sizes. Always replace a sewing machine needle when it becomes dull, bent, or rough. A damaged needle can cause stitching problems and harm fabric. Some people insert a new needle when they begin a project.

Types of Needles

Several types of sewing machine needles are available. These are shown in *Fig. 4-2* below.

- **Universal or general-purpose needle.** Has a sharp point and is designed for most woven and knitted fabrics.
- **Ballpoint needle.** Designed for knits and stretch fabrics; slightly rounded tip allows the needle to slip between fabric yarns.
- **Stretch needle.** Specially designed to prevent skipped stitches when sewing on synthetic suede and elastic knitwear.
- **Leather needle.** Has a wedge-shaped point designed to pierce leather, vinyl, and heavy nonwoven fabric.
- **Twin (double) and hemstitch (wing) needles.** Available for decorative stitching.

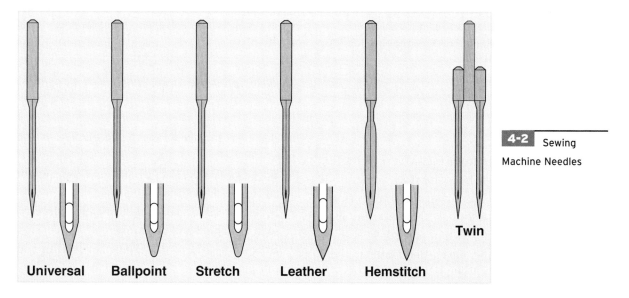

4-2 Sewing Machine Needles

Universal   Ballpoint   Stretch   Leather   Hemstitch   Twin

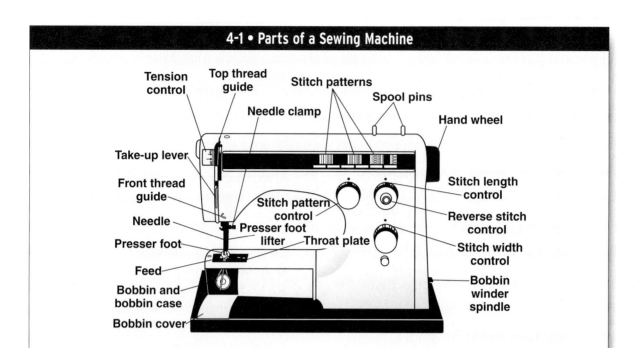

Figure 4-1: Parts of a Sewing Machine. Labels: Tension control, Top thread guide, Stitch patterns, Needle clamp, Spool pins, Hand wheel, Take-up lever, Front thread guide, Stitch pattern control, Needle, Presser foot lifter, Throat plate, Presser foot, Feed, Bobbin and bobbin case, Bobbin cover, Stitch length control, Reverse stitch control, Stitch width control, Bobbin winder spindle

- **Bobbin.** Holds the bottom, or bobbin, thread.
- **Bobbin case.** Holds the bobbin in the machine and regulates the tension of the bobbin thread; may be removable or stationary.
- **Bobbin cover or slide plate.** Covers the bobbin and bobbin case in the machine; may be a small, hinged cover that flips open or a sliding cover.
- **Bobbin winder.** Spindle, latch, and tension discs used to wind thread onto a bobbin.
- **Feed dog or feed.** Teeth that move the fabric under the presser foot, advancing the fabric one stitch at a time.
- **Foot or knee control.** Regulates the starting, running, and stopping of the machine by the amount of pressure applied to the control (not shown).
- **Hand wheel.** Controls the movement of the take-up lever; can be turned by hand to raise or lower needle.
- **Hand-wheel knob.** Small knob inside the hand wheel; stops the needle from moving while a bobbin is being wound (not shown).
- **Needle.** Comes in different types and sizes; must be inserted firmly into the shaft called a needle bar.
- **Needle clamp.** Holds the needle firmly in the machine; loosened and tightened by a screw.
- **Power and light switch.** Turns on the machine and the light (not shown).
- **Presser foot.** Holds the fabric against the feed dog as you stitch.

Needle Sizes

Needle sizes range from 6 (for very delicate fabrics) to 20 (for very heavy fabrics). Some foreign manufacturers use a different numbering system for needles. Although their needles are numbered 60 to 125 (shown in parentheses), the same rules apply. The lower the number, the finer the needle is. The lighter and finer the fabric, the finer the needle should be. See *Fig. 4-3* on page 458.

- **Size 9 (70) or 11 (75).** For fine, lightweight fabrics, such as chiffon and voile.
- **Size 14 (90).** For medium-weight fabrics, such as flannel and corduroy.
- **Size 16 (100) or 18 (110).** For heavier and thicker fabrics.

- **Presser-foot lifter.** Raises and lowers the presser foot.
- **Reverse button or lever.** Button or lever that allows backward stitching.
- **Spool pins.** Hold spool of thread.
- **Stitch-length control.** Regulates the length of the stitch.
- **Stitch patterns.** Show the selection of stitches available on the machine.
- **Stitch-pattern control.** Regulates the selection of different stitching patterns, including zigzag, stretch stitch, and decorative stitches.
- **Stitch-width control.** Regulates the width of zigzag stitching and positions the needle for straight stitching.
- **Take-up lever.** Controls the amount of thread pulled from the spool to the needle for each stitch; moves up and down as you stitch.

- **Tension control.** Regulates the tension placed on the needle thread by tightening or loosening the tension discs that the upper thread passes through.
- **Thread guides.** Help guide upper thread from spool to needle without tangling.
- **Throat or needle plate.** Located directly under the needle and surrounds the feed dog; usually has seam width guidelines to help keep stitching straight.

Note: Machines vary from model to model. See your owner's manual for the names and locations of the parts and special features of your machine.

Thread

The type and weight of your fabric also determines what thread to use. See *Fig. 4-3* on page 458. In general, for lightweight fabrics use a fine needle, fine thread, and short stitches. For heavier fabrics, use a coarser needle, heavier thread, and longer stitches. Except for special decorative stitching, always use the same type of thread in the needle and bobbin.

CHANGING NEEDLES

To change a sewing machine needle, follow these steps:
1. Raise the needle to the highest position by turning the hand wheel.
2. Loosen the thumbscrew on the needle clamp.
3. Remove the old needle, being sure to notice its position. The long groove on the needle should face the side from which you thread the needle.
4. Insert the top of the needle firmly up into the needle clamp.
5. Tighten the thumbscrew securely.

PREPARING THE BOBBIN

The **bobbin** holds the bottom thread in a sewing machine. Most bobbins must be removed from the bobbin case in order to be wound. Some machines, however, have a bobbin winder built into the bobbin case for easy rewinding. Keep extra bobbins in your sewing box to avoid winding one color thread over another.

Winding the Bobbin

Refer to the machine's manual for specific instructions for winding a bobbin. Here is a common method used.
1. Loosen the hand-wheel knob to stop movement of the needle.
2. Insert the end of the thread through a hole in the bobbin.
3. Wrap the thread securely around the bobbin several times.
4. Place the bobbin on the bobbin winder.
5. Hold the end of the thread until the bobbin starts winding.

4-3 • Choosing Thread, Needle Size, and Stitch Length			
FABRIC	**THREAD**	**NEEDLE SIZE**	**STITCH LENGTH**
Delicate fabrics: chiffon, fine lace, silk	polyester, polyester/cotton, silk	9 (70)	4-16
Lightweight fabrics: batiste, crepe, organdy, taffeta	polyester, polyester/cotton, silk	11 (75)	12-14
Medium-weight fabrics: gingham, poplin, linen, fine corduroy, lightweight wool, velveteen	polyester, polyester/cotton, mercerized cotton, silk	14 (90)	10-12
Medium-heavy fabrics: denim, corduroy, gabardine, woolens, sailcloth	polyester, polyester/cotton, mercerized cotton, silk, heavy duty	16 (100)	10-12
Heavy fabrics: canvas, coatings, fake fur, upholstery fabrics	polyester, polyester/cotton, heavy duty	18 (110)	8-10
All knits and stretch fabrics	polyester, polyester/cotton	ballpoint or stretch	10-14 or special stretch stitch
Leather and suede	polyester, polyester/cotton, heavy duty	leather	8-10
Decorative topstitching on fabrics	any	twin or hemstitch	8-12

Be sure the bobbin winds evenly. See *Fig. 4-4*. If necessary, gently guide the thread with your finger. If the bobbin winder doesn't have an automatic shut-off, wind the bobbin only about three-quarters full. Cut the thread with scissors, and remove the bobbin from the winder. Tighten the hand-wheel knob.

Inserting the Bobbin

To insert the bobbin, begin by opening the slide plate that covers the bobbin case. For a built-in bobbin case, simply insert the bobbin directly into the case. For a removable bobbin case, take the case out of the machine and insert the bobbin. Be sure the thread unwinds in the right direction. Check the manual for specific instructions. Insert the bobbin case back into the machine.

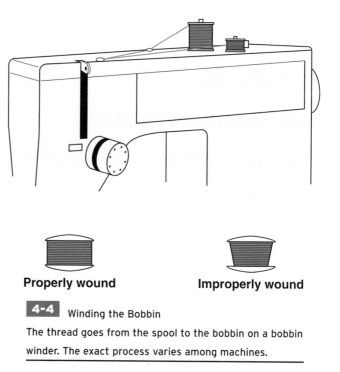

Properly wound   **Improperly wound**

4-4 Winding the Bobbin

The thread goes from the spool to the bobbin on a bobbin winder. The exact process varies among machines.

Pull the bobbin thread gently to see whether there is a slight **tension**, or tightness, on it. If it unwinds too easily, check the threading of the bobbin case again. Then close the slide plate.

THREADING THE MACHINE

Threading a machine may look difficult at first, but the general procedure is simple and the same for all machines. See *Fig. 4-5*. The thread goes from the spool pin through a thread guide to the tension discs. Then it goes to the **take-up lever**, which controls the amount of thread that pulls from the spool. The thread continues down through additional thread guides and to the needle. **Thread guides** direct the thread and keep it from tangling. Study the illustration in the manual for your machine.

Tension Discs

Be sure to check the threading of the tension discs. Raise the presser foot and pull the thread gently to look for slight tension. If the thread unwinds too easily or without any resistance, try once more to pass the thread around the tension discs. The thread should be placed between two of the discs and then brought up and caught on a hook or spring on the tension discs. Always thread the tension discs before you thread the take-up lever.

Thread Guides

The placement of thread guides differs among machines. The location of the last thread guide tells you in which direction to thread the needle. See *Fig. 4-6*. If the thread guide is on the right, thread the needle from the right. If the guide is on the left, thread the needle from the left. If the guide is on the front of the needle bar, thread the needle from front to back.

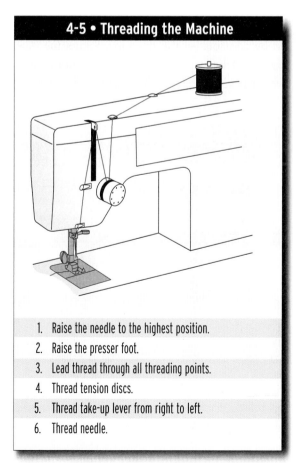

4-5 • Threading the Machine

1. Raise the needle to the highest position.
2. Raise the presser foot.
3. Lead thread through all threading points.
4. Thread tension discs.
5. Thread take-up lever from right to left.
6. Thread needle.

4-6 The thread must pass through the thread guides before going through the needle.

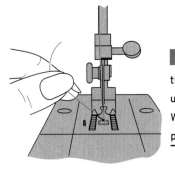

4-7 The bobbin thread must be pulled up before you can sew. Where should it be placed?

Pull out at least 3 inches (7.5 cm) of thread from the needle. This will prevent the thread from pulling out of the needle as it is raised and lowered.

Raising the Bobbin Thread

After the bobbin and needle have been threaded, bring the bobbin thread up through the hole in the needle or throat plate. See *Fig. 4-7*. To do this, hold the needle thread in your left hand. With your right hand, turn the hand wheel slowly toward you until the needle enters the throat plate. Continue turning until the needle rises and brings up a loop of the bobbin thread. Pull up the loop to bring the end of the bobbin thread out. Pull both thread ends under the presser foot and toward the back of the machine so the threads won't tangle as you start to stitch.

ADJUSTING THE MACHINE

How does a sewing machine work? As the needle thread intertwines with the bobbin thread, a **lockstitch** forms. See *Fig. 4-8*. This intertwining of threads creates a stitch that doesn't pull out or unravel when a loop or loose thread is pulled.

To get the best stitch for each fabric, make different adjustments. You can change the type of stitch, length of stitch, tension, and pressure.

Always check your owner's manual and pretest the adjustments by stitching on a scrap of the same fabric. Use a double thickness of fabric to imitate sewing actual seams.

Adjusting Stitch Type

Although any garment can be constructed with a straight stitch, most machines offer other stitches, including zigzag, stretch, and decorative stitches. See *Fig. 4-9*. The stitch is usually regulated by controls on the machine. Sometimes specialty stitches are controlled by separate discs, which are inserted into the machine.

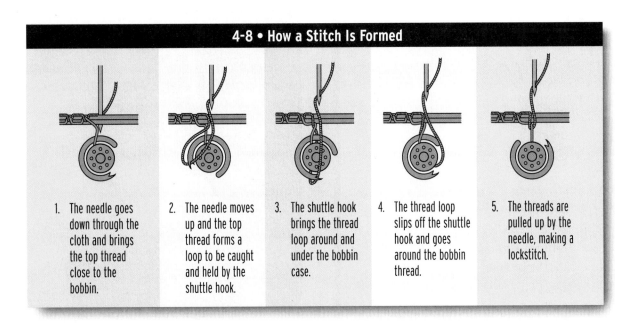

4-8 • How a Stitch Is Formed

1. The needle goes down through the cloth and brings the top thread close to the bobbin.

2. The needle moves up and the top thread forms a loop to be caught and held by the shuttle hook.

3. The shuttle hook brings the thread loop around and under the bobbin case.

4. The thread loop slips off the shuttle hook and goes around the bobbin thread.

5. The threads are pulled up by the needle, making a lockstitch.

4-9 Although a straight stitch is typical, some special situations might call for a decorative stitch.

4-10 • Stitch-Length Conversion	
Some sewing machines show stitch length in millimeters rather than stitches per inch.	
STITCHES PER INCH	MM EQUIVALENT OF STITCH LENGTH
24	1
13	2
9	3
6	4
5	5

Adjusting Stitch Length

The numbers on the stitch-length control are based on either English or metric measurement. See *Fig. 4-10.* Numbers from 6 to 20 indicate the number of stitches per inch. Numbers from 1 to 5 indicate the length of stitch in millimeters. For example, the number 4 indicates that each stitch is 4 mm long, or about 6 stitches per inch.

Stitch length should match fabric type and stitching purpose, as indicated below.

- **Regular stitching.** Choose a medium-length stitch for most fabrics. This is 10 to 12 stitches per inch (or a stitch length of 2 to 2.5 mm). For lightweight fabrics, use a shorter stitch. For heavier fabrics, use a longer stitch.
- **Machine basting.** Use the longest stitch possible, for easy removal. Basting is 6 to 8 stitches per inch (or a stitch length of 3 to 4 mm).
- **Reinforcement stitching.** Use very short stitches to prevent stretching or pulling in certain areas. This is 15 to 20 stitches per inch (or a stitch length of 1 to 1.5 mm).

Adjusting Tension

A properly balanced stitch has two threads that lock in the center between the two layers of fabric. If the stitches are too tight or too loose, adjust the tension.

Check the tension by examining sample stitches sewn on a double layer of fabric. See *Fig. 4-11.* If the top thread lies flat on the surface of the fabric and loops show on the top, then the top tension is too tight. Turn the tension dial to a lower

4-11 Although the stitches are balanced in the top drawing, they're not in the others. How would you correct each situation?

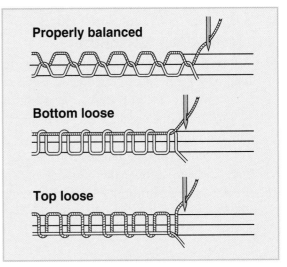

Properly balanced

Bottom loose

Top loose

number. If the bottom row of stitching is flat along the bottom layer of fabric with loops showing on the surface, then the top tension is too loose. Turn the dial to a higher number.

Keep adjusting and testing to get the proper balance. Test the tension balance by pulling the fabric until the stitching breaks. If one thread breaks first, the tension on that thread is tighter.

Adjusting Pressure

The **presser foot** holds fabric against the **feed dog**, which moves the fabric forward. Correct pressure between these two parts moves the two layers of fabric smoothly under the needle. If one layer of fabric feeds faster than the other, the fabric will ripple. If the pressure is too great, one layer of fabric may be longer than the other after the seam is sewn. When the pressure is correct, both layers of fabric feed smoothly under the needle. The result is an evenly stitched seam.

Some machines have a pressure regulator that can be adjusted. Refer to your manual.

USING THE SEWING MACHINE

With practice, you can control sewing machine speed. Use light pressure on the knee or foot control. Experiment with slowly increasing and decreasing speeds. Learn how to start slowly, build up speed, and slow down toward the end.

Guidelines on Stitching

1. Before you start to stitch, raise the take-up lever and the needle to the highest position. This will prevent the upper thread from pulling out of the needle when you begin. Be sure both threads are pulled back behind the presser foot to prevent tangled stitches.
2. Place the fabric under the presser foot. Put the bulk of the fabric to the left of the needle.
3. Position the stitching line directly under the needle.

SEWING TIP

Straight and curved stitching. If your needle plate doesn't have guideline markings, place a piece of masking tape ⅝ inch (1.5 cm) from the needle to act as a guide for regular seams. Stitching curves takes more practice. Draw curved lines on fabric scraps and practice stitching until you can sew them smoothly.

4. To begin stitching, turn the hand wheel to lower the needle into the fabric. Then lower the presser foot. Gradually apply pressure on the knee or foot control to stitch at a slow, even speed.
5. When you stop stitching, turn the hand wheel to raise the take-up lever and needle to the highest point. Raise the presser foot. Gently slide the fabric toward the back of the machine. Don't pull the fabric forward because you could bend the needle. Clip the threads.

Stitching Straight

Your first attempts at stitching may not produce perfectly straight rows. Learn to guide the fabric with your hands, without pulling or pushing. Keep one hand in front and one hand behind the presser foot to guide the fabric smoothly. See *Fig. 4-12.*

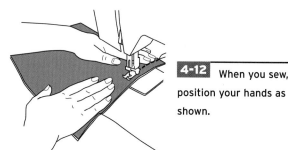

4-12 When you sew, position your hands as shown.

Use the guideline markings on the throat or needle plate to help keep the rows of stitching straight. Line up the edge of the fabric with the guideline for the seam width you're sewing. Keep your eyes on this marking instead of watching the needle.

Stitching Problems

Frequently the cause of stitching problems is incorrect threading. If rethreading the machine doesn't correct a problem, check the needle and the tension setting. Refer to *Fig. 4-13* for solutions to specific stitching problems.

4-13 • Correcting Stitching Problems

SKIPPED STITCHES

- Replace dull or bent needle.
- Rethread machine.
- Check size and type of needle for fabric.
- Loosen upper thread tension.
- Check needle position.

PUCKERING

- Loosen upper tension.
- Replace dull or bent needle.
- Use same type of thread in needle and bobbin.
- Loosen pressure on presser foot.
- Shorten stitch length.

THREAD BREAKS

- Check threading of machine.
- Replace needle.
- Check size of needle.
- Check thread for knots or unevenness.
- Begin stitching at a slower speed.

NEEDLE BREAKS

- Carefully guide the fabric through the machine; do not pull it.
- Check needle position.
- Tighten presser foot.
- Use fewer layers of fabric.

MACHINE JAMS

- Check for loops of matted thread under stitching.
- Check bobbin for caught thread.
- Check needle position.
- Check machine threading.

MACHINE DOESN'T SEW

- Check on/off switch.
- Tighten hand-wheel knob.
- Check electrical cord.
- Check knee or foot control.

BUNCHING OF THREAD

- Pull thread ends behind presser foot and hold when starting to stitch.
- Rethread machine.

SEWING MACHINE ACCESSORIES

Many machines come with accessories. Some are described below.

- **Straight-stitch foot.** Has a narrow opening and is used for sewing straight stitches.
- **Zigzag foot.** Has a wide opening to allow for the sideways needle motion of zigzag and special stitches; works for straight stitches too.
- **Zipper foot.** Can be adjusted to the right or left side of the needle for stitching close to zipper teeth or cording.
- **Buttonhole foot.** Has markings for measuring buttonhole stitches.
- **Blindstitch-hem foot.** Guides the fabric for a blindstitch hem.

SEWING MACHINE CARE

Routine care keeps a sewing machine in top working condition. How often is cleaning needed? That depends on how often the machine is used. Lint from fabric collects around the bobbin and needle bar and can eventually clog the machine. Many people clean their machine before starting a new project. In the sewing laboratory, your instructor will give you guidelines.

Always unplug the machine before cleaning. Use a soft cloth to remove lint or fuzz from the machine base and needle bar. Use a soft brush to gently clean the bobbin and bobbin case. If possible, remove the entire bobbin case mechanism, following the directions in the manual. Wipe away old oil with a cloth.

Many new machines are designed to never need additional oil. The oil is permanently imbedded in the machine. Never oil such machines. If your machine does require oil, the manual will show the specific areas to be oiled. Use only high-grade sewing machine oil. Wipe the machine with a cloth to remove any drips or excess oil. Then plug it in and stitch on a fabric scrap to be sure excess oil is removed. Machine oil stains fabric and is very difficult to remove.

COMPUTERIZED MACHINES

Computerized sewing machines are state of the art for sewers. Although expensive, they make sewing easier and more creative. See *Fig. 4-14.*

Many computerized machines feature push-button commands and large, easy-to-read LCD panels that display stitches. Just press a button to select a stitch. The machines also automatically adjust tension and pressure settings.

Special stitches, with some that do embroidery, are stored in a computerized machine's memory. Hundreds of stitch programs are possible, including alphabets, monograms, buttonhole styles, and decorative stitches. Machines can be programmed to combine stitches into unique patterns or to sew them in single units.

Some machines have sewing advisory LCD panels that give information and tips. You can even get instructions in eight different languages.

Using the command ball as a pencil, you can draw your own design on the screen of some machines. One machine has a separate embroidery unit that attaches to the machine and can be connected to a personal computer. You create your own design on the computer and download it to the sewing machine, which then stitches the design. You can store your original designs in the machine's memory. You can also download embroidery designs from the Internet to a personal computer and then transfer them to the machine.

4-14 Computerized Sewing Machine

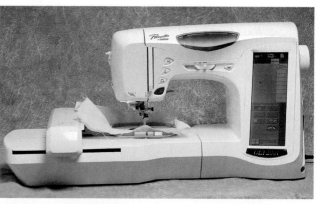

Using a Serger

THE SERGER, also called an overlock machine, is a special sewing machine that can stitch, trim, and overcast a seam all at the same time. Moreover, it's twice as fast as a conventional machine. See *Fig. 5-1*.

Because a serger can handle thicker threads than a conventional machine, it can create special effects on seams and edges. It also does a special edge finish, called a narrow rolled hem.

The serger can't replace a conventional machine. It can't make buttonholes, insert a zipper, or do embroidery. Using both machines, however, allows you to make clothes with the same sewing techniques used for ready-to-wear.

Sergers are described by the number of threads they use. Machines may be three-, four-, five-, and eight-thread machines. Each thread sits on a separate **spool pin** on the serger. Although an eight-thread serger doesn't use all threads at the same time, it can create all the versions of a serger stitch. A serger may have one or two needles. Only the needle thread penetrates the fabric when serging.

PARTS OF A SERGER

Fig. 5-2 shows the parts of a serger. Instead of a bobbin, the serger has two **loopers**, called the upper looper and the lower looper. See *Fig. 5-3* on page 466. The two looper threads come up from underneath the needle plate. The upper looper thread appears on the top of the fabric, the lower looper thread on the underside. The two looper threads interlock at the fabric edge.

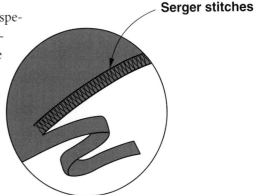

Serger stitches

5-1 A serger can trim, stitch, and overcast in just one step.

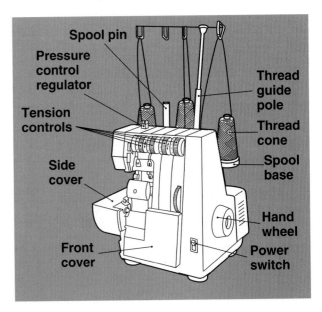

5-2 Parts of a Serger

How does a serger differ from a conventional machine?

- Spool pin
- Pressure control regulator
- Tension controls
- Side cover
- Front cover
- Thread guide pole
- Thread cone
- Spool base
- Hand wheel
- Power switch

SAFETY TIP

Never sew over pins with a serger. The knives will cut through a pin, which dulls the blades. The pin fragments can cut your face, hurt your eyes, or damage the inner workings of the machine. If pins are needed to hold the fabric pieces together, place them 1 inch (2.5 cm) away from the edge. A glue stick or basting stitches can also be used.

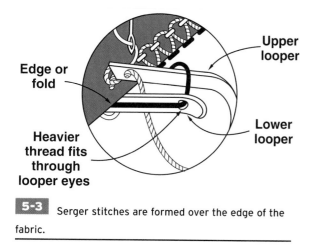

5-3 Serger stitches are formed over the edge of the fabric.

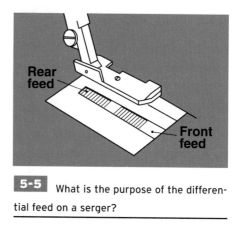

5-5 What is the purpose of the differential feed on a serger?

On the right side of the needle plate are moveable and stationary knives. See *Fig. 5-4*. These trim off the excess fabric before the stitch is formed. Most machines have knives that are retractable so you can serge without cutting the fabric.

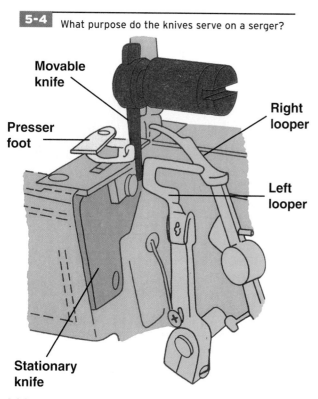

5-4 What purpose do the knives serve on a serger?

Some sergers have a **differential feed**, which is two sets of feed dogs that move the fabric through the machine at different speeds. See *Fig. 5-5*. This can be used to gather one layer of fabric to a straight piece of fabric. It can also prevent puckered seams on lightweight, silky fabrics and prevent wavy seams on stretchy knits.

STITCH VARIATIONS

Some sergers create only one or two stitch variations; others perform several. An eight-thread machine can create all of the stitches. Here are different types of serger stitches.

- **Three-thread serger stitch.** This basic stitch is formed with one needle and two looper threads. See *Fig. 5-6*. All three threads interlock at the fabric edge. With this stitch, you can stitch and overcast a seam, finish the fabric edges of a conventional seam, and hem.

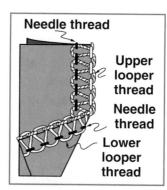

5-6 Three-Thread Serger Stitch

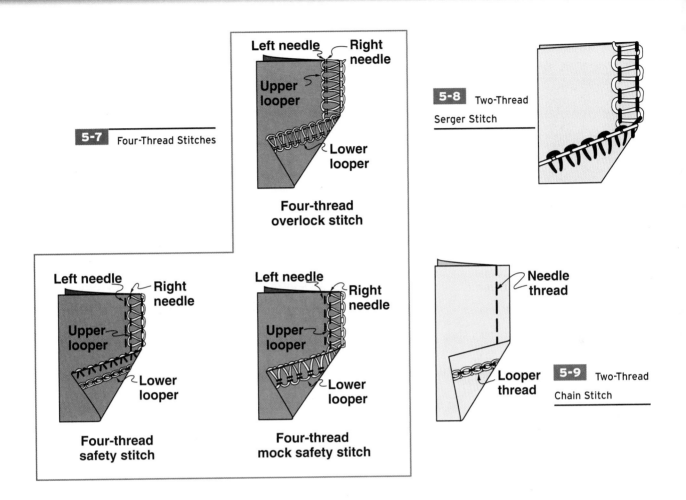

5-7 Four-Thread Stitches

Left needle — Right needle

Upper looper

Lower looper

Four-thread overlock stitch

Left needle — Right needle

Upper looper

Lower looper

Four-thread safety stitch

Left needle — Right needle

Upper looper

Lower looper

Four-thread mock safety stitch

5-8 Two-Thread Serger Stitch

Needle thread

Looper thread

5-9 Two-Thread Chain Stitch

- **Four-thread serger stitch.** By adding an extra row of stitches, this stitch is more durable than the three-thread. It uses two needles and two loopers. One variation is the four-thread safety stitch, which consists of a two-thread serger stitch and a two-thread chain stitch. It is recommended for woven fabrics, because the chain stitch may break if the fabric is stretched. The four-thread mock safety stitch, another variation, can be used for both knits and wovens. These stitches are shown in *Fig. 5-7*.

- **Two-thread serger stitch.** This stitch is created by one needle and one looper thread. See *Fig. 5-8*. The two threads interlock at the fabric edge. The needle thread forms a V on the underside of the fabric. The stitch is used mainly as a seam finish on a conventional seam or as an edge finish.

- **Two-thread chain stitch.** This stitch is formed by one needle and one looper. See *Fig. 5-9*. Since it doesn't overcast the edge, it can't make a conventional seam. If the cutter can be disengaged, the chain stitch can be used for decorative topstitching. Only a few sergers offer this stitch.

- **Five-thread serger stitch.** This stitch combines a two-thread chain stitch with a three-thread serger stitch. The more threads involved, the more durable the seam.

- **Rolled hemstitch.** As a variation of the three-thread serger stitch, this stitch creates a narrow row of short, dense stitches. See *Fig. 5-10* on page 468. With a bulk-free hem, this edge finish is often used on placemats, napkins, ruffles, scarves, and garment hems. On some sergers, you can switch to the rolled

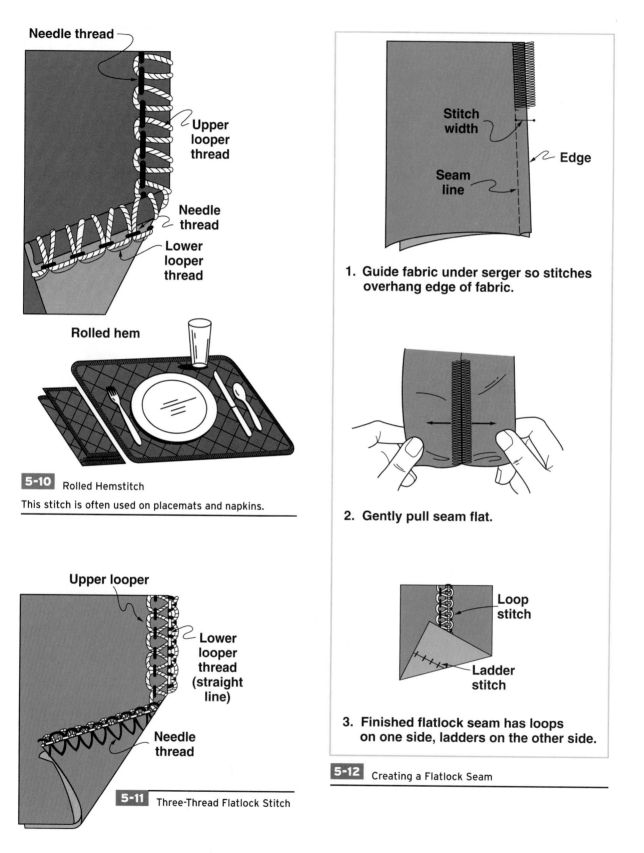

Needle thread

Upper looper thread

Needle thread

Lower looper thread

Rolled hem

5-10 Rolled Hemstitch

This stitch is often used on placemats and napkins.

Upper looper

Lower looper thread (straight line)

Needle thread

5-11 Three-Thread Flatlock Stitch

Stitch width

Edge

Seam line

1. **Guide fabric under serger so stitches overhang edge of fabric.**

2. **Gently pull seam flat.**

Loop stitch

Ladder stitch

3. **Finished flatlock seam has loops on one side, ladders on the other side.**

5-12 Creating a Flatlock Seam

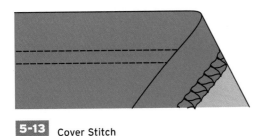

5-13 Cover Stitch

SERGER TENSION

Each thread that forms a serger stitch has a tension control. Thus, you can adjust the tension separately for each looper and each needle. In general, the heavier the thread, the looser the tension should be.

To create a balanced stitch, adjust the tension whenever you change fabric, thread, stitch width, or stitch length. The upper and lower looper threads should hug the top and bottom of the

hemstitch by changing the dials. On others, the needle plate and/or presser foot must be changed.

- **Flatlock stitch.** Use this stitch to create a decorative outside seam with two or three threads, depending on the machine. See *Fig. 5-11*. The stitch forms loops on the fabric top; a ladder stitch forms on the underside after the fabric is pulled flat. See *Fig. 5-12*. The stitch is reversible because you can plan to have either the loops or the ladder stitches show on the outside of the fabric.

- **Cover stitch.** This stitch uses one looper and two or three needles for decorative hemming or topstitching. See *Fig. 5-13*. Two or three parallel rows of stitching form on one side of the fabric. On the other side, one set of loops intersects with the needle threads. The stitch is reversible. Because it has some stretch, this stitch is often used for knits.

As you can see, the serger is capable of several versatile stitches. Some uses for these stitches are shown in *Fig. 5-14*.

5-14 Sergers sew seams as well as hems. They can also be used for decorative seams that show on garments, as on a vest or jacket. Another use is creating stretchable seams, such as those needed for a pullover top with ribbing at the wrists.

Overlock seam

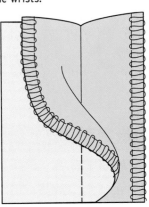

Conventional seam with overlock finish

Blindstitch hem

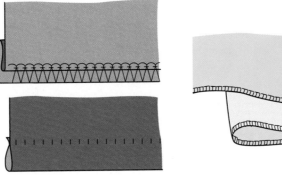

Narrow rolled hem

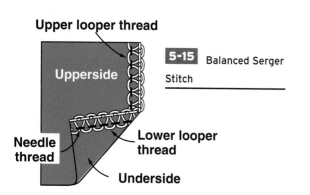

5-15 Balanced Serger Stitch

seam and meet exactly at the edge. See *Fig. 5-15*. If one thread is pulled to the other side of the fabric or overhangs the fabric edge, the tension needs adjustment.

The needle thread should look like a line of straight stitching on the top of the fabric, with only tiny loops on the underside. If the tension is too tight, the seam will pucker. If too loose, the seam will spread apart when gently pulled. Always check the tension by serging on a fabric swatch before starting a project.

If problems occur while sewing, incorrect tension or another condition could be the source. *Fig. 5-16* shows some possible problems and solutions.

5-16 • Correcting Serging Problems

SKIPPED STITCHES

- Replace dull or bent needle.
- Check size and type of needle.
- Loosen upper looper tension.
- Rethread machine.

LOOPS FORM AT EDGE OF FABRIC

- Check threading at tension disks, take-up lever, thread guides.
- Increase looper tension.
- Check knife alignment.

MACHINE JAMS

- Serge a thread chain at end of seam so thread will not get caught under presser foot.
- Insert fabric in front of needle and knife.

THREAD BREAKS

- Check threading sequence.
- Check thread spool or cone.
- Loosen tension of thread.
- Replace dull or bent needle.
- Try a different thread.

STITCHES PULL THROUGH TO RIGHT SIDE OF FABRIC

- Increase needle thread tension.
- Check threading at tension disks and thread guides.
- Replace dull or bent needle.
- Use wider stitch width.
- Check knife alignment.

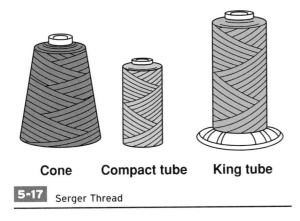

Cone   Compact tube   King tube

5-17 Serger Thread

SERGER THREADS AND ACCESSORIES

Conventional polyester or polyester/cotton thread can be used for general sewing. Because the serger sews faster and uses more threads in each seam, however, some special threads are helpful.

- **Polyester or polyester/cotton serger thread.** Similar to conventional all-purpose thread; slightly finer and comes on large cones or tubes. See *Fig. 5-17.*
- **Woolly nylon thread.** Soft, fuzzy thread that stretches when sewn; good for serging swimwear and lingerie and giving a narrow rolled hem an attractive, "filled in" appearance. Woolly nylon thread is used in loopers; all-purpose serger thread is used in needles.
- **Decorative threads.** Various threads that include metallic, pearl cotton, silk or rayon ribbon that is $\frac{1}{16}$ inch wide (1 to 2 mm), and crochet cotton; used in loopers to create special effects. Because loopers have large eyes, a wider range of decorative threads can be used on a serger than on a conventional sewing machine. Regular serger thread is used in the needles.

The following special notions help ensure smooth stitching with a serger:

- **Adapter cones.** Fit over spool pins to hold the large thread cones and prevent them from vibrating while the machine is on.
- **Spool caps.** Fit over the top of standard thread spools to hold them in place on the spool pins. See *Fig. 5-18.* Always place the spool with the notch down to prevent the thread from catching in the notch and breaking.
- **Thread nets.** Fit over thread spools to keep thread from unwinding too quickly.
- **Tweezers and a loop threader.** Helpful for threading the machine.

SERGER CARE

As the knife trims the fabric, it creates a great deal of lint. For good performance, keep the serger lint-free. Use the small brush that comes with the machine to remove lint from the area around the knife and loopers. Canned, compressed air is also good for cleaning and can be purchased at fabric, sewing machine, and camera stores. Follow what the instruction manual says about oiling the serger.

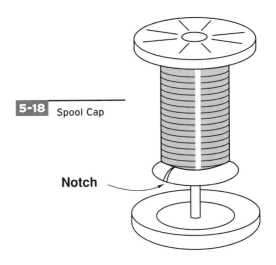

5-18 Spool Cap

Notch

Identifying Sewing Equipment

Peeople who sew regularly collect various tools and equipment, some needed for routine tasks and some for special purposes. As your skills and interest grow, you can add to your sewing supplies, but for now you'll probably need only a few basic items. Check with your instructor to find out what those are.

Sewing equipment can be divided into six groups, according to purpose. You'll be using tools to help you measure, pin, cut, mark, stitch, and press as you learn to sew.

MEASURING TOOLS

Your sewing box won't be complete without measuring tools. Most of these tools have scales in both English and metric. The three essential measuring tools are a tape measure, a sewing gauge, and a yardstick or meterstick. *Fig. 6-1* shows the measuring tools listed below.

- **Tape measure.** This flexible tape is 60 inches (150 cm) long. With it, you can take body measurements and measure fabric; keep the tape neatly rolled in a sewing box. See *Fig. 6-1***A**.
- **Sewing or seam gauge.** With a 6-inch (15-cm) scale, this gauge measures short lengths, such as hem and seam widths. You can set a marker on the gauge for the width to be measured. See *Fig. 6-1***B**.
- **Yardstick or meterstick.** To check grain lines and mark hemlines, this 36-inch (91.5-cm), rigid, measuring stick is useful. It may be wood, metal, or plastic. See *Fig. 6-1***C**.
- **Transparent ruler.** The ability to see through this device makes it useful for measuring and marking buttonholes, pleats, tucks, and bias strips. See *Fig. 6-1***D**.
- **Hem gauge.** Made of metal or plastic, this tool marks straight or curved hems. See *Fig. 6-1***E**.
- **Skirt marker.** This device is used to measure and mark hemlines with either pins or chalk. See *Fig. 6-1***F**.

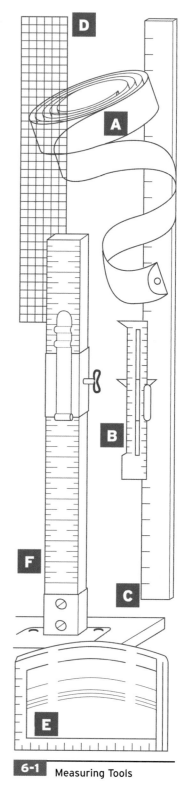

6-1 Measuring Tools

PINNING TOOLS

For many stages of sewing, you'll need pins. See *Fig. 6-2.* Use them to hold patterns to fabric, to hold two layers of fabric together while stitching, and to mark hemlines. To avoid damaging the fabric, pins should be sharp, slender, and smoothly finished.

- **Silk pins.** Made of stainless steel or brass, silk pins can be used with most fabrics. See *Fig. 6-2***A**.
- **Ballpoint pins.** These are silk pins with rounded points that allow them to slip easily between strands of yarn, preventing fabric snags. Use them on knitted fabrics. See *Fig. 6-2***A**.
- **Ball-head pins.** These pins have colorful, round, plastic or glass heads, which make them easy to see and pick up. See *Fig. 6-2***B**.
- **T-pins.** Distinguished by a large T-shaped head, these pins work well on loosely woven, bulky, or pile fabrics. See *Fig. 6-2***C**.

Pincushions

Pincushions come in many different styles. The pins in *Fig. 6-2* have been placed in one com-

SAFETY TIP

Follow these safety suggestions when using sewing equipment.
- To prevent accidental swallowing, never hold pins in your mouth.
- Don't place pins in the clothes you're wearing. Forgotten pins might cause injury or be dropped and later picked up by a child.
- Keep shears and scissors closed when not in use.
- Pass a sharp object handle-first to another person.
- Keep all tools in your sewing box when not in use.

6-2 A pincushion provides a safe way to store pins conveniently. How would you use the pins shown?

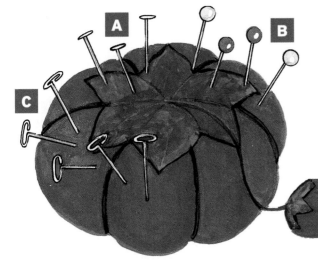

mon pincushion style. Another style has an elastic or plastic band for wearing around your wrist. Others use an adhesive backing to attach to the sewing machine. Magnetic pincushions hold pins securely, even when tipped over. When turned upside down, one style in the shape of a bowl picks up scattered pins.

CUTTING TOOLS

Cutting tools are essential for sewing. Two basics that you'll need are shears and scissors. **Shears** have long blades and two handles with different shapes. They are used for cutting out fabric. **Scissors**, which are smaller than shears, have two handles with the same shape. Use them to trim and clip fabric and cut threads. Scissors and shears need to be sharp since dull blades make it very difficult to cut accurately.

The list on the following page summarizes the cutting tools you may use in sewing. They're shown in *Fig. 6-3.*

- **Dressmaker's shears.** The bent handles on these shears allow fabric to lie flat on the table as you cut. Results are more accurate when you don't lift up the fabric while cutting. One handle fits your thumb and the other handle, with its different shape, fits several fingers. Blades are usually 7 to 8 inches (18 to 20 cm) in length. Quality shears have an adjustable screw so you can change the cutting action of the blades. See *Fig. 6-3***A**.
- **Sewing scissors.** These scissors have small round handles and blades 4 to 6 inches (10 to 15 cm) in length. The blades are different widths. Sewing scissors are easier to handle than shears for detail work. Use them to trim seams, clip curves, and cut into corners. See *Fig. 6-3***B**.
- **Pinking or scalloping shears.** With these shears, you can finish a seam edge or other raw edge on firmly woven fabrics. The zigzag or scallop design helps to prevent raveling. These are not for cutting out fabric pieces because the uneven edge is difficult to follow when stitching. Instead, pink or scallop the seam edges after the seams are stitched. See *Fig. 6-3***C**.
- **Embroidery scissors.** These small scissors are only 3 to 4 inches (7.5 to 10 cm) in length, with very pointed blades. Use them for such detail work as cutting buttonholes and ripping stitches. See *Fig. 6-3***D**.
- **Seam ripper.** You can remove stitches with the small blade on one end of this pen-shaped gadget. The blade lifts the thread away from the fabric before cutting. Be careful not to cut the fabric. See *Fig. 6-3***E**.
- **Thread clipper.** This tool has spring-action blades for clipping thread ends or stitches. See *Fig. 6-3***F**.

SEWING TIP

Keeping tools sharp. Sewing tools won't stay sharp if you use them to cut paper (other than pattern tissue), string, and other objects. At home, keep a pair of household shears handy for other cutting jobs. To have your shears or scissors sharpened, check with a fabric store or hardware store.

- **Rotary cutter.** The round, retractable blade on this tool makes it resemble a pizza cutter. Crafters and quilters like the straight, clean cuts they can make through multiple layers of fabric. The cutter must be used with a special "self-healing" mat. See *Fig. 6-3***G**.

MARKING TOOLS

Marking tools transfer symbols and lines from pattern pieces to fabric. Accurate markings help make construction easier. The marking equip-

6-3 Cutting Tools

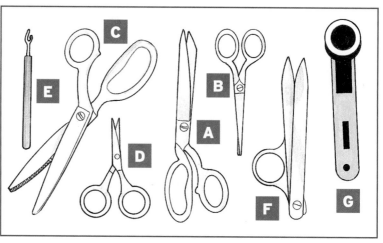

ment you choose depends on the fabric. These tools are shown in *Fig. 6-4*.

- **Fabric marking pen.** Because of this pen's disappearing ink, you can mark on the right or wrong side of fabric. With some pens, the ink marks disappear when treated with water. With others, the ink evaporates, usually in less than 48 hours. See *Fig. 6-4***A**.
- **Tracing wheel.** When you run this wheel over dressmaker's tracing paper, the marks transfer to fabric. Use a smooth-edged wheel for delicate fabrics, and a saw-toothed wheel for most others. Special waxed carbon paper for tracing is available in several colors. Washing or dry-cleaning the fabric removes the tracing marks. See *Fig. 6-4***B** and **C**.
- **Tailor's chalk.** These small squares or pencils will mark fabrics. The markings can be brushed away or will disappear when pressed with an iron. See *Fig. 6-4***D** and **E**.
- **Ordinary thread.** Make simple hand-sewn stitches to mark construction lines on fabric.

SPECIAL SEWING ITEMS

Here are some special items for faster and easier sewing.

- **Disappearing basting thread.** Dissolves in the wash or when you iron over it with a damp press cloth.

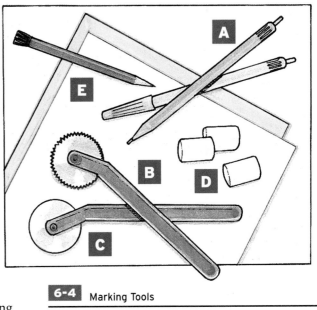

6-4 Marking Tools

- **Liquid seam sealant.** Prevents cut edges from fraying when you apply this colorless liquid to fabric or ribbon.
- **Stabilizer.** Adds temporary body and support to fabric; particularly useful for machine embroidery and machine appliqué work. One type of stabilizer can be torn away after the work is finished. Another type dissolves when washed or sprayed with water.

STITCHING TOOLS

Although machine stitching nearly completes most projects, some hand sewing may be needed. All sewing boxes need a variety of needles and at least one thimble. Some other possibilities are also listed here. See *Fig. 6-5* on page 476.

- **Needles.** Needles should have sharp points and smooth eyes to avoid snagging fabric or splitting thread. Sizes range from 1 (coarse) to 12 (fine). The smaller the number, the larger the needle is. For most hand-sewing tasks, use a size 7 or 8 needle. Use a finer needle on delicate fabrics and a coarser needle on heavy fab-

Marking pens. Ironing over the marks made by some fabric marking pens may permanently set the ink. Be sure to remove the marks before pressing the area.

rics. Some packages contain only one size; others contain a variety. The lengths and shapes of the needle eye vary. Needles called sharps are all-purpose, medium-length needles with a small eye and sharp point. Embroidery and crewel needles have larger eyes and are easier to thread. Specialty needles are available for heavy-duty fabrics and crafts. See *Fig. 6-5***A**.

- **Thimble.** This tool will help protect your finger when sewing by hand. Made of metal or plastic, thimbles come in different sizes. Small indentations on the top and sides help hold the end of the needle as you push it through the fabric. See *Fig. 6-5***B**.
- **Needle threader.** This small device has a thin metal wire that helps thread a needle. See *Fig. 6-5***C**.
- **Glue stick.** Use this fast, easy way to temporarily hold two layers of fabric together. Be sure the glue is thoroughly dry before stitching through it. See *Fig. 6-5***D**.
- **Basting tape.** This narrow, double-faced tape holds two layers of fabric together or a zipper in place for stitching. See *Fig. 6-5***E**.
- **Bodkin.** A bodkin resembles a large, blunt needle. Pull cord, elastic, or tape through casings with it. See *Fig. 6-5***F**.
- **Loop turner.** A long metal rod with a hook, this tool turns bias tubing right side out. See *Fig. 6-5***G**.

- **Pointer.** This wooden tool has one pointed end for pushing out sharp corners, as on a collar point. The other end is rounded for holding seams open for pressing. See *Fig. 6-5***H**.

PRESSING EQUIPMENT

A garment takes on a professional finish when carefully pressed. You should press as you sew and also when a garment is complete. Three essential items are an iron, ironing board, and press cloth. Pressing equipment is shown in *Fig. 6-6*.

- **Iron.** Needs a wide temperature range for all fabrics. A combination steam-and-dry iron gives best results. See *Fig. 6-6***A**.

SEWING TIP

Thimbles. Using a thimble may seem awkward at first. Choose one that fits your middle finger well. Try dampening the end of your finger. The suction will hold the thimble firmly in place.

- **Ironing board.** Level and sturdy surface with a tight fitting cover and smooth padding. A silicone-treated cover helps prevent scorching and sticking.
- **Press cloth.** Lightweight cloth that protects certain fabrics from developing a shine, or glossy marking, and from scorching. Dampen a press cloth to create steam for special pressing techniques. You can use a clean cloth or handkerchief as a press cloth. See *Fig. 6-6***B**.
- **Tailor's ham.** A firm, round cushion used to press curved areas of a garment, such as darts and curved seams. See *Fig. 6-6***C**.
- **Sleeve board.** A small ironing board about 20 inches (51 cm) long; used to press narrow areas, such as sleeves, that don't fit over the end of a regular ironing board. See *Fig. 6-6***D**.
- **Seam roll.** A long, firm tubular cushion used to press long seams and small curved areas. A seam line can be pressed without having the imprint of the seam allowances showing through on the right side of the fabric. See *Fig. 6-6***E**.

SEWING TIP

Irons. Handle an iron carefully. If you drop it, the thermostat control, which regulates the temperature, can be damaged. Avoid ironing over pins since they can scratch the soleplate, or bottom, of an iron. When using fusible interfacings or fusible webs, make sure the adhesive doesn't touch the iron. Drain any water from an iron before storing.

- **Point presser.** A narrow wooden surface with a pointed end for pressing collar points. Other edges can be used for pressing curved and straight edges. See *Fig. 6-6***F**.

STORING EQUIPMENT

By keeping sewing equipment together in a box or basket, you'll always be able to find what you need. A measuring tape can be folded and held with a rubber band. Needles may be kept in original containers or placed in a pincushion. Small boxes or plastic bags can hold small items, such as thimbles, chalk, buttons, and other fasteners.

Spilling a box of pins is frustrating, yet it happens easily. Using a pincushion helps prevent such accidents. You may want to store a large supply of pins in a container but keep the ones you use regularly in a pincushion.

Taking care of your equipment through good organization helps ensure that items last longer and don't get lost.

6-6 Pressing Equipment

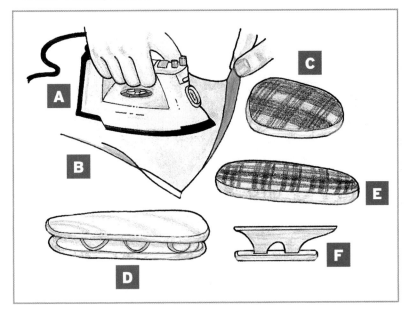

Review

SUMMARY

- All sewing machines operate in a similar manner. (Lesson 4)

- Choose needles and thread according to fabric type. (Lesson 4)

- Needles should be replaced when dull, bent, or rough. (Lesson 4)

- Adjusting the machine produces the best stitch. (Lesson 4)

- Controlling sewing machine speed comes with practice. (Lesson 4)

- The serger can stitch, trim, and overcast a seam at the same time. (Lesson 5)

- A serger creates different stitches with three, four, five, or eight threads. (Lesson 5)

- Special equipment and tools are used for measuring, pinning, cutting, marking, stitching, and pressing. (Lesson 6)

RECALLING THE FACTS

1. If you have a specific question or problem with your sewing machine or serger, what should you do? (Lesson 4)

2. When choosing a machine needle and thread, what should you consider? (Lesson 4)

3. Why is the long groove on a sewing machine needle significant? (Lesson 4)

4. What three recommendations would you make for winding and inserting a bobbin? (Lesson 4)

5. What does thread guide location tell you about threading a machine? (Lesson 4)

6. What causes a lockstitch to form? (Lesson 4)

7. What stitch length is recommended for regular stitching on most fabrics? (Lesson 4)

and Activities

8. Before you start to stitch, what two things should you do to prevent tangled stitches? (Lesson 4)

9. Where are the hands placed when stitching with a conventional machine? (Lesson 4)

10. What are three features of computerized sewing machines? (Lesson 4)

11. What three tasks does a serger do at the same time? (Lesson 5)

12. Why does a serger have a looper instead of a bobbin? (Lesson 5)

13. Why shouldn't you sew over pins with a serger? (Lesson 5)

14. Name the three essential measuring tools. (Lesson 6)

15. How should you use and store pins safely? (Lesson 6)

16. What is the difference between scissors and shears? (Lesson 6)

17. Why is a thimble useful? (Lesson 6)

18. Name the three essential items needed for pressing. (Lesson 6)

APPLYING KNOWLEDGE

1. **Sewing machine use.** Wind the bobbin on a conventional sewing machine. Then thread the machine and stitch a row of regular stitches, basting stitches, and reinforcement stitches.

CREATIVE SOLUTIONS

In your clothing class the student sitting next to you has sewn a seam for the tie he is making. He turns the fabric over and sees that the seam has little loops of thread that stick up and run the entire length of the seam. He doesn't know what happened and asks you for help.

Think Creatively

What might have happened? How would you help him solve the problem?

2. **Serger use.** Thread a serger and adjust the tension for each looper and needle. Then sew the stitches that the machine can create.

3. **Safety poster.** Create a poster of safety tips for using sewing machines, sergers, and equipment.

4. **Equipment costs.** Visit a fabric store to research the price of tools and equipment. Identify the basic tools a beginning sewer would need and determine their total cost.

Getting Ready
to Sew

Understanding Patterns

OFTEN PEOPLE ARE SO eager to see their completed sewing project that they rush the process. Before you begin to sew, think about how helpful an organized approach can be.

STAYING ORGANIZED

What can you do to save time and energy before and during a sewing project? Keep these ideas in mind:

- Gather all the notions and supplies you'll need. Check the list on the back of the pattern envelope.
- Double-check the steps to take. Verify the layout before cutting. Before stitching, make sure fabric pieces are pinned together correctly. Be sure the fit is correct before continuing.
- Press after each construction step. Pressing some areas after stitching can be difficult.
- Fit as you go. Minor adjustments made during construction are easier than a major alteration at the end.

PATTERNS AND THEIR PARTS

Your most helpful assistant throughout a sewing project will probably be the pattern. Like a blueprint, a pattern has all the instructions you need to construct a project. Following the pattern is one more way to stay organized as you sew.

Before beginning a project, read the pattern carefully. Every pattern consists of the three parts shown in *Fig. 7-1*: an envelope, a guide sheet, and tissue pattern pieces. Each item contains valuable information.

Pattern Envelope

On the front of the pattern envelope is a drawing or photograph of the design. Several garment views may be shown to give you a selection of styles. From the illustrations, you can see how the garment fits—whether it's slim or full on the body.

The envelope front lists the pattern number, size, and price. Sometimes a label indicates that the pattern is "Easy" or "Includes an Estimated Sewing Time." A special feature of the pattern may be mentioned. For example, whether a pattern is a designer fashion, sewing lesson, or craft project might be noted.

As you learned earlier, the reverse side of the pattern envelope shows how the garment looks from the back and lists the amount of fabric and notions needed. See *Fig. 1-3* on page 442.

Guide Sheet

The **guide sheet** gives step-by-step information for cutting, marking, and sewing. See *Fig. 7-2* on page 482. On the front are cutting layouts and general information, including how to lengthen and shorten a pattern. The reverse side has sewing directions. By referring regularly to the pattern guide sheet, you're less likely to have to rip out and redo stitches.

7-1 How are the three parts of a pattern used?

SEWING TIP

Guide sheet. Always keep your guide sheet handy for quick reference through layout and construction. By circling the cutting layout you're using, you'll always focus on the right one at each glance and be less likely to copy something incorrectly from a different layout.

7-2 You'll use the guide sheet from start to finish when sewing with a pattern.

Cutting Layouts

The **cutting layout** is a diagram that shows how to arrange pattern pieces on fabric. See *Fig. 7-3*. This diagram makes it easier to recognize and find the pattern pieces you need. Select the diagram that matches your particular design view, pattern size, and fabric width and nap. Separate layouts may be provided for fabrics with and without nap. A separate cutting layout may be included for interfacing and lining.

Sewing Directions

Step-by-step sewing directions appear on the back of the guide sheet. For patterns with several views, the directions may continue to one or more additional sheets. As you follow the directions, you'll want to be sure you follow the steps that apply to the view you're making.

A **fabric key** shows how shading and texture indicate the right and wrong sides of fabric and any interfacing or lining. Some construction details may be enlarged to show the specific sewing procedure clearly.

Pattern Pieces

Each pattern piece is marked with a number or letter and with a specific name, such as collar or sleeve. The number of fabric pieces to be cut is also printed on the pattern piece.

The symbols and lines on the pattern pieces serve as guides during cutting and sewing. Some pattern pieces have many markings; others have only a few. Learn to recognize and understand these symbols and lines. See *Fig. 7-4* on page 484.

PATTERN PREPARATION

Remember to handle pattern pieces carefully because they tear easily. Follow these steps to prepare the pattern pieces:

1. Remove the entire pattern from the envelope.
2. On the guide sheet, circle the cutting layout you'll use.
3. Select the pattern pieces for the view you're sewing.
4. Fold the rest of the pattern pieces and put them back into the envelope.

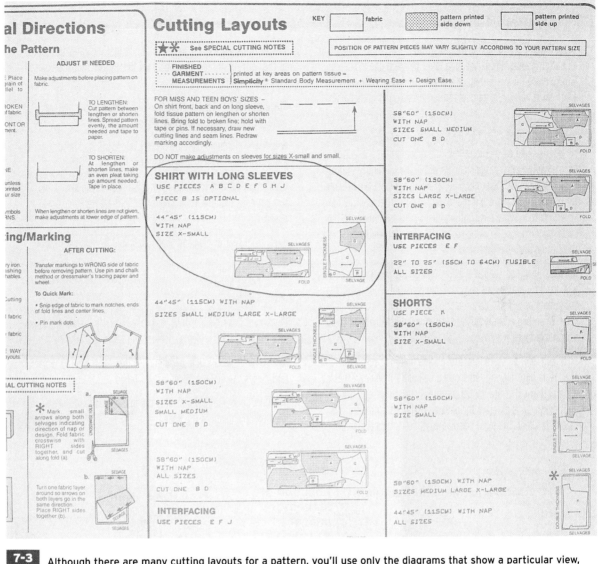

al Directions

he Pattern

ADJUST IF NEEDED

Place grain of llel to

Make adjustments before placing pattern on fabric.

OKEN f fabric.

ONT OR ment.

TO LENGTHEN: Cut pattern between lengthen or shorten lines. Spread pattern evenly, the amount needed and tape to paper.

NE

unless rinted r size

TO SHORTEN: At lengthen or shorten lines, make an even pleat taking up amount needed. Tape in place.

ymbols RNS.

When lengthen or shorten lines are not given, make adjustments at lower edge of pattern.

ing/Marking

AFTER CUTTING:

ry iron. shing hables.

Transfer markings to WRONG side of fabric before removing pattern. Use pin and chalk method or dressmaker's tracing paper and wheel.

Cutting

To Quick Mark:

fabric

• Snip edge of fabric to mark notches, ends of fold lines and center lines.

fabric

• Pin mark dots.

WAY ayouts:

IAL CUTTING NOTES

a.

✳ Mark small arrows along both selvages indicating direction of nap or design. Fold fabric crosswise with RIGHT sides together, and cut along fold (a).

b.

Turn one fabric layer around so arrows on both layers go in the same direction. Place RIGHT sides together (b).

Cutting Layouts

✶✶ See SPECIAL CUTTING NOTES

KEY ☐ fabric ▨ pattern printed side down ☐ pattern printed side up

POSITION OF PATTERN PIECES MAY VARY SLIGHTLY ACCORDING TO YOUR PATTERN SIZE

┄ **FINISHED GARMENT MEASUREMENTS** printed at key areas on pattern tissue = **Simplicity** ® Standard Body Measurement + Wearing Ease + Design Ease.

FOR MISS AND TEEN BOYS' SIZES – On shirt front, back and on long sleeve, fold tissue pattern on lengthen or shorten lines. Bring fold to broken line; hold with tape or pins. If necessary, draw new cutting lines and seam lines. Redraw marking accordingly.

DO NOT make adjustments on sleeves for sizes X-small and small.

SHIRT WITH LONG SLEEVES

USE PIECES A B C D E F G H J

PIECE B IS OPTIONAL

44"45" (115CM)
WITH NAP
SIZE X-SMALL

44"45" (115CM) WITH NAP
SIZES SMALL MEDIUM LARGE X-LARGE

58"60" (150CM)
WITH NAP
SIZES X-SMALL
SMALL MEDIUM
CUT ONE B D

58"60" (150CM)
WITH NAP
ALL SIZES
CUT ONE B D

INTERFACING
USE PIECES E F J

58"60" (150CM)
WITH NAP
SIZES SMALL MEDIUM
CUT ONE B D

58"60" (150CM)
WITH NAP
SIZES LARGE X-LARGE
CUT ONE B D

INTERFACING
USE PIECES E F

22" TO 25" (55CM TO 64CM) FUSIBLE
ALL SIZES

SHORTS
USE PIECE K

58"60" (150CM)
WITH NAP
SIZE X-SMALL

58"60" (150CM)
WITH NAP
SIZE SMALL

58"60" (150CM) WITH NAP
SIZES MEDIUM LARGE X-LARGE

44"45" (115CM) WITH NAP
ALL SIZES

7-3 Although there are many cutting layouts for a pattern, you'll use only the diagrams that show a particular view, size, and fabric width and nap.

---

5. Cut apart any pattern pieces printed together on one large piece of tissue paper. You need not trim away extra tissue paper from around the pieces. This will be cut off as you cut out the fabric.

6. Write your name on the guide sheet, the pattern envelope, and all the pattern pieces.

7. Smooth out pattern pieces. If necessary, press them with a cool, dry iron. Wrinkled pattern pieces make it very difficult to cut fabric accurately.

8. On a multisized pattern, mark cutting lines for your size with a felt-tip pen, as shown in *Fig. 7-5* on page 485.

Grain line. Heavy, solid line with an arrow at each end; appears on all pattern pieces not placed on a fold. The grain line indicates how to place the pattern piece on grain. To do this, the grain-line arrow must be exactly parallel to the selvage unless otherwise noted.

Cutting line. Heavy line that outlines pattern pieces. Sometimes a scissors symbol on the line shows the proper cutting direction. Occasionally a cutting line appears within the pattern to indicate a shorter hemline, lower neckline, or lining cut from the same pattern piece. If the pattern is multisized, major pattern pieces have several cutting lines. Each cutting line is marked to indicate the corresponding size. To avoid confusion, use a felt-tip pen to mark the cutting lines for your size.

Notches. Diamond-shaped symbols that extend beyond the cutting line; used for matching seams and joining garment pieces. Always cut around notches to create fabric extensions that can be clearly seen. When two or more notches are grouped together, cut them as a single block.

Stitching line, or seam line. Broken line that indicates where to sew. Seam lines may not be shown on all pattern pieces, especially on patterns that are multisized. The width of the seam allowance, however, is listed in the general directions on the front of the guide sheet. The most common width is $5/8$ inch (1.5 cm).

Center front and center back. Solid line that indicates the center of the garment. If brackets appear on this line, it should be placed on a fold.

Place on fold. Bracketed grain line that indicates the pattern edge is to be placed exactly on the fold.

Fold line. Solid line that shows where fabric will be folded to form a finished edge, such as a hemline or cuff.

Dots, squares, and triangles. Symbols used to help match and join garment sections, especially areas that are gathered or eased.

Dart. Triangular or diamond shape indicated by dots and two broken lines.

Buttonholes. Solid lines that show the exact locations and lengths of buttonholes.

Placement lines. Single, solid, or broken lines that show the exact locations of pockets, pleats, zippers, and trims.

Adjustment lines. Double parallel lines that show where the pattern pieces can be lengthened or shortened.

Hemline. Solid line that indicates the finished edge of the garment and the depth of the hem.

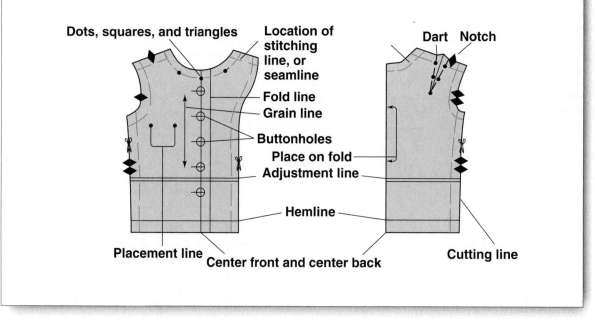

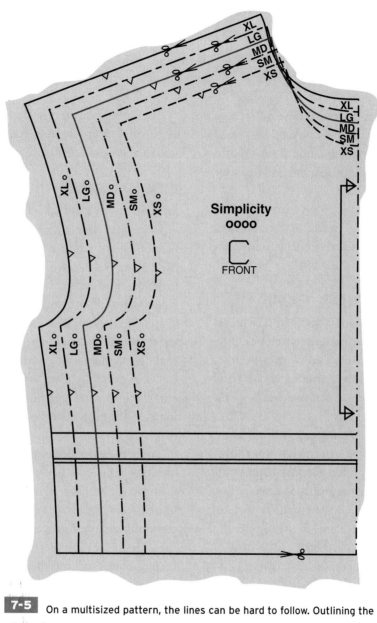

Simplicity
oooo

C
FRONT

7-5 On a multisized pattern, the lines can be hard to follow. Outlining the size you want on the pattern makes cutting easier and reduces the chances of error.

Adjusting a Pattern

FEW PEOPLE HAVE exactly the same measurements as those listed on a pattern. Therefore, some minor adjustments may be needed.

For loosely fitted garments, minor differences in measurements can be overlooked. For fitted garments, your measurements should correspond very closely to the body measurements for your pattern size.

Before laying pattern pieces on fabric, check to see whether the pattern needs to be adjusted. After the fabric is cut, it's too late to add extra inches to any part.

UNDERSTANDING EASE

Pattern sizes are designed for the body measurements listed on the pattern envelope. Only such garments as bodysuits and swimsuits, however, measure exactly the same as those body measurements. Most garments have wearing ease added to the pattern.

As you read earlier, wearing ease is the amount of fullness added to a pattern to allow for movement and comfort. For fitted garments, most patterns have the following amounts of ease:

- About 1 inch (2.5 cm) at the waistline.
- 2 to 2½ inches (5 to 6.5 cm) at the hips.
- 2½ to 4 inches (6.5 to 10 cm) at the bust or chest.

For fuller garments, designers have added extra fullness to create a particular style or silhouette. This is called design ease.

COMPARING MEASUREMENTS

Compare your own measurements to those listed on the pattern envelope. Make a chart like the one in *Fig. 8-1*, which lists both sets of measurements for bust or chest, waist, hip, and back or side length. If any measurements are not the same, enter the plus or minus difference in your chart. When complete, the chart shows where to make adjustments and how much to take in or let out. For example, if your waistline is 1 inch (2.5 cm) larger than the pattern size, you will have to increase the pattern pieces at the waistline a total of 1 inch (2.5 cm).

Some measurements are not listed on the pattern envelope. For these, measure the actual pattern pieces. Be sure to measure only from seam line to seam line. Since seam lines are not marked on multisized patterns, draw them in before you measure the pattern pieces. Most seam lines are ⅝ inch (1.3 cm) in from the cutting line. Check the

8-1 • Personal Measurements Chart			
	MY OWN MEASUREMENTS	**PATTERN MEASUREMENTS**	**+ OR -**
Bust/Chest			
Waist			
Hip			
Back/Side Length			

general directions on the front of the guide sheet. Do not include any darts, pleats, tucks, or overlapping edges. For total width, measure both the front and back sections and then double the amount. For length, measure only from seam line to hemline. Do not include the hem allowance.

PATTERN ADJUSTMENTS

The two most common pattern adjustments are for length and width. Be sure you make them on both front and back pattern pieces. As you do so, check that grain lines remain straight. Also, redraw any darts or design details. Blend sizes by drawing a new cutting line that tapers from the smaller to the larger size.

When making pattern adjustments, accuracy is critical. If you make an error of just ¼ inch (6 mm) at each side seam of a pants pattern, for example, it will become a 1-inch (2.5-cm) error when all four seam allowances are added together.

Adjusting Length

Many patterns have adjustment lines for length printed on the pattern pieces. Other patterns are altered at the lower edge. See *Figs. 8-2* and *8-3*.

- **Lengthening at the adjustment line.** Cut the pattern apart at the adjustment line. Place

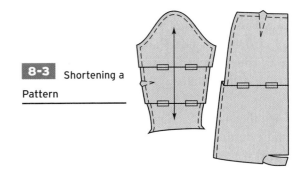

8-3 Shortening a Pattern

paper under the opening and spread the pieces the necessary amount. Keep cut edges parallel across the entire opening, verifying this with a ruler. Also check that the center-front line and grain line are straight. Tape pattern pieces in place. Redraw the cutting line along the outer edge. Redraw any darts or design details. For pants, first adjust crotch length and then adjust overall length.

- **Lengthening at the lower edge.** Tape paper to the edge of the pattern. Measure down the necessary amount and draw a new cutting line parallel to the lower edge. Extend the cutting lines along the side edges.
- **Shortening at the adjustment line.** Measure up from the adjustment line the necessary amount to be shortened and draw a line. Fold the pattern along the adjustment line and bring the fold up to exactly meet the new line. Check the grain line. Tape the fold in place. Redraw cutting lines and any darts or design lines.
- **Shortening at the lower edge.** Draw a new hemline above the original line. Redraw the cutting lines.

Adjusting Width

A total width adjustment of 2 inches (5 cm) or less can be made at the side seams. Because a garment has two side seams and four side-seam allowances, the amount to be adjusted on the front pattern piece is ¼ of the total amount.

For example, to increase the waistline by 2 inches (5 cm), you add ½ inch (1.3 cm) to the

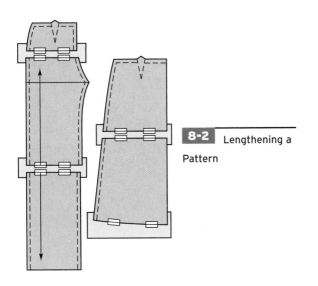

8-2 Lengthening a Pattern

side seam of the front pattern piece and ½ inch (1.3 cm) to the side seam of the back pattern piece. Thus, each side seam increases 1 inch (2.5 cm), and the total waistline increases 2 inches (5 cm).

Width adjustments larger than 2 inches (5 cm) require cutting and spreading or overlapping the pattern pieces. For these, check the procedure in an alteration book or a detailed sewing book.

Methods for increasing and decreasing pattern width are shown in *Fig. 8-4* and described here.

- **Increasing pattern width.** Tape paper along the pattern piece edge. Measure out ¼ of the necessary amount at the area to be widened. Redraw cutting lines and seam lines, tapering gradually. For a waistline, taper side seams up to the armhole or down to the hipline. Be sure to make the same adjustments

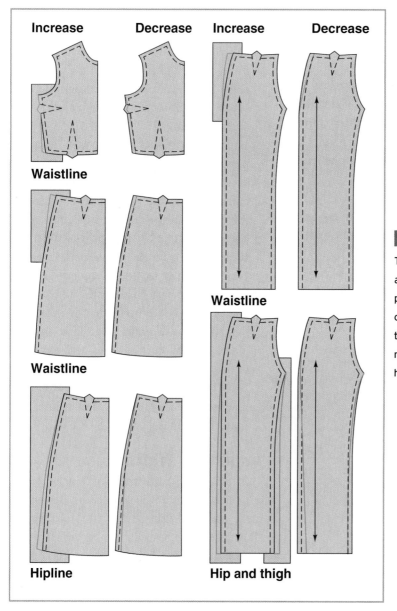

8-4 Adjusting Width on a Pattern These diagrams show how to increase and decrease the width of pattern pieces. On the pattern for a top, the changes are made at the waistline. On the skirt and pants, changes can be made at the waistline as well as the hip.

on the waistband pattern. For the hipline, continue the adjustments down to the hemline to retain the original shape of pants or skirt. Above the hipline, taper side seams in to meet the original waistline. For pants thigh, add ¼ of the amount to each inseam and side seam, extending the lines straight down to the hem edge.

- **Decreasing pattern width.** Measure in ¼ of the necessary amount on each pattern piece. Redraw the cutting lines and side seams, tapering gradually. For a waistline, taper the side seams up to the armhole or down to the hipline. For a waistband, fold ½ of the necessary amount out of each side seam marking. For the hipline, taper cutting lines and side seams up to the original waistline and straight down to the hemline. For pants thigh, take in ¼ of the amount on the inside seam and side seam, redrawing the lines straight down to the hemline.

Blending Sizes

Multisized patterns are helpful to people who are a different size on top and bottom. For example, a person might have a size 10 bust and size 12 hips. To blend two sizes, draw a new cutting line that gradually tapers out from the smaller size to the larger size. See *Fig. 8-5.*

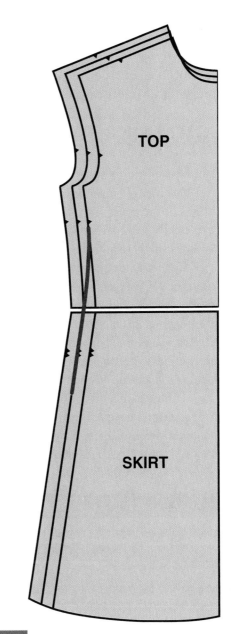

8-5 When blending two sizes on a multisized pattern, draw a new cutting line. Taper gradually from one size to the other.

Preparing Fabric

ALTHOUGH YOU MAY BE eager to cut out the pattern, fabric preparation steps should not be overlooked. These steps help fabric pieces go together more easily and promote a proper fit when the completed garment is worn and laundered.

STRAIGHTENING FABRIC ENDS

When fabric is cut from a bolt, the cut may not be straight. Uneven edges make it hard to check the straightness of the grain.

If you can clearly see the individual crosswise yarns, cut along a single yarn from one **selvage** to the other. See *Fig. 9-1* to learn about selvages and other fabric terms. If you can't see the crosswise yarns, clip the selvage and pull one crosswise yarn, gently pushing the fabric along the yarn. The pulled yarn leaves a mark you can use as a cutting line. See *Fig. 9-2*. If the yarn breaks in the middle of the fabric, cut up to the broken point, pick up the end of the yarn, and continue pulling.

Knitted fabrics don't have a thread that can be pulled. Straighten the ends by cutting along one crosswise row of loops. First, baste across the fabric, following one row of loops. Then use the basting as a cutting line. See *Fig. 9-3*.

PRESHRINKING FABRIC

By **preshrinking**, you wash or dry-clean the fabric to prevent or minimize later shrinkage. Preshrinking also helps remove some fabric finishes that cause stitching problems on lighter weight, woven, and knitted fabrics. The method you choose depends on how the finished garment will be cleaned. Check the fabric care instructions.

9-2 Cutting along Pulled Yarn

9-1 • Fabric Terms

Selvages. Two, finished, lengthwise edges on fabric; usually stiffer than the rest of the fabric. Avoid placing pattern pieces over the selvage when laying out the pattern.

Lengthwise grain. Grain that runs in the same direction as the selvage; usually the strongest and sturdiest direction of the fabric. Most garments are cut with the lengthwise grain running vertically, or up and down, for more strength and durability during wear. Directions referring to straight grain or grain line mean the lengthwise grain.

Crosswise grain. Grain that runs across the fabric from one selvage to the other; usually has a slight amount of give or stretch.

Bias grain. Grain that runs diagonally across the fabric; any direction other than lengthwise or crosswise. Fabric cut on the bias has more stretchability than fabric cut on the straight grain. Folding the fabric at a 45-degree angle so the crosswise grain is parallel to the selvage creates true bias, which has the most stretch.

Wales or ribs. Lengthwise chains of loops in knitted fabric. They correspond to the lengthwise grain of woven fabrics.

Courses. Crosswise rows of loops in knitted fabrics. In most knits, the crosswise loops have the most stretch.

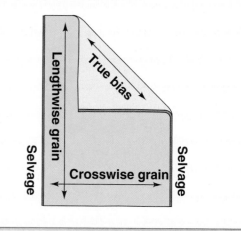

9-3 Basting Knit Fabric

A

9-4 When you fold your fabric in half lengthwise, it will look like one of these. Which one needs to be straightened? Why?

B

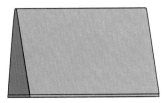

- **Washable fabrics.** Simply wash the fabric in the machine with other clothes. For fabrics that ravel easily, first machine zigzag the raw edges. Dry either in a tumble dryer or lay flat, keeping the edges square.
- **Hand-washable fabrics.** Fold the fabric and place in hot or warm water for 30 minutes. If the fabric cannot be tumble-dried, lay flat to dry.
- **Fabrics to be dry-cleaned.** Take the fabric to a professional dry cleaner or a self-service dry cleaner for preshrinking.

STRAIGHTENING GRAIN

Fabric is **off-grain** when the crosswise and lengthwise yarns are not at right angles. This may happen during the finishing process or when the fabric is rolled onto the bolt. If the fabric isn't straightened before cutting, the finished garment may pull or twist to one side of your body or the hemline may hang unevenly.

Check to see whether your fabric needs straightening. Fold the fabric in half lengthwise and match the selvages accurately. If the crosswise ends match exactly and are at right angles to the selvage, the fabric is straight. The fold should be smooth and wrinkle-free. If the edges don't match or the fabric puckers when you try to line up the edges, the fabric is not straight. See *Fig. 9-4.*

To straighten the fabric, pull it on the true bias. Open up the fabric and pull the two opposite corners that are too short. See *Fig. 9-5.* If necessary, ask someone to help you. Refold the fabric to check whether you have pulled enough.

Most fabrics can be realigned by pulling. If the yarns became off-grain during the finishing process, however, the grain may be locked in position permanently. The fabric must be used as is.

PRESSING FABRIC

Press your fabric to remove all wrinkles. Wrinkled fabric cannot be cut accurately. Check to be sure the center fold can be pressed out of the fabric. If the fold doesn't press out with a steam iron and a damp press cloth, it won't come out with washing or dry cleaning. This sometimes occurs with knits and permanently finished fabrics. Plan a special cutting layout to avoid the fold line.

9-5 To straighten fabric grain, pull the fabric on the true bias between the corners that are closer together. Can you straighten the grain correctly if you haven't straightened the ends first?

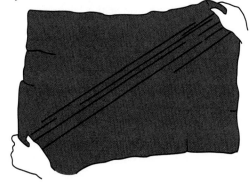

Laying Out a Pattern

Circle the cutting layout for your particular view, size, and fabric width. If your fabric has a nap, pile, shading, or one-way design, use the with-nap layout. You'll use the least amount of fabric while still having all the pieces match.

FINDING THE RIGHT SIDE

For many fabrics, the right side is obvious due to the nap, pattern, or print. On other fabrics, however, the right side may be difficult to determine. One clue is the way the fabric is folded or rolled on the bolt. Cottons and linens usually have the right side out on the bolt. Wools and most other fabrics are folded with the right side toward the inside.

Fold one edge back and compare the two surfaces. The right side may be shinier or have a more pronounced weave, more nap, or a brighter, clearer print. Some plain-weave fabrics are the same on both sides. For knitted fabrics, stretch a crosswise cut edge. The edge will usually roll to the right side of the fabric.

If you are undecided, pick the side you like better. Then be sure to keep the same side throughout so the finished garment will not have any differences in color or sheen. To help identify the sides, mark the wrong side of the fabric with chalk marks or small pieces of masking tape.

FOLDING THE FABRIC

The cutting layout shows exactly how to fold the fabric. For most layouts, the fabric is folded with the right side in. The pattern pieces are placed on the wrong side of the fabric for ease in transferring markings. This also protects fabric from soil and dirt during handling.

Stripes, plaids, and prints should be folded with the right side out. Matching fabric design is easier this way. When cutting a single layer of fabric, place the fabric right side up.

Your fabric may need to be folded lengthwise, crosswise, double, or partial. See *Fig. 10-1*.

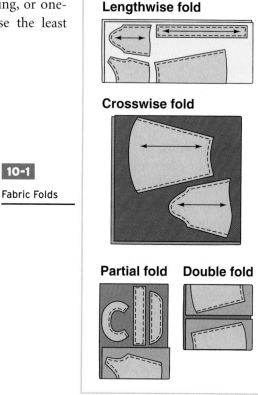

Lengthwise fold

Crosswise fold

10-1

Fabric Folds

Partial fold　**Double fold**

- **Lengthwise fold.** Fold fabric in half lengthwise with right sides together. Match selvages and ends.
- **Crosswise fold.** Fold fabric in half crosswise with right sides together. Match cut ends and keep the two layers of selvage even along each side. For napped fabrics, the nap must run in the same direction on both layers. Cut the fabric along the crosswise fold and turn the top layer around end to end. Match all edges.
- **Double fold.** Fold fabric twice along the lengthwise grain, right sides together. Usually the selvages meet in the center. This layout is often used for knitted fabrics.
- **Partial fold.** Fold fabric on the lengthwise grain, right sides together, only wide enough to fit the widest pattern piece.

After folding the fabric, smooth out any wrinkles by pulling both layers of fabric at the ends or sides. Don't try to smooth only the top layer with your hand, or the two layers will be off-grain. When the grain lines are straight, pin the two layers together along the edges. This prevents the fabric from shifting as you lay out the pattern pieces.

Always work on a large, hard surface so the full width of the fabric can be laid out without any fabric hanging over the sides. In school, use a long cutting table. At home, work on a large table, folding cutting board, or the floor. Don't use a bed because the fabric can easily shift on a soft surface.

PINNING THE PATTERN PIECES

Lay out all pattern pieces in the same position shown in the cutting layout. Most pattern pieces are placed printed side up on the fabric. Pattern pieces that are shaded on the layout should be placed with the printed side down.

An arrow or a "place-on-fold" bracket indicates the grain line on each pattern piece. Place every pattern piece exactly on the proper grain line. Never try to tilt or angle a piece to fit a smaller space. If you do, that section of the garment will not hang properly.

Place pins at right angles to the pattern edge, making sure the points don't go past the cutting line. Pin every 6 to 8 inches (15 to 20.5 cm) along folds and straight edges. On curved edges and slippery fabrics, place pins 3 to 6 inches (7.5 to 15 cm) apart.

Follow these steps for pinning the pattern pieces:

1. Start with large pattern pieces that go on the fold. Place the pattern fold line exactly along the fabric fold. Pin along the fold. Smooth the pattern away from the fold and pin diagonally into the corners. Then pin the remaining edges.

2. Next, pin pattern pieces that have a grain-line arrow. Place a pin at the end of each arrow, pinning through all fabric layers. Measure carefully from the point of each arrow to the fabric edge. See *Fig. 10-2*. If the measurements are not exactly the same, unpin one end and shift the pattern. Re-pin and measure again. Repeat until the grain line is straight. Smooth out the pattern in all directions from the grain-line arrow and pin diagonally into the corners. Finish pinning all edges.

3. Count the number of pieces on the cutting layout and compare to the number on the fabric. If any pattern pieces must be cut more than once to create four or more layers, be sure you have left the needed space. If two pieces must be cut from a single fabric layer, turn the pattern over when cutting the second piece. If a piece extends beyond the folded edge of the fabric, cut the other pieces first. Then unfold the fabric and cut the remaining pattern piece.

10-2 Checking the Grain Line

4. Double-check your layout. Are all pieces positioned correctly? Are the grain lines straight? Are there any special instructions for certain pattern pieces?

SPECIAL LAYOUTS

Special pattern layouts and extra fabric may be needed if you choose certain fabric designs. When laying these out, always place the largest pattern pieces on the fabric first. Visualize where the dominant lines or designs will fall on the body.

- **Napped fabrics.** Place all pattern pieces in the same direction. For a richer color in corduroy and velvet, lay out the pattern so the nap or pile runs up the garment. Use a with-nap layout. See *Fig. 10-3***A**.
- **Plaids.** Plaids can be even or uneven, depending on the repeat of the lines. Even plaids are the same in both vertical and horizontal directions. Use a without-nap layout. For uneven plaids, use a with-nap layout so all pattern pieces are laid in the same direction. Use the dominant line of the plaid for the center front and center back. Match plaids at side seams and sleeves. See *Fig. 10-3***B**.
- **Stripes.** For even stripes, use a without-nap layout. For uneven stripes, use a with-nap layout. For vertical stripes, place the dominant stripe at center front and center back. Match stripes at side seams and sleeves. Stripes will chevron, or meet on an angle, on bias seams. See *Fig. 10-3***C**.
- **Directional prints.** Use a with-nap layout. Match designs at seam lines. See *Fig. 10-3***D**.
- **Border prints.** Place all pattern pieces on the crosswise grain. Match hemline markings to the lower edge of the border design. Place other pieces in the space available above the design. See *Fig. 10-3***E**.

Match stripes, plaids, and prints by placing corresponding notches of the pattern pieces on the same line or design of the fabric. Be sure to match at the seam line, not at the cutting line.

10-3 | Special Layouts for Different Fabric Designs

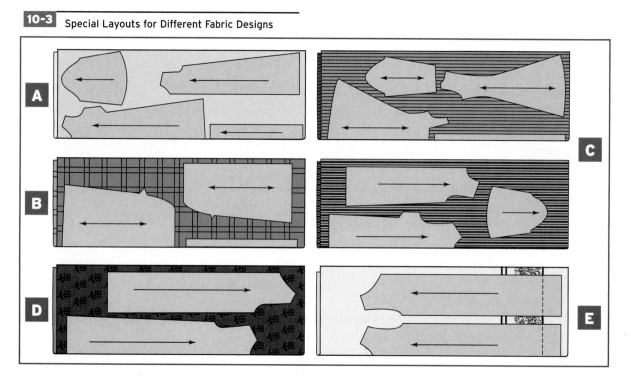

Cutting and Marking Fabric

ONCE YOU HAVE PINNED all pattern pieces to the fabric, you can cut them out. Then the lines and symbols on the pattern pieces must be transferred to the fabric. These markings will help you assemble the garment.

CUTTING ACCURATELY

Follow these guidelines when cutting out fabric pieces. See *Fig. 11-1.*

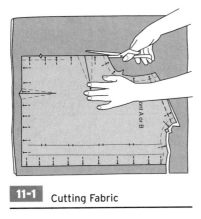

11-1 Cutting Fabric

- **Use bent-handled shears.** Cut with long, even strokes without closing the blades completely. Hold the fabric flat on the cutting surface with your other hand. Cut slowly and accurately. Never use pinking shears.
- **Cut directionally with the grain line.** Some patterns have a symbol printed on the cutting line or stitching line to show the direction to cut and stitch. If in doubt, cut from the widest point to the narrowest point.
- **Follow the correct cutting line on a multisized pattern.** Mark the cutting lines for your own size with a felt-tip pen to make them easier to follow, or trim the pattern pieces before laying them out.
- **Cut carefully around notches.** Use the tip of the shears for greater accuracy. Cut double and triple notches together with one long edge across the top. See *Fig. 11-2.*
- **Leave pattern pieces pinned to the fabric until you're ready to sew.** You'll need

to transfer construction markings to the fabric before unpinning.
- **Save all fabric scraps.** Use them to test marking methods, type and length of stitches, and pressing temperatures.

WHAT TO MARK

The lines and symbols on pattern pieces are important guides during construction. Before unpinning the pattern, transfer these marks to the fabric: darts, pleats, tucks, dots, and placement lines for buttonholes, buttons, pockets, and

11-2 Markings on a pattern tell you where to cut. How should you cut two notches that are together?

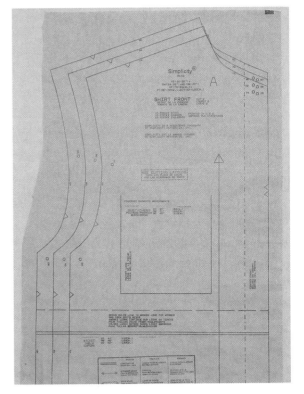

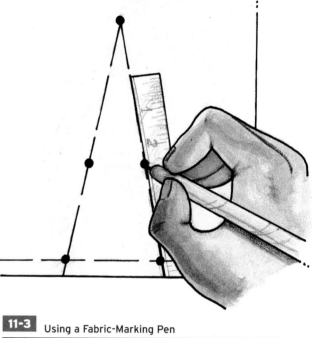

11-3 Using a Fabric-Marking Pen

any trims. You may also want to mark fold lines and center front and back lines.

Seam allowances and hemlines need not be marked. Seam allowances can be measured as you stitch by using the guides marked on the sewing machine. After the garment is made, hems are measured and turned under.

MARKING METHODS

Markings must be visible as you sew, but they should never show on the outside of a finished garment. Different marking methods may be used for different fabrics and types of marks.

Fabric-Marking Pens

Fabric-marking pens contain ink that removes with water or evaporates from fabric. Because the ink is removable, you can use these pens to mark on the right side of fabric. Follow this procedure. See *Fig. 11-3.*

1. Stick pins straight through the pattern and both fabric layers at all marking points.
2. Start at an outside edge of the pattern piece, and carefully separate the layers of fabric just enough to place an ink dot where the pin is inserted. Mark both layers of fabric.
3. Repeat, working toward the center of the garment section until all symbols are marked.

Tracing Wheel and Dressmaker's Tracing Paper

Marking with a tracing wheel is quick and useful for most fabrics. See *Fig. 11-4.* Use a saw-toothed wheel for most fabrics and a smooth-edged wheel for delicate fabrics. Tracing paper

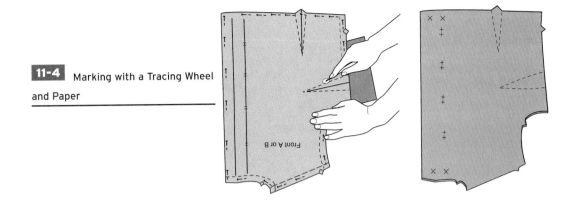

11-4 Marking with a Tracing Wheel and Paper

has a waxy surface on one side and is available in several colors. Pay close attention to whether marks are removable.

- **Papers that make permanent marks.** Use these only on the wrong side of fabric. Choose a color that is similar to the fabric color but still shows. Test on a fabric scrap to be sure the marks don't show on the right side. Use caution with light-colored and lightweight fabrics. To mark your garment, place the waxy side of the paper against the wrong side of the fabric.

- **Papers that make removable marks.** Use these on the right or wrong side of fabric. Test on a scrap of fabric to make sure the marks disappear. To mark your garment, place the waxy side of the paper against the right or wrong side of the fabric.

To mark fabric, use two layers of paper for a double layer of fabric. For small areas, fold the paper in half. Mark all symbols by guiding the tracing wheel over each line or symbol only once. Press down lightly on the tracing wheel. Mark dots with an X. Mark the end of a dart with a short line. For longer lines, use a ruler to keep lines straight.

Tailor's Chalk

Chalk markings can be made on most fabrics. Mark only the wrong side of the fabric with either a flat square of tailor's chalk or a chalk pencil. Be sure the edge or point is sharp so the markings are accurate. Follow this procedure. See *Fig. 11-5*.

1. Push a pin through both layers of fabric at each symbol. Carefully loosen the pattern and slip it over the pins. Be careful not to pull out any pins.
2. Make a chalk mark at each pin on the top layer of fabric.
3. Turn the fabric over and mark the other layer at each pin.

Chalk markings can be easily brushed off some fabrics, so handle carefully until all construction is complete.

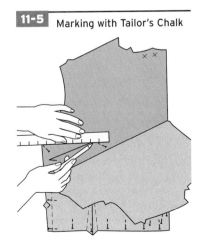

11-5 Marking with Tailor's Chalk

Review

SUMMARY

- Pattern information and instructions are provided on the envelope, guide sheet, and tissue pattern pieces. (Lesson 7)

- Body measurements should be compared to those on a pattern envelope to see if any adjustments are needed. (Lesson 8)

- Fabric may need straightening, preshrinking, or pressing. (Lesson 9)

- The cutting layout shows how to arrange pattern pieces on fabric. (Lesson 10)

- Each pattern piece should be placed on the proper grain line before pinning in place. (Lesson 10)

- Bent-handled shears are used to cut out pattern pieces. (Lesson 11)

- Construction lines and symbols can be marked with a fabric-marking pen, tracing wheel and dressmaker's tracing paper, or tailor's chalk. (Lesson 11)

RECALLING THE FACTS

1. For what specific reasons do you need a pattern guide sheet? (Lesson 7)

2. What are the lines and symbols on pattern pieces? Explain the purpose of each. (Lesson 7)

3. Why should pattern pieces be smoothed or pressed? (Lesson 7)

4. How do you widen a pattern? (Lesson 8)

5. How do you combine two different sizes on a multisized pattern? (Lesson 8)

6. Why are most garments cut with the lengthwise grain running vertically? (Lesson 9)

7. How can you preshrink washable fabric? (Lesson 9)

8. What does "off-grain" mean? (Lesson 9)

9. How can fabric grain be straightened? (Lesson 9)

10. How can you determine the right side of a fabric? (Lesson 10)

11. Why are some fabrics folded with right side in and some with it out? Give examples. (Lesson 10)

12. Why shouldn't you tilt or angle a pattern piece to save fabric? (Lesson 10)

13. Why do some fabrics require special pattern layouts? Give examples. (Lesson 10)

14. How can you know in which direction to cut a pattern piece? (Lesson 11)

and Activities

15. Describe how to cut around notches. (Lesson 11)

16. Why should you save fabric scraps? (Lesson 11)

17. List five construction lines and symbols that need to be marked and two that don't. (Lesson 11)

APPLYING KNOWLEDGE

1. **Measurements.** Compare your own measurements with the body measurements listed on a pattern envelope. Indicate any differences.

2. **Adjustment math.** Suppose you want to widen a pants pattern a total of $1\frac{1}{2}$ inches (3.75 cm). How much should you add to the front and back pieces?

3. **Marking techniques.** Use the three marking methods on different types of fabrics. Compare the results.

4. **Pattern preparation and adjustment.** Complete the following steps on your pattern: circle the layout diagram, select needed pattern pieces, write your name on all pattern parts, smooth out or press pattern pieces, and mark cutting lines on multisized pattern. Make any needed length or width adjustments on the pattern pieces.

5. **Layout, cutting, and marking.** Demonstrate the proper techniques for laying out, pinning, cutting, and marking fabric.

CREATIVE SOLUTIONS

A friend in your clothing class discovers she doesn't have quite enough fabric to lay out her pattern. She is discouraged as she shows you her partially laid out pattern and asks whether you have any ideas about what she might do.

Think Creatively

What suggestions can you give your friend that might help?

6. **Project management.** In Part 1 of the "Sewing and Serging Handbook," you planned a sewing project. Planning is the first step in the management process, as described on page 54. Now utilize the next two management steps, listed below, as you work on your project.
   a. **Get organized:** Write a timeline for your project. For example, when will you work on the project, and what tasks can you realistically accomplish at each session? Gather supplies and any other resources you need.
   b. **Implement your plan:** As you work on your project, check your progress against the timeline. Are you working efficiently and using your resources well? If not, make adjustments in order to be done on schedule.

PART 4

Basic Construction

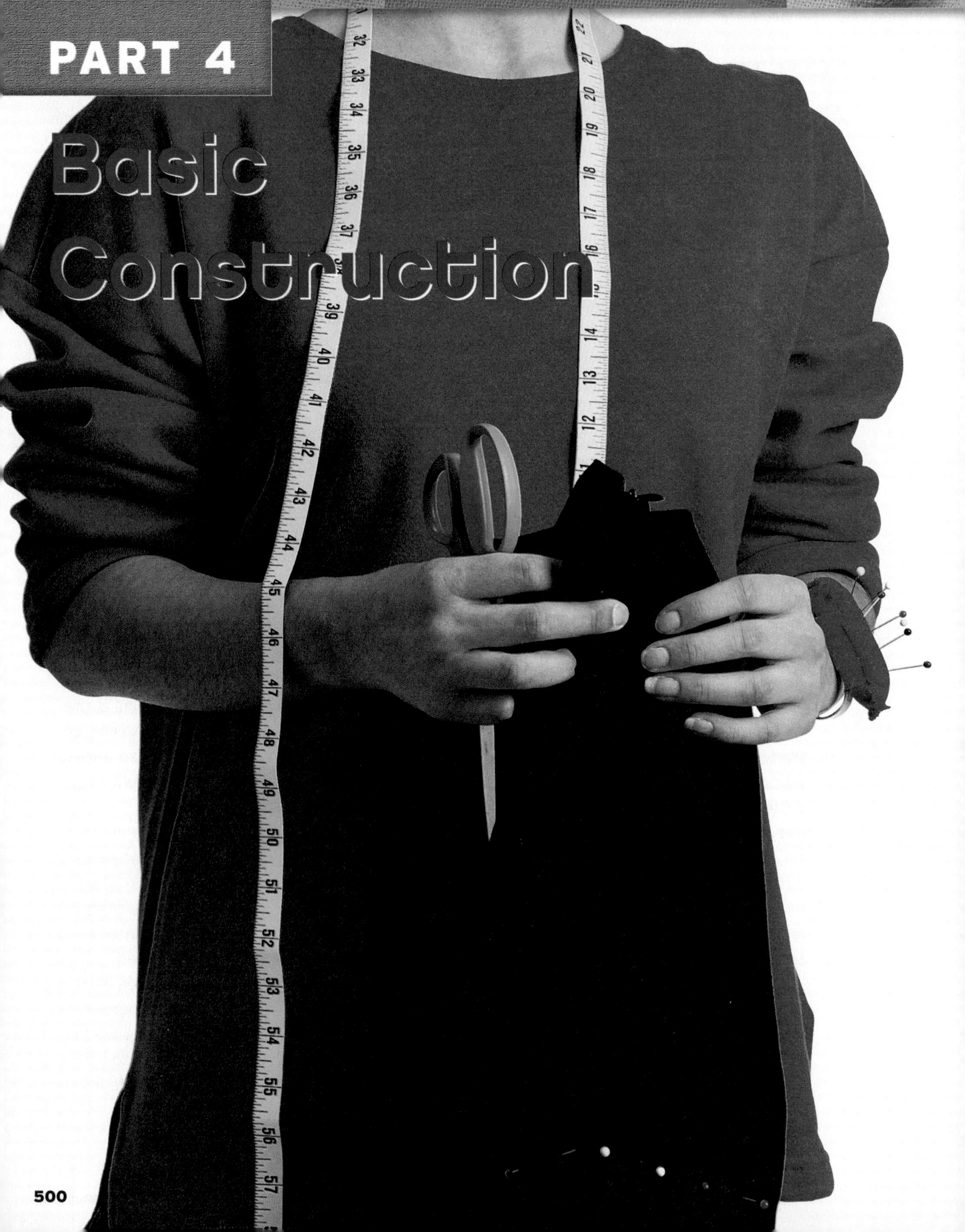

Stitching by Machine

FTER LAYING OUT your pattern and cutting and marking the pieces, you're ready to sew. Both machine and hand stitching are involved in most projects. The machine stitching described in this lesson is used on seams, darts, and facings. Machine stitches can also be used to finish seam edges, insert zippers, create buttonholes, and attach trims.

STITCH LENGTHS

The stitch length you choose depends on the purpose. A medium length is common for most stitching. Basting stitches are very long, while reinforcement stitches are very short. See *Fig. 12-1*.

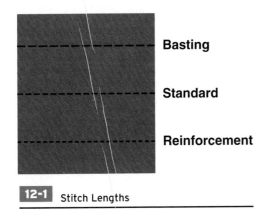

Basting

Standard

Reinforcement

12-1 Stitch Lengths

- **Standard stitching.** Use these stitches for permanent seams and construction details. For most fabrics, 10 to 12 stitches per inch (2 to 2.5 mm in length) work well. Finer fabrics take a shorter stitch of 12 to 15 stitches per inch (1.5

to 2 mm in length). Heavy fabrics need a longer stitch of 8 to 10 stitches per inch (2.5 to 3 mm in length).

- **Basting.** Machine basting temporarily holds two or more pieces of fabric together until they're permanently stitched. It can also be used on a single layer of fabric for easing, gathering, and marking guidelines. Use a very long stitch of 6 stitches per inch (2.5 cm in length). Decrease the upper tension one or two settings for easy removal of basting stitches.

- **Reinforcement stitching.** These stitches add strength to areas that will be trimmed or clipped close to the stitching. Use a very short stitch, 15 to 20 stitches per inch (2.5 cm in length), to hold the fabric yarns in place.

TYPES OF MACHINE STITCHING

To complete a project, you're likely to use a number of machine stitches, each with a specific purpose. Since you'll see the names often in directions, you'll want to become familiar with these stitches.

SEWING TIP

Stitching guidelines. As you stitch, keep your eyes on the fabric edge and guideline marking—not on the needle. Guide the fabric with your fingers, without pushing or pulling the fabric. As you come to a corner, curve, or the end of a seam, slow down the machine's speed. If you're having trouble with the tension or stitch quality, try a new needle. A good guideline is to use a new needle on every project.

- **Stay-stitching.** Prevents stretching as you handle fabric. This stitching is placed along bias and curved edges. See *Fig. 12-2*. It's added after fabric is marked and before pinning, basting, and permanent stitching. Stay-stitches belong on a single layer of fabric ⅛ inch (3 mm) away from the seam line and within the seam allowance. Use standard machine stitching and stitch directionally. Stay-stitching can act as a guideline for clipping and joining curved edges.

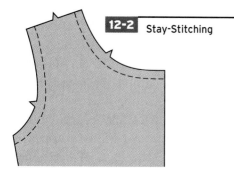

12-2 Stay-Stitching

- **Directional stitching.** Helps prevent a seam from stretching or changing shape as you stitch. Directional stitching is produced by stitching with, or in the same direction as, the fabric grain. See *Fig. 12-3*. To determine grain direction, run your finger along the fabric edge. The direction that smoothes the yarns

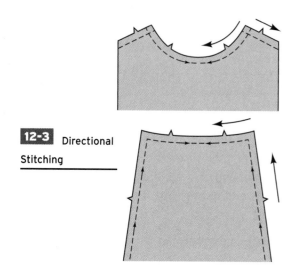

12-3 Directional Stitching

against the fabric is with the grain. Stitch in this direction. If you stitch from the wide part of a fabric section to the narrow part, you'll be stitching with the grain in most situations. Seams on straight grain can be stitched in either direction.

- **Standard seam stitching.** Produces a seam that is ⅝ inch (1.5 cm) wide. This stitching is used on almost all patterns. If another seam width is needed, it's marked on the pattern piece.

- **Backstitching.** Secures the ends of a row of stitching. To backstitch, begin stitching ½ inch (1.3 cm) in from the beginning of the stitching line. Stitch backward to the edge of the fabric; then stitch forward over the stitches you just made. See *Fig. 12-4*. Continue stitching the seam, and backstitch at the

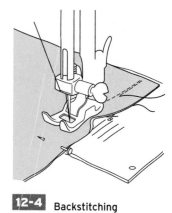

12-4 Backstitching

SEWING TIP

Stitch direction. On a conventional machine, the top fabric layer always feeds slightly faster than the bottom layer. Therefore, you should stitch with the grain whenever possible. With a serger, you can stitch a seam in any direction. The serger's presser foot has a firmer pressure, and the loopers interlock the threads across the fabric and along the length of the fabric. Thus, shifting is eliminated on most fabrics.

other end for ½ inch (1.3 cm) exactly over the first stitching.

- **Understitching.** Keeps the facing or the bottom layer of fabric rolled out of sight. You can create this stitch with standard stitching. Stitch from the right side, through the facing and seam allowances, ⅛ inch (3 mm) from the seam line. See *Fig. 12-5*.

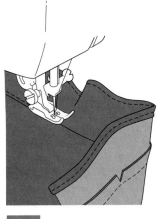

12-5 Understitching

- **Topstitching.** Provides decorative or functional stitching when placed on the outside of a garment. Topstitching outlines seams, secures facings, attaches pockets, stitches pleats, and holds hems. See *Fig. 12-6*. Using either matching or contrasting thread, stitch on the right side of the fabric with a slightly longer stitch length of 8 to 10 stitches per inch (2.5 cm in length). To keep topstitching even, use the edge of the presser foot, guideline markings, or sewing tape as a guide. See *Fig. 12-7*.

12-6 Topstitching on Garment

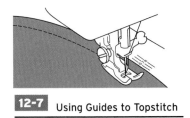

12-7 Using Guides to Topstitch

- **Edgestitching.** Holds fabric and seams tightly in place. This row of topstitching is placed very close to a finished edge. See *Fig. 12-8*. You can use edgestitching in many places, such as on zippers and neck edges.

12-8 Edgestitching

- **Stitch-in-the-ditch.** Holds two or more layers of fabric together at the seams. With this technique, you can secure neckline, armhole, or waistband facings, as well as fold-up cuffs. This row of standard machine stitching is placed on the outside of a garment in the groove of a seam line. On the outside, stitch directly in the seam groove through all layers of fabric. See *Fig. 12-9*.

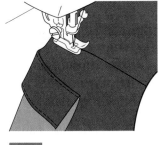

12-9 Stitch-in-the-Ditch

- **Zigzag stitching.** Used to finish seams, stitch buttonholes, attach cording and elastic, and create decorative designs. See *Fig. 12-10*. Both the length and width of a zigzag stitch can be adjusted. The stitch can range from very narrow and closely spaced for a satin stitch to very wide and far apart for a seam finish. Most machines can do zigzag stitching.

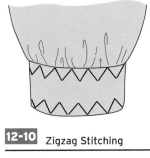

12-10 Zigzag Stitching

- **Specialty stitches.** Serve many purposes, especially decorative, when available on a

Stitching

For a smooth start, serge a 3- to 4-inch (7.5- to 10-cm) thread chain. See *Fig. A*. Then place the fabric in front of the presser foot, aligning the seam line with the needles. The presser foot can be left in the down position because the feed dogs will pull the fabric under the presser foot.

Always remove pins before the knife reaches them. See *Fig. B*. For long seams, place the pins at least 1 inch (2.5 cm) from the cut edge and parallel to the seam line. Then the pins will not come near the cutting blades. See *Fig. C*.

To end the stitching, serge off the fabric for about 5 to 6 inches (12.5 to 15 cm). This is called chaining off. Without raising the presser foot, bring the chain and the fabric around so the chain crosses in front of the knife. See *Fig. D*. Stitch for a few more seconds so that the knives automatically cut the thread chain.

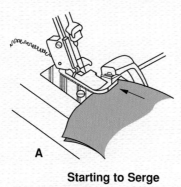

A

Starting to Serge

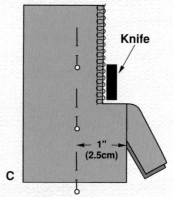

Knife

1" (2.5cm)

C

Placing Pins on Long Seams

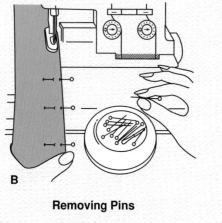

B

Removing Pins

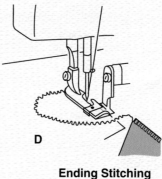

D

Ending Stitching

machine. Refer to your sewing machine manual for specific directions.

CHECKING THE MACHINE

Before you begin to sew, always check the machine. Practice sewing on two layers of scrap fabric to make sure everything is set correctly and working well. Here's a checklist to follow.

- Is the stitch length correct?
- Are stitches the correct width?
- Is the tension producing an even stitch?
- Is the needle smooth and straight?
- Has the needle been inserted properly?
- Is the presser foot firm and tight?
- Has the bobbin been inserted properly into the case?
- Was the wheel knob tightened after winding the bobbin?

UNIT CONSTRUCTION

With your machine in working order, you can start putting a project together. Many experienced sewers recommend **unit construction** for assembling a project. With this method, you complete individual parts as fully as possible before sewing them together. Because you work on small areas first, they're easier to handle and you can press each part before seams are added.

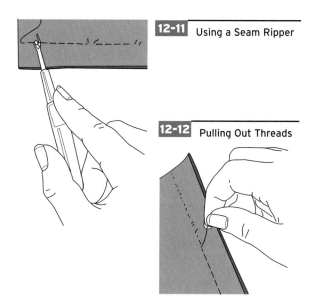

12-11 Using a Seam Ripper

12-12 Pulling Out Threads

Serging Techniques

Removing Stitches

Most serging involves more than two threads. To remove stitches, a seam ripper can be used to cut through the looper threads so the other threads pull free. Sometimes the needle threads can be gently pulled out, freeing the looper threads. Pulling on the looper thread at the end of the stitching line can unravel a serger chain stitch.

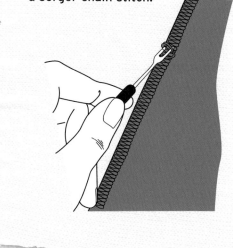

To do unit construction, first complete all staystitching. Next, sew any darts, gathers, tucks, or pleats on each piece. Such details as buttonholes and plackets can be completed on small sections. Interfacing can be applied. Then all pieces are carefully pressed before combining them.

REMOVING STITCHES

Mistakes do happen. To rip out stitches, use a seam ripper, thread clippers, or small scissors. Cut threads about every 2 inches (5 cm) along one side of the fabric. See *Fig. 12-11*. Pull the thread out on the other side, and then remove the short threads from the clipped side. See *Fig. 12-12*.

Stitching by Hand

Hand stitches are used primarily for finishing steps, such as hemming and sewing on fasteners. Hand stitches are also used for basting, reinforcement, and decorative stitching.

THREADING A NEEDLE

To thread a needle, unwind no more than 24 inches (61 cm) of thread. Longer lengths may tangle or knot as you sew. Use scissors to cut the thread at an angle so the end will slide easily through the eye of the needle. Biting or breaking the thread causes it to fray and makes it difficult to slip through the needle's eye.

Most hand sewing is done with a single thread. Make a knot in just one thread end. If you need a double thread, hold the two ends together as you tie the knot. *Fig. 13-1* shows how to tie a knot.

SEWING TIP

Needle threading. For easy needle threading, hold the needle against a white background to see the eye clearly. To use a needle threader, push the wire through the eye of the needle. Then insert the thread through the wire. Pull the wire back out of the needle, drawing the thread through the eye.

13-1 Tying a Knot

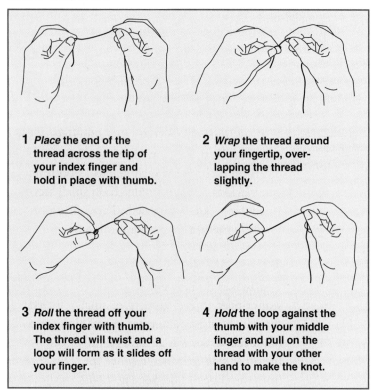

1 *Place* the end of the thread across the tip of your index finger and hold in place with thumb.

2 *Wrap* the thread around your fingertip, overlapping the thread slightly.

3 *Roll* the thread off your index finger with thumb. The thread will twist and a loop will form as it slides off your finger.

4 *Hold* the loop against the thumb with your middle finger and pull on the thread with your other hand to make the knot.

TYPES OF HAND STITCHING

For most hand stitches, hold the fabric so that you sew from right to left if you're right-handed. Left-handed sewers move from left to right.

To secure the beginning and end stitches, make a small knot or take two small stitches, one on top of the other, on the wrong side of the garment.

The following stitches are done by hand:

- **Basting stitch.** Hand basting is temporary stitching that marks or holds fabric layers together. Basting should be removed from the garment as soon as the permanent stitching is completed and no longer needed. There are two types of basting stitches. *Even basting* holds seams together for fitting or permanent stitching, such as basting sleeves into armholes. Make stitches about ¼ inch (6 mm) long and even on both sides of the fabric. See *Fig. 13-2. Uneven basting* marks or holds hems in place for stitching. Make 1-inch (2.5-cm) stitches on the top side of the fabric and short ¼-inch (6-mm) stitches on the underside. See *Fig. 13-3.* To save time, take several stitches with the needle before pulling the thread through.

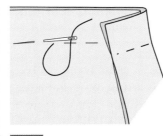

13-2 Even Basting Stitch

13-3 Uneven Basting Stitch

• **Running stitch.** This is the simplest hand stitch. Use it to gather, ease, tuck, quilt, and sew seams that have little or no strain on them. Make tiny, even stitches ¹⁄₁₆ to ¼ inch (1.5 to 6 mm) in length. See *Fig. 13-4.*

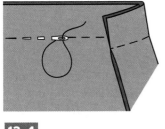

13-4 Running Stitch

• **Backstitch.** As one of the strongest hand stitches, backstitches repair machine-stitched seams and fasten thread ends securely. Use a tiny running stitch. To begin the backstitch, insert the needle at the end of

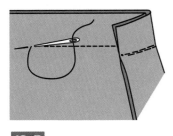

13-5 Backstitch

the previous stitch. Bring it out one stitch length in front of the thread. Keep inserting the needle in the end of the last stitch and bringing it out ahead of the thread. The stitches on the underside will be twice as long as those on the upper side. See *Fig. 13-5.*

• **Pickstitch.** This variation of the backstitch is used to insert zippers by hand and as a decorative stitch. The needle is brought back only one or two threads so that a very tiny stitch forms on the upper side. See *Fig. 13-6.*

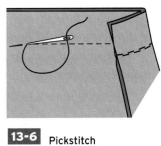

13-6 Pickstitch

• **Slip stitch.** Since it's almost invisible, the slip stitch can attach one folded edge to another piece of fabric, as on patch pockets, hems, linings, and trims. Slip the needle inside the fold of the upper fabric

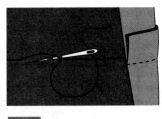

13-7 Slip Stitch

for ¼ inch (6 mm). Then pick up one or two threads of the under fabric directly below. Continue to take a stitch through the fold and then in the other fabric. See *Fig. 13-7.*

• **Overcast stitch.** You can prevent raw edges from raveling with this stitch. Make diagonal stitches over the edge of the fabric, spacing them evenly apart. See *Fig. 13-8.*

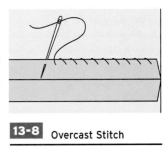

13-8 Overcast Stitch

Belt Carrier

To make belt carriers, set the serger for a narrow, rolled hemstitch. Without any fabric in the machine, serge a long chain of stitches. Thread the chain onto a hand-sewing needle. Working from the outside of the garment, insert the needle in the seam line. Gently pull the tail of the chain to the inside of the garment and tie a knot. Repeat for the other end of the chain.

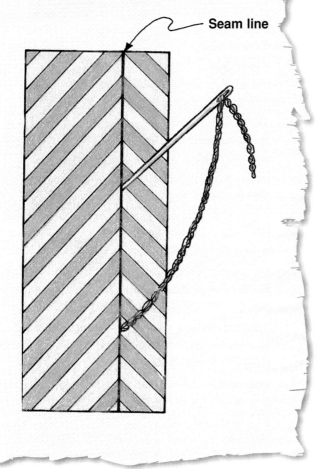

Seam line

- **Hemming stitch.** This slanted stitch finishes different hems, especially those with seam binding or a folded edge. Make a tiny stitch in the garment. Then bring the needle diagonally up through the folded edge of the fabric or the seam binding. Space stitches about ¼ inch (6 mm) apart. See *Fig. 13-9*.

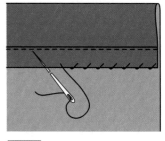

13-9 Hemming Stitch

- **Blindstitch.** Since it's barely visible from the garment's right side, the blindstitch is excellent for hemming and holding facings in place. It also allows movement without pulling. Fold the hem or facing edge back about ¼ inch (6 mm). Take a small stitch in the garment, catching only one or two threads. Then take a tiny stitch diagonally above in the hem or facing. Don't pull the stitches tight. Continue to form a very narrow zigzag stitch. See *Fig. 13-10*.

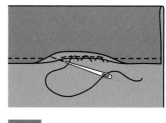

13-10 Blindstitch

- **Catchstitch.** This criss-cross stitch holds two layers of fabric together with flexibility. Use it to hem stretchy fabrics or attach sew-in interfacings. Stitch from left to right if you are right-handed. Make a small horizontal stitch from right to left in one layer of fabric a short distance from the edge. Then make another horizontal stitch just

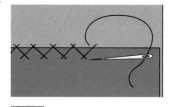

13-11 Catchstitch

over the edge and diagonally to the right on the other layer of fabric. The threads will cross each other between stitches. See *Fig. 13-11*.

- **Blind catchstitch.** This stitch is concealed between two layers of fabric. Fold the hem edge back about ¼ inch (6 mm). Make catch-stitches between the two layers. See *Fig. 13-12*.

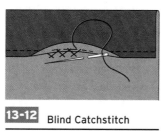

13-12 Blind Catchstitch

- **Cross-stitch.** This decorative stitch holds layers of fabric together. A series of cross-

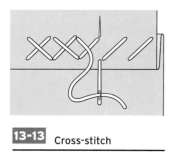

13-13 Cross-stitch

stitches is often used at the center back pleat of a jacket lin-ing. Make a series of horizontal stitches about ¼ to ⅜ inch (6 to 9 mm) wide, spaced as far apart as they are long, to form a diagonal design. Then reverse direction and continue making horizontal stitches at the same location as the previous stitches to form an X design. See *Fig. 13-13*. A *cross-stitch tack*

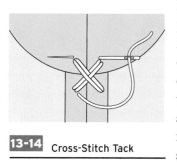

13-14 Cross-Stitch Tack

holds a facing edge in place at a seam line. Make a cross-stitch over the edge with-out allowing stitches to show on the out-side. Continue mak-ing several cross-stitches over the first one. See Fig. *13-14*.

- **Buttonhole stitch.** Making handworked buttonholes and attaching hooks and eyes are uses for this stitch. It also provides a decorative finish along the edge of a garment by placing stitches farther apart. Use a double thread. Begin by inserting the needle through the but-

tonhole slash and bringing it out on the right side of the fabric. Then loop the thread under the eye of the needle and under the point. Pull the needle out of the fabric and draw up the loop to form a knot along the but-tonhole edge. See *Fig. 13-15*.

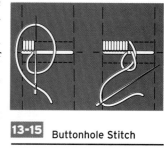

13-15 Buttonhole Stitch

- **Blanket stitch.** This stitch makes thread loops, eyes, and belt carriers, as well as bar tacks, French tacks, and a decorative finish along a fabric edge. Stitch from left to right, holding the fabric edge toward you. Point the needle toward you and insert it through the fab-ric from the right side. Keep the thread under the needle as the stitch is pulled up. See *Fig. 13-16*. Make a *thread*

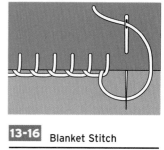

13-16 Blanket Stitch

loop, eye, or *belt carrier* by working blanket stitches over longer base stitches. Use a double thread. Take two or three stitches the desired length of the loop, eye, or carrier. Secure the ends with small backstitches. Be sure the base stitches are long enough for the button, hook, or belt to pass through. Then with the same thread, make closely spaced blanket stitches over the entire length of the base stitches. Secure with several small stitches on the underside of the fabric. See *Fig. 13-17* on page 510. A *French tack* holds a lining hem to a skirt hem or a coat hem at a seam line. Form them by working blanket stitches over several long stitches. See *Fig. 13-18* on page 510.

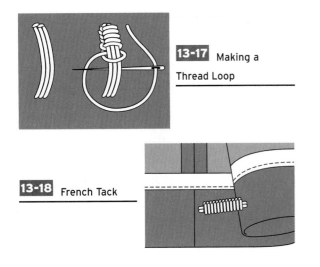

13-17 Making a Thread Loop

13-18 French Tack

• **Chain stitch.** This stitch also forms thread loops, eyes, and carriers. Use a double thread to form a series of loops. Secure the thread with several overlapping stitches on the underside. Then take a short stitch to form a loop on the right side. Slip your thumb and first two fingers through the loop. Reach through the loop with a finger and catch the thread to form

a new loop. See *Fig. 13-19.* Pull the new loop through the first loop and tighten so that the first loop forms a knot at the base of the thread chain. Keep forming new loops and sliding them down the thread evenly until the desired length. Slip the needle and thread through the last loop to end the chain. See *Fig. 13-20.* Stitch into the fabric and secure with small stitches on the underside.

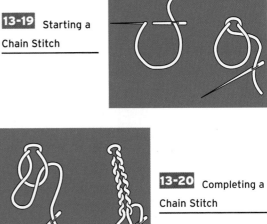

13-19 Starting a Chain Stitch

13-20 Completing a Chain Stitch

Pressing Fabric

SINCE PRESSING TAKES place throughout the sewing process, good pressing techniques are as necessary as good sewing skills. At the start, pressing ensures that both pattern and fabric are wrinkle-free for accurate cutting. Through every step of construction, pressing smoothes and shapes a garment.

If you keep pressing equipment near the sewing machine, you'll be less tempted to skip this step. An ironing board, a steam iron, and a press cloth are essential. A tailor's ham helps press curved areas. Other pressing equipment, although less essential, can make the job easier. (See *Fig. 6-6* on page 477.)

PRESSING BASICS

To press fabric correctly, use the following guidelines:

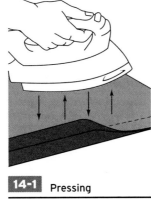

14-1 Pressing

- Press rather than iron. As you've read, the iron slides back and forth when ironing. This can cause the fabric to wrinkle and stretch, which makes pressing a better technique for garment construction. In pressing, the iron is lowered to the fabric, then raised up and lowered to a different spot. The heat and steam do most of the work, so heavy pressure isn't needed. See *Fig. 14-1*.
- Use the correct temperature setting. Set the temperature according to the fiber content of your fabric; however, don't use the cotton and linen settings for pressing because the fabric could scorch. If your fabric is a blend, use the setting for the most heat-sensitive fiber in the blend.
- Always test fabric for any reaction to heat, steam, and pressure. Press a scrap of fabric and check for damage or marks left by the iron. If the fabric sticks, puckers, or melts, the iron is too hot. Check to see whether the fabric holds water spots. Too much pressure can crush napped fabrics or create press marks on the right side.
- Press on the wrong side of the fabric whenever possible. Pressing on the inside prevents shine on the right side of the fabric. Also, seams can be seen clearly and pressed correctly.

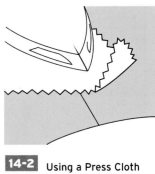

14-2 Using a Press Cloth

- When pressing on the right side of the fabric, always use a press cloth. Some areas, such as pleats and pockets, may have to be pressed on the outside of the garment. A press cloth prevents leaving shiny marks on fabric. See *Fig. 14-2*.
- Never press over pins. Pins leave an impression on fabric and may scratch the iron.
- Always press seams and darts before other seams are stitched across them. This reduces bulk in the finished garment.
- Press directionally with the grain of the fabric. This prevents stretching.
- Press seams flat before you press them open. Press one side and then turn the seam over and press on the other side. This allows the stitches to settle into the fabric. Puckers will be eliminated and the seam will be smoother when pressed open.

Pressing Seams

To press a serged seam, press the seam allowance flat on both sides. Then press the seam allowance to one side.

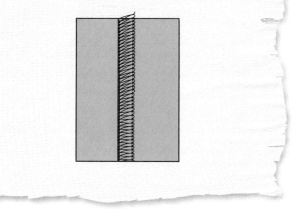

- Press curved areas over a curved surface. Use a tailor's ham to maintain the curved shape of the fabric.
- Prevent press marks on the right side of the fabric. Slip strips of paper or an envelope under the edges of seam allowances, darts, and pleats when pressing. This prevents imprints on the outside of the garment. See *Fig. 14-3.*

14-3 Using Strips of Paper

- Check the fit of the garment before you press any sharp creases, such as pleats.
- Don't overpress. Avoid heavy pressure and let the steam do the work. Use the tip of the iron in small places. Never press the fabric completely dry.

- When pressing an entire garment, start with small areas. First press the collar, cuffs, and other detail areas. Then press the small areas, such as sleeves and yokes. Finally, press the large flat areas of the garment.

PRESSING TECHNIQUES

Which pressing method to use depends upon whether the garment area is flat, curved, enclosed, gathered, or has fullness.

Flat Areas

Flat areas, such as straight seams, can be pressed flat on the ironing board.

1. Place the garment on an ironing board with both seam allowances to one side. Press the seam line to blend the stitches into the fabric.
2. Open up the fabric and place it over the ironing board. Press the seam allowances open, using your fingers and the tip of the iron to open the seam completely. Check on the right side to be sure the seam is perfectly smooth.

If a seam is to be pressed to one side, on a yoke or waistline, for example, first press the seam flat. Then press the seam allowances open. Finally, press the seam allowances toward one side.

SAFETY TIP

Use special care with an iron. Never touch a hot iron except on the handle. Keep your fingers and face away from the steam. Don't overfill the iron or the water can boil out. If recommended by the manufacturer, use distilled water. Always rest the iron on its heel, not flat down on the soleplate. Turn off and unplug the iron after each use. Some irons should be drained of water before storing.

Curved Areas

Darts and curved seams should be pressed over a curved tailor's ham to maintain their shape.

1. Press darts and seams flat to blend stitches into the fabric. Press the darts only up to the point, and not beyond, to prevent pressing in a crease.
2. Place the fabric wrong side up over a tailor's ham. Press the seams open; then press the darts to one side.

Enclosed Seams

Enclosed seams are on the edge of a collar, facing, or cuff. They should be pressed flat and then pressed open. This creates a sharper edge when the garment section is turned to the right side.

1. Press the seam flat to blend stitches.
2. Press the seam open. Use only the tip of the iron near the point or corner.
3. Turn right side out. Gently push out the corner or point.
4. Press the garment section flat on an ironing board, slightly rolling the seam to the underside. This helps prevent the seam from showing at the edge of the completed garment.

Gathered Areas

Gathers and ruffles should ripple softly below the seam line. The iron shouldn't pleat or crush them.

1. Press the seam allowances together to flatten the fabric above the seam line.
2. Slip the garment over the end of an ironing board. Turn the seam allowances away from the fullness.
3. Press directly up into the gathers with the point of the iron. Hold the seam allowance taut above the gathers by using your other hand to lift it slightly up from the ironing board. This helps prevent folds from pressing into the gathers at the seam line. See *Fig. 14-4*.

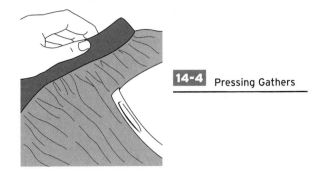

14-4 Pressing Gathers

Shrinking in Fullness

Sometimes you'll need to shrink in the fullness of a hem or sleeve cap.

1. Hold the iron above the fabric to allow steam to penetrate before pressure is applied. See *Fig. 14-5*.
2. Use your fingers to pat out any folds and flatten the fabric.
3. Press the edge of the fabric to shrink in fullness. Check to be sure the sleeve or hem looks smooth on the right side of the garment.

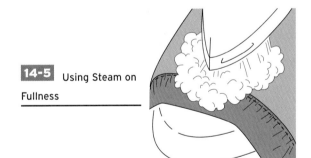

14-5 Using Steam on Fullness

FINAL PRESSING

If you press carefully while constructing your garment, only a light pressing will remove any final wrinkles caused by handling. This final pressing should be merely for touch-up. It should never be a cure-all for poor pressing during construction.

Making Darts

TRIANGULAR FOLDS OF fabric stitched to a point are called **darts**. They control fullness and give shape to fitted clothing. Darts should point to the fullest part of the body and end about 1 inch (2.5 cm) from the body curve to which they point. The two basic darts are single-pointed and double-pointed.

STITCHING DARTS

The following four basic steps produce single-pointed darts:

1. Fold the dart with right sides of the fabric together, matching stitching lines. Place one pin exactly at the point and other pins at the small dot markings.
2. Stitch from the wide end of the dart to the point. See *Fig. 15-1.*
3. Stitch the last two or three stitches as close to the fold line as possible. This creates a sharp point without any bubbles. Don't backstitch because it can cause puckering at the point.
4. Tie the thread ends in a knot or simply leave 1-inch (2.5-cm) thread ends, which won't pull out. See *Fig. 15-2.*

For double-pointed darts, start at the center and stitch to each point. Overlap stitching lines in the center about 1 inch (2.5 cm). Make one or more clips in the dart along the fold so it can be flat. See *Fig. 15-3.*

15-3 Double-Pointed Dart

PRESSING DARTS

Always press a dart before crossing it with another seam. Horizontal darts are pressed with the fold downward. Vertical darts are pressed with the fold toward center front or center back. See *Fig. 15-4.*

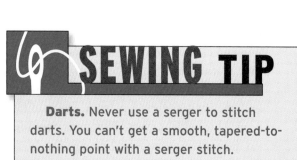

15-4 Pressing Directions on Darts

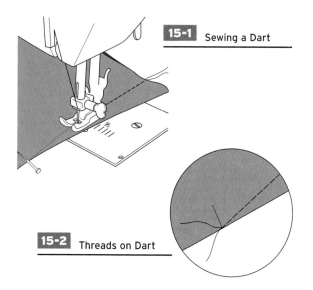

15-1 Sewing a Dart

15-2 Threads on Dart

SEWING TIP

Darts. Never use a serger to stitch darts. You can't get a smooth, tapered-to-nothing point with a serger stitch.

1. Press the dart flat, as stitched. See *Fig. 15-5*.

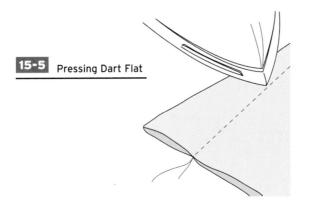

15-5 Pressing Dart Flat

2. Place the dart over a tailor's ham and press it to one side. See *Fig. 15-6*.

15-6 Pressing Dart to the Side

Wide darts or darts in heavy fabric should be pressed open. Refer to your pattern guide sheet. Slash the dart along the fold line to within 1 inch (2.5 cm) of the point. See *Fig. 15-7*. Trim the slash to ½ inch (1.3 cm) from the stitching line. Press the dart flat, as stitched. Then press the trimmed edges open and press the point flat. See *Fig. 15-8*.

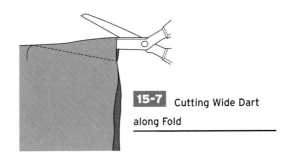

15-7 Cutting Wide Dart along Fold

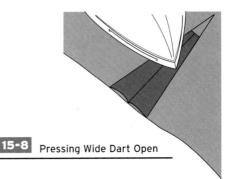

15-8 Pressing Wide Dart Open

Gathering and Easing Fabric

GATHERING AND EASING are methods that control fullness along a seam line. **Gathers** are soft folds of fabric formed by pulling up basting stitches to make the fabric fit into a smaller space. **Easing** allows fabric to be shaped over a curved area of the body. It's used when one edge of fabric is slightly longer than the other. Easing should not create any visible folds or gathers.

GATHERING

An area to be gathered is marked on the pattern with "gather" or "gathering line" on the seam line. Notches or dots mark the beginning and end of the area to be gathered. Usually fabric is gathered into ½ or ⅓ of its original width. It takes more yardage to create full gathers in lightweight fabrics than in heavier ones.

How to Gather

Gathers start with two parallel rows of machine basting. Then the bobbin threads are pulled from both ends to draw up the fabric. Finally the gathered fabric is stitched to the shorter length of fabric.

1. Adjust the stitch length for 6 to 8 stitches per inch (3 to 4 mm in length). Loosen the upper thread tension.

2. Stitch the first row of basting next to the seam line in the seam allowance. Leave the long thread ends. For long areas, start and stop stitching at the seams.

3. Stitch the second row ¼ inch (6 mm) away in the seam allowance. Leave the long thread ends. See *Fig. 16-1*.

16-1 Gathering Stitches

4. Pin the fabric edges, right sides together, matching notches, seams, and markings.

5. Pull up both bobbin threads from one end. Gently slide the fabric along the thread to gather half the section. Repeat at the other end until the gathered section is the proper length. See *Fig. 16-2*.

16-2 Pulling Up Gathering Stitches

6. Wrap the threads in a figure 8 around a pin to secure. See *Fig. 16-3*.

7. Distribute the gathers evenly and pin in place about every ½ inch (1.3 cm).

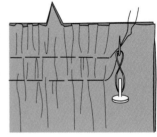

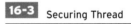

16-3 Securing Thread

8. Stitch with standard stitching along the seam line, gathered side up. See *Fig. 16-4*. Use your fingers to hold the gathers evenly on both sides of the needle to prevent any folds from catching in the seam.

SEWING TIP

Gathering fabric. When gathering fabric by machine, use a contrasting thread color in the bobbin. You'll see which thread to pull more easily.

Gathering

To gather lightweight to medium-weight fabrics, follow these steps:

1. Adjust the serger for a wide, three-thread stitch.

2. Serge a thread chain for gathering that is at least 6 inches (15 cm) longer than the edge to be gathered. Don't cut the chain. Gently run your fingers along the chain to smooth it out.

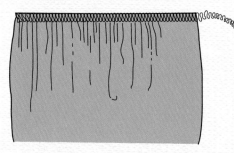

3. Raise the presser foot. Bring the chain under the presser foot and around to the front, then up and over the toe of the presser foot to the left of the knife. Lower the presser foot.

4. Serge along the fabric edge, encasing the chain in stitches. Don't serge off the fabric at the end. Instead, stop stitching. Raise the needle and presser foot. Turn the hand wheel several times and gently ease the fabric away from the presser foot. Cut the threads. Do not cut the gathering chain.

5. Pull up on the chain to gather the fabric.

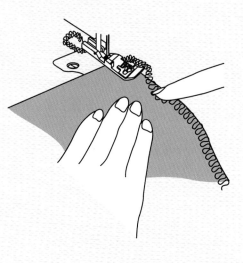

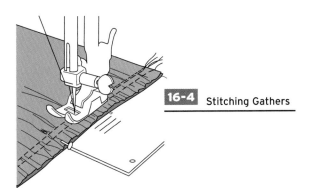

16-4 Stitching Gathers

For heavy fabrics, use a zigzag stitch over a narrow cord for easier gathering. Place a thin cord on the seam allowance, ¼ inch (6 mm) from the seam line. Zigzag over the cord, being careful not to catch the cord. Pull the cord ends to form gathers. Stitch along the seam line with the gathered side up. Remove the cord.

Pressing Gathers

To press gathers, follow these steps:

1. Press the seam allowances flat.
2. Lay the garment flat on an ironing board, with the seam allowances turned away from the gathers.
3. Press carefully up into the fullness with the tip of an iron on the wrong side of the fabric. Hold the seam allowances taut above the gathers to prevent folds from being pressed into the gathers at the seam line. (See *Fig. 14-4* on page 513.)

Shirring

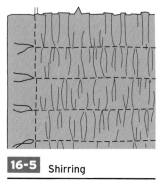

Shirring is formed by several rows of gathering. Use only on soft or lightweight fabrics. Stitch as many rows of gathering as desired and secure each row with a knot. Then stitch over the knots in the seam allowance. See *Fig. 16-5*.

16-5 Shirring

Using elastic thread in the bobbin makes elasticized shirring. Wind elastic thread on the bobbin by hand, stretching slightly. Use a long stitch, 6 to 8 stitches (3 to 4 mm in length) per inch. Stitch on the right side of the fabric, stretching the previously stitched rows as you sew each new row.

EASING

Easing is most often used at shoulder seams, sleeves, yokes, and waistbands. The most common eased seam is a set-in sleeve. The finished seam should look smooth, without any gathers or tucks.

Pin Basting

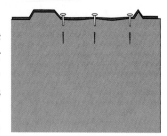

If one fabric edge is only slightly longer than the other, pin-baste the right sides of the fabric together, with the longer side on top. Place pins every ½ inch (1.3 cm) to keep fullness from shifting. See *Fig. 16-6*. Stitch with the longer side on top and gently ease in extra fullness as you stitch.

16-6 Pin Basting

Ease Stitching

To ease a greater amount of fullness, use one or two rows of ease stitching. Follow the techniques used for gathering. See *Fig. 16-7*.

1. Stitch close to the seam line with long machine stitches, extending the stitching slightly beyond the markings.
2. Stitch a second row ¼ inch (6 mm) away in the seam allowance for set-in sleeves.
3. Pin the fabric, right sides together, with the eased side up.
4. Pull up the thread between markings and distribute the fullness evenly.
5. Stitch with standard stitching along the seam line, being careful not to stitch in any folds or gathers.

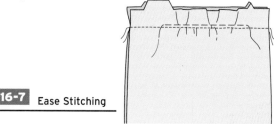

16-7 Ease Stitching

Sewing Plain Seams

A SEAM IS A LINE of stitching that holds two layers of fabric together. A plain seam is the standard seam used for most sewing. It is ⅝ inch (1.5 cm) deep and stitched with the standard stitch length for your fabric. Patterns are designed with standard seams unless stated otherwise. (For special types of seams, see pages 547-550.)

STITCHING A SEAM

For best results in stitching seams, always follow these steps:

1. Stay-stitch any bias or curved areas ½ inch (1.3 cm) from the cut edge.
2. Pin-baste the fabric layers along the seam line, with right sides together. Match fabric ends and notches; then pin. To keep the fabric edges even, place additional pins 5 inches (15 cm) apart. Insert pins at a right angle to the stitching line, with heads toward the seam allowance.
3. Raise the needle and take-up lever to their highest point by turning the hand wheel. Be sure thread ends are behind the presser foot to prevent the thread from pulling out or jamming when you start to stitch.
4. Position the fabric under the needle. Line up the fabric edge with the ⅝-inch (1.5-cm) marking on the right side of the needle plate. Place the fabric about ½ inch (1.3 cm) in from the end for backstitching. Turn the hand wheel to lower the needle into the fabric. Lower the presser foot.
5. Backstitch for ½ inch (1.3 cm) to the beginning of the seam line.
6. Stitch forward slowly and evenly to the end of the seam. Remove pins as you stitch.
7. Backstitch ½ inch (1.3 cm) to secure seam.
8. Remove the fabric by turning the hand wheel to raise the take-up lever and needle to their highest position. Lift the presser foot. Slide the fabric toward the back of the machine.
9. Clip threads at seam beginning and end.
10. Finish the seam edges if necessary.
11. Press the seam open.

Turning a Corner

To turn a corner in the middle of a seam, stitch to within ⅝ inch (1.5 cm) of the corner and stop with the needle in the fabric. Lift the presser foot and turn the fabric on the needle. Lower the presser foot and continue stitching in the new direction. See *Fig. 17-1.*

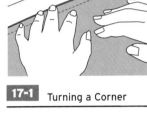

17-1 Turning a Corner

SAFETY TIP

When sewing with a conventional sewing machine, remove each pin just before it reaches the presser foot. A needle can bend or break if it hits a pin. Never place pins on the underside of the fabric. They can catch in the feed dog and break the machine needle or tear the fabric.

Never sew over pins with a serger. Pins can damage the knives and needle, and pin fragments could fly into your eyes or face. Instead, place pins at least 1 inch (2.5 cm) from the edge, parallel to the stitching line, or remove each pin before it reaches the knives.

To keep pins off the floor, place them in a pincushion as you stitch. Never place pins in your mouth or clothes.

Plain Seams

1. Pin the seam. Position the fabric in front of the presser foot. Match the stitching line on the fabric to the appropriate mark on the seam guide.

2. Serge a 4- to 5-inch (10- to 12.5-cm) thread chain. Then gently feed the fabric under the presser foot.

3. Serge off the fabric for 5 to 6 inches (12.5 to 15 cm). Bring the thread chain around to the front so the knife can cut it.

4. Secure the thread ends. Run your fingers along the thread chain to smooth it out. Tie the thread in a loose loop knot. Insert a pin through the center of the loop so the pin tip is next to the fabric edge. Pull the thread chain until the loop tightens into a knot at the pin tip. Remove the pin and clip the thread tails.

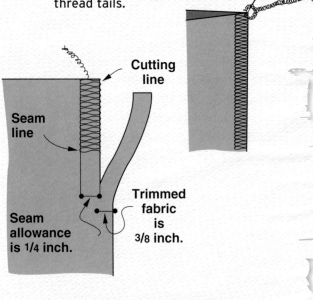

Cutting line

Seam line

Seam allowance is 1/4 inch.

Trimmed fabric is 3/8 inch.

Turning a Sharp Point

To turn a sharp point, such as the point of a collar, take one or two diagonal stitches across the corner. The extra stitch makes a thinner, neater corner when the point is turned to the right side. See *Fig. 17-2.*

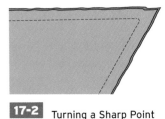

17-2 Turning a Sharp Point

To do this, stitch to the corner and leave the needle in the fabric. Raise the presser foot and turn the fabric diagonally. Lower the presser foot and make one or two stitches by turning the hand wheel. Leave the needle in the fabric, raise the presser foot, and turn the fabric to complete the corner. Lower the presser foot and continue stitching.

Reinforcing

To reinforce a sharp corner or point, such as a V-neckline or placket, use reinforcement stitches. Stitch again for about 1 inch (2.5 cm) on each side

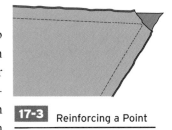

17-3 Reinforcing a Point

of the point. This helps prevent fabric yarns from pulling out of the seam after the fabric is trimmed and turned. See *Fig. 17-3.*

SPECIAL SEAM TREATMENTS

Some seams may need special treatment to reduce bulk in the seam allowance. Enclosed seams, such as those in necklines, collars, and cuffs, should lie flat and smooth. Curved seams and corners also need special treatment. You can reduce the bulk of a seam by trimming, grading, clipping, and notching.

Trimming

The seam allowances of enclosed seams should be trimmed to an even width, usually ¼ inch (6 mm). See *Fig. 17-4.* The corner of a seam allowance should be trimmed diagonally to remove extra thickness when the corner is turned. See *Fig. 17-5.* If the corner is very pointed, make an additional diagonal cut on each side of the point, trimming to ⅛ inch (3 mm). See *Fig. 17-6.*

Curved seams, such as the lower part of an armhole and the center back seam of pants are usually trimmed. These areas can be reinforced with two rows of stitching ¼ inch (6 mm) apart and then trimmed close to the second row of stitching. See *Fig. 17-7.*

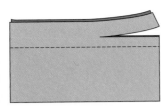

17-4 Trimming Seam Allowance

17-5 Trimming Diagonally

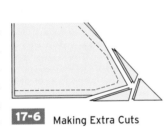

17-6 Making Extra Cuts

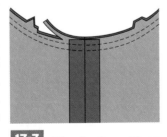

17-7 Trimming Curved Seam

Grading

Grading means to trim each layer of the seam allowance to a different width to reduce bulk. Enclosed seams in heavier fabrics should be graded. Seams with three layers of fabric, such as a collar stitched to a neckline, should also be graded.

Always grade a seam so that the widest seam allowance is next to the outside of the garment. This reduces press marks on the right side. To

grade, trim the seam allowances in half. Then trim the seam allowance toward the inside of the garment in half again. See *Fig. 17-8.* For three layers, trim each one slightly narrower.

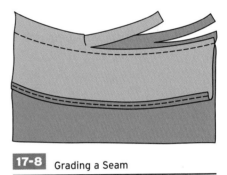

17-8 Grading a Seam

Clipping

On a curved seam, the seam allowances should be clipped to allow the curve to lie flat when pressed. **Clipping** means making tiny clips, or snips, in the seam allowance every ¼ to ½ inch (6 to 13 mm). Using the point of the scissors, clip to within ⅛ inch (3 mm) of the seam line or up to the stay-stitching line. The sharper the curve, the closer together the clips should be made.

Clipping is done after the seam is trimmed or graded. See *Fig. 17-9.*

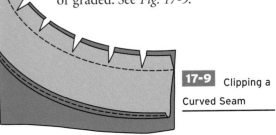

17-9 Clipping a Curved Seam

Sometimes an inward curve or corner must be clipped before stitching the seam. Stitch a row of reinforcement stitches just inside the seam line in the seam allowance. Clip up to the reinforcement stitches to allow the fabric to lie flat for stitching the seam.

Notching

Some curved seams have too much fabric in the seam allowance after being trimmed or graded. The extra fabric forms ripples and doesn't allow the seam to lie flat. These are usually outward curves that are turned and pressed to form an inward curve, as on the outer edge of a collar.

Notching means cutting out tiny wedge-shaped pieces of fabric from the seam allowances. See *Fig. 17-10*. Notch no closer than ⅛ inch (3 mm) to the seam line. When the seam is turned and pressed, the sides of the notches should meet.

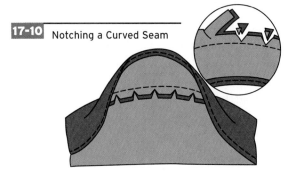

17-10 Notching a Curved Seam

PRESSING SEAMS

Seams should be pressed after they are stitched and before they are crossed by another seam. Check your pattern guide sheet to see whether the seam is to be pressed open or to one side.

First, press all seams flat to blend in the stitches. Then open the seam allowances and press again. If necessary, press both seam allowances to one side. Curved seams should be pressed over a tailor's ham. See *Fig. 17-11*.

Enclosed seams in a collar or cuff should be pressed open before turning. Use a point presser or sleeve board and press with the tip of an iron. Then turn the fabric to the right side and lay flat on an ironing board with the underside up. Roll edges in just until the seam shows and press lightly. This helps prevent the underside or facing from showing along the edge. See *Fig. 17-12*.

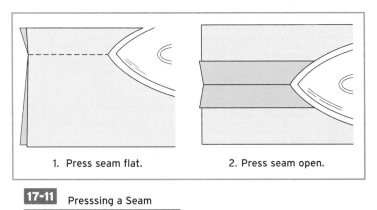

1. Press seam flat.　　2. Press seam open.

17-11 Presssing a Seam

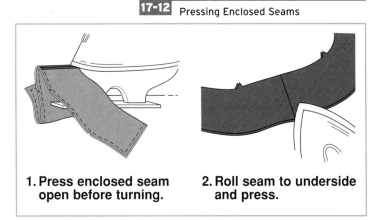

17-12 Pressing Enclosed Seams

1. **Press enclosed seam open before turning.**　　2. **Roll seam to underside and press.**

SEAM FINISHES

A seam finish is any method of sewing or trimming seam edges to prevent raveling. A seam finish is needed on woven fabrics, but not on most knitted fabrics. After the seams of a garment are stitched and pressed, a seam finish can be added.

Seam Finishing Methods

When finishing a seam, the method to use depends on the type of fabric and the reason for finishing the seams. Zigzag stitching and serging are the easiest and quickest methods.

- **Machine zigzag finish.** This is a fast and easy method for finishing fabrics that ravel. Set the zigzag setting for medium width and length. For loosely woven or heavy fabrics, use a wide stitch. Zigzag along the edge of each seam allowance. See *Fig. 17-13*.

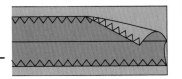

17-13 Machine Zigzag Finish

- **Pinked finishes.** Most firmly woven fabrics can be trimmed with pinking shears. See *Fig. 17-14*. Pinking doesn't prevent raveling entirely. For more protection, stitch ¼ inch (6 mm) from each edge before pinking. Press the seam open.

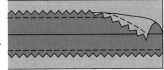

17-14 Pinked Finish

- **Hand-overcast finish.** Although very time-consuming, this method is sometimes used for sheer or delicate fabrics. Make overcast stitches by hand over the edge of the seam allowances. See *Fig. 17-15*.

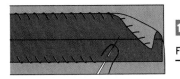

17-15 Hand-Overcast Finish

Serging Techniques

Seam Finishes

To finish a conventional seam, use a two-thread or three-thread serger stitch. As you serge, the knife should skim the edge of the fabric so nothing is trimmed from the seam allowance except a few loose threads. Finish the edges of the fabric before stitching the seam.

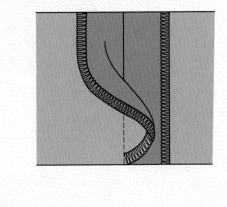

- **Hemmed finishes.** This method forms a narrow, single-fold hem along the edges of the seam allowances. It is also called a clean finish or a turned-and-stitched finish. Use this method on lightweight to medium-weight fabrics. The finish is attractive on unlined jackets. Turn the edges under ¼ inch (6 mm) and press. Stitch close to the folded edge. See *Fig. 17-16*.

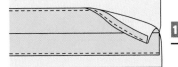

17-16 Hemmed Finish

Applying Facings

To finish a raw edge, such as a neckline or armhole, **facings** are used. The facing piece may be separate or cut in one with the garment. A facing is turned to the inside for a smooth finish. Facings should not be visible from the outside. Three basic facings are used.

- **Shaped facing.** A separate pattern piece is provided for shaped facing. The shape of the piece is the same as the area to be covered. After stitching, the facing is turned to the inside of the garment. See *Fig. 18-1*. A shaped facing is also called a fitted facing.

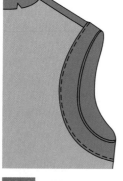
18-1 Shaped Facing

- **Extended facing.** This facing is an extension of the garment pattern piece, so both are cut as one. See *Fig. 18-2*. The facing is then folded to the inside. It is used along a front or back opening.

18-2 Extended Facing

- **Bias facing.** This is a strip of bias fabric stitched to the garment and turned to the inside. See *Fig. 18-3*. It's used mostly for very bulky or sheer fabrics. Purchased bias tape or bias strips cut from fabric can be used.

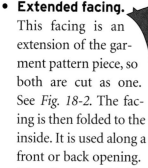

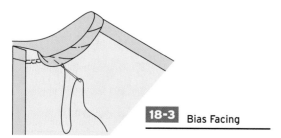
18-3 Bias Facing

STITCHING SHAPED AND EXTENDED FACINGS

Both shaped and extended facings are attached to a garment in the same way. The facing pieces must be stitched together at the ends before attaching to the garment. Then the facing is understitched to prevent the facing from rolling to the outside of the garment. Finally, the facing edge is fastened at each seam allowance. Apply facing according to the steps that follow.

Constructing the Facing

1. Stay-stitch the notched edge.
2. Pin the right sides of the facing pieces together at the ends, matching notches.
3. Stitch the seams, trim, and press them open.
4. Finish the outside edge of the facing with a zigzag, hemmed, or serged finish. See *Fig. 18-4*. (Also see the seam finishes on page 523.)

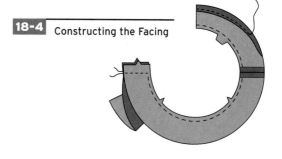
18-4 Constructing the Facing

Attaching the Facing

1. Pin the facing to the garment edge, right sides together. For extended facing, turn the facing to the right side along the fold line.
2. Stitch the seams. See *Fig. 18-5*. Trim or grade seam allowances; trim corners. Clip curved areas. See *Fig. 18-6*.

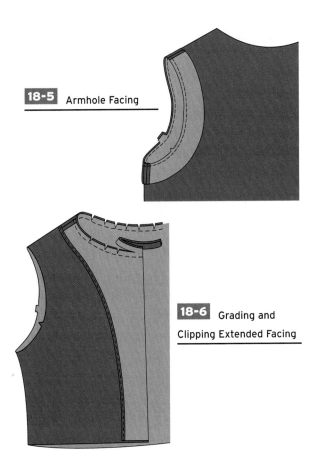

SEWING TIP

Hemmed finish. For a hemmed finish on facing, first stay-stitch ¼ inch (6 mm) from the outside on the unnotched facing edge. The stay-stitching line makes it easier to turn the hem under. Knitted fabrics don't need a finish; however, a row of stay-stitching around the outer edge helps the facings hold their shape better.

18-5 Armhole Facing

18-6 Grading and Clipping Extended Facing

2. Machine-stitch close to the seam line from the right side of the facing through all seam allowances. See *Fig. 18-7.* Gently pull the fabric on each side of the seam line to keep it flat.

3. Turn the facing to the inside and press. An alternative is to top-stitch the garment edge from the outside instead of under-stitching.

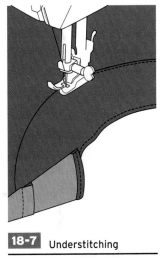

18-7 Understitching

3. Press the seam allowances open; then press them toward the facing.

4. Turn the facing to the garment inside. Press along the seam line, rolling the seam slightly toward the facing side.

Understitching the Facing

1. Open the facing out flat, with seam allowances toward the facing.

SEWING TIP

Clipping. If you've clipped the seam allowance, check frequently as you understitch to make sure the small wedges of fabric don't get folded under while stitching. If the garment edge will be topstitched, facings don't need to be tacked in place.

Facings

A serger can finish facing edges. If the faced edge is straight or a gradual curve, use the serger to attach the facing to the garment. The serger stitch creates very narrow seam allowances that need no trimming, grading, notching, or clipping.

1. Serge facing sections together at the shoulder seams. To reduce bulk, press the seams in the opposite direction of the garment shoulder seams.

2. Serge-finish the outer edge of the facing.

3. Pin the facing to the garment edge. If the faced edge has an opening, fold both the garment and facing to the inside at the opening edge and pin.

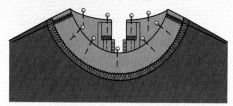

4. Serge along the neckline seam.

5. Press the seam allowances toward the facing.

6. Understitch with a conventional sewing machine.

Tacking Facing at Seams

The edge of the facing should be tacked, or fastened, at each seam allowance. See *Fig. 18-8.* Use a hemming stitch, blindstitch, cross-stitch tack, or stitch-in-the-ditch method. Another method is to fuse the facing and garment seam allowance together with a small piece of fusible web, following the manufacturer's directions.

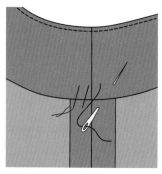

18-8 Tacking Facing at Seam

STITCHING BIAS FACINGS

For a bias facing, open out one long edge of bias tape. Then follow these steps:

1. Pin the crease line of the tape along the seam line of the garment, right sides together.

2. Stitch the seam line. See *Fig. 18-9.* Trim, grade, and clip the seam allowances.

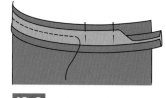

18-9 Stitching Bias Facing

3. Fold the bias tape to the garment inside and press.

4. Slip-stitch the edge in place. See *Fig. 18-10.*

18-10 Slip-Stitching Bias Facing

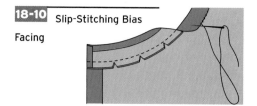

Making Casings

ACLOSED TUNNEL OF FABRIC that holds a piece of elastic or a drawstring inside is called a **casing**. Casings are used at sleeve edges, necklines, waistlines, and hemlines to help control fullness. The elastic or drawstring makes the garment adjustable. A casing is much easier to construct than a waistband or a cuff and thus is used in many easy-to-sew patterns.

Casings can be sewn with headings. A **heading** is a width of fabric between the casing and the edge of the garment. A narrow heading has a more tailored appearance. A wider heading creates a ruffled edge. See *Fig. 19-1*.

The two basic types of casing are self-casing and applied casing.

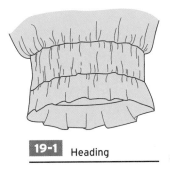

19-1 Heading

SELF-CASING

Similar to a hem, a self-casing is formed by folding over the edge of the garment and stitching in place. Use the following steps:

1. Turn the raw edge under ¼ inch (6 mm) and press. See *Fig. 19-2*.

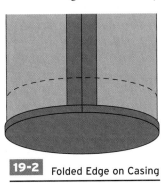

19-2 Folded Edge on Casing

2. Turn the casing to the inside of the garment along the fold line and pin in place. Press the outer edge of the casing.

3. Stitch close to the inner, pinned edge of the casing. Leave a 2-inch (5-cm) opening at the side seam or center back to insert the elastic. See *Fig. 19-3*. If the casing has a header, stitch around the heading line.

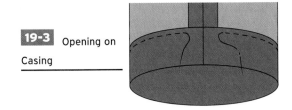

19-3 Opening on Casing

APPLIED CASING

An applied casing can be sewn to the edge of a garment or inside a garment. An example of the latter is the waistline casing in a jumpsuit.

Make applied casing by sewing single-fold bias tape or a separate strip of fabric to the garment. The length of the tape or fabric strip should be ½ inch (1.3 cm) longer than the finished casing. The width of the strip should be 1 inch (2.5 cm) wider than the width of the elastic. The pattern guide sheet may include cutting instructions or a separate pattern piece for the casing. Fold in the long edges of the fabric strip ¼ inch (6 mm) and press before you begin.

Applying to Garment Edge

To sew casing to the garment edge, use the following steps:

1. Pin one edge of the casing to the garment, with right sides together. Fold back the ends. See *Fig. 19-4*.

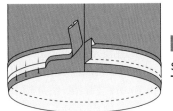

19-4 Pinning and Stitching Casing

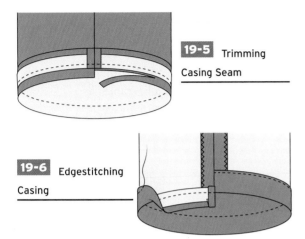

19-5 Trimming Casing Seam

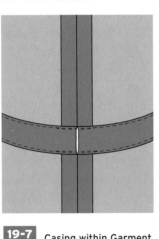

19-6 Edgestitching Casing

2. Stitch a ¼-inch (6-mm) seam. Trim. See *Fig. 19-5*.
3. Turn the casing to the inside of the garment and press.
4. Edgestitch the other casing edge to the garment. See *Fig. 19-6*.

Applying within Garment

To sew casing within the garment, follow these steps. See *Fig. 19-7*.

1. Pin the casing to the garment, using the placement markings on the pattern. Turn the casing ends under so the folds meet without overlapping.

19-7 Casing within Garment

2. Edgestitch along both long edges of the casing.

ELASTICS

Elastics are varied, including special types for swimwear and lingerie. The pattern recommends the proper elastic width to use. Elastic should be about ⅛ inch (3 mm) narrower than the finished

casing so it can be pulled through easily. If the casing is too wide, the elastic may twist and roll inside the casing when the garment is worn.

The guide sheet should give directions for cutting the right length of elastic. If not, measure your body at the casing position and add 1 inch (2.5 cm) for overlapping the elastic ends.

To insert the elastic, follow these steps:

1. Pull the elastic through the casing with a safety pin, being careful not to twist it. See *Fig. 19-8*. Let the ends extend several inches at the opening.

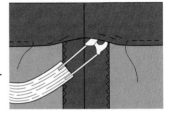

19-8 Pulling Elastic through Casing

2. Overlap the ends ½ inch (1.3 cm) and pin together. Try the garment on to check fit and adjust the elastic if necessary.
3. Stitch the overlapped ends securely by machine. See *Fig. 19-9*.

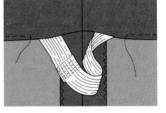

19-9 Stitching Elastic Ends

4. Finish the opening of the self-casing by completing the edgestitching, stretching the elastic as you stitch. Finish the opening of the applied casing by slip-stitching along the folded ends. See *Fig. 19-10*.

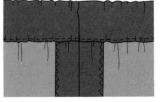

19-10 Finishing Casing

DRAWSTRINGS

Drawstrings can be made from cord, tubing, braid, and ribbon. You'll need an opening in the garment to pull the drawstring through to the outside or inside. See *Fig. 19-11*. The opening can be two button-

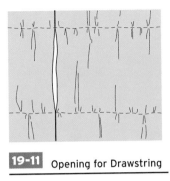

19-11 Opening for Drawstring

holes or a slit in a seam and should be reinforced with a small piece of fabric or fusible interfacing.

Make buttonhole openings in the outer fabric before the casing is stitched. See *Fig. 19-12*. A

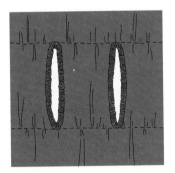

19-12 Buttonhole Openings for Drawstring

seam opening is made as you stitch the seam. Leave the seam open between markings, and reinforce the opening with backstitching. Use a safety pin to pull the drawstring through the casing. The ends of the drawstring can be knotted to prevent it from pulling out of the casing when washing and wearing.

SEWING TIP

Drawstrings. To prevent a drawstring from pulling out of the casing, stitch the drawstring to the casing at the center back.

Applying Elastic to Lingerie

1. Leave one garment seam open.

2. Divide and mark the garment edge into quarters or eighths. Divide and mark special lingerie elastic into quarters or eighths.

3. Pin the elastic to the right side of the fabric, with the straight edge of the elastic along the fold line.

4. Position the straight edge of the elastic next to the knife. Serge a couple of stitches to anchor the elastic. Be careful not to cut the elastic.

5. Continue serging, using the flatlock stitch. Hold the elastic up against the presser-foot toe, slightly off the fabric. As you stitch, stretch the elastic to fit between the pins. Remove the pins as you come to them.

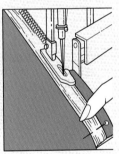

6. Pull on the elastic until the decorative edge is turned up and the seam is flat.

7. To finish, serge the remaining seam with a serger stitch.

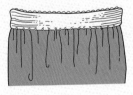

Applying Fasteners

YOU CAN CHOOSE from many fasteners to close garments securely. They include hooks and eyes, snaps, special nylon tapes, buttons, and zippers. Some fasteners are decorative as well as functional. A combination of fasteners may be used on the same closing of a garment—such as a hook and eye above a zipper or a snap with a button.

The pattern envelope recommends fasteners for your garment. Usually snaps, hooks and eyes, and buttons are attached by hand. Use a double strand of thread. Always secure the stitches with a knot or tiny backstitches.

HOOKS AND EYES

Hooks and eyes come in many sizes and types. Small hooks and eyes are used most often at necklines. Large covered hooks and eyes are available for jackets and coats. Special heavy-duty hooks and bars are designed for waistbands on pants and skirts. The hooks are strong and flat so they won't slide out of the bar. See *Fig. 20-1.*

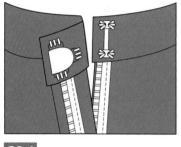

20-1 Heavy-Duty Hook and Bar

Hooks are typically sold with two kinds of eyes—a round eye for edges that meet and a straight eye for edges that overlap. A thread eye may be used in place of a metal eye to make it less noticeable. Use either a blanket stitch or a chain stitch.

Edges That Meet

A hook with a round eye is the right choice for edges that meet. To attach the hook, follow these steps. See *Fig. 20-2.*
1. Position the hook ⅛ inch (3 mm) from the edge.
2. Stitch around each loop with a buttonhole or overcast stitch. Sew only to the facing fabric.

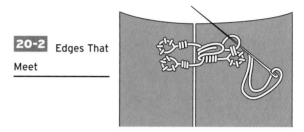

20-2 Edges That Meet

No stitches should show on the right side of the garment.
3. Slide the needle between the fabric layers to the end of the hook. Take three or four stitches across the end of the hook to hold it flat against the fabric. Secure the threads.

To attach the round eye, follow these steps:
1. Match the garment edges.
2. Position the eye so the loop extends ⅛ inch (3 mm) beyond the edge. When the hook and eye are each attached, the garment edges should meet exactly.
3. Stitch around each loop with buttonhole or overcast stitches. Sew only to the facing fabric. Secure the threads.

Edges That Overlap

A hook and a straight eye are used for edges that overlap. The hook is placed on the overlap side, following these steps. See *Fig. 20-3.*
1. Place the hook on the underside of the overlap at least ⅛ inch (3 mm) from the edge.

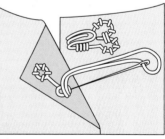

20-3 Edges That Overlap

2. Stitch around each loop with buttonhole or overcast stitches. Be sure no stitches show on the garment's right side.
3. Stitch across the end of the hook to hold it flat against the fabric. Secure the threads.

Use a straight eye on the under lap side according to this procedure:
1. Overlap the edges.
2. Mark the position of the eye by placing a pin in the fabric under the bend of the hook.
3. Stitch the eye in place with buttonhole or overcast stitches around each loop. Secure the threads.

SNAPS

Snaps hold overlapping edges together where there isn't much strain. Sizes vary. Small snaps are used at necklines or cuffs. Heavy gripper snaps are good for children's clothes and sportswear. Large covered snaps are available for jackets and coats.

Snaps have two sections—a ball and a socket. The ball half is sewn to the overlap. The socket half is sewn to the under lap. See *Fig. 20-4*. Use this procedure:

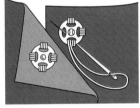

20-4 Sewing on Snaps

1. Center the ball half of the snap over the marking on the underside of the overlap. Be sure it's at least ⅛ inch (3 mm) from the edge.
2. Sew three or four stitches through each hole, using either an overcast or buttonhole stitch. Carry the thread under the snap from one hole to the next. Stitch only through the facing, making sure the stitches don't show on the right side of the garment. Secure the threads.
3. Mark the position for the socket half of the snap. Overlap the edges and push a pin

SEWING TIP

Snap location. When sewing on snaps, first stitch the ball half in place. Then rub tailor's chalk on the ball. Overlap the fabric and press the ball against the fabric to mark the position of the socket half of the snap.

through the ball of the snap and into the under lap.
4. Place the socket half over the marking. Hold it in place by inserting a pin through the center hole of the socket and into the fabric.
5. Stitch in place in the same manner as the ball half, except stitch through all layers of the fabric.

HOOK-AND-LOOP TAPE

Hook-and-loop tape is a special nylon-tape fastener that comes in strips or precut round or square shapes. One side has tiny hooks; the other has a looped pile. When pressed together, the two sides interlock until pulled apart. See *Fig. 20-5*. Hook-and-loop tape can be used on overlapping edges.

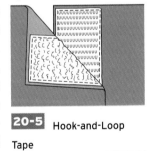

20-5 Hook-and-Loop Tape

It is excellent for sportswear, children's clothes, home furnishings, and craft items.

To stitch hook-and-loop tape, follow these steps:
1. Cut the strips to the desired length.
2. Place the loop half on the underside of the overlapping edge.
3. Position the hook half directly underneath on the under lap.
4. Machine-stitch around both tapes.

BUTTONHOLES AND BUTTONS

Buttons and buttonholes can be used on all types of overlapping edges, including collars, cuffs, center fronts and backs, pockets, and waistbands. These strong fasteners are able to withstand much pulling and strain. Besides being functional, buttons and buttonholes can add a decorative accent to a garment.

Buttonholes should always be completed before buttons are sewn in place. Traditionally, buttonholes are made on the right front side of garments for females. For males, they are placed on the left front side.

Buttons come in a wide variety of sizes, shapes, and designs. The pattern envelope lists the button size to use, stated in fractions of an inch. A button's size is the measurement of its diameter.

Buttons should be sewn with a double strand of thread. Heavy-duty thread can be used for extra strength on heavier garments.

Buttonhole Types

The three types of buttonholes are described below.

- **Machine-stitched buttonholes.** A zigzag machine stitch makes these buttonholes when the garment is completed. See *Fig. 20-6*. Machine-stitched buttonholes can be used on almost all fabrics.

20-6 Machine-Stitched Buttonhole

- **Hand-stitched buttonholes.** These are made with a buttonhole stitch. They are used primarily on fabrics that are too lightweight or too loosely woven to machine-stitch.
- **Bound buttonholes.** With strips of fabric for the opening, these buttonholes are made in the garment before the facing is attached. See *Fig. 20-7*. Bound buttonholes used to be very popular on tailored garments. Today even expensive ready-to-wear garments feature machine-stitched buttonholes. Some couture designers, however, still use bound buttonholes on their garments.

20-7 Bound Buttonhole

Buttonhole Placement

The location of each buttonhole is indicated on the pattern pieces. If you have adjusted the length of your pattern, changes may be needed. Re-space the buttonholes evenly between the top and bottom buttonholes on the pattern. Sometimes a buttonhole may have to be added or omitted.

Buttonholes should extend a little beyond the button placement marking to allow for the shank of the button.

- **Horizontal buttonholes.** Begin these ⅛ inch (3 mm) beyond the button marking toward the fabric edge. See *Fig. 20-8.*

20-8 Horizontal Buttonholes

- **Vertical buttonholes.** Begin these ⅛ inch (3 mm) above the button marking. Vertical buttonholes are often used on shirt bands or for a row of small buttons. See *Fig. 20-9.*

20-9 Vertical Buttonholes

If you choose a larger button size than the pattern recommends, double-check the buttonhole placement. Be sure the buttonholes are sewn far enough from the edge of the garment to prevent buttons from extending beyond the edge when the garment is buttoned.

Buttonhole Length

Adding the following three measurements determines buttonhole length: the diameter of the button; the thickness of the button; and ⅛ inch (3 mm) to allow for fabric thickness. The pattern piece has buttonhole markings that match the recommended button size and fabric type. If you choose a different button size, you'll have to adjust the buttonhole length.

Buttonhole Markings

Machine-stitched buttonholes are placed on the right side of the fabric. Be sure to choose a marking method that won't leave a permanent line on the outside of the garment. Several lines should be marked. See Fig. 20-10.

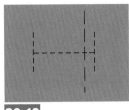

20-10 Lines to Mark for Buttonholes

- **Centerlines.** Must meet when the garment is fastened.
- **Short lines.** Indicate the ends of each buttonhole.
- **Long lines.** Indicate the length of each buttonhole.

Machine-Stitched Buttonholes

Before making any buttonholes on a garment, always do a sample buttonhole on a piece of scrap fabric. Many sewing machines have a built-in buttonhole attachment. Others are operated manually by changing the zigzag-stitch width. Check to be sure the bobbin has plenty of thread. Rethreading in the middle of a buttonhole is difficult. Follow these steps to complete a buttonhole:

1. Mark the location of the buttonhole on the right side of the garment. See *Fig. 20-11.*
2. Stitch the buttonhole, following instructions in the sewing machine manual.
3. Place a pin across each end of the buttonhole to prevent cutting through the end stitching. See *Fig. 20-12.*
4. Cut the buttonhole opening, using small, sharp scissors. Insert the scissors blade in the center of the buttonhole and cut carefully from the center in both directions.

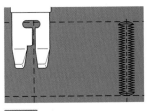

20-11 Placing Foot over Buttonhole Mark

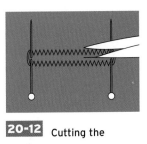

20-12 Cutting the Opening

Button Placement

After the buttonholes have been created, you can sew on the buttons. Mark their placement through the buttonhole openings rather than using the pattern. This ensures that each button will correspond to the actual buttonhole location. Follow these steps:

1. Overlap fabric edges with the buttonhole on top. Match centerlines or overlap lines.
2. Place a pin through the buttonhole, ⅛ inch (3 mm) from the end, along the centerline.
3. Slip the buttonhole over the head of each pin and separate the garment sections. See *Fig. 20-13.* Be careful when doing this step.

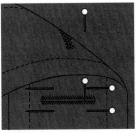

20-13 Marking Button Location

Attaching Sew-Through Buttons

Sew-through buttons have holes, or "eyes," in the face of the button. Buttons used only for decoration can be sewn flat against the fabric. Buttons used with a buttonhole should be attached with a thread shank. The shank allows the buttonhole to fit smoothly between the button and the under fabric. The length of the thread shank is determined by the thickness of the fabric. To attach this type of button, follow these steps:

1. Using small backstitches, secure a double thread at the button marking.
2. Place a toothpick, heavy pin, or similar object on top of the button.
3. Bring the needle up through one hole, over the toothpick, and down through the second hole. See *Fig. 20-14*. Continue to make several stitches through the button and fabric. If the button has four holes, repeat the stitching at the other pair of holes. End the stitching with the needle and thread under the button.

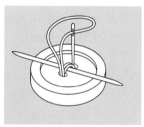

20-14 Attaching Sew-Through Button

4. Remove the toothpick and pull the button to the top of the thread loop.

5. Wind the thread tightly around the stitches under the button to form a thread shank. See *Fig. 20-15*. Fasten the thread securely in the fabric under the button.

20-15 Making a Shank

Shank Buttons

These buttons have a metal or plastic loop on the back of the button. Thread is stitched through the shank to attach the button to the fabric, as described below. See *Fig. 20-16*.

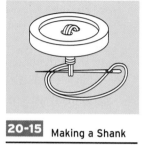

20-16 Attaching Shank Button

1. Using backstitches, secure a double thread at the marking.
2. Stitch through the shank and fabric with four or five small, even stitches.
3. Fasten the thread securely in the fabric under the button.

SEWING TIP

Button reinforcement. Sometimes buttons need reinforcement on heavy fabric or in areas of extra strain. Sew a small, flat button to the wrong side of the garment as you stitch the sew-through or shank button in place.

Putting in Zippers

ZIPPERS COME IN different types, weights, and lengths. The most common is the conventional zipper, which has a stop at the bottom. Such specialty zippers as invisible, separating, decorative, and heavy-duty are also available. The pattern envelope recommends the zipper type and length for a project.

ZIPPER PREPARATIONS

Before putting in a zipper, several actions should be taken.

- Check the zipper package. If the zipper tape is 100 percent polyester, press the tape to remove any folds. If the tape is not 100 percent polyester, preshrink the zipper.

- Stay-stitch any curved or bias seam lines to prevent stretching.

- If seam allowances are less than ⅝ inch (1.5 cm), stitch seam tape to the edge for extra width.

- Check the pattern guide sheet to see whether the zipper should be stitched before or after any facing is attached.

- Check the length of the zipper opening, or placket. Place the zipper teeth, or coils, ¾ inch (2 cm) from the top edge of the fabric. If a fastener will be sewn above the zipper, place the zipper 1 inch (2.5 cm) below the top edge. Mark the fabric where the coils end at the bottom of the zipper.

- To shorten a zipper, machine zigzag or whipstitch across the coils in one place to form a new bottom stop. Cut away the zipper ½ inch (1.3 cm) below the stitching.

- Stitch the garment seam below the zipper marking, using a regular machine stitch. Backstitch ¼ inch (6 mm) to secure the seam.

- To prepare the zipper opening, machine-baste it closed. Be sure to match plaids and stripes carefully. Press the seam open. After the zipper has been put in, you can clip the basting threads every inch (2.5 cm) for easier removal.

APPLYING A ZIPPER

Zippers can be sewn in several ways, known as applications. Zippers are typically applied with machine stitching, which requires a zipper foot attachment for stitching close to the zipper. If sewing a zipper by hand, use a pickstitch. Always stitch both sides of a zipper in the same direction to prevent any wrinkles or puckers in the zipper placket.

To choose the right application method, refer to the pattern guide sheet. Application instructions are also in the zipper package. The most common applications are for centered, lapped, and fly-front zippers. A different procedure is used for invisible zippers.

Centered Zipper Application

For a centered zipper application, follow these steps:

1. Machine-baste the seam and press open.

2. Place the zipper face down on the open seam allowance. Center the zipper coils exactly on top of the basted seam. Hold the zipper in place with hand basting or sewing tape. See *Fig. 21-1*.

3. Spread the garment flat, right side up. Mark the bottom zipper stop with a pin. Attach the zipper foot.

21-1 Basting Centered Zipper

4. Begin stitching at the lower end of the zipper on the right side of the fabric. Stitch across the end,

pivot, and stitch up along one side ¼ inch (6 mm) from the basted seam.

5. Begin again at the lower end and stitch the other side in the same manner.

6. Pull the thread ends at the bottom to the wrong side of the fabric and knot.

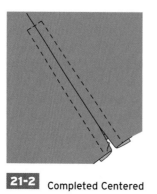

21-2 Completed Centered Zipper

7. Remove the machine basting and press. See *Fig. 21-2*.

Lapped and Fly-Front Application

To apply a zipper with the lapped or fly-front application, follow these steps:

1. Machine-baste the seam and press open.

2. Open the zipper. Place it face down on the back seam allowance with the coils at the seam line. Pin, baste, or tape in place.

3. Machine-stitch through the zipper tape and seam allowance only, from the bottom to the top of the zipper. Use the zipper foot to stitch close to the zipper's edge. See *Fig. 21-3*.

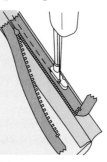

21-3 Stitching First Lap

4. Close the zipper and turn it face up. Smooth the fabric away from the zipper, forming a narrow fold between the zipper coil and the basted seam.

5. Machine-stitch close to the fold, beginning at the lower end of the zipper. Sew through the folded seam allowance and zipper tape only. See *Fig. 21-4*.

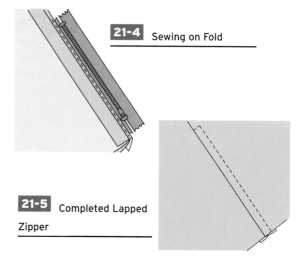

21-4 Sewing on Fold

21-5 Completed Lapped Zipper

6. Open out the fabric and place the zipper face down on the front seam allowance. Turn the tab up and pin in place.

7. Machine-baste through the tape and seam allowance only, starting at the top of the zipper. This will hold the zipper in place for the final stitching.

8. Stitch from the right side of the garment, beginning at the lower end of the zipper. Stitch across the bottom, pivot, and stitch up the lap side. Stitching should be ⅜ to ½ inch (1 to 1.3 cm) from the seam. See *Fig. 21-5*.

9. Pull the thread ends to the wrong side of the fabric and knot.

10. Remove the basting stitches and press.

Invisible Zippers

An invisible zipper is a special zipper that looks like a plain seam on the outside of the garment. All you see is a small pull-tab at the top of the seam. Generally, if your pattern calls for a zipper, you can choose conventional or invisible.

An invisible zipper is applied before the rest of the seam is stitched. You'll need a special zipper foot, usually available where you purchase the zipper. This foot holds the zipper coil upright during stitching so you can stitch very close to the coil, making the zipper invisible on the outside of the garment. To apply an invisible zipper, follow the directions provided in the zipper package.

Putting in Hems

A HEM FINISHES THE bottom edge of a shirt, jacket, sleeve, skirt, or pants leg. Hem lengths follow fashion trends, but a length that flatters body proportions is best.

A well-made hem should not be noticeable. Stitches should not show on the outside of the garment, and the hem edge should be flat and smooth. In addition, the garment should hang evenly around your body.

Hems can be an important part of the garment design. A decorative binding or topstitching adds special interest to a hemline.

Hems are made in ways that depend on the garment's fabric and design. Turning the raw edge of fabric to the inside of the garment, however, is the most common way to make a hem. The edge of the hem is held in place by hand stitching, machine stitching, or fusing. To finish a hem, follow these four basic steps:

1. Mark the hem length.
2. Turn up the hem.
3. Finish the hem edge.
4. Attach the hem to the garment.

MARKING HEM LENGTH

Your garment should hang on a hanger for at least 24 hours before the hem is marked. This allows any bias areas of the garment to stretch and prevents the hemline from sagging. Put on the garment with the clothes and shoes to be worn with it. Fasten all openings and any belt. Stand in normal posture with your weight on both feet. For complete accuracy, have someone else mark the hem for you. You should remain standing still, and the person doing the marking should move around you.

- **Skirts and dresses.** Use a yardstick, meterstick, or skirt marker. Be sure to keep the marker at a right angle to the floor. Place pins or mark with chalk every 3 or 4 inches (7.5 or 10 cm) around the hemline. Turn the hem to

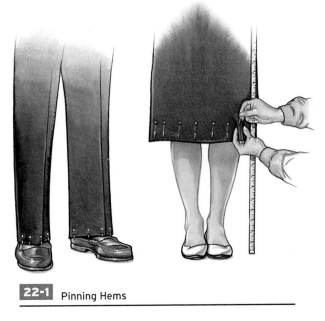

22-1 Pinning Hems

the inside along markings and pin to check the length. Readjust if necessary. See *Fig. 22-1*.
- **Pants.** Fold the fabric edge under and pin. The front of pants should just touch the top of the shoe; the back should be about ½ inch (1.3 cm) longer than the top of the shoe. See *Fig. 22-1*.
- **Jackets.** Fold the fabric under along the hemline markings and pin. Adjust the length according to body proportions. Be sure the hem is even around the entire body.
- **Sleeves.** Bend the arm so the hand is in the center of the waistline. Fold the sleeve edge under until it just covers the wrist bone. Pin in place.

TURNING UP HEM

After the hemline is marked, the hem must be trimmed to the proper width and any extra fullness eliminated.

Trimming Hem Width

Your pattern recommends the proper width for the finished hem. Most hems are 2 to 3 inches (5 to 7.5 cm) wide. This gives added weight to the hemline and helps it fall evenly.

The width of the hem, however, depends on the flare of the garment and the fabric weight. A curved edge takes a narrower hem than a straight edge. Knitted and heavier weight fabrics may have a narrower hem too. Sheer fabrics usually have a narrow rolled hem or a very deep hem.

To trim hem width, follow these steps:

1. Fold the hem up along the marked line.
2. Measure an even distance from the folded edge with a sewing gauge or small ruler.
3. Mark the desired hem width with chalk. See *Fig. 22-2.*

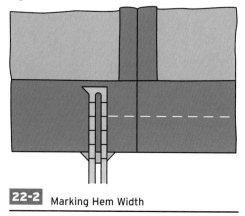

22-2 Marking Hem Width

4. Trim away any excess fabric.
5. Remove any pins and lightly press the fold of the hem.

Eliminating Hem Fullness

If the garment is flared, the turned-up hem will be wider at the upper edge than the garment. Follow these steps to ease this fullness in to fit flat against the garment:

1. Machine-baste ¼ inch (6 mm) from the hem's upper edge.
2. Turn the hem up and pin at each seam and at the center.

3. Use a pin to pick up a stitch of the bobbin thread. See *Fig. 22-3.* Gently pull the thread toward a seam to ease in extra fabric.

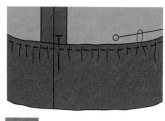

22-3 Easing in Hem Fullness

4. Press the hem allowance to shrink out the fullness.

On fabrics that cannot be eased, remove the extra fullness by tapering the seam line below the hem. See *Fig. 22-4.* Take the same amount off each seam. Remove the original stitching and trim the seam allowances to remove bulk. Press the seam open.

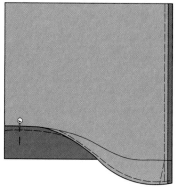

22-4 Tapering Seam Allowance

FINISHING THE HEM EDGE

The hem finish depends on the fabric and the garment. The same finishes used for seams can also be used for hems. (See the seam finishes on page 523.)

If the fabric ravels, a finish that prevents this problem is needed. Most knits don't need a finish. If you want to cover the edge of the hem, you can use seam tape, bias tape, lace, or other decorative trim.

- **Machine zigzag finish.** Used for all fabric weights. Zigzag close to the fabric edge or serge the edge with a serger stitch. See *Fig. 22-5.*

22-5 Machine Zigzag Hem Finish

- **Seam tape, bias tape, or lace finish.** Used on all fabrics. Place the tape or trim ¼ inch (6 mm) over the raw edge and stitch, overlapping the ends. See *Fig. 22-6.*

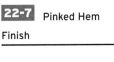

22-6 Seam Tape Hem Finish

- **Pinked finish.** Used for more firmly woven fabrics. Pink the edge or stitch ¼ inch (6 mm) from the edge and then pink. See *Fig. 22-7.*

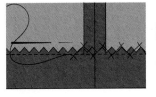

22-7 Pinked Hem Finish

22-8 Hemmed Finish

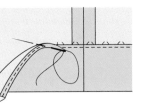

- **Hemmed finish.** Used for lightweight to medium-weight fabrics. Turn the raw edge under ¼ inch (6 mm) and stitch. See *Fig. 22-8.*

ATTACHING HEM TO GARMENT

The hem can be attached to the garment by hand stitching, machine stitching, or fusing. Each method has advantages and disadvantages.

Hand-Stitching a Hem

To hem by hand, use a single thread. Make sure the stitches don't show on the outside of the garment. Keep the stitches slightly loose so the fabric doesn't pull or ripple. (See Lesson 13, pages 506-510, for specific directions on different stitches.)

- **Blindstitch.** Used with all fabrics and hem finishes. This stitch shows less than others and allows for movement without pulling.

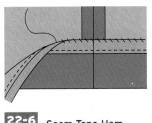

Serging Techniques

Hems

The serger can finish the raw edge of a hem that will be stitched to the garment by hand or machine.

1. Plan the hem allowance with at least ¹⁄₁₆ inch (1.2 mm) of extra fabric that can be trimmed off during serging.

2. Serge along the raw edge of the hem allowance, and secure the thread chains.

3. Complete the hem by folding up the hem allowance and hand-stitch or topstitch on the conventional machine.

A blind hem can be stitched with a serger. Some sergers have a special blind-hemming foot to help guide the fabric.

1. Turn up the hem allowance as for a hand-sewn hem.

2. Fold the garment back ¼ inch (6 mm) from the raw edge of the hem allowance and pin in place. Press the hem.

3. Serge along the raw edge so the needle just catches the fabric fold.

4. Open the garment out until the stitches lie flat. Press on the wrong side to set the stitches and ease in the fullness.

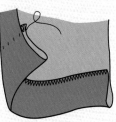

- **Hemming stitch.** Used to stitch a hem with seam tape or lace finish.
- **Catchstitch.** Good for hemming knits and stretch fabrics. This stitch can be done at the hem edge or as a blind catchstitch inside the hem.
- **Slip stitch.** Used to join a folded edge, such as a hemmed finish, to the garment. This stitch is excellent for narrow, hand-rolled hems.

Machine-Stitching a Hem

Machine stitching can be used for both invisible and decorative stitching. It's a fast, easy way to complete a garment or other sewing project.

Some machines have a built-in blindstitch. Fold the garment back ¼ inch (6 mm) below the hem edge. Machine-stitch so the straight stitches fall on the hem allowance and single zigzag stitches just catch the garment along the fold line. See *Fig. 22-9*.

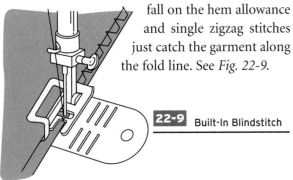

22-9 Built-In Blindstitch

Topstitching can attach the hem and decorate the garment at the same time. Fold the hem to the desired width. For woven fabrics, turn the raw edge under ⅜ inch (1 cm) and press. Stitch close to the upper edge. Knitted fabrics can be stitched single thickness and then trimmed close to the stitching. Use two or more rows of stitching for a more decorative finish. Be sure to keep the rows straight and parallel. See *Fig. 22-10*.

22-10 Attaching Hem with Topstitch

Fusing a Hem

With fusible web, you can hold two layers of fabric together for hemming. Place fusible web between the garment and hem about ¼ inch (6 mm) below the top of the hem. This helps prevent the hem outline from showing on the garment's right side. Also, it keeps any web from accidentally touching the iron and sticking to it. Press to fuse, following the manufacturer's directions. See *Fig. 22-11*.

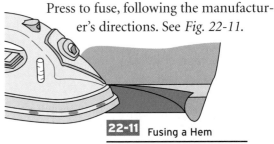

22-11 Fusing a Hem

To alter a fused hem, press the area with steam until the two fabric layers can be gently pulled apart.

SPECIAL HEM TECHNIQUES

Some hems require special hemming techniques. These include a rolled hem, a faced hem, and a hem with a pleat.

Rolled Hem

A narrow, rolled hem works well on lightweight to medium-weight fabrics. Use it to hem scarves, ruffles, sashes, blouses, evening clothes, lingerie, tablecloths, napkins, and curtains. The hem can be stitched by hand or machine as described in the steps that follow.

Hand-Rolled Hem

1. Machine-stitch ¼ inch (6 mm) from the raw edge and trim close to the stitching.
2. Roll the edge between your thumb and forefinger until the stitching is concealed.

22-12 Slip-Stitching Hand-Rolled Hem

Rolled Hems

The serger can roll fabric to the underside as a hem is stitched, creating a professional appearance. The lower looper tension is tightened to produce the rolled edge. Use a rolled-hem presser foot, if needed.

1. Plan at least a ½-inch (1.3-cm) hem allowance.

Hemline

½ inch (1.3 cm)

2. Do a test swatch and adjust tension settings until the hem rolls properly. Tighten the lower looper tension and loosen the upper looper tension if the lower looper thread forms large loops on the underside.

3. Serge along the hemline with the garment right side up.

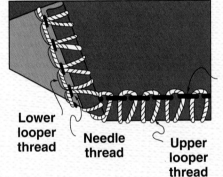

Needle thread

Lower looper thread

Needle thread

Upper looper thread

3. Slip-stitch the hem in place, completing one small section at a time. See *Fig. 22-12.*

Machine-Rolled Hem

1. Mark the hemline ⅛ inch (3 mm) longer than the desired finished length. Fold the fabric up along the hemline. Don't press.

2. Stitch as close as you can to the fold. Trim the hem allowance close to the stitching, using embroidery scissors. See *Fig. 22-13* on page 542.

3. Press the hem allowance up along the stitching line. See *Fig. 22-14* on page 542. As you press, roll the stitching line just to the inside of the garment.

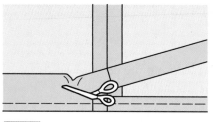

22-13 Trimming Hem Allowance

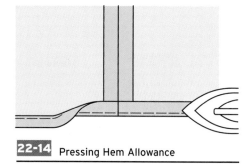

22-14 Pressing Hem Allowance

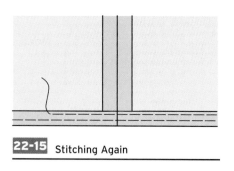

22-15 Stitching Again

4. Stitch again close to the first fold. See *Fig. 22-15*.

Faced Hem

When there's not enough fabric for the hem allowance, a hem may be faced. Facings are also used when the hem edge is an unusual shape, such as scallops, or the fabric is very heavy or bulky. Purchase bias hem facing or cut your own fabric facing and follow these steps:

22-16 Slip-Stitching Faced Hem

1. Pin the facing to the garment, with right sides together and ends overlapped.
2. Stitch a ¼-inch (6-mm) seam.
3. Turn the facing to the inside of the garment and slip-stitch in place. See *Fig. 22-16*.

Hem with Pleat

This technique helps create sharp pleats:

1. Clip the seam allowance above the hem area.
2. Press the seam allowance open below the clip and trim to reduce bulk. See *Fig. 22-17*.
3. Complete the hem.
4. Press the pleat with the seam on the fold edge.
5. Edgestitch along the fold through all thicknesses of the hem. See *Fig. 22-18*.

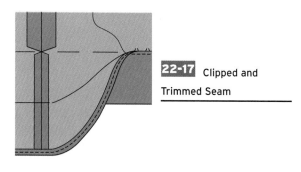

22-17 Clipped and Trimmed Seam

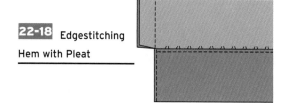

22-18 Edgestitching Hem with Pleat

Checking the Fit

ONE OF THE NICEST compliments someone who sews can receive comes when people can't tell a garment was made personally. In other words, the item doesn't have any telltale signs that it was handmade. Puckers, visible stitches, uneven areas, and poor fit just aren't there. How can you prevent these?

Besides taking the time to follow directions and sew carefully, you can also check the fit as you go. Don't wait until your garment is done to try it on. By then it may be too difficult or impossible to make necessary changes. Instead, check the fit as sewing progresses. Try on the garment as soon as the major seams are joined. Stand in front of a full-length mirror to make your analysis. See *Fig. 23-1*

As you take note, begin at the top and work your way down. The fit at the top affects the fit of the lower part of the garment. A wrinkle or a break line in the fabric indicates a problem. Make any necessary fitting changes. Try the garment on again, making sure any problem has been corrected before going on to other steps.

CHECKLIST FOR EVALUATION

The following checklist will help you evaluate the fit of your garment:

- Does the neckline lie smooth, with no pulling or gapping?
- Does the collar roll evenly?
- Are the collar points identical?
- Do the shoulder seams rest smoothly over the shoulders?
- Do the darts taper toward the fullest part of the body?
- Do the sleeves hang straight from the shoulders to the elbow?
- Are the center front and center back seams in the center of the body and perpendicular to the floor?
- Do the side seams hang straight?
- Does the buttoned closing lie flat without any gapping?
- Is the waistline seam at the natural waistline just above the hipbone and not too snug?
- Is the crotch length comfortable for sitting?
- Is the fit of pants or skirt smooth through the hips and thigh area, with no wrinkles or extra fabric?
- Are hemlines even and parallel to the floor?
- Can you stand, sit, stretch, and bend comfortably?

23-1 When you check the fit of a garment as you sew, you'll be pleased with the results when your project is done.

Review

SUMMARY

- Machine stitching is used for the major seams and construction techniques needed to make a garment. Hand stitching takes care of finishing steps. (Lessons 12 and 13)

- Pressing should be done after each step of construction. (Lesson 14)

- Darts, gathers, and easing are used to control fullness. (Lessons 15 and 16)

- Curved and enclosed seams may need to be trimmed, graded, clipped, or notched. (Lesson 17)

- Facings finish necklines, front openings, and armholes. (Lesson 18)

- Casings hold elastic or a drawstring. (Lesson 19)

- Fasteners can be both functional and decorative. (Lesson 20)

- Zipper type determines how it is applied. (Lesson 21)

- Hems must be marked, turned up, finished along the edge, and attached to the garment. (Lesson 22)

- The fit of a garment should be checked as it's constructed. (Lesson 23)

RECALLING THE FACTS

1. Name at least six machine stitches and explain how they're used. (Lesson 12)

2. What is the width of a standard seam? (Lesson 12)

3. What is the basic purpose for each of these hand stitches: basting stitch; backstitch; pickstitch; slip stitch; overcast stitch; and blindstitch? (Lesson 13)

4. What is the difference between pressing and ironing? (Lesson 14)

5. Why is pressing after each construction step necessary? (Lesson 14)

6. Why should curved areas be pressed over a tailor's ham? (Lesson 14)

7. In what directions should horizontal darts and vertical darts be pressed? (Lesson 15)

8. What is the difference between easing and gathering? (Lesson 16)

9. When pin-basting a seam, how far apart should the pins be placed? (Lesson 17)

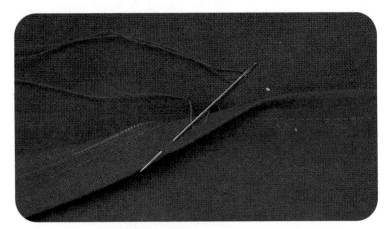

and Activities

10. When grading a seam, which seam allowance should be the widest? (Lesson 17)

11. Why are curved seams often clipped? (Lesson 17)

12. What is the difference between shaped and extended facings? (Lesson 18)

13. Why are self-casings easier to make than applied casings? (Lesson 19)

14. Why do hooks and eyes have both straight and round eyes? (Lesson 20)

15. If you choose buttons wider than the pattern suggests, what must happen? (Lesson 20)

16. Why should you stitch both sides of a zipper in the same direction? (Lesson 21)

17. What are the four basic steps in finishing a hem? (Lesson 22)

18. If a hem has too much fullness, what can you do? (Lesson 22)

19. Why should you check the fit of a garment throughout construction? (Lesson 23)

APPLYING KNOWLEDGE

1. **Comparing time.** Try putting on a facing, finishing a hem, or completing another procedure on both a serger and conventional machine. Compare the time each machine takes. Which machine is faster for the task you chose?

2. **Sewing samples.** Make samples of the following techniques: different stitches, darts, gathering and easing, seams and seam finishes, facings, casings, fasteners, and hems. Use hand stitching, machine stitching, and serger stitching where appropriate. Mount samples on heavy paper and write a description of each technique.

3. **Project evaluation.** To complete the sewing project begun in Part 1 of the "Sewing and Serging Handbook," you used the management process that was described on page 54. Planning, organizing, and implementing were steps in the process. Evaluation is the last step. Think about your project and efforts, and explain how successfully you followed your management plan. Also evaluate your success with construction techniques. What, if anything, would you have done differently?

CREATIVE SOLUTIONS

In clothing lab, you hear a sound of dismay from a student close by. While using a seam ripper to remove stitches, he accidentally cut the fabric. In frustration, he looks over at you, shrugs his shoulders, and says, "Now what?"

Think Creatively

After looking at the fabric, you see that the rip runs parallel to the seam that he was taking out. What suggestions can you offer to this student?

Special Sewing Techniques

Sewing Special Seams

When sewing, you may have occasion to use something different from a plain seam. Seams can enclose the seam allowance and create decorative effects. Some seaming techniques are needed to stitch special areas.

SELF-FINISHED SEAMS

Self-finished seams enclose the seam allowances as the seam is stitched. They provide a more attractive appearance and strengthen seams. Self-finished seams include the French seam, flat-felled seam, double-stitched seam, and narrow serged seam.

French Seam

A French seam works well on sheer fabric because no raw edges show through. The seam looks like a plain seam on the garment's outside and a narrow tuck on the wrong side. This seam can be used on straight seams but isn't flexible enough for curved seams. Here's how the seam is created.

1. Pin the wrong sides of the fabric together.
2. Stitch $\frac{3}{8}$ inch (9 mm) from the raw edges. Trim the seam allowances to $\frac{1}{8}$ inch (3 mm). Press the seam allowances open.
3. Fold the fabric along the seam line with right sides together. Press.
4. Stitch $\frac{1}{4}$ inch (6 mm) from the folded edge. The two seams, $\frac{3}{8}$ inch and $\frac{1}{4}$ inch (9 mm and 6 mm), combine to make a $\frac{5}{8}$-inch (1.5-cm) seam. See *Fig. 24-1*.

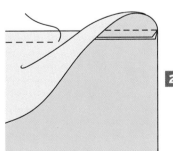

24-1 French Seam

Flat-Felled Seam

You'll find this sturdy and durable seam on shirts, jeans, sportswear, pajamas, and other garments. Two rows of stitching show on the outside of the garment. Contrasting thread can be used as an accent. Follow these steps to make the seam:

1. Pin the wrong sides of the fabric together.
2. Stitch a $\frac{5}{8}$-inch (1.5-cm) standard seam. Press open.

Serging Techniques

Narrow Rolled Seam

A narrow rolled seam is especially good for lingerie fabrics and laces, which are sheer and lightweight.

1. Pin the wrong sides of the fabric together.
2. Adjust the serger for a narrow rolled hem with a 1.5- to 2.5-mm stitch length and a balanced tension.
3. Serge the seam.

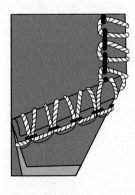

Reinforced Seam

In areas of stress, combining a serged seam with one sewn conventionally creates a stronger seam.

1. Stitch the seam on a conventional machine, using a straight stitch.
2. Press the seam allowances flat, as they were stitched.
3. Serge the edges together, using the two-thread serger stitch, ⅛ inch (3 mm) from the seam line.

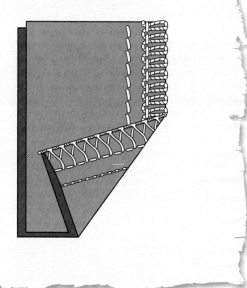

3. Press both seam allowances to one side.
4. Trim the under-seam allowance to ⅛ inch (3 mm).
5. Fold in the edge of the upper seam allowance ¼ inch (6 mm). Place it over the trimmed seam allowance. Press.
6. Stitch close to the folded edge through all thicknesses. See *Fig. 24-2*.

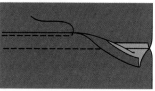

24-2 Flat-Felled Seam

Double-Stitched Seam

As described below, this seam works well on curved seams, such as armhole or crotch seams.

1. Stitch a ⅝-inch (1.5-cm) standard seam, with right sides of the fabric together.
2. Stitch again about ⅛ inch (3 mm) from the seam line in the seam allowance. A narrow zigzag stitch can be used for this second row of stitching.
3. Trim the seam allowances close to the stitching. See *Fig. 24-3*.

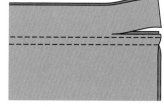

24-3 Double-Stitched Seam

DECORATIVE SEAMS

Decorative seams create special effects with topstitching or cording. They give a sporty, tailored, or contrasting finish to a garment. Decorative seams include the topstitched seam, welt seam, lapped seam, and piped or corded seam.

Topstitched Seam

Topstitching holds bulky seam allowances flat and emphasizes the seams of a garment. Topstitching can be done on one or both sides of a seam. Follow these steps:

1. Stitch a ⅝-inch (1.5-cm) standard seam. Press the seam allowances open.
2. Topstitch along each side of the seam, through both layers of fabric. Keep stitching a straight and equal distance from the seam line. See *Fig. 24-4*.

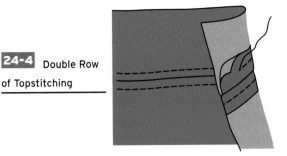

24-4 Double Row of Topstitching

As an alternative, you can press both seam allowances to one side as indicated on the pattern. Topstitch through all three layers of fabric. See *Fig. 24-5.*

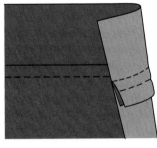

24-5 Single row of Topstitching

Welt Seam

Because it's less bulky than the flat-felled seam, a welt seam gives a tailored finish on heavier fabrics. Follow these steps:

1. Stitch a ⅝-inch (1.5-cm) standard seam, with right sides of the fabric together. Press the seam open.
2. Press both seam allowances to one side.
3. Trim the seam allowance against the garment to ¼ inch (6 mm).
4. Stitch from the outside through the garment and the wider seam allowance. Keep stitching an even distance from the seam line. See *Fig. 24-6.*

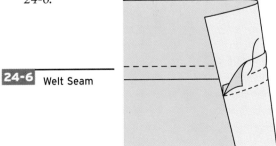

24-6 Welt Seam

Serging Techniques

Topstitched Seam

A serged seam can be topstitched once or twice for a sporty look. Press the serged seam to one side. Then topstitch on a conventional machine.

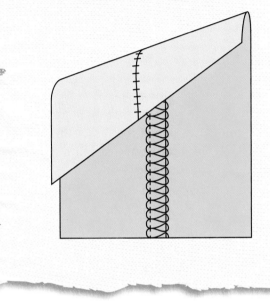

Lapped Seam

With this seam, one piece is lapped over the other and topstitched in place. It is often used with natural or synthetic leather and suede. Follow these steps to make a lapped seam:

1. Turn the seam allowance under on the section to be lapped. Press. For leather and suede, trim away the seam allowance.
2. Lap the folded or trimmed edge over the other piece at the seam line, wrong side to right side.
3. Edgestitch along the folded or trimmed edge. See *Fig. 24-7.*

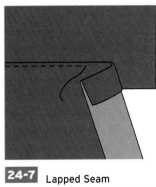

24-7 Lapped Seam

Flatlock Seam

A flatlock seam is a good choice for straight seams on knit fabric.

- The traditional flatlock seam is formed by using the two-thread serger stitch.

- A mock flatlock seam is created with the three-thread serger stitch. Loosen the needle tension almost as much as possible, and tighten the lower looper tension. When the serger is properly adjusted, the needle thread forms a V on the underside of the fabric. The lower looper thread forms a straight line along the fabric edge.

- For both types of flatlock seams, serge the seam. Then gently pull on the layers until the fabric lies flat and the cut edges meet. The stitch will have a ladder-like appearance on one side of the garment and loops on the other.

4. Topstitch again ¼ inch (6 mm) from the edge.

Piped or Corded Seam

Piping is a narrow band of fabric stitched into a seam to accent the seam line or outer edge of a garment. As the procedure below describes, piping can be inserted into a seam while it is stitched. Cording covered with bias strips of fabric may also be used.

1. Pin the piping or cording to the right side of one fabric section along the seam line. Be sure the piping or cording is facing the garment and the seam allowance is toward the edge of the fabric.

2. Stitch close to the seam line in the seam allowance, using a zipper foot.

3. Pin the second piece of fabric over the piping or cording, with right sides together.

4. Stitch along the seam line through all thicknesses, using a zipper foot. See *Fig. 24-8.*

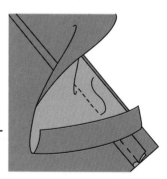

24-8 Piped Seam

Making Tucks and Pleats

Tucks and pleats are folds of fabric that control fullness or add design interest. They are folded and then pressed or stitched in place.

TUCKS

The narrow folds of fabric on **tucks** may be stitched part way or the entire length. The width of the tucks and the spacing between them varies according to design. See *Fig. 25-1*. The pattern indicates narrow pin tucks by a series of fold lines. Wide tucks usually have both fold and stitching lines indicated. Follow the pattern guide for stitching directions. The basic steps are as follows:

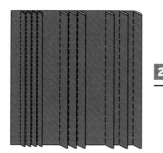

25-1 Tucks

1. Mark the stitching and fold lines for each tuck. To save time, use clips to mark the ends of stitching lines, and notches to mark the ends of fold lines.
2. Fold the fabric along the fold lines, matching stitching lines.
3. Stitch each tuck from the side that will be seen after the tuck is pressed flat. Keep stitching straight and even. See *Fig. 25-2*.

SEWING TIP

Adding tucks. You can add your own tucks to a garment by tucking the fabric before cutting out the pattern pieces. Be sure to purchase extra fabric to allow for the tucks.

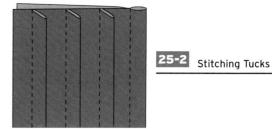

25-2 Stitching Tucks

4. Press each tuck flat, as stitched. Then press each tuck to one side, as shown on the guide sheet. See *Fig. 25-3*.

25-3 Pressing Tucks

PLEATS

Pleats are folds of fabric that are wider than tucks and stitched or pressed in place. A garment may have one single pleat or a series. Pleats can be pressed sharp along the edges or fall in soft folds. For a more tailored look, they can also be stitched.

The way pleats are turned creates various effects. See *Fig. 25-4*. On knife pleats the folds are turned in one direction. Turning two pleats toward each other makes box pleats and inverted pleats. Follow the guide sheet for specific instructions on folding, pressing, and stitching pleats. Some basic steps are provided here.

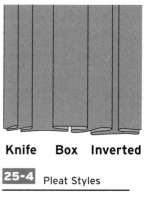

Knife   Box   Inverted

25-4 Pleat Styles

Tucks

Tucks can be stitched on the serger. Mark and fold the fabric the same as for conventional tucks.

- For pin tucks, adjust the serger for the narrow rolled hemstitch.
- For wider tucks, use the three-thread or four-thread serger stitch. Disengage the knife, or keep the fold slightly to the left of the knife so the fabric is not cut.
- For decorative tucks, use metallic thread, embroidery floss, pearl cotton, or narrow ribbon in the upper looper.

Folding Pleats

1. Mark the fold line and placement line for each pleat. If the pleats are to be made from the right side, clip and notch the ends of the lines or mark with a fabric marking pen.

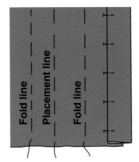

25-5 Folding a Pleat

2. Fold the fabric, matching the fold and placement lines, and pin. See *Fig. 25-5*. An arrow on the pattern piece shows the direction to fold.
3. Stay-stitch the pleats along the upper seam line.

Pressing Pleats

1. Press pleats gently from the inside of the garment. If the pleats leave an impression on the fabric, slip strips of paper under each fold before pressing. See *Fig. 25-6*.

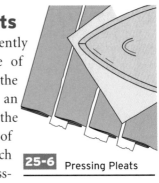

25-6 Pressing Pleats

2. Turn the garment to the right side.
3. Press the pleats in place, using a press cloth. For soft pleats, press lightly. For sharp pleats, use plenty of steam and a damp press cloth.
4. Let the pleats dry on the ironing board.

Stitching Pleats

Pleats may be topstitched or edgestitched for a smoother appearance. Stitching also holds the pleats in place. For pleats that are edgestitched and topstitched, do edgestitching first.

Edgestitching, described here, gives a sharper crease along the outer or inner fold of a pleat. See *Fig. 25-7*.

1. Complete the hem.
2. Stitch from the bottom of the pleat to the top as close to the fold as possible.

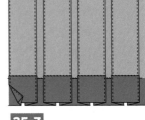

25-7 Edgestitching Pleats

3. Repeat on the other fold of the pleat, if desired.

Topstitching is stitched only part way, usually between the waist and hip areas. Use this technique. See *Fig. 25-8*.

1. Topstitch from the right side through all thicknesses. Begin at the hip; don't backstitch. Stitch to pleat top.
2. Pull threads to the under side and tie.

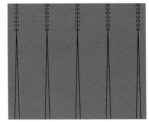

25-8 Topstitching Pleats

Applying Interfacings

INTERFACING IS A LAYER of fabric that is placed between the facing and the outer fabric of a garment. See *Fig. 26-1*. As part of the inner construction, interfacing provides shape and support for the outer fabric, although it shouldn't show on the outside.

Interfacing gives shape to collars, cuffs, and waistbands. It prevents edges on necklines and front closings from stretching and gives added body to a belt, bag, or hat. Sometimes a separate pattern piece is provided for interfacing. If not, the interfacing is cut from the facing, collar, cuff, or waistband pattern piece.

Special woven, knitted, and nonwoven interfacing fabrics are available in many types and weights. Sew-in interfacings are stitched by machine or by hand to the garment. Fusible interfacings are fused directly to the fabric with an iron, using a combination of heat, steam, and pressure. Always follow the manufacturer's fusing directions carefully.

When choosing interfacing, always drape the garment fabric over the interfacing. How do the two fabrics look and feel together? Check to be sure they are compatible in weight and fiber content. Also make sure the fabrics take the same cleaning and pressing methods.

SEW-IN INTERFACING

To use sew-in interfacing, cut the interfacing pieces according to the directions on the guide

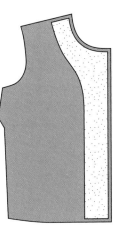

26-1 Interfacing adds shape to parts of a garment and keeps fabric from stretching.

sheet. Lightweight to medium-weight interfacing can be stitched into the seam of a garment. Follow these steps:

1. Pin the interfacing to the wrong side of the garment or facing.
2. Machine-baste ½ inch (1.3 cm) from the fabric edge.
3. Trim the interfacing close to the stitching. See *Fig. 26-2*.
4. Catchstitch the interfacing by hand along a folded edge, such as an extended facing or cuff.

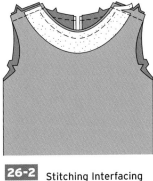

26-2 Stitching Interfacing

SEWING TIP

Interfacings. Usually the interfacing should be slightly lighter in weight than the outer fabric. Remember that some fusible interfacings are crisper after fusing. Always pretest on a scrap of fabric to be sure you like the results.

SEWING TIP

Minimizing bulk. To minimize bulk, trim either sew-in or fusible interfacing diagonally at corners. Trim just inside the point where the seam lines meet. Also trim off any hem allowances on the interfacing pieces before stitching or fusing to the garment fabric.

FUSIBLE INTERFACING

Before applying fusible interfacing to garment sections, test the fusing process on a scrap of fabric. If the interfacing leaves an outline along the edge, then fuse it to the facing rather than the garment. Follow these steps:

1. Trim any corners or hem allowances. For medium-weight interfacings, trim away all seam allowances.
2. Place the adhesive side of interfacing on the wrong side of the fabric, matching the cut edges of the interfacing to the seam lines.
3. Fuse in place, using a press cloth and following the fusing directions. See *Fig. 26-3*.

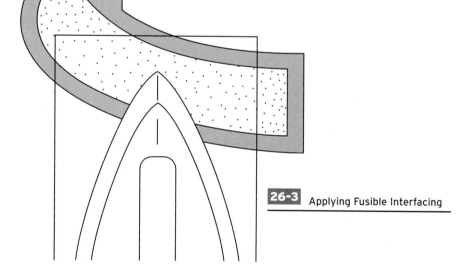

26-3 Applying Fusible Interfacing

Putting in Linings

A LINING IS A LAYER of fabric attached to the inside of a garment. See *Fig. 27-1*. It is constructed separately from the outer garment and then joined at one or more major seams. A lining gives an attractive appearance to the inside of a garment and helps prevent the outer fabric from stretching and wrinkling. Some coat linings are backed with a napped finish or insulation for added warmth. A lining may have a center back pleat to allow for movement.

Lining fabrics are firmly woven and have a smooth, slippery texture. To choose a lining fabric, always drape the garment fabric over the lining fabric. Check to see how the two fabrics look and feel together.

- Is the lining too soft or too crisp for the shape you want?
- Does the color show through or change the color of the outer fabric?
- Do the two fabrics have compatible fiber content?
- Can both fabrics be cleaned in the same manner?
- Do they require pressing?

CUTTING AND STITCHING

Some linings are cut from the same pattern pieces as the outer fabric. A coat or jacket pattern, however, might have separate pattern pieces for lining.

Follow the pattern guide sheet to stitch the lining pieces together. Seam finishes aren't needed on the outer fabric or the lining unless the fabric

27-1 A lining gives support to a garment and adds a finished look.

ravels easily. Use machine or hand stitching to attach the lining to the garment along the facing or the waistline seam.

HEMMING

Some linings are hemmed separately; others are sewn to the garment. See *Fig. 27-2*. Coat, skirt, and dress linings are usually hemmed separately. Make the lining hem ½ to 1 inch (1.3 to 2.5 cm) shorter than the outer garment. (See "Putting in Hems" on page 537.) For coats, use French tacks to hold the hems together at the seam lines.

Jacket, sleeve, and pant linings are usually attached to the garment hem, as described here.

1. Match the folded hem edges of the lining and garment.
2. Pin the folded edge of the lining at least ½ inch (1.3 cm) above the garment edge, creating a small tuck that allows for movement.
3. Slip-stitch the edge of the lining to the garment hem.

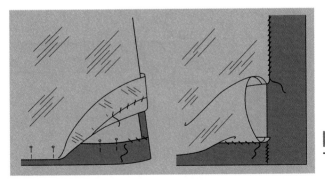

27-2 Hemming the Lining

Lining Hemmed Separately   Attaching Lining to Hem

Sewing Collars

THERE ARE MANY different collar styles. Four collar styles are basic. See *Fig. 28-1.*

- **Flat collar.** Lies flat against the garment. Both upper and lower collars are cut from the same pattern piece.
- **Rolled collar.** Stands up at the back of the neck and then turns down to create a rolled edge around the neck. It can be cut with a one-piece upper collar and a two-piece under collar that is slightly smaller. Another way is to cut the entire collar as one piece and fold it at the outer edge.
- **Shirt collar.** Has a separate stand, or band, that attaches the collar to the neckline.
- **Standing collar.** Forms a band that stands straight up or folds over to create a turtleneck.

Because a collar is close to your face and attracts attention, it should be well made and carefully pressed. The collar should have the following qualities: circles the neck smoothly without rippling; has front points or curves with identical shape; and has an under collar that doesn't show along the edge. A rolled collar and a shirt collar should cover the neck seam in back.

Interfacing gives collars added shape and support. It is usually stitched or fused to the under collar. If the outer fabric is lightweight, however, the interfacing can be stitched to the upper collar to prevent the seam allowances from showing.

To make a collar, construct it first and then attach it to the garment.

CONSTRUCTING THE COLLAR

To construct a collar, first cut out the collar and any facings. The upper and under collar may be cut from the same or separate pattern pieces. Some collars are cut from one piece of fabric and folded lengthwise. After cutting, follow these steps:

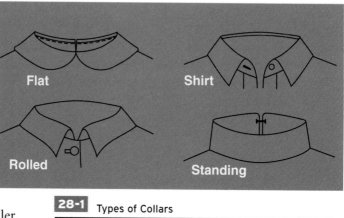

28-1 Types of Collars

1. Stitch or fuse the interfacing to the wrong side of the under collar. For a one-piece collar, catchstitch the interfacing along the fold line if the interfacing hasn't been fused. Stitch the center back seam of the under collar, if necessary. Press the seam open and trim.
2. Pin the collar sections with right sides together. Follow the pattern guide sheet for specific directions.
3. Stitch the outer seam of the collar. Strengthen the corners or points with short reinforcement stitches.
4. Trim and grade the seam allowances. See *Fig. 28-2.* Trim the corners close to the stitching for crisp, sharp points. Clip or notch curved areas. Press the seam open, using a point presser.

28-2 Trimming and Grading Seam Allowances

5. Turn the collar to the right side. See *Fig. 28-3.* Gently pull out the points. (To prevent poking a hole in the fabric, don't push the points out with scissors.)

28-3 Turning the Collar

6. Press the outer seam, rolling slightly to the collar's underside.
7. Understitch the under collar to the seam allowances to help prevent it from showing at the edge, or topstitch around the edge of the collar.

For a shirt collar, stitch the collar band to the upper collar and the under collar at the inner edge. See *Fig. 28-4*. Trim, grade, clip, notch, and press the seams.

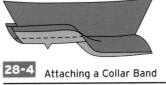

28-4 Attaching a Collar Band

ATTACHING THE COLLAR

A collar may be stitched to a garment with no facing, a partial neckline facing, or complete facing. Use the directions in your pattern guide sheet. The following steps are basic:

Collar without Facing

This method is used for shirt collars and standing collars.
1. Stay-stitch the garment neckline and clip.
2. Pin the under collar or band to the neckline, right sides together, matching all markings.
3. Stitch the seam, trim, and clip. Press the seam toward the collar. See *Fig. 28-5*.

28-5 Attaching Collar to Neckline

4. Turn in the seam allowance of the upper collar or band. Press. Trim the seam allowance to ¼ inch (6 mm).
5. Pin the folded edge over the neckline seam. Machine-stitch close to the edge, or slip-stitch by hand. See *Fig. 28-6*.

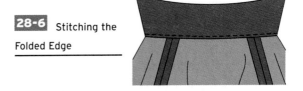

28-6 Stitching the Folded Edge

Collar with Partial Facing

This method is used for flat and rolled collars.
1. Stay-stitch the garment neckline and clip.
2. Pin the collar to the neckline, matching notches and markings.
3. Machine-baste the collar to the neck edge between the front openings and shoulder markings. Machine-baste the under collar only to the back neck edge between shoulder markings. See *Fig. 28-7*.

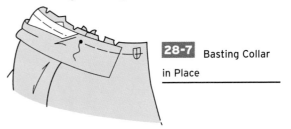

28-7 Basting Collar in Place

4. Pin the front facings to the neckline, with right sides together. Match all the markings. Clip the neck edges through all layers at both shoulder markings.
5. Stitch the neck seam as basted, being careful not to catch the free edge of the collar back. See *Fig. 28-8*. Trim, grade, and clip the seam allowances.

28-8 Stitching Neck Seam

Serging Techniques

Collar

Use this method for a collar with a partial or full neckline facing.

1. Follow Steps 1 to 5 for "Collar with Neckline Facing" to prepare facing, baste the collar to the neckline, and pin the facing to the neckline.
2. Serge the neckline seam.
3. Follow Steps 7 to 9 to turn, understitch, and tack the facing.

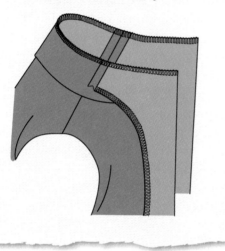

6. Turn the facing to the inside and press.
7. Understitch the facing to the neckline seam allowances.
8. Turn under ⅝ inch (1.5 cm) on the raw edge of the collar back. Press. Trim to ¼ inch (6 mm). See *Fig. 28-9*.
9. Slip-stitch the folded edge of the collar over the back neck seam. Tack the facing to the shoulder seam allowances.

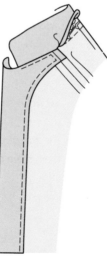

28-9 Turning Collar Edge Under

Collar with Neckline Facing

1. Stitch facing sections together. Trim and press the seams. Finish the outer, unnotched edge of the facing.
2. Stay-stitch the garment neckline and clip.
3. Pin the collar to the neckline, matching notches and markings.
4. Machine-baste the collar to the neck edge. See *Fig. 28-10*.

28-10 Basting Collar to Neck Edge

5. Pin the facing to the neckline, with right sides together. Match markings and seam lines.
6. Stitch the neckline seam. Trim, grade, and clip seam allowances. See *Fig. 28-11*.

28-11 Stitching Neckline Seam

7. Turn the facing to the inside and press.
8. Understitch the facing to the neckline seam allowances. See *Fig. 28-12*.

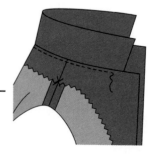

28-12 Understitching and Tacking

9. Tack the edge of the facing to the shoulder seam allowances.

Sewing Sleeves

BECAUSE SLEEVES ARE SO different, they are sewn with varied techniques. Sleeves can be finished at the bottom edge with a hem, facing, casing, or cuff. There are three basic sleeve styles. See *Fig. 29-1*.

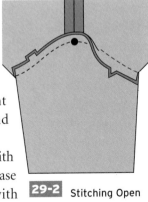

Set-In

Kimono

Raglan

29-1 Sleeve Styles

- **Set-in sleeve.** Joined to a garment by an armhole seam that circles the arm near the shoulder.
- **Raglan sleeve.** Has a front and back diagonal seam that extends from the neckline to the underarm.
- **Kimono sleeve.** Cut in one piece with the front and back of the garment.

SET-IN SLEEVE

Although it's the most common sleeve style, a set-in sleeve is also the most difficult to sew. A set-in sleeve nearly always measures more than the armhole that holds it. With extra fullness, the sleeve fits well over the top curve of the arm and allows movement.

Some set-in sleeves are very full across the cap, or top, of the sleeve. This fullness must be eased into the seam without any gathers or puckers. Other sleeves, on a tailored shirt, for example, have a short sleeve cap that is only slightly larger than the armhole.

The two techniques for sewing a set-in sleeve are the open-sleeve and the closed-sleeve methods.

Open-Sleeve Method

The open-sleeve method is fast and easy but can only be used for sleeves that need little easing. Tailored shirts, sports shirts, and shirts with dropped shoulders are examples.

With this method, the sleeve is first stitched to the armhole. See *Fig. 29-2*. Then the side and underarm seams are stitched in one continuous seam. Because the sleeve and garment seams remain open while the sleeve is attached, this method is also called the flat construction method. Follow these steps:

1. Match the sleeve to the garment, right sides together, and pin.
2. Stitch the seam with the sleeve side up. Ease in any fullness with your fingers as you sew.

29-2 Stitching Open Sleeve to Garment

3. Stitch a second row of stitching ⅜ inch (1 cm) from the outer edge. Trim close to the stitching. Press the seam allowances toward the garment. Alternatives: topstitch on the outside of the garment ¼ to ⅜ inch (6 to 9 mm) from the seam on the body side, or serge to finish the seam.

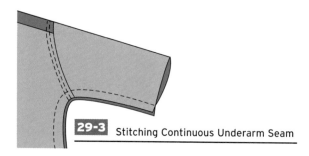

29-3 Stitching Continuous Underarm Seam

4. Match and pin the side seam and underarm sleeve seam.

5. Stitch the seam from the bottom of the garment to the end of the sleeve in one continuous line of stitching. See *Fig. 29-3*. Press the seams open. Alternatives: trim the seam allowances and zigzag together, or serge the seam.

Closed-Sleeve Method

Use the closed-sleeve method for sleeves with extra fullness across the sleeve cap. With this method, the underarm seam of the sleeve and the side seam of the garment are first stitched separately. Then the sleeve is attached to the armhole. Because the sleeve is completed before stitching to the armhole, this method is also called the unit method of construction. Follow the directions in your pattern guide sheet. These are the basic steps:

1. Using about 8 stitches per inch (3 mm in length), machine-baste close to the ⅝-inch (1.5-cm) seam line within the seam allowance. Stitch around the top of the sleeve between the notches. If the sleeve cap is full, the pattern guide sheet will recommend a second row of machine basting ⅜ inch (1 cm) from the outer edge. See *Fig. 29-4.*

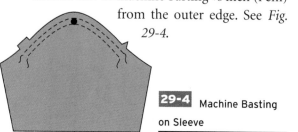

29-4 Machine Basting on Sleeve

2. Stitch the underarm seam of the sleeve, and stitch the garment side seam separately. Press seams open.

3. Pull up the bobbin thread ends of the machine basting until the sleeve cap fits the armhole. Adjust the fullness evenly between the notches.

4. Turn the garment wrong side out. Turn the sleeve right side out and slip it inside the armhole.

5. Pin the sleeve to the garment, with right sides together. Match the underarm seams, shoulder markings, and notches. Adjust the fullness. Place pins at right angles to the seam line so they can be easily removed as you sew. See *Fig. 29-5.*

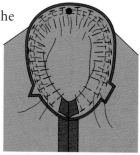

29-5 Pinning and Adjusting Fullness

6. Stitch the sleeve to the armhole with the sleeve side up. This allows you to control fullness and prevents tucks or puckers from forming. See *Fig. 29-6.*

7. Reinforce the armhole seam with a second row of stitches ⅜ inch (1 cm) from the outer edge. Trim close to the stitching or serge to finish the seam. Some armhole seams are reinforced only in the underarm section. Stitch from notch to notch.

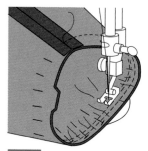

29-6 Stitching Sleeve to Armhole

8. Press the seam allowances together from the sleeve side, using the side of the iron. See *Fig. 29-7.* Do not press the seam from the right side of the garment. An armhole seam is sup-

posed to be gently curved. Turn the seam allowances toward the sleeve.

RAGLAN SLEEVE

29-7 Pressing Seam Allowances

A raglan sleeve is loose fitting and comfortable to wear. A shoulder dart or seam shapes the sleeve over the shoulder area. Follow these steps to make this sleeve:

1. Stitch the shoulder dart or seam. Slash and press open. See *Fig. 29-8*.

29-8 Dart in a Raglan Sleeve

2. Pin the diagonal seams of the sleeve to the garment, with right sides together. Match notches, markings, and underarm seams.
3. Stitch the seams. See *Fig. 29-9*.

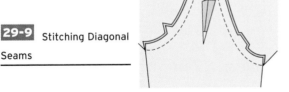

29-9 Stitching Diagonal Seams

4. Reinforce the underarm section between the notches by stitching again, ⅜ inch (1 cm) from the outer edge, or serge to finish the seam.
5. Clip at the end of the second row of stitching. Trim the underarm seams. Press the seams open between notches and neckline.
6. Stitch the underarm seam of the sleeve and side seam, and press open. See *Fig. 29-10*. Alternatives: trim the seam allowances and zigzag together, or serge the underarm seam of the sleeve and side seam.

Serging Techniques

Sleeves

For sweatshirts and similar sportswear knit garments, use the two-thread flat-lock or three-thread, mock, flatlock stitch to join the sleeve to the garment. (See Steps 3 and 4 for the "Raglan Sleeve.") Use the three-thread or four-thread serger stitch to serge the underarm seam.

29-10 Stitching Underarm Seams

KIMONO SLEEVE

This is the easiest sleeve for a beginner because it's simply an extension of the garment front and back. Here's the procedure. See *Fig. 29-11*.

1. Stitch the shoulder seam, right sides together. Press open.

29-11 Stitching a Kimono Sleeve

2. Stitch the underarm seam.
3. Reinforce the underarm seam with a second row of stitching ⅜ inch (1 cm) from the outer edge. To give the seam extra strength, sew a piece of seam tape over the curved underarm seam, stitching through all layers.
4. Clip the curve of the seam, but don't clip the seam tape. Press the seam open, or trim the seam and zigzag the seam allowances together. You can also serge to finish the seam.

Sewing Cuffs

CUFFS GIVE A tailored finish to the end of a sleeve. They have three basic styles: fold-up, band, and buttoned. See *Figs. 30-1, 30-2,* and *30-3*. Some cuffs are interfaced. Follow your pattern guide sheet and the information on interfacings.

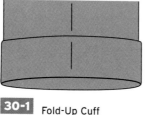

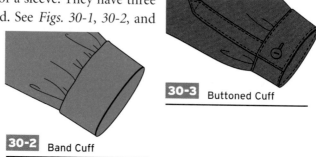

30-3 Buttoned Cuff

30-2 Band Cuff

30-1 Fold-Up Cuff

FOLD-UP CUFF

A fold-up cuff is actually a deep hem at the bottom of a sleeve or pant leg, but it's folded to the right side of the garment. You can create this cuff with the following procedure:

1. Finish the lower edge of the fabric with a zigzag, hemmed, or bound finish. (See the seam finishes on page 523.)
2. Turn the cuff to the inside along the fold line and pin.
3. Hem by hand or use machine stitching. See *Fig. 30-4*.

30-4 Hemming a Fold-Up Cuff

4. Turn the lower edge of the garment to the right side along the hemline to form a cuff.
5. Tack or stitch-in-the-ditch to hold the cuff in place at each seam. See *Fig. 30-5*.

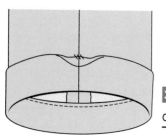

30-5 Tacking Fold-Up Cuff

BAND CUFF

A band cuff has no side opening, so it must be large enough for your hand to slip through easily. Follow these steps to make the cuff:

1. Interface the cuff, if desired.
2. Fold the unnotched seam allowance of the cuff to the inside and press. Trim the seam allowance to ¼ inch (6 mm).
3. Pin the notched edge of the cuff to the bottom edge of the sleeve, right sides together, matching markings. Adjust fullness.
4. Stitch the seam with the sleeve side up. Trim, grade, and press the seam allowances toward the cuff. See *Fig. 30-6*.

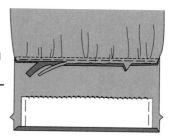

30-6 Stitching Band to Sleeve

5. Stitch the sleeve and cuff seams. Trim the cuff and press the seams open. See *Fig. 30-7*.

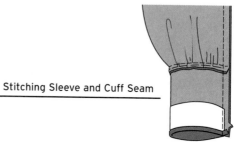

30-7 Stitching Sleeve and Cuff Seam

6. Fold the cuff in half along the fold line, wrong sides together.
7. Pin the folded edge of the cuff over the seam line. Topstitch from the right side or slip-stitch the edge in place. See *Fig. 30-8*.

30-8 Stitching Cuff in Place

BUTTONED CUFF

A buttoned cuff fits snugly around the wrist and fastens with a button or other fastener. There must be an opening in the sleeve to allow the cuff to slide over the hand. The opening, called a placket, is sewn before attaching the cuff.

Sewing Sleeve Plackets

A **placket** is a slit at the wrist, neck, or waist of a garment to make it easier to put on and take off. The three most common sleeve plackets are faced, continuous lap, and banded plackets. See *Fig. 30-9*. The pattern guide sheet gives complete directions for making the placket for a particular garment. Basic procedures are covered here.

Faced Placket

A faced placket forms a split opening that can be used on a sleeve or neckline.
1. Finish the edge of the placket facing.
2. Center the placket over the opening, with right sides together.

3. Stitch along the stitching lines, using short reinforcement stitches. Take one small stitch across the point. See *Fig. 30-10*.

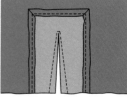

30-10 Stitching a Faced Placket

4. Slash carefully up to the point.
5. Turn the facing to the inside and press. See *Fig. 30-11*.

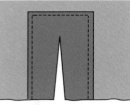

30-11 Completed Faced Placket

Continuous Lap Placket

A continuous lap is a narrow binding that overlaps at the opening. It can be used on sleeves or the waistline of pants, skirts, and shorts.
1. Stay-stitch the placket opening along the stitching lines, using reinforcement stitches. Take one small stitch across the point.
2. Slash carefully up to the point. See *Fig. 30-12*.

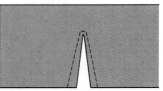

30-12 Stitching Placket Opening

30-9 Sleeve Plackets

Faced   Continuous Lap   Banded

Open the slash until the line of stitching is almost straight.

3. Cut a fabric strip 1½ inches wide (3.8 cm) and twice the length of the slash. Pin the fabric strip to the slashed edge, matching the right side of the strip to the wrong side of the sleeve so that the stitching line is ¼ inch (6 mm) from the edge of the strip. The fabric edges will not match.

4. Stitch along the first row of stitching. See *Fig. 30-13*. Press the seam allowances toward the fabric strip.

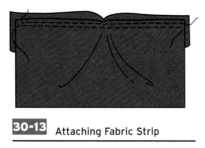

30-13 Attaching Fabric Strip

5. Turn in the raw edge of the fabric strip ¼ inch (6 mm) and pin over the seam. Topstitch in place. See *Fig. 30-14*.

30-14 Topstitching Fabric Strip

6. Press the front portion of the lap to the inside and baste in place across the lower edge of the opening. See *Fig. 30-15*.

30-15 Completing the Lap

Banded Placket

A banded placket gives a tailored finish to a sleeve. It is similar to the neckline placket used on a shirtfront. The placket can be one or two pieces.

1. Reinforce the opening with stitching.

2. Slash and clip into the corners. See *Fig. 30-16*.

3. Stitch under the lap to the back edge of the opening, following directions in the guide sheet. See *Fig. 30-17*.

4. Stitch the overlap to the front edge of the opening. See *Fig. 30-18*.

5. Overlap the placket and stitch at the upper edge. Stitch through all thicknesses across the point and around the edges. See *Fig. 30-19*.

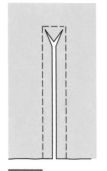

30-16 Opening for Banded Placket

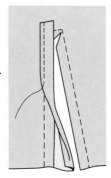

30-17 Adding the Underlap

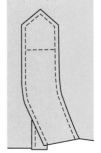

30-18 Adding the Overlap

30-19 Completing the Overlap

Sewing Buttoned Cuff

Some buttoned cuffs are cut in one piece and folded lengthwise. Others are cut in two pieces and stitched along the outer edge. Follow these steps to sew the cuffs:

1. Complete the sleeve opening.
2. Interface the cuff, if desired.
3. Fold the long, unnotched edge of the cuff to the inside and press. Trim to ¼ inch (6 mm). See *Fig. 30-20.*

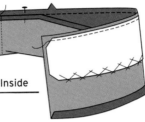

30-20 Folding Cuff to Inside

4. Stitch the ends of the cuff, right sides together, or stitch the cuff sections together along the outer edge. Trim and grade the seams and press. Turn the cuff to the right side.
5. Pin the cuff to the gathered sleeve edge, right sides together, matching notches and markings. For a shirtsleeve, the cuff edges will be even with the placket edges. For other sleeve openings, the cuff will extend beyond the back edge of the placket.

6. Stitch the seam. Trim, grade, and clip the seam allowances. Press the seam allowances toward the cuff. See *Fig. 30-21.*

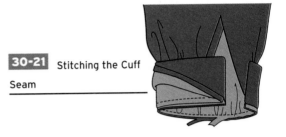

30-21 Stitching the Cuff Seam

7. Place the folded edge of the cuff over the seam and extension end. Topstitch in place from the right side. If desired, topstitch the outer edge of the cuff.
8. Make machine buttonholes and attach the buttons. See *Fig. 30-22.*

30-22 Adding Button and Buttonhole

Sewing Pockets

POCKETS CAN BE FUNCTIONAL, decorative, or both. A pocket concealed in a side seam is purely functional, while a patch pocket is both functional and decorative. Before adding a pocket, check the location to be sure the placement is correct for your height and size. You may have to raise or lower it for convenience or for better proportion.

Pocket styles vary. Some are located inside the garment and open through a seam or slash. Others are stitched on the outside of the garment. Some may have a flap covering the top of the pocket.

Three pockets that are easy to make are the in-seam pocket, the patch pocket, and the front hip pocket. See *Figs. 31-1, 31-2,* and *31-3.*

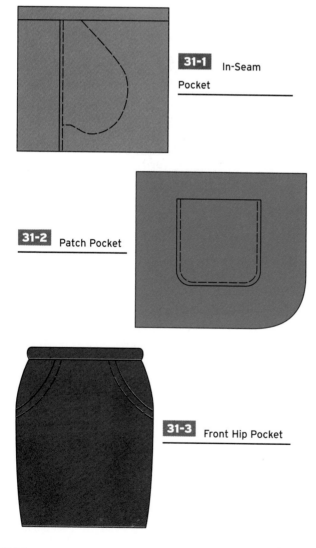

31-1 In-Seam Pocket

31-2 Patch Pocket

31-3 Front Hip Pocket

IN-SEAM POCKET

As the easiest to make, the in-seam pocket is simply attached to the side seam of the garment. It can be cut as part of the garment front and back, or it can be cut from a separate pattern piece and stitched to the seam. If the outer fabric is bulky or heavy, cut the pocket pieces from lining fabric. All construction is done on the inside of the garment, as you'll see in the following steps:

1. If the pocket is cut separately, stitch the pocket pieces to the front and back opening, right sides together. Press the seam allowances toward the pocket pieces.

2. Pin the garment front to the garment back, matching markings at the seam line and pocket.

3. Stitch directionally along the seam and around the pocket in one step. Use reinforcement stitches at the corners. Press the seam allowances flat. See *Fig. 31-4.*

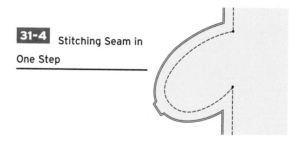

31-4 Stitching Seam in One Step

4. Turn the pocket toward the front of the garment. Clip the back seam allowance above and below the pocket so the seam allowances of the garment can be pressed open.

5. If necessary, finish the seam allowances. See *Fig. 31-5.*

SEWING TIP

Reinforcing in-seam pockets. When making an in-seam pocket, you may want to reinforce the pocket opening to prevent stretching. Stitch a piece of seam tape or twill tape along the front and back fold line or seam line. As an alternative, you can fuse a strip of interfacing along the opening edge of the pocket.

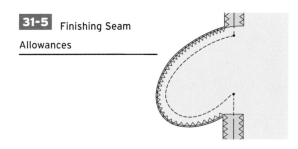

31-5 Finishing Seam Allowances

PATCH POCKET

Patch pockets are made from the same fabric as the garment and stitched to the outside by machine or hand. If using a plaid, stripe, or printed fabric, match the pocket to the garment, or cut the pocket on the bias for a special design effect.

When making a pair of patch pockets, be sure both pockets are the same size and shape. Attach the pockets to the garment evenly.

Patch pockets may have straight or curved sides and be lined or unlined. A lining is needed for fabrics that stretch or sag. Fabrics that are firm enough to hold their shape can be used without a lining. Sometimes a flap is stitched above the pocket.

The instructions that follow outline procedures for making different patch pockets.

Unlined Patch Pocket

1. Turn under the top edge of the pocket hem ¼ inch (6 mm), press, and stitch.
2. Turn the hem to the right side of the pocket along the fold line, and pin.

3. Stay-stitch around the pocket on the seam line, beginning at the fold line of the hem. Stay-stitching acts as a guide for turning and pressing the edges and corners.
4. Trim and grade the seam allowances. Trim the upper corners diagonally. See *Fig. 31-6.* Turn the hem right side out and press.

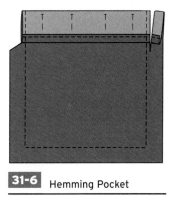

31-6 Hemming Pocket

5. Fold in the seam allowances along the stitching and press. Square corners must be **mitered**, made to fit together with a precise right angle at the corner; curved edges must be notched. These procedures are described in the following sections.
6. Stitch the edge of the hem to the pocket by hand, or topstitch from the right side. See *Fig. 31-7* on page 568.
7. Pin the pocket to the garment. Topstitch around the edge of the pocket, or slip-stitch in place. Reinforce the corners by backstitch-

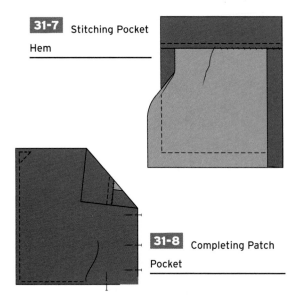

31-7 Stitching Pocket Hem

31-8 Completing Patch Pocket

ing or by stitching a small triangle or square. See *Fig. 31-8*.

Mitering Square Corners

Miter square corners to eliminate bulk and form a flat, smooth right angle.

1. Open out the seam allowances.
2. Trim each corner diagonally to ¼ inch (6 mm) from the fold.
3. Fold the corner in diagonally and press. See *Fig. 31-9*.

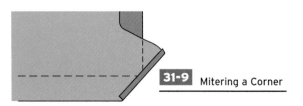

31-9 Mitering a Corner

4. Refold the seam allowances on both sides of the corner to form a square edge, and press again.

Curving Edges

Extra fabric must be eased in when pocket edges are curved. Follow these steps. See *Fig. 31-10*.

1. Machine-baste around the curved edges ½ inch (1.3 cm) from the outer edge.
2. Pull on the bobbin thread until the seam allowance curves in and lies flat.
3. Trim and notch the seam allowance to eliminate bulk and puckers.
4. Press.

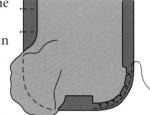

31-10 Making Curved Pocket

Lined Patch Pocket

1. Pin the upper edge of the lining to the upper edge of the pocket, right sides together.
2. Stitch on the seam line, leaving a 1-inch (2.5-cm) opening in the center for turning. See *Fig. 31-11*. Press the seam toward the lining.

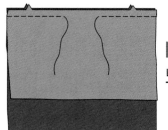

31-11 Attaching Lining to Pocket

3. Fold the pocket, right sides together, along the upper fold line.
4. Pin and stitch the lining to the pocket around all three sides. Trim and grade the seam allowances. See *Fig. 31-12*. Clip the corners and notch the curved areas.
5. Turn the pocket right side out through the opening. Roll the seam slightly toward the lining and press.

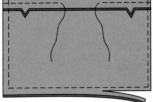

31-12 Stitching Lining to Pocket

31-13 Slip-Stitching the Opening

6. Slip-stitch the opening closed. See *Fig. 31-13*.
7. Pin the pocket to the garment, and topstitch or slip-stitch in place.

Pocket Flap

If a pocket flap is planned, follow these steps to add one:

1. Interface the outer half of the flap.
2. Fold the flap in half, right sides together, and stitch the end seams, or pin two flap sections together and stitch around the outer edge. Trim and grade the seam allowances. See *Fig. 31-14*. Notch any curved areas.

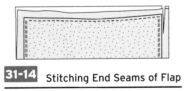

31-14 Stitching End Seams of Flap

3. Turn the flap right side out and press.
4. Pin the flap above the pocket, with the outer side of the flap against the outside of the garment. Match the seam line of the flap to the placement line on the garment.
5. Stitch through all thicknesses. Trim the seam allowance next to the garment close to the stitching. See *Fig. 31-15*.

Serging Techniques

Curved Patch Pocket

The following technique makes the seam allowances curl to the inside of a curved patch pocket:

1. Set the machine for the widest three-thread serger stitch. Adjust the tensions so the needle is normal, the upper looper slightly tight, and the lower looper slightly loose.

2. Serge around the outside edge of the pocket, with the needle just inside the seam line. When you reach the curved area, tighten the needle tension. When you are past it, set the needle tension back to normal.

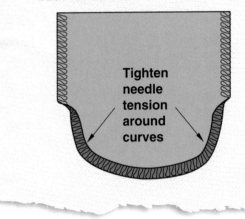

Tighten needle tension around curves

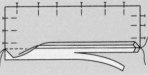

31-15 Attaching Flap to Pocket

6. Fold under the long edge of the upper seam allowance, turning the ends in diagonally. Pin over the trimmed edge and edgestitch. See *Fig. 31-16* on page 570.

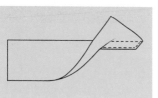

31-16 Completing
the Flap

7. Turn the flap down and press.
8. Slip-stitch the upper corners of the flap to the garment to hold in place.

FRONT HIP POCKET

Front hip pockets are often used on pants and shorts. This diagonal or curved pocket attaches to the waist and side seams. Because the back section of the pocket is part of the main garment at the front of the hip, it must be cut from the garment fabric. The inside front section of the pocket can be cut from the same fabric or a lining fabric. Follow these steps to make the pocket:

1. To prevent stretching, reinforce the upper edge of the pocket with interfacing or seam tape. See *Fig. 31-17*.

31-17 Reinforcing
Pocket Edge

2. Pin the front edge of the garment to the front pocket section, right sides together. Stitch, trim, and grade the seam. See *Fig. 31-18*. Press.

31-18 Stitching Front Pocket to Garment

3. Understitch or topstitch the seam to prevent the pocket from rolling to the right side of the garment. See *Fig. 31-19*.

31-19 Understitching Seam

4. Pin the back section of the pocket to the front section, right sides together. Stitch around the seam line, being careful not to catch in the garment front. Press the seam flat. Finish the raw edges with zigzag stitching. See *Fig. 31-20*.

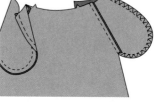

31-20 Attaching Front
to Back

5. Pin and stitch the side seams, catching in the back section of the pocket as part of the garment front.
6. Finish the waistline according to the pattern directions. See *Fig. 31-21*.

31-21 Finished Waistlines
and Hip Pockets

Finishing Waistlines

Tʜᴇ ᴡᴀɪsᴛʟɪɴᴇ ᴏꜰ ᴀ garment can be finished with a waistband, facing, or casing. Most waistlines fall at the natural waistline. Some garments, however, may have a raised or lowered waistline, depending on the design.

WAISTBANDS

A waistband is a strip of fabric attached to the waistline of pants, skirts, or shorts. Both straight and curved waistbands are attached to the garment in the same way. A straight waistband, however, usually has a fold along the upper edge, while a curved, or shaped, waistband has a seam.

To allow for movement and comfort, the waistband should be about 1 inch (2.5 cm) larger than the waistline. It shouldn't fit too tight. Easing or gathering the garment onto the waistband allows for the body's curve below the waistline.

Usually the zipper is inserted before the waistband is applied. A side opening is always on the left side, and the waistband laps from front to back. If the opening is in the front, the waistband overlaps in the same direction as the lapped zipper application. If the opening is in the center back, the waistband laps left over right.

Interface a waistband to prevent stretching and wrinkling. Usually the side that will be on the outside of the garment is interfaced. Follow pattern directions.

Plain Waistband

A plain waistband is stitched to the right side of the garment, turned to the inside, and stitched by hand.

1. Interface the waistband.
2. Turn in the seam allowance on the unnotched edge of the waistband and press. Trim the seam allowance to ¼ inch (6 mm). See *Fig. 32-1*.
3. Pin the waistband to the garment, right sides together. Match the notches and ease the garment to the waistband between markings. Check that the extension is on the correct side of the opening.

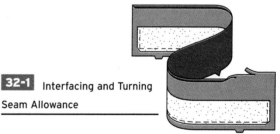

32-1 Interfacing and Turning Seam Allowance

SEWING TIP

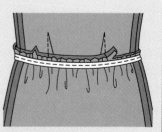

Stays. A stay, or support, can be stitched over the waistline seam to prevent stretching. Cut the stay from seam tape, twill tape, or grosgrain ribbon, making it the same length as the waistline measurement of the garment. To attach the stay, pin it to the seam allowance on the bottom section of the garment, with one edge along the waistline seam. Machine-stitch just above the waistline seam through the stay and seam allowances. Trim the seam allowances even with the stay. Zigzag the upper edge of the stay and the seam allowances together.

Serging Techniques

Plain Waistband

With heavyweight or bulky fabrics, it may be helpful to eliminate a layer of fabric at the waistline seam of a plain waistband. Serge along the unnotched edge of the waistband, trimming off the ⅝-inch (1.5-cm) seam allowances. When turning the waistband right side out, place the serged edge so that it meets the waistband seam on the inside of the garment.

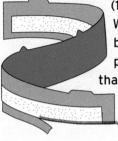

4. Stitch the waistband to the garment along the seam line. Trim the interfacing close to the stitching. Trim and grade the seam allowances; clip if necessary. Press the seams flat and then up toward the waistband. See *Fig. 32-2*.

32-2 Attaching the Waistband

5. Fold the ends of the waistband, right sides together as shown in *Fig. 32-2*. Pin carefully, being sure the folded edge exactly meets the seam line.
6. Stitch both ends. Trim and grade the seam allowances. Clip the corners, and press.
7. Turn the waistband right side out. Pin the folded edge over the seam.
8. Slip-stitch the waistband in place, continuing across the extension. See *Fig. 32-3*.
9. Attach the fasteners.

32-3 Slip-Stitching Waistband

Topstitched Waistband

A topstitched waistband is stitched to the wrong side of the garment, turned to the outside, and topstitched in place.

1. Interface the waistband.
2. Turn in the unnotched edge of the waistband along the seam line and press. Trim to ¼ inch (6 mm). See *Fig. 32-4*.

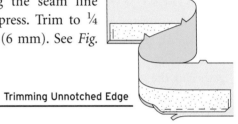

32-4 Trimming Unnotched Edge

3. Pin the right side of the waistband to the wrong side of the garment, matching notches and markings. Check to be sure the waistband will flip over so the right side is on the outside of the garment.
4. Stitch the seam. Grade the seam allowances so the widest layer is toward the outside of the garment. See *Fig. 32-5*. Clip if necessary. Press the seam allowances up toward the waistband.

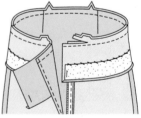

32-5 Stitching and Grading Seam

5. Stitch the ends of the waistband, with right sides together. Trim, grade, and clip the corners. Press. See *Fig. 32-6*.

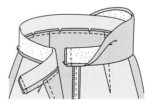

32-6 Stitching Waistband Ends

6. Fold the waistband over the seam line to the right side of the garment. Press and pin.

7. Topstitch along the bottom edge of the waistband close to the fold. See *Fig. 32-7.*

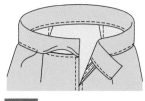

32-7 Topstitching Waistband

8. Attach the fasteners.

WAISTLINE FACING

A facing finishes a waistline edge, allowing the finished edge of a garment to rest right at the natural waistline. Prevent stretching by interfacing the waistline seam according to the pattern directions.

1. Apply fusible interfacing to the facing sections or sew-in interfacing to the garment edge.

2. Prepare the facing, and finish the outer edge with serger stitching, zigzag stitching, or a hem.

3. Stitch the facing to the garment, right sides together. Match seams, notches, and markings. Trim, grade, and clip the seam allowances. See *Fig. 32-8.* Press the seam allowances toward the facing.

32-8 Stitching Facing to Garment

4. Understitch the facing to the seam allowances. See *Fig. 32-9.*

5. Turn the facing to the inside of the garment and press. Tack at the seams with small cross-stitches.

32-9 Understitching Facing

6. Turn under the ends of the facing at the garment opening. Slip-stitch to the zipper tape. See *Fig. 32-10.*

Attaching Waistbands

1. Fold the waistband in half lengthwise, with right sides together.

2. Stitch across the ends, using a conventional machine. On the under-lap side, pivot and stitch along the waistline seam, ending at the dot. Clip at the dot, and trim the ends.

3. Turn the waistband right side out, and press.

4. Pin both edges of the waistband to the outside of the garment, matching notches and markings.

5. Serge the waistline seam, with garment side up. Press the seam toward the garment.

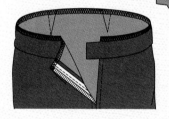

32-10 Finishing Facing Ends

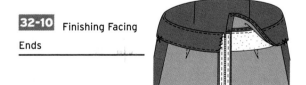

WAISTLINE CASING

A casing can be made at the waistline edge of a garment or within a garment. Use it with either elastic or a drawstring. (See Lesson 19 on page 527.)

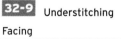

Applying Bias Bindings

A STRIP OF FABRIC CUT on the true bias is used to make **bias bindings**. When attached to the edge of a garment or other item, they cover the raw edge and create decorative trimming. Because bias bindings are flexible, they can be used on curved as well as straight edges.

Bias bindings have a number of uses: as a substitute for the facing or hem on a neckline, armhole, or hemline; as an edge finish for placemats, pillows, backpacks, wall hangings, and other items; and as piping or tubing for trim, loops, ties, shoulder straps, and belts.

The pattern guide sheet gives cutting and stitching directions for self-fabric bindings. The pattern envelope may list single-fold or double-fold bias tape to use as binding. Sometimes fold-over braid trim can also be used. Ready-made bindings come in different widths and colors to match or contrast with your fabric.

CUTTING BIAS STRIPS

The method you use to cut bias strips depends on the length you need. The two methods are described here.

Continuous Bias-Strip Method

Use this method to create long bias strips:

1. Cut a square or rectangular piece of fabric.
2. Fold one corner on the true bias by matching the crosswise grain to the lengthwise grain. Cut the fabric along the fold line. See *Fig. 33-1.*

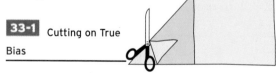

33-1 Cutting on True Bias

3. Mark parallel lines the desired width for the bias strip on the wrong side of the fabric. Unless the pattern states otherwise, use a 1½-inch (3.8-cm) width. Cut away the remaining fabric. See *Fig. 33-2.*

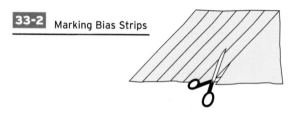

33-2 Marking Bias Strips

4. Pin the fabric, right sides together, to form a tube. Be sure one strip width extends beyond the edge at each end of the tube.
5. Stitch a ¼-inch (6-mm) seam and press open.
6. Cut along the marked line at one end to create a continuous bias strip of fabric. See *Fig. 33-3.*

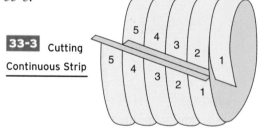

33-3 Cutting Continuous Strip

Cut-and-Piece, Bias-Strip Method

For smaller lengths, you can cut individual strips and stitch them together.

1. Fold the fabric diagonally, matching crosswise grain to lengthwise grain, to find the true bias.
2. Mark the bias strips on the wrong side of the fabric. Cut apart. See *Fig. 33-4.*

33-4 Cutting Bias Strips

3. Pin the ends of the strips, right sides together, matching the straight grain. Strips will form a right angle. See *Fig. 33-5.*

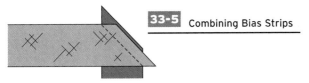
33-5 Combining Bias Strips

4. Stitch a ¼-inch (6-mm) seam along the straight grain of the fabric. Press the seam open. See *Fig. 33-6.*

33-6 Pressed Seam

ATTACHING BINDING

Bias strips can be attached with a one-step or two-step method. Always follow the directions in the pattern guide sheet. Special techniques create smooth curves and sharp corners.

One-Step Method

Use the one-step method to attach double-fold bias tape and fold-over braid, which have one edge folded slightly wider than the other. Slip the binding over the edge of the fabric and stitch in place with one row of machine stitching.

1. Trim away the seam allowance from the edge to be bound.
2. Slip the binding over the raw edge with the wider edge on the wrong side of the garment. Turn the ends under, overlapping if necessary, and pin.
3. Machine-stitch close to the edge of the binding through all layers. See *Fig. 33-7.*

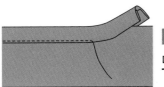
33-7 Attaching Double-Fold Bias Tape

Two-Step Method

Use the two-step method for single-fold bias tape and bias strips you cut yourself. The pattern gives directions for cutting self-fabric strips. Usually the bias strip is four times the finished binding width. After stitching one edge of the binding to the fabric, fold the binding over the fabric edge and stitch again by machine or hand.

1. Trim away the seam allowances from the fabric edge.
2. Pin the edge of the binding to the fabric, with right sides together.
3. Stitch an equal distance from the edge, according to pattern directions. See *Fig. 33-8.* For single-fold bias tape, stitch along the crease line of the binding.

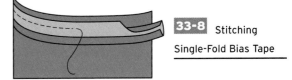
33-8 Stitching Single-Fold Bias Tape

4. Turn the binding over the seam allowance and pin.
5. Slip-stitch or machine-stitch in place. See *Fig. 33-9.*

33-9 Stitching Tape in Place
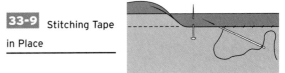

Alternative: stitch the binding to the wrong side of the garment. Flip the binding to the right side of the garment and edgestitch in place.

Stitching Curves

Pre-shape the binding with a steam iron before stitching to the fabric.

1. Lay the tape on top of the pattern piece, shaping to fit the curve.
2. Press with steam to shrink out excess fullness and prevent puckers. See *Fig. 33-10.*

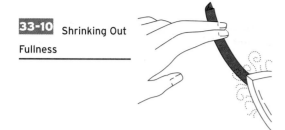

33-10 Shrinking Out Fullness

Stitching Outward Corners

1. Stitch the binding to one edge, ending exactly where the seam lines meet. See *Fig. 33-11*.

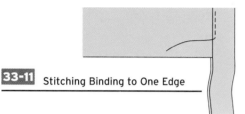

33-11 Stitching Binding to One Edge

2. Fold the binding diagonally at the corner, forming a neat diagonal fold, or miter, on both sides of the binding at the corner. Pin the binding along the other edge of the fabric. See *Fig. 33-12*.

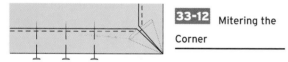

33-12 Mitering the Corner

3. Stitch the binding, starting at the corner and continuing along the other edge. For the two-step method, finish by stitching the inside edge of the binding in place. For wider bindings, edgestitch or slip-stitch along the mitered folds to secure. See *Fig. 33-13*.

33-13 Edgestitching a Mitered Corner

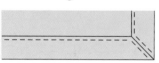

Stitching Inward Corners

1. Reinforce the corner with small machine stitches.
2. Clip into the corner. See *Fig. 33-14*.
3. To finish, choose one of the following:

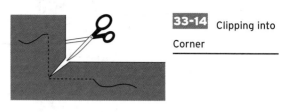

33-14 Clipping into Corner

For the one-step method. Slip the binding over one edge and stitch to the clip. Form a neat miter at the corner. Slip the binding over the other edge and continue stitching. See *Fig. 33-15*. Edgestitch along the mitered fold if necessary. See *Fig. 33-16*.

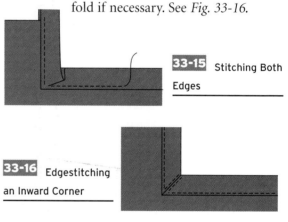

33-15 Stitching Both Edges

33-16 Edgestitching an Inward Corner

For the two-step method. Stitch the binding to the edge up to the clip. Spread the fabric at the clipped corner to form a straight edge and continue stitching. See *Fig. 33-17*. Fold the binding over the edge, mitering the corner. Finish by stitching the inside edge by hand or machine. See *Fig. 33-18*.

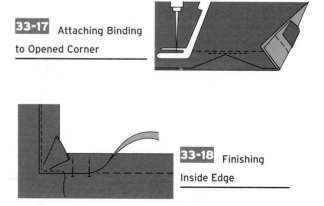

33-17 Attaching Binding to Opened Corner

33-18 Finishing Inside Edge

PIPING

Piping accents the seam line or outer edge of a garment. This narrow band of fabric stitched into a seam is sometimes used around a neckline, at the edge of a collar or cuff, or along a yoke seam.

1. Cut a bias strip of fabric twice as wide as the finished piping, plus 1¼ inches (3.2 cm) for seam allowances.
2. Fold and press the strip lengthwise, with wrong sides together.
3. Pin the piping to the garment's right side, with cut edges even.
4. Machine-baste just inside the seam line in the seam allowance. See *Fig. 33-19.* Clip the seam allowance of the piping around curves.
5. Pin and stitch the seam. See *Fig. 33-20.*

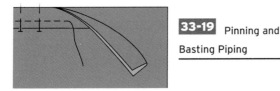

33-19 Pinning and Basting Piping

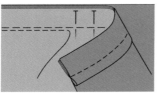

33-20 Pinning and Stitching Seam

Corded Piping

Piping can encase cable cord to create a thicker trim.

1. Fold a bias strip over cable cord, with the cording on the inside of the fabric.
2. Stitch as close as possible to the cord, using a zipper foot. See *Fig. 33-21.*

33-21 Stitching Close to Cording

3. Pin the corded piping to the garment's right side so the stitching rests on top of the seam line.
4. Machine-baste just inside the stitching line in the seam allowance. Clip around curves.
5. Pin and stitch the seam line, working with the corded section on top so you can see the basting stitches. Use a zipper foot. Place the stitches up close to the cord so the basting stitches are in the seam allowance. See *Fig. 33-22.*

33-22 Stitching Corded Seam

TUBING

Tubing is a strip of fabric stitched and turned right side out so the seam allowances are inside the tube. Use it for straps, loops, and belts.

1. Cut a bias strip of fabric two times the finished width of tubing plus seam allowances.
2. Fold the fabric in half lengthwise, with right sides together.
3. Stitch, stretching the bias slightly as you sew. At the end, slant the stitches out toward the raw edge to make the tube easier to turn. See *Fig. 33-23.*

33-23 Stitching Tubing

4. Trim the seam allowances the same width as the tubing. For heavier fabrics, trim the seam allowances closer to the stitching.
5. Turn the tubing by attaching a heavy thread to the wide end of the seam. Pull, using a large needle, bodkin, or loop turner. See *Fig. 33-24* on page 578.

Tubing

Tubing can be made easily on the serger.

1. Serge a thread chain at least 2 inches (5 cm) longer than the bias strip. Run your fingers along the chain to tighten the stitches.

2. Pull the chain around to the front of the presser foot and center it lengthwise on the right side of the bias strip. Fold the strip so the cut edges meet and the chain is next to the fold.

3. Serge the raw edges together, being careful not to cut the inside chain. Remove the strip from the serger.

4. Pull gently on the thread tail to turn the tubing right side out.

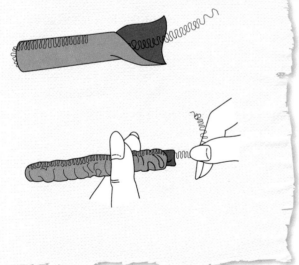

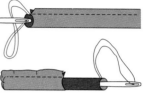

33-24 Turning Tubing

Corded Tubing

Corded tubing is filled with cable cord for added fullness and strength.

1. Cut a bias strip wide enough to fit around the cord plus seam allowances.

2. Cut the cording twice the length of the bias strip plus 1 inch (2.5 cm).

3. Fold the bias strip over one end of the cord, with right sides together and edges even.

4. Stitch across the cord and bias strip at the center of the cording.

5. Stitch the long edge close to the cord, stretching the bias slightly, using a zipper foot. Trim the seam allowances. See *Fig. 33-25*.

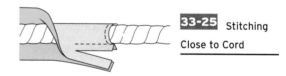

33-25 Stitching Close to Cord

6. Turn the right side out by gently pulling the fabric down over the cord and working the fabric along with your hands. See *Fig. 33-26*. Trim off any excess cording.

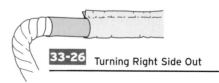

33-26 Turning Right Side Out

Adding Ruffles

RUFFLES DECORATE GARMENTS, accessories, and home decorating items. They can accent the edge of a neckline, collar, cuff, or hem. See *Fig. 34-1*. They also decorate curtains and pillows and form the dust ruffle around a bed.

 **34-1** Decorative Ruffles

The amount of fullness built into a ruffle depends on the ruffle's width. To keep them from looking skimpy, wide ruffles need more fullness than narrow ones.

The two basic ruffles you'll learn to make are straight and circular.

STRAIGHT RUFFLES

A straight ruffle is made from a straight strip of fabric that is gathered along one edge and stitched into a seam or to a fabric edge. Straight ruffles can also be gathered down the center or off-center and stitched to the outside of a garment or curtain.

The outer edge of a ruffle can be finished with a narrow hem stitched by hand or machine. On lightweight and sheer fabrics, the ruffle may be cut twice the desired width and folded lengthwise to create a double thickness.

Follow these steps to make a straight ruffle:

1. Cut a straight piece of fabric that is two to three times the length of the edge or area to which the ruffle will be stitched.
2. Stitch and gather the ruffle along the upper edge. See *Fig. 34-2*.

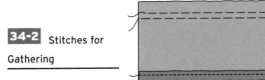 **34-2** Stitches for Gathering

3. Pin the ruffle to the edge of the garment, adjusting fullness evenly.
4. Stitch the ruffle in place, with the ruffle on top to prevent stitching tucks into the seam. See *Fig. 34-3*.

34-3 Stitching Ruffle

You can cover the gathering stitches on double-edge ruffles by putting a trim, such as rickrack, on top of the stitches. See *Fig. 34-4*.

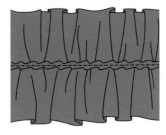 **34-4** Attaching Rickrack to Double-Edge Ruffle

CIRCULAR RUFFLES

Stitching two or more circles of fabric together creates a circular ruffle. The ruffle fits smoothly along the edge joined to the garment and ripples softly on the outer edge of the ruffle.

1. Cut out circles, following the directions on the pattern.

Serging Techniques

Ruffles

Use the serger to finish the outer edge of a ruffle with a narrow rolled hem. Then use a serger stitch to attach a straight ruffle or a circular ruffle to the garment.

2. Stitch the circles together, with narrow seams, to form the ruffle. Finish the outer edge of the ruffle with a narrow hem. (Sometimes the ruffle is cut as two layers and stitched together at the outer edge. Then it is trimmed, clipped, and turned right side out.)

3. Stay-stitch the inner edge of the ruffle ½ inch (1.3 cm) from the edge. Clip up to the stay-stitching. See *Fig. 34-5*.

34-5 Stay-Stitching and Clipping Inner Edge

4. Stay-stitch the garment edge to prevent stretching.

5. Pin and stitch the ruffle to the garment, right sides together. Press the seam allowances flat, and trim.

6. Finish the inside edge with facing or a double row of stitching. See *Fig. 34-6*.

34-6 Attaching Ruffle to Garment

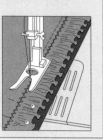

Adding Trims

T RIMS COME IN MANY shapes, sizes, and colors. Rickrack, braid, ribbon, lace, eyelet, piping, and fringe are all examples of trims. Fabric appliqués can also be used for trimming.

Trims should be coordinated to the design of a project and its fabric. Be sure the trim you select can be washed or dry-cleaned in the same manner as the fabric that will hold the trim. Preshrink washable trims by soaking them in hot water for 30 minutes. You can leave them wrapped around the cardboard, which should be bent slightly to allow for any shrinkage. Let them dry before using.

Three basic methods allow you to apply trim: the flat method, edging method, and inserted method.

FLAT METHOD

The flat method can be used with any trim that is finished on both sides, such as braid, ribbon, and rickrack. Use narrow trims for curved areas. Before stitching in place, shape the trim by pressing it with a steam iron. Then follow these steps to apply the trim:

1. Pin the trim along the placement line.
2. Stitch along one edge, both edges, or through the center. Rickrack should be stitched with a straight row of stitching down the center. See *Fig. 35-1.*

 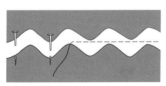

35-1 Attaching Rickrack

3. Miter the corners by stitching the outside edge up to the corner. Lift the presser foot, pivot, and continue stitching in the new direction. Fold the trim diagonally at the corner and pin. See *Fig. 35-2.*
4. Stitch the inside edge of the trim. Stitch the mitered fold, if necessary. See *Fig. 35-3.*

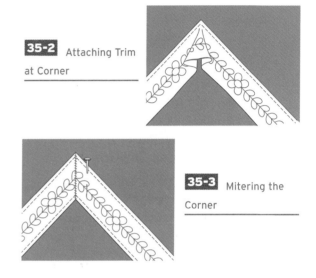

35-2 Attaching Trim at Corner

35-3 Mitering the Corner

EDGING METHOD

Use the edging method for trims with only one finished edge, such as piping, gathered lace, gathered eyelet, and fringe. The trim can be stitched to the edge of a garment or inserted into a seam.

To stitch the trim to the edge of the garment, follow these steps:

1. Pin the trim along the edge or seam line, with right sides together. Be sure the trim is toward the garment.
2. Stitch close to the trim, using a zipper foot if necessary. See *Fig. 35-4.*

 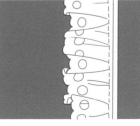

35-4 Stitching Close to Trim

3. Finish the edge by turning the seam allowance to the inside and topstitching

Trims

You can use the serger to apply a straight-edge trim, such as lace, to the edge of a garment.

1. Trim the edge of the garment so there is a $\frac{5}{8}$-inch (1.5-cm) seam or hem allowance.

2. Place the lace and fabric right sides together, with the straight edge of the lace $\frac{1}{2}$ inch (1.3 cm) from the raw edge of the fabric. Pin or use a glue stick to hold the lace in place.

3. Serge with the lace side up, using a two-thread or three-thread serger stitch, a flatlock stitch, or a rolled hemstitch. Keep the edge of the trim slightly to the left of the knife. Press the seam allowance toward the garment.

A serger can also be used to insert lace with two straight edges. Use either a flatlock stitch or a rolled hemstitch. For the flatlock method, place the lace and fabric right sides together. For the rolled-hem method, place them wrong sides together. After serging, open out the garment section so the lace lies flat; press.

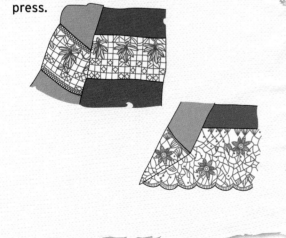

through all thicknesses. See *Fig. 35-5*. You can also finish the edge with a facing.

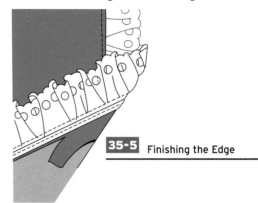

35-5 Finishing the Edge

To stitch trim into a seam, place the other section of fabric on top of the trim, with right sides together. Stitch the seam and trim in one step. See *Fig. 35-6*.

35-6 Stitching Trim into Seam

INSERTED METHOD

The inserted method works well on any straight section of a garment, such as down the front of a shirt or blouse or around the bottom of a jacket or skirt. It cannot be used for curved areas. Choose flat trims, such as lace or eyelet. Follow these steps:

1. Cut the fabric along the placement line.

2. Turn under each fabric edge $\frac{1}{2}$ the width of the exposed trim. Press the edges. See *Fig. 35-7*.

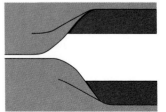

35-7 Turning Fabric Edges Under

3. Place the flat trim under the folded edges of fabric.
4. Edgestitch through all thicknesses. See *Fig. 35-8.*

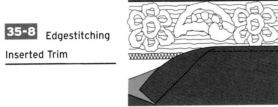

35-8 Edgestitching Inserted Trim

FINISHING ENDS

Several methods are possible for finishing the ends of trims to create a neat appearance.

- Stitch the trim to the fabric before stitching the seams so the ends will be hidden in the seam. See *Fig. 35-9.*

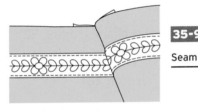

35-9 Ends Hidden in Seam

- Turn the ends to the wrong side and slip-stitch. See *Fig. 35-10.*

35-10 Slip-Stitching on Wrong Side

- Taper the ends into the seam line. See *Fig. 35-11.*

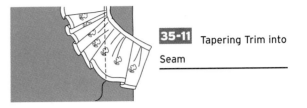

35-11 Tapering Trim into Seam

- For overlapping ends, fold one end under ¼ inch (6 mm). Overlap the folded end and stitch in place. See *Fig. 35-12.*

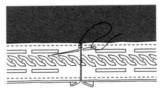

35-12 Overlapping Ends

- For heavy trims, fold both ends under ¼ inch (6 mm), so the ends just meet. Stitch in place. See *Fig. 35-13.*

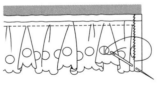

35-13 Joining Folded Trim Ends

PART 5

Review

SUMMARY

- Special seams can enclose a seam allowance or create a decorative effect. (Lesson 24)

- Tucks and pleats control fullness or add design interest. (Lesson 25)

- Interfacings and linings help shape and support the outer fabric. (Lessons 26 and 27)

- The four basic collars are flat, rolled, shirt, and standing. (Lesson 28)

- The three basic sleeves are set in, raglan, and kimono. They can be finished with a hem, facing, casing, or cuff. (Lessons 29 and 30)

- Three popular pocket styles are in-seam, patch, and front hip. (Lesson 31)

- A waistline can be finished with a waistband, facing, or casing. (Lesson 32)

- Some garments are trimmed with bias binding. Others are decorated with ruffles or trims. (Lessons 33, 34, and 35)

RECALLING THE FACTS

1. Why might you use a flat-felled seam instead of a French seam? (Lesson 24)

2. Why are seams sometimes topstitched? (Lesson 24)

3. What is the difference between tucks and pleats? (Lesson 25)

4. What should you do before applying fusible interfacing to garment sections? (Lesson 26)

5. What should you consider when choosing lining fabric? (Lesson 27)

6. Describe four basic collars. (Lesson 28)

7. To which side of a collar is interfacing usually applied? (Lesson 28)

8. How can you make crisp, sharp points on a collar? (Lesson 28)

9. Describe three basic sleeves. (Lesson 29)

10. Why is a kimono sleeve easy to sew? (Lesson 29)

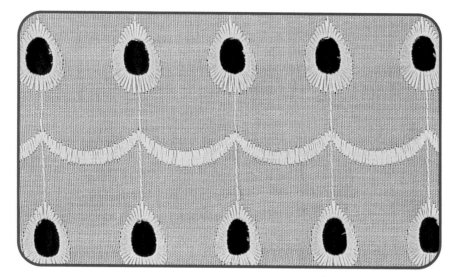

and Activities

11. Describe three basic cuffs. (Lesson 30)

12. Why is a placket added to a sleeve? (Lesson 30)

13. How do you miter the corners on a pocket? (Lesson 31)

14. How is the direction of a waistband overlap determined? (Lesson 32)

15. What are bias bindings? (Lesson 33)

16. What is the difference between piping and tubing? (Lesson 33)

17. How do straight and circular ruffles differ? (Lesson 34)

18. Describe the three methods used to apply trims. (Lesson 35)

APPLYING KNOWLEDGE

1. **Construction features.** Look at actual garments or photos from magazines and catalogs. Identify such construction features as tucks; pleats; waistbands; and varied styles of collars, sleeves, plackets, cuffs, pockets, and bias bindings.

2. **Decorative trims.** Using fashion magazines and catalogs, collect photos that show decorative trims used on garments. Describe the construction method used to apply each trim.

3. **Samples.** Sew samples of the following: self-finished seams, decorative seams, tucks, pleats, bias bindings, tubing, and trims. Make mini-samples of a flat or rolled collar, set-in sleeve, cuff, in-seam pocket, patch pocket, waistband, and ruffle. How might you improve your samples?

4. **Project.** Construct a garment that has a collar, sleeves, and pockets. Evaluate each of the special sewing techniques used in the project.

5. **Serging.** If a serger is available, use it to stitch a sample collar, sleeve, pocket, or waistband.

CREATIVE SOLUTIONS

A student in clothing class is making an outfit for a young family member who is nearly two years old. She wants to use her creativity to give the garment a unique look and is willing to take the time and make the effort to do something special.

Think Creatively

While talking with you about her sewing project, the student asks whether you have ideas about her project's design. What might you suggest?

GLOSSARY

Chapter numbers and Sewing and Serging Handbook part numbers are shown in parentheses. These indicate where terms are located.

A

abrasion. Worn spot that can develop when fibers rub against something. (11)

absorbent. Able to take moisture. (11)

adaptive design. Type of design that reduces the effort needed to put on and take off garments and promotes independence for people with disabilities. (21)

adornment. Decorations that express uniqueness and creativity and bring admiration and recognition. (1)

agitator. Center post in a top-loading washing machine; jiggles clothes during the wash and rinse cycles to loosen dirt and get out soil. (15)

alterations. Modifications that change a garment in some way. (19)

application form. Information document filled out by a job applicant for a potential employer. (22)

appliqué. Cutout pieces of fabric applied as a decoration. (16)

appropriate. Suitable; for clothing, suitable or acceptable to wear. (2)

aptitude. Natural talent and capacity for learning particular skills. (22)

arbitration. Settlement of a dispute by a person or panel that hears each party and issues a decision. (20)

assembly line. System by which each worker specializes in a certain task in order to manufacture a product; items pass from worker to worker for step-by-step completion. (8)

asymmetrical. Design of a garment with visually different sides; balanced by design elements with various visual "weights." (10)

atelier (a-tul-YAY). Designer's workroom. (7)

avant-garde (ah-vahn-GARD). Ahead of fashion (French). (6)

B

balance. One of the five design principles; concerns whether the spaces on both sides of a central line, real or imagined, appear equal. (10)

balance of trade. Comparison of the value of a country's imports and exports. (25)

barter. Trading goods, services, ideas, and techniques without the use of money. (5)

bias bindings. Cover raw edges and create decorative trims when sewing a garment; made from a fabric strip cut on true bias. (Part 5)

blends. Yarns that are made with a combination of different fibers. (12)

bobbin. Sewing machine accessory that holds the bottom thread in the machine. (Part 2)

body language. Nonverbal messages, consisting of eye contact, facial expressions, posture, arm and leg positions, and distance from others. (4)

bolts. Rolls of fabric. (Part 1)

boutique. Specialty store that features very fashionable or unique designs. (17)

budget. Plan or schedule used by an individual or family to control spending and cover all expenses. (3)

C

career path. Series of related jobs within a field of work. (22)

casing. Closed tunnel of fabric that holds a piece of elastic or a drawstring inside. (Part 4)

cellulose. Main component of such plants as cotton and flax; produced by dissolving the fibrous inner bark of mulberry trees. (5)

chain. Large retail company with stores in many cities and towns all over the country. (8)

classics. Certain styles that stay in fashion for a long time. (6)

clipping. Making tiny clips, or snips, in the seam allowance every ¼ to ½ inch (6 to 12 mm). (Part 4)

collection. Group of clothes designed and produced by a designer for a specific season. (7)

colorfast. Fabric that doesn't fade, whether it's been washed or exposed to chlorine or sunlight. (13)

color scheme. Plan for using a color or a combination of colors to decorate a room or put together an outfit. (9)

comparison shopping. Looking at the quality, price, and usefulness of similar items to find the best value for your money. (18)

complementary colors. Colors that are directly opposite each other on the color wheel. (9)

compromise. Helpful communication tool when resolving disagreements; settlement comes through give-and-take. (3, 19)

computer-aided design (CAD). Software programs used to create fashion designs; take the place of hand sketching. (7)

conformity. When an individual complies with certain standards, attitudes, or practices followed by the group. (4)

consignment shop. Shop that sells garments supplied by multiple sellers; pays the seller a percentage of the selling price after selling. (16)

contractors. Companies that specialize in sewing certain garments, according to a manufacturer's designs and specifications and for a specific price. (8)

converters. Companies or individuals who serve as middle agents between textile mills and apparel manufacturers. (8)

copy. Words and sentences used in advertising to help promote a product; in fashion, communicates a fashion message. (8)

cost per wearing. Method of determining what each wearing of a garment costs; computed by adding purchase price to the cleaning costs and dividing by the number of wearings. (19)

counterfeit. Items (in fashion, garments and accessories) made with unauthorized use of registered trade names or trademarks. (25)

couture (koo-TOOR). Designing, making, and selling of high-fashion clothing; French word for dressmaking. (7)

couturiers (koo-TOOR-ee-ays). Designers who make fashionable, custom-made clothes. (7)

cover letter. Introductory letter that requests a meeting or interview with a potential employer and shows a person's written communication skills, as well as personality. (22)

cowl. Softly draped neckline on dress or blouse. (6)

creativity. Ability to use imagination to come up with an original idea or product. (17)

credit card. Purchasing method that allows the cardholder to buy and receive merchandise, but pay for it later. (20)

croquis (kro-KEY). Preliminary fashion design sketch. (7)

culture. Collected ideas, skills, beliefs, and institutions of a society at a particular time in history. (2)

customs. Long-established practices that regulate social life in a community of people. (2)

cutting layout. Diagram that shows how to arrange pattern pieces on fabric when sewing a garment. (Part 3)

D

darts. Triangular folds of fabric stitched to a point when sewing a garment. (Part 4)

debit card. Used to make a money payment; amount transfers electronically from a person's checking account to the store's account via computer. (20)

decorative seams. Special effects made with topstitching or cording when sewing a garment. (Part 5)

delegate. To assign responsibilities to another person. (3)

department store. Large store with merchandise grouped into areas according to specialty. (17)

design ease. Extra fullness built into clothes by the designer to create a particular style or silhouette. (Part 1)

detergents. Cleaning agents that remove soil from fabric and prevent it from returning. (15)

differential feed. Two sets of feed dogs on a sewing machine; move the fabric through the machine at different speeds. (Part 2)

disability. Condition that hinders a person's functioning in some way. (21)

discount store. Store where merchandise is sold at less than full retail price. (17)

domestic. For any country, the products that originate there and the companies that reside there. (25)

draping. Arranging fabric into graceful folds and attractive lines. (7)

dress code. Set of rules that describe acceptable or required clothing. (2)

dry cleaning. Process that uses special liquids containing organic solvents to clean fabrics without water. (15)

dyes. Compounds that color fabrics. (13)

E

easing. Allows fabric being sewn to be shaped over a curved area of the body. (Part 4)

economical. Describes purchasing techniques that help a person save money. (17)

emphasis. One of the five design principles; focal point of a design; draws attention. (10)

entrepreneur (AHN-truh-pruh-NUR). Someone who organizes and manages his or her own business. (24)

entry-level job. Job requiring little or no special training or experience; where learning on the job is typical. (22)

enzymes. Special proteins that control chemical activity. (14)

ethics. Moral principles and values that guide a person's actions. (23)

expectations. As related to clothing, thoughts about what is reasonable for people to wear. (2)

exports. Products sent out from one country to others. (25)

F

fabric care symbols. Symbols on garment labels that show in a visual way the special care needed for fabrics. (14)

fabric key. Shows how shading and texture indicate the right and wrong sides of fabric and any interfacing or lining; located on a pattern guide sheet. (Part 3)

facings. Finish a raw edge on a garment, such as a neckline or armhole. (19, Part 4)

fad. Fashion that is very popular for a short time. (6)

family life cycle. Basic stages through which a family goes during its existence. (3)

fashion. Style that is popular at a given time. (6)

fashion cycle. "Life-time" of each fashion; has four stages: introduction, growth, maturity, and decline.

fashion merchandising. Critical component of fashion industry; retailers display, advertise, promote, and sell items, choosing techniques they hope will entice people to buy. (8)

fashion promotion. All the efforts to inform people about what's new in fashion and to convince them to buy. (8)

feed dog. Teeth on a sewing machine that move the fabric under the presser foot, advancing the fabric one stitch at a time. (Part 2)

fiber. Basic unit that makes fabric. (11)

filament yarns. Yarns made entirely of filament fibers, which are the long, continuous fibers measured in yards or meters. (12)

filling yarns. Crosswise yarns in fabric. (12)

finance charge. Fee added for use of credit. (20)

finishes. Special treatments applied to improve a fabric's appearance, texture, or performance. (13)

flexibility. Willingness to adapt to new opportunities and situations. (23)

forecasting services. Services that predict color, fabric, and fashion trends two or more years in advance. (8)

franchise. Right to sell a company's goods or services in a given area. (24)

freelance. Selling work or services without earning a regular salary from any employer; freelancers charge by the job or the hour. (24)

free trade. Movement of goods that are not restricted by tariffs or quotas between countries. (25)

fusible webs. Network of bondable fibers used to hold two layers of fabric together. (Part 1)

G

gathers. Soft folds of fabric formed by pulling up basting stitches to make the fabric fit into a smaller space. (Part 4)

generic name. Fiber name for a general classification of fibers of similar composition. (11)

global sourcing. When a company manufactures or purchases goods at a lower cost in another country of the world. (25)

grading. To trim each layer of the seam allowance to a different width to reduce bulk. (Part 4)

grain. Direction that yarns run in woven fabric. (12)

gray goods. Name for fabric that lacks color when it first comes from the loom. (13)

guide sheet. Step-by-step information for cutting, marking, and sewing fabric pieces together. (Part 3)

H

harmony. One of five design principles; a visual effect created when design elements complement each other. (10)

haute couture (oht koo-TOOR). Dressmaking industry that creates the most fashionable, expensive, and exclusive designer clothing. (7)

heading. Width of fabric between the casing and the edge of a garment; may be included when sewing casing. (Part 4)

heritage. Cultural background and ethnic traditions handed down from ancestors. (2)

hidden costs. Expenses for customer carelessness, theft, and returns; included in the price of merchandise. (20)

hues. Precise way to describe colors, using the specific names that identify them, such as red, green, and blue. (9)

I-J

image ads. Advertisements that use emotional appeals to tempt a consumer to buy. (18)

imports. Goods that come into a country from foreign countries. (25)

impression. Image that forms in the minds of others. (4)

impulse buying. Making unplanned purchases; often not based on knowledge and reasoning. (18)

individuality. Total combination of characteristics that set one person apart from another. (4)

Industrial Revolution. Period in history characterized by rapid changes that resulted from the invention of power-driven machines. (5)

information ads. Advertisements that include information about the product. (18)

initiative. Desire and willingness to plan and carry out a task. (23)

inseam. Inside leg measurement on pants, from the crotch to the hemmed edge. (19)

intensity. Brightness or dullness of a color. (9)

interfacing. Piece of fabric placed between the outer fabric and facing to prevent stretching, add shape, or add crispness to a certain area. (Part 1)

intermediate color. Combination of a primary color with a neighboring secondary color on the color wheel. (9)

interview. Meeting with potential employer to discuss the details of the job and the qualifications of the applicant. (22)

inventory. List of items on hand, as in products in a store or garments in a wardrobe. (17)

ironing. Process of removing wrinkles from clothes with an iron, using heat, slight pressure, and possibly moisture with a gliding, back-and-forth motion. (15)

K

kimono sleeve. Sleeve style that is cut in one piece along with the garment front and back. (6)

knitting. Looping yarns together to make fabric. (12)

knock-offs. Less expensive versions of high-fashion design. (7)

L

laundering. Washing fabric by hand or machine with a soil-removing product. (15)

leadership. Ability to guide or influence others. (23)

licensing. Giving legal permission to use your name to promote a product. (7)

line. One of the five design elements; series of points connected to form a narrow path. (10) Designer's clothing collection. (8)

lining. Fabric used to finish the inside of a garment; constructed separately and then joined at one or more major seams. (Part 1)

lockstitch. Type of stitch that does not pull out or unravel when a loop or loose thread is pulled. (Part 2)

logo. Identifying symbol of manufacturer. (18)

loopers. Two parts of a serger (upper and lower loopers) that hold the threads; like the bobbin on a sewing machine. (Part 2)

luster. Fabric sheen created by the amount of reflected light. (11)

M

management process. Useful tool that helps people plan how to use resources to achieve goals. (3)

mandatory. Required by law. (18)

manufactured fibers. "Test tube" fibers developed during scientific experimentation. (11)

market week. Time when designers and manufacturers introduce their new fashion lines. (8)

marketing. Aspect of fashion industry concerned with developing, promoting, and selling products. (8)

mass-produced. Making many garments at the same time, with machines doing most of the work. (8)

maternity clothes. Clothes designed for wear by pregnant women. (21)

media. Method of communicating messages to a large audience, as through magazine and television advertising. (1)

mediation. Settling a dispute with the help of a neutral third party. (20)

mentor. Advisor or role model, often on job. (23)

microfibers. Extremely thin fibers recently developed through fiber research. (11)

mitered. Made to fit together with a precise right angle at the corner; makes sharp corners and eliminates bulk when sewing garments. (Part 5)

modesty. Belief about the proper way to cover the body with clothes. (1)

money order. Purchased document stating that money is to be paid to a particular person or store named on the form. (20)

multiple roles. More than one role, including inside and outside the family, such as son, volunteer, and student. (3)

multisized. Printed with several sizes on the same pattern tissue. (Part 1)

N

nap. Soft and fuzzy surface on a fabric; created by raised, short fiber ends. (13)

natural fibers. Fibers that come from natural sources, such as plants and animals. (11)

networking. Talking to people to get information or advice, often about jobs. (22)

nonverbal messages. Communication without words. (4)

notching. Cutting out tiny wedge-shaped pieces of fabric from the seam allowances to remove bulk and make seams lie smooth. (Part 4)

notions. Small items that become a permanent part of the garment, such as thread and seam tape. (Part 1)

O

off-grain. When crosswise yarns in fabric are not at right angles to lengthwise yarns. (Part 3)

off-price retailers. Stores that sell brand-name and designer merchandise at reduced prices. (17)

off-shore production. When domestic companies manufacture merchandise in foreign countries. (25)

OSHA. Occupational Safety and Health Administration; government organization that establishes, revises, and enforces safety and health standards for workers. (25)

outlet. Stores that sell only the brands produced by the designer, manufacturer, or factory that owns the store. (17)

overlock seam. Special combination of stitches that join the fabric and finish the seam edges in one sewing operation; creates a narrow seam allowance and prevents fraying. (19)

P

parliamentary procedure. Way of conducting a meeting properly and leading group discussions in an orderly way. (23)

patchwork. Sewing craft in which small fabric shapes are sewn together to create a new, decorative fabric. (16)

pattern. Contains all the instructions needed for constructing a sewing project. (Part 1)

peer group. Group of people with a similar background, social status, and age. (1)

peer pressure. Peer group's push to conform. (4)

personality. Individual's unique combination of mental, emotional, and social qualities. (4)

pigments. Substances that are in items and that absorb some light rays and reflect others, causing the items to be seen in varying colors. (9)

pile. Raised surface of loops or yarn ends on fabric. (12)

pill. When tiny balls of fiber form on fabric. (11)

piping. Narrow band of fabric stitched into a seam to accent the seam line or outer edge of a garment. (Part 5)

placket. Finished slit in fabric at the wrist, neck, or waist of a garment to make it easier to put on and take off. (Part 5)

pleats. Folds of fabric, which are wider than tucks and stitched or pressed in place. (Part 5)

ply. Identifies the number of yarn strands twisted together to make a thicker yarn; ply yarns may have two or more single yarns twisted together. (12)

portfolio. Set of drawings, photos, written articles, and samples that exemplify a person's work or skills; useful for presentation when seeking a job. (22)

preshrinking. To cause a fabric to contract in order to prevent or minimize shrinkage after the finished garment is washed or dry-cleaned. (Part 3)

presser foot. Holds the fabric against the feed dog on a sewing machine. (Part 2)

pressing. When iron is lowered to the fabric, then raised up and lowered to a different spot; often used for touch-up pressing. (14, Part 4)

pret-a-porter (PRET-a-por-TAY). Deluxe, ready-to-wear, French fashion collections; more practical and less expensive than couture. (7)

pretreating. Method of cleaning heavily soiled area on fabric just before laundering in order to give it extra attention. (14)

prewash soil-and-stain remover. Substance that is effective in dissolving oily, greasy, or heavily soiled stains on fabric. (14)

primary colors. Three basic colors from which all other colors are made: red, yellow, and blue. (9)

printing. Transfer of color to the surface of a fabric to form a pattern. (13)

priorities. Ranking the importance of different items or options. (3)

prioritize. To rank items so you know which ones are most important. (17)

procrastinate. To put off doing something. (23)

profit. Amount of money remaining after subtracting the cost of goods or supplies and operating expenses from a business's income. (24)

proportion (scale). One of five design principles; describes how separate garment parts relate to each other and to the whole in size. (10)

prosthesis (prahs-THEE-sus). Artificial device used to replace a limb on the human body. (21)

punctuality. Arriving on time. (23)

Q

quality. Superior characteristics; in fashion, good fabric and good workmanship. (19)

quota. Set amount of specific merchandise that a country's government allows to be imported. (25)

R

raglan sleeve. Sleeve style formed with a front and back diagonal seam that extends from the neckline to the underarm. (6)

ready-to-wear. Clothing made in advance for sale to any purchaser. (5)

recalled. When notice is given by a manufacturer that a product needs to be returned for repair or replacement. (20)

recycle. To reclaim items for another use; in interest of the environment. (16)

redesign. To change an existing garment to make it suitable for more wear. (16)

references. Names, addresses, and telephone numbers of people who will speak positively about your personal character and qualifications for a job. (22)

resale store. Store that specializes in used or secondhand clothing. (17)

resilient. Able to spring back into shape after crushing or wrinkling of fabric. (11)

resource. Means used to reach a goal or manage life. (3)

resourceful. Able to identify all the means and methods for accomplishing goals. (17)

résumé (REH-zuh-may). Detailed summary of a person's education, work experience, and job-related activities. (22)

retail. Sale of goods in small quantities to consumers. (8)

retro. Clothing style of an earlier time. (6)

rhythm. One of the five design principles; effect produced by design elements, carrying the eye through a regular repeated pattern. (10)

roles. Different positions people have in society, such as daughter, student, and employee. (2)

royalty. Fee and a percentage of profits; paid when licensing occurs in fashion industry. (7)

S

scissors. Cutting tool that is smaller than shears and with both handles the same shape. (Part 2)

seam allowance. Extra fabric inside the garment between the seam line and the fabric edge. (19)

seam finish. Any method that stitches or trims seam allowances to prevent fraying. (19)

secondary color. Combination of equal amounts of two primary colors on the color wheel. (9)

self-concept. Image you have of yourself. (4)

self-finished seams. Seams that enclose the seam allowances as the seam is stitched. (Part 5)

self-motivated. Able to set goals and work independently. (24)

selvage. Self-edge formed by the filling yarn when it turns to go back in the other direction as fabric is created; the two finished lengthwise edges of fabric. (12, Part 3)

set-in sleeve. Sleeve style created by joining the sleeve to the garment with an armhole seam that circles the arm near the shoulder. (6)

shade. Darker color that results when black is added to a color. (9)

shadowing. Accompanying a person at work to learn about job responsibilities. (22)

shape. One of five design elements; outline or silhouette of a garment, forms when one or more lines come together to enclose an area. (10)

shears. Cutting tool with long blades and two handles that are shaped differently. (Part 2)

shirring. Method of gathering fabric with several rows of gathers. (Part 4)

silhouette. Outline or shape of a garment that forms when one or more lines come together to enclose an area. (10)

sloper. A basic pattern that has been used successfully by a designer for a particular body shape; the basis for a new pattern design. (7)

snags. Loops of yarn that pull out of a fabric. (16)

society. Group of individuals who live together in a particular area, sometimes as a nation or community. (1)

solvent. Substance that dissolves another substance. (15)

sourcing. When a company chooses where to manufacture or purchase goods. (25)

space. One of the five design elements; area inside shape. (10)

specialty store. Store that carries limited line of merchandise, such as clothing, accessories, or fabrics. (17)

spool pins. Hold spools of thread on a sewing machine. (Part 2)

spun yarns. Yarns made of staple fibers, the short fibers measured in inches or centimeters. (12)

standards. Guidelines and principles that set forth what's suitable to wear. (2) Specific models of quality or performance against which products are judged. (20)

status. Person's position or rank within a group. (1)

status symbols. Items worn to give the wearer a special feeling of importance or wealth; may be names, initials, or symbols of fashion designers, sports figures, and other celebrities on clothes and accessories. (1)

stereotype. Simplified or standardized image of a person or group. (4)

stretch gauge. Guide on pattern; shows how much knit fabric must be able to stretch. (Part 1)

style. Characteristics that distinguish one particular item of clothing from another. (6)

sumptuary laws. Regulations that controlled what each social class could wear during the Middle Ages. (5)

sweatshops. Name applied to early clothing factories because of dark, airless, uncomfortable and unhealthful working conditions. (5)

symmetrical balance. Design of a garment that has identical spaces on each of two sides. (10)

T

take-up lever. Controls the amount of thread pulled from the spool to the needle for each stitch; moves up and down as you stitch on a sewing machine. (Part 2)

target audience. Specific group of potential customers. (24)

tariff. Tax on imported items. (25)

teamwork. Work done cooperatively, rather than individually, by several associates. (23)

technology. New developments brought about by increasing scientific knowledge. (5)

tensile strength. Ability to withstand tension or pulling. (11)

tension. Tightness of thread when sewing on a machine. (Part 2)

texture. Describes the surface characteristics that determine the look and feel of an object, such as fabric. (10)

texturing. Process using chemicals, heat, or special machinery to turn straight, rod-like filaments into coiled, looped, or crimped yarns. (12)

thread guides. Parts on a sewing machine that help guide upper thread from spool to needle without tangling. (Part 2)

tint. Lighter color that results when white is added to a color. (9)

toxic. Poisonous, as in the lead in paint, a special danger for young children who tend to put things in their mouth. (20)

trademark. Identifying mark used by manufacturer or retailer to distinguish its products from those of the competition. (18)

trade names. Names, as for fibers, registered as trademarks and protected by law. (11)

trade-off. Exchange of one item for another. (19)

tubing. Strip of fabric stitched and turned right side out so the seam allowances are inside the tube. (Part 5)

tucks. Folds of fabric that control fullness or add design interest. (Part 5)

tumble dry. Drying a garment in a tumble dryer at the specified setting—high, medium, low, or no heat. (14)

U

unit construction. Completing individual parts of a garment as fully as possible before sewing them together. (Part 4)

V

value. The degree of lightness or darkness of a color, which was created by the amount of white or black added. (9)

values. Person's or family's beliefs about what's important, desirable, or worthwhile. (1)

verbal messages. Communication that uses words. (4)

versatile. Having multiple capabilities or functions, as when a garment can be worn for more than one activity. (17)

vintage. Fashions from earlier decades. (17)

W

wardrobe plan. Guide for making future additions to a wardrobe. (17)

warp yarns. Yarns that run the length of a fabric. (12)

warranty. Manufacturer's pledge of assurance about a product's quality or performance. (18)

wearing ease. Amount of fullness needed for movement and comfort when wearing a garment. (Part 1)

weaving. Interlaces two yarns that are at right angles to each other. (12)

wholesale. Price paid by stores to manufacturers when buying goods to sell. (8)

X-Y-Z

yarns. Fibers twisted together or laid side by side. (12)

CREDITS

Interior Design: Bill Smith Studio
Cover Design: Bill Smith Studio
Cover Photography: Ken Karp

Special thanks to Art MacDillo's Gary Skillestad, Marshall Greenberg, Jeff Stoecker, and Jo-Ann Fabrics & Crafts for their assistance with art and photographs in the *Sewing and Serging Handbook.*

INDEX

S

Safety tips
in children's clothes, 362
with iron, 512
for sergers, 465
with sewing equipment, 473
for sewing machine, 463
with sewing machine, 519
Sailcloth, 231
Sailor collar, 105
Saint Lauren, Yves, 130, 408
Sales
evaluating, 329
types of, 328–29
Sales associate, 374
Sales promotions, 321–22
Sales representative, 74
Samples, making, 140
Sander, Jil, 118, 130
Sari, 38, 40
Sateen, 231
Satin, 231
Satin weave, 223
Scale, 185–86, 591
Scalloping shears, 474
Scheduling, 57
Schiaparelli, Elsa, 130
Scissors, 473, 474, 592
Screen printing, 237
Seam(s)
decorative, 548–50
pressing, 522
restitching, 287, 288
sewing special, 547–50
special treatments for, 520–22
stitching, 519–20
Seam allowance, 337, 592
Seam finish, 338, 523, 592
Seam gauge, 472
Seam ripper, 474
Seam roll, 477
Seam tape, 450
Seasonal colors, 167
Seasonal storage, 263
Secondary colors, 161, 592
Second-generation fibers, 204
Seconds, 329
Security, store, 346
Seersucker, 231
Selections, evaluating, 332–41
Self-adornment, 64
Self-casing, 527
Self-concept, 65–66, 592
Self-dressing, children, 363
Self-finished seams, 547, 592
Self-motivation, 405, 592
Selvages, 219, 490, 592

Separating zipper, 448
Serger
care, 471
parts of, 465–66
removing stitches, 505
safety tip, 465
stitching by, 504
stitch variations, 466–69
tension, 469–70
threads and accessories, 470–71
using, 465–71
Serging techniques
applying elastic to lingerie, 529
attaching waistbands, 573
belt carrier, 508
collar, 558
curved patch pocket, 569
facings, 526
flatlock seam, 550
hems, 539
narrow rolled seam, 547
plain seams, 520
plain waistband, 572
pressing seams, 512
reinforced seam, 548
rolled hems, 541
ruffles, 580
sleeves, 561
topstitched seam, 549
trims, 582
tubing, 578
tucks, 552
Set-in sleeve, 106, 559–60, 592
Seventeen, 146
Sewing direction, 482
Sewing equipment, 472–77
Sewing gauge, 472
Sewing machine, 87, 455–64
accessories, 464
adjusting, 460–62
adjusting pressure, 462
adjusting stitch length, 461
adjusting tension, 461–62
care of, 464
changing needles, 457
choosing needle and thread for, 455–57
computerized, 464
guidelines on stitching, 462
needle sizes for, 456
parts of, 456–57
preparing bobbin, 457–58
safety tips, 463
safety with, 519
stitching by, 501–3, 505
stitching problems, 463
stitching straight, 462–63

tension discs for, 459
thread guides for, 459–60
threading, 458–60
Sewing machine operator, 152
Sewing projects, staying organized, 481
Sewing skills in fabric selection, 445–46
Sew-in interfacing, 451, 553
Sew-through buttons, 449
Shade, 162, 592
Shadowing, 382, 592
Shank buttons, 449, 534
Shantung, 231
Shape, 177, 179, 180, 181, 592
retention of, 198, 218
Shaped facing, 524
Shears, 592
Sheath dress, 107
Shelves, 263
Shift dress, 107
Shipping and receiving clerks, 153
Shirring, 518, 592
Shirt collar, 556
Shirt styles, 109
Shirtwaists, 88
Shoe bags, 262
Shoes, 69, 292
Shoplifting, 345, 346
Shopping
as entertainment, 32
multiple options for, 30–31
Shrinkage control, 240
Shuttle, 221
Silhouette, 179, 592
Silk, 199, 202–3, 215, 219, 271
identifying in lab, 210
Silk pins, 473
Silk thread, 448
Singer Sewing Machine Company, 87
Size ratios, 174
Sizes
blending, 489
children's, 361–62
finding correct, 333–35
on garment label, 326
selecting correct, for pattern, 441
Sizing, 240
Skills
developing, 380–81
identifying, 379–80
level of, in pattern selection, 441
Skin tones, 166
Skirt marker, 472
Skirts
length of, 101–2
styles of, 110
Sleeve board, 477
Sleeve plackets, 563–64

Terrycloth, 223, 231
Textile chemist, 246
Textile converters, 138, 246
Textile Fiber Products Identification Act (TFPIA) (1958), 197, 325, 353
Textile fibers, 196–211
Textile industry, 135–37
Textile mills, 136–37
Textiles
    dyeing, 235–36
    preserving, 89
    printing, 237, 239
    production of, 244–47
Texture, 181–82, 219, 593
    in children's clothes, 363–64
    illusion and, 182
Textured yarns, 217
Texture finishes, 239–40
Texturing, 216–17, 217, 593
Thimbles, 476
Third-generation fibers, 204
Thread(s), 475
    choosing, 447–48
    color of, 447
    disappearing basting, 475
    serger, 470–71
    for sewing machine, 457
Thread clipper, 474
Thread guides for sewing machines, 459–60, 593
Thread nets, 471
Three-thread serger stitch, 466
Tie-dye patterns, 238
Tie-dying fabric, 238
Tilaka, 64
Tint, 162, 593
Topstitched seam, 548–49
Topstitched waistband, 572–73
Topstitching, 290, 503, 540
Toxic, 427, 593
Toxic Substances Control Act, 427
T-pins, 473
Tracing wheel, 475, 496
Trade agreements, 423
Trade associations, 147
Trademark Counterfeiting Act (1984), 423
Trademarks, 326, 593
Trade name, 197–98, 593
Trade-off, 341, 593
Trade publications, 146-147
Traditional retailers, 144
Training and education, 381–82
Transparent ruler, 472
Travel, packing for, 429

Travel and entertainment cards, 350
Trench jacket, 113
Triacetate, 203, 206, 209
Triadic color scheme, 165
Tricot, 225, 226, 231
Trimming, 521
Trims, 582
    adding, 285–86, 582–84
    choosing, 449–50
    selecting, 121
Trouser zipper, 448
Truth-in-Lending Law, 351, 355
T-shirts, 91, 93
Tubing, 577–78, 578, 593
Tubular shape of clothes, 179, 180
Tucks, 551, 552, 593
Tulle, 231
Tumble dry, 593
Tunic, 81
Tunic shirt, 109
Turban, 38
Tuxedo, 46
Tuxedo collar, 105
Tuxedo jacket, 113
Tuxedo shirt, 109
Tweed, 231
Tweezers, 471
Twentieth century, fashions of, 90–93
Twill tape, 450
Twill weave, 222–23
Twin (double) needles, 455
Twisting, 219
Two-thread chain stitch, 467
Two-thread serger stitch, 467
Two-way zipper, 448
Tyler, Richard, 130

U

Ultra detergents, 268
Understitching, 503
Understitching facing, 525–26
Ungaro, Emanuel, 130
Union label, 326
Union of Needletrades, Industrial, and Textile Employees (UNITE), 143, 326
Unions, role of, 143
Unisex look, 92
Unit construction, 505, 593
Universal needle, 455
Unlined patch pocket, 567–68

V

Valentino, 131
Value-added network (VAN), 425

Values, 26, 41–42, 162, 593
    family, 53
Velour, 223, 231
Velvet, 219, 223, 231
Velveteen, 223, 231
Verbal messages, 62, 593
Versace, Gianni, 131
Versatile, 593
Vertical buttonholes, 532–33
Vertical lines, 176
Victoria (Queen of England), 86
Victoria's Secret, 425
Vicuna, 203
Video cameras, 345
Vintage fashions, 313, 593
Vinyl, 231
Vionnet, Madeleine, 131
Virtual dressing rooms, 333
Virtual fitting room, 47
Visual displays, 146
Vittadini, Adrienne, 131
Vogue, 146
Voile, 222, 231
Voluntary information, 326
Von Furstenberg, Diane, 131

W

Waistline casing, 573
Waistline facing, 573
Waistlines, 571–73
Wales, 224, 490
Wang, Vera, 131
Wardrobe
    evaluating your, 303–7
    expanding, 308–15
Wardrobe chart, 304
Wardrobe consultant, 298
Wardrobe plan, 307, 593
Warm-up pants, 111
Warp knits, 225, 226
Warp yarns, 219, 221, 235, 593
Warranty, 326, 593
Washability, 199, 339
Washable fabrics, 491
Wash cycle, 274–75
Washers, 270–71
Waterproof, 241
Water repellent finish, 241
Water softeners, 270
Watt, James, 86
Wearable electronics, 225, 226
Wearing ease, 444, 486, 593
Weaving, 219, 221–24, 593
Web-site designer, 435
Web sites, 411